THE ROUTLEDGE HANDBOOK OF URBAN LOGISTICS

The Routledge Handbook of Urban Logistics offers a state-of-the-art, comprehensive overview of the discipline of urban and city logistics. The COVID-19 pandemic and the rise in internet shopping in particular have placed new demands on urban logistics which require innovative technological and policy responses. Similarly, the necessity for sustainable urban logistics offers both a challenge and opportunity for development and seeks to address traffic congestion, local air quality, traffic-related degradation, the use of energy, safety aspects and noise.

Featuring contributions from world-leading, international scholars, the chapters examine concepts, issues and ideas across five topic areas that reflect the increasingly diverse nature of current research and thinking in urban logistics: transport modes, urban logistics sectors, technical analysis, policy, and sustainability. Each chapter provides an overview of current knowledge, identifies issues and discusses the relevant debates in urban logistics and the future research agenda.

This handbook offers a single repository on the current state of knowledge, written from a practical perspective, utilising theory that is applied and developed using real-work examples. It is an essential reference for researchers, academics and students working in all areas of urban logistics, from policy and planning to technology and sustainability, in addition to industry practitioners looking to develop their professional knowledge.

Jason Monios is Professor of Maritime Logistics at Kedge Business School, Marseille, France. His research revolves around three key areas: maritime transport (port system evolution, collaboration and integration in port hinterlands, port and shipping governance and policy, institutional and regulatory settings), intermodal transport (corridors, dry ports, terminal development, business models and logistics strategies, also including urban logistics) and sustainability and environmental concerns (maritime sustainability, decarbonisation and environmental policy, green ports, climate change adaptation, autonomous and electric vehicles). He has led numerous research projects on these topics with a total budget of over €1 m and contributed to many others. He has worked with national and regional transport authorities and authored technical reports with UNCTAD, UN-ECLAC and the World Bank. He has over 100 peer-reviewed publications, including 7 books. The most recent Stanford/Elsevier ranking placed him in the top 2% of logistics researchers globally, and in 2022, his work on climate change adaptation was cited in the IPCC report.

Lucy Budd is a human geographer and Professor of Transport Management at Leicester Castle Business School, De Montfort University, UK. She is Co-Editor-in-Chief of *Research in Transportation Business and Management* and is an Editorial Board member of the *Journal of Transport Geography*, the *Journal of Air Transport Management*, the *Journal of Transportation Planning and Technology*, *Transport Policy* and *Transport Reviews*. Her research interests comprise aspects of urban transport policy and operations, including equity and sustainability. She has published over 100 papers and edited 14 books in the area of transport management.

Stephen Ison is Professor of Transport Policy in Leicester Castle Business School at De Montfort University, Leicester, UK. He has published widely in the area of economics and transport policy. He has edited, authored or co-authored twenty books, and published over 140 peer-reviewed journal papers. He is a member of the Scientific Committee of the World Conference on Transport Research, Founding Editor of the journal *Research in Transportation Business and Management* (Elsevier), Associate Editor of *Transportation Planning and Technology* and book series co-editor of *Transport and Sustainability* (Emerald). He is on the Editorial Board of *Transport Policy* and *Transport Economics and Management*.

THE ROUTLEDGE HANDBOOK OF URBAN LOGISTICS

Edited by
Jason Monios, Lucy Budd and Stephen Ison

LONDON AND NEW YORK

Cover image: Getty/Michael H

First published 2023
by Routledge
4 Park Square, Milton Park, Abingdon, Oxon OX14 4RN

and by Routledge
605 Third Avenue, New York, NY 10158

Routledge is an imprint of the Taylor & Francis Group, an informa business

© 2023 selection and editorial matter, Jason Monios, Lucy Budd and Stephen Ison; individual chapters, the contributors

The right of Jason Monios, Lucy Budd and Stephen Ison to be identified as the authors of the editorial material, and of the authors for their individual chapters, has been asserted in accordance with sections 77 and 78 of the Copyright, Designs and Patents Act 1988.

All rights reserved. No part of this book may be reprinted or reproduced or utilised in any form or by any electronic, mechanical, or other means, now known or hereafter invented, including photocopying and recording, or in any information storage or retrieval system, without permission in writing from the publishers.

Trademark notice: Product or corporate names may be trademarks or registered trademarks, and are used only for identification and explanation without intent to infringe.

British Library Cataloguing-in-Publication Data
A catalogue record for this book is available from the British Library

ISBN: 978-1-032-14857-1 (hbk)
ISBN: 978-1-032-14858-8 (pbk)
ISBN: 978-1-003-24147-8 (ebk)

DOI: 10.4324/9781003241478

Typeset in Bembo
by codeMantra

CONTENTS

List of Figures ix
List of Tables xi
List of Contributors xiii

Introduction 1

1 Introduction to Urban Logistics: Key Challenges and Current Debates 3
   Jason Monios, Lucy Budd and Stephen Ison

2 The Role of Urban Logistics in the City Economy 13
   Michael Browne and Sam McLeod

PART A
Transport Modes 25

3 Road Transport and Urban Logistics 27
   Maja Piecyk and Julian Allen

4 The Use of Rail and Water in Urban Logistics 45
   Allan Woodburn

5 Cycle Logistics: Sustaining the Last Mile 59
   Jonathan Cowie and Keith Fisken

6 Drones: The Scope for Integration into Multi-modal Urban Logistics Services 72
   Matt Grote, Andy Oakey, Aliaksei Pilko, Angela Smith and Tom Cherrett

7 Integrating Freight and Passenger Transport for Urban Logistics   91
   Silvio Nocera, Francesco Bruzzone and Federico Cavallaro

PART B
Urban Logistics Sectors   **105**

8 Parcel Deliveries as a Pioneer for Climate Neutrality: The Case of
   Ecozone in Mechelen (Belgium)   107
   Koen Mommens and Cathy Macharis

9 Urban Logistics and Retailing   121
   Leigh Sparks

10 Dark Stores as a Post-Pandemic Omnichannel Strategy: Implications
   for Urban Logistics   134
   Heleen Buldeo Rai

11 Food Logistics   147
   Eleonora Morganti

12 Healthcare and Urban Logistics   159
   Liz Breen, Sarah Schiffling and Ying Xie

13 Construction and Urban Logistics   175
   Russell G. Thompson, Oleksandra Osypchuk and Stanisław Iwan

PART C
Technical Analysis   **187**

14 Facility Locations in Urban Logistics   189
   Takanori Sakai, Adrien Beziat and Adeline Heitz

15 Multi-echelon Urban Distribution Networks: Models, Challenges
   and Perspectives   208
   *Imen Ben Mohamed, Olivier Labarthe, Yann Bouchery,
   Walid Klibi and Gautier Stauffer*

16 Computing Technology and Its Applications in Urban Logistics   225
   Lóránt Tavasszy and Hans Quak

17 Small Containers for Evolving Logistics in Changing Cities   238
   Michael G. H. Bell, Veronica Schulz and Shengda Zhu

PART D
Policy — 249

18 Policy and Planning for Urban Logistics — 251
    Laetitia Dablanc

19 Policy Acceptability and Implementation in Urban Logistics — 267
    Edoardo Marcucci, Valerio Gatta and Ila Maltese

20 The Role of Road Pricing and Incentives in Urban Logistics Management — 282
    Oriana Calderón, José Holguín-Veras and Stephen Ison

21 Urban Consolidation Centres — 295
    Emine Zehra Akgün and Jason Monios

22 Success Factors for Urban Logistics Pilot Studies — 305
    Andisheh Ranjbari, Anne Goodchild and Elizabeth Guzy

PART E
Sustainability — 321

23 Climate Change and Urban Logistics — 323
    Maria Attard

24 Decarbonizing Road Freight and Alternative Fuels for Urban Logistics — 333
    Genevieve Giuliano and Sue Dexter

25 Urban Logistics in the Global South — 351
    Nora Mareï

26 Urban Logistics in Megacities — 364
    Quan Yuan and Zhiwei Yang

27 The Gig Economy and Urban Logistics — 375
    Geraint Harvey, Naveena Prakasam and Refat Shakirzhanov

28 Gender Diversity in Urban Logistics — 387
    Anicia Jaegler, Salomée Ruel, Nadine Kafa and Lucy Budd

29 Post-Pandemic Impacts of COVID-19 on Urban Logistics — 395
    John R. Bryson

Index — *407*

FIGURES

2.1	Simplified supply chain and interaction with policy levels	17
4.1	Estimated number of weekly loaded freight train services (by commodity) and share of train service provision to, from and within London (2010–2020, each January)	50
4.2	Active rail freight terminals in Greater London in 2019	51
4.3	Inland waterway freight in London (2011–2020)	53
5.1	E-commerce as a share of total retail sales, United Kingdom	62
5.2	Changes in the total number of vehicle registrations, LGV, rigids and articulated vehicles (artics), 1994–2020 (1994 = 100)	63
5.3	The retailer urban freight market (simplified)	65
6.1	Medium Versapak loaded into the drone used in the chemotherapy medicine case study for the Isle of Wight	75
6.2	Locations of the 14 GP surgeries serviceable by drone	84
8.1	E-commerce penetration rate by region	108
8.2	Structure of stakeholder groups in e-commerce	110
8.3	Map of city center of Mechelen with zone with vehicle restriction in gray	112
8.4	Mode choice for consumers in business-as-usual and implementation case	114
8.5	Distance traveled by consumers to pick up their parcel for the business-as-usual and implementation case	114
8.6	Yearly external cost in euro for business-as-usual and reorganization (implementation case) with differentiation for the external cost parameters	117
10.1	Supply, delivery and parking activities at Getir's dark store	143
10.2	Number of delivery vehicle departures and arrivals per hour for Getir's dark store at Rue Popincourt in Paris	143
10.3	Number of orders per hour for Getir's dark store at Rue Popincourt in Paris	144
11.1	The urban food transport system and its stakeholders	148
12.1	Sustainability development goals and healthcare logistics	160
13.1	(a) Permanent unloading area next to the Eiffel Tower in Paris. (b) Permanent unloading area next to the Sagrada Familia in Barcelona	181
13.2	(a, b) Permanent unloading area in Oslo	181
13.3	Construction materials storage on a canal in Stockholm	182

Figures

14.1	Logistics facilities in Japan (left: a multi-story facility in a suburban area, mainly for cross-docking; right: a parcel delivery centre in an urban area)	191
14.2	Logistics facility typologies proposed by Heitz et al. (2017, 2019)	192
14.3	Trends in spatial distribution of logistics facilities	194
14.4	(a) Population density by municipality and (b) location of logistics facilities in France	196
14.5	Logistics Sprawl in the Tokyo Metropolitan Area	198
14.6	Chanteloup Prologis 2 freight village in Moissy-Cramayel, France, 2022	199
14.7	The Rungis wholesale market	201
14.8	A modern multi-story logistics facility in the coastal area (left) and a delivery center in the central business district (right)	202
14.9	Zoning plan, extracted from the Paris urban local plan, 2013	203
15.1	Typical distribution networks	209
15.2	Examples of cyclo-logistics solutions	214
15.3	Example of web distribution in urban zones	216
16.1	Conceptual framework for this chapter	226
16.2	New business value of physical-digital integration in logistics	228
17.1	Reallocation of road space to a bike lane in suburban Sydney	243
17.2	(a) The metre cube box. (b) Ferry berthing and gangway in foreground	245
18.1	"Logistics perimeters" in the Paris 2016 zoning ordinance	259
21.1	Diagrammatic representation of the location of UCCs in relation to the city and surrounding distribution centres	297
22.1	Seattle microhub location	307
22.2	Three installations of parcel lockers in (a) a residential condominium, (b) a commercial building and (c) a surface parking lot	309
22.3	Sample site plan developed for the street use permit application for the sidewalk locker installation	311
22.4	Sample elevation plan developed for the street use permit application for the sidewalk locker installation	312
22.5	Examples of marketing materials developed for the parcel lockers with assistance from local organizations: (a) flyers, (b) sandwich boards and (c) postcards	314
22.6	The cargo e-bike and trailer (EP1 smart pallet) used in the Seattle pilot	317
23.1	CO_2 concentrations (a) over 10,000 years and (b) over 800 thousand years	325
23.2	Share of electrically chargeable vans, buses and trucks in new vehicle sales in the EU-27, 2018–2020	329
24.1	Dar es Salaam projected growth of informal settlements if past trends continue	334
24.2	Global transportation CO_2 emissions	335
24.3	Alternatives for decarbonizing urban freight	336
24.4	Volvo VNR regional class 8 heavy-duty electric truck	341
24.5	Sample electric and hydrogen truck LCA system flow diagram and boundary	343
24.6	Results of LCA comparing HD truck powertrains on CO_2e	344
24.7	California's truck decarbonization policies	347
25.1	Photographs of the surroundings of the "Mosquée marocaine" market, January 2020	358
26.1	Typical examples of logistics facility clusters in the Shanghai Metropolitan Area	368

TABLES

2.1	Hierarchy of logistics sustainability measures	18
2.2	Major urban logistics research programmes	20
2.3	Urban logistics research networks	21
3.1	Categories and examples of urban road freight transport initiatives	35
3.2	Indicative assessment of how initiatives can potentially affect the negative impacts of urban road freight transport operations	36
4.1	Number of flows, number of trains and tonnage estimates for construction rail freight in London (by direction of flow and commodity, 2019)	52
5.1	Main vehicles used in cargo bike logistics	60
5.2	Cycle logistics, operational characteristics	61
5.3	Cargo bike contribution to wider economic, social and environmental goals	64
6.1	Features of the Project Lima shared airspace concept	81
7.1	First–last mile costs	92
7.2	Identification of KPIs for IPFT	97
7.3	Freight transport on urban light rail tracks	99
8.1	External costs for transport used in the model	115
10.1	Omnichannel store concepts in terms of setting and offering, in comparison to the traditional store	136
10.2	Omnichannel store concepts in terms of operations, in comparison to the traditional store	136
11.1	Examples of food digital services	151
16.1	Digitalised innovations in urban logistics	230
16.2	Role of advanced computing technology in the PI	232
16.3	Role of advanced computing technology in control of urban logistics in the city	233
16.4	Role of advanced computing technology in digital twins	235
18.1	Ranking of EU countries for the efficiency of low-emission zones for urban logistics	254
18.2	Example of use of ANPR cameras' data in Rotterdam, the Netherlands	262
21.1	Services that may be offered at a UCC	297
21.2	Supportive policies that may incentivise use of a UCC	301

Tables

24.1	Summary of alternative fuel trucks, compared to conventional diesel	339
24.2	Medium-duty truck/van (classes 3–6) parity between electric and diesel powertrains	340
24.3	Cost comparison of different powertrains for class 8 truck (day cab) based on 2021 prices	342
24.4	National/US state truck decarbonization policies	345
24.5	Local truck decarbonization policies	346
28.1	Gender pay gap in selected logistics occupations, UK, 2021	390

CONTRIBUTORS

Emine Zehra Akgün holds a PhD in logistics and supply chain management, specifically focussing on urban freight transportation, urban consolidation centres and governance of freight activities in cities. She is now a Lecturer at the Business School at Edinburgh Napier University and extending her research activities to investigate public sector innovation, smart cities and urban innovation in the context of public sector organisations. She studied for her PhD at the Transport Research Institute of Edinburgh Napier University. She worked with local authorities, regional and national transport organisations in Scotland, England, and Sweden to investigate public policy-making in the domain of urban freight transport. So far, she has published her research in several well-known journals in transport policy and logistics such as *Transport Policy* and *International Journal of Logistics: Research and Applications*. Recently, she contributed to the research project investigating the role of science, technology and innovation in sustainable urban development in a post-pandemic world, which was published by the United Nations (UNCTAD Secretariat) in 2022.

Julian Allen is a Senior Research Fellow at the University of Westminster, where he also contributes to the MSc Logistics and Supply Chain Management course. His main current research interests include urban road freight transport operations, online shopping and its transport implications, the role of transport policy in addressing negative impacts of freight transport, the relationship between logistics land and freight transport activity, and the history of road freight transport. He has worked on European Commission-funded projects on urban freight transport including BESTUFS, BESTUFS II and CITYLAB, as well as on freight transport and logistics projects supported by the UK Engineering and Physical Sciences Research Council (EPSRC), Transport for London, the UK Department for Transport and the UK Government Office for Science. He is currently working on two EPSRC-funded projects: 'Centre for Sustainable Road Freight' and 'Decarbonising UK Freight Transport'.

Maria Attard is Professor of Transport Geography and Director of the Institute for Climate Change and Sustainable Development at the University of Malta. She is Co-Editor-in-Chief of *Research in Transportation Business and Management*, Associate Editor of *Case Studies on Transport Policy* and sits on the editorial board of the *Journal of Transport Geography*, among others. Between 2002 and 2008, she was a Consultant to Malta's government and helped develop the first white paper on transport policy (2004) and implement the 2006 Valletta Strategy including park-and-ride, pedestrianisation and road pricing (2007). She also supported the planning for the 2011 public transport reform. She sits on the Steering Committee of the WCTR and is a Cluster co-chair for NECTAR.

Michael G. H. Bell is Professor of Ports and Maritime Logistics in the Institute of Transport and Logistics at the University of Sydney Business School since 2012. Prior to this, he was for 10 years Professor of Transport Operations at Imperial College London where he established the Port Operations Research and Technology Centre. He graduated from Cambridge University with a BA in Economics, then obtained an MSc in Transportation and a PhD in Freight Distribution from Leeds University. His research and teaching interests span city logistics, ports and maritime logistics, transport network modelling, traffic engineering and intelligent transport systems. Michael is the co-founder of the International Symposium on Transport Network Resilience (INSTR) in 2001 and is currently the convenor of its International Scientific Committee. He also serves on the International Advisory Committee of the International Symposium on Transport and Traffic Theory (ISTTT) and was its convenor from 2009 to 2015. Michael is the author of many papers and books, including *Transportation Network Analysis*, published in 1997. For 17 years, he was an Associate Editor of *Transportation Research B*, the leading transport theory journal, and is now an Editorial Board Editor. He was also an Associate Editor of *Maritime Policy & Management* and is currently an Associate Editor of *Transportmetrica A*.

Imen Ben Mohamed is an Assistant Professor at Emlyon Business School in Lyon. Her research interests focus on analytics-based decision-making and combinatorial optimization techniques and their applications to supply chain management problems as urban logistics and omnichannel retailing. She holds a PhD in Applied Mathematics and Scientific Computing from the University of Bordeaux and Inria, and a Master's degree in Operational Research. Before joining Emlyon, she was a Post-Doctoral Researcher in the centre of excellence for supply chain at Kedge Business School where she was involved in several industrial research projects such as Sephora and La Poste. In 2021, she received the 2nd Prize for the best PhD thesis in logistics and transport from GT2L working group and EU/ME.

Adrien Beziat is a Senior Researcher at the Laboratory of Production Systems, Logistics, Transport Organizations and Work (SPLOTT), at Gustave Eiffel University in Paris, France. His work primarily deals with the environmental impacts of city logistics. His current research interests are the development of agent-based modelling frameworks for urban logistics to conduct socioeconomic assessments of public policy and innovative delivery schemes, as well as the analysis of urban distribution systems' environmental impacts through Life-Cycle Assessments. He received his Ph.D. degree from Paris-East University in 2017. His thesis topic was on the social cost of road congestion caused by urban freight transport in the Paris Region. Before joining Gustave Eiffel University, he was a post-doctoral researcher for three years at the Transport Urban Planning Economics Laboratory (LAET), in Lyon, France, where he published several papers on urban freight and urban waste management systems.

Yann Bouchery is an Associate Professor in Operations Management and a member of the Center of Excellence in Supply Chain at Kedge Business School. He holds a PhD in Industrial Engineering from Ecole Centrale Paris (France) obtained in 2012. Before joining Kedge Business School in 2019, he spent two years at Eindhoven University of Technology (The

Netherlands) and five years at EM Normandie. His research interests focus on sustainable operations management and green logistics.

Liz Breen is the current Director of the Digital Health Enterprise Zone, an innovation facility based at the University of Bradford. She is also a Professor of Health Service Operations in the School of Pharmacy and Medical Sciences, having previously been a Senior Lecturer in the School of Management. Liz has held leading roles in multiple National Institute for Healthcare Research (NIHR) funding bids including the Yorkshire and Humber Patient Safety Translational Research Centre. Liz's research focusses on improvement in healthcare eco-systems to improve access to medicines and patient safety. Specific projects include analysis of disruptions in the pharmaceutical supply chain, vaccine supply chains, application of circular economy principles to medicines and the impact of the COVID-19 pandemic on community pharmacies. Liz has also undertaken extensive media engagement discussing the creation and deployment of COVID-19 vaccines within the United Kingdom and globally. This work has been cited in key media outlets such as *The Guardian*, *Time Magazine* and *Forbes*.

Michael Browne is a Professor at the University of Gothenburg. His main research focus is on urban logistics, and he provides academic leadership in the Urban Freight Platform, a University of Gothenburg and Chalmers initiative supported by the Volvo Research and Education Foundations (VREF). He is also a member of the Center of Excellence for Sustainable Urban Freight Systems led by Rensselaer Polytechnic Institute. He is committed to engaging practitioners and policy-makers with the research community on all aspects of logistics impacting future urban goods transport.

Francesco Bruzzone is a Research Fellow in transport planning at the IUAV University of Venice (Italy) and a PhD candidate in the Department of Urban and Regional Development at the Polytechnic University of Turin (Italy). Francesco graduated in 2018 in urban and territorial planning at the IUAV University of Venice and has since worked on these topics and participated on behalf of the IUAV University of Venice in three EU-funded projects on sustainable commuting and the first–last mile. His main research interests include equity in transport, the first–last mile issue, and innovation in transport planning and appraisal.

John R. Bryson has held research and teaching posts at the Universities of St Andrews, Cambridge, Wales and most recently at the University of Birmingham where he is Professor of Enterprise and Economic Geography. His research focusses on understanding people and organisations in place and space and the ways in which place-based adaptation occurs including understanding barriers and enablers to adaptation. Much of his research has focussed on developing an integrated approach to understanding city-regions. His recent books include *Service Management: Theory and Practice* (Palgrave, 2020), *Ordinary Cities, Extraordinary Geographies: People, Place and Space* (Edward Elgar, 2021) and *Living with Pandemics: Places, People and Policy* (Edward Elgar, 2021).

Heleen Buldeo Rai is a Senior Researcher at the Mobilise research group of the Vrije Universiteit Brussel. Supported by a fellowship from Research Foundation – Flanders, she specialises in e-commerce, urban logistics and sustainability. Heleen obtained a PhD in Business Economics at the MOBI research group of the Vrije Universiteit Brussel in 2019 in Brussels, Belgium and carried out post-doctoral research at the Logistics City chair of the

Gustave Eiffel University, Paris, between 2020 and 2022. Her doctoral thesis is titled 'Environmental Sustainability of the Last Mile in Omnichannel Retail'. Heleen has authored several scientific publications and published a best practice guide on sustainable e-commerce supply chains in 2021. The book was awarded by Platform Innovation in Marketing in 2022.

Oriana Calderón obtained her PhD in Transportation Engineering at Rensselaer Polytechnic Institute in Troy, New York. She works as a researcher at the Center for Infrastructure, Transportation, and the Environment (CITE) at the same university. Her main research interest is transportation economics, focused on freight modelling to foster sustainable urban deliveries. Other research areas are related to humanitarian logistics, in specific purchase patterns of critical supplies during disasters. She holds a Master of Business Administration (MBA) from Universidad ICESI, a Bachelor of Industrial Engineering from Universidad del Valle, and a Bachelor of Economics from Universidad del Valle in Cali, Colombia. She has industry experience in different supply chain roles in manufacturing companies. She has also worked as a Teaching Assistant at Rensselaer Polytechnic Institute and Universidad del Valle. She is a member of the Transport Economics and Land Use Committee of the Pan-American Society of Transportation Research (PANAMSTR). She promotes equity and access for women in the transportation industry through her board position as president of the Women in Transportation Seminar (WTS)-RPI Student Chapter (2022–2023).

Federico Cavallaro is an Associate Professor in Transport Engineering and Planning at the Department of Architecture and Arts of Università Iuav di Venezia. His scientific interests range from transport planning to transport economics. The main research themes include the performances of public and freight transport, integrated passenger-freight transport, evaluation of external costs, transport policies, mobility planning and transport operations in low-demand areas, territorial accessibility and equity. His research is documented in more than 70 national and international scientific contributions.

Tom Cherrett is a Professor of Logistics and Transport Management and the Director of the Transportation Research Group at the University of Southampton. His main areas of research are in (i) last-mile logistics systems and operations; (ii) drone logistics particularly with relevance to medical deliveries; (iii) optimisation of city logistics systems and practices; (iv) waste logistics practices and operations (recyclate and residual), having over 180 Journal and conference papers published across a variety of academic and industry publications. He has received over £16m of research funding since 2011 and is an active member of the Chartered Institute of Logistics and Transport, sitting on the Freight and Logistics Policy Group. He has spoken at many logistics and transport management events both nationally and internationally and provided evidence to the Transport Select Committee and other government bodies. He has been lecturing in Logistics and Transport Management for over 20 years.

Jonathan Cowie is a Lecturer in Transport Economics and a member of the Transport Research Institute at Edinburgh Napier University. He has an active research interest in supply-side economics of both public and freight transport modes, and has published many articles and book chapters in these areas. He is the author of *The Economics of Transport* and joint editor of the *Routledge Handbook of Transport Economics*. He is the principal investigator in the EU-funded research project 'Sustainable freight flow hubs' (Surflogh), which runs until 2023.

Contributors

Laetitia Dablanc, an urban planner, is a Professor at the Gustave Eiffel University, Paris, where she heads the Logistics City Chair. She leads the Young Initiative of the World Conference of Transport Research Society. Her areas of research are freight transportation, freight and the environment, urban freight and logistics, freight policies and spatial issues related to logistics. She received a PhD in Transportation Planning from Ecole des Ponts-ParisTech, and a Master's degree in City and Regional Planning from Cornell University. She was initially trained in policy analysis and economics at Science Po Paris. Dr Dablanc has authored or co-authored numerous publications on freight transportation and urban logistics.

Sue Dexter is an Urban Planning and Development PhD candidate at the University of Southern California studying sustainable goods movement, urban spatial structure and transportation technologies to reduce carbon emissions. Her dissertation investigates life cycle impacts of alternative fuel heavy-duty cargo vehicles on greenhouse gas emissions and fleet operational impacts arising from their implementation. Formerly she was a Programme/Project Manager at Toyota Motor North America, specialising in large-scale distribution and system development projects. Sue has a Master's degree from the London School of Economics in Operational Research with an emphasis on network optimization.

Keith Fisken works on strategy development and on several projects for the South East of Scotland Transport Partnership (SEStran). He is working on a number of logistics projects included the EU-funded SURFLOGH, BLING & CONNECT projects, work involved overseeing an Edinburgh pilot project into sustainable logistics as well as developments in 'smart' contracts through blockchain technology. He is currently studying at Edinburgh Napier University for an MSc in Transport Planning and Engineering. He has extensive commercial experience with a Master's degree in marketing from the University of Sydney (Australia). Prior to working with SEStran, he worked in the global alcohol industry for over 20 years in the United Kingdom, Europe and Australia.

Valerio Gatta is Associate Professor of Applied Economics at Roma Tre University, where he teaches 'Sustainability, Economic Development and Transport', 'Economic Development' and 'Digitalization, Preference and Policy Intervention', and he is responsible for the PhD programme 'Sustainable Transport Policy'. He is Editor-in-Chief of journal *Research in Transportation Economics* and is co-director of Transport Research Lab (TRElab). He has an extensive research experience, based on international and national funded research projects, in innovative transport solutions especially in urban freight, linked to decision-making processes and sustainability, with particular reference to stated preference and discrete choice modelling. Advanced methods and models for planning, policy acceptability, behavioural change analysis and socioeconomic/environmental impact assessment are at the core of his academic path. His main research interests are: sustainable mobility solutions, participatory policy planning and making, quantitative data collection for behavioural analysis, ex-ante policy evaluation, demand modelling and willingness to pay analysis. He has been involved in several international funded research projects such as: MOVE21 – Multimodal and interconnected hubs for freight and passenger transport contributing to a zero-emission 21st century; LEAD – Low-Emission Adaptive last-mile logistics supporting 'on-demand economy' through Digital Twins; CITYLAB – City Logistics in Living Laboratories; SEFIRA – Socio Economic implications for Individual Responses to Air pollution policies in EU.

Contributors

Genevieve Giuliano is a USC Distinguished Professor of Public Policy and Ferraro Chair in Effective Local Government at the Sol Price School of Public Policy, University of Southern California. Her research focus includes relationships between land use and transportation, transportation policy analysis, and travel behaviour. Her current research includes the examination of e-commerce and travel behaviour, curb management, and new mobility options for low-income communities. She has published over 200 papers. Professor Giuliano is a past Chair of the Executive Committee of the Transportation Research Board, a National Associate of the National Academy of Sciences and an RSAI Fellow in Regional Science. She is the recipient of several awards, most recently the Walter Isard award for distinguished scholarship contributions from the North American Regional Science Association. She is a frequent participant in National Research Council policy studies.

Anne Goodchild leads the University of Washington's academic and research efforts in the area of supply chain, logistics and freight transportation. She is Professor of Civil and Environmental Engineering and serves as the Founding Director of both the Supply Chain Transportation & Logistics online Master's degree programme and the Supply Chain Transportation & Logistics Center, the latter of which launched the Urban Freight Lab (UFL) in 2016 to bring together the public and private sectors to address the challenges of the urban freight system by engaging in innovative research. Under Goodchild's leadership, the UFL coined the increasingly used term 'Final 50 Feet' and defined it as the last leg of the supply chain for urban deliveries – including finding parking, moving items from a delivery vehicle, navigating traffic, sidewalks, intersections, bike lanes and building security, and ending with the recipient. In addition to being key to customer satisfaction, this final segment is both the most expensive (where an estimated 25–50% of total supply chain costs are incurred) and most time-consuming part of the delivery process – and ripe for improvement. One of the hurdles in the final 50 feet is that many different parties are involved – city departments of transportation, delivery carriers, property owners, residents and consumers – making a collaborative effort between sectors essential for developing mutually beneficial solutions.

Matt Grote is a Research Fellow at the University of Southampton, where he has been part of the Transportation Research Group since 2012. His research interests are primarily concerned with the impacts of transport systems on the environment, in particular the impacts of atmospheric emissions and practical methods for their mitigation. His doctoral thesis was on the development of emissions models for road traffic. His recent areas of research included: atmospheric emissions from aircraft in the global airline industry; provision of electric vehicle charging infrastructure in urban areas; mitigation of the impacts of delivery and servicing activities; and future developments in the domains of urban traffic control and transport modelling. Currently, his work is focussed on the potential for integrated logistics involving the use of drones (Unmanned Aerial Vehicles, UAVs) alongside traditional last-mile delivery solutions as part of the E-Drone project (www.e-drone.org) based around the transportation of pathology samples and medicines in the UK National Health Service (NHS). Prior to entering academia, Matt worked for fifteen years as a pilot for a large, global airline, giving him extensive practical experience in aviation operations. Matt obtained a BEng in Aeronautical Engineering from the University of Bristol (1995) and an EngD in Transport and the Environment from the University of Southampton (2017).

Elizabeth Guzy directs the transformative research, and engagement with industry and the public sector of the Urban Freight Lab (UFL) at the University of Washington, which is an innovative partnership bringing together private industry, academic researchers and public transportation agencies to solve urban freight management problems that overlap private and public spaces and have wide-ranging benefits. She supports the UFL in building professional networks and developing benchmarked best practices in support of industry productivity and building sustainable communities. She managed the UFL's microhub pilot project and assisted with the installation and management of the public parcel locker pilot project in downtown Seattle. Ms Guzy holds Master's degrees in Urban Planning and Public Health from the University of Colorado.

Geraint Harvey is DANCAP Private Equity Chair in Human Organization and Professor of HRM at Western University, Ontario. Harvey's research has focussed on the changing nature of work. Harvey has been commissioned to undertake research by a variety of international organisations, and his findings have been published in a range of media.

Adeline Heitz is an Associate Professor at the Conservatoire National des Arts et Métiers (CNAM) in Paris and a researcher at LIRSA laboratory. She is co-director of the Master in urban planning and in charge of a bachelor degree in transport and logistics at CNAM. Her work deals with the development of city logistics, the issues and impacts of the location of logistics and industrial activities on urban development, employment and public policies. She has published on the rise and evolution of urban logistics and its consequences for urban planning. Adeline Heitz received his Ph.D. degree from Gustave Eiffel University (ex-Paris-East University) in 2017. Her thesis topic was on Logistics in Metropolitan Area: metropolitan structure and planning issues focusing the Paris Region. Before joining CNAM, she was a post-doctoral researcher for two years at Gustave Eiffel University, Paris, France, where she published several papers on public policies and urban planning regarding urban logistics.

José Holguín-Veras is the William H. Hart Professor and Director of the Volvo Research and Educational Foundations Center of Excellence for Sustainable Urban Freight Systems, and the Center for Infrastructure, Transportation, and the Environment at Rensselaer Polytechnic Institute. He is the recipient of numerous awards, including the 2013 White House's Transportation Champion of Change Award, the 1996 Milton Pikarsky Memorial Award, and the 2001 National Science Foundation's CAREER Award. He is one of the most widely published and cited freight researchers in the world. His research interests are in the areas of freight transportation modelling and economics, and humanitarian logistics. His work has opened the door to new paradigms of freight systems that increase economic efficiency and environmental justice. His research has led to major changes in transportation policy and substantial improvements in the ability to improve urban freight systems. His work on humanitarian logistics has played an influential role in disaster response procedures, and has led to deeper insight into how best to respond to large disasters and catastrophic events. He is the President of the Pan-American Society of Transportation Research. He is a member of numerous technical committees and editorial boards of leading journals. He received his PhD from The University of Texas at Austin in 1996; an MSc from the Universidad Central de Venezuela in 1984; and a BSc from the Universidad Autónoma de Santo Domingo in 1982.

Stanisław Iwan is an Associate Professor at the Maritime University of Szczecin. He is the Dean of the Faculty of Engineering and Economics of Transport and the Head of the Department of Management and Logistics. He has more than 15 years of research experience in transport and logistics. His areas of research include city logistics, transport systems telematics, logistics telematics, utilising artificial intelligence in transport and logistics, utilising simulation tools in transport and logistics as well as knowledge management. He has co-authored over 150 papers, monographs and chapters in monographs (in Polish and in English). His work has been published in journals, such as *Transportation Research Part D, Sustainable Cities and Society, International Journal of Shipping and Transport Logistics, Energies, Sustainability and others*. He has had key leadership roles in numerous city logistics projects, founded under prestigious European research programmes including C-LIEGE (Clean Last Mile Transport and Logistics Management for Smart and Efficient Local Governments in Europe), GRASS (GReen And Sustainable freight transport Systems in cities), 'Analysis of information needs of heterogeneous environment in sustainable urban freight', NOVELOG (New cOoperatiVe business modEls and guidance for sustainable city LOGistics), and Low Carbon Logistics, EUFAL (Electric Urban Freight And Logistics). He is the organiser and the Chair of Scientific Committee of the International Conference Green Logistics for Greener Cities.

Anicia Jaegler is a Full Professor at Kedge Business School. She received a Diploma in Engineering and a PhD from the École des Mines de Saint-Etienne, France, and an HDR (post-doctoral diploma) from the CRETLOG of the University Aix-Marseille, France. Between 2018 and 2021, she was the Head of the Operations Management and Information Systems Department at Kedge Business School and since 2021, Associate Dean for Inclusivity and Sustainability. In 2020, she received the second award at the Global Women Supply Chain Leaders in the category Supply Chain Academic Excellence. Her current research focusses on manufacturing and sustainable supply chain management.

Nadine Kafa is an Assistant Professor in Supply Chain Management and Information Systems and a member of the Center of Excellence in Supply Chain at Kedge Business School. She holds a PhD in Industrial Engineering specialised in Supply Chain Management. from the University of Paris. Her research focusses on supply chain analytics, sustainable supply chain and multi-criteria decision making. As a member of the Center of Excellence in Supply Chain, she is involved in a number of research projects on subjects related to supply chain management in collaboration with industrial partners such as La Poste, Sephora, ID logistics and Stelia Aerospace. She has published articles in international journals such as *Transportation Research Part E: Logistics and Transportation Review* and *British Food Journal*.

Walid Klibi is a Professor of Supply Chain and Operations Management at Kedge Business School (France) since 2011, and a member of the Center of Excellence in Supply Chain (CESIT) of Kedge Business School. He obtained his PhD in Business Administration, specialised in Supply Chain Management, at Laval University in Canada in 2009. He holds since 2020 a Habilitation degree in Applied Mathematics at the University of Bordeaux in France. His research work focusses on supply chain design, resilience, omnichannel distribution and urban logistics networks, carried out in partnership with several international companies. He is also co-author of more than 30 articles in international academic and professional journals and a book which is intended for an academic and professional audience. Most of his work is carried out in collaboration with affiliated schools and international colleagues. He is currently a research affiliate at the MIT Center for Transportation and Logistics and a member of the Physical Internet Lab at GeorgiaTech.

Olivier Labarthe is an Associate Professor in Supply Chain Management and a member of the Center of Excellence in Supply Chain at Kedge Business School. His research interests include agent-based modelling and simulation of supply networks and the deployment of the Physical Internet for sustainable urban logistics. Recently, he co-supervised the InViCy project (cyclo-logistics in urban environments), with the French postal service and parcel delivery La Poste Group (project funded by The French Agency for Ecological Transition). He received his PhD in Administrative Sciences and Computer Science from Laval University (2006) and Aix-Marseille III University (2006), respectively.

Cathy Macharis is a Professor at the Vrije Universiteit Brussel. She leads the Mobilise research group and brings together research on sustainability at the university. Cathy teaches courses in supply chain management and sustainable mobility and logistics. She is specialised in the assessment of policy measures and innovative concepts in the field of sustainable logistics and urban mobility. She is the chairwoman of the Brussels Mobility Commission.

Ila Maltese is a Lecturer at the University of Milan, Polytechnic University of Milan, and Roma Tre University, where she teaches Microeconomics and Economic Principles, and research associate at Roma Tre University and Bocconi University. After graduating in Economics from Bocconi University with a thesis in Urban Economics, she obtained a PhD in Urban Projects and Policies at the Polytechnic University of Milan. She is currently involved in the Transport Research Lab (TRElab), an interdisciplinary group of leading academics working on transport research at Roma Tre University. Her research focusses on innovative and sustainable solutions for urban freight distribution, and she has participated in several research projects. She also works on behavioural changes in e-grocery and e-commerce, active travel and sustainable mobility at tourism destinations. She is research fellow and project manager of the EU-funded project 'L-3D, a new dimension of participation", which aims to increase the stakeholder involvement in public policy decision-making processes for urban logistics using new technologies and innovative communication techniques.

Edoardo Marcucci is Professor of Economic Policy at the Department of Political Sciences of Roma Tre University and Professor of Transportation Economics at the Department of Logistics, Molde University College in Norway. He has an extensive research experience in innovative transport solutions, especially in urban freight, linked to decision-making processes and sustainability, with particular reference to survey designs and discrete choice modelling techniques. Advanced methods and models for planning, policy acceptability, behavioural change analysis and socioeconomic/environmental impact assessment are at the core of his academic research. His research, based on international networks and relevant academic collaborations, has produced more than 100 publications mostly in peer-reviewed journals and with an international co-authorship. He is Editor-in-Chief of 'Research in Transportation Economics'. He is also co-director of Transport Research Lab (TRElab), an independent, cutting-edge experimentation environment where academics, policy-makers, entrepreneurs and citizens work together to co-create effective, efficient and sustainable transport solutions. As Co-Director of TRElab, he served as scientific coordinator of the urban logistics section of the SUMP (Sustainable Urban Mobility Plan) of Rome.

Nora Mareï is a geographer (PhD from Nantes University). She is a Research Fellow at CNRS (Prodig research team) and a Lecturer at the Sorbonne University (Paris 1). She specialises in urban transport and logistics issues in the Global South, especially in the Mediterranean area (Morocco, Spain), in West Africa (Mauritania, Senegal) and in the Middle East (Egypt). Her current research is about contemporary territorial dynamics in the context of globalisation and focusses on cities, macro-regional (or multi-state) processes, and port and logistics infrastructures. She is currently leading a comparative research project on logistics transitions in both Global North and Global South cities (ANR Trans-Log, 2022-2026). She is the author of numerous publications available on her contact page (https://www.prodig.cnrs.fr/nora-marei/).

Sam McLeod is an experienced researcher and policy professional, currently affiliated with the University of Western Australia. Sam is currently working as a political advisor and has previously been employed in professional planning consultancy and in academic research teams. Sam holds formal qualifications in urban and regional planning and project management.

Koen Mommens is a Research Professor at the Mobilise research group at Vrije Universiteit Brussel. He leads a team of 15 researchers working on sustainable logistics within the group. His research includes the impact of different cargo-types (e.g. containers and pallets) on the modal shift to rail and inland waterways. He has developed the LAMBTOP (GIS model) and TRABAM (agent-based model). The latter model is a freight transport model for Belgium integrating both logistic service provider behaviour and external cost calculations on individual vehicle level. Koen has published in the most important peer-reviewed journals in his research field. He was involved in over 50 projects, for governments and large enterprises.

Eleonora Morganti is an Assistant Professor in Urban Food Consumption, Distribution and Sustainability at the University of Leeds, sharing her work between the Institute for Transport Studies and the School of Food Sciences and Nutrition. Her research focusses on the last mile for food and the effects of new consumption and purchasing habits on the urban freight system. The food supply sector represents her main field of study, comparing different Food Hubs in urban areas in Europe and the Americas. Prior to moving to England, Eleonora worked at the French Institute of Science and Technology for Transport, Development and Networks (IFSTTAR) in Paris, exploring ways to enhance the transition towards low-carbon transport in city logistics. She conducted study visits in various countries including the United States, Italy and Argentina. Eleonora is Strategy Leader for Global Supply Chains at Global Food and Environment Institute (GFEI) at the University of Leeds.

Silvio Nocera is Professor of Transport Engineering and Planning at the Università Iuav di Venezia in Venice, Italy. His research interests are quite extensive, spanning the economic evaluation of transport systems, the external costs of transportation (he delved particularly deep into the evaluation of carbon dioxide and its effects on global warming), high-speed railways, demand responsive transport systems, freight, intermodal and integrated transport, intelligent transport systems, and transit quality evaluation. Silvio has published studies widely, and his most recent work was published in major journals. He belongs to the top 2% percentile of the most cited authors in the field of *Logistics & Transportation* in the last two Elsevier-Stanford University world surveys, and serves on the editorial boards of several international journals, including *Transportation Research Interdisciplinary Perspectives*, *Research in Transportation Business and Management*, and *Case Studies on Transport Policy*.

Andy Oakey is a Transport and Logistics Researcher at the University of Southampton, working in the Transportation Research Group since 2019, having supported their projects in 2018. With a Civil Engineering background, his research methods typically combine technical quantitative, qualitative and strategic approaches, giving a holistic perspective. His past work includes investigating the reintroduction of pavement porters to decongest London's last-mile freight system as part of the Freight Traffic Control 2050 project. More recently, his research has been scoping the capabilities of drones in medical logistics in the United Kingdom as part of his doctoral thesis and the Solent Future Transport Zone and E-Drone research projects. Andy obtained a BEng in Civil Engineering from the University of Southampton (2018) and is currently undertaking a PhD, also at the University of Southampton (expected completion in 2023).

Oleksandra Osypchuk is currently completing a PhD at Czestochowa University of Technology in the Faculty of Management. The title of her doctoral dissertation is 'Supply Logistics in Construction Companies and Sustainable Urban Freight Transport'. The main goal of the dissertation is to analyse and critically assess the current state of supply logistics in selected construction companies and its impact on the operation of modern cities. The implementation of her research goal provided an opportunity to develop a comprehensive model of supply logistics for construction companies, which allows them to reduce their negative impacts. In the future, she plans to expand and continue research in the field of construction and city logistics. For last 6 years, Oleksandra has also been an Assistant Lecturer at the Faculty of Economics and Transport Engineering at the Maritime University of Szczecin. She conducts classes in the area of management and logistics. She is a member of the GRASS-NEXT project (GReen And SuStainable – kNoewledge EXpanded freight Transport in cities, project financed under the Norwegian Financial Mechanism 2014–2021) and the EntreAction! project (EntreAction: An Innovative Case-to-videostory Approach in Entrepreneurial Education, project financed by the Erasmus+ programme). Her research interests include urban logistics, urban freight transport, construction and sustainable development.

Maja Piecyk is a Professor in Logistics at the University of Westminster. She is a former Deputy Director of the Centre for Sustainable Road Freight, an EPSRC-funded research centre between Westminster, Heriot-Watt and Cambridge Universities. Her research interests focus on the environmental performance and sustainability of freight transport operations. Much of her current work centres on city logistics, CSR, GHG auditing of businesses and forecasting of long-term trends in energy demand and environmental impacts of logistics. Maja is a Fellow of the Higher Education Academy. She is currently leading the University of Westminster's input to the EPSRC-funded Centre for Sustainable Road Freight and Decarbonising the UK's Freight Transport network. Her recent projects include: Freight Traffic Control 2050, the Volvo Centre of Excellence in Sustainable Urban Freight Systems and CityLab: City Logistics in Living Laboratories, among others.

Aliaksei Pilko is a Researcher in the Computational Design and Engineering group at the University of Southampton. Having both an academic and practical background in aviation, his research centres on uncrewed aerial systems' safety and integration into existing airspace structures. His past work involved the use of agent-based models to determine airspace capacity and conflict risk in different airspace structures with heterogenous agents. Currently, his work is focussed on the computational quantification of air and ground risks posed by UAVs and the subsequent design of mitigation strategies against this, as part of the E-Drone medical logistics research project. He achieved his BEng in Aerospace Engineering at the University of Southampton (2020) and has continued to pursue his PhD at the same institution (expected completion in 2024).

Naveena Prakasam is a Lecturer in Organisational Behaviour and Human Resource Management at Southampton Business School, University of Southampton. Naveena's primary area of research interest is in leadership studies with a focus on authentic leadership, as well as critical and diverse approaches to leadership. Naveena is also interested in inclusion/exclusion in organisations. Her areas of research extend to the digital context in which she has investigated populist responses to leadership, inclusion/exclusion in digital media platforms.

Hans Quak works as a Senior Research Scientist at the Dutch research institute TNO (Sustainable Transport and Logistics). He is also Professor of Applied Sciences Smart Cities and Logistics at the Breda University of Applied Sciences (BUas) at the Academy for Built Environment and Logistics. After obtaining his PhD in 2008 from the RSM Erasmus University with his thesis 'Sustainability of Urban Freight Transport', he has been working on a range of projects in the field of urban logistics and sustainable logistics for various clients (varying from EU, the Dutch Top Sector Logistics, companies and authorities). He has (co) authored several reports, papers and book chapters on urban freight transport, logistics and (local) policy in these areas. In recent years, the transition to zero-emission city logistics has formed the central issue of this practice-oriented research, from the perspective of policy, technology and logistics operations. Hans is a member of the Steering Committee for Cities of the Top Sector Logistics.

Andisheh Ranjbari is Assistant Professor of Civil and Environmental Engineering at Pennsylvania State University, and her research focusses on urban freight, shared mobility and public transit. Prior to joining Penn State, Dr Ranjbari served as the Director of the Urban Freight Lab (UFL) at the University of Washington, a public–private research partnership with about 20 private company members and public agency partners, focussed on developing and testing solutions around urban freight management and operation problems. Dr Ranjbari completed her PhD in Transportation Engineering at the University of Arizona and her MSc in Transportation Engineering and BSc in Civil Engineering in her native Iran. Along with her academic experience, Dr Ranjbari also worked as a transportation modeller at multiple transportation agencies in the United States.

Salomée Ruel is an Associate Professor at Kedge Business School in Information Systems Management and Supply Chain Management, and belongs to the Sustainability excellence centre. She holds a PhD and a Habilitation in Management Sciences specialised in Supply Chain Management. In 2014, she received the 'FNEGE-AIRL Daniel Tixier' thesis prize for the best thesis in Logistics and Supply Chain Management. Her research focusses on supply chain strategy, inter-organisational relations, information systems, digitalization, dynamic capabilities (agility, resilience, visibility, viability) and gender diversity in SCM. She has published articles in prestigious scientific journals such as *International Journal of Production Economics*, *International Journal of Production Research*, *Annals of Operations Research* and *International Journal of Physical Distribution & Logistics Management*. She is the treasurer of the AIRL-SCM Scientific Association.

Takanori Sakai is an Associate Professor at the Department of Logistics and Information Engineering, School of Marine Technology, Tokyo University of Marine Science and Technology (TUMSAT). Takanori's research interest lies in urban freight transportation and logistics. His current research subjects are the locational dynamics of logistics land use and advanced urban and transportation simulations for evaluating land use, smart transportation systems, and novel transportation policies. Takanori obtained a Ph.D. degree from the Department of Urban Planning and Policy at the University of Illinois at Chicago (UIC) in 2017. Prior to joining TUMSAT, he was a Senior Postdoctoral Associate at the Singapore-MIT Alliance for Research and Technology, MIT's research institute in Singapore. He has an extensive record of research in transport studies and received the Best Paper Awards in the Transportation Research Board (TRB) Urban Freight Transportation Committee (AT025) in 2017 and 2018. He is currently serving as a committee member of the TRB Freight Transportation and Logistics Committee (AT015).

Sarah Schiffling is Assistant Professor of Supply Chain Management and Social Responsibility at Hanken School of Economics, Helsinki, Finland. She is also the Deputy Director of the Humanitarian Logistics and Supply Chain Management Research Institute, HUMLOG. The centre works extensively with humanitarian organisations around the world on issues such as medical supply chains in the COVID-19 pandemic, cash-based assistance for refugees, delivery of humanitarian assistance to conflict zones and others. Sarah's own research interests include complexity in supply chains, trust and distrust in supply chain relationships, cash-based interventions, pharmaceutical supply chains and the effects of transport disruptions. Sarah frequently delivers lectures, talks and panel discussions on humanitarian logistics and supply chain management topics to audiences of students, academics, practitioners and policy-makers. Her recent publications include papers in the *International Journal of Operations & Production Management*, *Annals of Operations Research* and *International Journal of Production Research*. In addition, she writes for general audiences and often contributes to media coverage on supply chain topics around the world.

Veronica Schulz is a PhD Student at the Institute of Transport and Logistics Studies (ITLS) at the University of Sydney Business School in Australia since 2022. She has received numerous scholarships including the Australian Government's Research Training Program Stipend Scholarship in 2022. Prior to this, she obtained a Bachelor of Music (BMus) from the Sydney Conservatorium of Music in 2019 majoring in clarinet performance. She then graduated from the University of Sydney Business School with a Master of Commerce (MCom) in 2021 majoring in logistics and supply chain management. In 2021, she completed her MCom dissertation in ITLS investigating the feasibility of integrating freight and passengers on public ferries. She also has practical experience in marketing and public transport. Veronica's teaching and research interests are in city logistics, port logistics, business operations management and sustainability.

Refat Shakirzhanov is a Postgraduate Research Student and Graduate Teaching Assistant at Swansea University. His PhD research explores discourses of work and work-based subjectivities within cultural and creative employment domain, with a particular focus on the discourses of 'enterprise' in community and participatory arts practice in Wales. This builds upon the topic of his MSc dissertation into experiences of job insecurity within the UK performing arts sector. Previously, Refat worked extensively in the global supply chain and logistics industry. His professional experience fuelled his deep interest in understanding social dynamics in non-standard forms of employment and raising awareness of labour conditions in the contemporary workplace.

Angela Smith is a Research Fellow within the E-Drone research team and is based at Bournemouth University. Her research is focussed on the sociological aspects of planning for future transport provision and how we can actively link research with practice. In 2018, she was part of the team of researchers tasked with gathering evidence for the UK Government Office for Science 'Future of Mobility' report for which she reviewed evidence relating to factors affecting transport mode choice. She completed her PhD in 2019 in the area of transport use in rural tourism. Her thesis used the lens of social practice theory to examine how visitors used transport to reach and travel around a case study area, producing a framework for the appraisal of transport provision in rural tourism destination areas. Her background is within transport planning, and she has worked in the public and private sectors since 2004 on diverse project types including the transport impact assessment of rail and road logistics facilities and the development and implementation of sustainable travel strategies for new and existing communities.

Leigh Sparks is the Deputy Principal at the University of Stirling with specific responsibility for education and students. He is also Professor of Retail Studies. He was a geography undergraduate at the University of Cambridge and completed his PhD in Retail Employment at the University of Wales. He has been Professor of Retail Studies at Stirling since 1992, a Visiting Professor at Florida State University from July 2000 to July 2001 and Visiting Professor at the University of Tennessee from June to December 2006. He is well known for his research into aspects of retailing with work undertaken on behalf of public and private clients, for the research councils and for other funding bodies. He has authored and edited a number of books, including a leading volume in its fifth edition on Retail Logistics and Supply Chains. He has published over 125 refereed journal articles as well as many practitioner, trade and newspaper pieces, and runs a Scottish retailing blog www.stirlingretail.com. He is the Chair of Scotland's Towns Partnership, the 'go-to' body for Scottish Government on matters to do with Scotland's towns and town centres. He was a member of the External Advisory Group for the Scottish Government's National Town Centres Review and of the Expert Advisory Group investigating the lessons of the horsemeat scandal for the Scottish Government. Most recently he chaired and wrote the Scottish Government's review of the Town Centre Action Plan ('A New Future for Scotland's Town Centres') and was a member of their Social Renewal Advisory Board and the Ministerial Executive group developing a National Retail Strategy. He is a Fellow of the Royal Society of Edinburgh (FRSE).

Gautier Stauffer is an Associate Professor in the faculty of Business and Economics (HEC Lausanne) at the University of Lausanne. His research focusses on the use of integer programming and combinatorial optimization techniques to solve challenging operations and supply chain management problems. He owns a PhD from EPFL (Lausanne), he was a Postdoc at MIT and, prior to joining HEC Lausanne, he worked as a Researcher or Professor at IBM research (Zurich), University of Bordeaux, Ensimag (Grenoble) and Kedge Business School (Bordeaux).

Lóránt Tavasszy is a Full Professor in Freight Transport & Logistics at the Delft University of Technology (TU Delft). He studied Civil Engineering and completed his PhD research in 1996 on Multimodal Freight Transport Models for Europe. Between 1996 and 2016, he worked with the Dutch national research institute TNO as researcher, manager and principal scientist and held part-time chairs at the University of Nijmegen and TU Delft. His research and education relate to freight transportation modelling at urban, national and global levels. He represents the TU Delft as core research partner in the VREF global Center of Excellence for Sustainable Urban Freight Solutions (CoE-SUFS). His online course with the partners of this network was completed by almost 10,000 students since its launch in 2019. Professor Tavasszy currently chairs the Scientific Committee of the World Conference for Transport Research Society and is a member of several national and international professional committees.

Russell G. Thompson is Professor in Transport Engineering at the University of Melbourne. He leads the Physical Internet Lab at the University of Melbourne and is Vice-President of the Institute for City Logistics based in Kyoto. Russell was a leader of the Volvo Global Center of Excellence in Sustainable Urban Freight Systems (CoE-SUFS), 2013–2020. Russell's main research interests are in network modelling and the simulation of urban freight systems. Currently, Russell is actively involved in several urban freight projects in Melbourne and Sydney including High Productivity Freight Vehicles, Urban Consolidation Centres and the effects of COVID on urban distribution patterns. He is currently conducting research studies investigating the benefits of the Physical Internet, parcel lockers, logistics sprawl, collaborative freight systems, road pricing, urban consolidation centres and multi-modal freight systems. He has also contributed to a number of international studies relating to urban freight, including the European Union's Best Urban Freight Solutions (BESTUFS) project and the OECD report on urban distribution. He has co-authored 10 books and over 150 refereed publications. Russell co-edited a book, '*City Logistics: Mapping the Future*' (CRC Press, 2015), that presents a range of innovative solutions to increase the efficiency and improve the sustainability of freight in cities.

Allan Woodburn has more than 25 years' experience of rail freight research and consultancy, including his PhD which focussed on the role of logistical structure in the development of rail freight services in Great Britain. For 13 years, he was Course Leader for the MSc Logistics and Supply Chain Management course at the University of Westminster (London). Allan has published widely in international peer-reviewed journals, written several book chapters, and presented his research findings at both academic and industry conferences. The focus of his work has been on rail freight policy, operations and sustainability, together with trend analysis of the British rail freight market. Since 1997, Allan has compiled an annual database of rail freight service provision, giving considerable insight into the evolution of the privatised rail freight market. He has also been involved in many other freight and logistics projects, giving him a detailed understanding of freight mode choice within the supply chain. Allan has carried out projects for various clients including the Department for Transport (DfT), Centre on Regulation in Europe (CERRE), United Nations Economic Commission for Europe (UNECE), Transport for London (TfL) and Government Office for Science. He led the freight mode choice component of the Green Logistics research project funded by the Engineering and Physical Sciences Research Council (EPSRC). Several projects have involved innovative data collection and analysis techniques relating, for example, to the analysis of container train capacity provision and utilisation.

Ying Xie is a Professor in Supply Chain Analytics at Cranfield University, UK. Her research interests cover machine learning, big data analytics, forecasting, decision support system, supply chain modelling and simulation, supply chain digitalisation and circular economy. She specialises in healthcare supply chain, international shipping, port management and sustainable aviation supply chain. Ying has successfully won and completed many research and consultancy projects, totalling more than £1 m, including projects from EPSRC, Innovate UK, ERDF, EU Horizon, Health Education England and industries. Ying has worked with

NHS to reduce pharmaceutical waste and develop green pharmaceutical supply chain. Commissioned by Health Education England, Ying examined population health prevalence in East England and supported multi-year healthcare workforce plan; she is also working with Ocado Technology to develop digital twins-enabled ecosystem for social care and healthcare. Ying is a Board Member of the Strategy Advisory Board for Digital Supply Chain Innovation Hub, Digital Catapult. This is a £10m programme funded by UKRI, and it draws another £10m investment from the private sector.

Zhiwei Yang is a Doctoral Candidate in the Department of Traffic Engineering, College of Transportation Engineering, Tongji University, Shanghai. He holds a BSc in Traffic Engineering and an MSc in Engineering from Hefei University of Technology. He is co-author of several scientific papers published in indexed journals. In his research, he concentrates on sustainable logistics and urban mobility, especially in the spatiotemporal distribution of logistics facilities, freight trip generation and urban freight activities.

Quan Yuan is a Research Professor at Urban Mobility Institute, Department of Traffic Engineering, College of Transportation Engineering, Tongji University, Shanghai. He earned his PhD from the University of Southern California in 2018. His research interests lie in freight transportation planning and management, transportation emissions and freight transportation modelling.

Shengda Zhu is an Honorary Associate at the Institute of Transport and Logistics Studies (ITLS). Shengda obtained his PhD degree from ITLS in 2020, and his thesis was focussed on vertical integration between container shipping lines and terminal operators. His main research interest is adopting economic methods in transport studies. Shengda's research area covers maritime transport, city logistics, sustainable transport and emerging technologies in transport.

Introduction

1
INTRODUCTION TO URBAN LOGISTICS

Key Challenges and Current Debates

Jason Monios, Lucy Budd and Stephen Ison

Introduction

The transport of goods takes place at all levels, from small parcels carried on foot, by cart or bike to super tankers each transporting hundreds of thousands of tonnes of oil across the ocean. Bulk goods such as iron ore for steel used in construction and manufacturing are shipped worldwide to provide inputs for heavy industry and the production of consumer products, while finished goods are then transported in containers by ships to ports around the world. Large volumes of these containers are then transported by road, rail and barge to distribution centres and warehouses on the edges of urban areas, which is where the complexity of urban logistics begins. According to the International Transport Forum (2021), the movement of freight amounted to 145,229 billion tonne-kilometres (tkm) in 2019, producing 3,233 million tonnes of CO_2. This means that freight transport was responsible for 42% of all transport emissions worldwide. Only 3% of global freight transport tkm are performed at the urban level, yet this activity is responsible for 20% of greenhouse gas emissions for the sector. Moreover, these levels are predicted to increase, with demand for freight transport forecast to more than double by 2050. The complex and fast-changing nature of urban logistics makes this *Routledge Handbook of Urban Logistics* both timely and highly relevant.

The urban environment presents many challenges to the management of freight flows. Networks are more complex, space restrictions prevent the economies of scale enjoyed by ships and trains and sometimes even trucks, and goods and people compete for limited space. In this context, a range of goals, desires, policies and uses for urban space interact with each other, such as housing, essential services, leisure and business. Given that 55% of the global population live in urban areas, a level that is predicted to increase to 68% by 2050 (United Nations Department of Economic and Social Affairs, 2018), these issues already affect the majority of the world's population and will affect an increasing proportion in the future. Around 12% of urban dwellers reside in 33 megacities (defined as having over 10 million inhabitants), and the majority of these megacities are located in the Global South. Moreover, as the majority of growth in urban areas is expected to occur in lower-income countries, several challenges linked to this growth, such as unplanned urban sprawl, congestion, pollution and waste, will need to be faced. In all cities, the capacity of public institutions to manage the urban space and balance competing needs is already important and will become increasingly central in future, particularly in the context of the regulation of negative environmental impacts.

At the outset, it is important to provide definitions of key terms, as 'transport', 'logistics' and 'supply chain management' are often used interchangeably and/or erroneously. *Transport* refers to the physical movement of goods, where the focus is mostly on the economics and the operational issues of the different modes of transport, although transport scholars also consider the governance of the system, business models in the industry and the interactions of public and private actors in organising these complex systems. Transport is rarely demanded for its own sake, being what is called a *derived demand*, used for the movement of goods from A to B. *Logistics* is a broader topic, and while transport remains the largest task within logistics, there is also a need to consider the role of warehouses, their location and organisation, and the management of inventory moving through the system. Thus, logistics occupies itself not just with the transport of boxes and containers but considers the goods themselves: how many and of what type should be ordered, how far in advance, where should they be stored and in what condition, and when brought to the store, including the management of packaging and waste. Finally, *supply chain management* is a larger field again, which treats all of these questions in the broader scope of the entire system of production and distribution, from raw materials to final product, focussing on value management and partner relationships from upstream suppliers to downstream customers. Defining the term *urban* is considerably more complex, as there is no globally consistent quantitative minimum threshold for a town or city. The 2018 study by the United Nations Department of Economic and Social Affairs took data from 233 countries and noted that the levels given in national figures represent a large range of minimum urban population levels from 200 to 50,000 inhabitants. The emphasis of this *Handbook of Urban Logistics* is on the movement and intermediate handling and storage of goods at the urban level, the end point of most supply chains and the location of most of the stores and customers.

Urban logistics is, however, not solely related to the movement of goods quickly or cheaply. The chapters in this *Handbook* reveal that there are many issues to be explored that impact the optimal means of transporting, storing and selling goods as they move from warehouse to store to home. These include the operational aspects of the various transport modes, the specificities of different logistics sectors and the technical evolutions and strategies for optimisation. These various aspects of the urban logistics realm are then influenced by, and themselves influence, public policies relating to issues of road space, emissions, noise and safety, reaching even further into the fabric of modern life in such respects of employment legislation, inclusivity and recently the COVID-19 pandemic.

Following this introduction, the *Handbook* commences with Chapter 2 on the role of urban logistics in the city economy by Michael Browne and Sam McLeod. Their chapter sets the scene for the succeeding chapters by introducing the nature of urban logistics as it responds to economic conditions, adapts to policy and regulation and evolves according to technological opportunities. They highlight the complexity of the field which aims to optimise operations at the same time as seeking to become more sustainable, both of these aims mediated through a range of public and private actors. After that chapter, the *Handbook* is divided into five key topic areas, although there is inevitable overlap and cross-referencing between them.

The key topic areas are:
A   Transport Modes
B   Urban Logistics Sectors

C   Technical Analysis
D   Policy
E   Sustainability

A   Transport Modes

The core activity of logistics is the transport of goods at all levels, from raw materials to inputs to production to finished products to stores and homes. At the urban level, road is dominant, including both heavy trucks and smaller vans, while the use of rail and water in the urban space is limited due to the short distances and fragmentation of flows. Shifts towards lower-carbon cities are driving electrification and increases in other types of movement such as cargo bikes and drones. These alternative modes are complemented by attempts by public transport services to make better use of their capacity by incorporating freight and passengers.

In Chapter 3, Maja Piecyk and Julian Allen provide an overview of road transport, which is the dominant transport mode in urban logistics. The authors identify the key features of road freight transport at the urban level, its regulation by traffic authorities, the developments and challenges it faces and the efforts being made to address these challenges and particularly to reduce the negative impacts.

In Chapter 4, Allan Woodburn examines the use of rail and water as transport modes in urban logistics. The author points out that while such modes are often overlooked at the urban level, they can play an important role in the functioning of cities and, crucially, can help to mitigate against some of the negative consequences of urban freight transport activity. The chapter presents a review of the opportunities and difficulties associated with increasing the role of rail and water in urban logistics as well as considering how these modes can be better integrated with road transport.

In Chapter 5, Jonathan Cowie and Keith Fisken discuss the critical factors which either inhibit or contribute to the successful establishment and operation of cycle logistics. The authors highlight the main economic barriers to successful operation and the main factors that lead to its success. The chapter shows that the key success factors for cycle logistics are full employment and acceptance of the triple bottom line (economic, social and environmental), the importance and motivation of key staff, strong partnership working, and an aim to provide complementary, rather than competing, freight services. A limiting factor identified by the authors is the extent to which such operations can be scaled up, which, without stronger policy interventions, is likely to remain a significant issue in the medium and longer terms.

In Chapter 6, Matt Grote, Andy Oakey, Aliaksei Pilko, Angela Smith and Tom Cherrett explore the use of drones (or Uncrewed Aerial Vehicles – UAVs) in urban logistics. The authors discuss how drones have been seen as a potential new logistics mode that could improve point-to-point journey times while also helping to reduce the use of road transport and the associated emissions. Their analysis reveals that the majority of the use of drones in other sectors (such as surveying and photography) involves keeping the drone in the sight of the operator, whereas going beyond this limit requires specific permissions and is one of the key reasons why largescale commercial drone operations are not yet prevalent anywhere in the world except for some medical use cases in Africa.

In Chapter 7, Silvio Nocera, Francesco Bruzzone and Federico Cavallaro consider the potential for integrating freight and passenger transport in urban logistics. They discuss the operational, socioeconomic and environmental benefits obtainable with the integration of passengers and cargo flows, as well as the policy and normative implications for local regulators and planners. Their analysis compares the sharing of public transport vehicles, the sharing of public transport infrastructure (such as tram and subway rails), and the sharing of transit-dedicated public space (such as public transport stops, stations and squares) and also explores the challenges and the efforts to regulate combined passenger/freight mobility.

B   Urban Logistics Sectors

In order to obtain a full understanding of the complexities of urban logistics, it is essential to understand the different types of demand and the operational needs of the various sectors. Parcels are the most familiar sector, given the growth in e-commerce, yet retail and fashion stores continue to dominate shopping areas and have particular needs for their goods. E-commerce in all its forms is rapidly changing the notion of the traditional high street, from parcel delivery to local hubs to dark stores. In addition, the complexity of services provided in cities means that significant demand for transport comes from service sectors, including food, healthcare and construction, each of which has their own needs such as temperature-controlled delivery or safety requirements.

In Chapter 8, Koen Mommens and Cathy Macharis present an overview of the parcels sector, which is one of the most recognisable types of urban logistics, given the growth of e-commerce and home delivery. They note that parcel deliveries are still dominated by diesel trucks, and they present the results of a study to compare this current approach with alternatives such as electric vehicles and cargo bikes, along with the use of micro hubs and a network of lockers. Their analysis reveals the potential for significant carbon emission savings, both from the logistics operations as well as the travel behaviour of consumers.

In Chapter 9, Leigh Sparks covers the specific features of the retail sector. The chapter demonstrates that retailing logistics has become a highly sophisticated operation over recent decades, and identifies the pressures on urban systems and the complications of urban delivery to stores, as well as discussing how trends for fast fashion, online sales and omnichannel retailing have increased and added costs and complexity. The author discusses how concerns over the environmental impact of fashion and retail logistics and recent disruptions to supply chains (such as Brexit, COVID-19 and shipping and labour shortages) have exerted further pressure on retail systems. Looking to the future, the author discusses how the sector may respond to a combination of influences, including the disruptions of recent years, the operational constraints on the supply chain and increasing environmental pressures.

In Chapter 10, Heleen Buldeo Rai examines how e-commerce and dark stores have transformed the retail landscape and what this means for urban logistics. The chapter charts how, in an attempt to remain relevant in the e-commerce era, traditional retailers converted to multichannel and omnichannel models, in which they combine online and offline retail channels. Stores are now multifunctional hubs, acting as showrooms, collection points, returns facilities, micro-warehouses and micro-fulfilment centres. New models include 'warestores' (with a part of the store dedicated to fulfilment only) and 'dark stores' (with the entire store temporarily or permanently dedicated to fulfilment only), thus altering the way they interact with urban logistics operations.

In Chapter 11, Eleonora Morganti describes the sector of food logistics. This chapter provides an overview of the recent evolution of the four main stakeholders in the urban food transport system: the food transport industry, the food distribution channels, households and the city government. The linkages and the interactions among these stakeholders are illustrated and discussed in the context of urban logistics, pointing out many specific features of this sector, such as distinct handling procedures, temperature-controlled transport, a high number of receivers (supermarkets and food outlets), small volumes, high-frequency and non-homogeneous transport units (pallets, parcels and boxes). The author's analysis reveals that receivers, both businesses and households, set increasingly high performance standards that must be met, including shorter time windows, no minimum order amount and higher frequency of deliveries, all of which impact on the availability and choice of transport type.

In Chapter 12, Liz Breen, Sarah Schiffling and Ying Xie highlight that the healthcare sector is the largest employer in many urban areas, providing vital services to the population at hospitals, doctors' surgeries, pharmacies and a wide range of other settings. Service provision is facilitated by complex logistics operations, involving the processing of people, goods and high volumes of information and is also governed by legislation and policy. The chapter demonstrates a differentiation between routine logistics such as regular deliveries to pharmacies that can be planned in advance and emergency logistics such as ambulances that have to operate in a highly agile manner. The authors discuss how the particular challenges of urban areas such as traffic congestion can hinder logistics operations to the detriment of patients, in addition to considering the many specificities of the sector's needs, such as temperature-controlled transport and disposal of medical waste through reverse logistics chains.

In Chapter 13, Russell G. Thompson, Oleksandra Osypchuk and Stanisław Iwan explain that the storage and transport of materials for construction projects is essential for the development of urban areas. They demonstrate that new residences, offices, retail and industrial developments as well as infrastructure projects generate a large amount of construction activity and that improving efficiency, sustainability and reliability are major challenges in construction logistics. This chapter considers how construction-orientated city logistics initiatives are being implemented, including urban consolidation centres, construction delivery plans, night deliveries and inland waterways. Trends and issues related to the implementation of advanced technologies, including building information systems and intelligent transport systems, are also described.

C Technical Analysis

Given the complexities of managing the competing demands of urban logistics, technical analysis is needed to resolve and optimise these issues. One of the key questions in logistics is how many distribution centres, depots and warehouses are optimal and where they should be located, as more facilities could reduce transport costs but increase total logistics costs. Linked to these decisions is the management and optimisation of vehicle routing between these facilities and to the final destinations at stores or customer homes. Digitalisation is increasing in all parts of modern life and its use in urban logistics allows for better use of mobile assets as well as higher levels of customer service. In order to resolve both old challenges of space limitations as well as new challenges of improved flexibility to adapt to complex supply chains, new processes are continually being proposed and tested, such as new types of containers to facilitate enhanced multimodality in the urban space.

In Chapter 14, Takanori Sakai, Adrien Beziat and Adeline Heitz provide an overview of facility locations in urban logistics. They show that compared with other land-use types in cities, such as home, work, school and leisure, logistics land use has unique characteristics. Due to logistics being a network-based activity, the areas used for logistics facilities are intermediate points for commodity flows. The authors highlight the key influences on these locations such as the trend in spatial distribution (e.g. logistics metropolitan concentration, logistics sprawl, logistics clustering, the growth in proximity logistics and spatial hysteresis), the production of externalities and the evolution of policies for logistics facility locations. Their analysis also highlights the challenges ahead for sustainable logistics land use in urban environments.

In Chapter 15, Imen Ben Mohamed, Olivier Labarthe, Yann Bouchery, Walid Klibi and Gautier Stauffer analyse multi-echelon urban distribution network models. The chapter presents and discusses existing location and routing models that have been studied in the last decade, in which a special focus is given to integrated and multi-echelon models suitable for the urban context. Given the new challenges to the urban logistics landscape (e.g. the COVID-19 pandemic, the rapid expansion of e-commerce and increased attention to sustainability), the extension of these models is discussed and the challenge of their adequacy and solvability is raised. Emerging challenges and major organisational paradigms are also shared to propose perspectives for future research.

In Chapter 16, Lóránt Tavasszy and Hans Quak consider computing technology and its applications in urban logistics. They discuss how advances in this technology have allowed paper-based administrations to become digitalised and enriched logistics systems with various new capabilities, such as automated sensing, connectivity and communication, data analytics and automated decision-making. They show that the impact of digitalisation on logistics business is being felt in three ways: through increased availability of transport assets and products, through general improvements in service levels and through new digitally integrated services like e-commerce. The authors discuss current concepts such as cyber-physical systems, physical internet, industry 4.0 and logistics 4.0. The chapter provides a systematic overview of the recent and upcoming innovations in computing technology and discusses how these are reshaping the urban logistics landscape.

In Chapter 17, Michael G. H. Bell, Veronica Schulz and Shengda Zhu discuss the use of small containers for evolving logistics in changing cities. They show how the growing expectations of on-demand and same-day delivery are increasing the volume of small shipments circulating in cities, while, at the same time, the urban streetscape is changing, with road space reallocation to active transport and the rapid rollout of bike lanes. The authors review previous attempts at co-modality (the use of public transport to carry cargo) and propose a new kind of city container with the footprint of the Europallet to support the growth of city logistics. They present a feasibility study for a co-modal scheme involving these city containers and the ferry network in Sydney, Australia and draw conclusions about the potential for this kind of scheme.

D Policy

While to some degree public policy is more often directed at the movement of people, aiming to ensure high-quality public transport and dealing with the challenges of congestion and emissions on public roads, in more recent times public actors are becoming more involved in questions of freight transport. At the urban level, policy-makers seek to ensure that local businesses are supported by free flow of their goods, while at the same time aiming to reduce issues of congestion and emissions in this concentrated space where residents also live and work. Thus, policy-makers introduce certain regulations that apply to all vehicles such as road charging or low-emission zones, as well as specific freight-related policies such as managing loading bays, supporting urban consolidation centres and introducing public parcel lockers.

In Chapter 18, Laetitia Dablanc analyses policy and planning for urban logistics, by discussing policies that, directly or indirectly, aim to reduce its negative impacts (e.g. pollution, energy consumption, congestion, accidents) and increase its positive impacts (e.g. provision of urban jobs, promotion of the economic vitality of cities, service innovation). Policy interventions from the local to the national level are discussed, from which the author develops nine best practices: freight consultation forums, low- and zero-emission zones, the promotion of clean delivery vehicles, road pricing, off-hour deliveries, kerbside management, urban planning, support for innovative start-ups and new methods for freight data collection.

In Chapter 19, Edoardo Marcucci, Valerio Gatta and Ila Maltese explore the role of policy acceptance and implementation in urban logistics, focussing on stakeholder engagement, stakeholder preferences and process replicability. In this chapter, they aim to shed light on a complex set of activities, organised and managed by different and potentially conflicting stakeholders, whose consequences impact citizens, sometimes unaware of the role they also play within the whole system. They argue that it is essential to start from the perspective of *ex-ante* policy acceptability, whereby decision-makers can assess and identify the most prominent and sustainable interventions.

In Chapter 20, Oriana Calderón, José Holguín-Veras and Stephen Ison provide an overview of the role of road pricing and initiatives relating to urban logistics management aiming not only to make urban activity more efficient but also to contribute to sustainable cities. The authors summarise the economics of road pricing, discuss its advantages and disadvantages, review current road pricing measures, discuss the use of incentives as an alternative to road pricing and examine the lessons learned from implementations that have taken place. Finally, the authors suggest potential road pricing measures for urban logistics that allocate the externalities to the agent causing them, and also discuss considerations for the design or reforming of freight road pricing schemes in an era of technological and climate change.

In Chapter 21, Emine Zehra Akgün and Jason Monios consider the role of urban consolidation centres (UCCs) in urban logistics. They show how UCCs are usually initiated by local authorities to mitigate problems concerning air quality, congestion and road safety, but their implementation requires collaboration between various stakeholders with different objectives and priorities, the main ones being local authorities, logistics service providers (LSPs) and retailers. Their analysis concludes that a successful UCC usually requires a commitment of financial support over at least the medium term, allowing time for the system to mature and collaborative service offerings to be developed.

In Chapter 22, Andisheh Ranjbari, Anne Goodchild and Elizabeth Guzy identify success factors for urban logistics pilot studies. They evaluate potential urban logistics solutions such as parcel lockers, deploying street parking sensors, setting up and operating a multi-service micro hub and collaborating in a cargo e-bike implementation. From a review of these initiatives, they develop five types of success factors: identifying the right location, securing required permits and agreements, collaboration between involved parties, engaging local agencies and community associations in marketing and advertising efforts, and establishing regulations and processes for new strategies and technologies.

E Sustainability

Sustainability is no longer the optional "add-on" it may once have been, but a minimum level of quality and liveability towards which cities are increasingly aiming. Moreover, sustainability is increasingly recognised as covering more than just the environment, but social and economic issues as well. In this section, the authors consider first of all the challenge of climate change and decarbonisation options for urban logistics, whether that involves switching to zero-carbon fuels or alternative modes of transport. The authors also consider some specificities of urban logistics in megacities and in the Global South, recognising that not all cities are the same and a geographically differentiated perspective is required when discussing the urban level. In addition, when focussing on the transport of goods, it must be recognised that the vehicles do not (yet) drive themselves, and questions of employment conditions and inclusivity are essential yet frequently overlooked aspects of sustainable cities. Finally, the unavoidable question of the effect of the COVID-19 pandemic, which impacted our daily lives and habits and questioned the permanence of our supply chain structures at all levels, is considered.

In Chapter 23, Maria Attard approaches the important topic of climate change and urban logistics, in which she argues that the consequences of inaction are too negative to ignore and every sector, including that of logistics, has to adapt. In this chapter, the author reviews the literature on climate change and identifies the potential impacts of climate change on the urban level, and then discusses the contributions of urban logistics to the management of mitigation measures in an attempt to reduce the burden of emissions from the sector, as well as shift the sector to alternative, more sustainable, modes of transport.

In Chapter 24, Genevieve Giuliano and Sue Dexter explore the decarbonisation of road freight and the potential for alternative fuels for urban logistics. While arguing that goods movement is essential for both people and the economy, and demand for goods movement will continue to grow, the authors focus primarily on the decarbonisation of medium and heavy-duty trucks. They evaluate a broad range of technology and policy solutions, with a particular focus on alternative fuels as the strategy with both the greatest potential and greatest risks.

In Chapter 25, Nora Mareï considers urban logistics in the Global South. As the majority of research on urban logistics has addressed the Global North, this chapter analyses how logistics strategies are implemented in cities that are faced with strong demographic and spatial growth but suffer from a lack of planning, organisation and compliance with development and urbanism standards. The author argues that a logistics transition must work alongside an urban transition, and thus may require a modification of production and consumption systems in countries of the Global South.

In Chapter 26, Quan Yuan examines urban logistics in megacities, identifying a relationship between logistics activities and urban structure. The chapter summarises the major factors driving the trends in which logistics facilities and vehicles are organised in megacities, and discusses how such trends affect urban areas in terms of environmental and social externalities. In this analysis, the author incorporates the perspectives of both public and private sectors and identifies best practice in the United States, Europe and Asia that aim to reduce conflicts and improve the sustainability of urban logistics in megacities.

In Chapter 27, Geraint Harvey, Naveena Prakasam and Refat Shakirzhanov consider the gig economy and urban logistics. The authors consider the nature of work in this sector and how it is defined and regulated, with a specific analysis of three urban logistics organisations: Uber, Deliveroo and Amazon Flex. The authors explain why this type of work is often considered to be false self-employment, and they also consider the future of work in this sector and whether the success of gig economy firms is predicated upon the continuation of this quasi-employment model.

In Chapter 28, Anicia Jaegler, Salomée Ruel, Nadine Kafa and Lucy Budd cover gender diversity in urban logistics. The analysis shows that despite studies demonstrating that gender diversity improves business outcomes, the urban logistics sector globally is overwhelmingly male-dominated. The authors point out that there has been little academic research into the opportunities for, benefits of, and challenges to achieving greater gender diversity in urban logistics. Therefore, in this chapter, the authors elucidate the key benefits of gender diversity in the workforce, highlight the challenges to achieving gender diversity and equality in the urban logistics sector and, finally, offer practical recommendations as to how urban logistics can become more gender-equal and benefit from a more diverse talent pool.

In Chapter 29, John R. Bryson reviews the post-pandemic impacts of COVID-19 on urban logistics. The chapter reveals that the pandemic has challenged existing systems and processes as well as accelerating pre-pandemic trends, while at the same time forcing governments and companies to focus on improvisations and recovery processes. The chapter explores the pandemic and its impacts on urban logistics by highlighting processes of continuity and change, while also considering the role of urban logistics in the context of the post-pandemic city.

Conclusion

The diversity of subjects covered in this *Handbook* shows that urban logistics is a complex and rapidly changing field. Not only are the foundational elements such as transport modes constantly evolving, but new demands for good movements are emerging, as are new methods for managing and processing both the goods and, increasingly, the information. The need to address the negative impacts of urban logistics is now firmly on the agenda, a challenge that is only exacerbated by social, cultural and political trends and unexpected events such as the COVID-19 pandemic and the ever-more unavoidable impacts of climate change. As editors, our aim has been to address all of these issues and to strike a balance between informing our readers while at the same time opening up new debates and looking to the future. No doubt some issues have been overlooked, inevitable with such a broad subject as urban logistics, which touches on all aspects of our lives. Nevertheless, we are pleased with the outcome. We feel it will make a major contribution to the study and understanding of urban logistics.

Acknowledgements

Finally, we would like to add that an edited book is only as good as the input of the contributors. We thank all of the authors for giving their time and for sharing their best work with us, and for responding to editor demands for revisions and updates and most of all for keeping to the tight deadlines. All three editors have found the experience rewarding and took great pleasure working with all of the contributors. We hope you are as pleased as we are with the outcome.

This *Handbook* would not have been possible without the support of Routledge throughout the process. We would specifically like to thank Guy Loft for the initial discussion, Alex Atkinson for commissioning the book and Manjusha Mishra for guiding us through the production process.

References

International Transport Forum (2021). ITF Transport Outlook 2021. OECD Publishing. https://www.oecd-ilibrary.org/transport/itf-transport-outlook-2021_16826a30-en

United Nations Department of Economic and Social Affairs (2018). World Urbanization Prospects: The 2018 Revision, United Nations. https://population.un.org/wup/Publications/Files/WUP2018-Report.pdf

2
THE ROLE OF URBAN LOGISTICS IN THE CITY ECONOMY

Michael Browne and Sam McLeod

Introduction

The movement of goods through and within cities fundamentally reflects how economies have evolved to support production and consumption, and to maintain standards of living. Patterns in urban logistics are continually evolving – responding to market competition and prevailing economic conditions, adapting to policy and regulation and capitalising on emergent technological opportunities. Since these freight flows are influenced by a myriad of complex and ever-changing systems – right up to the complex political and geographical dynamics that shape economics – gaining insight into urban logistics requires a broad and multidimensional view, and an openness to other fields of study and unexpected discoveries. This is especially important in informing how the future of urban logistics and urban economies can be made more efficient and sustainable, and illustrates the importance of multi-disciplinary studies in freight and logistics.

In this chapter, the aim is to chart foundational principles in the study of logistics. Through doing so, we aim to empower readers with a summary of the major ideas spanning freight and logistics research. The chapter seeks to address four questions: what is urban logistics, why are there common problems in urban logistics, what can be done to improve urban logistics and what might be next for urban logistics?

What Is Urban Logistics?

Urban logistics is the movement of goods in cities. Urban logistics often receives particular research focus, since the impacts of freight in urban areas are typically the most concentrated and visible. The passage of cargo within cities, mainly through the last mile of supply chains or individual trips, tends to produce the greatest environmental and social impacts, while also representing a large proportion of the total cost of transporting something (Allen et al., 2018). In this chapter, the last mile may refer to the final leg of transport of goods from a business to a consumer (B2C), from a consumer to a business (C2B – such as returns or waste collection), or from one business to another (B2B). Urban logistics can also encompass transportation to deliver services (Cherrett et al., 2012).

Many elements of urban logistics are characterised by heterogeneity – this extends to vehicle types and sizes, products carried, services provided by transport operators, origins and destinations of trips, and the logistics activities associated with different types of land use. In many cases, the city centre typically receives more research and policy attention than more peripheral areas. However, a narrow focus on the city core can be problematic, since developing an understanding of the flows of goods into and out of cities commonly requires a more coherent spatial view, to ascertain how trip and activity patterns relate to wider logistics structures and economic factors. The structure of urban logistics reflects the broader composition of systems of production. In turn, these structures are shaped by bases of competition, within a political-institutional context. Supply chains are highly dynamic at every scale because shippers (i.e. suppliers or businesses dispatching freight), carriers (the organisation managing logistics) and any sub-contractors compete[1] in their market segment to reduce costs and attract customers. These market participants may seek to innovate in ways that may not appear to optimise their supply chain. For instance, a supermarket may operate inefficient delivery services at a loss to gain market share or have vehicles out on the road as mobile outdoor advertising.

Two fundamental realities often characterise competition in logistics. Firstly, private freight and logistics operators usually cause negative impacts (such as noise, pollution, congestion, resource depletion and safety hazards – see Chapters 18 and 19) on other parties (such as neighbours, other travellers, the general public, on environments and ecosystems and on people intergenerationally) – but these impacts do not typically impose any direct cost for the operator or their customer (Mostert and Limbourg, 2016). In totality, these negative externalities cause enormous harm and economic damage and are a principal reason for government logistics regulation.

Secondly, many parts of supply chains exist in markets with low barriers to entry. Employment driving trucks or in the manual handling of goods may be highly substitutable, and – especially where under-regulated and/or commodified through market platforms – vulnerable to *the iron law of wages*.[2] In recent years, the proliferation of market platforms and crowdsourced delivery services (for instance, see Castillo et al., 2018) has only exacerbated hyper-competitive markets for urban logistics. Similarly, employment in manufacturing may be relocated to the lowest cost locations, though typically on a longer time span. This means that interventions or initiatives which add to costs and prices without creating well-recognised benefits are not likely to be durable.

Over the long run, competition and innovation have significantly reduced transport costs (Glaeser and Kohlhase, 2003), and improved the quality of service available to customers. Shippers, in particular, have capitalised on improvement in logistics to be able to offer "free" shipping, and increasingly quick and "instant" deliveries (Dablanc et al., 2017). Competition-based zero-price shipping and returns, and rapid delivery – while convenient for consumers – disincentivises more efficient shopping behaviour, such as consolidating purchases into one larger delivery.

Why Are There Common Problems in Urban Logistics?

Urban logistics issues are strikingly similar in many cities around the world (see Chapters 25 and 26). Similarly, many local or regional authorities struggle to implement initiatives to improve urban logistics that prove to be sustainable over the long term. In each case, there may be several explanations for this. Many urban logistics problems also relate to much broader issues of resource depletion, environmental degradation, economic equity and human rights.

Firstly, logistics impacts both transport and land-use patterns, resulting in complex dynamics and lock-in effects. Today, logistics has significantly de-localised consumer markets, by enabling trade – even for low volumes of consumer goods – to occur seamlessly across borders. These changes in the structure of logistics have significant and complex implications for urban land use (McKinnon, 2009). This is particularly the case as supply chains can be surprisingly sensitive to the price of land across the supply chain, and intolerant of many planning regulations imposed on land that may be used for logistics activity. As supply chains have become more globalised, many cities have seen logistics facilities relocate to low-cost and less-regulated peri-urban land, termed *logistics sprawl* (Aljohani and Thompson, 2016; Dablanc, 2014). Concurrently, many operators have reduced storage in retail or warehousing spaces, towards storing goods in transit, including in vehicles out for delivery (McLeod and Curtis, 2020; Rodrigue et al., 2001, p. 6). This may mean that logistics activity consumes more capacity on transport networks, and occupies more public land for parking and loading. Relatedly, the reconfiguration of logistics has also seen waves of change for urban retail land uses. The disruption of conventional retail by e-commerce over recent decades (see Chapter 10) is the latest wave of change, threatening the viability of many legacy retail models and land-use formats (Dolega and Lord, 2020).

Aside from land use, the true magnitude and economic cost of other negative external costs of logistics are often concealed or highly uncertain (see Chapters 18, 23 and 24). For instance, logistics contributes to air pollution, including greenhouse gases, with transportation constituting about a quarter of total energy-related CO_2 emissions (IPCC, 2015) – the full long-term impacts of which are incompletely known. Similarly, road and rail logistics vehicles tend to contribute to background noise, exposure to which is increasingly recognised as a significant public health issue (Khreis et al., 2016, p. 254). The contribution of logistics to traffic crash events is also highly diffuse and potentially irregular. Further, the impacts of logistics on the desirability of walking and cycling, and urban severance effects, are difficult to measure. The quantification of the total public health and amenity harms caused by urban logistics is exceptionally challenging, though they have an immense economic effect (Bickel et al., 2006, p. 398; Mindell and Karlsen, 2012). In turn, the diffuse and varied nature of these negative external costs may mean that they do not result in the immediate formation of political forces to address them. However, since they exert a significant economic toll, externalities should always be considered as a cost of logistics activity, and wherever possible these costs should be integrated into prices paid by customers through the supply chain.

Unfortunately, some forms of logistics activity – and the other manufacturing work involved through the goods supply chain – may exploit workers through low pay or poor conditions to increase cost competitiveness (see Chapters 27 and 28). Depending on how it is structured, the reliance of some forms of urban logistics on the exploitation of labour may be similarly obscured. Globalisation is widely recognised as a mechanism to devalue labour, and logistics has become increasingly less labour-intensive as technology has increased productivity. In particular, the emergence of market platforms, and their business model of constantly auctioning tasks based only on price, presents a threat to the employment standards of a wide scope of people working in logistics. This is especially the case where market platforms may compete with existing logistics businesses, which may be based on fairer standards. Market platforms may also exclude the workforce from having an active voice in how logistics services are managed. Taking this to increasing extremes, some of today's dominant market players in logistics have structured their business models to minimise operational employment to only very low-skill roles, performed by highly substitutable workers. These workers have no power to negotiate on increasingly precarious contract structures, which place costs on workers. This precarity is increasingly recognised as an impediment to economic development, and a cause of increasingly volatile politics (Lonergan and Blyth, 2020; Piketty, 2014).

Addressing the problems associated with urban logistics is challenging because identifying, developing, and implementing effective policy is exceedingly difficult. The regulation of logistics spans every level of government, and is commonly fragmented across many portfolios and agencies (McLeod and Curtis, 2020). Many authors have noted the wide range of stakeholders engaged in urban logistics (Bjørgen et al., 2021; Marcucci et al., 2017). Not surprisingly, the wide range creates complexities including difficulty in reaching agreement about priorities for action in both the long term (e.g. planning for future needs) and the shorter term (e.g. regulating freight movements). This makes it challenging to find simple solutions that can be implemented quickly.

Logistics activity almost always benefits from some form of subsidy, even if it may take the form of government provision of public infrastructure, or tolerance of negative externalities. At the most macro international level, the structure of supply chains today is highly globalised, with countries and regions generally having to exhibit some degree of specialisation to compete in their international trade. This is influenced by national trade and industrial policy, participation in supranational organisations and agreements, currency dynamics, labour and natural resource costs, infrastructure and capital and regulatory structures in each country (McLeod et al., 2019). At the regional level, state and regional governments may shape freight and logistics activity through many policy settings – primarily through economic policy and infrastructure provision. Governments themselves may seek to regulate or compete internationally in ways that do not appear to optimise long-run results. For instance, a regional government may compete with other regions to host industrial activity through their investments in infrastructure. While this may improve capacity, it does not improve the relative competitiveness of any region if every regional government is forced into making similar investments to remain competitive (Taylor, 1992). There are several examples of savvy private-sector enterprises shopping between governments in order to influence policy and achieve direct or indirect subsidies. Regional governments who aim to complete based on laxness of regulation risk trading the health and welfare of their population in exchange for less mature industrial activity (McLeod and Browne, Forthcoming).

Cities have a regional importance, and this can be especially true in the case of gateway cities with a major port or airport, or those which act as hubs within freight networks. Understanding the role played by cities in terms of nodes on major trade corridors is important and an area that is receiving more attention (Closs and Bolumole, 2015). As noted in this chapter, there is considerable competition for space within cities (see Chapter 14), which has implications for the role of cities as hubs in freight networks. There are inherent complexities and conflicts in attempting to intensify and expand the role of logistics hubs when there are already constraints on land use and an increased focus on densification within city planning. Freight activities for gateway functions provide employment and economic benefits, but there are also clear environmental trade-offs and studies increasingly point out social equity issues in terms of the location selected for logistics activities such as transhipment, storage and transport.

Local authorities often manage the most acute and obvious impacts of urban freight – especially parking and local traffic concerns – though they may exercise the most narrow degree of power, and have the most significant challenges resourcing freight and logistics initiatives (Lindholm and Blinge, 2014). Understanding freight and logistics is also complicated by operators' reluctance to share information or insight, which they may consider to be a competitive advantage or commercial-in-confidence (Lindawati et al., 2014).

The power of logistics operators to evolve supply chain structures around regulatory settings can fundamentally challenge the power of regulations. Rather than respond as policy-makers intended, logistics operators may simply continue to search for an alternative source of competitive advantage, especially one for which another party bears the costs. There is also the potential for rebound effects – where more efficient, low-cost innovations result in greater realisation of demand, thereby eroding overall actual benefits (IPCC, 2015).

What Can Be Done to Improve Urban Logistics?

While developing schemes to address logistics problems can be challenging, there remains immense scope to improve urban logistics (see Chapters 18–22), and the increasingly broad streams of research into freight and logistics offer insights into how to do so. Urban logistics may also benefit from emergent technologies and the transition towards renewable economies. Through this, the innovative capacity of participants in logistics markets is an immense resource, especially if it can be directed towards macro-level sustainability concerns. However, in the same way, the disruptive power of private-sector operators – especially if they exhibit a degree of monopolism or excessive corporate consolidation – can represent a barrier to facilitating economically resilient, low-impact, sustainable logistics systems.

Logistics studies have long retained a focus on operational optimisation. However, since urban logistics is shaped by decisions across the entire supply and value chains, examining logistics issues at this larger scale, and through the lens of different fields and disciplines, holds the most promise for achieving structural improvements in the economic efficiency of logistics systems (Strale, 2019). The public sector can use regulatory power to set controls and minimum standards for freight and logistics – especially at the local level, where regulators may set rules for captive delivery markets (Ville et al., 2013). If regulations are enforceable, these can transform the market by establishing fair rules and parameters to competition, preventing operators from using externalities to subsidise their activity.

As a highly simplified representation, the interface between a typical product supply chain, the urban logistics components of the supply chain, and the way that different levels of policy may interact with logistics activity is represented in Figure 2.1. Local delivery and the end customer component of the supply chain are captive to local regulations,

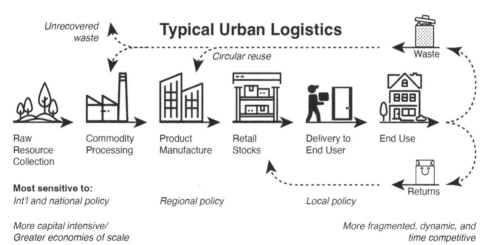

Figure 2.1 Simplified supply chain and interaction with policy levels
Source: The authors

whereas mass production at the start of supply chains may relocate to find more lax regulatory settings – meaning that only national or international policy may be effective. This figure also demonstrates the potential for more circular economies (Geissdoerfer et al., 2018) to localise re-use, which has significant potential for expanding the use of city – rather than international – logistics.

At the macro level of global production systems, locational competition based on the laxness of environmental controls, labour conditions, safety standards or taxation may influence production location choices and supply chain structures. Expanding the use of global minimum standards holds much promise for reducing regulatory evasion and improving urban logistics. Supranational and international standards, certification schemes, auditing, and alliances built on implementing sustainability principles can provide frameworks for building supply chains that have minimal external costs. Consumer-facing certification schemes (such as the Forest Stewardship Council FSC mark, the Australian GECA Standard, and ISO 14001 and 14024) may also be effective at providing the opportunity for citizens to make informed and conscious choices between products and their corresponding supply chains. All of these measures may confer an advantage for products adopting more circular production systems. However, the use of marketing standards or corporate self-certification (which may only reflect lax standards) risks providing consumers with a false impression about the structure and sustainability of the product's supply chain.

In terms of the transportation component of urban logistics, there is a generally agreed hierarchy of types of measures to improve sustainability, set out as Table 2.1. However, care must be taken to avoid assumptions about the overall efficiency and actual benefits of measures intended to improve urban logistics. For instance, economies of scale that may come with centralised production, plus the significant energy intensity advantage of maritime transport over land transport, may make longer supply chains more efficient than geographically shorter ones (Mathers et al., 2014). Accordingly, applied research should be a foundational part of freight policy-making.

Urban logistics can benefit immensely from cooperation between the public and private sectors. The role of the public sector in providing forms of subsidy to urban logistics should be recognised – different forms of subsidy may be much more visible than others. For example, generalised road spending effectively subsidises road freight, even if the infrastructure spending is primarily motivated or justified on the basis of passenger transport capacity. In contrast, public involvement in urban consolidation centres (see Chapter 21) is a highly visible form of logistics subsidy (Ville et al., 2013) – even

Table 2.1 Hierarchy of logistics sustainability measures

Type of measure	Related initiatives
Avoidance (or Reduction)	At the macro level: Reducing total consumption, circular economies
	At the operational level: Consolidation, backloading, local production or stockpiling, co-location, prevention of failed delivery attempts
Substitution (Modal Shift)	Intermodality, substitution of road transport for rail or maritime shipping, use of cargo cycles, swapping consumer trips for direct delivery
Efficiency Improvements	Use of cleaner and more autonomous vehicles, fuel substitution, pavement porters, safer vehicle design

Source: The authors, see also IPCC (2015)

though it may deliver a better overall economic outcome than road spending when negative external costs are fully considered. We contend that public investments in greener urban logistics should be recognised as delivering benefits well beyond delivery efficiency.

Governments may also strive to improve their capacity and maturity as a leading participant in the systems of urban logistics. Generally, policy-makers may do so through: collaboration between levels of government (vertical integration); collaboration between agencies (horizontal integration); providing funding and participating in relevant research and development; internal capacity-building – especially in the professional development of staff; deploying participatory frameworks, methods and tools; applying inter-jurisdictional learning; and facilitating policy diffusion and transfer (Hull, 2008; Marsden and Stead, 2011).

As this chapter has identified, developing coherent urban logistics policies has been a major challenge for cities. But there have been promising developments, particularly in the last decade. Freight and logistics research has increasingly turned to participatory methods to involve operators and stakeholders in policy-making (Lindholm and Browne, 2013; Marcucci et al., 2017). There has also been a growing wealth of practical logistics research programmes illustrating the value of collaboration across government, academia and private enterprise (Allen et al., 2007). For instance, the initial focus of the concept of Sustainable Urban Mobility Plans (an initiative emerging from research supported by the European Commission) focussed on passenger transport and personal mobility. Increasingly, European cities are widening the scope of these plans to include freight transport and logistics – resulting cases in the development of Sustainable Urban Logistics Plans (SULPs). For instance, the EU project ENCLOSE (Ambrosino et al., 2014) and the NORSULP project in Norway (TØI, 2019) have focussed on the development of SULPs. The CIVITAS research programme (van Rooijen and Quak, 2014) proposed six categories of measures/initiatives that are likely to be relevant for many cities: stakeholder engagement; regulations; market-based initiatives; land-use planning; new technology-driven measures; and 'ecologistics' awareness-raising measures.

Policy-makers seeking to implement practical initiatives to address freight and logistics issues in cities now have access to a large and growing body of knowledge to draw upon. Research activity on freight and logistics issues has seen a significant focus towards examining urban issues over the last two decades. Increasingly, research projects have sought to examine evidence and test practical initiatives within multiple cities. Major examples of such research projects, initiatives and programmes from around the world are listed in Table 2.2. To our knowledge, the European Union and the United States have the strongest tradition of establishing large, multi-city urban logistics research projects.

A number of freight and logistics research networks also continue to facilitate research cooperation and dissemination, often serving as a bridge for researchers to relate their local research to the global corpus of knowledge. These networks are found at the global level (see Table 2.3). Many of these networks are co-funded by governments, academic institutions, and commercial organisations, and can be particularly valuable given the associated potential for knowledge and policy translation and transfer.

While the growing body of published knowledge and the continued work of these international networks provides a strong base for informing proactive measures to improve urban logistics, most cities will continue to face significant challenges putting theory into practice. As noted in this chapter, cities are complex and heterogeneous, and the combination of measures required to address freight issues will vary from one city to another. This means that

Table 2.2 Major urban logistics research programmes

Project/Initiative	Objectives
Best Urban Freight Solutions (BESTUFS) thematic network funded by the European Commission 2000–2008.	To identify, describe and disseminate information on best practices, success criteria and bottlenecks of urban freight transport solutions; and develop enhanced networking between those engaged in urban logistics activities.
The Transferability of Urban Logistics Concepts and Practices from a World Wide Perspective (TURBLOG) project took place between 2009 and 2011 and aimed at supporting research implementation and translation.	Strong focus on sharing experiences between Europe and Latin America.
CITYLAB (2011–2016) was supported by the EU CIVITAS initiative.	The approach was built around creating innovation by means of living labs in cities.
The United States' National Cooperative Freight Research Program (NCFRP) Project 38 (2012–2014) delivered NCFRP Report 33 – Improving Freight System Performance in Metropolitan Areas.	A major research project to develop a planning guide report (Holguín-Veras et al., 2015).
European Union's Horizon 2020 research and innovation programme Urban Logistics as an On-Demand Service (ULAADS) project has focussed on the urban last mile, and is ongoing.	Focussed on establishing local collaboration in practical urban logistics solutions in several cities in Europe.
ICLEI's EcoLogistics project (2017–2021) supported by the German Federal Ministry for the Environment, Nature Conservation and Nuclear Safety (BMU) through the International Climate Initiative (IKI). Involving 9 cities in Argentina, Colombia, and India.	Focuses on capacity building among governmental and non-governmental actors to promote low-carbon and more sustainable urban freight transport through local action and national support.

Source: Compiled by the authors

planning solutions need to be carefully customised by city authorities – which in many cases lack resources, and are not necessarily strongly-focussed on urban logistics (Lindholm and Blinge, 2014). Relatedly, many lessons from other cities can be difficult to transfer because of the specific differences between cities – and, also to some extent, because of local attitudes and the generic 'not invented here' problem.

These factors may slow down the speed of change in devising ways to integrate urban logistics into the liveability strategy of a city. However, the growing focus on how to create and support change – for example, the roadmaps for urban logistics created by ALICE/ERTRAC (2015) – combined with the increased awareness of the importance of robust business models for initiatives and projects, does point towards promising opportunities. As outlined, combining policies, strategies and initiatives between the public and private sectors is essential to shape better approaches to urban logistics planning. Academic and applied researchers are getting closer to creating the tools and models needed to provide deeper insights into how different policies can be combined and the consequences of these actions. Such tools and models also require a more coherent and sustained commitment to develop a framework for data collection related to urban logistics.

Table 2.3 Urban logistics research networks

Network	Summary
World Conference on Transport Research Special Interest Group in Urban Goods Movement.	Launched 1995 and continues to provide a platform for sharing research insights on a global basis by means of conferences, seminars and workshops.
Standing Committee on Urban Freight Transportation (AT025) of the Transportation Research Board (TRB).	The committee provides a link between researchers and practitioners – the TRB conference is increasingly international.
Institute for City Logistics (ICL) was established in Kyoto, Japan, in 1999.	The Institute is a focal point for sharing research findings bringing together academics and practitioners to exchange knowledge, experience and information mainly through a bi-annual conference.
The Volvo Research and Educational Foundations (VREF) initiative on Urban Freight 2012 to present.	The VREF initiative has supported a major programme of research and outreach that has enhanced urban logistics knowledge considerably. The structure has involved research centres that have developed networks conducting both research and working on how the research can be applied by practitioners and policy-makers.

Source: Compiled by the authors

What Might Be Next for Urban Logistics?

The coming years are likely to herald significant change and transformation of urban logistics. Even if structural, long-term globalisation continues, patterns in urban logistics are likely to continue to evoke, potentially at an increasingly rapid pace. The response to the crises of climate change, resource depletion, geopolitical tensions and economic equity will involve the reorientation of supply chains and the transformation of urban logistics. Many events of recent years starkly reveal the vulnerability of 'highly optimised' lean supply chains, and the presumption towards low stockholding and just-in-time supply chains may now be broken. Similarly, as this chapter has identified, the economic impacts of costs being passed to other parties create political pressures that are increasingly likely to challenge the status quo. So, what might be in transit for the future of urban logistics?

At the most basic level, technology will likely continue to facilitate productivity improvements and cost efficiency for urban logistics, especially if greater use of renewable energy might power an increasing share of goods transportation. Much like many other areas of transport policy, especially for frontiers such as electric and automated vehicles, considerable caution should be taken towards promising technologies which may solve individual problems while missing – or exacerbating – others. Critically, we contend that every improvement in efficiency must be seen primarily as an opportunity to address and rectify significant negative external costs before any direct cost savings are passed on to lower the prices paid by consumers. This recognises the inequity of negative costs borne by others, and the risk of rebound effects. Whether this is achieved might depend on the effectiveness of government policy-making, as discussed in the previous section.

The rise of circular economies holds potential for urban logistics, because previously split flows of waste and production may become increasingly connected, challenging import models (see Figure 2.1). Similarly, the potential for reshoring is significant, including for reasons of: national security, supply surety; economic self-sufficiency; and local employment. Advances in manufacturing technology, consistent environmental regulation across countries, and circular forms of production may also support the ability of post-industrial cities to return to manufacturing a greater share of the goods they consume. With the continued expansion of automation, the future of employment is also likely to push human involvement out of more logistics activity.

Looking toward these potential futures, it is critical that researchers and practitioners continue to develop the improved analytical approaches needed to understand and address these complex issues. There are many signs that this work is becoming more widespread (such as through the research programmes and networks described in this chapter). For instance, work continues to examine the relationship of cities and land use in wider supply chains. More locally, there has been growing interest in the scope to develop better analytical approaches for optimising urban logistics activities, such as in hubs and loading spaces (such as including examining use and availability and pricing options). This is promising, recognising the fundamental challenges of competition, heterogeneity and complexity, and managing issues of priority and allocation as have been explored in this chapter.

Conclusions

In this chapter, we have sought to define urban logistics, and chart its wide-ranging economic impacts. In doing so, we have explored the foundational reasons why cities worldwide face similar challenges in ensuring urban logistics contribute positively to economic activity and human welfare. Examining urban freight in this way demonstrates how issues of urban logistics go far beyond the narrow domains of transportation, or commerce, or operations, or city planning. We contend that the study of urban logistics must tie together knowledge about a range of issues, and be based on a strong understanding of the forces which incentivise supply chain structures (see McLeod and Curtis, 2020). Developing policies and strategies to reshape or reform urban logistics also depends on examining the important cross-sectoral and inter-disciplinary issues that surround the entire supply chain.

As we have outlined, urban logistics is likely to see a period of accelerating change and transformation. Indeed, change is urgently needed to improve the efficiency and sustainability of the urban logistics systems we depend on to support living standards. With the control and shape and direction of this change being shared across many different fields, domains and sectors, everyone involved in urban logistics has the potential to deliver improvements.

Notes

1 In a highly integrated supply chain, the shipper and carrier(s) may be the same entity.
2 Widely attributed to Lassalle.

References

ALICE/ERTRAC, (2015). *Urban Freight Research Roadmap.* ALICE/ERTRAC, Brussels.
Aljohani, K., and Thompson, R.G., 2016. Impacts of logistics sprawl on the urban environment and logistics: Taxonomy and review of literature. *Journal of Transport Geography 57,* 255–263. http://dx.doi.org/10.1016/j.jtrangeo.2016.08.009

Allen, J., Piecyk, M., Piotrowska, M., McLeod, F., Cherrett, T., Ghali, K., Nguyen, T., Bektas, T., Bates, O., Friday, A., Wise, S., and Austwick, M., (2018). Understanding the impact of e-commerce on last-mile light goods vehicle activity in urban areas: The case of London. *Transportation Research Part D: Transport and Environment 61*, 325–338. https://doi.org/10.1016/j.trd.2017.07.020

Allen, J., Thorne, G., and Browne, M., (2007). *BESTUFS Good Practice Guide on Urban Freight Transport*. BESTUFS, Karlsruhe.

Ambrosino, G., Guerra, S., Pettinelli, I., and Sousa, C., (2014). The role of logistics services in smart cities: The experience of ENCLOSE project, in: *Proceedings of 19th International Conference on Urban Planning, Regional Development and Information Society*. Presented at the 19th International Conference on Urban Planning, Regional Development and Information Society, CORP–Competence Center of Urban and Regional Planning, Vienna, 1029–1034.

Bickel, P., Friedrich, R., Link, H., Stewart, L., and Nash, C., (2006). Introducing environmental externalities into transport pricing: Measurement and implications. *Transport Reviews 26*, 389–415. https://doi.org/10.1080/01441640600602039

Bjørgen, A., Fossheim, K., and Macharis, C., (2021). How to build stakeholder participation in collaborative urban freight planning. *Cities 112*, 103149. https://doi.org/10.1016/j.cities.2021.103149

Castillo, V.E., Bell, J.E., Rose, W.J., and Rodrigues, A.M., (2018). Crowdsourcing last mile delivery: Strategic implications and future research directions. *Journal of Business Logistics 39*, 7–25. https://doi.org/10.1111/jbl.12173

Cherrett, T., Allen, J., McLeod, F., Maynard, S., Hickford, A., and Browne, M., (2012). Understanding urban freight activity – key issues for freight planning. *Journal of Transport Geography 24*, 22–32. http://dx.doi.org/10.1016/j.jtrangeo.2012.05.008

Closs, D.J., and Bolumole, Y.A., (2015). Transportation's role in economic development and regional supply chain hubs. *Transportation Journal 54*, 33–54. https://doi.org/10.5325/transportationj.54.1.0033

Dablanc, L., (2014). Logistics sprawl and urban freight planning issues in a major gateway city, in: Gonzalez-Feliu, J., Semet, F., Routhier, J.-L. (Eds.), *Sustainable Urban Logistics: Concepts, Methods and Information Systems*. Springer, Berlin, 49–69.

Dablanc, L., Morganti, E., Arvidsson, N., Woxenius, J., Browne, M., and Saidi, N., (2017). The rise of on-demand 'Instant Deliveries' in European cities. *Supply Chain Forum: An International Journal 18*, 203–217. https://doi.org/10.1080/16258312.2017.1375375

Dolega, L., and Lord, A., (2020). Exploring the geography of retail success and decline: A case study of the Liverpool City Region. *Cities 96*, 102456. https://doi.org/10.1016/j.cities.2019.102456

Geissdoerfer, M., Morioka, S.N., de Carvalho, M.M., and Evans, S., 2018. Business models and supply chains for the circular economy. *Journal of Cleaner Production 190*, 712–721. https://doi.org/10.1016/j.jclepro.2018.04.159

Glaeser, E.L., and Kohlhase, J.E., (2003). Cities, regions and the decline of transport costs. *Papers in Regional Science 83*, 197–228. https://doi.org/10.1007/s10110-003-0183-x

Holguín-Veras, J., Amaya-Leal, J., Wojtowicz, J., Jaller, M., González-Calderón, C., Sánchez-Díaz, I., Wang, X., Haake, D.G., Rhodes, S.S., Frazier, R.J., Nick, M.K., Dack, J., Casinelli, L., and Browne, M., (2015). National Cooperative Freight Research Program, Transportation Research Board, National Academies of Sciences, Engineering, and Medicine, 2015. *Improving Freight System Performance in Metropolitan Areas: A Planning Guide*. Transportation Research Board, Washington, D.C. https://doi.org/10.17226/22159

Hull, A., (2008). Policy integration: What will it take to achieve more sustainable transport solutions in cities? *Transport Policy 15*, 94–103. https://doi.org/10.1016/j.tranpol.2007.10.004

IPCC, (2015). Transport, in: Edenhofer, O. (Ed.), *Climate Change 2014: Mitigation of Climate Change*. Cambridge University Press, 599–670.

Khreis, H., Warsow, K.M., Verlinghieri, E., Guzman, A., Pellecuer, L., Ferreira, A., Jones, I., Heinen, E., Rojas-Rueda, D., Mueller, N., Schepers, P., Lucas, K., and Nieuwenhuijsen, M., (2016). The health impacts of traffic-related exposures in urban areas: Understanding real effects, underlying driving forces and co-producing future directions. *Journal of Transport & Health 3*, 249–267. https://doi.org/10.1016/j.jth.2016.07.002

Lindawati, van Schagen, J., Goh, M., and de Souza, R., (2014). Collaboration in urban logistics: Motivations and barriers. *International Journal of Urban Sciences 18*, 278–290. https://doi.org/10.1080/12265934.2014.917983

Lindholm, M., and Browne, M., (2013). Local authority cooperation with urban freight stakeholders: A comparison of partnership approaches. *European Journal of Transport and Infrastructure Research, 13*(1). https://doi.org/10.18757/EJTIR.2013.13.1.2986

Lindholm, M.E., and Blinge, M., (2014). Assessing knowledge and awareness of the sustainable urban freight transport among Swedish local authority policy planners. *Transport Policy 32*, 124–131. https://doi.org/10.1016/j.tranpol.2014.01.004

Lonergan, E., and Blyth, M., (2020). *Angrynomics*. Agenda Publishing, Newcastle upon Tyne.

Marcucci, E., Le Pira, M., Gatta, V., Inturri, G., Ignaccolo, M., and Pluchino, A., (2017). Simulating participatory urban freight transport policy-making: Accounting for heterogeneous stakeholders' preferences and interaction effects. *Transportation Research Part E: Logistics and Transportation Review 103*, 69–86. https://doi.org/10.1016/j.tre.2017.04.006

Marsden, G., and Stead, D., (2011). Policy transfer and learning in the field of transport: A review of concepts and evidence. *Transport Policy 18*, 492–500. http://dx.doi.org/10.1016/j.tranpol.2010.10.007

Mathers, J., Wolfe, C., Norsworthy, M., and Craft, E., (2014). *The Green Freight Handbook*. Environmental Defense Fund.

McKinnon, A., (2009). The present and future land requirements of logistical activities. *Land Use Policy 26*, Supplement 1, S293–S301. http://dx.doi.org/10.1016/j.landusepol.2009.08.014

McLeod, S., and Browne, M., Forthcoming. *Planning for the Sustainability of Freight and Logistics: Strategic Guiding Principles for Regional Policy*.

McLeod, S., and Curtis, C., (2020). Understanding and planning for freight movement in cities: Practices and challenges. *Planning Practice & Research 35*, 201–219. https://doi.org/10.1080/02697459.2020.1732660

McLeod, S., Schapper, J.H.M., Curtis, C., and Graham, G., (2019). Conceptualizing freight generation for transport and land use planning: A review and synthesis of the literature. *Transport Policy 74*, 24–34. https://doi.org/10.1016/j.tranpol.2018.11.007

Mindell, J.S., and Karlsen, S., (2012). Community severance and health: What do we actually know? *Journal of Urban Health 89*, 232–246. https://doi.org/10.1007/s11524-011-9637-7

Mostert, M., and Limbourg, S., (2016). External costs as competitiveness factors for freight transport — A state of the art. *Transport Reviews 36*, 692–712. https://doi.org/10.1080/01441647.2015.1137653

Piketty, T., (2014). *Capital in the Twenty-First Century*. Harvard University Press.

Rodrigue, J.-P., Slack, B., and Comtois, C., (2001). The paradoxes of green logistics. Presented at the *World Conference on Transport Research (WCTR)*, Citeseer.

Strale, M., (2019). Sustainable urban logistics: What are we talking about? *Transportation Research Part A: Policy and Practice 130*, 745–751. https://doi.org/10.1016/j.tra.2019.10.002

Taylor, L., (1992). Infrastructural competition among jurisdictions. *Journal of Public Economics 49*, 241–259. https://doi.org/10.1016/0047-2727(92)90022-8

TØI, 2019. Prosjekt: NORSULP [WWW Document]. Transportøkonomisk institutt. URL https://www.toi.no/norsulp/ (accessed 6.26.22).

van Rooijen, T., and Quak, H., (2014). City logistics in the European CIVITAS initiative. *Procedia - Social and Behavioral Sciences*, Eighth International Conference on City Logistics 17-19 June 2013, Bali, Indonesia *125*, 312–325. https://doi.org/10.1016/j.sbspro.2014.01.1476

Ville, S., Gonzalez-Feliu, J., and Dablanc, L., (2013). The limits of public policy intervention in urban logistics: Lessons from Vicenza (Italy). *European Planning Studies 21*, 1528–1541. https://doi.org/10.1080/09654313.2012.722954

PART A

Transport Modes

3
ROAD TRANSPORT AND URBAN LOGISTICS

Maja Piecyk and Julian Allen

Introduction to Road Freight Transport in Urban Areas

The OECD (2002) defines a road as a 'line of communication (travelled way) using a stabilised base other than rails or air strips open to public traffic, primarily for the use of road motor vehicles running on their own wheels'. The earliest roads yet discovered, built from wooden logs, date back approximately 6,000 years, while roads built from stone have been in existence for more than 4,000 years, with networks of such roads in common use in ancient Egypt, Greece and Rome.

In urban areas, the road is commonly divided into the carriageway (also referred to as the roadway and highway) on which vehicles operate and the footway (also referred to as the pavement or sidewalk) on which pedestrians walk. In many towns and cities in developed countries, the point where the carriageway and footway meet is known as the kerb, and acts as a division between them. The kerb is typically raised above the height of the carriageway and the roadside of the kerb is used for vehicle stopping and other vehicle travel purposes (such as cycle lanes). Kerbs were used in cities in ancient Rome and can be seen in situ to this day in Pompeii (Poehler, 2017). However, the modern widespread usage of kerbs and well-surfaced footways first began in 18th-century London in efforts to modernise and beautify urban areas and improve road safety (White, 2010).

Both the carriageway and the footway are used for road freight transport. Various types of motorised and non-motorised vehicles are used to provide road freight transport in urban areas by travelling on the carriageway. Traditionally, the most commonly used have been heavy goods vehicles (usually over 3.5 tonnes gross weight – both articulated and rigid vehicles) and light goods vehicles (also referred to as light commercial vehicles and, more generally, as vans). In addition, other road vehicles used for freight transport include cars, motorcycles, mopeds and bicycles. More recently, the use of cargo cycles has been increasingly rapidly, which can be either manual or electrically assisted. Their use has been growing especially fast in larger cities (Mejia, 2021). Research and trials are also being carried out into connected autonomous vehicles (CAVs) for the transportation of goods, which will eventually replace the need for human drivers (Oxbotica, 2017; Paddeu et al., 2019).

In developing countries, powered two-wheelers (motorcycles, scooters and mopeds) and powered three-wheelers are also commonly used for urban freight transport, especially last-mile deliveries (Shah, 2018). In India, for example, these vehicles account for approximately 80% of total vehicles sold annually. The vast majority of these are powered two-wheelers, with approximately 20 million sold in 2018–2019, and accounting for approximately 60% of road vehicle fossil fuel consumption. It is estimated that approximately 637,000 powered three-wheelers were sold in India in 2019/2020 and that 20% of the 1.5 million three-wheelers fleet is used for goods transport (Anup and Yang, 2020; Auto Punditz, 2020; Gadepalli, 2009; Goldstein Market Intelligence, 2020; Kumar and Bhat, 2021; Sinha, 2021). In addition, in some urban areas in developing countries, carts are used to move goods either drawn by hand (i.e. humans on-foot) or by animals including horses, donkeys and oxen (Dablanc, 2009; Herzog, 2010).

Walking, on footways rather than on carriageways (also referred to as on-foot portering), is also used in dense urban areas. Walking includes deliveries operations carried out entirely on foot (such as delivery rounds by postal staff), as well as the part of the urban freight transport operation between the vehicle and the delivery or collection point. Robot droids have also recently been developed and are being tested and trialled for providing urban goods movement on footways but have many development challenges to address (Kapser and Abdelrahman, 2020; World Economic Forum and McKinsey and Company, 2021).

Urban road freight transport is essential to the economic prosperity and liveability of towns and cities. It consists of two types of operation: (i) those in which the movement and delivery/collection of goods is the primary purpose, and (ii) those in which the provision of servicing activities (but which also involve the movement of goods, tools and equipment to carry out the servicing task) is the primary purpose. Servicing activities are often overlooked in considerations of urban freight transport, but are equally important to urban functioning and lifestyle. Examples of such servicing activities include the work of engineers working for utility, telecommunications companies, plumbers, electricians, air conditioning and lighting engineers, carpenters, glaziers, roofers, builders, pest controllers, cleaners, security system providers, property maintenance personnel, surveyors, caterers and gardeners. While those providing these services may carry goods as part of their work, they are also likely to carry tools and equipment that are necessary for the services they provide (Anderson et al., 2001).

Road is by far the most commonly used mode for urban freight transport given its connectivity to commercial and residential buildings, which no other mode can provide. For example, in Greater London, approximately 89% of all goods lifted in 2012 were transported by HGV, in the Paris region 90% of all goods lifted in 2006 were transported by HGV, and in the New York Metropolitan Transportation Council (NYMTC) region 88% of all goods lifted in 2012 were transported by HGV (Allen et al., 2014; New York Metropolitan Transportation Council, 2017; Smart Freight Centre, 2017).

The most common forms of urban road freight transport in terms of the quantity of goods and services provided are conducted by motorised commercial goods vehicles (i.e. rigid and articulated heavy goods vehicles and light goods vehicles). In London, for example, light and heavy goods vehicles accounted for 17% and 3% of total motorised road traffic in 2020, respectively (Department for Transport, 2021a). Similarly, in Paris goods vehicles accounted for 20% of motorised road traffic in 2017 (Dablanc and Nicol, 2017).

As well as urban goods movement by road being carried out by freight transport operators and other commercial and public sector organisations, it is also performed by private individuals conveying their retail purchases from the point of purchase or collection (such as a locker bank or collection point) to their homes. However, this urban goods movement by private individuals is typically overlooked by policy-makers.

The types of products most commonly transported in urban goods movement by road (either by weight or volume) include: food and drink, non-food retail products, construction materials, post and parcels, and waste. In 2014, bulk construction materials accounted for approximately 30% of all tonnes lifted by HGVs on London journeys, while food and drink, waste and mail and parcels accounted for 25% and 20%, respectively (Allen et al., 2014). Some products are supplied from one commercial or public sector organisation to another (referred to as business-to-business transactions), while others, especially those that involve private consumers purchasing goods online, are supplied from a commercial organisation to a private individual or between two private individuals (referred to as business-to-consumer and consumer-to-consumer transactions, respectively). The growth in online shopping is resulting in substantial increases in urban goods movements carrying out these so-called 'last-mile deliveries' of groceries, parcels and packages containing non-food retail items, and meals ordered from restaurants, cafes and fast-food takeaways.

Operating Patterns for Urban Freight Transport by Road

The choice of vehicle type and the pattern of vehicle operation road-based urban goods movements depends on several factors including: the type, size and weight of product, the shipment size, the origin and destination locations of the journey, and the delivery lead time and service level agreements. Some vehicle operations involve single-drop work in which the vehicle collects goods at one location and delivers the entire load to the destination location. Other vehicle operations involve multi-drop work in which the vehicle stops at several or many locations to make deliveries and/or collections as part of its journey.

The geographical coverage of urban road freight transport journeys also varies depending on where the journey commences and ends. Some journeys take place wholly within an urban area, whereas others, while making deliveries and/or collections in an urban area have either an origin, destination or both outside of the urban area.

Surveys of goods vehicle deliveries and collections in urban areas in the United Kingdom over the last twenty years (over the period 1996–2015) have shown light goods vehicles are the dominant vehicle type, responsible for 40-65% of all vehicles loading and unloading depending on survey location, followed by rigid HGVs (approximately 20–50%) and articulated HGVs vehicles (usually 20% unless an industrial survey location). Cars accounted for less than 5% of vehicle deliveries in the majority of UK surveys, as did other vehicles (including motorcycles, bicycles and pedestrians) (Cherrett et al., 2012; Transport for London, 2015a, 2015b, 2015c, 2015d; Systra, 2017). However, the use of motorcycles, cargo cycles, bicycles and cars has grown rapidly in the years since these surveys took place due to growth in the demand for online shopping and the journeys this generates that originate at restaurants, fast-food takeaways, so-called 'dark kitchens' and grocery outlets offering online ordering and home delivery services. In the case of grocery and meals deliveries, a sizeable proportion of these take place in the evening and at weekends, thereby altering the profile of freight activity in these locations over the course of the day and week (Allen et al., 2021).

Delivery of goods in an urban area typically involves a vehicle stopping at the kerbside to load/unload, a small proportion of deliveries take place with the vehicle stopped off-street, if such facilities are available at the receiver's location. UK surveys of high streets and other busy commercial locations have found that 75% or more of goods vehicles making collections and deliveries stop at the kerbside, increasing to 90% or more in central urban locations where off-street stopping space is rarely available. Deliveries and collections in industrial areas of towns and cities often in outer urban locations tend to be more likely to involve off-street loading/unloading (Cherrett et al., 2012; Systra, 2017).

For all kerbside deliveries and collections, goods need to be conveyed across the footway between the vehicle and the building served. This can involve the driver simply carrying the goods if they are lightweight and not bulky. However, in many cases, drivers make use of manual handling equipment such as barrows, roll cages and pallet trucks to convey goods across the footway.

Research has identified that goods vehicle dwell times are influenced by a range of factors including: the distance from the goods vehicle to the premises being served, the type of product and whether or not the goods are unitised, the size of the delivery and the weight of the goods, the means of getting goods off the vehicle and conveying them to the premises, the number of people performing the delivery, the checking procedures necessary by the receiver and the proof of delivery requirements (Allen et al., 2000). Analysis of UK urban freight surveys has indicated that for freight planning in urban areas, approximately 30 minutes should be allowed for the average articulated HGV delivery, 20 minutes for deliveries by rigid HGVs, and 10 minutes for delivery by LGV (Cherrett et al., 2012).

Various urban freight studies from a range of countries have indicated insufficient provision of kerbside space for loading/unloading in totality and by time of day, poorly located kerbside loading/unloading in relation to the businesses served, the effect that lack of enforcement has on illegal car parking in loading/unloading space and on illegal use of the kerbside by goods vehicles (Alho et al., 2018; Chen et al., 2017; Dezi et al., 2010; Ezquerro et al., 2020; Intermodality, 2004; Jaller et al., 2013, Silva et al., 2020; Urban Freight Lab, 2019; Wenneman et al., 2015). All of these factors lead to higher rates of illegal goods vehicle loading/unloading at the kerbside.

Goods vehicle drivers may discover on arrival at the building or street where delivery/collection is scheduled to take place that no kerbside loading space is available. This can result in the driver stopping illegally or having to circulate in the hope that space becomes available or in an effort to find somewhere else to stop. A study in Seattle estimated 'cruising' time of 2.3 minutes per goods vehicle journey as the driver tried to locate a legal stopping space (Dalla Chiara and Goodchild, 2020). This can also lead to disruption to urban businesses and other receivers if, as a result, delivery is delayed or unable to take place when intended.

For urban freight operations in which providing a servicing activity is the main purpose, the time spent by the person providing the service at the location at which it is provided is often substantially greater than for delivery/collection work, varying according to the type of service. A study of service trips in American cities found that service vehicles typically account for 30–65% of total parked vehicle-hours per mile-day of all goods vehicles, while these trips only account for 6–25% of all motorised freight trips, reflecting their relatively long dwell times at the kerbside compared with goods deliveries (Holguín-Veras et al., 2021). Despite the importance, growth and prevalence of servicing activities and their related vehicle use, the requirements of these vehicles have generally been overlooked in kerbside stopping regulations and treated in the same way as car parking.

Road Freight Transport Trip Generation in Urban Areas

Urban freight transport activity occurs due to the demand for goods and services by businesses, public sector institutions and private individuals in towns and cities. Freight trip generation rates vary by land-use type. Survey results indicate that certain types of retailer, including grocery stores selling fast-moving consumer goods, hot food takeaways, restaurants and cafes, hotels, pubs, chemists, opticians and charity shops generate more freight vehicle activity than others (Cherrett et al., 2012; Transport for London, 2015a, 2015b, 2015c, 2015d). The type of supply chain that the business is part of also impacts the number of freight vehicle trips, with independent retailers using a range of suppliers tending to generate more trips than chain stores which receive deliveries from a single distribution centre thereby allowing more consolidated goods flows (Allen et al., 2000). Research in New York identified the substantial freight transport activity generated by large multi-tenanted office buildings and other establishments with either large numbers of workers or large physical areas. It was estimated that 56 multi-tenanted buildings generated approximately 4% of the city's total goods vehicle activity. Establishments located in geographical areas with the top 0.5% of commercial floorspace in terms of its freight trip generation accounted for 37% of the city's goods vehicle activity (Jaller et al., 2015).

Journeys involving urban goods movement often begin and/or end at a commercial freight facility. Such facilities include depots, warehouses, logistics hubs/fulfilment centres, and intermodal terminals. These freight facilities are often among the greatest generators of goods vehicle activity. Intermodal terminals in urban areas at which road-based goods vehicles collect or deliver goods to be transported in the rest of the supply chain by non-road modes include seaports, airports and rail freight terminals.

Many urban areas are net importers of goods given the number of retail, leisure and commercial businesses, public facilities (such as schools and hospitals) and residents (i.e. they import more goods than they export). The economic structure and land-use patterns in an urban area will determine whether, and the extent to which, an urban area is a net importer of goods. Those urban areas with small manufacturing sectors and industrial land uses are likely to be among the greatest net importers of goods. In Greater London in 2020, 38% more tonnes of freight travelled inbound by HGV than travelled outbound, while in the New York Metropolitan Transportation Council (NYMTC) region in 2012, 168% more tonnes of freight travelled inbound by HGV than travelled outbound (Department for Transport, 2021b; New York Metropolitan Transportation Council, 2017).

Urban road traffic levels, kerb space availability and journey reliability are typically worse the more central the location. This makes the provision of goods and services by road freight transport especially challenging in such locations. Lorry parks and rest areas also need to be provided in urban areas to enable drivers to take legally required rest breaks and overnight stops.

Developments and Challenges in Urban Freight Transport by Road

Forecasts foresee the demand for urban freight transport services growing over the coming years as a result of increasing urbanisation and population growth unless freight initiatives are implemented to counteract this. In 1950, 30% of the world's population lived in urban areas. By 2018, this had increased to 55%, and urbanisation is expected to continue with 68% of the world's population forecast to be living in urban areas by 2050 (United Nations Department of Economic and Social Affairs, 2018). For example, the population of Amsterdam is likely to increase by 20% by 2032, with jobs increasing by 30% by 2040. In London, the population is predicted to increase by 50,000–70,000 people per year, resulting in a 20% increase in population by 2050 (Greater London Authority, 2021; World Economic Forum, 2020). One study estimates that goods vehicle activity in the top 100 cities globally will grow, on average, by 36% between 2020 and 2030, leading to a 32% increase in greenhouse gas emissions from these vehicles and contributing to rising traffic levels and journey times

(World Economic Forum, 2020). Another modelling exercise predicts that if the international community adheres to its current climate initiatives and continues its economic practices of past decades then urban freight transport tonne-kilometres will be, respectively, 11% and 94% greater in 2030 and 2050 than in 2020. In terms of greenhouse gas emissions from urban freight transport these will be, respectively, 11% lower and unchanged in 2030 and 2050 compared with 2020 (International Transport Forum, 2021).

There are several developments and challenges facing road freight transport operations in urban areas. These are listed below and then discussed in turn.

- Demand for road and kerbside space;
- Growth in demand for online shopping and last-mile delivery services and urban freight transport services as a whole;
- Demand for logistics land in urban areas – to provide last-mile deliveries and switch to cleaner operations and avoid logistics sprawl;
- Lack of availability of zero-emission vehicles and charging/refuelling infrastructure;
- Shortages in vehicle drivers and other logistics personnel.

In many cities, there is a growing competition for carriageway and kerbside space. This has come about through increasing levels of car ownership and usage over recent decades, together with more recent efforts by policy-makers to promote active travel by bus, bicycle and walking through the reallocation of space to bus and cycle lanes together with improved and widened footways, and low traffic neighbourhoods which close residential streets to through motorised traffic. In addition, the road and kerbside are also being put to other uses by policy-makers to support community health and well-being, taking account of place as well as movement functions, through the introduction of bike and e-scooter cycle hire docking stations, cycle parking facilities, electric vehicle charging points and bays, car clubs to reduce the number of vehicles owned and parked, parklets (also known as pocket parks) to provide green, social spaces and outdoor gyms, as well as to support businesses through street eating and drinking facilities (sometimes known as 'streateries') during the COVID-19 pandemic. A report by the International Transport Forum (ITF) has recognised how the use of road and kerb is changing internationally, noting that it is, 'an increasingly contested piece of urban real estate' (International Transport Forum, 2018, p.11). This has been referred to as a shift from a 'Car-oriented city' to a 'Sustainable mobility city' and a 'City of Place' (Jones, 2018).

As the roadway and kerbside become increasingly in-demand and contested spaces, this is placing ever-greater pressure on urban road freight transport operations, both in terms of journeys and their reliability, and the stopping space available for loading/unloading. International research has demonstrated that knowledge of road space use, especially the kerbside, is typically poor among policy-makers with them having insufficient data and metrics to understand its current usage and how its allocation could be changed to improve its efficient use. This results in carriageway and kerbside space being allocated in a piecemeal fashion, often without a coherent strategy (Butrina et al., 2020; Diehl et al., 2021; International Transport Forum, 2018; POLIS and ALICE, 2021).

Online shopping and the delivery of these orders to consumers, the vast majority of whom live in urban areas, has been growing rapidly internationally over the last twenty years. During the COVID-19 pandemic, online shopping has increased at an unprecedented rate in many countries, resulting in far more goods deliveries, especially of groceries, non-food packages and parcels, and ready-to-eat meals (pwc, 2021). Freight trip generation rates at the urban depots, fulfilment centres, logistic hubs, restaurants, fast-food takeaways and 'dark kitchens' from which these delivery journeys originate can be substantial and are resulting in rapid growth in commercial urban freight activity (Piecyk et al., 2021). There has been a concomitant reduction in retail sales from physical stores in urban locations over this period, which has accelerated during the COVID-19 pandemic. This has resulted in the quantity of goods being supplied to physical retailing, drinking and dining, and other leisure outlets declining. However, unless such outlets close on a permanent basis, this does not mean that they will receive fewer goods vehicle visits. Instead, they may still require vehicle deliveries and collections to take place at the same frequency that they did previously. It is only the quantity of goods delivered or collected per vehicle visit that will have changed.

De-industrialisation in American and European cities since the 1960s has resulted in a major decline in industrial land use, which is a major generator of freight activity. As a result of de-industrialisation, together with urban land prices and changes in logistics strategy including the spatial centralisation of stockholding, many large modern warehouses are now situated on the edge of, or outside, urban areas close to the motorway network (Cidell, 2010; Dablanc and Rakotonarivo, 2010; Dablanc et al., 2014, 2016; Hesse, 2008). Spatial centralisation of stockholding has been adopted by manufacturers and retailers in order to achieve cost savings in their supply chains. This has led many supply chains to make use of fewer, large-scale national and regional distribution centres that serve a far larger geographical area, which reduces total stockholding requirements in the supply chain (McKinnon, 2009). In addition, increases in imported goods passing through seaports have led to large modern warehouses being located on major roads near ports.

Despite this movement of much large-scale warehousing out of urban areas in developed countries, the recent sizeable growth in online shopping and the related goods delivery requirements has led to a substantial demand for so-called logistics hubs and fulfilment centres. These are often relatively small facilities from which grocery and non-food last-mile vehicle deliveries to consumers can be despatched. However, urban land prices, which have been driven up by residential and commercial office demand, can put rental prices beyond many logistics and road freight transport operators. These facilities are important in terms of their potential to allow these last-mile deliveries to be carried out using low and non-polluting methods including electric vans, cargo cycles and even on-foot porters in dense urban areas. Therefore, policy-makers are investigating the ways in which they can help protect such land for this use and help these companies to acquire its use (Cross River Partnership and Steer, 2020; Piecyk and Allen, 2017; Transport for London, 2019a).

While there is a growth in electric vans and electrically assisted cargo cycles being used for urban freight, the overall number as a proportion of all goods vehicles remains low. For instance, in the United Kingdom, only 0.5% of all vans were electrically-powered at the end of June 2021 (Department for Transport, 2021c). One of the important factors in company uptake of electric vans is urban HGVs is the recharging infrastructure required. At present, the provision of rapid rechargers at the kerbside and in other public locations remains low. In addition, the cost of electricity connection upgrades and vehicle recharging infrastructure in urban depots and other warehouses together with legal and ownership issues when such sites are rented rather than owned is an important deterrent to the uptake of electric vehicles. Zero-emission alternatives for HGVs at the heaviest end of the weight profile making deliveries and collections in urban areas are likely to remain technologically and commercially challenging in the nearest future, especially for those vehicles travelling to/from urban areas from depots located further away. However, some operators are already using transition, lower GHG fuels such as for instance biomethane.

Shortages in drivers and other logistics and freight transport personnel, both nationally and in urban areas in many countries, have been growing in severity in recent years. This has been especially exacerbated by the COVID-19 pandemic and the demand for online shopping and last-mile delivery services by consumers this has resulted in (IRU, 2021; Keckarovska, 2021; Piecyk and Allen, 2021).

Initiatives to Improve Urban Freight Transport by Road

Despite the contribution it makes to the prosperity and liveability of urban areas through the goods and services that it provides, urban road freight transport also imposes negative impacts (see Chapters 18, 23 and 24). The impacts of urban road freight transport operations include:

- road traffic impacts – the contribution motorised goods vehicles make to road traffic levels and the consequences that they can have on traffic flow when waiting for kerbside space to load/unload and when they ingress and egress to and from this kerbside space and off-street facilities;
- greenhouse gas emission impacts – due to fossil fuel consumption by motorised goods vehicles;
- local air quality impacts – pollutants (especially oxides of nitrogen and particulate matter) emitted by fossil-fuelled motorised goods vehicles result in health impacts for those breathing this polluted air;
- safety impacts – from collisions between goods vehicles and other, especially vulnerable, road users (i.e. pedestrians and cyclists) which result in injuries and fatalities;
- noise disturbance impacts – from the noise that is generated by the use of motorised goods vehicles and the handling of goods between vehicles and delivery/collection points.

The environmental and safety impacts are related to the levels of road freight vehicle activity, but also depend on other factors including driver and company behaviour, vehicle type/design, and vehicle and operating regulations. Once zero-emission goods vehicles have been fully implemented this will address the greenhouse gas and local air quality impacts associated with their use. However, although electric vans are now being manufactured and are being used in small numbers it will take at least a decade or more until they represent the majority of these vehicles used in urban areas in the highest developed countries, and even longer elsewhere. In the case of HGVs, the time scales involved will be much longer given the technological, infrastructural and commercial viability challenges with both fuel and vehicle provision.

In the time period until these zero-emission vehicles are fully deployed, their greenhouse gas and local air quality impacts arising can only be limited through the use of less-polluting fuels, improved vehicle design/maintenance, and changes to goods vehicle operations (including the practices of vehicle drivers, the freight companies they work for, their customers and others in the supply chain including building owners and managers). Efforts can be made to minimise goods vehicle activity in urban areas by making freight operations as efficient as possible. In addition, products requiring collection and delivery can be transported by the least harmful road-based vehicles or by non-road modes where viable, goods vehicle journeys can be retimed to outside peak traffic times and through traffic can be routed so as to avoid sensitive areas. Both public and private sector stakeholders have important roles to play in achieving these changes.

The range of initiatives that can alter the impacts of urban road freight transport can be summarised in the eleven categories shown in Table 3.1, which also provides examples of the initiatives included in each of these categories. The first six of these categories are specifically taken by the national and urban governments, while the other five can be influenced and taken by a range of stakeholders including government, road freight transport operators, retailers, private individuals, receivers of goods and services, and vehicle manufacturers.

Table 3.2 provides an indicative assessment of the traffic, social and environmental impacts of urban road freight transport that each of these categories of initiative can influence.

Table 3.1 Categories and examples of urban road freight transport initiatives

Categories of initiative	Examples of initiatives
Road traffic management	<ul><li>Vehicle weight and size access restrictions</li><li>Lorry routes</li><li>Access time restrictions</li><li>Variable use of road space by time of day</li><li>Use of urban traffic management and control systems</li><li>Goods vehicle operator licensing</li><li>Vehicle construction and use regulations</li></ul>
Kerbside parking and loading/unloading management	<ul><li>Provision of kerb loading/unloading space</li><li>Kerb loading/unloading time controls</li><li>Off-street loading/unloading space in major new developments</li><li>Enforcement of kerb parking and loading restrictions</li></ul>
Removing constraints on delivery/collection times	<ul><li>Reviewing and, where appropriate revoking, planning permission, environmental health officer and other legislative time constraints imposed on buildings or streets</li></ul>
Planning and land-use policy	<ul><li>Mixed-use developments</li><li>Safeguarding of logistics land</li><li>Zoning of logistics land use</li><li>Requirement for logistics facility as part of new builds over a certain size</li><li>Use of public land for sustainable logistics hubs</li><li>Freight transport plans for construction projects/new buildings</li></ul>
Pricing and taxation	<ul><li>Road user charging</li><li>Parking & loading/unloading charges</li><li>Fuel tax</li><li>Subsidies for zero-emission vehicles and charging infrastructure</li></ul>
Road infrastructure design	<ul><li>Design and geometry of features including roundabouts, road junctions and loading bays</li><li>Use of quieter road surfaces</li></ul>
Logistics operations management	<ul><li>Load consolidation</li><li>Locker banks and collection points</li><li>Company collaboration</li><li>Retiming of deliveries and collections</li></ul>

(Continued)

Table 3.1 Conitnued

Categories of initiative	Examples of initiatives
Information use and provision	• Freight traffic signing and mapping • Provision of road works and closure information • Vehicle routeing and scheduling systems • Telematics systems • Parking space booking systems • Driver training • Voluntary schemes to promote and share safe, clean freight transport operations
Behavioural change of those sending and receiving goods	• Procurement frequency and order size • Requested delivery lead time • Collaborative procurement
Use of lower carbon and less-polluting fuel sources	• Engine emission standards • Low-Emission Zones • Vehicle refuelling infrastructures • Use of electric LGVs and biomethane for HGVs (and electric or hydrogen in future) • Use of cargo cycles, bicycles and on-foot porters
Vehicle design and energy efficiency	• Vehicle safety design requirements for urban operations • Vehicle maintenance • Aerodynamics and low rolling resistance tyres to save energy • Lightweighting of vehicles, improved steering systems and use of double-deck trailers

Table 3.2 Indicative assessment of how initiatives can potentially affect the negative impacts of urban road freight transport operations

Categories of initiative	Road traffic impacts	Greenhouse gas impacts	Local air quality impacts	Safety impacts	Noise disturbance impacts
Road traffic management	✓	✓	✓	✓	✓
Kerbside parking and loading/unloading management	✓	✓	✓	✓	✓
Removing time constraints on delivery times at buildings/in streets and areas	✓	✓	✓	0/X	0/X
Planning and land-use policy	✓	✓	✓	✓	✓
Pricing and taxation	✓	✓	✓	0	0
Road infrastructure design	✓	✓	✓	✓	✓
Logistics operations management	✓	✓	✓	✓	✓
Information use and provision (for journey planning)	✓	✓	✓	0/✓	0/✓
Behavioural change of those sending and receiving goods	✓	✓	✓	✓	✓
Use of lower carbon and less-polluting fuel sources	0	✓	✓	0	✓
Vehicle design and energy efficiency	0/✓	✓	✓	✓	✓

Source: Authors' own indicative assessment

A tick indicates a potential positive influence, a cross indicates a potential negative influence and a zero indicates no change. It has been assumed that if road traffic impacts are reduced, given that the vast majority of motorised goods vehicles currently use fossil fuels, this will result in associated improvements in greenhouse gas emissions and local air quality, due to reduced fossil fuel consumption. In the case of safety and disturbance impacts, these have been assessed in their own right rather than assuming that they are linked to goods vehicle traffic levels.

In addition to the initiatives shown in Table 3.2, the use of non-road modes can also be employed. However, as previously discussed, this is difficult to achieve for many urban freight transport operations and is not discussed in this chapter.

As indicated in Table 3.2, road traffic management and kerb space-management initiatives can be used to reduce the various impacts of urban road freight transport operations. However, it is important to note that if initiatives in these two categories are not deployed with road freight transport in mind but instead with prioritising other carriageway users and kerbside space uses, they can result in an increase in the impacts of these operations, as well as contributing to them becoming less efficient and reliable and more expensive (POLIS and ALICE, 2021).

Some urban authorities encourage the uptake of less-polluting goods and other vehicles through the implementation of Low-Emissions Zones either in city centre locations or across the entire urban area. A few urban authorities are going further with efforts to implement Zero-Emission Zones in specific areas or streets. Examples include schemes in Shenzen in China and Santa Monica in the United States, and plans in many Dutch cities, and in the City of London and the London Borough of Hackney (Transport Decarbonisation Alliance, C40 Cities and POLIS, 2020).

National and urban governments frequently urge road freight operators to improve vehicle load consolidation, retime deliveries to outside peak traffic hours and to make use of cargo cycles. While each of these three approaches can help to reduce these and other impacts, it is important to note that their implementation and uptake are subject to barriers and limitations. Previous research into, and trials of, physical consolidation centres serving urban areas in several countries has shown the public sector funding requirements, lack of goods throughput and stakeholder collaboration, and the misallocation of costs and benefits between supply chain partners that hinder them and often result in their failure (Akgün et al., 2020; Allen et al., 2012; Browne et al., 2005; Peter Brett Associates and WYG, 2019; Steer, 2019). Instead, improvements in vehicle load consolidation are more likely to be successfully achieved within companies' own supply chain operations and through operational collaboration between companies. However, the latter, while offering much potential, requires that legal and organisational barriers concerning competition law, commercial sensitivity about data sharing and issues of trust are addressed (White et al., 2017).

Substantial efforts have been made over a period of twenty years to promote the retiming of deliveries in the United Kingdom, with various guidance documents and protocols produced. However, this has led to few changes in existing planning and environmental health conditions that prevent it from taking place at specific sites, while other commercial barriers to its implementation also frequently exist (Browne et al., 2006). Commercial challenges to delivery retiming have limited the uptake of such schemes in New York (Holguín-Veras et al., 2017a).

Cargo cycles have an important role to play in urban freight transport, but are limited to the movement of specific types of lightweight, non-bulky goods (such as meals, and some parcels and other lightweight products) and are only likely to prove economic and competitive over relatively short distances from an urban hub to a delivery point in dense, busy central urban locations (Element Energy, 2019). In addition, the use of cargo cycles is not currently covered by the same operating regulations as motorised goods vehicles to ensure driver and public safety. The shortage of affordable urban logistics land from which these vehicles can operate and where they can be stored and recharged overnight is also a substantial barrier to their greater uptake (Cross River Partnership and Future City Logistics, 2020).

Various examples of innovative land-use and planning policies with respect to urban road freight transport exist. In Paris, such efforts include the development of a 'logistics hotel' by a public-private sector partnership, a zoning ordinance that encourages the development and use of logistics land, the provision of underground car park space and other unused public land for logistics activities in central areas, and the requirement for new buildings in key locations to include a logistics facility as part of the development permission (Dablanc and Nicol, 2017; Dablanc, 2021). In the United States, national tools and guidance have been made available to better assess the impacts that land-use decisions have on road freight transport activity and incorporate freight into land-use planning (Federal Highway Administration, 2012; Holguín-Veras et al., 2015, 2017b). In London, efforts have been taken to safeguard logistics land through strategic land-use planning, encourage mixed-use development that includes logistics facilities, identify and publicise available sites for sustainable logistics hubs, and to introduce the need for freight transport plans for construction projects and new buildings as part of the planning process (e.g. see Cross River Partnership and Steer, 2020; Mayor of London, 2021; Transport for London, 2019a).

Data and information have a key role to play in improving the efficiency of urban freight transport operations (Transport Decarbonisation Alliance, 2019). This includes companies using vehicle routeing and scheduling software to minimise distance travelled while maintaining service levels and harnessing vehicle telematics data to monitor and improve driver performance. Urban authorities can provide appropriate and up-to-date road signing information for drivers, while also providing data on road works and closures to companies for them to utilise in their journey planning. Companies can enter into data-sharing agreements with urban authorities to provide them with anonymised vehicle-tracking data to help inform freight planning and road and kerbside space-management strategies. Bookable parking systems using apps and sensors are already available for car users and this technology can be applied to goods vehicles to help reduce vehicle circulation through the securing of loading/unloading space prior to arrival. This would be especially helpful in the case of deliveries of large, heavy, bulky loads. Several publications are available that present and discuss the development of urban freight transport strategies and the specific actions that policy-makers and company actions can take to reduce the negative impacts of urban freight transport (e.g. Allen et al., 2007; Allen and Browne, 2016; Giuliano et al., 2013; Holguín-Veras et al., 2015; POLIS and ALICE, 2021; Rhodes et al., 2012; Smart Freight Centre, 2017; Transport Decarbonisation Alliance, 2019; World Economic Forum, 2020).

In some cities and countries subsidies have been made available to encourage the uptake of electric LGVs (Transport Decarbonisation Alliance, 2019). In some cities such as Oslo, London and New York, tolls and road user charging systems have been implemented to help manage road traffic levels (Broaddus et al., 2015; Holguín-Veras et al., 2015). With the gradual shift away from vehicles powered by fossil fuels the time will come when all national and urban governments need to consider how best to implement road user charging schemes to compensate for lost fuel duty and to manage urban road traffic (see Chapter 23). In some cities, goods vehicle users already pay to load/unload in busy central urban areas.

The consideration of whether to adopt this approach in other cities and to widen its approach across the urban area will arise as suitable proven technology becomes more widely available. However, in approaching pricing and taxation matters with respect to road freight transport, policy-makers will need to give serious consideration to the economic importance of this activity and the contribution it makes to urban prosperity and liveability. Given its derived demand and essential nature, together with the level of competition between operators resulting in them often not being able to pass on such cost increases to their customers, road freight operations do not respond to such price signals in anything like the same way as car users, instead acting as a means of revenue raising (Holguín-Veras et al., 2015). In addition, such pricing, unless carefully planned, could have unintended, inequitable impacts on small freight operators and other small businesses using their services.

The implementation of locker banks and collection point networks can help to make the deliveries of online shopping safer and more efficient by removing the need for goods vehicles to make deliveries to consumers' homes and thereby reduce operations in residential areas as well as incur high rates of failed deliveries associated with these operations. By working with industry, urban authorities can seek to ensure that such facilities are agnostic and located in close proximity to public transport and other key hubs, thereby encouraging consumers to use public transport rather than cars when collecting their goods and to trip chain where possible (Transport for London, 2019b). Advice to consumers as how best to carry out such online shopping and collections also helps to minimise the overall transport-related impacts of online shopping (Centre for Sustainable Road Freight, 2021; Transport for London, 2021).

Further efforts to reduce the impact of freight transport to and from building sites in London through the provision of training and a wide range of modification to logistics operations led by Transport for London in partnership with major construction companies provides helpful insights as to how the negative effects of this crucial but high-intensity road freight transport activity can be reduced (Allen and Piecyk, 2021).

In London, recent efforts have been made by the Mayor to improve the safety of HGV operations through the introduction of so-called Direct Vision Standards that require vehicles operating in the city to meet design guidelines concerning driver visibility (Transport for London 2019c). Voluntary membership schemes that promote and disseminate good practice in driver safety and fuel use, such as the Fleet Operator Recognition Scheme (FORS) and the Construction Logistics and Community Safety (CLOCS) scheme established in London also provide a useful template for other city authorities (CLOCS and Transport for London, 2020; FORS, 2020).

While partnership working between policy-makers and the road freight transport industry is not itself one of the eleven initiatives listed in Table 3.1, it can play an important role in addressing existing urban freight transport problems and impacts as well as in shaping a wide range of future policies and road/kerbside plans and designs. Various examples exist of such freight partnerships between the public and private sectors and their achievements (Allen et al., 2010; Browne et al., 2019; Lindholm and Browne, 2013).

Conclusion

This chapter provided an overview of road freight activities in urban areas. For the time being, the vast majority of delivery and collection of goods in towns and cities in the coming years are likely to continue to be made during working hours, direct from company warehouses and depots (located in suburban or ex-urban locations) to the point of delivery/collection, in LGVs and HGVs, albeit increasingly ones that are not diesel powered. This transition period to zero-emission goods vehicles may persist for a considerable period of time, especially in the case of larger, heavier HGVs that operate over longer distances to urban areas, given the technological, recharging/refuelling infrastructure and commercial viability challenges involved. During this transition period, there is a need for urban policy-makers, road freight transport operators and all associated stakeholders including consumers to focus on initiatives that can achieve greenhouse gas emissions and air pollutant improvements together with reductions in other impacts of urban freight transport through operational and consumer behaviour change.

Future technology developments are likely to ultimately result in the deployment of connected autonomous goods vehicles in urban areas (i.e. driverless vehicles) as well as pavement drones. Even though humans can currently perform deliveries to front and back doors, crossing roads and climbing stairs far more cost effectively and efficiently than robots, these technologies are developing rapidly and are sure to have a strong presence in the future urban landscape.

References

Akgün, E., Monios, J. and Fonzone, A. (2020) Supporting Urban Consolidation Centres with Urban Freight Transport Policies: A Comparative Study of Scotland and Sweden. *International Journal of Logistics: Research & Applications*, 23(3), 291–310. http://dx.doi.org/10.1080/13675567.2019.1679743

Alho, A., Silva, J., Sousa, J. and Blanco, E. (2018) Improving Mobility by Optimizing the Number, Location and Usage of Loading/Unloading Bays for Urban Freight Vehicles, *Transportation Research Part D*, 61, 3–18. http://dx.doi.org/10.1016/j.trd.2017.05.014

Allen, J., Tanner, G., Browne, M. and Jones, P. (2000) A Framework for Considering Policies to Encourage Sustainable Urban Freight Traffic and Goods/Service Flows – Summary Report, London: University of Westminster. http://home.wmin.ac.uk/transport/projects/u-d-summ.htm

Allen, J., Thorne, G. and Browne, M. (2007) BESTUFS Good Practice Guide on Urban Freight, BESTUFS project. http://www.bestufs.net/download/BESTUFS_II/good_practice/English_BESTUFS_Guide.pdf

Allen, J., Browne, M., Piotrowska, M. and Woodburn, A. (2010) Freight Quality Partnerships in the UK – An Analysis of Their Work and Achievements, Green Logistics Report, University of Westminster.

Allen, J., Browne, M., Woodburn, A. and Leonardi, J. (2012) The Role of Urban Consolidation Centres in Sustainable Freight Transport, *Transport Reviews*, 32(4), 473–490. https://doi.org/10.1080/01441647.2012.688074

Allen, J., Browne, M. and Woodburn (2014) London Freight Data Report: 2014 Update, report for Transport for London, University of Westminster. https://content.tfl.gov.uk/london-freight-data-report-2014.pdf

Allen, J. and Browne, M. (2016) Success Factors of Past Initiatives and the Role of Public-Private Cooperation, Deliverable 2.3, Report Prepared for the CITYLAB Urban Freight project. https://www.citylab.soton.ac.uk/deliverables/D2_3.pdf

Allen, J., Piecyk, M., Cherrett, T., Juhari, M., McLeod, F., Piotrowska, M., Bates, O., Bektas, T., Cheliotis, K., Friday, A. and Wise, S. (2021) Understanding the Transport and CO_2 Impacts of On-Demand Meal Deliveries: A London Case Study, *Cities*, 108, 102973. https://doi.org/10.1016/j.cities.2020.102973

Allen, J. and Piecyk, M. (2021) Construction Logistics Briefing Report, Centre for Sustainable Road Freight. https://www.csrf.ac.uk/wp-content/uploads/2021/12/CUED-C-SRF-TR-15-Construction-Industry-SRF-Report-Final-Draft.pdf

Anderson. S., Allen, J., and Browne, M. (2001) Service-Related Vehicle Activity in Urban Areas. In Taniguchi, E. and Thompson, R. (eds.), *City Logistics II, Institute for City Logistics*, Japan, 335–350.

Anup, S. and Yang, Z. (2020) New Two-Wheeler Vehicle Fleet in India for Fiscal Year 2017–18, Working Paper 2020-08, International Council for Clean Transportation (ICCT). https://theicct.org/sites/default/files/publications/India-2W-fuel%20consumption-2017-18.pdf

Auto Punditz (2020) Three Wheeler Sales Statistics India – FY2020, 23 April, Auto Punditz. https://www.autopunditz.com/post/three-wheeler-sales-statistics-india-fy2020

Broaddus, A., Browne, M. and Allen, J. (2015) Sustainable Freight: Impacts of the London Congestion Charge and Low Emissions Zone, *Transportation Research Record*, 2478(1), Freight Systems, 1–11. https://doi.org/10.3141/2478-01

Browne, M. Sweet, M. Woodburn, A. and Allen, J. (2005) Urban Freight Consolidation Centres, report for the Department for Transport, University of Westminster. https://ukerc.rl.ac.uk/pdf/RR3_Urban_Freight_Consolidation_Centre_Report.pdf

Browne, M., Allen J., Anderson, S. and Woodburn, A. (2006) Night-Time Delivery Restrictions: A Review. In Taniguchi, E and Thompson, R (eds.), *Recent Advances in City Logistics*, Elsevier, 245–258.

Browne, M., Brettmo, A. and Lindholm, M. (2019) Stakeholder Engagement and Partnerships for Improved Urban Logistics. In Browne, M., Behrends, S., Woxenius, J., Giuliano, G. and Holguin-Veras, J. (eds.) *Urban Logistics: Management, Policy and Innovation in a Rapidly Changing Environment*, Kogan Page, 257–273.

Centre for Sustainable Road Freight (2021) Online Shopping Policy Briefing Series: Consumer actions, Centre for Sustainable Road Freight. https://www.csrf.ac.uk/wp-content/uploads/2021/11/SRF-Online-shopping-Actions-for-Consumers.pdf

Chen, Q., Conway, A. and Cheng, J. (2017) Parking for Residential Delivery in New York City: Regulations and Behavior, *Transport Policy*, 54, 53–60.

Cherrett, T., Allen, J., McLeod, F. Maynard, S., Hickford, A. and Browne, M. (2012) Understanding Urban Freight Activity – Key Issues for Freight Planning, *Journal of Transport Geography*, 24, 22–32. https://doi.org/10.1016/j.jtrangeo.2012.05.008

Cidell, J. (2010) Concentration and Decentralization: The New Geography of Freight Distribution in US Metropolitan Areas, *Journal of Transport Geography*, 18, 363–371. https://doi.org/10.1016/j.jtrangeo.2009.06.017

CLOCS and Transport for London (2020) Construction Logistics Planning Guidance, CLOCS. https://constructionlogistics.org.uk/wp-content/uploads/2020/03/CLP-Guidance-by-CLOCS-March-2020-v1.5.pdf

Cross River Partnership and Future City Logistics (2020) Enabling Last Mile Cycle Logistics, Cross River Partnership. https://crossriverpartnership.org/wp-content/uploads/2020/06/Enabling-last-mile-cycle-logistics-FINAL-vPUB-May-2020.pdf

Cross River Partnership and Steer (2020) The Potential for Urban Logistics Hubs in Central London, Cross River Partnership. https://crossriverpartnership.org/wp-content/uploads/2021/01/Central-London-Hubs_Final-report.pdf

Dablanc, L. (2009) Freight Transport for Development Toolkit: Urban Freight, Transp. Res. Support World Bank. https://thedocs.worldbank.org/en/doc/899601433866450683-0190022009/render/UrbanTransporturbanfreight.pdf

Dablanc, L. and Rakotonarivo, D. (2010) The Impacts of Logistics Sprawl: How Does the Location of Parcel Transport Terminals Affect the Energy Efficiency of Goods' Movements in Paris and What Can We Do About It?, *The Sixth International Conference on City Logistics. Procedia Social and Behavioral Sciences*, 2(3), 6087–6096. https://doi.org/10.1016/j.sbspro.2010.04.021

Dablanc, L., Ogilvie, S. and Goodchild, A. (2014) Logistics Sprawl: Differential Warehousing Development Patterns in Los Angeles, California, and Seattle, Washington. *Transportation Research Record: Journal of the Transportation Research Board*, 2410, 105–112. https://doi.org/10.3141/2410-12

Dablanc, L., Blanquart, C., Combes, F., Heitz, A., Klausberg, J., Koning, M., Liu, Z., de Oliveira, L. and Seidel, S. (2016) CITYLAB Observatory of Strategic Developments Impacting Urban Logistics, Deliverable 2.1, CITYLAB project. https://www.citylab.soton.ac.uk/deliverables/D2_1.pdf

Dablanc, L. and Nicol, M-A. (2017) Logistics and Land Use Planning: The Example of Paris, CoESUFS Perr-to-Peer Program, 21 June. https://coe-sufs.org/wordpress/peer-to-peer-exchange-program/webinar18/

Dablanc, L. (2021) So Many New Warehouses in Paris Today: Why?, Presentation, 1 December, Delft University of Technology. https://www.lvmt.fr/wp-content/uploads/2021/12/Presentation-TU-Delft-Dablanc.pdf

Dalla Chiara, G. and Goodchild, A. (2020) Do Commercial Vehicles Cruise for Parking? Empirical evidence from Seattle, *Transport Policy*, 97, 26–36. https://doi.org/10.1016/j.tranpol.2020.06.013

Department for Transport (2021a) TRA0206: Motor Vehicle Traffic (Vehicle Kilometres) by Vehicle Type, Region and Country in Great Britain, Department for Transport. https://assets.publishing.service.gov.uk/government/uploads/system/uploads/attachment_data/file/981979/tra0206.ods

Department for Transport (2021b) RFS0122: Goods Lifted and Goods Moved by Region and Country of Origin and Destination, Department for Transport. https://assets.publishing.service.gov.uk/government/uploads/system/uploads/attachment_data/file/1006664/rfs0122.ods

Department for Transport (2021c) All Vehicles (VEH01) Data on All Licensed and Registered Vehicles, Department for Transport. https://www.gov.uk/government/statistical-data-sets/all-vehicles-veh01

Dezi, G., Dondi, G. and Sangiorgi, C. (2010) Urban Freight Transport in Bologna: Planning Commercial Vehicle Loading/Unloading Zones, *Procedia – Social and Behavioral Sciences*, 2(3), 5990–6001. https://doi.org/10.1016/j.sbspro.2010.04.013

Diehl, C., Ranjbari, A. and Goodchild, A. (2021) Curbspace Management Challenges and Opportunities from Public and Private Sector Perspectives, *Transportation Research Record*, 2675(11), 1413–1427.

Element Energy (2019) Cycle Logistics Study, Final Report for Cross River Partnership, Cross River Partnership. https://crossriverpartnership.org/wp-content/uploads/2019/03/20190520_Element-Energy_Cycling-logistics-study_FINAL-REPORT-1.pdf

Ezquerro, S., Moura, J. and Alonso, B. (2020) Illegal Use of Loading Bays and Its Impact on the Use of Public Space, *Sustainability*, 12(5915). https://doi.org/10.3390/su12155915

Federal Highway Administration (2012) *FHWA Freight and Land Use Handbook*, FHWA-HOP-12-006, U.S. Department of Transportation. https://ops.fhwa.dot.gov/publications/fhwahop12006/

FORS (2020) Fleet Operator Recognition Scheme Standard, version 5.1, FORS. https://www.fors-online.org.uk/cms/wp-content/uploads/2021/03/FORS-Standard_v5.1.indd-4-march-2021.pdf

Gadepalli, R. (2009) Two and Three Wheelers in India, Final Report for International Council for Clean Transportation (ICCT) & The Institute for Transport and Development Policy (ITDP), Innovative Transport Solutions (iTrans) Pvt. Ltd. https://www.researchgate.net/publication/290691439_Two_and_Three_Wheelers_in_India

Giuliano, G., O'Brien, T., Dablanc, L. and Holliday, K. (2013) Synthesis of Freight Research in Urban Transportation Planning, National Cooperative Freight Research Program Report 23, Transportation Research Board. http://www.trb.org/Publications/Blurbs/168987.aspx

Goldstein Market Intelligence (2020) India Three Wheeler Market Outlook, Goldstein Market Intelligence. https://www.goldsteinresearch.com/report/india-three-wheeler-industry-market-analysis

Greater London Authority (2021) Trend-Based Population Projections, *GLA*. https://data.london.gov.uk/dataset/trend-based-population-projections

Herzog, B. (2010) Urban Freight in Developing Cities, *GTZ*. http://transferproject.org/wp-content/uploads/2017/09/Urban-Freight-in-Developing-Cities.pdf

Hesse, M. (2008) *The City as a Terminal: The Urban Context of Logistics and Freight Transport*, Ashgate.

Holguín-Veras, J., Amaya-Leal, J., Wojtowicz, J., Jaller, M., González-Calderón, C, Sánchez-Díaz, I., Wang, X., Haake, D., Rhodes, S., Hodge, S., Frazier, R., Nick, M., Dack, J., Casinelli, L. and Browne, M. (2015) Improving Freight System Performance in Metropolitan Areas, *NCFRP 33, TRB*. http://www.trb.org/Main/Blurbs/172487.aspx

Holguín-Veras, J., Wang, C., Sánchez-Díaz, I., Campbell, S., Hodge, S., Jaller, M. and Wojtowicz, J. (2017a) Fostering Unassisted Off-Hour Deliveries: The Role of Incentives, *Transportation Research Part A: Policy and Practice*, 102, 172–187. https://doi.org/10.1016/j.tra.2017.04.005

Holguín-Veras, J., Lawson, C., Wang, C., Jaller, M., González-Calderón, C., Campbell, S., Kalahasthi, L., Wojtowicz, J. and Ramirez-Rios, D. (2017b) Using Commodity Flow Survey and Other Microdata to Estimate the Generation of Freight, Freight Trip Generation, and Service Trips: Guidebook, NCFRP Report 37, *Transportation Research Board*. https://www.trb.org/Publications/Blurbs/175283.aspx

Holguín-Veras, J., Kalahasthi, L. and Ramirez-Rios, D. (2021) Service Trip Attraction in Commercial Establishments, *Transportation Research Part E*, 149. https://doi.org/10.1016/j.tre.2021.102301

Intermodality (2004) IMT J0015 Business Survey Report, report to Bexley Council, Intermodality.

International Transport Forum (ITF) (2021) *ITF Transport Outlook 2021*, OECD Publishing. https://www.oecd-ilibrary.org/transport/itf-transport-outlook-2021_16826a30-en

IRU (2021) New IRU Survey Shows Driver Shortages to Soar in 2021, 8 March, IRU. https://www.iru.org/resources/newsroom/new-iru-survey-shows-driver-shortages-soar-2021

Jaller, M., Holguín-Veras, J., and Hodge, S. D. (2013) Parking in the City, *Transportation Research Record*, 2379, 46–56. https://doi.org/10.3141/2379-06

Jaller, M., Wang, X. and Holguín-Veras, J. (2015) Large Urban Freight Traffic Generators: Opportunities for City Logistics Initiatives, *The Journal of Transport and Land Use*, 8(1), 51–67. https://doi.org/10.5198/jtlu.2015.406

Jones, P. (2018) Urban Mobility: Preparing for the Future, Learning for the Past, Project Summary and Recommendations for Cities, CREATE project. https://discovery.ucl.ac.uk/id/eprint/10058850/1/Jones%20et%20al%202018%20Preparing%20for%20the%20future%2C%20learning%20from%20the%20past.pdf

Kapser, S. and Abdelrahman, M. (2020) Acceptance of Autonomous Delivery Vehicles for Last-Mile Delivery in Germany – Extending UTAUT2 with Risk Perceptions, *Transportation Research C*, 111, 201–225. https://doi.org/10.1016/j.trc.2019.12.016

Keckarovska, V. (2021) European Driver Shortages, Transport Intelligence. https://www.ti-insight.com/briefs/europes-road-freight-market-short-of-more-400000-drivers/

Kumar, P. and Bhat, A. (2021) Electrification of 3-Wheeler Cargo Segment in India: Potential & Challenges, 12 May, WRI India. https://wri-india.org/blog/electrification-3-wheeler-cargo-segment-india-potential-challenges

Lindholm, M. and Browne, M. (2013) Local Authority Cooperation with Urban Freight Stakeholders: A Comparison of Partnership Approaches, *EJTIR*, 13(1), 20–38. https://doi.org/https://doi.org/10.18757/ejtir.2013.13.1.2986

Mayor of London (2021) *The London Plan: The Spatial Development Strategy for Greater London*, Greater London Authority. https://www.london.gov.uk/sites/default/files/the_london_plan_2021.pdf

McKinnon, A. (2009) The present and future land requirements of logistical activities, *Land Use Policy*, 26: S293–S301. https://doi.org/10.1016/j.landusepol.2009.08.014

Mejia, A. (2021) Sustainable Transport: A Sourcebook for Policymakers in Developing Cities, GTZ. https://sutp.org/publications/delivering-sustainability-urban-freight-in-developing-cities/

New York Metropolitan Transportation Council (2017) 2018–2045 Regional Freight Plan, *NYMTC*. https://www.nymtc.org/Portals/0/Pdf/RTP/Plan%202045%20Final%20Documents/Plan%202045%20Individual%20Appendices/Appendix%208_Regional%20Freight%20Plan.pdf

OECD (2002) Road, in Glossary of Statistical Terms, OECD. https://stats.oecd.org/glossary/detail.asp?ID=4005

Oxbotica (2017) UK First: Autonomous Grocery Delivery Trials in Greenwich, press release, 28 June, Oxbotica. https://www.oxbotica.com/insight/uk-first-autonomous-grocery-delivery-trials-in-greenwich/

Paddeu, D., Calvert, T., Clark, B. and Parkhurst, G. (2019) New Technology and Automation in Freight Transport and Handling Systems, Evidence Review: Future of Mobility, Government Office for Science. https://assets.publishing.service.gov.uk/government/uploads/system/uploads/attachment_data/file/781295/automation_in_freight.pdf

Peter Brett Associates and WYG (2019) London Freight Consolidation Feasibility Study, Final Report, Transport for London. http://content.tfl.gov.uk/london-freight-consolidation-feasibility-study.pdf

Piecyk, M. and Allen, J. (2017) Land Availability in London, Logistics and Transport Focus, November, 38–40.

Piecyk, M., Allen, J., Woodburn, A. and Cao, M. (2021) Online Shopping and Last-Mile Deliveries, Briefing Report, Centre for Sustainable Road Freight. https://www.csrf.ac.uk/wp-content/uploads/2021/11/SRF_Online-Shopping-Full-Report-Final-Jan-2021.pdf

Poehler, E. (2017) *The Traffic Systems of Pompeii*, Oxford University Press.

POLIS and ALICE (2021) Guide for Advancing Towards Zero-Emission Urban Logistics by 2030, ALICE-ETP and POLIS. https://www.etp-logistics.eu/wp-content/uploads/2021/12/POLIS_ALICE_Guide-Zero-Emission-Urban-Logistics_Dec2021-low.pdf

pwc (2021) The global consumer: Changed for good, Global Consumer Insights Pulse Survey June 2021, pwc. https://www.pwc.com/gx/en/consumer-markets/consumer-insights-survey/2021/gcis-june-2021.pdf

Rhodes, S., Berndt, M., Bingham, P., Bryan, J., Cherrett, T., Plumeau, P. and Weisbrod, R. (2012) Guidebook for Understanding Urban Goods Movement, National Cooperative Freight Research Program Report 14, Transportation Research Board. http://www.trb.org/Publications/Blurbs/166828.aspx

Shah, J. (2018) Two- and Three-Wheelers: A Guide to Sustainable Mobility Solutions for Motorcycles, *GTZ*. https://sutp.org/publications/two-and-three-wheelers-a-policy-guide-to-sustainable-mobility-solutions-for-motorcycles/

Silva, K., da Silva Lima, R., Alves, R., Yushimito, W. and Holguin-Veras, J. (2020) Freight and Service Parking Needs in Historical Centers: A Case Study in Sao Joao Del Rei, Brazil, *Transportation Research Record*, 2674(11), 352–366. DOI: 10.1177/0361198120943888

Sinha, A. (2021) Electric Two- and Three-Wheelers Are Everywhere in India, 6 May, The Third Pole. https://www.thethirdpole.net/en/energy/electric-three-wheelers-two-wheelers-driving-indias-electric-vehicle-transition/

Smart Freight Centre (2017) Developing a Sustainable Urban Freight Plan – A Review of Good Practices, Smart Freight Centre. https://www.smartfreightcentre.org/pdf/Developing-a-Sustainable-Urban-Freight-Plan-a-review-of-good-practices-SFC-Final-June2017.pdf

Steer (2019) Evaluation of Freight Consolidation Demonstrator Projects, Transport for London. https://content.tfl.gov.uk/steer-assessment-of-demos-report-oct-2019.pdf

Systra (2017) Freight Travel Demand Surveys: Data Report, Draft report for Transport for London.

Transport Decarbonisation Alliance (2019) Zero Emission Urban Freight, Transport Decarbonisation Alliance. http://tda-mobility.org/wp-content/uploads/2019/05/TDA-Zero-Emission-Urban-Freight.pdf

Transport Decarbonisation Alliance, C40 Cities and POLIS (2020) How-to Guide on Zero-Emission Zones for Freight, Transport Decarbonisation Alliance. https://www.polisnetwork.eu/wp-content/uploads/2020/12/ZEZ-F_How-to-Guide_low.pdf

Transport for London (2015a) TfL High Street Freight Survey Project: Acton High Street, Case Study Summary, Transport for London.

Transport for London (2015b) TfL High Street Freight Survey Project: Camden High Street, Case Study Summary, Transport for London.

Transport for London (2015c) TfL High Street Freight Survey Project: Kingsland High Street, Case Study Summary, Transport for London.

Transport for London (2015d) TfL High Street Freight Survey Project: Stratford High Street, Case Study Summary, Transport for London.

Transport for London (2019a) Freight and Servicing Action Plan, Transport for London. http://content.tfl.gov.uk/freight-servicing-action-plan.pdf

Transport for London (2019b) The Mayor and TfL Launch Major Plan to Help Freight Deliver for Londoners, press release, 7 March, Transport for London. https://tfl.gov.uk/info-for/media/press-releases/2019/march/the-mayor-and-tfl-launch-major-plan-to-help-freight-deliver-for-londoners

Transport for London (2019c) HGV Safety Permit Guidance for Operators Entering London, Transport for London. https://content.tfl.gov.uk/hgv-safety-permit-guidance-for-operators-entering-london2.pdf

Transport for London (2021) TfL Encourages Londoners to Adopt Green Shopping Habits This Black Friday and Festive Season, press release, 24 November, Transport for London. https://tfl.gov.uk/info-for/media/press-releases/2021/november/tfl-encourages-londoners-to-adopt-green-shopping-habits-this-black-friday-and-festive-season

United Nations Department of Economic and Social Affairs (2018) World Urbanization Prospects: The 2018 Revision, United Nations. https://population.un.org/wup/Publications/Files/WUP2018-Report.pdf

Urban Freight Lab (2019) The Final 50 Feet of the Urban Goods Delivery System: Tracking Curb Use in Seattle, University of Washington. http://depts.washington.edu/sctlctr/sites/default/files/research_pub_files/Final-50-Feet-Tracking-Curb-Use-in-Seattle.pdf

Wenneman, A., Habib, K. and Roorda, M. (2015) Disaggregate Analysis of Relationships Between Commercial Vehicle Parking Citations, Parking Supply, and Parking Demand, *Transportation Research Record*, 2478, 28–34. https://doi.org/10.3141/2478-04

White, J. (2010) City Rivalries and the Modernisation of Eighteenth-Century London 1720–1770, *Literatur in Wissenschaft und Unterricht*, 43(2/3), 83–102. ISSN 0024-4643

World Economic Forum (2020) The Future of the Last-Mile Ecosystem: Transition Roadmaps for Public- and Private-Sector Players, World Economic Forum. http://www3.weforum.org/docs/WEF_Future_of_the_last_mile_ecosystem.pdf

World Economic Forum and McKinsey and Company (2021) Efficient and Sustainable Last-Mile Logistics: Lessons from Japan, Briefing Paper, WEF. https://www3.weforum.org/docs/WEF_Future_Last_Mile_Delivery_Japan_and_World.pdf

4
THE USE OF RAIL AND WATER IN URBAN LOGISTICS

Allan Woodburn

Introduction

Frequently, consideration of urban freight transport is limited to road freight, even if this is not always made explicit, and non-road modes such as rail and water tend to receive limited attention. For example, in developing a methodology for evaluating the environmental performance of urban freight transport, Muñoz-Villamizar et al. (2020) make no mention of the potential for non-road modes to impact the outcome. Behrends (2017) points out that intermodal rail freight and urban logistics tend to be viewed as separate areas of study, with little overlap, and the same is true for other types of rail freight and for water freight. However, these non-road modes offer potential for greater urban transport efficiency and sustainability and, in some cities at least, already play an important role. While rail and water are rarely able to offer end-to-end freight journey opportunities, particularly when serving urban freight requirements, they can help to reduce the dominance of road freight in some circumstances. For example, they are often well placed to cater for trunk flows, leaving road to handle the 'last mile' to the destination (or, indeed, the 'first mile' from the origin).

Freight flows in an urban area, by whatever transport mode, can be categorised as follows:

- Flows to/from/within an urban area to satisfy its freight transport needs;
- Flows starting or finishing at a freight terminal within a city, but not directly serving the city (e.g. at a city port);
- Flows transiting an urban area.

Given the book's focus on urban logistics, this chapter considers mainly the first of these flow types, though the others are discussed where relevant. The main focus is on urban rail freight, given most major cities have a more extensive rail network than waterway system, though waterborne freight is also considered. Good-quality datasets relating to the use of rail and water at the city level rarely exist. In the United Kingdom, for example, official statistics relating to rail freight moved (measured in tonne kilometres) are disaggregated by commodity, with seven different commodity groups (ORR, 2022). However, there is no geographical disaggregation, even to regions, never mind the level of individual cities. When such data exist, it tends to be the result of individual studies rather than regularly published information, so usually only a snapshot is provided. Typically, therefore, it is challenging to ascertain a clear picture of non-road freight activity within a city. That said, the following section considers the reasons in favour of the use of rail and water freight, followed by the identification of examples of the use of these modes in urban logistics and a more detailed consideration of the use of these modes in the context of a specific large city, London (in the United Kingdom). Finally, there is a review of the opportunities and barriers associated with urban rail and water freight activity.

Why Consider Rail and Water Freight?

One of the main benefits of these non-road modes is their ability to reduce the negative consequences of freight transport activity by removing goods vehicles from the road network. While dependent on the circumstances of a particular flow, both rail and water freight are typically far more energy efficient than road haulage and, given the increasing focus on climate change, they tend to have greenhouse gas (GHG) emissions at least 75% lower per tonne-kilometre than for road haulage (EEA, 2022). Local air pollution impacts are of great importance to large urban areas, given the high population density and associated transport activities, and they again tend to be worse per unit of activity for road than for rail and water (U.S. EPA, 2015; EEA, 2022). Wider benefits of the use of non-road modes rather than road haulage include reductions in road network congestion, less damage to road infrastructure from heavy vehicles, fewer serious and fatal accidents, and increased economic output for a region or country (see, for example, Oxera, 2015).

It is generally the case that these benefits of rail and water over road haulage are greatest for longer-distance freight flows but, with the right conditions, the non-road modes can play a part within urban areas too. It should be noted, though, that the energy mix for the freight modes varies considerably by location and over time and can have a major impact on the relative benefits of the different freight modes. For example, while electric rail freight has been far more common for many years in Europe than in North America, reducing local air pollution and, possibly, GHG emissions (dependent on how the electricity is generated), the more recent growth worldwide of non-fossil-fuel urban road haulage is likely to have narrowed the gap in environmental performance between rail and road.

Examples of Rail and Water Use in Urban Logistics

Unsurprisingly, most of the literature relating to rail and water freight focuses on these modes in the context of long-distance freight flows, playing to their key strengths. That said, there are examples relating specifically to the urban context, with key issues including:

- The composition of freight transport activity within an urban area;
- The availability and capability of appropriate rail and water networks and terminals;
- Public policies towards non-road modes in urban areas.

These issues vary considerably between different countries and, indeed, cities, and are discussed further when considering opportunities and barriers for non-road modes. This section aims to provide examples that demonstrate the breadth of rail and water use in urban logistics rather than to set out an exhaustive list. Examples from London are excluded here, given that the chapter provides a specific London case study.

Rail Freight in Urban Logistics

The use of rail in urban logistics can take different forms, but fundamentally it falls into one of two categories, with the vast majority being the first type:

- Dedicated rail freight services;
- Carrying freight on passenger rail services.

In many cases, urban rail freight is simply the standard use of rail which happens to serve an origin and/or a destination within a city. Typically, this will be for the manufacturing or construction sectors, but port activity can be a major source of rail freight in some cities, though generally with a focus on a wider hinterland rather than serving the city itself. Given the unremarkable nature of these types of flows, examples in the literature tend to focus on less traditional rail freight use within urban areas.

A 'good practice' example of rail delivering consumer goods into a major city can be found in Paris (Eltis, 2015a). Monoprix, a large French retailer, commenced using rail in 2007 for deliveries from two distribution centres around 30 kilometres outside Paris into a terminal next to Bercy station in the city centre. The train carries non-perishable goods (e.g. household products, beauty products, soft drinks and textiles) and operates each weekday evening, with the goods then transhipped to road vehicles for delivery to 90 central Paris stores the following morning Alessandrini et al. (2012).

In Kawasaki City, Japan, a rail-borne flow of containerised waste materials has operated since the mid-1990s over a distance of just 23 kilometres, from the loading terminal in the city to a waste disposal centre just to the south (Diziain et al., 2014). A range of waste materials, including general waste, incinerated ash, and cans and bottles are carried. Rail can also be used for special construction projects, such as the rebuilding of Birmingham New Street station in the United Kingdom between 2010 and 2015 (Modern Railways, 2011, 2013). Poor road access led to a shuttle service for construction products and waste materials being established to link to rail sidings around three kilometres away. A similar use of rail took place in Prague, Czech Republic, during the rebuilding of the main station.

Self-contained urban rail systems (e.g. metros, trams) are a common feature of large urban areas. They tend to cater to even more intensive passenger service provision than do "mainline" suburban systems, and their self-contained nature means that freight options tend to be limited to niche services over short distances. While the overwhelming majority of such systems have no freight activity, there are some current or recent examples, such as the Dresden CarGoTram in Germany, the Zürich Cargo Tram and E-Tram in Switzerland and waste collection on the New York subway, in the United States, using modified vehicles. The Dresden tram operated from 2001 to 2020, supplying automotive components to Volkswagen's 'transparent factory' near the city centre from a distribution centre in a logistics zone around five kilometres from the factory (Arvidsson and Browne, 2013; Railway Gazette, 2021). The CarGoTram ended because the factory switched to producing a different vehicle model, with a revised supply chain to support it. In Zürich, the Cargo Tram commenced operation in 2003 as a non-commercial municipal waste service and has since expanded to incorporate an E-Tram which collects electrical and electronic waste; around 425 tonnes of waste are collected each year, representing 3.2% of Zürich's bulk waste (Arvidsson and Browne 2013; Tramways and Urban Transit, 2021). Proposals for cargo trams in other European cities, such as Amsterdam, Barcelona, Frankfurt, Paris and Vienna, appear to have been abandoned. In New York, overnight waste collections are carried out on the subway system, using 11 dedicated trains (Behiri et al., 2018). In Kyoto, Japan, accompanied parcels are carried using regular vehicles on a light rail route into the city prior to the morning peak period, with deliveries made by electric bicycles (Diziain et al., 2014).

While historically a regular feature (e.g. Red Star Parcels in the United Kingdom until 2001), the carriage of freight on passenger rail services is little discussed in the literature and seems to be fairly uncommon nowadays, though there are some examples. In Mumbai, India, 150,000 lunch boxes are collected from homes and transported to offices in the morning, with the empty boxes being moved back from offices to homes in the late afternoon (Ravichandran, 2005). Boxes arrive at the origin railway station and are sorted based on their destination. The entire operation is highly time sensitive, with collections from homes typically taking place around 08:30-09:00. The boxes arrive at the destination station by around 11:30 and deliveries are made by 13:00. The lunch boxes are accompanied by the Dabbawallahs on the train journey, each one having responsibility for up to 30 boxes. The high frequency of train services, generally around one per minute, is crucial to the operation. In Sapporo, Japan, a pilot project took place in 2010 with goods carried in hand carts on regular off-peak metro trains into the city centre (Kikuta et al., 2012). It is likely that there are many other examples that go unreported – see below for details of some small-scale flows on long-distance passenger trains into London.

Waterborne Freight in Urban Logistics

In countries with a relatively dense inland waterway system (e.g. Bangladesh, Belgium, Netherlands), inland waterways have a higher than average mode share, with barges often being used to satisfy urban freight requirements. In Bangladesh, for example, limitations in the land transport networks mean that inland waterways are used quite extensively, with a network of 12 inland ports used for freight, together with approximately 800 smaller loading/unloading facilities (UNESCAP, 2021). A mix of formal and informal barge activity is used to move a wide range of commodities, including agricultural produce and industrial materials to and from urban areas. In Brazil, Divieso et al. (2021) identified flows of general cargo and containers in a number of major cities, with urban goods and perishable products handled in Belém.

As with rail, it can be difficult to separate the waterborne freight activity serving a city from the presence of a (sea or inland) port in a city but which has a more strategic function for the wider area it serves. This is particularly the case in countries like Belgium, the Netherlands and parts of France and Germany which are well connected both by sea and inland waterways. Two of Germany's inland cities, Berlin and Duisburg, demonstrate this overlap between the urban and regional functions. Duisport in Duisburg is a strategic inland port, connected via the Rhein (Rhine) river to the major seaport of Rotterdam (Duisburger Hafen, 2022) and is a European rail hub for intercontinental trains to/from China. As a trimodal hub, considerable use is made of rail and water as part of integrated supply chain solutions. Of particular relevance to urban freight activity, many manufacturers and logistics companies are co-located with the transport terminals, allowing them to use non-road modes directly to their sites. In Berlin, BEHALA (2022) operates three river ports, two of which are also rail-connected. The largest, Westhafen, is a logistics hub located in the inner city, with a high degree of integration between water, rail and road. For example, DHL containers arriving in Berlin are transhipped at Westhafen and delivered by road within the city, some by electric vehicle.

Focusing explicitly on urban freight requirements, the Netherlands provides some good examples. In Amsterdam, with its dense canal network, DHL uses a boat (referred to as a 'floating service centre') in the city centre to distribute parcels to bike couriers who make the customer deliveries (DHL, 2022). Introduced in 2010, the electric Beer Boat in Utrecht makes use of the city's canals to deliver to more than 60 hospitality businesses located along the canals (Eltis, 2015b).

A more typical example of water freight can be found in Ghent, Belgium, though with some unusual characteristics to make it work in such a historic city with lots of low bridges over the waterways (Eltis, 2015c). Barges were modified to enable them to fit under the bridges, allowing them to move building materials to, and industrial waste from, the construction site, linking to a consolidation centre outside the city centre. This is part of a Belgium-wide 'Distribuild' initiative to establish a network of construction consolidation and distribution centres.

Summary of Key Points Relating to Current Rail and Water Use

While these examples of rail and water use in urban logistics demonstrate the variety of existing types of non-road activity, they provide mostly isolated, novel examples, often linked to publicly-funded research and development initiatives or companies proactively furthering their corporate social responsibility (CSR) agenda. In addition to the traditional uses of rail and water, moving large volumes of goods into, out of and around urban areas, specific examples have shown that there can also be applications involving smaller volumes such as retail products and parcels. Overall, though, the examples offer limited insight into the overall use of these modes at a city level; the next section attempts to remedy this gap in awareness.

Case Study: London

This section focuses on London, United Kingdom, making use of a combination of published material and original research to offer insight into the use of rail and water in a major city. It first considers the rail freight situation, followed by water activity.

Rail Freight in London

For a time, the urban transport authority (Transport for London (TfL)) published a London Freight Data Report which included data relating to the non-road modes; the last report was published in 2014 (TfL, 2014). The annual tonnage handled by rail each year from 2004 to 2012 fluctuated between 6 and 7.5 million tonnes, the majority of which was brought by rail into London. In 2012, the final year for which there were data, 6.68 million tonnes were handled, 71% of which was inbound to London, 19% was outbound from London and 10% was internal to London. It is noteworthy, given that rail is generally perceived to be suited to longer-distance flows, that approximately 10% of London's rail freight tonnage over the entire 2004–2012 period was internal to London so, by definition, short distance.

While the TfL report did not identify the nature of these flows, original research, in the form of an annual database of rail freight service provision (each January), offers considerable insight into the characteristics of London's rail freight activity. The database is constructed by corroborating a range of reliable sources, including open-access data made available by Network Rail (the British rail infrastructure manager), rail freight company information, online rail enthusiast forums, etc., allowing the identification of individual freight trains

Allan Woodburn

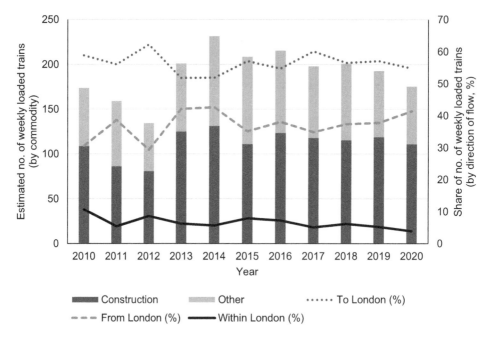

Figure 4.1 Estimated number of weekly loaded freight train services (by commodity) and share of train service provision to, from and within London (2010–2020, each January)

Source: Author's annual rail freight database

operated. Given that many freight trains tend to operate more sporadically than do passenger trains, estimates of typical service frequencies are then made. Figure 4.1 presents two key annual trends for 2010–2020, based on the estimated number of loaded freight trains serving London per week:

- by commodity, broken down into the dominant construction flows and other commodities; and

- by direction of flow, whether inbound to London, outbound from London, or wholly within London.

Given that service provision is estimated at a particular point each year, care needs to be taken when interpreting the data. Perhaps not surprisingly, however, it is evident that the 'typical' freight train serving London is an inbound flow of construction materials, most commonly bulk aggregates (i.e. stone or sand). As with the official tonnage data for the earlier period, there were notable fluctuations from year to year, although less so from 2013 to 2019. Almost two-thirds of service provision in 2020 was related to construction traffic but, given that these trains have average loads much higher than for the other London flows, the share of tonnage handled is likely to be considerably higher. In 2020, the key flow types, based on service provision rather than tonnage, were as follows:

- Inbound flows of stone, particularly from two regions with major quarries (i.e. South West and East Midlands) – approx. 50 trains per week;

- Outbound flows of spoil/industrial waste – approx. 22 trains per week;
- Two-way flows of Royal Mail traffic – approx. 20 trains per week;
- Outbound flows of containerised domestic waste – approx. 16 trains per week;
- Outbound flows of vehicles and two-way flows of automotive components – approx. 16 trains per week;
- Inbound flows of sand – approx. 15 trains per week.

These six groups of flows accounted for almost 80% of London's rail freight service provision. The remainder included other flows of sand, plus trains of cement, concrete blocks, recycled aggregates and unitised retail goods.

Figure 4.2 shows a map of the rail freight terminals in London that were active in 2019, a clear majority of which act only as receiving locations, particularly when it comes to those dedicated to construction traffic. Of the 33 terminals, some of them co-located at strategic railheads, 27 were dedicated to construction flows, with three domestic waste terminals and just one terminal each for automotive, intermodal and mail traffic. The three domestic waste terminals acted solely as origins for rail-borne traffic, while the other three non-construction terminals catered for two-way rail flows; by contrast, most of the construction terminals were solely destinations.

Focusing on construction rail freight activity, a typical train carrying 1,500 tonnes is equivalent to 75 lorry loads, reducing vehicle kilometres and GHG emissions by around 75%, as well as reducing local air pollution in urban areas (RFG and MPA, 2019). 'Jumbo'

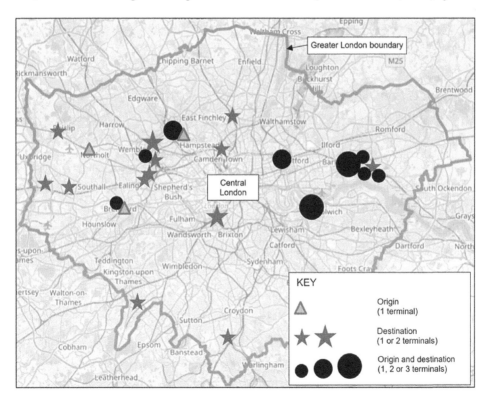

Figure 4.2 Active rail freight terminals in Greater London in 2019

Source: Based on survey data; base map from openstreetmap.org (© OpenStreetMap contributors)

aggregates trains operating into London from quarries in South West England carry more than 3,000 tonnes per train. Some large new infrastructure projects in London have made use of rail (and indeed water) to deliver materials to and remove waste from railheads in the city. Examples have included the London 2012 Olympics site and the Crossrail tunnel, while an ongoing project in the 2020s is the new High Speed 2 (HS2) railway line. In some cases, the use of non-road modes has been mandated in the project agreement, with the aim of reducing the freight transport impacts of the project.

To better understand the nature of London's construction-related rail freight a detailed survey was conducted in 2019. Using open-access data, details of all construction trains serving London terminals that year were recorded. This was supplemented by observation surveys to assess the typical payload of each flow. Table 4.1 presents the key findings for loaded trains, showing the number of unique origin-destination flows, the number of loaded trains and the tonnage estimates. Despite being based on a different data-collection method to the earlier TfL statistics, it appears that there has been a big increase in the tonnage of construction materials handled at London terminals over the last decade or so. The relative importance of flows to London, from London and within London has remained fairly consistent, with the 2019 survey data suggesting that 73% of the tonnage is inbound, 20% is outbound and 7% is wholly within London.

Excluded from the discussion of London rail freight activity thus far are several niche flows of high-value and/or time-sensitive goods on long-distance passenger trains. For example, live seafood is transported from Inverness, in the far north of the United Kingdom, to central London using the Caledonian Sleeper passenger train, with last-mile delivery to restaurants and hotels by road, using electric vehicles (Keltic Seafare, nd). Similarly, InterCity Railfreight works with long-distance passenger train operators to move a range of products including seafood and medical supplies into London (Intercity Railfreight, nd).

Finally, there is considerable transit traffic on London's rail network, which is not serving London's freight requirements *per se*, but is significant in that it uses scarce network capacity and competes for train paths with freight trains serving London. These transit flows exist for various reasons, including the geography of the rail network, the location of freight terminals just beyond London's boundary, and the lack of route capacity or capability elsewhere. For example, the North London Line, which runs east-west just north of the city centre, typically caters for around 25 transiting container trains per day in each direction to/from East Coast ports, plus several trains carrying other products.

Table 4.1 Number of flows, number of trains and tonnage estimates for construction rail freight in London (by direction of flow and commodity, 2019)

Direction of flow	To London	From London	Within London	Total
No. of origin-destination flows	49	13	7	**69**
No. of loaded trains	4,454	1,188	411	**6,053**
Tonnage estimates (million tonnes)	6.34	1.75	0.60	**8.69**

Source: Compiled from survey of open-access real-time data and observation surveys

Water Freight in London

The use of water for freight flows serving London is more limited than the rail freight activity, not least because there is less water-related infrastructure available. That said, according to PLA (2020), there are 31 freight terminals on the River Thames within Greater London. Figure 4.3 shows the annual inland waterway tonnage handled, defined as freight moved between terminals on the River Thames, typically barge traffic. Some of the downstream wharves also handle maritime traffic, though statistics explicitly showing this element within London's boundaries are not provided.

As with rail freight, most traffic handled at the river terminals is construction- and waste-related, including for large projects such as the Tideway sewer currently under construction, but a small number of specialist wharves handle commodities such as vehicles and automotive components, scrap metals and recyclables, raw sugar, timber and petroleum products. London also has a limited canal network, but at present, there is very little use of the canals for freight.

Integration of Water and Rail Freight Flows

While there is a tendency to view either rail or water as an alternative to road haulage, and for much of the time it is the case, some of the London rail and water flows already discussed are integrated. One example is marine-dredged aggregates, which are transferred up the River Thames to rail-connected wharves for onward rail movement followed, typically, by 'last-mile' road haulage, demonstrating good integration of the freight modes. Indeed, all the 'within London' and some of the 'from London' rail freight activity shown in Table 4.1 has arrived at the origin rail terminal (either Angerstein, on the south side of the river, or Dagenham, on the north side) by water. Another example of integration is the vehicles imported by water through the Ford terminal at Dagenham, for onward movement by rail within Britain.

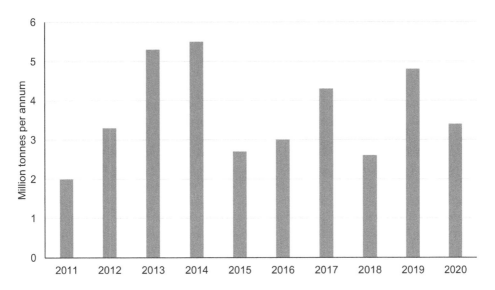

Figure 4.3 Inland waterway freight in London (2011–2020)
Source: Based on PLA data (2021 and earlier years)

Summary of Non-road Freight Activity in London

Rail and water freight already play a considerable role in London for certain commodities and in certain supply chains, particularly forward flows of construction materials and reverse flows of waste (both industrial and domestic), but this role is often overlooked despite being fundamental to the functioning of London's economy. It is evident that such use of non-road modes removes considerable heavy goods vehicle activity from the city's road network, with consequent economic, environmental and social benefits. However, there is very limited use of rail and water in key supply chains involving, for example, retail goods or parcels in London. Reflecting London's limited manufacturing activity, there is little non-road activity related to industries other than the construction sector.

Opportunities and Barriers for Greater Use of Rail and Water in Urban Logistics

This section first considers the opportunities for greater use of non-road modes for urban freight movements, followed by an assessment of key barriers to such change.

Opportunities

While there may be opportunities for rail and water to increase their role in the movement of bulk commodities, the relevant issues are generally well understood and do not necessarily have a specific urban dimension. Using the earlier example of London, new construction-related rail flows have begun when opportunities have arisen, though there may well be latent demand for rail and water freight dependent on the constraints within a particular urban environment. Four interrelated opportunities form the basis of the discussion in this section:

- The considerable challenges associated with decarbonising freight activity;
- Incorporating freight mode choice into supply chain reconfiguration;
- Growth in e-commerce and parcels deliveries;
- Favourable urban transport and land-use planning policies.

There is a growing urgency to find solutions to decarbonise freight transport, not least in urban areas, with considerable attention focused on the harm done by traditional heavy goods vehicles (HGVs). Opportunities arise from both the public policy and private sector business perspectives, though in reality the two are closely related. Public policy measures to promote decarbonisation and the 'green' agenda have gathered pace in recent years, with greenhouse gas (GHG) emissions targets becoming ever more stringent. Freight modal shift is used by companies to demonstrate their efforts to decarbonise their supply chains and show their commitment to CSR. In addition to 'sticks' to limit the use of traditional road freight, there is a role for 'carrots' to encourage the use of non-road modes. Technologies to allow the decarbonisation of modally-integrated, end-to-end freight transport flows already exist (d-fine, 2022).

There are obvious opportunities to take freight mode integration into account when urban supply chains are being reconfigured, with the aim of increasing the use of non-road modes. Much attention is devoted to 'last-mile' urban logistics, focusing on issues such as collection points and fossil-free deliveries (Bosono, 2020), but relatively little consideration is given to reconfiguring the flows into the urban area. The types of solutions proposed for the 'last mile' often require the final stage of the supply chain to be altered by adding a break-bulk location, perhaps introducing a local distribution or consolidation centre and providing an opportunity to rethink the transport mode used to bring the goods into the city.

The typical current scenario whereby an HGV comes into the city to make one or more customer deliveries could be replaced by rail (or water) for the trunk movement into an urban distribution/consolidation centre, with final delivery on foot, by cargo bike, or by non-fossil-fuel van or lorry. This is similar to the longstanding use of rail for mail and parcels traffic to and from urban areas, such as in the United Kingdom (as seen in the London case study above) and elsewhere, except this has typically involved the use of traditional goods vehicles within the urban area rather than more sustainable alternatives. In the United Kingdom, Royal Mail traffic is now handled at dedicated terminals away from passenger stations, rather than the previous practice of using passenger stations themselves, but mail is loaded and unloaded within the station area in other countries (e.g. in the Czech cities of Olomouc and Ostrava).

Focusing specifically on consumer goods, which are responsible for a large proportion of urban freight flows, the growth in e-commerce and associated home delivery may provide opportunities for fulfilment models which make use of rail for the trunk haul of consolidated loads of parcels into a city and, in appropriate circumstances, even for distribution within the urban area (Villa and Monzón, 2021). For example, in principle, a 'zero emissions' B2C (business-to-customer) fulfilment option could involve the use of rail for the trunk haul from a distribution centre to an urban area, with the 'last-mile' delivery carried out by sustainable road-based options. This growth in small-volume freight may provide further opportunities for the integration of passenger and freight activity in urban areas, for instance making use of spare capacity on passenger trains at off-peak times to deliver parcels to collection points at local stations. The combination of regular service provision, fast transit times and good penetration of urban areas (with potential, say, for direct access to a network of station-based collection points) may be an attractive rail-based option in the face of greater constraints on the use of traditional road options.

Similarly, where water routes penetrate the urban area, there may be potential to link barges with 'last-mile' sustainable road freight. The Port of London Authority (PLA, 2020) markets the River Thames as a congestion-free and sustainable way for light freight (e.g. e-commerce) to reach central London, although as was seen above that existing freight uses are mainly for traditional bulk commodities. The examples from elsewhere, set out above demonstrate that water freight can play a greater role given the right conditions.

Behrends (2017) concluded that urban transport planning can have a considerable impact on the suitability of rail freight in urban areas, with urban transport needing to adapt to take account of the benefits of switching mode. To have maximum effect, rail- and water-friendly policies need to be developed as part of a holistic package of measures aimed at reducing the negative impacts of urban logistics. Potential interventions can be categorised as: land-use planning measures; infrastructure measures; market-based and regulatory measures; new technologies; and management measures. One of the key challenges in densely developed urban areas, typically with high land costs, is identifying sufficient land for logistics purposes, but this is often magnified when it comes to finding land connected to the rail or water network. Paris, France, is an exemplar that combines a number of the interventions in its 'logistics hotel' concept at La Chapelle International on the edge of the city centre (Baron and Khodadad-Saryazdi, 2019; Sogaris, 2020). As part of the development of an eco-district, the innovative concept unusually incorporates logistics space in a development that also includes offices, sports facilities, a restaurant and an urban farm. Even more unusually, the 'logistics hotel' has a direct rail connection, as a result of its location adjacent to one of Paris's arterial rail lines. Planned integration of rail (and water) facilities is vital to ensuring that urban areas can be served by these non-road modes.

Finally, it may be expected that a continuing trend towards urbanisation, particularly in developing economies, and the challenges that this brings may provide greater impetus to find innovative solutions which include the use of rail and water.

Barriers

Almost without exception, urban areas are blessed with a dense road network that provides 'go anywhere' freight opportunities, subject to any physical or regulatory barriers. By contrast, the more limited rail and water networks restrict the possibilities for modal shift from road. If non-road modes are to play a greater role in urban logistics, more terminal capacity to load and unload wagons and barges will inevitably be required. Existing terminals may not be capable of handling new flows; for example, it is unlikely that an existing construction or waste terminal will be able to cater for parcels traffic. Both the expansion of existing terminals and the provision of new ones are challenges in densely-populated areas, where space is at a premium and land costs are high. Logistics activities typically suffer from limitations of access and space in urban areas (Bosono, 2020), often made worse for rail and water by the more limited infrastructure in the first place.

Despite offering a means to reduce total road freight activity within urban areas, with the associated economic, environmental and social benefits this brings, there is often opposition to rail and water freight in cities. As Behrends (2017) noted, rail terminals cause environmental impacts which may make them unpopular with local residents and politicians, and the same can be true of water freight facilities. Depending on the nature of the terminal activity, there may be concerns including noise, air pollution and contamination, vibration and smells. Terminals handling construction and waste materials are likely to cause more concern than those for parcels-type activities, the latter handling lighter-weight, quieter trains with fewer terminal-related issues. Nevertheless, terminals may have restrictions on their operations (e.g. operating curfews or noise limits) and new terminals may be vetoed in the planning process, particularly in residential districts of cities. Concerns are sometimes raised about night-time freight activity on railway lines themselves, with some countries (e.g. Germany) installing sound barriers alongside the lines to reduce the disturbance to nearby residents.

There may also be opposition from urban authorities or passenger train operators to the allocation of network capacity to rail freight rather than passenger trains, particularly where network utilisation is high and capacity is scarce. This is particularly the case with mixed-use rail systems dominated by passenger activity, as in most European countries. Where capacity is made available for freight operations, there may be inflexibility in the provision of train paths, leading to inefficient freight outcomes or even the abandonment of plans to use rail. For example, unlike passenger train services, very few of the construction flows identified in the London case study operated every weekday, and some operated only sporadically. This poses challenges for the efficient use of the rail network – should paths for such freight trains be included in the timetable on a daily basis, but often unused, or only on specific days, which then restricts the flexibility for the train to operate when supply chain circumstances dictate? When disruption occurs, passenger trains are often prioritised over freight services, causing supply chain disruption and uncertainty.

Finally, when considering the mode choice decision-making process for freight customers, it can be challenging to overcome inertia and the often poor perception of the service attributes of non-road modes, particularly for those who are used to road-only transport options. When reviewing the freight mode choice literature, Holguín-Veras et al. (2021) found that the most commonly cited modal attributes influencing the choice of mode were freight rate, transit time, and reliability, with shipment size and commodity type being the commodity attributes most identified. Given the particular challenges of delivering in urban areas, there may be considerable apprehension about changing away from road freight, particularly if supply chain reconfiguration is required, potentially with extra time and cost involved. This adds emphasis to the need to consider urban freight mode choice in a holistic way, with a mix of incentives to use rail or water and disincentives to use road when there is a viable alternative.

Conclusion

This chapter has set out a range of examples of the use of rail and water in urban logistics, together with an assessment of the opportunities and barriers associated with the use of these non-road modes in an urban environment. While many of the examples in the literature relate to rare and/or innovative uses of rail and water freight, the case of London shows that, there at least, these non-road modes are used mainly for more traditional types of flows with characteristics which play to their modal strengths (e.g. volume, distance, regularity of flow). It is likely that this holds true more generally, with most urban flows being bulk in nature and largely taking place in a routine and unnoticed manner. Generally speaking, rail and water could, and should, play a greater role in urban logistics, but achieving change often requires considerable effort among a range of stakeholders and, particularly, a supportive policy environment.

References

Alessandrini, A., Delle Site, P., Filippi, F. and Salucci, M.V. (2012), Using rail to make urban freight distribution more sustainable, *European Transport/Trasporti Europa*, 50, 5

Arvidsson, N. and Browne, M. (2013), A review of the success and failure of tram systems to carry urban freight: the implications for a low emission intermodal solution using electric vehicles on trams, *European Transport/Trasporti Europei*, 54 (2013), 5

Baron, M.L. and Khodadad-Saryazdi, A. (2019), Public and public-private cooperation in building resilient urban logistics: The case of 'La Chapelle International Paris', in: Gonzalez-Feliu, J., Chong, M., Vargas Florez, J., & Padilla Solis, J. (eds.), *Handbook of Research on Urban and Humanitarian Logistics*, pp. 1–21, IGI Global

BEHALA (2022), Berliner Hafen- und Lagerhausgesellschaft mbH (BEHALA) website, https://www.behala.de/en/ [accessed on 08/06/22]

Behiri, W., Belmokhtar-Berraf, S. and Chu, C. (2018), Urban freight transport using passenger rail network: Scientific issues and quantitative analysis, *Transportation Research Part E: Logistics and Transportation Review*, 115 (2018), 227–245

Behrends, S. (2017), Burden or opportunity for modal shift? – Embracing the urban dimension of intermodal road-rail transport, *Transport Policy*, 59 (2017), 10–16

Bosono, T. (2020), Urban freight last mile logistics – challenges and opportunities to improve sustainability: A literature review, *Sustainability*, 12, 8769

d-fine (2022), Zero-carbon combined transport: Technology and efficiency analysis of zero-carbon road-rail combined transport, Report on behalf of International Union for Road-Rail Combined Transport (UIRR), May, d-fine

DHL (2022), On the way to zero emission in urban areas, https://www.dhlexpress.nl/en/way-zero-emission-urban-areas [accessed on 08/06/22]

Divieso, E., Lima Júnior, O.F. and De Oliveira, H.C. (2021), The use of waterways for urban logistics: The case of Brazil, *Theoretical and Empirical Researches in Urban Management*, 16(1), 62–85

Diziain, D., Taniguchi, E. and Dablanc, L. (2014), Urban logistics by rail and waterways in France and Japan, 8th International Conference on City Logistics, Procedia – *Social and Behavioral Sciences*, 125(2014), 159–170

Duisburger Hafen (2022), Company website, https://www.duisport.de/ [accessed on 08/06/22]

EEA (2022), Transport and Environment Report 2021: Decarbonising Road Transport – The Role of Vehicles, Fuels and Transport Demand, European Environment Agency (EEA), Copenhagen

Eltis (2015a), Sustainable deliveries of goods in Paris (France), *Eltis: The Urban Mobility Observatory*, https://www.eltis.org/discover/case-studies/sustainable-deliveries-goods-paris-france [accessed on 29/05/22]

Eltis (2015b), Utrecht's sustainable freight transport (The Netherlands), *Eltis: The Urban Mobility Observatory*, https://eltis.org/discover/case-studies/utrechts-sustainable-freight-transport-netherlands [accessed on 08/06/22]

Eltis (2015c), Using waterways to transport construction materials in Ghent (Belgium), *Eltis: The Urban Mobility Observatory*, https://eltis.org/discover/case-studies/using-waterways-transport-construction-materials-ghent-belgium [accessed on 08/06/22]

Holguín-Veras, J., Kalahasthi, L., Campbell, S., González-Calderón, C.A. and Wang, X. C. (2021), Freight mode choice: Results from a nationwide qualitative and quantitative research effort, *Transportation Research Part A: Policy and Practice*, 143(2021), 78–120

Intercity Railfreight (nd), Great partnerships, https://www.intercityrailfreight.com/partnerships/ [accessed on 23/05/22]

Keltic Seafare (nd), Live seafood next day delivery throughout the UK, https://kelticseafare.com/restaurant-delivery/ [accessed on 23/05/22]

Kikuta, J., Ito, T., Tomiyama, I., Yamamoto, S. and Yamada, T. (2012), New subway-integrated city logistics system, *The Seventh International Conference on City Logistics, Procedia – Social and Behavioral Sciences*, 39 (2012), 476–489

Modern Railways (2011), John Lewis anchors Birmingham Gateway, 68(751), 82–84

Modern Railways (2013), All change at New Street, 70(777), 68–72

Muñoz-Villamizar, A., Santos, J., Montoya-Torres, J. R. and Velázquez-Martínez, J. C. (2020), Measuring environmental performance of urban freight transport systems: A case study. *Sustainable Cities and Society*, 52, 101844

ORR (2022), Data Portal, Office of Rail and Road (ORR), https://dataportal.orr.gov.uk [accessed on 23/05/22]

Oxera (2015), What is the contribution of rail to the UK economy? Report prepared for the Rail Delivery Group (RDG), September, Oxera, Oxford

PLA (2020), Port of London Authority Handbook 2020, Port of London Authority (PLA), https://issuu.com/andybullen1/docs/port_of_london_authority_handbook_2020 [accessed on 23/05/22]

PLA (2021), Annual Report & Accounts 2021, Port of London Authority (PLA), https://www.pla.co.uk/Media-Centre/Annual-Report-and-Accounts-2021 [accessed on 23/05/22]

RFG and MPA (2019), Cutting Carbon and Congestion: Rail Freight and Mineral Products working together to build Britain, Rail Freight Group (RFG) and Mineral Products Association (MPA), http://www.rfg.org.uk/wp-content/uploads/2019/10/RFG-MPA-Construction-brochure-August-2019-Final.pdf [accessed on 23/05/22]

Railway Gazette (2021), CarGoTram freight tram service comes to an end, 19 January, *Railway Gazette*, https://www.railwaygazette.com/light-rail-and-tram/cargotram-freight-tram-service-comes-to-an-end/58270.article [accessed on 02/06/22]

Ravichandran, N. (2005), World class logistics operations: The case of Bombay Dabbawallahs, W.P. No. 2005-09-01, Indian Institute of Management

Sogaris (2020), Chapelle international, https://www.sogaris.fr/fiche/chapelle-international/ [accessed on 13/06/22]

TfL (2014), London Freight Data Report: 2014 Update. Prepared by University of Westminster for Transport for London (TfL)

Tramways and Urban Transit (2021), Zurich's cargo tram, 22 December 2021, *Tramways and Urban Transit*, http://www.tautonline.com/zurichs-cargo-tram/ [accessed on 02/06/22]

UNESCAP (2021), Mainstreaming inland waterways into national logistics network: National experience of Bangladesh, Working Paper, December, United Nations Economic and Social Commission for Asia and the Pacific (UNESCAP)

U.S. EPA (2015), SmartWay Vision 2020: A new era of freight sustainability, United States Environmental Protection Agency (U.S. EPA), Washington, DC

Villa, R. and Monzón, A. (2021), Mobility restrictions and e-commerce: Holistic balance in Madrid Centre during COVID-19 lockdown, *Economies*, 9(2), 57

5
CYCLE LOGISTICS
Sustaining the Last Mile

Jonathan Cowie and Keith Fisken

Introduction

This chapter focuses on identifying the critical elements in the successful, i.e. profitable, operation of cycle logistic services in the urban freight market. The focus is specifically on 'profit' because the freight market (in virtually all of its different variants and modes) operates almost exclusively along free market principles. In other words, there is very little intervention by public authorities with regard to economic (quantitative) regulation, through for example the setting of carriage rates, restricting market entry or (going back in time…) specifying a 'duty of carriage', i.e. a legal requirement to accept all items presented for transport at fixed rates. As a result, the critical factors in cycle logistics are those that have a direct effect (either positively or negatively) on commercial profit.

The chapter begins with defining cycle logistics in terms of a formal specification, the characteristics of the main types of vehicles used and operating ranges. It will then consider the main reasons for employing cargo bikes in the urban freight market, before discussing the key factors behind, and main inhibitors to, the modes of successful implementation into urban supply chains. The chapter then finishes with a look at the main areas that offer future potential for further employment of cargo bikes, reflections and conclusions.

What Is Cycle Logistics?

A general definition of 'logistics', certainly within a business context, would be the management and operationalisation of the movement of consumer and intermediate goods from the point of manufacture to the point of consumption. In defining cycle logistics, it would therefore seem to follow that this is where this task is partly or wholly undertaken by cargo bike. This is generally confirmed by Schliwa et al. (2015: 52), who formally defined cycle logistics as:

> …*the use of human-powered or electrically-assisted standard bicycles, cargo bikes and cargo tricycles for the transport of goods between A and B, primarily in urban areas.*

In terms of this chapter therefore, this is the general definition that will be used. As such, it follows that services are likely to operate over the last mile[1] and hence require to be serviced through some form of hub located near the final delivery point. This therefore may include an element of consolidation. There is thus a degree of crossover between cargo bike operations and UCCs (see Chapter 24), but it should be stressed that in the context of cycle logistics, the primary purpose of such hubs is to support operations rather than consolidated final deliveries.

Technical Equipment

In order to give some overview/context to the type of equipment used in the production of cargo bike services, Table 5.1 provides basic details concerning the main types of vehicles used.

Whilst Table 5.1 presents the basic characteristics of the respective vehicles, what these figures represent can best be described as the operational optimum. A clear example of this relates to the maximum payload. In the case of cargo bikes, whilst in theory, heavier weights could be carried, from an operational perspective this then runs into various issues; manoeuvrability is severely compromised resulting in slower speeds, and at an even more basic level, hill starts on difficult surfaces (e.g. cobblestones) become challenging to say the least.[2] One final issue is in regard to cargo tricycles, trikes with higher payloads are now coming onto the market, quoted at around 300–400 kg, but to our knowledge, there is currently little or no publicly available data on the operational experience with these machines. The extent to which such technical maximum weights convert to the operational optimum therefore is yet to be established.

In commercial operation, it should also be noted that both cargo bikes and cargo tricycles are heavily adapted from those bought from the supplier, and in the case of tricycles, are often built from the frame upwards. Without going into technical specifics, alterations are based on operational considerations rather than operational capabilities, with adaptations normally centred around electro-power assist motors, drive chains, braking systems and wheels. In all cases, these are aimed at improving the durability of components, rather than achieving weight reductions. Nevertheless, some 'off-the-shelf' models of similar qualities are now beginning to appear on the market, but at the time of writing, these are prohibitively expensive for any commercial operator.

Operating Range

Operating range may be considered to be an issue with cargo bikes, clearly longer distances become unfeasible/uneconomic hence, as highlighted above, there exists a strong need to

Table 5.1 Main vehicles used in cargo bike logistics

	Bicycles	*Cargo bikes*	*Cargo tricycles*
Defining properties	2 wheels, backpack	2 wheels, cargo box	3 wheels, cargo box
	Unassisted	E-assisted	E-assisted
Max payload	15–20 kg	60–70 kg	200Kgs
Capacity (volume)	0.12 m^3	0.3–0.6 m^3	1.5 m^3
Applications	Document delivery	Small/medium parcel	Larger items
	Fast food	Fresh/market garden produce	Cool box
	Point-to-point		

Source: Developed from Schliwa et al. (2015)

Table 5.2 Cycle logistics, operational characteristics

Average distance (km)	18.00
Longest round (km)	29.93
Shortest round (km)	7.27
Average speed (kph)	14.25
Average no. of stops	18
Highest no. of stops	48
Lowest no. of stops	2

support operations from a hub near the final delivery point. In order to give some overview of operational ranges and properties, Table 5.2 presents operational data from a cycle logistics operator in Edinburgh. This is based on the period covering the first half of December 2021, where deliveries consisted of 19 rounds over six days. All of these were for a single client.

As shown in Table 5.2, the average distance covered per round was 18.00 kilometres at an average speed of 14.25 kph. The Table however shows the adaptability of the mode, in that round length varied from a shortest distance of 7.27 km to the longest at 29.93 km, although half fell in the range between 14 and 21 km.

In terms of the area covered, this generally represents the northern and central areas of Edinburgh, and measured around 43 km², although there did exist several corridors running out from what could be considered the core area. The furthest delivery point away from the hub was just under 6 km. What the figures also suggest is a need to establish a critical mass, as that ultimately is what builds up a feasible area to be served. One off relatively distant deliveries are simply not an option, i.e. not economically feasible, hence the need for complementarity of operations.

There is also a need to consider how 'operating' range is defined, particularly in relation to economic feasibility. Given the pricing structure of deliveries, what is feasible to an operator is one where they will not lose any money. To considerably simplify the equation, if in a given area a single delivery can be guaranteed per round, then that effectively increases the size of the operating area. In most cases, operators will make little return from such deliveries, but on delivery rounds where there is more than one drop off to such areas, this then becomes economically feasible and hence within the operating range. As such, there is a direct link between the operating range and economic feasibility. In terms of cycle logistics however, there is clearly a maximum size of area that can be serviced from a single hub, and whilst there is no other evidence to collaborate this, the case study in Edinburgh would appear to represent such a maximum. In order to service the southern and western areas of Edinburgh therefore, this would require establishing a second hub.

Why Do We Need Cycle Logistics?

When examining the issue of cycle logistics, it is worth considering the backdrop to it, particularly recent developments and trends in the urban freight market. The demand for transport services is a derived demand, in other words, good/services are demanded in order to achieve some other purpose. In the case of freight transport, the primary demand (consumer needs) creates a secondary demand (i.e. derived) for the transportation of these goods and associated services. This is no better illustrated than in the case of the urban freight market with the rise of online shopping, figures for which are shown in Figure 5.1.

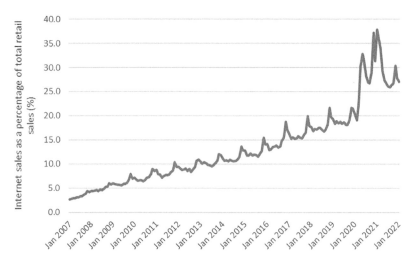

Figure 5.1   E-commerce as a share of total retail sales, United Kingdom
Source: Drawn from ONS statistics (Office for National Statistics, 2022)

What Figure 5.1 shows is internet sales as a percentage of total retail sales, plotted per month, hence including seasonal fluctuations. What this illustrates, certainly up to January 2020, is a very clearly defined trend, rising from a starting point of 2.7% of all sales in January 2007, up to 20.2% by January 2020. In terms of the annual average increase in share of sales, this represents around a 1.5% (compounded) increase every year. The figures in the latter years can clearly be related to COVID-19 restrictions, and whilst still early to predict, suggests that the longer-term effect of which was a single-step increase of around 6–7%, with the underlying trend continuing post-COVID. Whilst this is the primary demand, these trends also represent a significant change in the delivery of goods to the final customer, with the last stage of the supply change increasingly being less towards the retailer and more towards the final customer. In other words, this represents an element of de-centralisation of the final delivery point, and one that is far more fragmented and geographically dispersed. As a consequence, this has contributed to a significant increase in the use of light goods vans (LGVs). For Great Britain, this is illustrated in Figure 5.2.

Figure 5.2 illustrates a significant increase in the total number of registrations in LGVs, a small increase in artics and a small decline in rigids. Whilst clearly not all of the increase in LGVs can be attributed to the retail sector, the underlying trends are certainly consistent with e-commerce patterns. In simple terms, there were twice as many LGVs on the roads in 2020 as there were in 1994, a significant increase and far stronger growth than for example in car registrations. Figure 5.2 also suggests that whilst towards the end of the period the growth rate had begun to slow down, it was nevertheless still on an upwards trajectory. Furthermore, Allen et al. (2017) highlight that in 2015, LGV kilometres accounted for 74% of total goods vehicle activity across Great Britain, which indicates that at that point in time, it was by far the most used vehicle type in transporting goods.

Added to increased e-commerce, Dablanc et al. (2017) also allude to the idea of 'on-demand' instant deliveries. The authors highlight that the emergence of numerous app-based services, instantly connecting consignors, couriers and customers, has led to the existence of 'instant' deliveries, which they define as where delivery occurs within two hours. As such, this almost certainly will be local in nature, delivered by a smaller vehicle (i.e. 3.5 tons or less), and generally occur point to point within the urban environment.

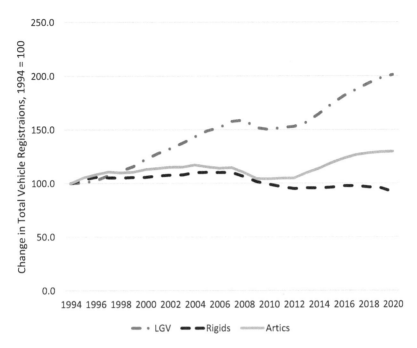

Figure 5.2 Changes in the total number of vehicle registrations, LGV, rigids and articulated vehicles (artics), 1994–2020 (1994 = 100)
Source: Drawn from DfT (2021)

What all of the above means is that the level of road-based activity over the last mile of the supply chain has increased significantly over the last twenty years due to the rise of e-commerce and the longer-lasting effects (on consumer behaviour) of the associated lockdowns and social restriction measures as a consequence of the COVID-19 pandemic. Given the impact this has had on traffic levels, intrusion of public space, and finally the global climate change debate, it would appear to suggest that ways need to be found to lessen the externalities of this activity. Utilising more sustainable modes (and supply chain systems) offers one potential solution, hence the importance (and potential rising importance) of cycle logistics. As an example, Allen et al. (2012) highlight that delivery over the last mile involving cargo tricycles can result in significant reductions in terms of CO_2 emission per parcel (in the order of 55%), overall improvements in vehicle load factors and reductions in vehicle kilometres. To that, Assmann et al. (2020) add that the employment of cargo bikes in last-mile deliveries could reduce greenhouse gas, particulate matter and nitrogen oxide emissions significantly, but importantly that such decreases are dependent upon the appropriate citing of supporting logistical hubs. Furthermore, Schliwa et al. (2015) highlight the key areas in terms of economic, social and environmental goals where cargo bikes can make a significant contribution. These are shown in Table 5.3.

Table 5.3 provides a comparison of relative contributions to each of the goals highlighted for diesel and electric vans, as well as cargo bikes. What it clearly suggests is that whilst diesel vans make a negative contribution to all three areas, a modal shift to electric vans whilst making positive contributions to environmental goals, does little in terms of wider economic and social objectives. Furthermore, if unchecked, at best many of these issues will remain unresolved, and in fact, are more likely to worsen significantly. Cargo bikes on the

Table 5.3 Cargo bike contribution to wider economic, social and environmental goals

Sustainability		Mode of transport		
Impacts		Diesel vans	Modal shift to electric vans	Modal shift to cargo cycles
Economic Goals	Traffic congestion	−	0	+
	Delivery time	−	0	+
	Infrastructure costs	−	0	+
Social goals	Reduction of accidents	−	0	+
	Reduction of vehicles	−	0	+
	Liveability	−	0	+
	Use of public space	−	0	+
Environmental Goals	Reduction of pollutants	−	+	+
	Reduction of CO_2 emissions	−	+	+
	Reduction of noise	−	+	+
	Conservation of energy	−	−	+

Source: Adapted from Schliwa et al. (2015)

other hand offer the potential to make positive contributions to all three areas. The simple conclusion from Table 5.3 is that in order to make any kind of progress, there are considerable advantages to making greater use of cargo bikes in the urban freight market.

Cycle Logistics in the Urban Context

At this point, it is useful to introduce the idea of cycle logistics in the urban context that operates at two different levels, which in simple terms can be defined by the form of the business organisations that operate them. In basic terms, these can be categorised as:

- Fully integrated: in this case, cycle logistics are fully integrated into well-established, well-defined and clearly branded urban logistics supply chains. This would mainly consist of parcel and courier service (PCS) providers, and hence be part of an international logistics network.
- Independent: in this sector, cycle logistics operates both partially within fully integrated supply chains and partially outside of them, and functions almost exclusively at the local level.

The small level of research that exists on the topic has exclusively focused on the independent sector, but nevertheless, many of the findings have clear implications for the fully integrated sector.

Beginning with the whole market, estimates of cycle logistics as a viable carrier in the urban freight market tend to suggest that it offers a great deal of potential. As an example, Lenz and Riehle (2014) highlight that cycle freight can form around 25% of city centre commercial traffic in the medium term, whilst Schliwa et al. (2015) cite other studies that suggest this figure could be considerably higher, at around 51%. In both cases however, no detail is given as to the evidence base from which these estimates were derived, and both figures, particularly the latter, would appear to be on the high side.

At this point, it is useful to highlight that the urban freight market is often mistakenly considered as a single entity, as in, one market, however the reality is that it is made up of multiple markets each serving different sectors of the local economy. This relates to both business-to-business items (B-2-B) and business-to-customer items (B-2-C). Within the context of this chapter however, such complexities are of a scale that a whole text could be devoted to it, and in fact, many of these aspects are covered elsewhere in this *Handbook* (see Chapters 2, 15 and 18). In order to better define the issue in the context of cycle logistics, the urban freight market can be simplified by applying the division by Allen et al. (2000) of the retail urban supply chain system into three sub-sections, namely centralised, de-centralised and hybrid. A (vast!) simplification of these is given in Figure 5.3.

The first, a centralised goods supply system, is where businesses receive goods from a single point of dispatch. This is represented by Retailer 1 in Figure 5.3, hence all deliveries come from a single source. These are likely to be larger stores that belong to some form of retail chain. Note that in terms of consolidation of loads, this occurs at the supplier level, and once consolidated, deliveries are then made to the retailer. Based on the Dutch experience, research by van Rooijen and Quak (2010) would suggest that in terms of the percentage of stores that belong to this category in the urban context, this represents around 75% of the sector. The second sector, a de-centralised goods supply system, is where retailers receive goods from several points of dispatch which could include a variety of different suppliers. This is represented in Figure 5.3 by Retailer 3, where all deliveries are received from a variety of suppliers (S2 to S5). In this simplified example, there will be no geographic-specific consolidation of loads, rather vehicle capacities will determine delivery runs that could be spread over large geographical areas. Finally, a hybrid goods supply system is where a significant proportion of core goods deliveries come through a centralised supply system, but this is augmented by goods received through de-centralised networks. This is represented by Retailer 2 in Figure 5.3, and hence most deliveries are from a single source (or in reality, a few key sources), supplemented by one-offs and special deliveries from secondary suppliers. This could also be augmented by one-off deliveries from the key supplier as a result of customers requiring items before the next main delivery.

As can be implied from the figures given in Table 5.1, any potential role for cycle logistics in the urban supply chain is likely to be over the last mile, involve some element of consolidation of loads and supported by a hub located near the centre in order to create a feasible

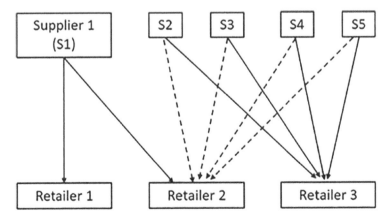

Figure 5.3 The retailer urban freight market (simplified)
Source: Authors

area. For the centralised supply chain, which includes retail chains who control their own inventories, transport operations and terminals, Olsson and Woxenius (2014) highlight that such supply chains are basically efficient because comparatively large lorries can be used and are often fully loaded. This would suggest therefore, there are few if any efficiency gains to be made by adding a further link in the supply chain in the form of last-mile deliveries, i.e. there is no role for cargo bikes in this sector. Consistent with this view, Browne et al. (2005) argue that from a logistical viewpoint, the major potential beneficiaries of specific last-mile delivery services are independent and small retailers combined with operators making small multi-drop consignments. In other words, retailers that are part of de-centralised and to a lesser extent hybrid urban supply chain systems. It is these sectors therefore, where the full potential of cargo bikes can be realised. As stated however, in the retail sector this tends to be a small proportion of the overall market. Using the figures given above, this would only represent a maximum of around 25% of the market.

To a large extent this figure is confirmed by Lajos Sárdi and Bóna (2021), who found that of 375 stores interviewed in Budapest city centre, 29% highlighted that cargo bikes could be used for some of their deliveries, although this consisted of a mix between deliveries from suppliers, home deliveries and inter-store transfers. Importantly however, the assessment was based purely on weight and load characteristics and did not consider operational practicalities or economic feasibility. Taking all of the above into account, a top-end estimate of current market potential for cargo bikes would be around a 25% share, but probably more realistically somewhere between 15% and 20%. Note however that in many respects this is entirely dependent upon both the absolute size of the retail market in a given location and its structure in terms of centralised, de-centralised and particularly hybrid supply chains.

Cycle Logistics as a Viable Business Model

Given the size of the potential market outlined in the previous section, the main issue with regard to cargo bikes is the extent to which this potential can be realised. As a consequence, this section will consider the key issues behind cycle logistics as a viable business model in the urban freight market. All that follows however focuses on the independent sector and begins with a look at the published research on the issue.

In terms of studies into cycle logistics in the urban environment, there really have only been two of note. In the first, Maes and Vanelslander (2012) identified only 14 cycle logistics providers in Belgium, and of these even a high number were relatively recent start-ups, a fact in itself that may raise questions over the commercial sustainability of such enterprises. Furthermore, only one (Ecopostale) had any formal link with a recognised logistics provider (at the time, TNT), as most attempts at co-operation had terminated due to the fact that the tariffs on offer (from the providers) were below operators' costs. This reinforces the fact that where such services exist, these generally operate essentially at the local level. This is also reflected in the business segments in which the mode was used, which the authors found to be mainly postal/package services delimited by time constraints, hence primarily point-to-point that had a demand that required to be met over a highly restricted time horizon. Total market size was estimated to be €550k, which applying a generous 3% inflation rate since that time would still only equate to an average revenue in today's terms of just under €58k gross per operator. Many were one-person businesses and operated as sole traders.

The second was a more extensive study undertaken by Lenz and Riehle (2014), who examined 38 cycle logistic companies across Europe. Again, most were found to be single person or small enterprises, and the use of cargo bikes was very much a clear expression of company philosophy. The main challenges to such providers were found to be primarily the perception of customers as regards the modes viability as a freight carrier, and to a lesser extent poor infrastructure provision. As regards the first point, this is something that our own research has identified as a constraining factor, but in doing so it is perhaps difficult to separate the mode from the provider. In other words, it may not be the viability of the mode, but rather confidence in the provider. As stated, such companies tend to be small in nature and relatively recently established.

One final point to note from this general discussion is that cycle logistics is a rapidly developing area, and hence even what may be considered 'recent' research into the topic may be at best dated, and at worst, the findings no longer valid.

Critical Factors to 'Success' and Main Constraints

As regards specific critical factors with regard to the success of, and barriers to, cycle logistics as a viable business model, our own research has identified three key areas, which are discussed below. All of these are related to the idea of establishing a commercially viable critical mass. In simple terms, this is key to the success of any such operation.

Bottom Up Versus Top Down (Or Start Things from Scratch...)

Within the independent sector, one key issue is an approach to cycle logistics that establishes operations from the bottom up. To clarify, many initiatives involving last-mile deliveries, including those provided by cargo bike, are implemented by the local authority, normally through funded operations of its own or as part of a more general (externally funded) pilot project. In other words, such initiatives are implemented from the top downwards, and inevitably established on top of what is not only an existing urban freight network system, but one that over time has been largely developed along free market principles based upon a highly competitive road freight sector (Cowie, 2017). As a result, costs are minimised and profit margins extremely low, resulting in carriage rates that are difficult, if not impossible, for any new initiative to match. In some senses this reflects an approach from the top down that fails to understand the realities of urban freight operations. The poor success rate of these initiatives tends to corroborate this fact – our own work suggests that even a 3% success rate may be viewed as extremely optimistic.

In the cases studied in the course of our own research, the model of establishment can be clearly identified as 'bottom up'. In one particular example, the initial business was established through what can only be described as a modified form of the door-to-door salesperson approach. Specific sectors were identified, particularly legal practices and local printers, and potential clients approached directly by the company, which at the initial stage constituted a one-person sole trader. In a second case, the business was initially established on the basis of what can be best described as odd jobs combined with short-term contract work, in the latter case normally in the form of a pilot initiative supported by the local authority. In both examples, a key element of the business model has been to define 'the last mile' in multidimensional terms. As stated, clearly the role of cargo bikes in the urban freight market is over 'the last mile' and needs to be supported by a hub near the centre. As highlighted earlier however, this should not be confused with a UCC, as the prime purpose is not to consolidate loads but rather to support operations. As such, 'the last mile' is not a one-dimensional peripheral to centre, but rather includes point-to-point (the only mile), an element of consolidation and (as will be seen later), the first mile.

These basic approaches to business have subsequently been complemented by increasing levels of partnership working, at which point it can be considered to be a viable business model.

Complementarity Rather Than Competition (Partnership Working)

This may seem an obvious critical factor to 'success', and whilst establishing a stand-alone independent cycle logistics provider may be possible, sustaining and developing that business in the medium to longer term becomes difficult. In fact, even initially establishing the business needs some form of financial support. Where the business is more likely to be successful when partnerships or strong working relationships are formed with existing logistics providers, and it is through these collaborations where the independent sector links into the fully integrated one. This is only likely to occur however, where there are clear operational advantages in using cargo bikes.

One key area where cycle logistics has potential advantages over other modes, particularly in the urban context, is a higher level of accessibility to the final delivery point. Jaller et al. (2013) highlight that parking represents a major challenge for drivers attempting to pick up or deliver goods within cities, with the problem being particularly acute in older cities characterised by narrower streets. As an example, in a study based on a pilot initiative undertaken by UPS in five German cities, Lenz and Riehle (2014) found that avoiding the requirement to repeatedly search for a parking space was stated by the firm as a major advantage of the cargo bike over the traditional van. Further evidence is provided by Allen et al. (2017) who conducted a survey of van delivery rounds in Central London. The results showed that in an 8-hour run, on average the vehicle was parked for 62% of the time. Furthermore, whilst the total distance covered by the van was on average 11.9 km, each driver walked 7.94 km, in other words almost two-thirds of the distance that they drove. What this results in is very slow average speeds, and from a highly critical perspective, only a 40% utilisation rate of the main capital input factor (the van). Given that this research was London based, this is perhaps an extreme case, but it does nevertheless present cycle logistic operators with an opportunity to offer a viable complementary service to an existing urban logistics provider. In our own experience, this is normally in the area of smaller packages, hence the PCS delivers the larger items, and the cycle logistics provider the smaller packages. This overcomes the issue of 'stop/start' type nature of delivery rounds, and significant cost savings can be made.

Importance of Company Culture and Key Individuals

Closely related to these ideas is the importance of company culture, and in this context, it specifically relates to a strong commitment to providing a more environmentally sustainable solution for last-mile logistics. The whole success of any such initiative is directly tied into the commitment, skills and drive of key personnel within cycle logistic operators to meeting these wider objectives. In many senses, such individuals are not solely motivated by profit, but by wider social and environmental goals, ideas consistent with Elkington's triple bottom line (Elkington, 1999).

Whilst clearly the case in the independent sector, these ideas easily transfer to the fully integrated sector through the importance of company culture/philosophy, where there is clear evidence that such attitudes are changing in this direction.

Current Constraints

As regards current constraints, Schliwa et al. (2015) guard their findings as to the potential of cycle logistics by putting forward a number of barriers with respect to the development of the mode, in both sectors in fulfilling its full potential. Specifically, these relate to the issue of mixing parcels from larger delivery companies in one vehicle, customer confidence in the mode and finally the lack of an active freight transport policy aimed specifically at the encouragement of cycle logistics. As regards the first point, this is what we would term as one of the main aspects of the more general issue of 'private' goods, and relates to the branding of packages/deliveries. Specifically, in this case, many carriers, both large and small, are reluctant to leave the final mile to a non-branded vehicle, whether that be a cargo bike or not; even where branding is not an issue, carriers are very reluctant to pass responsibility for the final delivery to a third party. As regards customer confidence in the mode, our early work also identified this as a major issue (Cowie and Fisken, 2019), but one that now appears to be rapidly changing. In the first instance, attitudes do appear to be shifting and potential clients more open to the idea of cycle logistics. In the second case, it may be argued that the mode has moved, or at the very least is moving, past the point of 'proof of concept' and emerging as a viable mode in the urban freight market, and this fact is now receiving greater recognition by potential clients.

As regards an active freight transport policy, it has also become evident through our own experience that the commercial success of cycle logistics operations is strongly tied to progressive local policy measures in the area of green urban logistics. Nevertheless, policy development in this area could at best be described as limited. Kiba-Janiak (2017), for example, in a study of twelve cities found that very few could be described as having a high level of urban freight policy maturity. In other words, in the vast majority of cases, very little attention was paid to urban freight in policy documents. Akgün et al. (2019) add that one key limiting factor is a lack of finance, or to be more exact, a lack of budget, to pursue a pro-active urban freight policy. As such, to date, this lack of policy development represents a ceiling on what can be achieved by cargo bike logistics in the urban context. There are however clear signs that this is an area that is now seeing some change. As an example, in the Netherlands over 40 municipalities have signed the National Green Deal Zero Emission City Logistics (GD-ZES), in doing so declaring themselves in favour of emission-free city logistics by 2030. Low-emission zones are another example that, whilst to date have had a limited impact on the urban freight sector in terms of modal shifts, is an expanding area of policy that offers the potential to improve (in relative terms) the economics of cargo bike logistics and hence lead to its increased use in the urban environment.

Future Prospects

Future possible developments surround the issue of the first, rather than the last, mile, specifically the consolidation of consignments from retailers where these have been purchased through freight auctions or other associated platforms. As a consequence, one retailer may have a variety of consignments for different PCS providers. The whole issue of collections is particularly problematic for these companies, as whilst deliveries are pre-planned, the need for collections tends to arise in the course of delivery runs. This can be highly disruptive to schedules and result in significant increased costs. This is where cycle logistics providers have achieved some success, where these collections can be consolidated over the first mile, and hence the PCS carrier collects from one single point, resulting in significantly reduced costs associated with such activities.

A second potential growth area surrounds the idea of 'the only mile', which is strongly related to the concept of the localisation of freight. This is particularly relevant to the independent sector, and indeed could be argued to be a key element in establishing the business, in other words, the need to link into and make strong connections with local businesses. In the early stages however, this has been on the basis of providing point-to-point services. Where considerable potential exists is to develop the market further where the carrier offers the opportunity to link up local businesses with local clients, through the offer of a 'one-stop shop' (and delivery) option. This is particularly relevant with regard to high-end/specialist consumable markets, and with regard to cycle logistics, we are seeing considerable development of these markets and logistical concepts.

Reflections, Summary and Conclusions

The first clear conclusion from the chapter is that cycle logistics is an area that has seen rapid development over the last ten to fifteen years, and at a rate of progress that is unlikely to abate in the near future. Whilst this chapter has mainly concentrated on the independent sector, we are now seeing clear examples of expanding and sustained cycle logistic operations within the integrated sector, with leading PCS providers such as DHL, Fedex and DPD to name but three investing heavily in the mode.

In terms of key factors to the successful employment of cargo bikes in the urban environment, to a lesser extent, this has been based on the provision of point-to-point services on time-limited lightweight consignments. Undoubtedly however, where greater progress has been made is through the use of cargo bikes to complement existing urban freight operations and certainly in the initial stages, employed where there is a clear operational advantage. In terms of constraints, the main ones to date can best be described as low perceptions of mode capabilities and public policies that have generally avoided the issue of the full social cost of urban freight operations. In both of these areas however, there is clear evidence that attitudes are changing.

To conclude, there is no doubt that the image of cargo bikes on the street in terms of both independent and fully integrated sectors will become an increasingly common site over the course of the next five to ten years. Don't watch this space, just wait for your next delivery….

Acknowledgements

For their enthusiasm and valuable insights on the subject, the authors wish to express their kind thanks to Charlie Mulholland and Rob King at Zedify, as well as our partners on the EU North Sea Region Surflogh project in the province of Drenthe and cities of Borås, Groningen and Mechelen.

Note

1 In order to clarify, the 'last mile' is not a literal mile, but rather the generic term used for the short-range final leg of the supply chain. This idea is developed further later in the chapter.

References

Akgün, E. Z., Monios, J., Rye, T., and Fonzone, A. (2019). Influences on urban freight transport policy choice by local authorities. *Transport Policy*, 75, 88–98. https://doi.org/10.1016/j.tranpol.2019.01.009

Allen, J., Anderson, S., Browne, M., and Jones, P. (2000). A framework for considering policies to encourage sustainable urban freight traffic and goods/service flows: summary report. In *Transport*

Studies Group (Issue March). http://westminsterresearch.wmin.ac.uk/7720/%5Cnhttp://westminsterresearch.wmin.ac.uk/7724/

Allen, J., Browne, M., Woodburn, A., and Leonardi, J. (2012). The role of urban consolidation centres in sustainable freight transport. *Transport Reviews, 32*(4), 473–490. https://doi.org/10.1080/01441647.2012.688074

Allen, J., Piecyk, M., Piotrowska, M., McLeod, F., Cherrett, T., Ghali, K., Nguyen, T., Bektas, T., Bates, O., Friday, A., Wise, S., and Austwick, M. (2017). Understanding the impact of e-commerce on last-mile light goods vehicle activity in urban areas: The case of London. *Transportation Research Part D: Transport and Environment, 61*, 325–338. https://doi.org/10.1016/j.trd.2017.07.020

Assmann, T., Lang, S., Müller, F., and Schenk, M. (2020). Impact assessment model for the implementation of cargo bike transshipment points in urban districts. *Sustainability (Switzerland), 12*(10), 4082–4101. https://doi.org/10.3390/SU12104082

Browne, M., Sweet, M., Woodburn, A., and Allen, J. (2005). *Urban Freight Consolidation Centres Final Report* (Issue March).

Cowie, J. (2017). Competition and complementarity in road freight: Key drivers and consequences of a dominant market position, In Cowie, J. and Ison, S.G., (eds), *The Routledge Handbook of Transport Economics*. Aldershot: Routledge, 348–367.

Cowie, J., and Fisken, K. (2019). Delivering on Sustainable Logistics by thinking inside the Box – a case study of a successful business model. Scottish Transport and Applications Research (STAR) Conference, 1–14.

Dablanc, L., Morganti, E., Arvidsson, N., Woxenius, J., Browne, M., and Saidi, N. (2017). The rise of on-demand 'Instant Deliveries' in European cities. *Supply Chain Forum, 18*(4), 203–217. https://doi.org/10.1080/16258312.2017.1375375

Department for Transport (DfT) (2021). *Transport Statistics Great Britain 2021*. London: Department for Transport.

Elkington, J. (1999). *Cannibals with Forks*. London: Capstone.

Jaller, M., J. Holguin-Veras and S. Hodge (2013). Parking in the city: Challenges for freight traffic. *Transportation Research Record, 2379*, 46–56.

Kiba-Janiak, M. (2017). Opportunities and threats for city logistics development from a local authority perspective. *Journal of Economics and Management, 28*, 23–39. https://doi.org/10.22367/jem.2017.28.02

Lajos Sárdi, D., and Bóna, K. (2021). A geometrical structure-based new approach for city logistics system planning with cargo bikes and its application for the shopping malls of Budapest. *Applied Sciences, 2021*, 3300. https://doi.org/10.3390/app11083300

Lenz, B., and Riehle, E. (2014). Bikes for urban freight? *Transportation Research Record: Journal of the Transportation Research Board, 2379*(1), 39–45. https://doi.org/10.3141/2379-05

Maes, J., and Vanelslander, T. (2012). The use of bicycle messengers in the logistics chain, concepts further revised. *Procedia - Social and Behavioral Sciences, 39*, 409–423. https://doi.org/10.1016/j.sbspro.2012.03.118

Office for National Statistics. (2022). *Retail industry - Office for National Statistics*. Retail Industry. https://www.ons.gov.uk/businessindustryandtrade/retailindustry

Olsson, J., and Woxenius, J. (2014). Localisation of freight consolidation centres serving small road hauliers in a wider urban area: Barriers for more efficient freight deliveries in Gothenburg. *Journal of Transport Geography, 34*, 25–33. https://doi.org/10.1016/j.jtrangeo.2013.10.016

Schliwa, G., Armitage, R., Aziz, S., Evans, J., and Rhoades, J. (2015). Sustainable city logistics - Making cargo cycles viable for urban freight transport. *Research in Transportation Business and Management, 15*, 50–57. https://doi.org/10.1016/j.rtbm.2015.02.001

van Rooijen, T., and Quak, H. (2010). The sixth international conference on city logistics local impacts of a new urban consolidation centre – The case of. *Procedia – Social and Behavioral Sciences, 2*(3), 5967–5979. https://doi.org/10.1016/j.sbspro.2010.04.011

6
DRONES
The Scope for Integration into Multi-modal Urban Logistics Services

*Matt Grote, Andy Oakey, Aliaksei Pilko,
Angela Smith and Tom Cherrett*

Introduction

First emerging in the late 2010s, commercial operations of Uncrewed Aerial Vehicles (UAVs, commonly known as drones) have been expanding ever since across a number of sectors for purposes such as surveillance and security, photography and video, infrastructure and agriculture inspection, mapping and surveying, assisting emergency services, humanitarian aid provision and environmental monitoring (Rana et al. 2016; Lin et al. 2018; Darvishpoor et al. 2020; Sah et al. 2021; Gao et al. 2021; Grote et al. 2021a). Typically, these applications are predominantly lower-risk services involving drones flown within Visual-Line-of-Sight (VLOS) of a manual safety pilot.

For some time, logistics services (i.e., payload delivery) have been postulated for drones, both in urban areas and beyond, and particularly in healthcare settings, offering potential benefits such as reductions in service times, energy consumption, harmful atmospheric emissions and numbers of van/truck-based trips, as well as improved access to locations that are hard to reach by existing surface transport modes (e.g., crossing waterways or where road infrastructure is poor/limited/congested). To date however, very few large-scale commercial examples have been established worldwide (Rana et al. 2016; Scott and Scott 2017; Goodchild and Toy 2018; Lin et al. 2018; Wright et al. 2018; Aurambout et al. 2019; Eichleay et al. 2019; Sah et al. 2021; Grote et al. 2021a). In order to be viable for logistics purposes, drones need to fly over distances that take them out of visual contact with the operator, known as operations Beyond-Visual-Line-of-Sight (BVLOS). Such operations entail higher risks due to concerns associated with communications reliability, air risk, ground risk, remote platform health monitoring and reliance on appropriately trained personnel to oversee activities (e.g., mission commanders, safety pilots, loaders), particularly when flying over densely populated urban areas.

With a focus on medical use cases and using first-hand experience of operating BVLOS flights, this chapter will discuss the practical realities of integrating drones into existing urban logistics supply chain infrastructures, specifically:

   i Public acceptance of drones for urban logistics purposes.
   ii Payload capabilities of drones relative to the service demand.

iii Adherence to client quality assurance requirements when transporting sensitive payloads.
iv Implications of dangerous goods regulations for drone payloads.
v Implications of air and ground risks on route planning and optimisation.
vi Mechanisms for integrating drones alongside crewed aircraft in shared airspace.
vii Overall service reliability given weather conditions and minimal risk routing.
viii Cost implications of utilising drones as part of multi-modal urban logistics supply chains.

Public Acceptance of Drones for Urban Logistics Purposes

Public acceptance is a dominant theme within the discourse around emerging drone technology and the use cases to which the technology might be applied, such as for urban logistics purposes. In general, the paradigm of public acceptance has developed from models of the willingness to accept and use emerging technologies, initially used within the context of Information Technology (Stilgoe and Cohen 2021). Venkatesh et al. (2003) provide a detailed overview of models which seek to understand and quantify behavioural intentions with respect to the use of technologies, taking account of factors such as attitudes towards the technology, subjective norms, ease of use and perceived usefulness. There is however some criticism that a focus on acceptance positions the public as reactive to change rather than providing for a wider spectrum of feedback and co-creation opportunities (Batel et al. 2013; Stilgoe and Cohen 2021). Stilgoe and Cohen (2021) argue for a shift towards exploring what is acceptable rather than making acceptance a target and consider that emerging transport technologies such as automated vehicles are currently not well-defined, making it unclear what the public is being asked to accept.

Polls and surveys have sought to determine the prevailing issues which may act to reduce public acceptance of drones, finding that the potential for loss of privacy, safety risks and security issues are the most cited areas of concern, followed by noise, environmental impacts, including visual intrusion and impacts on wildlife (Smith et al. 2022). Closer scrutiny of these studies, however, reveals that ambiguity exists as to the extent of these concerns when related to the use of drones specifically for logistics. This ambiguity has resulted from the conflation with broader drone uses such as for building inspection and photography, alongside the use of prompting within questions which actively problematises drones amongst what is a largely disengaged public (Smith et al. 2022).

The extent to which various potential impacts will be manifest will be dependent on the drone's technical capabilities, deployment scenario and the local context within which the drones would operate. For instance, privacy impacts will be dependent upon the proximity and frequency of drone flights to locations with greater sensitivities such as residential areas (Klauser and Pedrozo 2017; Tan et al. 2021). Measures such as pixilation of any video footage captured during operation, limited sound recording, and data use and storage protocols will limit the scope for actual loss of data privacy. Concerns could still prevail however as concepts of privacy may extend to the physical presence of the drone (Boucher 2016; Bajde et al. 2017), with the potential that the public will draw upon existing social representations of drones formed around heuristics such as hobby drones and media references. Potential safety and noise impacts are also highly context-dependent, and the development of urban logistics use case scenarios and trials can provide opportunities to explore the potential implications of deployment with stakeholders.

The use of drones for what may be a social benefit, such as medical deliveries, is considered by some agencies as an initial step in achieving wider acceptance of the use of drones in logistics (the reader is referred to European Union Aviation Safety Agency (EASA) (2021c) and UK Research and Innovation (UKRI) (2021) as examples). The advantages of using drones for the transportation of medical items have been demonstrated in developing countries, with Zipline providing an established medical drone delivery in Rwanda (Ling and Draghic 2019). Here, drones provide significant delivery time advantages for blood products in the face of limited surface transport links and/or challenging geographies.

Examples of deployment in medical settings within more developed countries are beginning to emerge, and studies have indicated that the public is more receptive to the use of drones for social good. However, Smith et al. (2022) caution that these findings are open to alternative interpretation and may reflect an underlying desire to contain the use of drones for narrowly defined purposes and therefore limit the potential impacts. There is also a tendency for respondents to provide socially desirable responses to healthcare uses, with organisations such as the UK's National Health Service (NHS) providing for wider social meanings (Antosa and Demata 2021). Greater readiness to accept drone logistics uses associated with health care therefore does not confer acceptance of deployment in other settings.

Payload Capabilities of Drones Relative to Service Demand

The majority of logistics studies have reflected on drones being used for the carriage of consumer goods parcels, replacing or supporting traditional delivery vehicles (e.g., vans/trucks/cargo bikes) that will have payload capacities far in excess of those typical for drones (Dorling et al. 2017; IEEE 2021; Ford 2022; Urban Arrow 2022). In many urban and inter-urban applications of drones for logistics purposes, such as blood stock or medicine transport (see case study box below), the goods are considerably more bespoke in nature than consumer parcels, and have to adhere to specific packaging standards that meet regulator and customer requirements as a result (MHRA 2017b; UPDWG 2022). These standards are typically stipulated to ensure that environmental factors such as temperature are maintained, and that goods are protected from damage (see subsequent section), particularly in the case of some products (e.g., diagnostic specimens) where dangerous goods regulations are observed (see the subsequent section).

Furthermore, based on the authors' practical experiences, to realise the benefits of drones over existing logistics modes, goods must be delivered in standard quantities, and not broken into an excessive number of smaller consignments (deliveries) to suit drone payload capabilities. Breaking a consignment into many smaller deliveries is likely to increase the overall costs and energy requirements of the drone due to repeat flights. Additionally, the potential time saving resulting from using drones in multi-modal logistics would be significantly reduced if only part of the delivery was completed in a faster time.

The need to carry heavier payloads will impact the energy consumption and flight range of drone platforms (Dorling et al. 2017; Consortiq 2022), with larger payload volumes likely to increase drone frontal area, regardless of whether payloads are carried in a hold or underslung, increasing the energy demand and decreasing the range for a given energy capacity (NASA 2021). As a result, copter-type vertical take-off and landing (VTOL) drones are unlikely to be capable of serving many use cases without intermediate refuelling/charging stops/battery changes, and many logistics applications will require a fixed-wing drone platform instead. This does not come without challenges as fixed-wing drones are typically larger in footprint than purely VTOL platforms, meaning that the number of safe and

Drones

Figure 6.1 Medium Versapak loaded into the drone used in the chemotherapy medicine case study for the Isle of Wight
Source: Authors

suitable landing sites to service customers is more limited, particularly in densely populated urban areas where open space is at a premium.

Should drones become prevalent in the logistics of a specific commodity, changes to industry packaging standards may occur to enable easier transport. For example, the national blood delivery network in Rwanda is almost entirely served by Zipline's drone platform (Ackerman and Koziol 2019), allowing the standard packaging to be designed around the platform used. However, until a tipping point in uptake/adoption is reached, it is unlikely that well-established industry standards will significantly change as it would be uneconomical to do so (Gobble 2020).

Adherence to Client Quality Assurance Requirements When Transporting Sensitive Payloads

It is vital that the quality assurance requirements of the client (or of the regulatory authority for the clients' industry) are satisfied when transporting sensitive payloads by drone. Logistics operators transporting medical goods in the United Kingdom must comply with the Good Distribution Practice (GDP) guidelines produced by the Medicines and Healthcare products Regulatory Agency (MHRA 2017a). These guidelines are intended to ensure that conditions experienced during transport do not adversely affect the stability of medicines or

> **Aseptic Cancer Medicine Case Study**
>
> The movement of short shelf-life aseptic cancer medicines from Portsmouth Pharmacy Manufacturing Unit, on the UK mainland, to St. Mary's Hospital, Isle of Wight, UK is currently completed by a combination of taxis and hovercraft in an end-to-end journey that takes a minimum of 1 hour 25 minutes but is subject to delays resulting from waiting times and road congestion. Trials are exploring the potential for drones to provide a more responsive transport service for these medicines. Regarding payload, a typical delivery consists of two boxes, each containing at least one medicine. The maximum dimensions of each medicine are 300 × 150 × 17 mm, with a mass of 1.1 kg. One box has a 2–8°C temperature range requirement (requiring one or more cool packs) and the other has an ambient temperature requirement.
>
> Based on these requirements, any drone being used to deliver these goods should be able to deliver at least one of the two boxes in a single flight as a minimum requirement. Furthermore, temperatures must be maintained, meaning validated industry-standard packaging and coolant must be used. The different temperature requirements also mean that the loads cannot be mixed.
>
> To satisfy these needs, a medium Versapak was selected (460 (L) × 305 (H) × 255 (W) mm, gross weight ~5 kg), which is an insulated medical carrier commonly used in transporting goods for the UK's NHS (e.g., medicines, pathology samples, vaccines) (Versapak 2021). An electric hybrid VTOL/fixed-wing drone with a 5 m wingspan (Figure 6.1) was used to transport the Versapak during the case study (University of Southampton 2022).

medical products (i.e., assurance that payload quality is not diminished by transport). Monitoring of the conditions during transport that affects stability is part of this process, ensuring the payload has remained within specification and highlighting any instances where this is potentially not the case. Usual approaches to stability testing for medicines are based on climatic conditions prevalent in the intended region of distribution and dispensing (Branch 2005; Bajaj et al. 2012), and therefore typical quality assurance specifications relate to temperature and humidity. Drones are an emerging urban logistics transport mode, and consequently, information regarding the extent to which platform design and operation could result in out-of-specification conditions is scarce (Grote et al. 2021a).

Drones are highly manoeuvrable, capable of rapid accelerations and decelerations that could exert considerable force on payloads, and are often propelled by multiple rotor systems, leading to concerns regarding how well vibration is controlled and/or balanced. It is reasonable to expect that the stability of most medicines is unlikely to be affected by these vibrations, given a history of successful transport onboard conventional aircraft. However, some medicines may be especially sensitive (e.g., monoclonal antibodies can aggregate and lose potency when shaken/dropped (Torisu et al. 2017)), and there is a need to potentially monitor vibration and shock during transport.

There have been a number of studies into drone in-flight environments and their effects on payload stability. Oakey et al. (2021) demonstrated that drone in-flight environments can subject payloads to a much wider range of vibration frequencies than would be experienced in other modes of transport, dependant on both the type of drone and the rigidity of payload packaging. Amukele et al. (2017) investigated the long-range transport by drone (258 km flown in 174 minutes) of biological samples, finding that stringent environmental controls were necessary to mitigate the effects of in-flight conditions (temperature, acceleration and vibration). Beck et al. (2020) investigated the possibility of delivering adrenaline auto-injectors (e.g., EpiPen) by drone (~10 km flown in 18 minutes), finding that the in-flight environment did not have any adverse effect.

In general, adherence to quality assurance requirements for drone payloads during transport is an area that requires considerable further research if the necessary evidence base to support the integration of drones into large-scale commercial logistics services is to be generated, particularly where sensitive payloads are concerned. As a specific example of the work required, establishing a register of potential vibration and g-force stresses and ranges is proposed for consideration by medical regulators, enabling potential risk to specific medical payloads to be quantified and managed. Ongoing or future research projects involving trials of drone logistics should be viewed as opportunities to build the necessary evidence base through monitoring and recording of in-flight conditions, and any associated impacts on payload quality.

Implications of Dangerous Goods Regulations for Drone Payloads

When integrated into multi-modal urban logistics services, drones may be required to transport payloads containing substances classified by the United Nations (UN) as Dangerous Goods (DG) when carried by air. In a healthcare setting, drone payloads containing items such as diagnostic specimens (i.e., pathology samples taken from patients), medicines, blood and organs for transfusion/transplant, medical devices and emergency equipment (e.g., defibrillators) have all been identified as likely to involve DG (Grote et al. 2021a).

Annex 18 to the Convention on International Civil Aviation (the Chicago Convention) (ICAO 2011) sets out the broad global principles governing the safe transport of DG by air. These have been expanded and published by the International Civil Aviation Organisation (ICAO 2020a) as the 'Technical Instructions for the Safe Transport of Dangerous Goods by Air' (known as the Technical Instructions; TI). The provisions of the TI detail the procedures and requirements for safe transport by air for each of the many (3,000+) substances classified as DG, including aspects such as quantity limits, packing instructions, documentation, loading, personnel training requirements, emergency response and leak/spill procedures. International civil aviation operations are obliged to comply with the TI, and domestic civil aviation operations are encouraged to do likewise (ICAO 2019).

Historically, the TI have developed exclusively from the perspective of application to crewed aircraft, particularly the operation of large, fixed-wing aeroplanes of the type typically used for the vast majority of airfreight. Consequently, there are no explicit references to drones within the provisions of the TI, leading to uncertainty and a lack of clarity for regulators and drone operators as to how the regulations should be interpreted and applied to this emerging mode of transport for urban logistics (Grote et al. 2021a).

Typically, the current process by which drone operators obtain approval to carry DG is by application to the National Aviation Authority (NAA) in the intended country of operation. Applications are considered based on case-specific risk assessments submitted by operators. DG approval is granted, even when full compliance with the TI is not necessarily achieved, as long as the NAA is satisfied that risks have been mitigated to an acceptable level (ICAO 2019; CAA 2021b; Grote et al. 2021a). In Europe, for example, drone operations are categorised as 'Open', 'Specific' or 'Certified', with carriage of DG only permissible in the more restrictive Specific or Certified categories. Regulations for the Certified category (i.e., full airworthiness type certification of aircraft similar to that for crewed aviation) are currently still under development. This means that, from a practical perspective, carriage of DG is only possible in the Specific category for now, with DG approval typically issued by NAAs as part of their overall case-specific operational authorisation assessment (CAA 2020; CAA 2021b; EASA 2021a). Hence, NAAs bear the responsibility for approving the application of (or deviation from) the TI in each case-specific situation without any explicit guidance relating to drones being available in the provisions of the TI, leaving the regulations open to interpretation by different NAAs.

Whilst case-specific DG approvals are a practical and expedient solution in the short term, with large-scale integration into logistics services, drones would become an increasingly prevalent mode for airfreight. Over the longer term, it would seem sensible to work towards revision of the TI explicitly to include drone operations, which would entail collaborative working across borders due to the international nature of the DG regulations.

Other transport modes (i.e., road, rail and maritime) are subject to their own DG regulations, but there is considerable overlap between each set (including those for air) due to shared principles based on the UN recommendations for transport of DG (UNECE 2021). In multi-modal urban logistics, operators need to ensure that the DG regulations applicable to each different mode by which a payload may be transported during a trip are satisfied. Road vehicles are the mode most likely to interact with drones, transporting payloads to/from landing sites, although foot porters or cycle couriers might be involved as well (Grote et al. 2021a). The DG regulations for road (UNECE 2017) specifically address road-air transshipment, stating that packages that do not entirely meet the requirements of the DG regulations for road are still acceptable for transport in road vehicles, as long as the packages conform to the TI. It seems prudent for logistics service providers always to check the specific regulations according to transport mode as part of best practice (Mohr 2021). Foot porters and cycle couriers are not subject to any specific DG regulations, but it would seem reasonable to assume that the transport of payloads in accordance with the DG regulations for air and road (plus any additional safety procedures stipulated by the organisations involved, such as health service organisations, cycle courier or porter service providers) would be sufficient (Grote et al. 2021a).

Broadly, the purpose of the TI is to ensure the safe transport of DG by air, protecting packages from damage, leaks or spills under the conditions typically encountered during routine aircraft operations. However, in late 2021/early 2022, the UK NAA developed a regime for designing and approving crash-protected containers specifically for DG carried by drones (CAA 2021a). The implication of this is an expectation that the protection for DG carried by drones will be beyond that for crewed aircraft, i.e., an expectation that, for drone operations, DG should be prevented from escaping into the surroundings not only during routine operations but also beyond that in circumstances up to and including a catastrophic aircraft crash. This is because, typically, drones are not certified to the same rigorous airworthiness standards as crewed aircraft (Grote et al. 2021a).

Implications of Air and Ground Risks on Route Planning and Optimisation

As with any method of transportation, there are inherent risks to operation, and integrating drones into multi-modal urban logistics services is no exception. At the time of writing, there are few commonly agreed design and manufacturing standards for small logistics drones, with the default position being case-specific reviews by the NAA before authorisation (i.e., case-specific operational authorisation) for operations involving any of the following: (i) flight BVLOS; (ii) aircraft with a Maximum Take Off Mass (MTOM) greater than 25 kg; (iii) flight greater than 400 feet (120 metres) above ground level; or (iv) aircraft with a maximum dimension greater than 3 metres being flown over assemblies of people (CAA 2020). Whilst this authorisation regime captures the majority of defects, it is neither perfect nor sustainable when scaled. Whilst progress continues to standardise and reduce the risk of the aircraft departing controlled flight as low as reasonably possible (ALARP), it must be recognised that this cannot achieve zero risk, particularly with the projections for large numbers of drones operating in our skies in the future.

Therefore, other means of reducing the direct risks to third parties (Third-Party Risks; TPR) posed by drones, be that to persons on the ground or to other aircraft in the air, must be sought. The next means of risk reduction that can be adopted relates to operational risk, i.e., changing the way the drone is operated in order to control the level of TPR exposure. This becomes particularly important for operations in and around urban areas, where the highest demand for logistics services is expected. To accomplish operational risk reduction, an ability to model and quantify the risk is necessary, and there are frameworks being developed to achieve this such as the Specific Operational Risk Assessment (SORA) (JARUS 2019).

Analysis of ground risk (i.e., the risk posed to third parties on the ground) is achieved through the estimation of the probability of an undesirable event (such as a fatality) occurring as a result of the drone losing control. Such modelling is complex both theoretically and computationally; however software has been developed to achieve this (Pilko and Tait 2021). The software produces a geospatial grid detailing the probability of a drone causing a fatality on the ground at all locations on the grid. This allows TPR exposure to be controlled simply by navigating the drone along different trajectories. Additional work has expanded the optimisation space from purely spatial to include the variation of TPR throughout the day due to time-fluctuating population densities, adding a temporal dimension to the optimisation (Pilko et al. 2022).

Analysis of air risk (i.e., the risk posed to other airspace users), either through direct collision or infringement of a protected volume of airspace around another aircraft, is considerably more difficult as it is a highly dynamic problem, therefore lending itself to agent-based and Monte Carlo methods.[1] Currently, the majority of drone logistics flights are confined to segregated airspace (i.e., designated areas of airspace from which all other aircraft are excluded) and the collision risk with conventional crewed aviation is therefore very low, only resulting from either party violating airspace. Despite this, full integration of drones into unsegregated (i.e., shared) airspace is desired by many operators (see subsequent section).

Simulation-based modelling of novel shared airspace structures has suggested that a 'layers' concept, where altitude is determined by flight direction, likely provides a suitable trade-off between rigid structure and reduction of collision risk (Sunil et al. 2015). Other methods have taken a data-driven approach by using transponder data to determine traffic density. The commonality is the arrival at a probability of infringing the protected volume around an aircraft, although the dimensions of this volume vary themselves.

These air risk probabilities can be superimposed on the same grid as the ground risk values to create a holistic risk environment. This can then be used as a cost-map for a variety of flightpath planning algorithms to plan trajectories that minimise TPR or ensure that it does not exceed a given value. This acceptable risk threshold will likely be set by regulators; however its current value is usually around 1e-7 fatalities per flight hour as a Target Level of Safety (Dalamagkidis et al. 2008).

Shared Airspace

Typically, the current approach to accommodating commercial drone operations within a country's airspace system, including for purposes such as development of drone urban logistics services, is for drone operators to apply to the NAA to reserve a specified volume of airspace exclusively for their intended drone flights, i.e., a Segregated Airspace Volume (SAV) that excludes all other airspace users (Grote et al. 2022). For example, drone operators in the United Kingdom apply to the Civil Aviation Authority (CAA; the UK's NAA) for activation of an SAV known as a Temporary Danger Area (TDA) (CAA 2020). This approach reduces the risk of mid-air collisions involving drones by enforcing complete segregation but represents considerable inconvenience for other airspace users forced to find alternative activity areas and/or routings and can cause high traffic density 'choke points' as aircraft are funnelled around SAVs (Grote et al. 2022).

Due to the expansion of commercial drone operations, which is likely to continue at pace if urban logistics services utilising drones flown BVLOS are to become commonplace, there is an increasingly urgent requirement for an alternative to SAVs whereby drones and crewed aircraft can be integrated harmoniously within the airspace system without unfairly disadvantaging either party, enabling this finite resource to be shared equitably (Alarcón et al. 2020; Hatfield et al. 2020; Merkert and Bushell 2020; Capitán et al. 2021). The global response to this requirement for shared airspace is known as the UAV Traffic Management (UTM) concept, an over-arching term used by the ICAO to describe the provision of services by which drones will be managed, controlled and integrated alongside crewed aircraft (CAA 2019; ICAO 2020b; Xu et al. 2020).

Ongoing developments in the UTM domain include: the European U-Space concept based on the Concept of Operations for European UTM Systems (CORUS) research project; development by the Federal Aviation Authority (FAA; the USA's NAA) and the National Aeronautics and Space Administration (NASA) of a UTM system to integrate drones into national airspace in the United States of America (USA); the UAV Operation and Management System (UOMS) under development in China; the UTM research agenda set by the UK Government's innovation accelerator for cities, transport and places; and UTM concepts being developed in Singapore by the Nanyang Technological University and in Japan by the Japan Aerospace Exploration Agency (JAXA) (CORUS Consortium 2019; CPC 2020; Hatfield et al. 2020; Xu et al. 2020; Bauranov and Rakas 2021).

However, UTM is recognised as a complex and challenging concept still in the early stages of development, reliant on emerging technology and regulatory environments. It has been suggested that necessary technologies (e.g., advanced Detect-And-Avoid, communication, navigation and surveillance systems) are currently too immature to enable safe operations. These factors indicate that the concept is realistically some years (~5+ years) away from the worldwide, large-scale implementation needed to accommodate the expansion of drone operations occurring today (ICAO 2020b; McCarthy et al. 2020; Bauranov and Rakas 2021; Grote et al. 2021b).

It is posited therefore that a shared airspace solution is required that can be implemented more quickly than UTM. For example, the Project Lima concept (under development in the UK by a consortium including the authors as part of the NAA's Innovation Sandbox programme) is proposed as a simpler alternative solution designed to be used in regions where population and air traffic densities are low (i.e., low ground and air risks) (Jelev 2021; Grote et al. 2021b). Such regions are likely to occur in remote locations that are hard to reach by existing surface transport modes, and therefore represent good opportunities for drone logistics operators to begin building incremental experience before expansion into busier urban areas. Project Lima shared airspace (Table 6.1) offers two principal benefits: (i) in the short term, the potential for the rapid development and implementation necessary to satisfy the growing demands of the commercial drone sector as a stopgap prior to full roll-out of UTM; and (ii) in the longer term, to provide a shared airspace solution for low traffic density and/or remote regions where UTM would be unnecessarily onerous for airspace users and/or technically difficult and costly to deliver.

An integral aspect of any shared airspace solution is likely to be a dependable Detect-And-Avoid (DAA) system for traffic deconfliction purposes (McCarthy et al. 2020; Grote et al. 2021b), typically based on Electronic Conspicuity (EC) equipment fitted onboard aircraft, where EC is an umbrella term used to describe devices that allow airspace users to be detected electronically. There are many different EC technologies on the market, and it is likely a standardised system will need to be agreed and mandated by regulators worldwide if global interoperability is to be achieved. The leading candidate appears to be Automatic Dependent Surveillance-Broadcast (ADS-B) because it is the system preferred by the FAA (the USA's NAA), who in 2020 mandated the carriage of ADS-B devices to enter most controlled airspace within the United States (FAA 2021), although it has been suggested that ADS-B suffers from a lack of bandwidth given the expected rise in the number of aircraft using the system, and that other EC technologies may therefore represent better options (Bauranov and Rakas 2021).

Resistance may well be encountered from other airspace users to the mandating of EC equipment carriage to enter shared airspace due to the additional equipment costs entailed

Table 6.1 Features of the Project Lima shared airspace concept

Feature
Designated zone in appropriate locations (i.e., low ground and air risks).
Guaranteed Secondary Surveillance Radar (SSR) transponder[a] reception coverage within the zone (although carriage of an SSR transponder is not a Project Lima airspace entry requirement).
Low latency and free promulgation of drone flight plans, along with real-time drone traffic status updates, which would be accessible via various connected flight-planning and navigation software applications (e.g., SkyDemon (2021) or similar) to all airspace users.
Assurance that drone operators would track crewed aircraft within the zone to ensure separation was maintained.
Requirement for drones to be capable of automatically avoiding any other Electronic Conspicuity (EC)[b] sources in the zone, providing an additional layer of safety should drone command links fail.
No additional costs and/or complex procedures for crewed aircraft, except the costs associated with fitting EC equipment.
Drones operating within the zone would be capable of automatically broadcasting regular position reports on a designated VHF frequency (VHF-Out). This would provide a further safety level, enabling crewed aircraft to maintain situational awareness that allows intervention should primary separation systems fail.
No requirement for an Air Navigation Service Provider (ANSP) to oversee and manage the zone because this would be unnecessary, costly and technically challenging in remote regions.

Source: adapted from Grote et al. (2021b).
a SSR transponders are traditional aviation transponders responsive to interrogation by the SSR system utilised by ATC worldwide.
b EC is an umbrella term for devices fitted to aircraft allowing airspace users to be detected electronically.

(Grote et al. 2022). One method to overcome this potential barrier could be for NAAs to offer financial incentives to encourage EC uptake. For example, the UK NAA has a scheme (open until March 2023) offering a 50% rebate (up to a maximum of £250) on the cost of EC equipment. Research by Merkert et al. (2021) points to another possible solution, with drone operators found to be willing to pay for access to shared airspace (e.g., A$7.09/hour to fly BVLOS). This means the drone industry could meet some/all of the cost burden of EC equipment on behalf of all shared airspace users through revenue generated by charging drone operators for access.

If drone urban logistics services are to become established, the problem of how best to integrate drones and crewed aircraft into shared airspace needs to be resolved. Airspace management policies are required that develop equitable regulatory and technology environments for shared airspace, and it would seem sensible for such policies to be inclusive, involving all stakeholders in co-development, as a way to ensure access to shared airspace is perceived as equitable by all and to minimise any resistance to implementation. It would also seem sensible for policy-makers to adopt an international perspective, pursuing solutions with international commonality wherever possible. The risk associated with implementing shared airspace solutions on a national rather than international basis is that a patchwork situation could develop composed of different country-specific regulations and procedures, which could impede the activities of multi-national logistics companies. Project Lima is a UK-centric concept at the moment, and would require increased awareness beyond the United Kingdom to become viable as an international solution (Grote et al. 2021b).

Overall Service Reliability Given Weather Conditions and Minimal Risk Routing

In developed nations, the reliability of traditional logistics services using vans/trucks is one of their key strengths. Aside from potential issues around staffing, severe traffic congestion and weather conditions (e.g., snow) (DfT 2021; HMG 2021), road freight vehicles themselves are considered to be generally quite reliable, which is in part due to the rigorous international standards helping to improve automotive manufacturing and quality control processes (e.g., IATF 16949) (IATF 2016). In contrast, the majority of drones currently used in a logistics setting are operating on an experimental basis (UPDWG 2022), and standards that govern their construction are still in their infancy, making them more susceptible to technical problems arising from less rigorous standards (AAIB 2021).

Regarding external factors such as weather, it is generally accepted that vans will operate in most conditions, with only extreme events (e.g., floods, heavy snow) negatively impacting performance. An exception to this being the quality of road surfaces in some developing nations, which can significantly impact the logistics efficiency of land transportation (Whalley 2016). In comparison, drone operations can be more limited by weather conditions. Wind, precipitation and temperature extremes can cause issues in terms of service reliability depending on severity (Ranquist et al. 2017; Gao et al. 2021). High winds are likely to affect: (i) the stability of flight; (ii) the speed of flight; and (iii) the range of the drone and whether a journey is achievable as a result. Precipitation and icing can affect the aerodynamics of the drone's surfaces, reducing its flight efficiency (Ranquist et al. 2017). Moisture from humidity and precipitation could damage a drone's electronics, causing a range of power, control or communication issues (Ranquist et al. 2017), whilst varying temperature levels can affect battery life (cold temperatures) or long-term durability (hot temperatures) (Warner 2015). Lightning can also present issues, with even some commercial aircraft sustaining damage following strikes, despite extensive engineering protection being in place (Sweers et al. 2012).

The limits of a given drone platform will largely dictate how resilient it is against weather, as identified by Gao et al. (2021), who suggested that weather resistance improved the average (median) global flyability for small (<25 kg) drones. With operating limits of −20 to 46°C, 14 m/s winds, and 50 mm/h of precipitation, the median flyability was 20.4 hours-per-day, if daylight hours did not affect flights, or 12.3 hours-per-day if they did. Whilst this may appear promising, a significant number of drone logistics use cases seek to connect areas that are coastal, or are separated by water (UPDWG 2022), meaning wind speeds are likely to be above average (Met Office 2021). Furthermore, other effects such as the North Atlantic Oscillation may induce stronger winds in areas of similar latitude to those otherwise deemed as flyable (Ottersen et al. 2001; Gao et al. 2021). Localised effects, such as turbulence, may also impact drone performance.

Gusting wind is another factor that is not often mentioned in literature but can have significant impacts on whether drones can be flown (Gao et al. 2021), most notably for VTOL platforms, which are significantly more vulnerable to gust effects during take-off and landing than fixed-wing platforms (Greif et al. 1972). Typical industry practice for large commercial fixed-wing aircraft (e.g., crewed airliners) is to ignore gust speeds when assessing operating limits for take-off and landing (BA 2011), though VTOL platforms are starting to face more stringent design guidance highlighting that gust effects must be considered (EASA 2021b).

In addition to the drone's capabilities, some NAAs may set environmental limits, or specify a legal requirement to maintain constant control of any remotely piloted aircraft (CAA 2021c), something that may be difficult in extreme weather. Furthermore, if any drone logistics system is operating in shared airspace, weather and visibility become significantly more important when determining service reliability and safety.

For multi-modal urban logistics involving drones to be reliable, in the event of non-flight due to weather, some form of contingency may be required, particularly if the cargo must be delivered (e.g., medical supplies). This may take the form of taxis, or other on-demand ground transportation systems; however, it is likely that the delivery will be significantly slower than the originally scheduled drone flight. In the case study described in the subsequent section, 19% of planned flights had to be substituted for taxi services due to the drone's assumed 10 m/s (19.4 knots) wind limit being exceeded, highlighting that service reliability could present a problem in some use cases.

Cost Implications of Utilising Drones as Part of Multi-modal Urban Logistics Supply Chains

Drones are often posited as having the potential to reduce costs when utilised as a part of multi-modal logistics supply chains (Goodchild and Toy 2018; Nesta 2018; Aurambout et al. 2019; Deloitte 2020; Moshref-Javadi et al. 2020; Sah et al. 2021; PwC 2021; Rejeb et al. 2021). However, recent research by the authors found that the cost benefits suggested by others may be difficult to realise in practice. A case study analysis (refer to Oakey et al. (2022) for further details) was undertaken investigating the use of drones to transport patient diagnostic samples from NHS General Practitioner (GP) surgeries to a central pathology laboratory located in a large urban area, as an alternative to business-as-usual (BAU) arrangements where samples are transported by van.

The case study was based on the 79 surgeries within the catchment area of the laboratory at Southampton General Hospital (SGH), located in Southampton, a city on the South coast

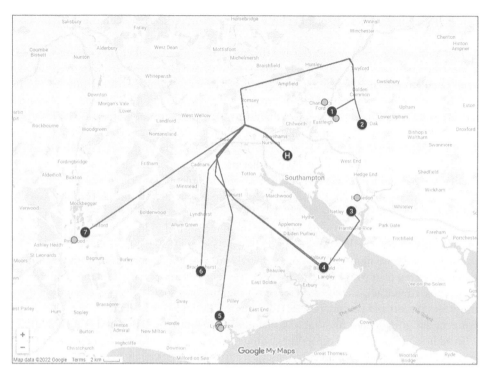

Figure 6.2 Locations of the 14 GP surgeries serviceable by drone

Note: Numbered circles indicate primary surgeries; smaller circles indicate satellite surgeries; H indicates Southampton General Hospital; lines indicate drone flightpaths

of the United Kingdom (population ~250,000), during March 2021. Fourteen surgeries were assessed as suitable for service by drone, constituted by: seven primary surgeries (sufficient open space nearby for drone landing and acceptably low-risk flightpath from/to SGH); plus seven secondary 'satellite' surgeries in close vicinity such that samples could be transferred by cargo bicycles for onward flights to SGH from primary surgeries (Figure 6.2). In instances where weather conditions (wind speed or precipitation rate) prevented drone flights, taxis were assumed as the replacement transport mode to provide service reliability. Cost estimates were based on a future scenario where drone operations are routinely automated, removing the need for safety pilots for take-off/landing and enabling mission commanders to manage multiple drones simultaneously.

Results suggested that to service the 14 surgeries by drone instead of a van was nearly four times more expensive (£2,964/week *cf.* £776/week). The impact on the overall sample collection service across all 79 surgeries was that, whilst beneficial reductions were achieved in van vehicle-kilometres (vkm), driving hours and tailpipe carbon dioxide (CO_2) emissions of 23%, 18% and 23%, respectively, the costs were increased by 56%, suggesting that an integrated drone collection service for patient diagnostics would be financially unsustainable. These results concur with an exploratory study by McKinnon (2016) into the practicality of drone logistics, which found that the introduction of widespread services was unlikely due to the limited value added over existing business-as-usual land-based logistics. There are also likely to be further costs associated with drone logistics (e.g., airspace management fees, DG training costs), which if included would make use of drones even more difficult to justify.

Drone transportation of samples does provide the scope for more frequent and expeditious deliveries compared to vans, which can lead to benefits such as: (i) improved flow of samples arriving for analysis, resulting in more efficient use of both laboratory staff and equipment time; (ii) shorter exposure of samples to in-vehicle conditions, which are potentially harmful (e.g., excessive temperature or vibration conditions) and could affect sample quality (Oakey et al. 2021); and (iii) reduced time from sample extraction to diagnosis. Emerging evidence from interviews by the authors with NHS practitioners suggests that there may be further advantages in providing for separation of some samples for fast-track analysis and improving the flexibility of collection services. These potential benefits have indirect value, and further research is required to quantify their value in monetary terms as a justification for the additional expense of introducing drones, e.g., using the Quality-Adjusted Life Year (QALY) approach, which is a metric commonly used for monetary evaluation of medical interventions (NICE 2013).

In general, it appears that the transport of time-critical and/or high-value payloads to/from hard-to-reach locations (e.g., crossing waterways or where road infrastructure is poor/limited/congested) may be the only circumstances where the additional costs of drones can be justified at present. This could have been a key factor in why large logistics operators, such as Amazon (Wired 2021) and DHL (sUAS News 2021), have recently suspended development programmes for routine parcel deliveries by drones.

Conclusions

Commercial drone operations are a relatively new addition to the aviation ecosystem and, as such, are associated with immature and evolving operational, regulatory and technology environments. The possibility of employing drones for urban logistics purposes has been widely recognised by practitioners, regulators, governments and academia around the world, and offers potential benefits such as reductions in service times, energy use and detrimental atmospheric emissions (Grote et al. 2021a). However, challenges remain if payload delivery by drone is to become widespread and routine in urban environments.

Integration and expansion of drones into multi-modal urban logistics services must be approached in a way that is acceptable to the public and endorsed by other airspace stakeholders if resistance is to be minimised and equitable solutions to challenges found. Operational, regulatory and technology frameworks must keep pace with the expansion if payloads (some of which may contain DG) are to be transported safely and with quality intact, whilst reducing to an acceptable level the risks posed both to other aircraft and to people on the ground. An international, rather than country-specific, approach is preferred so as not to impede the operations of multi-national logistics companies.

Ultimately, drones must be able to deliver an urban logistics service that is reliable and, maybe most importantly for commercial drone operators, cost-effective. In general, the need for cost-effectiveness suggests that drones may be best suited to logistics applications in circumstances involving high-value and/or time-critical payloads being delivered to locations that are difficult and/or expensive to reach by other, more traditional, logistics transport modes.

Note

1 Agent-based methods are commonly used for modelling of complex systems where the behaviours of individual agents are well defined and the focus is largely on the interactions of the agents,

where emergent behaviour can be observed. This can be used with Monte Carlo methods that are based around repeated random sampling to achieve statistically significant numerical results. These approaches can be combined by parameterising variables of the agent-based model and applying Monte Carlo sampling to construct distributions in output variable(s).

References

Ackerman E and Koziol M (2019) *The Blood is Here – IEEE Spectrum Magazine*, New York, USA: Institute of Electrical and Electronics Engineers.

Air Accidents Investigation Branch (AAIB) (2021) *AAIB Bulletin 3/2021*, Aldershot, UK: Air Accidents Investigation Branch.

Alarcón V, García M, Alarcón F, Viguria A, Martínez Á, Janisch D, Acevedo J J, Maza I and Ollero A (2020) 'Procedures for the Integration of Drones into the Airspace Based on U-Space Services', *Aerospace,* 7(9), 128.

Amukele T K, Hernandez J, Snozek C L H, Wyatt R G, Douglas M, Amini R and Street J (2017) 'Drone Transport of Chemistry and Hematology Samples Over Long Distances', *American Journal of Clinical Pathology,* 148(5), 427–435.

Antosa S and Demata M (2021) 'Get Covid Done: Discourses on the National Health Service (NHS) during Brexit and the Coronavirus Pandemic', *Textus, English Studies in Italy,* 2(2021), 47–65.

Aurambout J-P, Gkoumas K and Ciuffo B (2019) 'Last Mile Delivery by Drones: An Estimation of Viable Market Potential and Access to Citizens across European cities', *European Transport Research Review,* 11(1), 1–21.

Bajaj S, Singla D and Sakhuja N (2012) 'Stability Testing of Pharmaceutical Products', *Journal of Applied Pharmaceutical Science,* 2(3), 129–138.

Bajde D, Bruun M H, Sommer J K and Waltorp K (2017) *General Public's Privacy Concerns Regarding Drone Use in Residential and Public Areas*, Odense, Denmark: University of Southern Denmark and Aalborg University.

Batel S, Devine-Wright P and Tangeland T (2013) 'Social Acceptance of Low Carbon Energy and Associated Infrastructures: A Critical Discussion', *Energy Policy,* 58, 1–5.

Bauranov A and Rakas J (2021) 'Designing Airspace for Urban Air Mobility: A Review of Concepts and Approaches', *Progress in Aerospace Sciences,* 125, 100726.

Beck S, Bui T T, Davies A, Courtney P, Brown A, Geudens J and Royall P G (2020) 'An Evaluation of the Drone Delivery of Adrenaline Auto-Injectors for Anaphylaxis: Pharmacists' Perceptions, Acceptance, and Concerns', *Drones,* 4(4), 66.

Boucher P (2016) "You Wouldn't Have Your Granny Using Them': Drawing Boundaries Between Acceptable and Unacceptable Applications of Civil Drones', *Sci Eng Ethics,* 22(5), 1391–1418.

Branch S K (2005) 'Guidelines from the International Conference on Harmonisation (ICH)', *Journal of Pharmaceutical and Biomedical Analysis,* 38(5), 798–805.

British Airways (BA) (2011) *Flight Crew Procedures Manual – Part A (1)*, London, UK: British Airways.

Capitán C, Pérez-León H, Capitán J, Castaño Á and Ollero A (2021) 'Unmanned Aerial Traffic Management System Architecture for U-Space In-Flight Services', *Applied Sciences,* 11(9), 3995.

Civil Aviation Authority (CAA) (2019) *A Unified Approach to the Introduction of UAS Traffic Management (CAP 1868)*, Crawley, UK: Civil Aviation Authority.

Civil Aviation Authority (CAA) (2020) *Unmanned Aircraft System Operations in UK Airspace – Guidance (CAP 722)*, Crawley, UK: Civil Aviation Authority.

Civil Aviation Authority (CAA) (2021a) *Dangerous Goods RPAS Challenge Group - Terms of Reference*, Crawley, UK: Civil Aviation Authority.

Civil Aviation Authority (CAA) (2021b) *Fundamentals: Carriage of Dangerous Goods by Remotely Piloted Aircraft Systems (CAP 2248)*, Crawley, UK: Civil Aviation Authority.

Civil Aviation Authority (CAA) (2021c) *UK Consolidation – Regulation (EU) 2019/947 (as retained in UK law) (CAP 1789A)*, Crawley, UK: Civil Aviation Authority.

Connected Places Catapult (CPC) (2020) *Enabling UTM in UK*, London, UK: Connected Places Catapult.

Consortiq (2022) *Drone Payloads Vs. Performance: A Balancing Act* [Online], Hounslow, UK: Consortiq. Available at: https://consortiq.com/uas-resources/how-to-balance-your-drones-payload-performance [Accessed 21 January 2022].

CORUS Consortium (2019) *U-Space Concept of Operations: Enhanced Overview (Edn 01.01.03)*, Brussels, Belgium: SESAR Joint Undertaking.

Dalamagkidis K, Valavanis K P and Piegl L A (2008) 'On Unmanned Aircraft Systems Issues, Challenges and Operational Restrictions Preventing Integration into the National Airspace System', *Progress in Aerospace Sciences,* 44(7-8), 503–519.

Darvishpoor S, Roshanian J, Raissi A and Hassanalian M (2020) 'Configurations, Flight Mechanisms, and Applications of Unmanned Aerial Systems: A Review', *Progress in Aerospace Sciences,* 121, 100694.

Deloitte (2020) *Economic Benefit Analysis of Drones in Australia – Final Report*, Brisbane, Australia: Deloitte Access Economics Pty Ltd.

Department for Transport (DfT) (2021) *Road Traffic Estimates: Great Britain 2020*, London, UK: Department for Transport.

Dorling K, Heinrichs J, Messier G G and Magierowski S (2017) 'Vehicle Routing Problems for Drone Delivery', *IEEE Transactions on Systems, Man, and Cybernetics: Systems,* 47(1), 70–85.

Eichleay M, Evens E, Stankevitz K and Parkera C (2019) 'Using the Unmanned Aerial Vehicle Delivery Decision Tool to Consider Transporting Medical Supplies via Drone', *Global Health: Science and Practice,* 7(4), 500–506.

European Union Aviation Safety Agency (EASA) (2021a) *Easy Access Rules for Unmanned Aircraft Systems (Regulations (EU) 2019/947 and (EU) 2019/945)*, Cologne, Germany: European Union Aviation Safety Agency.

European Union Aviation Safety Agency (EASA) (2021b) *Means of Compliance with the Special Condition VTOL (MOC SC-VTO Issue 2)*, Cologne, Germany: European Union Aviation Safety Agency.

European Union Aviation Safety Agency (EASA) (2021c) *Study on the Societal Acceptance of Urban Air Mobility in Europe*, Cologne, Germany: European Union Aviation Safety Agency.

Federal Aviation Administration (FAA) (2021) *Automatic Dependent Surveillance-Broadcast (ADS-B)* [Online], Washington D.C., USA: Federal Aviation Administration. Available at: https://www.faa.gov/nextgen/programs/adsb/ [Accessed 08 December 2021].

Ford (2022) *Ford e-Transit (U.S.) Technical Specifications*, Dearborn, USA: Ford Motor Company.

Gao M, Hugenholtz C H, Fox T A, Kucharczyk M, Barchyn T E and Nesbit P R (2021) 'Weather Constraints on Global Drone Flyability', *Scientific Reports,* 11(1), 12092.

Gobble M M (2020) 'Identifying the Tipping Point', *Research-Technology Management,* 63(1), 62–67.

Goodchild A and Toy J (2018) 'Delivery by Drone: An Evaluation of Unmanned Aerial Vehicle Technology in Reducing CO_2 Emissions in the Delivery Service Industry', *Transportation Research Part D: Transport and Environment,* 61, 58–67.

Greif R K, Fry E B and Gossett T D (1972) *Effect of Stabilization on VTOL Aircraft in Hovering Flight (NASA Technical Note D-6900)*, Washington D.C., USA: National Aeronautics and Space Administration.

Grote M, Cherrett T, Oakey A, Royall P G, Whalley S and Dickinson J (2021a) 'How Do Dangerous Goods Regulations Apply to Uncrewed Aerial Vehicles Transporting Medical Cargos?', *Drones,* 5(2), 38.

Grote M, Pilko A, Scanlan J, Cherrett T, Dickinson J, Smith A, Oakey A and Marsden G (2021b) 'Pathways to Unsegregated Sharing of Airspace: Views of the Uncrewed Aerial Vehicle (UAV) Industry', *Drones,* 5(4), 150.

Grote M, Pilko A, Scanlan J, Cherrett T, Dickinson J, Smith A, Oakey A and Marsden G (2022) 'Sharing Airspace with Uncrewed Aerial Vehicles (UAVs): Views of the General Aviation (GA) community', *Journal of Air Transport Management,* 102, 102218.

Hatfield M, Cahill C, Webley P, Garron J and Beltran R (2020) 'Integration of Unmanned Aircraft Systems into the National Airspace System-Efforts by the University of Alaska to Support the FAA/NASA UAS Traffic Management Program', *Remote Sensing,* 12(19), 3112.

HMG (2021) *Letter to Industry – HGV Driver Shortage*, London, UK: HMG.

Institute of Electrical and Electronics Engineers (IEEE) (2021) *Robots – Your Guide to the World of Robotics – Zipline* [Online], New York, USA: Institute of Electrical and Electronics Engineers. Available at: https://robots.ieee.org/robots/zipline/ [Accessed 20 January 2022].

International Automotive Task Force (IATF) (2016) *IATF 16949:2016 – Technical Specification (1st Edition)*, Birmingham, UK: SMMT Industry Forum Ltd.

International Civil Aviation Organization (ICAO) (2011) *Annex 18 to the Convention on International Civil Aviation – The Safe Transport of Dangerous Goods by Air (4th Edition)*, Montreal, Canada: International Civil Aviation Organization.

International Civil Aviation Organization (ICAO) (2019) *Unmanned Aircraft Systems (UAS) for Humanitarian Aid and Emergency Response Guidance – U-AID*, Montreal Canada: International Civil Aviation Organization.

International Civil Aviation Organization (ICAO) (2020a) *Technical Instructions for the Safe Transport of Dangerous Goods by Air (Doc 9284), 2021-2022 Edition*, Montreal, Canada: International Civil Aviation Organization.

International Civil Aviation Organization (ICAO) (2020b) *Unmanned Aircraft Systems Traffic Management (UTM) – A Common Framework with Core Principles for Global Harmonization*, Montreal, Canada: International Civil Aviation Organization.

Jelev N (2021) *European Network of U-space Demonstrators – Lessons Learned from the Isles of Scilly (UK) BVLOS Airbridge*, Brussels, Belgium: Eurocontrol.

Joint Authorities for Rulemaking of Unmanned Systems (JARUS) (2019) *JARUS Guidelines on Specific Operations Risk Assessment (SORA) (Edition 2.0)*, Bern, Switzerland: Joint Authorities for Rulemaking of Unmanned Systems.

Klauser F and Pedrozo S (2017) 'Big Data from the Sky: Popular Perceptions of Private Drones in Switzerland', *Geographica Helvetica,* 72(2), 231–239.

Lin C A, Shah K, Mauntel L C C and Shah S A (2018) 'Drone Delivery of Medications: Review of the Landscape and Legal Considerations', *Am J Health Syst Pharm,* 75(3), 153–158.

Ling G and Draghic N (2019) 'Aerial Drones for Blood Delivery', *Transfusion,* 59(S2), 1608–1611.

McCarthy T, Pforte L and Burke R (2020) 'Fundamental Elements of an Urban UTM', *Aerospace,* 7(7), 85.

McKinnon A (2016) 'The Possible Impact of 3D Printing and Drones on Last-Mile Logistics: An Exploratory Study', *Built Environment,* 42(4), 617–629.

Medicines and Healthcare Products Regulatory Agency (MHRA) (2017a) *Rules and Guidance for Pharmaceutical Distributors 2017 (The Green Guide) (10th Edition)*, London, UK: Pharmaceutical Press.

Medicines and Healthcare Products Regulatory Agency (MHRA) (2017b) *Rules and Guidance for Pharmaceutical Manufacturers and Distributors 2017 (The Orange Guide) (10th Edition)*, London, UK: Pharmaceutical Press.

Merkert R, Beck M J and Bushell J (2021) 'Will It Fly? Adoption of the Road Pricing Framework to Manage Drone Use of Airspace', *Transportation Research Part A: Policy and Practice,* 150, 156–170.

Merkert R and Bushell J (2020) 'Managing the Drone Revolution: A Systematic Literature Review into the Current Use of Airborne Drones and Future Strategic Directions for Their Effective Control', *Journal of Air Transport Management,* 89, 101929.

Met Office (2021) *Where Are the Windiest Parts of the UK?* [Online], Exeter, UK: Met Office. Available at: https://www.metoffice.gov.uk/weather/learn-about/weather/types-of-weather/wind/windiest-place-in-uk [Accessed 20 January 2022].

Mohr N. 09 February 2021. *RE: Dangerous Goods by Air [email].* Personal communication to Grote M.

Moshref-Javadi M, Lee S and Winkenbach M (2020) 'Design and Evaluation of a Multi-trip Delivery Model with Truck and Drones', *Transportation Research Part E: Logistics and Transportation Review,* 136, 101887.

National Aeronautics and Space Administration (NASA) (2021) *The Drag Equation* [Online], Cleveland, USA: National Aeronautics and Space Administration. Available at: https://www.grc.nasa.gov/www/k-12/airplane/drageq.html [Accessed 21 January 2022].

National Institute for Health and Care Excellence (NICE) (2013) *How NICE Measures Value for Money in Relation to Public Health Interventions*, London, UK: NICE.

Nesta (2018) *Flying High: Shaping the Future of Drones in UK Cities*, London, UK: Nesta.

Oakey A, Grote M, Smith A, Cherrett T, Pilko A, Dickinson J and Ait Bihi Ouali L (2022) 'Integrating Drones into NHS Patient Diagnostic Logistics Systems: Flight or Fantasy?', *PLOS ONE,* 17(12), e0264669.

Oakey A, Waters T, Zhu W, Royall P G, Cherrett T, Courtney P, Majoe D and Jelev N (2021) 'Quantifying the Effects of Vibration on Medicines in Transit Caused by Fixed-Wing and Multi-Copter Drones', *Drones,* 5(1), 22.

Ottersen G, Planque B, Belgrano A, Post E, Reid P C and Stenseth N C (2001) 'Ecological Effects of the North Atlantic Oscillation', *Oecologia,* 128(1), 1–14.

Pilko A, Sóbester A, Scanlan J and Ferraro M. (2022) Spatiotemporal Ground Risk Mapping for Uncrewed Aerial Systems Operations. AIAA SCITECH 2022 Forum, 3–7 January 2022, San Diego, USA. American Institute of Aeronautics and Astronautics.

Pilko A and Tait Z (2021) *SEEDPOD Ground Risk*: Zenodo. https://doi.org/10.5281/zenodo.4776529.

PwC (2021) *Future Flight Challenge - Socio-economic study*, London, UK: PwC.

Rana K, Praharaj S and Nanda T (2016) 'Unmanned Aerial Vehicles (UAVs): An Emerging Technology for Logistics', *International Journal of Business and Management Invention*, 5(5), 86–92.

Ranquist E A, Steiner M and Argrow B. (2017) Exploring the Range of Weather Impacts on UAS Operations. 18th Conference on Aviation, Range, and Aerospace Meteorology, 22–26 January 2017, Seattle, USA. American Meteorological Society.

Rejeb A, Rejeb K, Simske S J and Treiblmaier H (2021) 'Drones for Supply Chain Management and Logistics: A Review and Research Agenda', *International Journal of Logistics Research and Applications*, 1–24, DOI: 10.1080/13675567.2021.1981273.

Sah B, Gupta R and Bani-Hani D (2021) 'Analysis of Barriers to Implement Drone Logistics', *International Journal of Logistics Research and Applications*, 24(6), 531–550.

Scott J E and Scott C H. Drone Delivery Models for Healthcare. 50th Hawaii International Conference on System Sciences (HICSS), 4–7 January 2017, Waikoloa, Hawaii, USA. University of Hawaii at Manoa.

SkyDemon (2021) *Welcome to SkyDemon* [Online], Frome, UK: SkyDemon. Available at: https://www.skydemon.aero/ [Accessed 4 January 2022].

Smith A, Dickinson J, Marsden G, Cherrett T, Oakey A and Grote M (2022) 'Public Acceptance of the Use of Drones for Logistics: The State of Play and Moving Towards More Informed Debate', *Technology in Society*, 68, 101883.

Stilgoe J and Cohen T (2021) 'Rejecting Acceptance: Learning from Public Dialogue on Self-driving Vehicles', *Science and Public Policy*, 48(6), 849–859.

sUAS News (2021) *DHL Parcelcopter Fails to Deliver* [Online]. Available at: https://www.suasnews.com/2021/08/dhl-parcelcopter-fails-to-deliver/ [Accessed 19 January 2022].

Sunil E, Hoekstra J, Ellerbroek J, Bussink F, Nieuwenhuisen D, Vidosavljevic A and Kern S. Metropolis: Relating Airspace Structure and Capacity for Extreme Traffic Densities. Eleventh USA/Europe Air Traffic Management Research and Development Seminar (ATM2015), 23–26 June 2015, Lisbon, Portugal. FAA/Eurocontrol.

Sweers G, Birch B and Gokcen J (2012) *Lightning Strikes: Protection, Inspection, and Repairs (Boeing Aero magazine – Qtr_04 12)*, Seattle, USA: The Boeing Company.

Tan L K L, Lim B C, Park G, Low K H and Yeo V C S (2021) 'Public Acceptance of Drone Applications in a Highly Urbanized Environment', *Technology in Society*, 64, 101462.

Torisu T, Maruno T, Yoneda S, Hamaji Y, Honda S, Ohkubo T and Uchiyama S (2017) 'Friability Testing as a New Stress-Stability Assay for Biopharmaceuticals', *Journal of Pharmaceutical Sciences*, 106(10), 2966–2978.

UAV for Payload Delivery Working Group (UPDWG) (2022) *MD3 – Medical Drone Delivery Database* [Online], Seattle, USA: UAV for Payload Delivery Working Group. Available at: https://www.updwg.org/md3/ [Accessed 4 January 2022].

UK Research and Innovation (UKRI) (2021) *Future Flight Vision and Roadmap*, Swindon, UK: UK Research and Innovation.

United Nations Economic Commission for Europe (UNECE) (2017) *ADR – European Agreement Concerning the International Carriage of Dangerous Goods by Road (ECE/TRANS/257)*, New York, USA: United Nations.

United Nations Economic Commission for Europe (UNECE) (2021) *Recommendations on the Transport of Dangerous Goods – Model Regulations – Vol I (22nd revised edition)*, New York, USA: United Nations.

University of Southampton (2022) *Research project: Solent Future Transport Zone (FTZ)* [Online], Southampton, UK: University of Southampton. Available at: https://www.southampton.ac.uk/engineering/research/projects/solent-future-transport-zone-theme-1.page [Accessed 15 March 2022].

Urban Arrow (2022) *Cargo L* [Online], Amsterdam, Netherlands: Urban Arrow. Available at: https://urbanarrow.com/business-bikes/cargo/cargo-l/ [Accessed 21 January 2022].

Venkatesh V, Morris M G, Davis G B and Davis F D (2003) 'User Acceptance of Information Technology: Toward a Unified View', *MIS Quarterly*, 27(3), 425–478.

Versapak (2021) *Medium Insulated Medical Carrier – Pathology (PYTB2)* [Online], Erith, UK: Versapak. Available at: https://www.versapak.co.uk/new-medium-insulated-medical-carrier-pathology [Accessed 25 January 2022].

Warner J (2015) *The Handbook of Lithium-Ion Battery Pack Design – Chemistry, Components, Types and Terminology*, Amsterdam, Netherlands: Elsevier.

Whalley O G (2016) *Bringing Paved Roads to the Hinterland (The World Bank Connections Series)*, Washington D.C., USA: The World Bank.

Wired (2021) *The Slow Collapse of Amazon's Drone Delivery Dream* [Online]. Available at: https://www.wired.co.uk/article/amazon-drone-delivery-prime-air [Accessed 19 January 2022].

Wright C, Rupani S, Nichols K, Chandani Y and Machagge M (2018) *What Should You Deliver by Unmanned Aerial Systems? (White Paper)*, Boston, USA: JSI Research & Training Institute.

Xu C, Liao X, Tan J, Ye H and Lu H (2020) 'Recent Research Progress of Unmanned Aerial Vehicle Regulation Policies and Technologies in Urban Low Altitude', *IEEE Access*, 8, 74175–74194.

7
INTEGRATING FREIGHT AND PASSENGER TRANSPORT FOR URBAN LOGISTICS

Silvio Nocera, Francesco Bruzzone and Federico Cavallaro

Introduction

Recent changes in passenger and freight mobility, such as growing urbanisation trends and the diffusion of e-commerce, exacerbate negative impacts in terms of congestion, safety, the environment, and quality of life (EC, 2020). The first and last miles (FLM) are considered to be critical legs of the transportation of passengers and goods owing to their high operational costs and impact on both natural and anthropic environments (Macioszek, 2018). In the context of FLM, mobility and logistics manage relevant issues in both dense urban cores and low-density rural or peri-urban areas. Urban operations pose additional challenges, such as competition for space among different users; uncoordinated operations; and restricted time windows, all generating impacts that can be negatively perceived by the urban community (Nocera et al., 2021), in a vicious circle that worsens the performance of transport operations with the contextual increase in traffic congestion as well as air and noise emissions. Currently, the movement of urban goods accounts for 20–30% of the total vehicle kilometres within metropolitan areas, and policy-makers and operators are struggling to improve operational efficiency while mitigating externalities (Rodrigue and Dablanc, 2021). To reduce the impact of urban logistic operations, authorities and decision-makers have formulated policies and regulations. Examples of promoted policies include reducing (or favouring, according to context) night time operations, dedicating idling spaces to freight vehicles, limiting operations to specific time windows during the daytime (such as off-peak morning hours) or to specific vehicles (such as zero-emission vehicles), and adopting taxation or incentives to regulate the sector (Savelsbergh and van Woensel, 2016). However, these policies are often uncoordinated and result in minor or counterproductive effects (Nocera et al., 2021).

This chapter presents urban mobility and logistics challenges with reference to FLM operations and indicates strategies that have been pursued with little or no positive results. This is followed by a discussion on an innovative paradigm for integrating passenger and goods transportation, which is referred to as "Cargo Hitching" (van Duin et al., 2019) or "Integrated Passenger Freight Logistics" (Bruzzone et al., 2021a) in previous literature, according to a concept that was first presented by the European Commission (EC) in its Green Paper on Urban Mobility (EC, 2007). Responding to the needs and indications of authorities, the EC suggested how a strong integration can improve mobility, logistics efficiency, and

DOI: 10.4324/9781003241478-9

sustainability (from environmental, operational, and socioeconomic perspectives) while promoting a socially acceptable approach. The basic principles and best practices of integrated passenger-freight transport (IPFT) for FLM are presented in this chapter to explore the origins and the potential of the concept. Finally, drivers for both their success and failure are discussed, focusing on achievable operational, environmental, and socioeconomic benefits as well as on the main constraints that currently interfere with the promotion of the management of the mobility system as an entirety, with a particular emphasis on operative and normative/regulatory limits.

Challenges of the Urban First–Last Mile

The FLM represents the set of links and services between an existing main transport service and its potential users; however, identifying where the FLM physically starts and ends is complicated. The FLM has various definitions in existing transport-related literature. Arvidsson et al. (2016) provided two separate explanations: one for goods and one for passenger transport. In the freight transport context, FLM is defined as the first–last part of the transport chain where goods are transported by a professional party to a customer location, which can include a home, retail store, drop-off point, or factory. Within the context of passenger transport, FLM is defined as the first and last leg of a journey by public transport, and often the journey from a transport hub to the destination. According to Wang et al. (2016), the FLM problem considers the analysis of travel services from a home or workplace to the nearest public transport stop or station (first mile) and vice versa (last mile). The first and last legs of a transport movement are significantly challenging from the perspective of a transport planner. Their identification and subsequent schematisation represent crucial phases of the process, the improvement of which is fundamental to ensure the success of a transport system while minimising operational costs and deriving negative externalities. FLM is a significant problem, particularly at the urban level, because it is often fragmented and uncoordinated, resulting in low utilisation of vehicles, excessive movement, high externalities, and an exacerbation of social conflicts. Existing literature agrees on the fact that FLM contributes to the increasing direct and indirect costs of a total trip chain. The percentages vary, ranging from 13% to 75% of the entire freight trip (Table 7.1).

Considering freight transport, the following three main factors contribute to the inefficiency of FLM: specific market requests (just-in-time deliveries, or the increasing fragmentation of retailers and consumers, resulting in low vehicle load rates, high mileage per vehicle, long idling times, and a high number of deployed vehicles), policy and regulation attempts (strict time windows for urban logistics operations, possibly leading to operational inefficiency), and physical constraints/real-time situations owing to the necessary coexistence of passenger and freight transport as well as the externalities generated by the mobility

Table 7.1 First–last mile costs

FLM costs compared to the total transport costs [%]	Source
75	Boyer et al. (2004)
25–40	Macharis and Bontekoning (2004)
13–75	Onghena (2008)
53	Goh et al. (2011)

Source: Nocera et al. (2021).

system, such as congestion or the lack of parking and idling areas (Bruzzone et al., 2021a; Nocera et al., 2021).

Similar issues exist for passenger transport. With reference to the generalised travel cost of users, the FLM in a trip completed with collective means is generally expensive, as it involves a considerable amount of disutility for passengers. The conventional transport modes for this stage of a trip are often relatively slow, are not flexible or reliable, and may not provide a direct connection for all passengers. This may lead to customers using private transport modes to complete the FLM or the entire journey, thus increasing congestion and contributing to the exacerbation of transport issues at an urban level, including air and noise pollution and social effects such as competition for roads and public spaces. In particular, the passenger FLM can be seen as a bottleneck; for instance, the time to get to an airport and perform check-in and boarding procedures can be longer than the flight time. The time to reach a train station or the waiting time for the connection could be longer than the travel time, particularly for high-speed trains. Therefore, the first and last legs of a journey, which are often the shortest in terms of distance, may be the longest in terms of travel time. Furthermore, the transport services of passengers and goods share the same infrastructure, predominantly in urban areas; however, they are considered different and independent systems by authorities and lawmakers. This aspect is more pronounced in policy, planning, and research (Arvidsson et al., 2016).

Various solutions for improving both the passenger and freight FLM have been explored by researchers and tested in real-life applications, aiming to increase the efficiency and overall sustainability of a specific leg of a trip (van Duin et al., 2019; Nocera et al., 2021). This increases the competitiveness of deliveries (for freight) and alternatives to private motorised transport (for passengers). Regarding urban logistics, a promising solution involves the creation of consolidation/distribution centres (Nocera and Cavallaro, 2017), where goods are redistributed and consolidated to optimise the final delivery, which can be performed by zero-emission vehicles, including cargo bikes. Acting on the delivery chain and routing processes by providing, for instance, specific time windows and reshaping the demand curve according to more convenient timing, allows for the reduction of negative externalities from urban logistics while enhancing its competitiveness (Boyer et al., 2009; Montoya-Torres et al., 2015). Considering the perspective of passenger operations, researchers and planners have been aiming to reduce the actual and perceived transfer time and cost required to cover the last leg of the journey, that is, from a transportation hub (an airport, a train, or a metro station) to the destination. The first batch of solutions that have been proposed focus on the urban shape, such as transit-oriented development or the remodelling of existing neighbourhoods, roads, and facilities to ensure faster and safer access to public transport for pedestrians and cyclists while discouraging the use of cars for short trips (Lesh, 2013). A different set of ideas for passenger FLM insists on the availability of options to cover the leg to and from a transport hub, aiming to provide faster, more frequent, and more personalised alternatives to conventional buses. In this regard, the authors have investigated the potential of flexible transport systems and demand-responsive transport (Charisis et al., 2018; Alho et al., 2020), as well as more innovative solutions, such as automated shuttles (Scheltes et al., 2017) or personal rapid transit (Vuchic, 1996; Mueller and Sgouridis, 2011). Recent technological advancements have enhanced the potential of flexible transit solutions (owing to easier booking, scheduling, and payments) including ridesharing and car-pooling options owing to web-based applications capable of reaching a wider public (Dimitrakopoulos et al., 2020; Bruzzone et al., 2021b). Shared transport options are not limited to cars, but include bike- (both station-based and free-floating) and scooter-sharing systems, all of which demonstrate the potential in shortening the last leg of a passenger trip (both in relation to the overall trip with the same means and in comparison with private cars).

Although most of the debated solutions proposed to improve passenger and freight FLM demonstrate the potential in resolving the most critical issues of urban passenger and freight transport, the coexistence of operations in dense, space-lacking urban environments requires further efforts toward higher financial and environmental sustainability. According to the EC and certain researchers, the separation of freight and passenger transport from a normative, regulatory, and planning perspective constitutes a significant constraint to further improve FLM. In the last decade, researchers have focused on options for overcoming the formal separation between the transport of passengers and goods, in particular within FLM, and integrating the two flows (Cavallaro and Nocera, 2021).

Integration of Passenger and Cargo Flows

Passenger-freight integration solutions have been tested in a small number of real-life applications, which is mostly because these strategies often fail to be utilised owing to their complexity and the amount of vertical and horizontal coordination required. However, less-demanding independent measures that have been promoted and tested have repeatedly proven to be ineffective, leading to the confidence that only vigorous efforts can yield effective results (Strale, 2014; Ardvisson et al., 2016). Existing literature stresses that an increasing capacity to integrate freight transport and other urban activities and the cooperation among stakeholders, whether public or private and impactful or impacted, can lead to a more economically and environmentally sustainable FLM. Herein, the IPFT for the urban FLM is presented and the main drivers for the success and failure of this system are examined. Evidently, this integration is complex and involves different stakeholders within not only the mobility system, but also the urban environment as an entirety.

The objective of IPFT is to "*design[ing] networks and related planning and scheduling policies to enable efficient and reliable delivery of each parcel*" (Jansen, 2014). This model envisions an integrated system in which passengers and goods share vehicles, infrastructure, urban space, or more than one of these simultaneously. The integrated system directly involves both the urban mobility system as a whole and the key stakeholders in city management and economy, including public administration, actors involved in the trading system (shopkeepers, carriers, and manufacturers), and residents. The IPFT should increase the viability, efficiency, and efficacy (or reliability) of operations by approaching passengers and freight transport from an integrated perspective (Ardvisson et al., 2016; Monios, 2019). Theoretically, the integrated approach leads to low direct and generated costs for all stakeholders involved, low environmental impacts, and high social value of transport operations. Such schemes must be accompanied by consistent policy and coherent planning; regulatory and policy aspects are crucial for determining the success for various instances and currently constitute the largest barrier to their diffusion (Bruzzone et al., 2021a). Spoor (2015) notes that regulatory constraints contribute to increasing delivery chain costs. Ghilas et al. (2013) identified the system as complex, in which several stakeholders interact, such as passenger door-to-door transportation, package transportation, and public fixed-line services, and presented different scenarios considering various integration levels. The capacity to establish a profitable cooperation is necessary for the success of an integration process. However, this is time-consuming and requires significant political effort. Timing-related issues, such as passenger sensitivity to travel times and their prioritisation over goods, time-limited availability of stores for receiving delivery, just-in-time deliveries, and the management of just-in-time orders through web platforms, are significant constraints to a worry-free integration (Fatnassi et al., 2015). Other relevant constraints are related to the spare transport capacity during certain times of the day or periods of the week, flexibility of scheduled transport, and reverse logistics, including both waste management and the return of empty rolls and containers.

Operationally, IPFT is not a new concept; outsourcing part of the delivery process is a common practice for long-haul air and rail operations, where mixed usage of one aircraft or train is not unusual (Ghilas et al., 2013). Therefore, the proposed tenet indicates the possible usage of the overcapacity of public transport to carry freight for short-haul FLM operations. The concept of shared passengers and freight urban transport systems has evolved from when it was introduced (EC, 2007), which is now not necessarily being limited to urban operations but attempting to encompass the passenger and freight FLM in general. Trentini and Mahléné (2010) provided a list of pioneering projects that focus on sharing public transport services, public road spaces, and existing urban areas. For its complete implementation, a full-scale IPFT system requires a consistent change in the operational model, including scheduling, fares, the entire pick-up, transfer and delivery process of goods, and physical changes to assets (vehicles and infrastructure). Before implementing this complex and resource-intensive strategy, local administrations and public/private companies (including goods manufacturing and delivering companies, passenger transport authorities, and service management agencies) should consider their domestic contexts.

In dense urban centres, benefits for passenger-freight FLM issues are not only financial (transport operators and agencies expect lower expenses) and environmental (as a consequence of less kilometres driven and less energy consumption), but also include better use of the urban space. In urban peripheries, the cost reductions resulting from the IPFT can allow for reinvestment of saved funds, thus guaranteeing additional, more frequent transit and delivery services. This positively reflects on the users' perception of the service and territorial cohesion; the feeling of isolation typical of several peripheries can be relieved and the attractiveness and competitiveness of such areas can be enhanced. The available literature demonstrates the potential of short-haul mobility operations. Jansen (2014), Spoor (2015), and Ghilas et al. (2016) demonstrate that the entire freight sector (manufacturers, shippers and carriers, and receivers) generally gains an economic advantage from load consolidation and FLM delivery by public transit. They stated that public transport operators obtain economic advantages when making their spare transport capacity available for transporting parcels and/or small goods. Moreover, public authorities may financially benefit from the improved sustainability of transit operations, which will require lower subsidies.

The innovative theoretical approach to mobility induced by the IPFT requires an adaptation of the regulatory setting; the norms, rules, and contracts must be revised to allow for and incentivise integrated transport on transit vehicles (Jansen, 2014). Furthermore, for both public and private infrastructural investments, at least one consolidation facility and certain pick-up and delivery locations at selected transit stops have to be made available to sort and transfer parcels on buses and to load/unload them during the service. In addition, it implies purchasing new low-impact vehicles to cover the last mile of freight transport and intervening in the existing public transport fleet to make it suitable for easy, rapid (particularly in loading/unloading operations), reliable, and safe transport of goods. An acceptance model (addressed to public administrations, private and public companies, and stakeholders of transport and logistics systems) needs to be merged with an integrated and broad business model, which should consider all phases of the innovation process (from theorisation and planning to implementation, monitoring, and evaluation). In this preliminary phase, the funding by public authorities and the design and implementation of pilot initiatives are fundamental. Rather than a radical change in the system, small-scale applications (restricted sector of an urban agglomeration) can be critical for testing the proposed models, which can allow the composition of an appropriate and reliable set of indicators and an operational model to facilitate broader diffusion.

Evaluation of Passenger/Freight Integrated Schemes

The evaluation of the potential (*ex-ante*) results and real performances (*in itinere* and *ex-post*) of IPFT systems remains to present an open debate. The limited number of real-life, wide-scale tests and applications, and the variety of the factors to be evaluated have thus far resulted in a dearth of academic research in this area.

However, limited contributions are available on the topic (Sampaio et al., 2019; Kiba-Janiak et al., 2021) that discuss both urban (Leijenhorst, 2014; Strale, 2014) and rural case studies (Jansen, 2014; Bakker, 2015; van Duin et al., 2019). A few of these publications adopt a qualitative approach to IPFT (e.g., through Delphi and stated preferences methods; see Cochrane et al., 2017), often supported by conceptual modelling (e.g., Kiba-Janiak et al., 2021) or computational approaches. Ghilas et al. (2013) provided a mixed-integer formulation for the "Pickup and Delivery Problem with Fixed Scheduled Lines", while Serafini et al. (2018) used discrete choice models to analyse stated preferences on crowdshipping using public transport.

When evaluating real-life or hypothetical IPFT case studies, the authors have diverged from conventional evaluation methods, such as cost-benefit and multi-criteria analyses, to embrace methodologies that are focused on the performance of integrated systems (Cavallaro and Nocera, 2021). Key performance indicators (KPIs) have been identified as promising tools for the assessment and evaluation of the IPFT potential and performance, particularly in terms of environmental, social, and operational impacts (Nathanail et al., 2016; Mazzarino and Rubini, 2019; Bruzzone et al., 2021a). The use of indicators to assess the efficiency and sustainability of transport operations traces back to the United Nations Conference on the Environment and Development in 1992. Since then, the literature regarding sustainability and related indicators has proliferated.[1] In general, Eboli and Mazzulla (2012) state that performance measurement can be defined as the assessment of an organisation's output as a product of the management of its internal resources (money, people, vehicles, and facilities) and the environment in which it operates. Performance measures are critical for assessing a transport system relative to community objectives, diagnosing problems, allocating resources, monitoring, and improving operations. Meyer (2001) used comprehensive classification categories, namely general performance indicators (population, trips, vehicle kilometres, and hours), effectiveness measures (service supply, quality of service, availability), and efficiency measures (cost efficiency, operating ratios, vehicle utilisation, labour productivity, energy use, and fares). Litman (2009) listed the following three general types of KPIs for transit operations: measures of service quality, indicators of outcomes, and indicators of cost efficiency. Similar classifications can be found by Carter and Lomax (1992) and Vuchic (2007). Other applications of KPIs have been used in transport practices, including accessibility (Vasconcelos and Farias, 2012; Lessa et al., 2019), sustainability and energy performance (Munira and San Santoso, 2017; Gustafsson et al., 2018), and safety (Castro-Nuño and Arévalo-Quijada, 2018). Regarding freight transport and the supply chain, a review by Gunasekaran and Kobu (2007) found that commonly identified components to be evaluated are related to the use of resources, operations, and flexibility. A similar approach was adopted by Chae (2009), who provided an agency-oriented perspective. Cavallaro et al. (2020)

defined specific KPIs, referred to as combined transport. Fu and Jenelius (2018) evaluated delivery reliability, driving, energy, and service efficiency of deliveries of goods at night by defining specific KPIs.

Formal and content-related aspects must be considered when defining the most suitable KPIs for IPFT. Referring to the former aspect, the performance criteria must be suitable, measurable, realistic, defensible, and universal to achieve objective and unbiased performance measures (Sinha and Labi, 2007). Referring to the contents, the operational, environmental, and social performances of the proposed IPFT settings may be a valid framework. Choosing indicators capable of evaluating the system from the multiple perspectives of operators (public transport, PT, and freight carriers), PT customers, residents and retailers, and different stakeholders and decision-makers is essential. To achieve an overview of the performance of IPFT, KPIs of two different temporal frameworks should be compared; namely A (the condition after the introduction of the IPFT scheme) and B (before introducing the scheme). Conditions A and B have to be temporally in close proximity, meaning that the introduction of structural changes to the context of the study and its infrastructural assets is not viable. Based on these assumptions, Bruzzone et al. (2021a) designed a set of suitable indicators to assess the operational, environmental, and social performances of IPFT systems (see Table 7.2).

Context-related (reflecting local peculiarities) or policy-related (strengthen the analysis of politically prioritised aspects) variations to the proposed set of indicators are possible, provided that the identified indicators follow the aforementioned formal and content-related requirements.

The capability of performance indicators to capture the potential impacts of IPFT systems is acknowledged in literature; however, assessment processes through KPIs are costly and time-consuming because they require a solid dataset for both conditions A and B. The difficulty of effectively evaluating (estimating prior to the IPFT implementation) the improvements and impacts generated by the IPFT are likely contributors to the general scepticism towards its implementation. The inadequacy of the regulatory setting combined with the institutional complexity that needs to be addressed indicates that the full-scale application

Table 7.2 Identification of KPIs for IPFT

Category	Indicator	Title	Description
Operational	I_1	Traffic variation	Average daily traffic variation between B and A
	I_2	Covered distance	Variation in distances covered by PT and freight vehicles between B and A
	I_3	PT load factor	Variation in load factor between B and A
	I_4	Freight service frequency	Variation in frequency of freight deliveries between B and A
Environmental	I_5	Energy used	Variation in energy requirements for performing operations between B and A
	I_6	Air pollution external costs	Variation in external costs due to polluting emissions between B and A
Social	I_7	Cost of labour	Variation in costs for human resources between B and A

Note: B and A are the conditions before and after the introduction of the IPFT service
Source: Bruzzone et al. (2021).

of IPFT systems requires significant political and institutional commitment as well as financial support from authorities at various levels. However, the available research emphasises the correctness of the EC's intuition that merging passengers and cargo flows in short-haul urban operations, and in FLM in particular, can lead to benefits and a reduction of negative externalities from the transport sector. Therefore, institutions and authors have continued to explore the topic and discuss regulatory settings, practical and operational implications, and planning and evaluation methods to increase the viability of the integrated systems. Within this context, several pilot projects and case studies can be identified, where transit vehicles and taxis and/or transport infrastructure (tracks and stations) are used for both goods and passenger mobility.

The next section briefly presents a selection of case studies and pilot applications, highlighting their potential and the measured impact when available, as well as the drivers preventing the consolidation within the FLM.

Case Studies

Despite the first IPFT studies typically dealing with urban environments, researchers and authorities have determined that there is potential for rural areas as well, where planners normally explore solutions to increase the financial sustainability of transit networks. Owing to the easy organisation, small dimensions, and fragmentation of rural operations, a discrete amount of literature and a few pilot projects have been promoted in these areas, particularly in Germany and the Netherlands. However, other initiatives have been designed, and in certain cases, are implemented in urban environments; these include the following three macro-categories: sharing transport infrastructure (mostly tram tracks), sharing public transport vehicles (buses and taxis), and simultaneously sharing both the infrastructure and vehicles. In dense urban environments, the focus is on the sharing the transport infrastructure, such as trams or light rail tracks, as the reduction of space allocated to public transport and logistics operations is often considered politically viable. On the contrary, the IPFT may worsen the level of service offered to passengers, for instance, due to additional stops, long dwell times, and reduction of spare capacity onboard.

Projects regarding the shared use of tram tracks are occasionally incentivised or accompanied by restricting policies against the circulation of trucks, such as time windows or emission policies. Freight transport on urban rails was commonly used prior to road transportation being developed; however, as in other rail freight businesses, the competition with road transport has been significantly unfavourable to rail services (Rodrigue et al., 2013). Nevertheless, a growing interest regarding the (re)use of light rail services for urban freight is observed as a response to concerns related to the social and environmental impacts of urban logistics (Arvidsson and Browne, 2013; Macharis, 2014; Strale, 2019; Pietrzak and Pietrzak, 2021). In this context, several rail experiences have been launched in Europe with various success implications, the most relevant being in Dresden, Zurich, Amsterdam, Vienna, Paris, and Saint-Etienne (see Table 7.3). In Dresden, the tram transports components for a local industry between two industrial sites near the city, avoiding the circulation of trucks (Metro Report, 2017). In Zurich and Vienna, the tram network is (or was: Vienna's project is on hold as of 2022) employed for special waste collection by using dedicated trailers that are to be attached to classic trams visiting a number of pick-up stops, which are equipped with double tracking to avoid interferences with the operations of passenger trams (Stadt Wien, 2005; TAUT, 2021; Stadt Zurich, 2022). In Amsterdam, a wide-scale project with 50 trams for parcel distribution was launched; however, it was halted after the pilot phase because it proved to be financially unsustainable without public support (Strale, 2014). Finally, in the French case studies, private retailers use decommissioned trams rather than trucks to replenish supermarkets (TramFret, 2022).

Masdar City's Freight Rapid Transit in the United Arab Emirates is a similar experiment in which the network is simultaneously used by freight and passenger vehicles. The pilot project, which involves three freight pods, is currently on hold due to the abortion of the planned expansion of the personal rapid transit network and the difficult interaction between the automated operations and "manual" loading/unloading and freight delivery to and from the stations.

Infrastructure sharing between passengers and goods appears to be promising only under certain conditions; Strale (2014) determines that only small-scale projects are successful

Table 7.3 Freight transport on urban light rail tracks

City	Type	Diffusion and frequency	History	Evaluation	Operator/Investor(s)
Dresden	Internal logistics of industry	Cross-city line	2000–2016; 2017-today	Verified financial benefits for Volkswagen, full compliance with policy requests (no trucks allowed)	Volkswagen, DVB Dresdner Verkehrsbetriebe
Zurich	Waste collection	Whole city; 3 trams	2003–today	Costly service (around 1,000€/day), but highly valuable for quality of life	ERZ Entsorgung und Reciclying Zurich, VBZ Verkehrsbetriebe Zurich
Amsterdam	Urban distribution	Whole city; 50 trams	2007–2009	Not available	Public funding
Vienna	Waste collection	Whole city	2005–currently on hold	Not available	Public funding
Paris	Internal logistics of retailer	One line from the city to a consolidation centre	2007–today	Not available	Private retailer (Monoprix)
Saint-Etienne	Urban distribution	Whole city	2011 (testing), 2016–today	No impact on regular passenger tram traffic, tangible environmental benefits	Private retailers (Carrefour/Casino), RATP/STIF Régie Autonome de Transports Parisiens/ Syndacat des Transports d'Île-de-France – Île-de-France Mobilités

Source: Authors

in terms of the actors involved or geographical extension. In contrast, settings involving a large-scale city distribution are rarely implemented, such as the project in Amsterdam. Similarly, Ardvisson and Browne (2013) highlight that light rail transport is less convenient than trucks for the same trip and that use of a light rail must be accompanied by attractive or exclusive services (evening delivery, temporary storage, and reverse logistics) as well as by restrictive policies toward truck access. Trentini and Mahléné (2010) emphasised that the sharing of tracks with passenger services generates issues, given the impossibility of stopping the latter during loading and unloading. The lack of flexibility offered by light rail has been found to be particularly penalising in urban environments, contributing to the difficult implementation of these systems (Alessandrini et al., 2012), which provide numerous benefits from environmental and social perspectives (Kuhn, 2002).

In addition to the idea of sharing transport infrastructure, which can include dedicated lanes and bays, bus rapid transit guideways, and right-of-way areas, the sharing of transit-related public spaces such as stations, stops, and redevelopment areas near transit can also be considered for the handling and storage of goods. The most relevant experiments in this field are constituted by the so-called "lockers" or "hubs" for parcels and mail, normally located at busy locations, including transit stops and stations. Other applications include the temporary allocation of transit-related space, for instance, for the organised distribution of groceries and goods or for events.

Conclusions

The combination of passenger and cargo flows for short-haul logistics operations in dense urban environments is a relatively new topic in transportation planning. Normative and regulatory systems, which consider logistics and passenger transport as distinct entities, require attention to allow wide-scale, real-life implementations of integrated passenger-freight mobility systems that are beyond pilot projects and testing.

However, the idea of combining passengers and cargo is increasingly recognised as a significant opportunity to enhance the financial, environmental, and social sustainability of the mobility system as a whole. Since the integration requested by the Green Paper on Urban Mobility (EC, 2007), researchers and authorities have been exploring the potential of these solutions aiming to improve the quality of the mobility system in both rural (where the feasibility of transit provision and the opportunities of residents and retailers are enhanced by reduced costs) and in particular, urban areas where the social acceptability of logistics operations grows while impacts diminish. Despite the need for an increased coordination between public and private stakeholders and the necessity of a non-negligible initial investment (to adapt the infrastructure and fleet and to design ad-hoc management tools and models), studies and/or tested projects reveal that small-scale urban applications succeed in their goals, whereas certain difficulties exist for citywide, large-scale attempts. Moreover, projects driven by a strongly interested private firm (such as CarGoTram in Dresden or TramFret in St. Etienne) and/or supported by policy restricting road traffic appear to more likely succeed and prove to be convenient for promoters and operators as well.

Without any structural changes to urban networks and regulatory systems, it is possible to effectively merge public transport and urban logistics operations even today, which would improve the operational, environmental, and social aspects. The future integration of the "combined mobility" perspective within European and local planning tools and processes can further enhance and legitimise the shared passenger-good mobility, providing planners and authorities with the right tools to incentivise the involved stakeholders and more effectively achieve the pursued policy objectives that more sectorial policies fail to reach.

Note

1 The topic is too vast to be presented in this section exhaustively. For a more detailed analysis, interested readers may refer to JRC (2009).

References

Alessandrini, A., Delle Site, P., Filippi, F., and Salucci, M.V., (2012). Using rail to make urban freight distribution more sustainable. *European Transport\Trasporti Europei* 50, 1–5.

Alho, A., Sakai, T., Oh, S., Cheng, C., Seshadri, R., Chong, W.H., Hara, Y., Caravias, J., Cheah, L., and Ben-Akiva, M., (2020). A simulation-based evaluation of a Cargo-Hitching service for E-commerce using mobility-on-demand vehicles. *arXiv preprint arXiv:2010.11585*.

Arvidsson, N., and Browne, M., (2013). A review of the success and failure of tram systems to carry urban freight: The implications for a low emission intermodal solution using electric vehicles on trams. *European Transport\Trasporti Europei* 54(Paper 5), 1–18.

Arvidsson, N., Givoni, M., and Woxenius, J., (2016). Exploring last mile synergies in passenger and freight transport. *Built Environment* 42, 523–538. https://doi.org/10.2148/benv.42.4.523

Bakker, J., (2015). Increasing delivery efficiency by Cargo Hitching: A case study. (Master thesis). *TU/e School of Industrial Engineering*.

Boyer, K.K., Prud'homme, A.M., and Chung, W., (2009). The last mile challenge: Evaluating the effects of customer density and delivery window patterns. *Journal of Business Logistics* 30, 185–201. https://doi.org/10.1002/j.2158-1592.2009.tb00104.x

Bruzzone, F., Cavallaro, F., and Nocera, S., (2021a). The integration of passenger and freight transport for first-last mile operations. *Transport Policy* 100, 31–48. https://doi.org/10.1016/j.tranpol.2020.10.009

Bruzzone, F., Scorrano, M., and Nocera, S., (2021b). The combination of e-bike-sharing and demand-responsive transport systems in rural areas: A case study of Velenje. *Research in Transportation Business & Management, Active Travel and Mobility Management* 40, 100570. https://doi.org/10.1016/j.rtbm.2020.100570

Carter, D.N., and Lomax, T.J., (1992). Development and application of performance measures for rural public transportation operators. *Transportation Research Record* 1338, 28–36.

Castro-Nuño, M., and Arévalo-Quijada, M.T., (2018). Assessing urban road safety through multi-dimensional indexes: Application of multicriteria decision making analysis to rank the Spanish provinces. *Transport Policy* 68, 118–129. https://doi.org/10.1016/j.tranpol.2018.04.017

Cavallaro, F., and Nocera, S., (2021). Integration of passenger and freight transport: A concept-centric literature review. *Research in Transportation Business & Management* 100718. https://doi.org/10.1016/j.rtbm.2021.100718

Cavallaro, F., Sommacal, G., Božičnik, S., and Klemenčič, M., (2020). Combined transport in the Alps: Reasons behind a difficult acceptance and possible solutions. *Research in Transportation Business & Management*, 35, 100461. https://doi.org/10.1016/j.rtbm.2020.100461

Chae, B. K., (2009). Developing key performance indicators for supply chain: An industry perspective. *Supply Chain Management: An International Journal* 14, 422–428. https://doi.org/10.1108/13598540910995192

Charisis, A., Iliopoulou, C., and Kepaptsoglou, K., (2018). DRT route design for the first/last mile problem: Model and application to Athens, Greece. *Public Transportation* 10, 499–527. https://doi.org/10.1007/s12469-018-0188-0

Cochrane, K., Saxe, S., Roorda, M.J., and Shalaby, A., (2017). Moving freight on public transit: Best practices, challenges, and opportunities. *International Journal of Sustainable Transportation* 11, 120–132. https://doi.org/10.1080/15568318.2016.1197349

Dimitrakopoulos, G.J., Uden, L., and Varlamis, I., (2020). *The Future of Intelligent Transport Systems*. Elsevier.

Eboli, L., and Mazzulla, G., (2012). Performance indicators for an objective measure of public transport service quality. *European Transport\Trasporti Europei* 51(Paper 3), 1–21.

EC, European Commission, (2007). *Green Paper: Towards a New Culture for Urban Mobility*. {SEC(2007) 1209}.

EC, European Commission, (2020). *Handbook on the external costs of transport: Version 2019 – 1.1. Ufficio delle pubblicazioni dell'Unione europea*, LU.

Fatnassi, E., Chaouachi, J., and Klibi, W., (2015). Planning and operating a shared goods and passengers on-demand rapid transit system for sustainable city-logistics. *Transportation Research Part B: Methodological, Optimization of Urban Transportation Service Networks* 81, 440–460. https://doi.org/10.1016/j.trb.2015.07.016

Fu, J., and Jenelius, E., (2018). Transport efficiency of off-peak urban goods deliveries: A Stockholm pilot study. *Case Studies on Transport Policy* 6, 156–166. https://doi.org/10.1016/j.cstp.2018.01.001

Ghilas, V., Demir, E., and van Woensel, T., (2016). The pickup and delivery problem with time windows and scheduled lines. *INFOR: Information Systems and Operational Research* 54, 147–167. https://doi.org/10.1080/03155986.2016.1166793

Ghilas, V., Demir, E., and van Woensel, T., (2013). Integrating passenger and freight transportation : Model formulation and insights, *BETA publicatie : Working Papers*. Technische Universiteit Eindhoven, Eindhoven.

Gunasekaran, A., and Kobu, B., (2007). Performance measures and metrics in logistics and supply chain management: A review of recent literature (1995–2004) for research and applications. *International Journal of Production Research* 45, 2819–2840. https://doi.org/10.1080/00207540600806513

Gustafsson, M., Svensson, N., and Anderberg, S., (2018). Energy performance indicators as policy support for public bus transport – The case of Sweden. *Transportation Research Part D: Transport and Environment* 65, 697–709. https://doi.org/10.1016/j.trd.2018.10.008

Jansen, T.A.M., (2014). Development of a design model for integrated passenger and freight transportation systems. (Master thesis). *TU/e School of Industrial Engineering*.

JRC, Joint Research Centre Institute for Environment and Sustainability, (2009). Indicators to assess sustainability of transport activities. *Office for Official Publications of the European Communities*. Luxembourg.

Kiba-Janiak, M., Thompson, R., and Cheba, K., (2021). An assessment tool of the formulation and implementation a sustainable integrated passenger and freight transport strategies. An example of selected European and Australian cities. *Sustainable Cities and Society* 71, 102966. https://doi.org/10.1016/j.scs.2021.102966

Kuhn, F., (2002). Bus rapid or light rail transit for intermediate cities? Presented at the URBAN MOBILITY FOR ALL. *Proceedings of the 10th International Codatu Conference*.

Leijenhorst, A., (2014). Cargo Hitching bij Binnenstadservice Maastricht [WWW Document]. URL http://essay.utwente.nl/65598/ (accessed 11.8.21).

Lesh, M.C., (2013). Innovative concepts in first-last mile connections to public transportation 63–74. In: *Urban Public Transportation Systems 2013*. 2013. 63–74. https://doi.org/10.1061/9780784413210.007

Lessa, D.A., Lobo, C., and Cardoso, L., (2019). Accessibility and urban mobility by bus in Belo Horizonte/Minas Gerais – Brazil. *Journal of Transport Geography* 77, 1–10. https://doi.org/10.1016/j.jtrangeo.2019.04.004

Litman, T., (2009). *A Good Example of Bad Transportation Performance Evaluation*. Victoria Transportation Policy Institute.

Macharis, C., Melo, S., Woxenius, J., and Lier, T. van, (2014). *Sustainable Logistics*. Emerald Group Publishing.

Macioszek, E., (2018). First and last mile delivery – Problems and Issues, in: Sierpiński, G. (Ed.), *Advanced Solutions of Transport Systems for Growing Mobility, Advances in Intelligent Systems and Computing*. Springer International Publishing, Cham, 147–154. https://doi.org/10.1007/978-3-319-62316-0_12

Mazzarino, M., and Rubini, L., (2019). Smart urban planning: evaluating urban logistics performance of innovative solutions and sustainable policies in the Venice lagoon—The results of a case study. *Sustainability* 11, 4580. https://doi.org/10.3390/su11174580

Metro Report, (2017). Freight trams to support electric cars production [WWW Document]. URL http://www.metro-report.com/news/single-view/view/freight-tram-to-support-electric-car-production.html (accessed 07/03/22).

Meyer, M., (2001). Measuring that which cannot be measured – at least according to conventional wisdom, in: *Transportation Research Board Conference Proceedings*. Presented at the Performance Measures to Improve Transportation Systems and Agency Operations Transportation Research Board; National Transit Institute; American Association of State Highway and Transportation Officials; and Federal Highway Administration.

Monios, J., (2019). Geographies of governance in the freight transport sector: The British case. *Transportation Research Part A: Policy and Practice* 121, 295–308. https://doi.org/10.1016/j.tra.2019.01.020

Montoya-Torres, J.R., López Franco, J., Nieto Isaza, S., Felizzola Jiménez, H., and Herazo-Padilla, N., (2015). A literature review on the vehicle routing problem with multiple depots. *Computers & Industrial Engineering* 79, 115–129. https://doi.org/10.1016/j.cie.2014.10.029

Mueller, K., and Sgouridis, S.P., (2011). Simulation-based analysis of personal rapid transit systems: Service and energy performance assessment of the Masdar City PRT case. *Journal of Advanced Transportation* 45, 252–270. https://doi.org/10.1002/atr.158

Munira, S., and Santoso, D.S., (2017). Examining public perception over outcome indicators of sustainable urban transport in Dhaka city. *Case Studies on Transport Policy* 5, 169–178. https://doi.org/10.1016/j.cstp.2017.03.011

Nathanail, E., Adamos, G., Mitropoulos, L., Gogas, M., Karakikes, I., Stanislaw, I., and Kiba-Janiak, M., (2016). *NOVELOG Project – Deliverable D3.1 – Integrated Assessment Framework for UFT Solutions*. (Deliverable No. D3.1). NOVELOG.

Nocera, S., and Cavallaro, F., (2017). A two-step method to evaluate the Well-To-Wheel carbon efficiency of Urban Consolidation Centres. *Research in Transportation Economics* 65, 44–55. https://doi.org/10.1016/j.retrec.2017.04.001

Nocera, S., Pungillo, G., and Bruzzone, F., (2021). How to evaluate and plan the freight-passengers first-last mile. *Transport Policy* 113, 56–66. https://doi.org/10.1016/j.tranpol.2020.01.007

Pietrzak, O., and Pietrzak, K., (2021). Cargo tram in freight handling in urban areas in Poland. *Sustainable Cities and Society* 70. https://doi.org/10.1016/j.scs.2021.102902

Rodrigue, J.-P., Comtois, C., and Slack, B., (2013). *The Geography of Transport Systems*, Third edition Routledge, London; New York.

Rodrigue, J-P., and Dablanc, L., (2021). What is city logistics? *City Logistics: Concepts, Policy and Practice*. Routledge. https://globalcitylogistics.org/

Sampaio, A., Savelsbergh, M., Veelenturf, L., and van Woensel, T., (2019). Chapter 15 - Crowd-based city logistics, in: Faulin, J., Grasman, S.E., Juan, A.A., Hirsch, P. (Eds.), *Sustainable Transportation and Smart Logistics*. Elsevier, 381–400. https://doi.org/10.1016/B978-0-12-814242-4.00015-6

Savelsbergh, M., and van Woensel, T., (2016). City logistics: Challenges and opportunities. *Transportation Science* 50, 579–590. https://doi.org/10.1287/trsc.2016.0675

Scheltes, A., de Almeida and Correia, G.H., (2017). Exploring the use of automated vehicles as last mile connection of train trips through an agent-based simulation model: An application to Delft, Netherlands. *International Journal of Transportation Science and Technology, Connected and Automated Vehicles: Effects on Traffic, Mobility and Urban Design* 6, 28–41. https://doi.org/10.1016/j.ijtst.2017.05.004

Serafini, S., Nigro, M., Gatta, V., and Marcucci, E., (2018). Sustainable crowdshipping using public transport: A case study evaluation in Rome. *Transportation Research Procedia, EURO Mini Conference on "Advances in Freight Transportation and Logistics"* 30, 101–110. https://doi.org/10.1016/j.trpro.2018.09.012

Sinha, K.C., and Labi, S., (2007). *Transportation Decision Making: Principles of Project Evaluation and Programming*. John Wiley & Sons.

Spoor, J.M., (2015). Replenishing nanostores in megacities for a consumer packaged goods company. (Master thesis). *TU/e School of Industrial Engineering*.

Stadt Wien, (2005) [WWW Document]. URL https://www.wien.gv.at/presse/2005/05/12/die-gueterbim-faehrt (accessed 07/03/22).

Stadt Zurich, (2022) [WWW Document]. URL https://www.stadt-zuerich.ch/ted/de/index/entsorgung_recycling/entsorgen/wo-wann-entsorgen/cargo-tram_und_e-tram.html (accessed 07/03/22).

Strale, M., (2014). The cargo tram: Current status and perspectives, the example of Brussels. *Transport and Sustainability* 6, 245–263. https://doi.org/10.1108/S2044-994120140000006010

Strale, M., (2019). Sustainable urban logistics: What are we talking about? *Transportation Research Part A: Policy and Practice* 130, 745–751. https://doi.org/10.1016/j.tra.2019.10.002

TAUT, Tramways and Urban Transit, (2021). Zurich's Cargo Tram. TAUT 1008, Dec. 2021.

TramFret 2022 [WWW Document]. Project TramFret.URL https://tramfret.com/ (accessed 07/03/22).

Trentini, A., and Mahléné, N., (2010). Toward a shared urban transport system ensuring passengers & goods cohabitation. *TeMA – Journal of Land Use, Mobility and Environment* 3. https://doi.org/10.6092/1970-9870/165

van Duin, R., Wiegmans, B., Tavasszy, L., Hendriks, B., and He, Y., (2019). Evaluating new participative city logistics concepts: The case of cargo hitching. *Transportation Research Procedia* 39, 565–575. https://doi.org/10.1016/j.trpro.2019.06.058

Vasconcelos, A.S., and Farias, T.L., (2012). Evaluation of urban accessibility indicators based on internal and external environmental costs. *Transportation Research Part D: Transport and Environment* 17, 433–441. https://doi.org/10.1016/j.trd.2012.05.004

Vuchic, V.R., (1996). Personal rapid transit: An unrealistic system. *The Urban Transportation Monitor*, 7.

Vuchic, V.R., (2007). *Urban Transit Systems and Technology*. John Wiley & Sons.

Wang, Y., Zhang, D., Liu, Q., Shen, F., and Lee, L.H., (2016). Towards enhancing the last-mile delivery: An effective crowd-tasking model with scalable solutions. *Transportation Research Part E: Logistics and Transportation Review* 93, 279–293. https://doi.org/10.1016/j.tre.2016.06.002

PART B

Urban Logistics Sectors

8
PARCEL DELIVERIES AS A PIONEER FOR CLIMATE NEUTRALITY

The Case of Ecozone in Mechelen (Belgium)

Koen Mommens and Cathy Macharis

Introduction

E-commerce is a fast-growing sector and one that has received an additional boost as a result of the COVID-19 pandemic with the obligatory closure of physical shops and lockdowns where people needed to stay in and work from home. E-commerce is here to stay. However, the parcel delivery operations are associated with nuisances (congestion, air pollution and double parking issues), especially in cities. In its White Paper for Transport, the European Commission sets the goal to achieve emission-free urban logistics by 2030 in the main European cities (European Commission, 2011). Within the field of urban logistics, parcel deliveries are often identified as a potential pioneer to make this transition toward emission-free deliveries.

This chapter consists of two main sections. The first one focuses on e-commerce in general, how are parcel deliveries organized, what is the impact of these deliveries and which solutions are there out there? The second section highlights the state-of-the-art case study of the Ecozone project in Mechelen. In this project, the largest parcel and postal operator of Belgium is organizing its parcel deliveries emission-free in the entire city.

E-commerce in General

E-commerce represented 21% of all retail sales worldwide in 2021, increasing from a share of 15% before the COVID-19 pandemic in 2019. The penetration rate of online sales varies for different regions around the globe, depending on internet access and payment facilities (see Figure 8.1). All regions are however indicating strong growth and estimations suggest that this growth will be continued in the coming years, despite the cooling down period after the pandemic that is currently seen in some regions (Morgan Stanley Research, 2022). By its fast growth and current organization, parcel logistics is setting challenges for retailers, logistic service providers and governments.

B2C e-commerce has multiple delivery options, and many studies exist on the consumer preferences for these options (Buldeo Rai, 2019; Molin et al., 2022). In general, home deliveries are most used as delivery option, including in Belgium. Exceptions are Poland, the

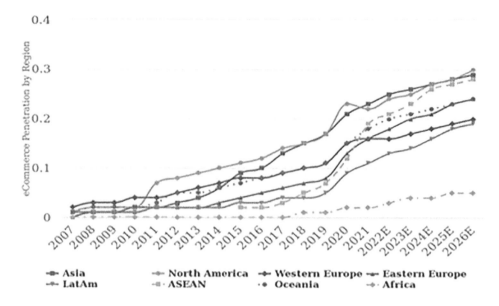

Figure 8.1 E-commerce penetration rate by region
Source: Morgan Stanley, 2022 based on Euromonitor, National Data Sources and Morgan Stanley Research estimates.

Baltic and Scandinavian countries, where lockers are the most used option. Manned pick-up points are another popular out-of-home delivery option. The COVID-19 pandemic made that many people shifted (obligatory) to working from home. It influenced transport demand toward home deliveries in disadvantage to out-of-home deliveries.

Fast and Free

The fast and free home delivery is the standard in the e-commerce market. It is offered as a service to consumers by E-retailers (Agatz et al., 2020). The free delivery however has as a consequence that consumers aren't aware of namely, the (internal and external) cost of the delivery. Consequently, there is no incentive for them to shift to more efficient and sustainable delivery options. Moreover, the free delivery decreases the economic margins for logistic service providers and increases the social pressure on the parcel logistics sector.

Fast deliveries are also a commercial strategy of the largest E-retailers (Rakuten Intelligence, 2019) and have implications on the entire e-commerce supply chain network. To enable next-day or even deliveries within a couple of hours after making the order, stocks should be available in proximity of the end consumers. Fast deliveries also don't leave room for much optimization and consolidation in the logistics organization. They consequently enhance the use of vans instead of more environmentally-friendly vehicles like cargobikes. Moreover, they increase the pressure on delivery men and women and their labor conditions (see Chapter 27).

Sustainability

To tackle climate change and meet the Paris Agreement, many regions and countries around the globe are developing action plans. In the European Union, the Fit for 55 program targets climate neutrality by 2050. Transport is the sector that is struggling the most in reducing its greenhouse gas emissions (European Commission, 2021). City distribution is identified as a pioneer in achieving emission-free logistics. The European Commission incorporated this in its White Paper of 2011 (European Commission, 2011). Even though the e-commerce deliveries currently account for only 3% of the CO_2 emissions of freight transport in the urban environment (Otten et al., 2016), much attention is being given to this sector.

Sustainability goes however beyond climate change. It considers people (social elements), planet (the physical/natural environment) and profit (the economic elements). This chapter will address the concept of sustainability from an external cost perspective (van Essen et al., 2019). An external cost is defined by Bickel and Friedrich (2005) as a cost that *"arises, when the social or economic activities of one group of persons have an impact on another group and when that impact is not fully accounted, or compensated for, by the first group."*

Last Mile and Global Supply Chain

Research on e-commerce has tended to focus so far mainly on the last mile. The last mile is often seen as the most challenging part of the supply chain, given its disproportional relationship between share of vehicle-kilometers in the supply chain and its share in logistic costs and environmental impact. Economically, Goodman (2005) states that 28% of the transport costs occur in the last mile, while for parcels Gevaers (2013) estimates that 13–75% of the total logistics costs are situated in the last mile. It should consequently not be a surprise that the different stakeholders are addressing this last mile to address sustainability. The societal and environmental impact of the last mile of parcel deliveries has also received a great deal of attention in the literature (Buldeo Rai et al., 2019; Carling et al., 2015; Edwards et al., 2010; Jaller and Pahwa, 2020; Van Loon et al., 2015; Wiese et al., 2012). The focus lies on the sustainability impact between the different delivery options; home deliveries and collection points or lockers. Recent attention is given on additional parameters influencing the sustainability impact. Mommens et al. (2021) researched the impact of the metropolitan, urban and rural environment – and related drop-, population- and socio-economic facility densities – on the impact of the different delivery options. OOH deliveries should be preferred in metropolitan and urban environments, while home deliveries are to be preferred in rural areas. Buldeo Rai et al. (2019) introduced the importance of the consumer, and omnichannel behavior in the sustainability equation. They showed that online purchases can be associated to lower CO_2 emissions than in-store purchases. However, once omnichannel behavior occurs, in-store purchases are to be preferred from a CO_2 perspective.

Yet, the largest E-retailers, representing the majority of parcels, are multinationals. They offer goods from all over the globe to the end-consumer. The e-commerce supply chain is consequently often a global one. There is little research on this international and intercontinental transport and its economic and sustainability impact.

Multiple Stakeholders

The decisions taken by e-commerce logistics and deliveries are not the subject of one stakeholder group. Multiple stakeholders have their role and importance. Therefore, stakeholder involvement and engagement are necessary to guarantee successful, efficient and sustainable parcel deliveries (Lindholm and Browne, 2013). Buldeo Rai (2019) identifies three stakeholder groups; the consumers, E-retailers and logistic service providers (see Figure 8.2).

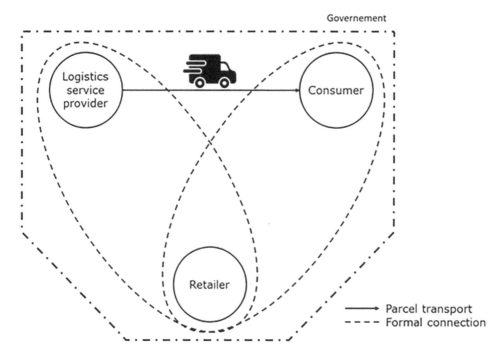

Figure 8.2 Structure of stakeholder groups in e-commerce
Source: Extension based on Buldeo Rai (2019).

Consumers are making several important decisions: decisions on the online purchase itself and the (online) place of the purchase, the decision on where the parcel will be delivered and the proper consumer transport movements related to the online purchase (pick-up of parcel, omnichannel behavior, eventual return). Regularly, the consumer can also choose between different delivery speeds. Research indicates that the consumer choices and behavior have a significant impact on the transport-related economic and sustainability performance of the parcel delivery (Buldeo Rai et al., 2019; Mommens et al., 2021).

The E-retailer are responsible for the delivery choices they offer to the consumers and the conditions (price, delivery speed) related to these delivery choices. A limited number of large E-retailers dominate this market. They offer free deliveries and fast deliveries to consumers as a service. Smaller E-retailers (need to) follow. Once the largest E-retailers are representing sufficient parcel volumes in a certain region, they tend to also take care of the parcel delivery itself. Examples are Amazon or recently Vinted installing own parcel lockers in Paris (France).

The third stakeholder group is the logistic service providers. They are organizing the delivery of the parcel to the end destinations. Generally, you have a large national parcel operator which is also providing postal services in the country. Next to that, you have several large international parcel operators with respective market shares (parcel volumes) in different countries. Lastly, a larger group of small logistics service providers are operating on a local – often city – level. In this last group, you have companies focusing on specific e-commerce segments, but also cargobike operators. The logistic service providers are responsible for the organization of the parcel deliveries: the vehicles used, the routes, the use and the location of distribution centers.

An additional stakeholder group to the structure presented by Buldeo Rai (2019) is the government. Especially local governments are having a significant impact on the parcel deliveries by the local measures – mainly restrictions on vehicle use, low-emission zones and parking.

Solutions

Macharis et al. (2014) identify five elements that require addressing in order to evolve toward sustainable logistics and sustainable parcel deliveries. They structure these elements along five "A's". The first one is Anticipation of new technologies, for example electric vehicles. The total cost of ownership of electric vans is becoming competitive with the conventional diesel vans, making electric vans a valuable sustainable alternative. Avoidance of transport via bundling or consolidation in (micro)hubs is the second A. Crowdsourced solutions offer the opportunity to save transport movements. Crowdsourced collection points (Akeb et al., 2018; Kedia et al., 2017) and especially crowdsourced deliveries (Buldeo Rai et al., 2017) showed less potential as the crowd in reality tends to still make dedicated trips to deliver their parcel(s). Microhubs are used more as consolidation hub for parcel deliveries. They are installed in many cities in Europe (Brussels, London, Chapelle, Paris, Bordeaux, Oslo, Gothenburg among others) and around the world (Montreal, Miami, New York City among others) (Katsela et al., 2022). The use of the microhubs allows consolidation for the incoming urban parcel flows, reduction of vehicle-kilometers (Vasiutina et al., 2021) and optimization of the final delivery in the city center via the use of sustainable transport modes. Act and shift is the third A. The shift to more sustainable modes of transport like cargobikes on the one hand. Microhubs are often combined with the use of cargobikes, bike-trailers (Ormond et al., 2019; Vasiutina et al., 2021) or to a smaller extent with electric vehicles (Clarke and Leonardi, 2017). On the other hand, you have the shift toward off-hours. This is hardly possible for home deliveries, but it is for OOH deliveries and parcel lockers in particular. A network of lockers was implemented and researched in multiple cities and countries (Morganti et al., 2014; Van Duin et al., 2020), with positive results in terms of sustainability, missed deliveries and efficiency gains for the logistic service provider, and substitution of car trips with soft modes (foot, bike) (McLeod et al., 2006). The fourth A is Awareness creation, which ideally and ultimately leads to behavioral change. An example is making consumers aware of the sustainability impact of different delivery options or their own transport behavior. The final A is Actor involvement, meaning that stakeholders should be considered to guarantee success. The above literature review illustrates that all case studies so far address one or two of the five A's. In many European cities, logistic solutions are implemented to increase the sustainability of parcel deliveries. Undeniably, these measures have a positive impact on global greenhouse gas emissions, local air quality and living quality. Yet, they don't reach their full potential as they remain limited to single or limited amount measures – cargobikes, electric vehicles, use of microhubs, locker network and consolidation centers. A simultaneous implementation of a large set of logistic solutions could create a new emission-free delivery system with interactions between the measures and a subsequent larger sustainability impact. Yet, such implementation requires innovation at all echelons of the distribution chain. Already, the implementation of one sustainable logistic solution entails a reorganization of the logistics processes of a logistic service provider (e.g. warehouse processes and routing). The simultaneous implementation of multiple interacting logistic solutions increases the complexity of the reorganizations. Success will require innovation and flexibility in the working processes in the different distribution and sorting centers, the mail centers, the work of the planners, the drivers and bikers. It requires a multi-actor approach, which is again rare (Kiba-Jania et al., 2021).

In the next section of this chapter, the implementation case in Mechelen is presented that tackles all five A's explained above.

Case Description

The largest postal and parcel logistic service provider of Belgium implemented an emission-free parcel delivery system for the medium-sized city of Mechelen (Belgium). The city has 87.000 citizens, a population density of 2.600 citizens per square kilometer and a parcel volume of almost 1 million parcels per year for this logistic service provider. The city of Mechelen has car/van/truck restrictions in the city center, where those vehicles cannot access the yellow zone between 11 am and 6 pm (Figure 8.3). Mechelen is situated near (35 km) and between two large cities (Antwerp and Brussels). The parcel distribution centers are located in those two cities. Parcels are brought to a local distribution center in Mechelen for the last mile.

Figure 8.3 Map of city center of Mechelen with zone with vehicle restriction in gray

The implementation was the result of a three-year process, starting with researching and configuring the concept. Next followed a stepwise approach in which measures were installed, tested and evaluated, after which adjustments were made. At first, a dense network of 49 unmanned lockers was installed in the city, resulting in one locker within the 400 m of every home address. Dedicated locker rounds – supply and pick-up combined – were organized on daily basis.

Next, all diesel vans were replaced by electric vans of different categories in Mechelen and the local distribution center was equipped with the necessary charging infrastructure. It represents an electric vehicle fleet of 63 vans. Electric vehicles have no tailpipe emissions and produce less noise nuisance, while having similar operational characteristics (capacity and speed) as conventional vans.

The shift to electric vehicles contributed to the zero-emission goal (Tank-To-Wheel), however, the logistic organization was still confronted with access limitations in the center. Therefore, as a next step, electric vans were replaced by bike-trailers. They enabled operation in the city throughout the day and their operations were supported by two microhubs in the city center to avoid trips to local distribution center located at the city outskirts.

As a fourth step, a machine was installed in the local distribution center to identify parcels with a Mechelen origin and destination. They represent approximately 10% of the parcel volume. Until then, all parcels were sent to the parcel distribution centers in Antwerp and Brussels. Via the use of this machine, 10% of the parcel volume of Mechelen could stay at the local distribution center, which enables other loads to be delivered, trips avoided or the use of smaller less-polluting vehicles.

The last step consisted of a reorganization of the mail and parcel delivery system in Mechelen by upgrading the bike rounds for postal (and letterbox-sized parcels) distribution to electric bike-trailer rounds. This enabled a reduction in the number of (electric) vans used and the amount of vehicle-kilometers traveled.

Consumer Movements

Buldeo Rai (2019) introduced the idea of including the consumer movements to pick-up their parcels in the sustainability analysis of e-commerce deliveries, and extended this idea to omnichannel behavior (see chapter 10). Meanwhile, research (Mommens et al., 2021; Zhang et al., 2018) indicate that the share of the consumer movements is not to be neglected and is heavily dependent on multiple variables among the urban/rural environment and the retail sector.

Consumer movements were in the case of Mechelen not only taken into consideration in the sustainability analysis, but they were also subject to improvement, even though the project was solely initiated by the logistic service provider. Consumer movements were obtained via a survey which was conducted before the implementation to capture the business-as-usual and during the implementation to capture the eventual transport behavior change of parcel consumers. Consumers were asked about their delivery preferences, their online purchase behavior and retours, the mode(s) of transport they use to pick up a parcel at the various delivery locations (collection point, postal office, lockers), the transport distance, dedicated visit to the pick-up point or combination with (purchase) activities at the pick-up point and if they had trip chaining behavior.

Significant differences were found between the business-as-usual and the implementation for the transport behavior of consumers. The first conclusion is that many consumers shifted from car use to foot to pick up their parcel. This is thanks to the installation of the dense locker network (with one situated maximum every 400 m of everybody's home; see Figure 8.4).

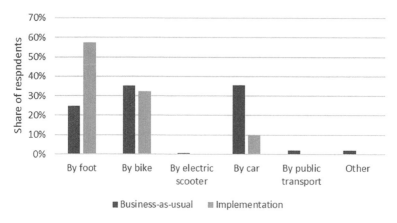

Figure 8.4 Mode choice for consumers in business-as-usual and implementation case

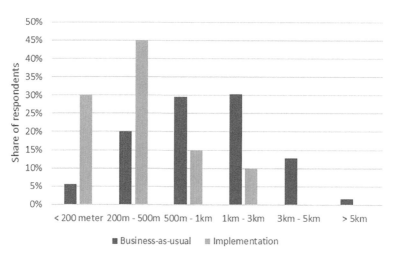

Figure 8.5 Distance traveled by consumers to pick up their parcel for the business-as-usual and implementation case

The effect is also visible in the distance that consumers travel to pick up their parcels. In the business-as-usual, this distance is mainly between 500 m and 3 km. During the implementation, this distance decreases to less than 500 m (Figure 8.5). Also, the traveled distances within a trip chaining pick-up are reduced significantly – majority less than 500 m, maximum 1 km compared to majority 500 m to 1 km and maximum above 5 km in the business-as-usual.

Methodology

The external costs were calculated to evaluate the implemented zero-emission parcel delivery system. The considered external cost parameters are congestion, air pollution, climate change, noise nuisance, well-to-tank processes, infrastructure and accidents. These are identified as being the most important external cost parameters for transport-related activities (van Essen et al., 2019). The main reference used in this research was the database of the

Table 8.1 External costs for transport used in the model

Congestion	Accidents
$EC_{congestion}$ = monetary value X vehicle kilometer$_{a,b,c}$	$EC_{congestion}$ = monetary value X vehicle kilometer$_{a,b}$
Air pollution	Noise nuisance
$EC_{congestion}$ = monetary value X vehicle kilometer$_{a,b,d}$	$EC_{congestion}$ = monetary value X vehicle kilometer$_{a,b,c}$
Climate change	Well-to-Tank
$EC_{congestion}$ = monetary value X vehicle kilometer$_{a,b,d}$	$EC_{congestion}$ = monetary value X vehicle kilometer$_{a,b}$
Infrastructure	
$EC_{congestion}$ = monetary value X vehicle kilometer$_{a,b}$	

a Stands for vehicle type (capacity, propulsion, euro emission norm, size, type).
b Represents the type of road.
c Indicates the moment of the day (night/day).
d Stands for the metropolitan, urban or rural environment.

Handbook of the External Costs of Transport (van Essen et al., 2019). This dataset considers the different parameters and their most important variables. To fill in those variables raw data on round level – vehicle type, propulsion, loading rate, travel time, vehicle-kilometers, round type, frequency – were used, originating from the logistic service provider. The Handbook does not consider electric cargobikes or bike-trailers. Literature is currently lacking in terms of providing robust external cost figures for these modes. Therefore, figures for electric scooters were used instead, originating from Litman et al. (2016) (Table 8.1).

In addition to the raw data, several assumptions were made to calculate the external costs. The first one is that Mechelen is a 100% urban environment (parameter *d*), following the Dijkstra and Poelman (2014) classification. The congestion level in Mechelen is based on data of the Vlaams Verkeerscentrum (Flemish traffic center) expressed in share of vehicle-kilometers in traffic circumstances: 78% free flow, 15% near capacity, 5% congested and 2% over capacity. Assumption three is that all parcel deliveries are performed during the daytime. Lastly, the proportion of vehicle-kilometers per road type is 0% motorway (given last mile), 15% trunk road, 20% urban road and 65% local road.

Results and Discussion

This section follows the same structure as the case description. First, the dense locker network was installed. From a logistics organization perspective, dedicated locker rounds were organized on a daily basis to supply and pick up from the parcel lockers. These rounds were more efficient than homedelivery rounds, but less efficient than rounds to manned collection points. This is also seen in the external cost per round type. The external cost of the last mile for a home delivery in Mechelen is 0,66€ per parcel, while this is 0,23€ per parcel for the locker round and 0,16€ per parcel for the manned collection points. The advantage of the proximity of the lockers is that they also generated a behavior change on the consumer side. In the previous section, one could also note re: modal shift – from car to foot – and the shorter travel distance to pick up the parcel. Both are caused by the consumers using the locker network. It results in a reduction of external costs for the consumer movement from 0,08€ per parcel in the business-as-usual to 0,007€ per parcel in the implementation case. This reduction is so significant that if both the external costs for the logistics part and consumer movement are combined, the locker delivery is most sustainable (0,24€/parcel), performing better than the manned collection points (0,29€/parcel) and home delivery (0,66€/parcel).

The shift to electric vehicles results solely in a limited reduction in external costs of 7%. This is mainly due to the relative importance of congestion costs – which are equal for both conventional diesel and electric vans. Electric vans reduce external costs for noise nuisance, climate change and air pollution. The limited reduction was an incentive for the logistics service provider to rethink the implemented solution and to consider a shift to bike-trailers and two supporting microhubs. This initially for the city center with its vehicle restrictions, given that the bike-trailers could operate in this zone during the entire day. Two electric vans were still used to deliver large parcels. Based on the average external cost per vehicle-kilometer in Mechelen, bike-trailers are 79% more sustainable than conventional diesel vans (business-as-usual) and 77% more sustainable than electric vans. The use of the microhubs additionally reduces the daily traveled vehicle-kilometers by 164. This resulted in an external cost per parcel of 0,31€ compared to the 0,48€ per parcel in the business-as-usual. The replaced electric vans were used by the logistic service provider in the larger region, with consequent sustainability gains which are out of the scope of this chapter.

The use of the machine at the local distribution center to identify the parcels with origin and destination Mechelen, and subsequently keeping those parcels at the local distribution center, enabled an optimization of loading rates, an avoidance of trips or the use of smaller less-polluting vehicles. It was not possible to collect the specific effects, yet rough estimations could be made based on the average external cost per parcel for the trips between the local distribution center and large distribution centers in Brussels and Antwerp. If one multiplies this average external cost per parcel with the volume which was kept in Mechelen, a yearly saving in external costs between 5.658 and 12.023€ was obtained.

Finally, the entire organization of parcel deliveries of the logistic service provider was changed based on the findings of the above implementations and their effects and impact on society, environment and the economics of the logistic service provider. The reorganization consisted of upgrading mail and parcel delivery bike rounds to electric bike-trailer rounds. This had multiple implications. In the logistics organization of the business-as-usual employees performed two rounds per day – one letter round by bike generally and generally one parcel round by van. With the bike-trailers, letters and parcels could be combined and via the use of the microhubs eventual refill could be optimized. By doing so, employees had to do one round per day. This first implication entails others: (1) by having one fixed round employees can increase social relations and customer service, (2) increase equity among employees as workload was distributed more equally, (3) reduce stress levels given that bike-trailers are not bound to the access restrictions which caused significant stress levels when vans were used instead, (4) better absorption of peak periods in parcels as the new organization increased flexibility by 10%, (5) better job accessibility given that no driving license is required for the bike-trailers and lastly (6) time gains were found thanks to reduction in parking issues. No jobs were lost during this reorganization.

Next to these social improvements for the employees – which in the field of last-mile parcel deliveries are put under severe economic and social pressure –sustainability gains were also found in terms of external costs (see Figure 8.6). The external costs for infrastructure, noise nuisance, air pollution and climate change are reduced to zero with the use of bike-trailers. Compared to the business-as-usual, the implementation of the reorganization reduced the external costs by 78%. Only well-to-tank increased compared to the business-as-usual, yet in monetary terms, this parameter is very small. The external cost per parcel of the reorganization is 0,10€, compared to the 0,48€ per parcel in the business-as-usual. On a yearly basis, this represents a saving of approximately 181,000 euros.

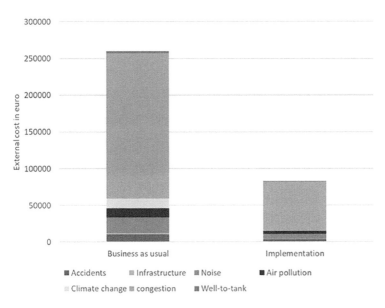

Figure 8.6 Yearly external cost in euro for business-as-usual and reorganization (implementation case) with differentiation for the external cost parameters

These positive results were an incentive for the logistic service provider to start implementing this new organization in other parts of cities in Belgium. The presented implementation can also be an example for other logistic service providers and the organization can be reproduced in other medium-sized cities. The concept should be researched on a metropolitan scale as a next step, and also cities with many height differences could pose some challenges.

The last mile is part of a larger supply chain, which for e-commerce is often international and even intercontinental. The delivery is – more than in other sectors – a commodity that is offered for free. That puts enormous pressure on the logistics service providers transporting parcels and the operators and operations in the last mile in particular given their disproportional share in the total logistics costs. This pressure also applies to the proposed implementation. Beyond the presented sustainable delivery system, one should also consider a larger evaluation of the e-commerce sector and its free deliveries. This is to encourage the realization of sustainable logistic solutions. One should also consider the largest players – most notably Amazon. The robustness of the presented solution in Mechelen will be the subject of further research.

Conclusions

E-commerce is a growing sector and one that has received an additional attention during the COVID-19 pandemic. The online sales and related deliveries of parcels are there to stay. However, with their growth, the sector and the related stakeholders are confronted with challenges, of which sustainability is central. Despite its global character, the focus on the impact of e-commerce is currently on its last mile, as consumers are confronted with the generated nuisances and pollution, governments are identifying the last mile of parcel deliveries as a front-runner in the shift toward zero-emission freight distribution and logistics service providers are confronted with high costs and increasing policy interventions.

Many solutions already exist (lockers, cargobikes and microhubs) and locally implemented. Still, citywide zero-emission parcel deliveries were not yet realized. Until in Mechelen – a medium-sized city in Belgium – the largest logistic service provider in the country implemented a zero-emission parcel and postal delivery system. The case was researched from a sustainability perspective via the calculation of transport-related external costs.

A stepwise approach was used to evaluate and adjust. First, a dense locker network was installed with one locker within 400 m of every citizens' home. This resulted in efficiency and sustainability gains for the logistic service provider and with a shift in mobility behavior of the consumers when picking up their parcels. Their transport-related external costs were reduced from 0,08€ per parcel to 0,007€ per parcel. Considering the external costs of both consumers and logistics operations, the lockers became the most sustainable delivery option in Mechelen. Next, the diesel vans were replaced by electric vans, with subsequent sustainability gains. The vehicles could however still not enter the city center between 11 am and 6 pm. Therefore, electric vans were replaced by bike-trailers. The operations of the bike-trailers are supported by two microhubs. The use of both reduced the external cost per parcel from 0,48€ in the business-as-usual to 0,31€. Finally, a reorganization was undertaken of the postal and parcel rounds in such a way that they could be combined with bike-trailers. This resulted in multiple social advantages for the employees – less stress, better equity and job accessibility. From a sustainability perspective, the reorganization led to a further reduction in external costs to 0,1€ per parcel. It represents a yearly saving in external costs of 181,000 euros in Mechelen. Additional savings were found by keeping the parcels with a Mechelen origin and destination in the local distribution center.

The concept and results are transferable to other medium-sized cities for parcel delivery companies and postal-parcel delivery companies in particular. The local vehicle restrictions are facilitating the implementation. Additional research is needed for larger cities and hilly cities.

References

Agatz, N.A.H, Fan, Y., and Stam, D., (July 21, 2020). Going green: the effect of green labels on delivery time slot choices. Available at SSRN: http://dx.doi.org/10.2139/ssrn.3656982

Akeb, H., Moncef, B., and Durand, B., (2018). Building a collaborative solution in dense urban city settings to enhance parcel delivery: an effective crowd model in Paris. *Transportation Research Part E Logistics Transportation Review, 119*, 223–233. https://doi.org/10.1016/J. TRE.2018.04.007.

Bickel, P., and Friedrich, R., (2005). *ExternE - Externalities of energy. Methodology 2005 update*, European Commission, Luxembourg.

Buldeo Rai, H., (2019). *Environmental sustainability of the last mile in omnichannel retail*. VUBPRESS.

Buldeo Rai, H., Mommens, K., Verlinde, S., and Macharis, C., (2019). How does consumers' omnichannel shopping behaviour translate into travel and transport impacts? Case study of a footwear retailer in Belgium. *Sustainability, 11* (9), 2534.

Buldeo Rai, H., Verlinde, S., Merckx, J., and Macharis, C., (2017). Crowd logistics: an opportunity for more sustainable urban freight transport? *European Transport Research Review, 9* (39).

Carling, K., Han, M., Håkansson, J., Meng, X., and Rudholm, N., (2015). Measuring transport related CO_2 emissions induced by online and brick-and-mortar retailing. *Transportation Research Part D Transport and Environment, 40*, 28–42. https://doi.org/10.1016/j.trd.2015.07.010.

Clarke, S., and Leonardi, J.J., (2017). Mayor of London agile parcels deliveries with electric vehicles—Central London trial—Final Report; Greater London Authority: London, UK.

Dijkstra, L., and Poelman, H., (2014). A harmonised definition of cities and rural areas: the new degree of Urbanisation Working Papers (Brussels).

Edwards, J., McKinnon, A., and Cullinane, S., (2010). Comparative analysis of the carbon footprints of conventional and online retailing: a "last mile" perspective. *International Journal of Physical Distribution and Logistics Management, 40*, 103–123.

European Commission, Directorate-General for Mobility and Transport, (2011). *White paper on transport: roadmap to a single European transport area: towards a competitive and resource efficient transport system*, Publications Office, https://data.europa.eu/doi/10.2832/30955

European Commission, (2021). Directorate-general for mobility and transport, EU transport in figures: statistical pocketbook 2021, Publications Office, https://data.europa.eu/doi/10.2832/27610

Gevaers, R., (2013). *Evaluation of innovations in B2C last mile, B2C reverse & waste logistics.* Universiteit Antwerpen.

Goodman, R.W., (2005). Whatever you call it, just don't think of last mile logistics. *Global Logistics & Supply Chain Strategies, 9* (12), 46–51.

Jaller, M., and Pahwa, A., (2020). Evaluating the environmental impacts of online shopping: a behavioral and transportation approach. *Transportation Research Part D Transport and Environment, 80.* https://doi.org/10.1016/j.trd.2020.102223.

Katsela, K., Güne, Ş., Fried, T., Goodchild, A., and Browne, M., (2022). Defining urban freight microhubs: a case study analysis. *Sustainability, 14*, 532. https://doi.org/10.3390/su14010532

Kedia, A., Kusumastuti, D., and Nicholson, A. (2017). Acceptability of collection and delivery points from consumers' perspective: a qualitative case study of Christchurch city. *Case Studies on Transport Policy, 5*(4), 587–595.

Kiba-Janiak, M., Marcinkowski, J., Jagoda, A., and Skowronska, A., (2021). Sustainable last mile delivery on e-commerce market in cities from the perspective of various stakeholders. Literature review. *Sustainable Cities and Society, 71*, 102984.

Lindholm, M., and Browne, M., (2013). Local authority cooperation with urban freight stakeholders: a comparison of partnership approaches. *European Journal of Transport and Infrastructure Research, 13* (1). https://doi.org/10.18757/ejtir.2013.13.1.2986

Litman, T. A., and Doherty, E. (2016). *Transportation cost and benefit analysis: techniques, estimates and implications.* Victoria.

Macharis, C., Melo, S., Woxenius, J., and Van Lier, T. (2014). *Sustainable logistics.* Bingley: Emerald Group Publishing.

McLeod, F., Cherrett, T., and Song, L., (2006). Transport impacts of local collection/delivery points. *International Journal Logistics Research Applications, 9*(3), 307–317. http://dx.doi.org/10.1080/13675560600859565

Molin, E., Kosick, M., and Van Duin, R., (2022). Consumer preferences for parcel delivery methods: The potential of parcel locker use in the Netherlands. *European Journal of Transport and Infrastructure Research, 22*(2), 183–200.

Mommens, K., Buldeo Rai, H., van Lier, T., and Macharis, C., (2021). Delivery to homes or collection points? A sustainability analysis for urban, urbanised and rural areas in Belgium. *Journal of Transport Geography, 94*, 103095.

Morgan Stanley Research, 2022. https://www.morganstanley.com/ideas/global-ecommerce-growth-forecast-2022.

Morganti, E., Seidel, S., Blanquart, C., Dablanc, L., and Lenz, B., (2014). The impact of e-commerce on final deliveries: alternative parcel delivery services in France and Germany. *Transportation Research Procedia, 4*, 178–190.

Ormond, P.A., Telhada, J., and Afonso, P., (2019). Evaluating the economic and environmental impact of the urban goods distribution by cargo cycles—A case study in São Paulo City. In Proceedings of the World Conference on Transportation Research 2019, Mumbai, India.

Otten, M., Meerwaldt, H., and den Boer, E., (2016). "De omvang van stadslogistiek". https://ce.nl/wp-content/uploads/2021/03/CE_Delft_4H63_De_omvang_van_stadslogistiek_Def.pdf

Rakuten Intelligence (2019). Forward deployed inventory: the future of e-commerce? www.rakutenintelligence.com

Van Duin, J., Wiegmans, B., Van Arem, B., and Van Amstel, Y., (2020). From home delivery to parcel lockers: a case study in Amsterdam. *Transportation Research Procedia, 46*, 37–44. https://doi.org/10.1016/j.trpro.2020.03.161

Van Essen, H., van Wijngaarden, L., Schroten, A., Sutter, D., Bieler, C., Maffii, S., Brambilla, M., Fiorello, D., Fermi, F., Parolin, R., and El Beyrouty, K. (2019) *Handbook of external costs of transport: version 2019.* CE Delft.

Van Loon, P., Deketele, L., Dewaele, J., McKinnon, A., and Rutherford, C., (2015). A comparative analysis of carbon emissions from online retailing of fast moving consumer goods. *Journal of Cleaner Production, 106*, 478–486. https://doi.org/10.1016/j.jclepro.2014.06.060

Vasiutina, H., Szarata, A., and Rybicki, S., (2021). Evaluating the environmental impact of using cargo bikes in cities: A comprehensive review of existing approaches. *Energies, 14*, 6462.

Wiese, A., Toporowski, W., and Zielke, S., (2012). Transport-related CO_2 effects of online and brick-and-mortar shopping: a comparison and sensitivity analysis of clothing retailing. *Transportation Research Part D Transport and Environment, 17*, 473–477. https://doi.org/10.1016/j.trd.2012.05.007.

Zhang, L., Matteis, T., Thaller, C., and Liedtke, G., (2018). Simulation-based assessment of cargo bicycle and pick-up point in urban parcel delivery. *Procedia Computer Science, 130*, 18–25. https://doi.org/10.1016/j.procs.2018.04.007.

9
URBAN LOGISTICS AND RETAILING

Leigh Sparks

Introduction

The importance of supply chains has become more generally recognised by businesses, the public and the media in recent years, partly due to major external shocks. The implications of the UK's Brexit referendum result are now being felt more clearly, most notably in the introduction of friction (paperwork, checking, borders) into supply chains. As predicted by many supply chain operators, disruption to the supply of products has been the consequence (Garcia-Lazaro et al., 2021; Moradlou et al., 2021). The COVID-19 pandemic produced extreme volatility in demand and supply leading to issues around panic-buying, stockholding and transport availability. Product shortages became more common and global supply chains have continued to be adversely affected by the pandemic. The inter-relationships between production, consumption, retailing and distribution have become more strained, generating additional disruption and costs. This has been further exacerbated by the war in Ukraine resulting in supply problems and price spikes in energy, including fuel, further affecting supply and, via price increases, demand. For many, the awareness of the potential fragility of supply chains has thus risen sharply, as has the understanding of our corporate and personal reliance upon them (Grant et al., 2021).

For retailers, their supply chain has become a key component of their operations (Fernie and Sparks, 2018). Historically reliant on producers and distributors, retailers were unable to easily provide the range, availability and prices required for their customers. They reacted to that over time by both, when legally permitted, taking more direct control of supply, and also by using their data and knowledge of consumer demand, and subsequently scale, to re-organise supply chains. This is evident across most sectors of retailing (Fernie et al., 2010; Sparks, 2010). Retailers' aim has been to produce a more efficient and effective supply of products to stores and customers and thus enhance the customer experience and in turn increase sales, satisfaction and consumer loyalty. This has resulted in a transformation of approach and operations in retailing, and especially in their supply chains.

This supply chain revolution has gone hand in hand with other retail changes. In many sectors, stores have increased in size and relocated away from central urban areas and onto decentralised retail parks and shopping centres. Purpose-built out-of-town retailing has considerable operating advantages, including simpler, separated, efficient logistics supply.

In the last two decades, there has been a further major structural change in the retail sector. The rise in the use of the internet and online shopping, to a point where it is now approximately 25% of all sales in the United Kingdom, has altered the channels of distribution, but has also generated new issues, including that of the scale of 'returns' of unwanted or unsuitable products, especially in the fashion sector.

Retail stores have historically been a key part of major urban centres. Recent trends of decentralisation and online retailing combined with cost pressures of operating in such sites (including logistics issues) have seen central urban retailing come under increased pressure. Previously the focal point of supply for many, urban stores are still significant, but their operations have become more marginal in many instances. For those that remain, pressures on their logistics have also grown. The transport issues of urban areas in particular have come more into focus and so urban retail logistics has become more significant.

Congestion and costs have become major issues for the supply of product. The environmental impact of human activity has been increasingly recognised (see Chapters 23 and 24). Retailers, as a focal point in the distribution of products to consumers, have been increasingly concerned over environmental sustainability. This is not all problematic, as within their own operations, there can be clear commercial benefits to actions, as for example in packaging and transport reduction. Efficient supply chains also hold less stock in the main, reducing wastage. However, sectors built on high short-term demands (and often at the cheapest possible cost) are prone to extractive models and to questions over practices (e.g., labour) and environmental sustainability. A system built on high levels of over-ordering and returns is environmentally questionable. In urban areas, traffic congestion and pollution have become human health issues. The very visibility of retail supply has made them a target for activists, as seen in recent UK demonstrations against fossil fuel and milk by Extinction Rebellion and Animal Rebellion. Over the last two decades or more there has thus been increased questioning of how our retail supply systems operate, for whose benefit and with what adverse effects (Khan and Richards, 2021; Wieland, 2021).

Retailing logistics has developed into a highly sophisticated operation over this period, attempting to match supply and demand whilst reducing costs and operating on a global basis. Pressures on urban systems and complications of urban delivery to stores, linked to the development of online sales and omni-channel retailing have increased and added costs and complexity. Concerns over the environmental impact of retail logistics and major recent disruptions to supply chains (such as Brexit, COVID-19 and capital infrastructure and labour shortages) have further pressured retail systems. Retail logistics generally and urban retail logistics specifically have thus begun to be re-assessed.

This chapter considers these issues. It begins with a review of logistics and supply chain management and a focus on retail logistics and supply chains. This is followed by a consideration of the main practical issues that have emerged in recent years. The final section provides a consideration of the implications of these recent changes and trends, with a focus on the future shape of urban retail logistics.

Logistics and Supply Chain Management

Over half a century ago, Peter Drucker (1962) described distribution as 'the economy's dark continent'. Businesses knew it was there but had an incomplete understanding of its size and shape and the activities undertaken. This hidden nature reflected the separate focus in economics on production and increasingly consumption, and the linkage of these was not well regarded. Some of this is derived from a functional view of the distribution process. There were varying foci including warehousing, transportation and inventory or stockholding. A great deal of effort was expended on making each of these functions work, but separately.

Drucker's comments helped generate a reconsideration of the nature of physical distribution and the bringing together of these separate silos. Aided by a stronger focus on the enabling opportunities in materials handling (pallets, roll cages, unit size standardisation) and in communications (especially data and information) a logistics approach began to emerge, producing efficiencies and synergies. There remained the issue however of the need to balance the costs and service levels in supplying products between producers and consumers.

The increasing focus on this logistics task took place within single organisations or perhaps a pair of businesses working together from different levels of supply (a single producer and a single retailer). There was an increasing realisation however that by considering an end-to-end supply system and sector-level agreements, more costs could be removed and a better service could be provided to the end consumer. The focus moved to supply chain management as an over-riding concept.

This can be illustrated by the well-documented case of the UK's leading (and one of the world's largest) food retailer, Tesco (Sparks, 2008). A major strategic change of direction in 1977 ('Operation Checkout' – Akehurst, 1984) saw the company realise the significance of product supply to stores, as their supply of products almost collapsed under a significant and rapid increase in consumer demand. In the decades that followed, Tesco took control of, radically redesigned and integrated a supply chain approach, recognised as world-leading in its effectiveness and efficiency (Evans and Mason, 2015; Sparks, 2018). This supply chain transformation was an integral component of them becoming the UK's leading food retailer in the 1990s (a position they maintain). Bringing together physical elements (distribution centres, warehouses, vehicles), handling elements (data, standardisation of sizes and equipment) and relationship elements (logistics service providers, end-to-end supply chains, reverse flows), Tesco delivered major cost and efficiency gains, which they used to support other strategic changes (store portfolio mix, consumer data use, variable store ranging). Some of this was aided in the 1980s by the focus on 'conforming' superstores, standardised out-of-town purpose-built operations and a withdrawal from smaller central urban stores. Predictability, standardisation of design and a new purpose-built distribution centre network drove major efficiencies. Their subsequent return to city and urban stores and their leadership of store- and fulfilment centre e-commerce complicated their supply systems but their learning proved critical to achieving sector-leading efficient performance (Sparks, 2018).

This brief and highly simplified description of a major long-term distribution transformation is provided to illustrate not only the relationship of logistics and supply chains but also the consistent and persistent emphasis of approach (see more broadly Lagorio and Pinto, 2021). The overall process has been one of simplification and standardisation. The aim of such systems, colloquially 'to get the right product to the right place at the right time' but to do it with the appropriate balance of costs and services, was shared and seen to benefit all. We can see this clearly in diverse sectors such as the car industry and the food retail sector, where the benefits of simplification and integration have been very apparent.

This stylised description of an 'ideal' supply chain cannot be delivered in all sectors or places though. It has also in the last twenty years especially been challenged by the altered demands of the customer and an awareness of some of the wider 'costs' of supply chains of this form. The search for scale and cost reduction, linked to globalisation for example, has produced long supply chains, often reliant on cheap labour in far-off places. Questions have therefore arisen over its ethics and environmental sustainability, even in less-turbulent times than those we are currently experiencing, where disruptions cause particular problems to this global model.

The ideal supply chain can be viewed as deriving from predictability of supply linked to predictability of demand, allowing flow-based systems structured around just-in-time operations. These 'flow-based' chains operate as a systemic regularity and are inherently smooth in their operations, leading to the ability to predict and deliver consistently. This was the case with the Tesco model, but even that came under pressure as retailing changed. In Tesco's case, their first-mover adoption of store based direct to home delivery via the internet, plus their move back into urban and convenience stores and their addition of non-food ranges all combined to complicate and make their supply chain more complex. A simple model of large trucks delivering to large purpose-built out-of-town stores in the 1980s altered to a complex model of vehicle delivery to small urban stores and people's homes in the 2000s (Sparks, 2018). This presents a major challenge, not least in urban retail logistics.

Retail Supply Transformations and Challenges

Since the late 1950s, therefore retailers have been focused on better serving the consumer and transforming the supply of product has been an integral part of that. Rather than focusing on the separate silos of transport or stockholding the aim has been to optimise across activities within logistics. This then began to drive optimisation across business and thus supply chains. As the information technology revolution advanced, so then data began to be a key component of organising and managing these supply chains. The more mundane aspects of standardisation and simplification were not neglected and indeed aided by the rise in the importance of data.

Retailers therefore became the controllers of many supply chains, deriving power and control from scale and knowledge. This, as noted above, reaches its apogee in the flow-based systems which provide for a lean approach built around predictability of supply and demand. By smoothing patterns and easing barriers, supply systems could deliver high quality at low cost but with predictable high service. A retail sector based around such principles and can operate really profitably. But, retail systems like this are prone to disruptions, some to the supply system and some to the demand system. This can be illustrated by the impact of so-called 'fast fashion'.

The Rise of 'Fast Fashion'

The fashion industry is a broad term for a very diverse range of businesses and activities. There is, and remains, the concept of high and luxury fashion with brands that have been present for decades, if not longer. Whilst this was focused on an elite market, increasing affluence in many societies has expanded the potential demand, driven also by increased lifestyle aspirations for many. The supply system is brand focused, with quality and exclusivity at its core. Given the retail price of such products, the supply emphasis is on quality and presentation.

Alternatively, there is mass fashion. For a long time in the United Kingdom, this was dominated by mid-market chains who catered for the bulk of the population. Marks and Spencer is a good example of this approach. The basis of their clothing offer was a dual-season system often designed 18 months to two years in advance and structured around basics and classics in Autumn/Winter and Spring/Summer collections. The supply system was geared around the design and production system on comparatively long lead times.

From the 1960s onwards, there was a degree of challenge to this approach as fashion and especially youth fashion expanded and became more significant. Designers and shops such as Mary Quant and Biba gained a significance beyond their sales. Businesses such as Laura Ashley also ate away at traditional models. The developments by George Davies of Next in the 1980s in the United Kingdom and the radical innovations in the initial Next Directory also signified a changing sense of what mainstream fashion could be.

In supply terms, the model was not that much altered, although with increasing globalisation and the opening-up of trade with countries such as China, this began to change. Production at a required level of quality could be provided at a much cheaper per unit cost by manufacturing away from the United Kingdom and especially in industrialising economies in East Asia. The fashion lead times allowed supply to be managed accordingly. The price differential gained, despite the cost and time of long international supply chains, proved a powerful competitive advantage.

In retail shop terms, there was also a revolution in location underway. Whilst shops in high streets within towns and cities still dominated, there was an emerging and then rapidly escalating movement to out-of-town sites. Whilst planned shopping centres had been mooted for some time, the 1990s saw an explosion of varying formats of out-of-town retailing which became increasingly embraced by mass fashion retailers.

The operational reasons behind this are clear in commercial terms. It is cheaper and easier to operate on a purpose-built, car-focused out-of-town site than on a more complex and expansive high street site. This can be especially true of the logistics of product moving and handling. Purpose-built sites normally allow for the separation of public and supply access. This separation also often permits flow-based handling within the stores from back storage and handling areas. The contrast between town centre and high streets can be stark. In such central stores, there may be restrictions on delivery times, limited or no back access or separation of retail and delivery 'traffic' and handling and space of delivery may be compromised by the nature of the building and/or the street. All of this adds effort and costs to the store operation, as well as reducing certainty. As consumers began to rely more heavily on private transport and to alter their shopping patterns accordingly, so this differential advantage increased.

These disparities between operations were however initially within a 'standard' range of fashion operational practices (Fernie and Grant, 2019). This began to change with the rise of so-called 'fast fashion' (Bhardwaj and Fairhurst, 2010) exemplified by the growth of chains such as Zara, H&M and Primark. There are a number of distinguishing features of fast fashion but at its heart is a faster linkage between consumer demand and production. Rather than fashion being season and production led as in the standard model, fast fashion is consumer and demand led around the idea of leading, capturing and responding to design trends. Rather than two 'seasons' or 'collections' per year, fast fashion focuses on a continuous refresh and adaptation to trends being experienced and evidenced in real time in the market. As such it is a total redesign of the distribution and production system. Rapid prototyping of product is followed by testing and then production on short lead times with flow-based logistics systems to stores and data capture, analysis and use on sales leading, if deemed necessary, to production alterations. New lines might be added on a weekly basis rather than as seasonal collections. The approach focuses on the demanding consumer with triangular relationships between retailing, logistics and production. All this is achieved both in rapid time but at a cost that undercuts the prior operating model. The result is a transformed sector focused on cheap, trendy, perhaps almost disposable product, reacting to and leading fashion developments in real time. For legacy or traditional retailers, this posed an existential threat showing up the lack of speed and flexibility, or indeed 'fashionability' in their distribution systems. Customers wanted their fashion to be up to date and they wanted it now.

One component of this change that can be overlooked is the rise of celebrity culture and information about celebrity behaviours and fashions. As print, visual and social media focused more on celebrities so an opportunity for businesses to link celebrity exposure to fast fashion became clear. An example of this was the development and growth of ASOS (which started out as A's Seen on Screen). In addition to exploiting the relationship to celebrity culture, and the desire to wear what celebrities/idols were wearing, or at least something that looked like it, ASOS were able to operationalise the emergence of the internet as a sales and distribution channel. The rise of the internet as a channel for clothes came relatively early and was readily adopted, but it has been based on some distinct characteristics.

First, the development of online clothes shopping was encouraged by retailers through the introduction of free delivery and/or free returns. Brought in to kick-start the purchasing online, the operation of free returns and in many cases, free delivery (although often only above a price point) has massively increased volumes. For retailers, this has led to some particular supply and delivery problems.

Secondly, and related to the concept of free returns, consumer behaviour altered to take advantage of the situation. Consumers began to 'over-order' by adding sizes and colours to their order and thus widening choice, in the knowledge they could freely return these products not needed or suitable. In some cases, this behaviour became extreme.

Thirdly, therefore in logistics terms fashion retailers became as involved in the returns industry as in the supply of product. Returns are logistical problems as the volume and variety of what is going to be returned when, is never that clear. Capital is tied up in stockholding and if a product is not on sale visibly to the consumer but remains in return transit or in warehouses waiting to be checked for re-sale then sales opportunities are being lost.

These are newly developed problems for retailers and have attained large dimensions, with return rates in fashion of over 50% being rumoured and the topic becoming a practical and research focus (Doung et al., 2021; Gustaffson et al., 2021). This makes the model challenging. At the same time however the rise of the internet as a consumer channel has been important for many retailers and they do not want to (nor could they in reality) end it. Focus has thus been on controlling returns, as for example in Zara's recent decision to charge for returns ('Zara starts charging shoppers for online returns – BBC News'). The sector is watching the impact of this carefully, though noting the powerful brand and store presence Zara has. More directly though these issues have stimulated fashion retailers to focus on multi or omni-channel integration whereby the online and the store experience is brought together especially in the areas of stockholding and availability. Online orders may thus be delivered from a central warehouse or a store (or reserved and collected from a store) and likewise returns could be posted or dropped off at a collection point which may or may not be the local store (see Chapter 12). At the heart of this are a centrally visible real-time stock system and a transport operation that can meet episodic and unpredictable demands. This adds to the complexity of store operations, but has fuelled the rise of parcel, express and courier services.

One of the debates in retailing in recent decades has been over the need for both physical stores and an online presence. Is the latter essential for current retailing? The example of Primark to date suggests that stores are critical and the internet less so. But other retailers have reduced their store portfolio dramatically as internet sales have risen. This relationship remains dynamic and often dependent on brand strength and consumer perception. Thus, whilst the number of stores has been in decline as internet sales have risen (and other factors also come into play), and the location of such stores has been altering, there is both a switch away from urban logistics need, but also an ongoing requirement, especially in central locations. The supply task though, especially for urban stores, has become more complex.

Despite the recent major shift towards online and internet retailing, shops remain a key component of retail infrastructure. Whilst more shops have moved to decentralised locations and the shop store portfolio for many retailers has been much reduced, shops in urban areas and in town centres or their high streets remain critically important to both retailers and consumers.

The description of supply chains and logistics above is broad and is provided at some length to illustrate the intersection of macro and specific trends which have created considerable issues for urban retail logistics. It is also heavily focused on the movement of data and information in the primary supply system. The complications for retailing is well recognised in the 'last-mile' problem (see Cardenas et al., 2017). The efficiencies in supply chains tend to derive from bulk movements between production and distribution centres. The retail purpose though is the sale of single – or small numbers of – items to final consumers. As such the bulk deliveries need to be broken down so as to be deliverable to stores and saleable to consumers. That process and the associated delivery costs of this are both complex and potentially expensive, giving rise to the phenomenon of the 'last-mile' delivery problem. How do retailers get products to their stores in the right quantity and quality and efficiently, effectively and cheaply? This store-by-store matching of supply with demand, smoothed by stockholding has been the focus of much academic and practical attention, given its criticality to businesses and consumers (Lauenstein and Schank, 2022, provide a systematic literature review). To an extent, the same issues persuade home delivery systems, though here the demand may be more manageable (Kiba-Janiak et al., 2021)

The approach to last-mile problems tends to focus on data availability to know what is going on and slick movement systems to be efficient and effective. In one sense this is nothing different to any store delivery. The complexity comes though when we consider this in a busy urban store. Issues that can arise in such cases include:

- The physical constraints of the shop and the storage area. Urban retail space may be expensive and thus storage space may be very limited to maximise selling space, so constraining stockholding;
- Building constraints such that a smooth in-store one-way delivery system may not be possible, with stores often having to take deliveries via the main consumer door;
- Delivery constraints including night time bans, permitted hours of operation, restricted vehicle sizes, no parking for unloading allowed, noise restrictions, and most recently staffing constraints;
- Potential increased volatility of demand in high-traffic urban areas and the consequent difficulty of maintaining adequate supply;
- Costs of operation for delivery including congestion charges, environmental levies as well as waste disposal and other refuse issues;
- Depending on the sector, high levels of unplanned returns to store, requiring storage and reverse logistics.

It is relatively straightforward to see how for many stores the costs and practicalities of urban retail distribution can be considerable. This applies not only to the multiple retailers, where it is magnified across their various urban locations, and where variability of restrictions amongst locations adds more complexity, but also to local independent retailers reliant on local or personal deliveries.

There is an additional point where multiple retailers are concerned. There is a balance to be struck (or trade-offs to be had) when delivery is required to a number of urban stores. This calculation will require consideration of the allowable size of vehicle, the relationship amongst vehicle size/capacity, store numbers and demand patters, time-based restrictions on combining store deliveries and the likelihood of urban congestion affecting timings. These are simply amongst the variables that need to be considered. The routing problems in last-mile deliveries to urban retail stores are legion. For a retailer, the potential to get it wrong in customer service and cost terms is considerable, especially with the global issues we currently face.

Current Challenges in Urban Retail Logistics

The earlier parts of this chapter have focused on long-run changes to the retail system and its supply. These have transformed the retail landscape and impacted the retail logistics operations, including in urban areas. These changes have operated at varying timescales and levels, but it could be argued that they are now coming to a head, providing a fundamental challenge to how retail and urban logistics are managed.

From a retail supply chain perspective, it has been recognised that key challenges are e-commerce and sustainability. Within these, the focus has been on key principles of pace, span, availability and information. Implications of this are that it is supply chains, not retailers alone that compete, focus should be on information movement before product movement and that business relationships really matter (Fernie and Sparks, 2018). Whilst the current disruptions are impacting operations, these broad issues and implications remain.

They find their major challenges in urban logistics. The concept of urban logistics itself is wide (Browne et al., 2018) as this *Handbook* demonstrates. Research has been disparate across a range of fields (see the review by Lagorio et al., 2016, as an example). Within this though, common themes can be discerned, with research, focusing on pollution/congestion, technology, routeing and inventory and changing capacities and behaviours.

Placing a retail focus on the broad urban logistics issues suggests that five areas can be identified as impacting this situation – the economic situation, retailing itself, place-based change, technology development and transport change. These can be considered in turn:

a) **Economic Situation:** As has been noted earlier, the economic certainties of the late 20th and early 21st centuries have been swept away. Brexit is a particularly British issue but has caused complex problems for the smooth and efficient supply of product to and from Europe. Disruptions have been felt to supply and to labour and transport availability.

   These issues have been exacerbated by the COVID-19 pandemic, which has impacted all countries and upset demand, supply and operations. Likewise, the war in Ukraine has impacted the supply of particular products, caused a focus on security of supply and spiked energy prices. Operations have become more marginal due to uncertainty and to spiralling costs. For many businesses, these are existential shocks and for many citizens and businesses life has become and will get more difficult.

   Overlaying all of this is climate change and the growing evidence that we are in a period of rapid and damaging climate impacts. This is forcing a reconsideration of how we manage and carry out many human activities. In the meantime, we need to cope with extremes of climate which again are disrupting patterns of supply and demand.

   This may seem somewhat distant from the issues of urban retail logistics, but in reality, it is not. The certainties that drove urban operations for many years are no longer in place and disruption is a key risk for operations, making problematic operations even more difficult or marginal.

b) **Retail Change:** The make-up of the retail sector, as outlined earlier, has also been altering. In the United Kingdom, there is too much physical retail space, and much of it is in the 'wrong' location. Development has added space and locations but has not removed sites at the same pace. The rise of the internet has compounded this.

There are thus fewer stores in operation, but these have arguably become more complex. Stores are no longer simply the place for a retailer–consumer transactional exchange. Now they are both a place of sale and return, a showcase/showroom of products and in some cases a point of distribution to the final consumer's home. This additional complexity has complicated logistics and supply. From being a 'simple' one-way system it is now responsible not only for two-way flows but for multiple places of distribution. Depending on the retailer and the sector, this applies to some or all of their stores, whatever the location. There is though a special place for central urban stores, especially with resident or visitor populations.

The nature of retailing and its adaptation to changing consumer patterns, behaviours and demands are driving changes in urban retail logistics.

c) **Place-based Change:** Society and economy as a whole has been decentralised and disaggregated over the last fifty years as a car-borne way of life was privileged. Retailing is an obvious component of this process but all facets of life have been subject to the pressures, e.g., cinemas, offices, football grounds, and schools are all now often located away from town and city centres.

This process has been seen as 'the death of the high street' and has been the subject of many reviews and reports and government involvement in a variety of ways. This 'death of the high street' narrative however is too narrow a construct. High streets are components of places and town and city centres. It is the relationship between people and places and the services and businesses they require that is important. As we have decentralised and disaggregated so, in many urban areas, business uses have reduced and footfall has fallen. Much depends on local circumstances but across the country, there has been an erosion of place.

There are many responses to this, and it is clear that the situation we are in is a choice we have made by the decisions and policies we have adopted (Sparks, 2021). Reversing this is not easy. This can be illustrated by considering some environmental responses to this crisis of place.

In the same way, as private vehicles have come to dominate decentralised activities, so too in urban areas, there is a crisis of road use and the accommodation with the private car that has been attempted over the last half-century. The result has been increased congestion and pollution. The environmental and health impacts of these results are now well known (see Chapters 23 and 24).

The response to such concerns has focused on restrictions on vehicles in urban areas. Congestion charges are an illustration of this but have been resisted in a number of places despite the impacts in London (see Chapter 23). Edinburgh's citizens, for example, voted against restrictions. Similarly, rising pollution in urban centres is being tackled by Low Emission Zones (LEZ). For businesses, there is concern that these LEZ require substantial extra cost to make vehicles suitable or buy a new vehicle fleet. There is also a sense that placing LEZ only in urban centres helps make business there less attractive compared to unrestricted, free parking-focused out-of-town operations. Workplace car parking levies, as in Nottingham, have cut private traffic (and made public and commercial traffic more reliable) but have a similar potential displacement effect (see Dale et al., 2019). Finally, partly as a result of lockdown in the pandemic, Low Traffic

Neighbourhoods (LTNs) saw roads and streets closed off to vehicles and the encouragement of alternative modes of transport and uses of the road surface. This too has become a focus for diverse opinion with proponents seeing better air quality, less congestion and more activity in safe, pleasant streets. Opponents claim businesses are harmed by having their deliveries and transport routes upset, increasing costs, and with no increase in local trade to compensate.

At the core of this place issue is the need to decide as a society what we value about towns and places and to support decision-making and planning accordingly. Do we value urban centres? If so, why are all the benefits, privileges and policies skewed in favour of non-central urban locations? For businesses, urban retail logistics is tough enough without incurring comparative additional costs of operation.

d) **Technological Change:** If we think of technological change in a computer technology sense then there has been a major transformation of capability and capacity. The internet is an obvious example as noted earlier. The revolution has been more than that alone though. Our capacity to record, store and use data has been massively enhanced. The internet, as in the Internet of Things, allows for enhanced interactions to assist flows and movements and to identify the status of almost any situation, e.g., as in Smart Cities.

In retail logistics terms, this enhanced capability has allowed retailers to better serve consumers. It does though place more demands on stockholding and the ability to react quickly through the supply system. A model based on internet orders for store-based home delivery needs to be able to resupply the store consistently and regularly in order to meet changing demand. This may lead retailers to question the size, shape and location of their stockholding points. Data has become ever more vital (e.g. Buldeo Rai and Dablanc, 2022).

e) **Transport Change:** There has been a move underway from petrol and diesel vehicles for delivery and towards hybrid and electric vehicles. As the capability of such vehicles increased in battery life and range amongst other dimensions, so they began to make more sense on both cost and climate response bases. This switch has received a further push with the rising cost of petrol/diesel but also the more obvious nature of climate issues. Against that currently is the rising price of electricity and continuing, though reducing, concerns over charging mechanisms and infrastructure. For these reasons and due to restrictions on congestion and pollution as noted above, electric vehicles are replacing fleets across businesses and other organisations. This is a benefit to urban areas and to retail logistics. Recent announcements by Tesco demonstrate the complete change underway as they replace their fleet with electric vehicles for urban store deliveries.

Congestion and the unreliability of local delivery cause issues for retailers. Given the volume of product moved to stores, this is simply the price of doing business. Whilst retailers will seek to increase efficiency and reduce costs, the basic model may be difficult to alter. This is not the case for delivery to the consumer's home. The internet has altered this end of the market and home delivery is now an accepted part of retailing, albeit one that is costly for retailers. At the same time, the consumer market has become hyper-local and time sensitive in some cases. The proliferation of courier delivery and motorbikes/scooters for food deliveries (takeaway but also convenience) has been well noted in recent years (see Chapters 8, 10, 11 and 27). More recently there has been increased interest in local environmentally friendly solutions such as e-bikes and cargo bikes, sometimes single business focused but increasingly there is interest in local consolidation mechanisms (see Chapter 5).

The increasing capacity of technology has also allowed testing of drones for home delivery and various types of automated robotic home delivery (see Chapter 6). The cost and acceptance of such approaches remain to be seen, but a switch from labour to capital makes sense in current circumstances and is seen elsewhere in retailing.

At one level these areas of interest have always been there, but there is a currently heightened attention to making urban retail logistics work effectively. Long-run changes have been exacerbated by major external disruptions leaving urban retail operations vulnerable without this focus. The retail drivers of e-commerce and sustainability are no different for urban logistics but the solutions are needed more urgently and could well be distinctive.

The Future

In the middle of a crisis, it is often felt that this is the most significant time and that decisions made (or not made) are pivotal. Currently, we are still living in the United Kingdom with the adverse impacts of Brexit, COVID-19, the war in Ukraine and an impending cost of living crisis. The impacts of climate change, our adherence to fossil fuels and the private car, behavioural and structural choices over decades and the ways in which we have chosen to value places and activities are all combining to challenge our patterns of life.

At one level these macro issues seem divorced from the consideration of urban retail logistics. This chapter however has attempted to argue that these large-scale and long-term changes are fundamental to understanding the current and future state of urban retail logistics. If there are no shops in a town centre then the urban retail logistics is different to the thriving retail high street of the past. If home delivery is the dominant model then the focus of urban delivery shifts. If changes produce a denser urban residential and organisational network (the 15-minute city for example), then urban retail logistics will need to adapt accordingly.

At the heart of the operation however the logistics issues remain unchanged. Retail logistics balances the provision of physical products to store and consumer in cost and service terms and does this by managing components of warehousing, inventory, transportation, handling and data/communications; both within a company or organisation's own operations but also with partners in the broader supply chain. The most effective and efficient models are based on good data utilised to deliver base flows of product and to react to altering demand.

Urban retail logistics has seen major disruption to the model. The impacts of economic retail, place and technological change have fragmented patterns of demand nationally and locally. Our capacity to respond via technology including transportation changes has been considerable but brings new cost and service challenges. Businesses and places need to manage these elements within this shifting landscape and under immense pressures, some more existential than others, but all currently enormously challenging. Urban retail logistics is becoming more complex and is likely to continue to be so. Some of the models/approaches currently under experimentation will fail, not only from internal reasons, but also from these external constraint, pressures and changes.

We have arrived at a point where our choices are making businesses marginal. This is clear in urban areas. As a society, we need to be able to resolve these tensions. The choices we make (Brexit disruption is an example) have major consequences. Doing nothing about climate change likewise has implications; as does a strong commitment to deliver change. Such macro issues will impact our patterns (and capabilities) for urban retail logistics, but in different directions. Businesses can only manage what they have control over and so efficient and effective stockholding, inventory management and delivery become ever more important to survival, whatever the constraints of operating in a single place or across multiple urban areas.

References

Akehurst, G. (1984) 'Checkout': the analysis of oligopolistic behaviour in the UK grocery retail market, *The Service Industries Journal*, 4, 189–242, DOI: 10.1080/02642068400000035

Bhardwaj, V. and Fairhurst, A. (2010) Fast fashion: response to changes in the fashion industry, *The International Review of Retail, Distribution and Consumer Research*, 20, 165–173, DOI: 10.1080/09593960903498300

Browne, M., Behrends, S., Woxenius, J., Giuliano, G., and Holguin-Veras, J. (eds) (2018) *Urban logistics: management, policy and innovation in a rapidly changing environment*. Kogan Page. London.

Buldeo Rai, H. and Dablanc, L. (2022) Hunting for treasure: a systematic literature review on urban logistics and e-commerce data. *Transport Reviews*, DOI: 10.1080/01441647.2022.2082580

Cardenas, I., Borbon-Galvez, Y., Verloinden, T, Van de Voorde, E., Vanelslander, T., and Dewulf, W. (2017) City logistics, urban goods distribution and last mile delivery and collection, *Competition and Regulation in Network Industries*, 18, 1-2, 22–43. DOI: 10.1177/1783591717736505

Dale, S., Ison, S.G., Frost, M., and Budd, L. (2019) The impact of the Nottingham workplace parking levy on travel to work mode share, *Case Studies on Transport Policy*, 7, 749–760.

Drucker, P. (1962) The economy's dark continent. *Fortune*, April, 265–270.

Duong, Q.H., Zhou, L., Meng, M., Van Nguyen, T., Ieromonachou, P., and Nguyen D.T. (2022) Understanding product returns: a systematic literature review using machine learning and bibliometric analysis, *International Journal of Production Economics*, 243, DOI: 10.1016/j.ijpe.2021.108340

Evans, B. and Mason, R. (2015) *The lean supply chain: managing the challenge at Tesco*. Kogan Page, London.

Fernie, J. and Grant, D.B. (2019) *Fashion Logistics: insights into the fashion retail supply chain*. Kogan Page, London. Second edition.

Fernie, J. and Sparks, L. (2018) *Logistics and retail management: emerging issues and new challenges in the retail supply chain*. Kogan Page, London. Fifth edition.

Fernie, J., Sparks, L., and McKinnon, A.C. (2010) Retail logistics in the UK: past, present and future, *International Journal of Retail & Distribution Management*, 38, 11/12, 894–914. DOI: 10.1108/09590551011085975

Garcia-Lazaro, A., Mistak, J., and Gulcin Ozkan F. (2021) Supply chain networks, trade and the Brexit deal: a general equilibrium analysis, *Journal of Economic Dynamics and Control*, 133, DOI: 10.1016/j.jedc.2021.104254

Grant, D.B., Banomyong, R., and Gibson, B.J. (2021) A brave new world for retail logistics and SCM in the 2020s and beyond, *International Journal of Logistics Research and Applications*, DOI: 10.1080/13675567.2021.1986477

Gustafsson, E., Jonsson, P., and Holmström, J. (2021) Reducing retail supply chain costs of product returns using digital product fitting, *International Journal of Physical Distribution & Logistics Management*, 51, 877-896. DOI: 10.1108/IJPDLM-10-2020-0334

Khan, R. and Richards, H. (2021) Fashion in 'crisis': consumer activism and brand (ir)responsibility in lockdown, *Cultural Studies*, 35, 2-3, 432–443. DOI: 10.1080/09502386.2021.1898028

Kiba-Janiak, M., Marcinkowski, J., Jagoda, A., and Skowronska, A. (2021) Sustainable last mile delivery on e-commerce market in cities for the perspective of various stakeholders. *Sustainable Cities and Society*, 71. DOI: 10.1016.j.scs.2021.102984

Lagorio, A. and Pinto R. (2021) Food and grocery retail logistics issues: a systematic literature review. *Research in Transportation Economics*, 87. DOI: 10.1016/j.retrec.2020.100841

Lagorio, A., Pinto, R., and Golini, R. (2016) Research in urban logistics: a systematic literature review. *International Journal of Physical Distribution and Logistics Management*, 46, 10, 908–931. DOI: 10.1108/IJPDLM-01-2016-0008

Lauenstein, S. and Schank, C. (2022) Design of a sustainable last mile in urban logistics – a systematic literature review. *Sustainability*, 14, 5501. DOI: 10.3390/su14095501

Moradlou, H., Reefke, H., Skipworth, H., and Roscoe, S. (2021) Geopolitical disruptions and the manufacturing location decision in multinational company supply chains: a Delphi study on

Brexit, *International Journal of Operations & Production Management, 41*, 2, 102–130. DOI: 10.1108/IJOPM-07-2020-0465

Sparks, L. (2008) Tesco: every little helps, Chapter (in Japanese) of Usui K (ed) *The history of top retailers in Europe*. Japan Society for the Study of Marketing History, Dhobunkan, Tokyo. (Chapter in English available from author)

Sparks, L. (2010) Supply chain management and retailing, *Supply Chain Forum: An International Journal, 11*, 4, 4–12. DOI: 10.1080/16258312.2010.11517242

Sparks, L. (2018) Tesco's supply chain management, Chapter 7 of Fernie, J. and Sparks, L. (eds) *Logistics and retail management: emerging issues and new challenges in the retail supply chain*. Kogan Page, London. Fifth edition, 183–219.

Sparks, L. (2021) Towns, high streets and resilience in Scotland: a question for policy? *Sustainability, 13*, 10, 5631. DOI: 10.3390/su13105631

Wieland, A. (2021), Dancing the supply chain: toward transformative supply chain management. *Journal of Supply Chain Management, 57*, 58–73. DOI: 10.1111/jscm.12248

10
DARK STORES AS A POST-PANDEMIC OMNICHANNEL STRATEGY

Implications for Urban Logistics

Heleen Buldeo Rai

Introduction

Years before the COVID-19 pandemic, growing online sales figures gave rise to announcements of the 'retail apocalypse' (Hagberg et al., 2017), predicting store closures and the 'death of distance' (Couclelis, 2004), rendering local stores redundant altogether. Today, e-commerce growth remains. Its transformative impact on the urban retail landscape is undeniable, although the extent of transformation is very different than anticipated. According to a global review published by the International Post Corporation in 2021, online purchases constitute approximately a quarter of consumer spending in countries such as South Korea, China and the United Kingdom. In the United States, online sales account for 20%, while most European countries are around 15%. Contemporary consumption does not rely solely on e-commerce, but rather on a combination of both online and 'offline' channels. Accordingly, the urban retail landscape has essentially become 'omnichannel' as well.

Omnichannel retail extends the 'multichannel' model, initially proposed by traditional retailers in an attempt to remain relevant in the e-commerce era (Neslin et al., 2006). While a retailer's physical store and 'virtual' webshop exist separately from one another in multi-channel retail, managing and optimising each channel independently, omnichannel retail integrates stores and webshops, managing and optimising activities across channels (Verhoef et al., 2015). The omnichannel retail model is best illustrated by services such as 'click-and-collect', enabling the collection of online purchases in store, 'ship-from-store', facilitating delivery of online purchases with store inventory, and 'return-in-store', allowing integration of online purchase returns into store inventory (Buldeo Rai et al., 2019).

Accelerated by pandemic-prompted lockdowns, business closures and physical distancing measures, the omnichannel model is now common practice among a range of stakeholders (Hänninen et al., 2020), from independent local stores, to large retail chains and international online marketplaces, and platform-based start-ups. Over the last two years, for example, the City of Paris created a map with hundreds of local retailers offering home delivery and click-and-collect services, Swedish furniture group IKEA launched automated collection points in London and mobile collection points in Antwerp, Chinese platform

AliExpress opened stores in various Spanish cities and meal delivery platforms Deliveroo and Uber Eats partnered with supermarket chains Carrefour and Casino.

In doing so, omnichannel retail has profoundly changed the role of the store (Hagberg et al., 2017). Rather than a supply chain destination heading towards imminent extinction, stores now serve as multifunctional hubs. They act as showrooms, collection points, returns facilities, micro-warehouses and micro-fulfilment centres (Alexander and Cano, 2020). Sheffi (2020) refers to 'dark stores', facilities that look like stores but are populated by staff who pick and pack online purchases, and 'warestores', spaces within stores that perform this fulfilment function. Alexander and Blazquez (2019) state that the role of the store is being redefined, although the future evolution of the format is uncertain.

Beyond a mere illustration of a transforming retail landscape, stores' multifunctionality has major implications for urban logistics, especially in relation to warestores and dark stores. These implications are poorly understood from a scientific perspective, despite the recent but relentless coverage of dark store developments in the popular and specialised press. In their review of three decades of retail research, Hänninen et al. (2020) envision a change to the entire logic of the store and refer to the many 'unique and radical reincarnations' to meet the expanding demands, impact and scope of the digital economy. Among five propositions for future research, the review calls to reimagine and redefine the store and to better acknowledge the role of delivery and transport (Hänninen et al., 2020).

This chapter responds to both gaps in research by focusing on dark stores in particular. It follows the evolution of the format as a lifeline for the retail sector during the first COVID-19-related lockdowns, its rapid rollout with the rise of 'quick commerce' and its potential as a post-pandemic retail strategy. To this end, the chapter applies a dual approach. First, a systematic analysis of international press articles published throughout 2021 by using the keyword 'dark store' in the Europresse database was conducted. Second, a transport intensity analysis of a dark store in Paris is presented, based on a two-day observation in February 2022. Building on the body of research on online and omnichannel retail, this chapter outlines the various ways in which stores operate in the retail landscape prior to that and presents concluding remarks on the implications for urban logistics thereafter.

Omnichannel Retail and the Store

A number of studies have investigated the impact of online and omnichannel retail on the store. The new concepts that they describe either modify the store setting, or propose a new type of setting (Hagberg et al., 2016). 'Showrooms' and 'click-and-collect' fall in the former category, while collection points (provided by third parties), 'click-and-drive' (organised at separate locations) and 'stores-on-wheels' (direct-to-consumer delivery) belong to the latter category.

Similarly, some of these new concepts alter stores' operational functions beyond their traditional focus on sales transactions, by modifying or adding supply, inventory, fulfilment, processing or delivery activities. Other concepts modify stores' experiences, mainly by implementing technological features such as intelligent fitting rooms, interactive digital screens and signage, self-service checkouts, wearable technologies and electronic personal shopping assistants (Alexander and Blazquez, 2019; Alexander and Cano, 2020; Hagberg et al., 2016). Such concepts include 'experience stores' and 'cashier-less stores'. Gauri et al. (2021) refer to 'retailtainment' or 'in-store experience-driven retail', while von Briel (2018) describes stores as key destinations for unique sensory shopping experiences. Table 10.1 presents an overview

Table 10.1 Omnichannel store concepts in terms of setting and offering, in comparison to the traditional store

	Modified store setting	New store setting
Operational offering	Showrooms, zero-inventory stores, digital assortment extension, digital shelf extension, virtual shelf expansion Buy online, pick-up in store (BOPIS/BOPS), click-and-collect, kerbside pick-up, reserve online, pick-up and pay in store (ROPS)	Click-and-drive, third-party access points, lockers, collection points, pick-up stations, delivery points
	Buy online and return in store	Stores-on-wheels
	Buy online, get it delivered from the store (BOGIDS), ship-from-store (SFS), warestores, dedicated stores as fulfilment nodes, dark stores	
Experimental offering	Experience stores, flagship stores, concept stores, pop-up stores, temporary stores, third places	
	Cashier-less stores	

Source: The author, based on Alexander and Blazquez (2019), Alexander and Cano (2020), Gauri et al. (2021), Hagberg et al. (2016, 2017), Hübner et al. (2022) and Sheffi (2020)

of different omnichannel store concepts found in literature and how they relate to traditional stores in terms of setting and offering, either focused on operations or experiences.

This chapter limits its discussion to omnichannel store concepts that modify settings as well as operations. When introduced in cities, they impact urban logistics activities as well. Of interest are urban goods transport activities in particular, in terms of upstream supply flows to the store, downstream delivery flows from the store, or both. Table 10.2 illustrates operational changes, as compared to traditional stores.

Table 10.2 Omnichannel store concepts in terms of operations, in comparison to the traditional store

	Supply	Inventory	Fulfilment	Processing	Delivery
Showrooms, zero-inventory stores, digital assortment extension, digital shelf extension, virtual shelf expansion	✓	✓	✗	✗	✗
Buy online, pick-up in store (BOPIS/BOPS), click-and-collect, kerbside pick-up, reserve online, pick-up and pay in store (ROPS)	✓	(✓)	(✓)	✓	✗
Buy online and return in store	✗	✓	✗	✓	✗
Buy online, get it delivered from the store (BOGIDS), ship-from-store (SFS), warestores, dedicated stores as fulfilment nodes, dark stores	✓	✓	✓	✓	✓

Source: The author, based on Alexander and Blazquez (2019), Alexander and Cano (2020), Gauri et al. (2021), Hagberg et al. (2016, 2017), Hübner et al. (2022) and Sheffi (2020)
Note: ✓ = concept implies definite change to logistical activity; (✓) = concept implies possible change to logistical activity; ✗ = concept implies no change to logistical activity

'Experience stores', which include 'flagship stores', 'concept stores', 'pop-up stores', 'temporary stores' and 'third places', modify the traditional store in their focus on experience, rather than mere transaction (Alexander and Cano, 2020). Their operations do not necessarily differ from traditional stores, except for 'showrooms' or 'zero-inventory stores'. Following this concept, stores hold inventory for consumers to experience the product assortment, but sales are exclusively fulfilled in and delivered from a dedicated warehouse (Gauri et al., 2021). Showrooms are an extreme variant of the 'digital assortment extension', 'digital shelf extension' or 'virtual shelf expansion' concept, in which retailers expand their store assortment with a more extensive one online, that is accessible through digital devices (Hübner et al., 2022). Discarding store inventory also relieves the necessity for regular supplies.

To reduce delivery costs and accelerate access to online purchases, retailers adopt strategies that allow consumers to buy online and collect their purchases in store or at kerbside (Gauri et al., 2021). 'Buy online pick-up in store' (abbreviated as 'BOPIS' or 'BOPS') or 'click-and-collect' enables demand transfers from webshops to stores. Online purchases are either fulfilled from store inventory or shipped to the store, along with regular supplies or in separate flows (Hübner et al., 2022). In response to the COVID-19 pandemic, collection at kerbside accelerated in particular (Gauri et al., 2021). Click-and-collect changes the organisation of stores and their surroundings, for example by reserving dedicated parking spaces, designating specific check-out lines or even creating separate entrances (Gauri et al., 2021). A variation to click-and-collect proposes 'reserve online, pick-up and pay in store' (ROPS), where products are reserved online but payment is only carried out upon collection (Hübner et al., 2022). Inversely, click-and-collect also allows exchange or return of online purchases in store with 'buy online and return in store' (Alexander and Blazquez, 2019).

Another way to regain competitive edge by leveraging stores, is to use them as alternative fulfilment locations. In this way, retailers provide the dual function of store shopping for 'offline' consumers and picking and packing to fulfil purchases for online consumers. Termed 'buy online, get it delivered from store' (abbreviated as BOGIDS) or 'ship-from-store', the concept notably enables fast deliveries, the day of purchase or even within hours (Gauri et al., 2021; Hübner et al., 2022). Sheffi (2020) distinguishes 'warestores', in which only a part of the store is dedicated to fulfilment, and 'dark stores', which are fully dedicated to fulfilment. To operationalise store fulfilment, Gauri et al. (2021) mention hiring specific staff for picking; implementing backroom robots to improve accuracy, transparency and productivity; partnering or acquiring delivery companies; and 'crowdsourcing'. Warestores to a lesser extent and dark stores to a greater extent impact on all store operations: from supply and inventory, over picking, packing and processing, to the organisation of deliveries.

Although omnichannel store concepts receive considerable attention in the retail literature (Alexander and Cano, 2020; Gauri et al., 2021; Verhoef et al., 2015), limited knowledge exists on how they relate to urban logistics (Hänninen et al., 2020). Nevertheless, the implications when transforming from a traditional supply chain structure with few large regional warehouses, to many small local warehouses are considerable. Especially following the pandemic-propelled surge of 'quick commerce', the consequences of fast local deliveries originating from a network of dark stores are already visible in cities around the world. With the promise of grocery deliveries within ten to twenty minutes, quick commerce reaches the most extreme end of what researchers have coined 'instant deliveries', or deliveries within two hours after purchase (Dablanc et al., 2017). The remainder of this chapter focuses on dark stores as urban logistics facility, outlining their development in operational, economic and spatial terms and estimating their transport implications.

Dark Stores in Operational, Economic and Spatial Terms
Systematic Analysis of the International Press

Using the keyword 'dark store' in Europresse resulted in 1,044 articles published in the international press throughout 2021, both popular and specialised. Europresse is a database giving access to more than 10,700 sources of local, regional and international information. The identified articles cover various languages for 38 countries in total, suggesting that 'dark store' has become universal as a term. Two notable exceptions: only one article in Chinese refers to dark stores, which Google Translate reproduced as 'behind-the-scenes stores', while German articles are absent, as they discuss the phenomenon mainly in terms of 'micro-hubs' or 'neighbourhood warehouses'. In essence, all terms refer to neighbourhood-level fulfilment centres, dedicated to online orders and local services, as opposed to facilities who serve cities as a whole.

Reporting on the subject remained modest and dominated by features from the United States and France in the first quarter of the year. Articles describe in particular the temporary or permanent decision of omnichannel chain retailers to 'turn' some of their stores 'dark'. Notable examples include Amazon, who temporarily converted several Whole Foods supermarkets in Los Angeles and New York into fulfilment centres, before opening its first Whole Foods dark store in Brooklyn in September 2020. Household goods retailer Bed Bath & Beyond turned a quarter of its stores dark. Supermarket chains Walmart, Kroger and Giant Eagle in the United States and Metro in Canada followed suit. In Paris, supermarket chain Franprix closed five of its stores located in empty office areas during lockdown, dedicating them to online orders before reopening them again to the public. It started testing a dark store in March 2021 out of the basement of one of its stores. Supermarket chain Monoprix has been operating a dark store since 2019 to prepare orders for Amazon.

Press coverage on dark stores accelerated quickly by mid-2021, with news focusing on the development of quick commerce, in Europe mostly and later on in the United States as well. Nonetheless, start-ups such as Yummy from Venezuela, Blinkit (formerly Grofers) and Zepto from India and Appetito from Egypt prove that quick commerce and its dark store model are actually global phenomena. In fact, the model finds its origins in Asia. In China in particular, instant grocery delivery is an established practice among consumers. For example, MissFresh runs dark stores in several Chinese cities since 2015, while Hema Fresh employs automated warehouses attached to supermarkets, labelled 'warestores' earlier in this chapter, since 2016. Both deliver fresh fruits, vegetables, meats and ready-to-eat foods to consumers in less than thirty minutes. The first reference of quick commerce in the 2021 press overview appeared in April, while the bulk of press coverage on dark stores concentrates in the last quarter of the year.

Dark stores' primary purpose and advantage over regular e-commerce warehouses is their ability to deliver fast. Coupled with consumers' pandemic-prompted online shopping habits and appreciation for online food offerings (UNCTAD, 2021) (see Chapter 11), this potential is what attracted a range of start-ups. Among the most successful are Gorillas founded in Germany in 2020, Gopuff from the United States (2013) and Getir from Turkey (2015). Dark stores serve neighbourhoods within a radius of two kilometres or about one square mile. They do so in ten to twenty minutes ("10-minute magic" as Grofers calls it). Quick commerce start-up JOKR says it uses a software that calculates how far an eight-minute ride on an electric bicycle is, then draws a 'polygon' around the store to show the coverage area. Indeed, all start-ups in the quick commerce business use two-wheelers to carry out their operations, including electric scooters and cargo-bicycles.

With about 2,000 product references available for purchase, quick commerce's offer is ten times smaller than traditional supermarkets (usually between 20,000 and 30,000 references). Some players therefore position themselves on impulse purchases and urgent needs, while others are vocal on their ambition to replace supermarkets altogether. About one-third of quick commerce's assortment comes from local producers, allowing them to negotiate favourable product prices. The Portuguese quick commerce start-up Bairro says to have direct contacts with multinational suppliers, such as PepsiCO and Unilever, and national suppliers alike. All start-ups stress the importance of their vertically integrated model, allowing control of process and technology along the entire value chain.

To deliver on their instant delivery promise for urban markets as a whole, dark stores are needed in numbers to succeed. For reference: three to four large warehouses serve a city like Delhi, compared to hundreds of dark stores. However, urban scarcity and cost of land are among the key reasons why warehouses have historically migrated ever further away from cities (Dablanc & Rakotonarivo, 2010). Unsurprisingly, urban space presents a challenge for the development of dark stores as well, particularly with population density being a key criterion in their location strategy. Some of the dark store requirements play a moderating role, including their size (small, overall between 200 m^2 and 400 m^2) and infrastructural needs (limited). Although they typically target 'A' markets, they do not necessarily need 'A' locations in those markets and prefer bystreets instead. Barely any reference is made in the press to dark stores' access necessities, to accommodate supply and delivery traffic. This stands in contrast to the rigorous requirements defined for micro-hubs, another type of urban logistics facility. To operationalise crossdocking activities, micro-hubs need a certain height, access for trucks, a turning area, among others, next to amenities that limit neighbourhood nuisances (Buldeo Rai, 2022).

Dark stores appear in various types of locations. In London, they include railway arches, light industrial parks and shopping centre basements. The most frequently used type of location is, however, former stores. Commercial vacancy rates have been growing in cities in general and have not improved post-pandemic. In New York, Buyk took over a variety of empty storefronts, including some that filed for bankruptcy last year. The fact that they are now occupied by dark stores seems to contribute to the negative sentiment of inhabitants and policy-makers about their development, fuelling dystopian images of the 'dark city'. "The last thing you want in a vibrant city centre are taped windows", says one article's interviewee. Another one states that "if we do nothing, they become zombie streets: where there is no life, where people just drive through". In Amsterdam, an Instagram page was launched sharing pictures of dark store nuisances (called 'stopdarkstoreswoonwijk' or 'stop dark stores residential area'). Next to complaints about noise and traffic safety, some fear that local stores are being pushed out. In New York, bodega owners raised concerns of ending up as the city's taxi drivers: once iconic parts of the streets, now largely replaced by platforms such as Uber and Lyft. A fundraising campaign for My Bodega Online was propelled, a delivery app developed by and for bodega owners.

In response to growing numbers of dark stores, some cities have suggested other locations to quick commerce players. In Paris, the local planning agency counted more than 80 dark stores within the city and its close surroundings (Apur, 2022). The city proposed underused underground car parks as alternative, as showcased by online supermarket Mon-Marche.fr. They equipped the space with cold rooms at five different temperatures and deliver groceries within the hour by cargo-bike to consumers in the west of Paris. In Amsterdam, the city estimated to have 28 dark stores operating by mid-December 2021. At the same time, companies such as BNP Paribas Real Estate are testing the dark store formula, converting some of their buildings in with a company specialising in this type of activity. This transformation can give commercially undesirable spaces a second chance, for example when windows are too small or locations are too far from pedestrian traffic. Many landlords however prefer to leave their premises empty rather than lowering their local face value and impacting their estimated rental value. It indicates that real estate conversions are not necessarily straightforward. Land values for commercial use are higher than those for logistics activities, which typically need more space. As a reference, Amazon added 371 new facilities with 119 million square feet of ground-level space in 2020 in the United States alone, working out at an average of 2.3 million square feet a week.

Despite relatively easy area and building requirements, setting up a dark store network requires significant capital. Adding to costs is the tendency of quick commerce start-ups to formally hire their employees, about five to fifteen per dark store, instead of relying on the 'gig economy'. In this way, the quick commerce model seems to diverge from meal delivery platforms, such as Deliveroo and UberEats, that precariously employ and pay their drivers by task instead of per hour (Dablanc et al., 2021). Quick commerce players also provide them with the necessary equipment and vehicles to carry out their operations. For example, the bicycles of Gorillas are branded and tracked, making them less likely to be stolen, thereby addressing a common grievance among gig economy drivers. Counter-sounds are registered nevertheless. For example, quick commerce start-up Cajoo pays no more than the minimum wage to their employees and relies on gig economy drivers for evening and night shifts. Also adding to capital needs, is quick commerce's high initial customer acquisition cost. As both service and brand are new, they are not embedded yet in consumer habits. Convincing consumers to download the app and make an order not only requires heavy online and 'offline' promotion, but also an offer that is on par with retail prices, does not charge for picking and keeps its delivery cost below two euros.

The breakdown suggests that the potential revenues are too limited to cover the high cost of operation, let alone of investment. Again compared to meal delivery platforms, McKinsey research lists several levers for profitability: restaurant commission fees; customer delivery fees; customer service fees; in-app advertising; and tips (Ahuja et al., 2021). Arguably, they also profit from restaurants' existing customer base and the more established traditions of taking out food and ordering in. Regardless, meal delivery platforms also remain unprofitable. Even more so now, as they are investing in 'dark kitchens', the delivery-only equivalent of dark stores for restaurants. For quick commerce players to succeed, it comes down to increasing basket size (between €20 and €30) as well as order frequency (more than once a week). Some players claim profitability, including Getir in home-market Turkey and GoPuff in markets where it has operated for more than eighteen months. Both businesses were created years before the current start-up boom, suggesting that there is long-term promise in the quick commerce model.

In addition, quick commerce start-ups have turned to venture capitalists to fund and accelerate their development. The goal is to adopt a pace that is faster than the competition. Raising almost US$ 14 billion by April 2021, it produced several so-called 'unicorns' along the way, or companies with an estimated market value of more than one billion dollars. Examples include Getir, becoming the second unicorn of Turkish origin; Daki, a Brazilian start-up reaching unicorn status within ten months of operation; and Gopuff, already founded in 2013. For comparison, supermarket chain Tesco, founded in 1919 and with 4,500 stores around the world, is worth £17 billion. In doing so, venture capitalists pursue a strategy of 'blitzscaling', describing a company racing to serve a global customer base before any of its competitors. As such, profitability is not their priority but securing spaces to create the best possible network in cities, is. It prompts references to micro-mobility developments a few years prior. Seemingly overnight, cities were 'flooded' with shared bikes and scooters from a range of providers, few of which are still active today. In the quick commerce market, consolidation has already started: Philadelphia-based Gopuff entered Europe by acquiring British players Dija and Fancy; Getir acquired Weezy in an attempt to solidify its position in the UK market; and Gorillas bought Frichti.

The press suggests a number of strategies that quick commerce players are putting in place to strengthen their business model. Partnerships are an important first one, illustrated by German supermarket chain Rewe's minority stake in Flink; French supermarket chain Carrefour's launch of 'Carrefour Sprint' in collaboration with Cajoo and UberEats; and by the involvement of supermarket chains Tesco in the United Kingdom, Jumbo in the Netherlands and Belgium and Casino in France in Gorillas. The deal with Tesco enables Gorillas to use spare space in supermarkets that once housed items now largely bought online, such as kitchen appliances. Tesco calls it 'co-located physical warehouses'. As important as these partnerships are financially, they are above all strategic. The interest is strong for both parties. While start-ups receive access to mature infrastructure, such as central purchasing units and logistics networks, traditional supermarket groups get insight into the technology behind instant grocery delivery. Emphasising the importance of this, Allianz Research estimates that European supermarkets are threatened almost €14 billion in sales and up to almost €2 billion in profits with every percentage of grocery sales moving online (Duthoit, 2021).

The development of quick commerce has inspired other players to develop their own dark stores. For example, supermarket chain Auchan operates a fifteen-minute grocery delivery service from the basement of their supermarket in Bordeaux (called 'the cave') and supermarket chain Carrefour launched an app called 'Bringo' from which it covers deliveries in a dozen neighbourhoods in Buenos Aires. There's also Sainsbury's Chop Chop, Ocado's Zoom and Tesco Whoosh in the United Kingdom. Online supermarkets La Belle Vie in Paris and Fresh Direct in New York also introduced an express delivery option next to their regular offering. Similar interest is found among meal delivery platforms. Deliveroo launched a grocery delivery service with dark stores in London called 'Deliveroo Hop'; Delivery Hero operates its quick commerce activities as 'Dmarts' and invested in Gorillas; DoorDash acquired Wolt and invested in Flink; Foodora launched its first dark store in Oslo with 'Foodora Market'; and Glovo already had eighteen dark stores in Spain, Italy, Portugal and Romania at the beginning of 2021. Quick commerce borrows from traditional retail as well, in their experiments with the franchise model (as pursued by Getir in Turkey, the United Kingdom and France), the development of private labels (as anticipated by Jiffy and JOKR, as launched by Frichti) and the introduction of a fidelity programme (as offered by Gopuff).

A second strategy to strengthen the quick commerce business model relies on technology and data. The start-ups use location intelligence and geospatial data to enhance their network of dark stores and predictive analytics to optimise their operations in terms of delivery and supply, among others. They collect consumer data as well, allowing to make necessary adjustments to their business model while creating adjacent business opportunities. This strategy is reminiscent of Amazon's origin story, which seemed focused on books at first but was all about data. As such, experts believe something similar is going on in the grocery sector. Venture capitalists might not be so interested in the delivery activities as in the business of using and selling data collected by the apps. Finally, a third strategy is based on the differentiation of services. Abu Dhabi-based Fenix combines ten-minute grocery delivery with its micro-mobility operations. Their dark stores, scattered around Reem Island, are used to fulfil groceries and charge the batteries of their e-scooters. It allows for the split of real estate costs between two businesses. Venezuela-based Yummy, Bengaluru-headquartered Ola and Dubai-based Careem combine instant grocery delivery and ridesharing, in a mission to create a 'super app' for their region. Super apps, as exemplified by the Chinese WeChat, aim to provide various consumer needs with one single app.

As quick commerce develops further, opposition against the model grows. The first proposal to adapt legislation came from Portugal in October 2021, proposing an update that responds to the 'new realities of commerce'. Some cities are taking a strong stance. Lyon, Paris and Amsterdam opposed dark stores for violating local zoning laws, by essentially conducting warehousing instead of commercial activities in areas or buildings where this is prohibited. An instruction published by the French government confirmed the importance of local zoning laws in the matter and clarified that customer reception distinguishes a warehouse from a store (Gouvernement, 2022). In response, some dark stores opened up their locations for click-and-collect, thereby meeting the requirement. New York introduced a bill, barring apps from advertising fifteen-minute delivery times, citing threats to driver and pedestrian safety. In March 2022, the urban planning department of the City of Paris organised a public meeting, explaining to citizens how to signal dark stores in their neighbourhood and on what basis. With quick commerce increasingly blending with traditional retail and traditional retail increasingly borrowing from quick commerce, the grounds for legal action will become only more difficult to distinguish and enforce. An updated view of retail is called for.

Observations of a Dark Store in Paris

Dark stores are scrutinised for their negative urban impact, but the extent of their impact is unclear. Some articles indicate the average number of daily orders required for dark stores to be viable: 1,100 to cover variable costs and 1,800 to cover fixed costs as well. These orders translate to the same number of deliveries in terms of departures and arrivals, unless several are consolidated on the same delivery. Reports from London suggest that drivers take two or three orders at a time. In an interview with The Twenty Minute VC podcast, JOKR's founder says that consolidation is easiest in a delivery window between fifteen and thirty minutes. Quick commerce's delivery promise is, however, faster. In addition, with the multitude of players present in the same city, service areas overlap. In Paris, New York and London, more than ten players are active. Both factors hinder efficient order consolidation. But not only deliveries impact the city, but also supplies. In the same interview, JOKR's founder envisions increasingly regular supplies of dark stores, to allow their assortment to evolve throughout the day depending on what consumers need. Dark stores also impact cities through their usage of space, having their vehicle fleet often parked next to or in front of the facility.

To identify the transport intensity of dark stores, a two-day observation was conducted in Rue Popincourt in the 11th arrondissement of Paris. Observations focused on Getir's dark store, situated in a former clothing store on the ground floor of a residential building. Several other dark stores are found in this area: Frichti at barely 63 metres walking distance; Gorillas; Cajoo; Zapp; and Gopuff in streets a bit further (Apur, 2022). In the week of the 21st of February 2022, data was collected for fifteen consecutive hours on weekdays (from 8 hours to 23 hours) and fourteen consecutive hours on weekend days (from 9 hours to 23 hours). To collect the data, a spreadsheet file was used based on the approach taken by Srinivas et al. (2019), who studied the intensity of use of three Amazon facilities in California. As such, we recorded the number of arrivals and departures of both supply and delivery vehicles, the number of units dropped off and shipped off and the number of vehicles parked in public space. Figure 10.1 shows three photographs of supply, delivery and parking activities at Getir's dark store.

Figure 10.2 shows the number of delivery vehicles' departing and arriving at Getir's dark store. Intensity of delivery transport is slightly higher during weekends (311 per day), compared to during the week (298 per day). It comes down to one departure or arrival every three minutes. Workers leaving on bicycle or scooter did not always return, suggesting staff sharing in Getir's network. Most deliveries concentrate on afternoon and evening. Deliveries decline after 22 hours during the week, while they increase again at this time during the weekend. Bicycle use is higher on the weekend, while scooter use is higher during the week. Delivery vehicles generally depart with several bags of groceries: 1.4 during the week and

Figure 10.1 Supply, delivery and parking activities at Getir's dark store
Source: Photos by Maxime Priet and Nathan Partouche, used with permission

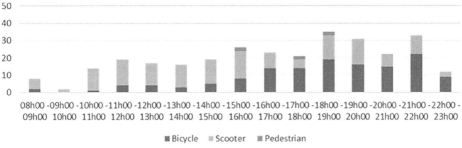

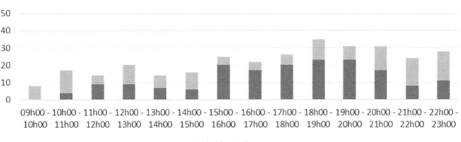

Figure 10.2 Number of delivery vehicle departures and arrivals per hour for Getir's dark store at Rue Popincourt in Paris

143

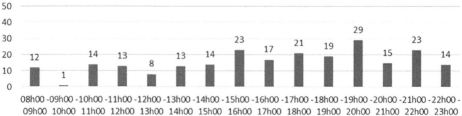
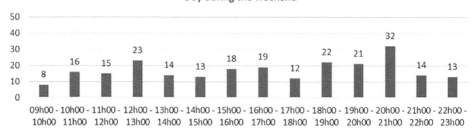

Figure 10.3 Number of orders per hour for Getir's dark store at Rue Popincourt in Paris

1.9 during the weekend. Given average basket sizes, we assume that one bag represents one order. With 1.5 orders per departure during the week and 2.2 during the weekend, scooters lend themselves better to consolidation than bicycles (respectively 1.2 and 1.6). We observed a worker carrying out deliveries on foot twice, bringing three bags of groceries the first time and seven bags the second time. Overall, we found a similar amount of orders for both observed days: 236 orders per day during the week and 240 orders per day during the weekend, see Figure 10.3. The numbers suggest that this particular dark store is not viable yet. Delivery transport is therefore likely to increase in the future, but not directly proportional to the number of orders, provided that order consolidation is sufficient.

Our observations suggest that dark stores are supplied regularly and in small quantities, but only during the week. We observed a van dropping off one pallet and a truck dropping off two pallets in the morning, as well as a van picking up four empty pallets in the evening. The parking spaces in front of the dark store are occupied by Getir's all-electric fleet of bicycles and scooters. As a consequence, the truck was forced to park on the streets during its unloading activities, thereby blocking the road completely for twenty minutes and creating a dangerous situation for residents passing on foot or by bike. During both week and weekend, an average number of five scooters occupied the parking spaces at the beginning and at the end of every hour of observation. For bicycles, we observed seven bicycles on average occupying the space, while this number was reduced to six during the weekend.

Conclusions on Dark Stores and Urban Logistics

This chapter presents the dark store model as a post-pandemic strategy for retail, by contextualising it against other concepts impacting settings and offerings of traditional stores and by illustrating it through the development of quick commerce. Pursued by a range of start-ups around the world, quick commerce relies on dark stores to propose instant grocery delivery, within ten to twenty minutes. The chapter demonstrates the intensive amount of transport for delivery (to a greater extent) and supply (to a lesser extent) that dark stores generate, as well as their significant use of parking space. Both impacts prompt careful management from urban policy-makers, among which opposition against the phenomenon is growing. Examples from Amsterdam, Lyon, New York and Paris are provided.

Nonetheless, fulfilment and delivery from stores will not remain limited to venture capital-backed quick commerce start-ups, nor to food retail (meals and groceries). Dark stores as a strategy concerns the retail sector as a whole. Pharmaceuticals are said to be the next in line offering instant delivery, supported by advancements in robotisation and automation that facilitate inventory, fulfilment and processing in store. Other segments are clothing and electronics, of which almost half are already bought online. What's more, with acquisitions and partnerships ongoing among various stakeholder types, retail is increasingly hybrid. Examples include a large online assortment with standard delivery from a warehouse, combined with dark stores providing instant deliveries and click-and-collect, or stores transforming from regular activities during the day to fulfilment and delivery during the night.

As such, the discussion about the details of urban management cannot be limited to rigidly categorising stores and warehouses or defining what constitutes an acceptable delivery promise. With so many eyes fixed on quick commerce and dark stores, it presents an opportunity to prioritise longstanding urban logistics topics on the research and policy agenda. Some of these topics include: providing and enforcing adequate space for loading and unloading activities; identifying appropriate locations for goods transport-intensive urban facilities and for storage of non-perishable goods; imposing and facilitating low emission and low noise regulations for goods vehicles; providing adequate charging infrastructure for goods vehicles; controlling and enforcing fair working conditions; facilitating and enforcing safe circulation of goods vehicles; and so on. Perhaps the widespread instant delivery trend, that requires storage to be local, can create an opportunity as well for urban consolidation centres to find a viable business model at last, something that has so far proved incredibly difficult.

Acknowledgements

Thank you to Maxime Priet and Nathan Partouche from Junior EUP UrbaConseil for collecting the data from observations.

References

Ahuja, K., Chandra, V., Lord, V., and Peens, C. (2021, September 22). Ordering in: The rapid evolution of food delivery. *McKinsey & Company*. https://www.mckinsey.com/industries/technology-media-and-telecommunications/our-insights/ordering-in-the-rapid-evolution-of-food-delivery

Alexander, B., and Blazquez, M. B. (2019). Futurising the physical store in the omnichannel retail environment. In W. Piotrowicz and R. Cuthbertson (Eds.), *Exploring omnichannel retailing*. Springer Nature Switzerland. https://doi.org/10.1007/978-3-319-98273-1

Alexander, B., and Cano, M. B. (2020). Store of the future: Towards a (re)invention and (re)imagination of physical store space in an omnichannel context. *Journal of Retailing and Consumer Services*, 55(101913). https://doi.org/10.1016/j.jretconser.2019.101913

Apur. (2022). *Drive piéton, dark kitchens, dark stores – Les nouvelles formes de la distribution alimentaire à Paris*. www.apur.org

Buldeo Rai, H. (2022, February 23). Micro facilities. *E-Commerce Mobilities Observatory*, 14(1). https://doi.org/10.3390/SU14010532

Buldeo Rai, H., Verlinde, S., Macharis, C., Schoutteet, P., and Vanhaverbeke, L. (2019). Logistics outsourcing in omnichannel retail: State of practice and service recommendations. *International Journal of Physical Distribution & Logistics Management*, *49*(3), 267–286. https://doi.org/https://doi.org/10.1108/IJPDLM-02-2018-0092

Couclelis, H. (2004). Pizza over the Internet: e-commerce, the fragmentation of activity and the tyranny of the region. *Entrepreneurship & Regional Development*, *16*, 41–54. https://doi.org/10.1080/0898562042000205027

Dablanc, L., Aguilera, A., Krier, C., Adoue, F., and Louvet, N. (2021). *Gig delivery workers in Paris.* https://www.lvmt.fr/wp-content/uploads/2021/06/Instant-delivery-Paris-survey-2021.pdf

Dablanc, L., Morganti, E., Arvidsson, N., Woxenius, J., Browne, M., and Saidi, N. (2017). The rise of on-demand 'Instant Deliveries' in European cities. *Supply Chain Forum: An International Journal*. https://doi.org/10.1080/16258312.2017.1375375

Dablanc, L., and Rakotonarivo, D. (2010). The impacts of logistics sprawl: How does the location of parcel transport terminals affect the energy efficiency of goods' movements in Paris and what can we do about it? *Procedia – Social and Behavioral Sciences*, *2*(3), 6087–6096. https://doi.org/10.1016/j.sbspro.2010.04.021

Duthoit, A. (2021). *European food retailers: The bitter digital aftertaste of the COVID-19 legacy.*

Gauri, D. K., Jindal, R. P., Ratchford, B., Fox, E., Bhatnagar, A., Pandey, A., Navallo, J. R., Fogarty, J., Carr, S., and Howerton, E. (2021). Evolution of retail formats: Past, present, and future. *Journal of Retailing*, *97*(1), 42–61. https://doi.org/10.1016/J.JRETAI.2020.11.002

Gouvernement. (2022). *Instruction du gouvernement Fiches techniques : modalités de régulation des dark stores.* https://www.cohesion-territoires.gouv.fr/sites/default/files/2022-03/Fiche modalites de regulation des dark stores-1.pdf?v=1647622828

Hagberg, J., Jonsson, A., and Egels-Zandén, N. (2017). Retail digitalization: Implications for physical stores. *Journal of Retailing and Consumer Services*, *39*, 264–269. https://doi.org/10.1016/j.jretconser.2017.08.005

Hagberg, J., Sundstrom, M., and Egels-Zandén, N. (2016). The digitalization of retailing: An exploratory framework. *International Journal of Retail & Distribution Management*, *44*(7), 694–712. https://doi.org/10.1108/IJRDM-09-2015-0140

Hänninen, M., Kwan, S. K., and Mitronen, L. (2020). From the store to omnichannel retail: Looking back over three decades of research. *The International Review of Retail, Distribution and Consumer Research*, *31*(1), 1–35. https://doi.org/10.1080/09593969.2020.1833961

Hübner, A., Hense, J., and Dethlefs, C. (2022). The revival of retail stores via omnichannel operations: A literature review and research framework. *European Journal of Operational Research*. https://doi.org/10.1016/J.EJOR.2021.12.021

International Post Corporation. (2021). *Global Postal Industry Report 2021 - A global review of industry performance and trends.*

Neslin, S. a., Grewal, D., Leghorn, R., Shankar, V., Teerling, M. L., Thomas, J. S., and Verhoef, P. C. (2006). Challenges and opportunities in multichannel customer management. *Journal of Service Research*, *9*(2), 95–112. https://doi.org/10.1177/1094670506293559

Sheffi, Y. (2020, November 24). How e-commerce is reinventing the humble warehouse. *Medium*.

Srinivas, S., Nishi, B., and Bradas, T. (2019). *Comparing the intensity of use of e-commerce facilities.*

UNCTAD. (2021). *COVID-19 And e-commerce: A global review.* https://unctad.org/system/files/official-document/dtlstict2020d13_en_0.pdf

Verhoef, P. C., Kannan, P. K., and Inman, J. J. (2015). From multi-channel retailing to omni-channel retailing. Introduction to the special issue on multi-channel retailing. *Journal of Retailing*, *91*(2), 174–181. https://doi.org/10.1016/j.jretai.2015.02.005

von Briel, F. (2018). The future of omnichannel retail: A four-stage Delphi study. *Technological Forecasting and Social Change*, *132*(August 2016), 217–229. https://doi.org/10.1016/j.techfore.2018.02.004

11
FOOD LOGISTICS

Eleonora Morganti

Introduction

With increased urbanisation and economic development, a large number of urban areas, and in particular megacities and large cities, are facing a variety of challenges including food access and poor air quality. One of the main challenges is to promote the transition to cleaner, non-fossil fuel technology in food transport while preserving diverse, affordable, and capillary food distribution across the urban areas. Though crucial, achieving these aims is difficult due to the constantly changing landscape in the urban food distribution and transport system.

A recent study by Li et al. (2022) provided a global overview of the carbon footprint of food miles, with emissions being 3.5–7.5 times higher than previous estimates. Global food-miles emissions account for 3.0GtCO2e, equivalent to nearly 30% of food-system emissions (transport and production) or 19% of total food-system emissions (transport, production and land-use change) (ibid.). Looking at the global food chains, domestic transport is the most critical segment (ibid.). This is due to the fact that food is usually delivered by large fleets of trucks and vans within a country and road transport features a much higher emission intensity per tkm than maritime shipping, mainly used for international food movements.

Recently, there has been more attention towards the issues associated with food transport; however the lack of data to detail domestic food transport and how food circulates in our cities, also called *last food miles*, impacts the path to urban sustainability. Additional issues are represented by the critical disruption experienced by the global food supply system in the last fifteen years. Price surges and shortages, resulting from the financial crisis of 2007–2008, the recession in 2022 and extreme weather events are examples. More recently, the COVID-19 pandemic and the subsequent recession have placed exceptional stress on food supply chains, with issues related to transport and logistics, as well as considerable shifts in demand. The consequences of the global food disruption have strongly affected, and still affect, consumers in city environments, where food access and food security have been seriously threatened (Béné 2020).

This chapter offers an overview of the recent evolution of the four main stakeholders in the urban food transport system: (i) the food distribution channels; (ii) the households; (iii) the food transport industry and (iv) the city government. The ongoing changes and the interactions between these stakeholders are illustrated from the food transport angle, in order to provide a better understanding of the implications for the city logistics sector. The following section provides the representation of the urban food transport system while the subsequent sections are respectively dedicated to the four stakeholders. The final section contains the conclusion and recommendations for relevant strategies linked to urban food transport and city logistics.

The Urban Food Transport System

The aim of the chapter is to identify and characterise four prominent stakeholders in the urban food transport and to explore the links amongst them. Research focuses on carriers, local authorities and end-receivers (Lindholm 2012). Based on the growing trends for home deliveries, in this chapter, the category of the end-receivers is divided into two different groups, namely: (i) businesses in the food distribution sector and (ii) households as they generate two different flows of food circulating throughout a city, with specific logistic needs.

As shown in Figure 11.1, the urban food transport systems revolve around four main stakeholders:

- *Food distribution channels* refers to the food supply. It explores how food distribution is organised in the city and its region and where people acquire food. The retailers, the food outlets, and the online food platforms are part of this stakeholder group;
- *Households* illustrates food consumption and demand. It investigates who is consuming what kind of food, and what are their purchase and consumption habits and their mobility patterns. This stakeholder is represented by the consumers and their preferences;

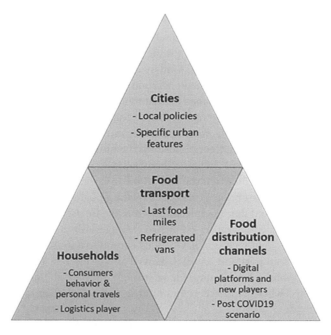

Figure 11.1 The urban food transport system and its stakeholders
Source: Author

- *Food transport* refers to carriers, transport and logistics operators delivering to the end-receivers both business outlets and private households. The *last food mile* is designed as the last stretch of delivery service to end-receivers;
- *Cities* comprise aspects related to both governance and specific urban settings. This stakeholder includes local authorities, policy-makers and decision-makers and the different departments involved in different ways in organising food provision for the community. Public health, clean air, urban planning, business support and waste management are among the services that are usually part of the implementation of an urban food transport plan at a municipal level.

Food Distribution Channels

Digital Platforms and New Players

The number and variety of distribution channels by which food is supplied to urban consumers have risen dramatically in recent years. Besides supermarkets, corner shops, vending machines, restaurants, cafes and traditional food outlets, more online options for food shopping have appeared in the urban food distribution system. 'Click and collect' services from corporate retailers, digital intermediary platforms and mobile applications (Dablanc et al. 2017), as well as dark kitchens and dark stores (see Chapter 10) are popular examples of new distribution schemes.

Dark kitchens – also known as ghost kitchens, cloud kitchens or virtual kitchens – are food services without a physical dining room but with a delivery-only menu. These alternatives to 'brick and mortar' restaurants are becoming more and more popular especially for large restaurant chains trying to maximise the amount of meals at reduced operational costs. Dark kitchens appear to be particularly successful in densely populated urban areas, where order volume is high and there are plenty of delivery drivers or riders to quickly move food (Hussey 2021). The label *dark kitchens* usually refers to new facilities; however it includes under-utilised existing restaurant kitchens that start new online menus under new names or are re-branded (Deloitte 2019).

A similar concept has been adapted to online grocery delivery operations. Dark stores, shadow warehouses or dotcom centres function as distribution centres exclusively for online shopping, just as a supermarket but not open to the public. It has been designed as an alternative to store-based fulfilment, to improve order accuracy and operational efficiency as well as allowing retailers to move inventory closer to residential areas (Wells 2021) and in areas not covered by brick and mortar stores. Dark stores usually feature artificial intelligence, robots and automation for retrieval systems, order fulfilment, picking, and delivery. It is a growing logistics service built by digital food delivery platforms in collaboration with retailers. In the United States, the supermarket chain Kroger, for example, has opened automated distribution centres powered by the British grocery fulfilment technology firm Ocado, while the retailer Albertsons built similar hubs in partnership with Instacart (ibid.).

The diffusion of dark kitchens and dark stores is linked to growth and transformation in the food service sector. In just a couple of decades, a growing share of the food delivery industry (for both prepared meals and grocery) has shifted from in-person and telephone-based ordering systems to websites and mobile applications, including ordering via smartphone and virtual assistant technology such as Amazon's Alexa and Google Assistant.

In competition with retailers and restaurants websites, digital intermediaries have made their appearance on the online food marketplace and they quickly became well-used platforms to access food in cities around the world. Originally structured as intermediary platforms to facilitate transactions between buyers (households) and sellers (restaurants and food outlets), these platforms rely on both technical infrastructure and organisational elements (Gawer 2014). They are able to collect a large volume of data on markets, consumers and then train algorithms to drive decision-making and generate increased revenue. Some platforms include options for delivery services and they develop algorithms to combine users and delivery operations, mainly via subcontracted bike riders and drivers.

Within the urban food distribution landscape, these third-party intermediary platforms appear to be a new relevant player shaping both food access and *last food mile* operations. They can be distinguished as two-sided or three-sided platforms (Deloitte 2019; Ecker and Strüver 2022):

- Two-sided platforms, or *aggregators* for online food ordering, have been developed since the early 2000s. They allow households to place orders with restaurants, presenting their menus and conveying orders in return for a fee (ibid.). Restaurants deliver the food through their own couriers or contractors. Examples include, Takeaway.com and HungryHouse.
- Three-sided platforms, or *gig platforms*, became more common in the second decade of the 21st century, adopting a platform-to-consumer-delivery-model. They include a third set of participants namely, independent delivery workers (see Chapter 27). Restaurants and retailers pay a fee to access the consumers and also the delivery workers who deliver the order (ibid.). Examples of these platforms, include Uber Eats and Deliveroo, for both prepared meals and grocery.

The trend of 'platformisation' for the online food distribution sector has been explored by various studies including the Deloitte (2019) and Lehdonvirta et al. (2020). The 'platformisation' is not uniform between countries, and in some European countries, food delivery industries were platformised to a much higher degree than in other countries, in terms of the share of the overall market that passes through platforms (ibid.). The nature of the platforms varies between countries, with some countries being platformised mainly by large global platforms like UberEats in Portugal, while in other countries local platform companies were stronger such as in Spain with Glovo and Germany with Delivery Hero (ibid.)

Some of these companies define themselves as technology companies (DoorDash 2021) or more often as food delivery services (see the websites of Deliveroo and Uber Eats). It appears clear that they cannot be classified as food transport couriers, since they usually own limited fleets and assets and they mostly subcontract the transport to delivery workers, who act as independent firms or entrepreneurs. In more general terms, it is possible to define the rise of these third-party intermediates as an institutional innovation in the urban food transport system, creating ways to 'strategically mobilise' data, people, and things thanks to the spread of information and communication technologies (ICT) (Meemken et al. 2022; Van dorm 2020 cited by Ecker and Strüver 2022).

Online food platforms are diverse and they differentiate by size, service, business model and range of products. They have evolved quickly receiving large amounts of investment, growing with the acquisition of other companies and becoming market leaders at both a national and international level. Only twenty years ago, in the early 2000s, platforms and third-party apps were leading to the rise in online orders for prepared meals, while the growth of online grocery shopping was driven mostly by the retailers' own websites and mobile services (Lehdonvirta et al. 2020). More recently, a large number of food retailers have

Table 11.1 Examples of food digital services

Sector	Firms				
Food deliveries (prepared meals)	Just Eat TakeAway Corporation (UK, Italy)	Uber Eats, Postmates (USA)	Zomato (India)	Delivery Hero, Foodpanda Foodora Glovo Talabat Yemeksepeti	Meituan Waimai (China)
Online fulfilment grocery	Ocado (UK)	Instacart (USA)	Grubhub (with Seamless and Eat24 – USA)	Amazon Fresh	Freshippo (China)
Meal in a box	HelloFresh (UK)	Blue Apron (USA)	Cook It (Canada)	My Food Bag (New Zealand)	
Ghost kitchens	CloudKitchens (USA)	DoorDash (USA)	Deliveroo Editions (UK)	Rebel Food (India)	Robin Food (Turkey)
Diet-specific service	Elite Sweets (USA, keto-friendly)	Allplants (UK, plant-based food)	Change Foods (USA, animal-free dairy)	Shiok Meats (Singapore, alternative protein)	Magic Spoon (low-carb cereals)
Super App	Getir (Turkey)		Grub (USA)	WeChat (China)	
Platform cooperatives/ Alternative platforms	CoopCycle (France, Worldwide)			Velofood (Austria)	

built partnerships with delivery platforms, to integrate scheduled home deliveries operated by their own fleet with subcontracted on-demand services. In the United Kingdom, this is the case with the Co-op, Asda, Sainsbury's and Morrisons, for example using Deliveroo and Uber Eats for rapid deliveries (Retail Gazette 2022).

Table 11.1 provides an overview of a selection of digital platforms and online food tech start-ups helping to define the online digital marketplace and the variety of players. Alongside the most well-known meal delivery platforms such as Just Eat, Uber Eats and Meituan Waimai, there is a large section of companies dedicated to online grocery fulfilments, most notably Ocado, Instacart and Freshippo. Another type of food service gaining popularity in Western economies is the meal in a box or meal kit, where consumers that subscribe to companies, such as Blue Apron, HelloFresh, Cook It Up and My Food Bag, receive pre-portioned ingredients for the selected recipe.

In the case of ghost kitchens, there are firms offering physical spaces for chefs and cookers to prepare and sell meals online, such as CloudKitchens, DoorDash Kitchens, Deliveroo Editions, Rebel Food and Robin Food. Looking at food tech start-ups, new niche marketplaces have been designed to address specific dietary needs and more sophisticated consumer's preferences. Among these, there is Elite Sweets selling gluten-free, keto-friendly donuts; Magic Spoon for sugar-based cereals with low-carb cereals; Allplants online vegan meal delivery platform; Shiok Meats designing alternative proteins and cell-based meat menus and Change Foods, for animal-free dairy products. Other new players can be classified as 'super app' (Chew 2022) such as Grab, Getir and WeChat that offer 'everything' including prepared meals, grocery, rides, loans and insurance in just one platform. Finally, it is worth mentioning initiatives that propose a business approach aligned with sustainability and the circular economy concept. It is the case of CoopCycle, which provides the software platform to local cooperatives to run their delivery businesses, and Velofood, a competitive Austrian delivery company not affiliated with big brands.

COVID-19 and Online Grocery Shopping

During 2019/2020, restrictions during the COVID-19 pandemic caused a major shift in the way people accessed food in cities and the lockdown accelerated online grocery shopping and home delivery orders. In all regions of the globe, the share of sales of food service from home delivery registered an upward trend, from 2% to 7% in 2009 to 6% to 16% in 2019, and then a steep spike in 2021 to 13% to 27% (Meemken et al. 2022). Global revenues for the online food delivery sector were about $90 billion in 2018, rose to $294 billion in 2021, and are expected to exceed $466 billion by 2026 (Statista 2021).

In the case of the United States, for example in December 2019, the market penetration of online groceries in the United States was circa 4% of overall sales; in 2021 it reached 14% and it is expected to reach in the region of 25% by 2030 (Aull et al. 2021). In May 2022, U.S. sales for meal delivery services grew 8% year-over-year (Bloomberg Second Measure 2022). Looking at U.S. consumers' meal delivery sales, DoorDash has 59% of the market, Uber Eats (and Postmates) accounts for around 28%, followed by Grubhub (including the subsidiaries Seamless and Eat24) with 13% (ibid.).

This acceleration reflects the success of large retailers, restaurants chains and digital platforms in that during the severe lockdown they quickly responded to the challenge and expanded their digital offer, their networks and fleet. At the same time however, serious difficulties were generated for small independent food outlets that relied on physical shopping. The lockdown restrictions on food retailing and catering services have created new barriers for all stakeholders and in particular for local independent businesses, with limited investment capacity to adapt to the new rules and to develop a stronger online presence (Haas et al. 2020).

Households

In cities, the consumer behaviour of the working population has evolved due to the work-life culture and the limited time available to physically shop in stores and malls. This busy lifestyle, combined with the spread of ICT, contributes to the rise of online shopping in general, with prepared meals and grocery delivery services quickly flourishing among urban communities (Das and Ghose 2019).

Among other factors, economic growth, urbanisation, increasing female labour market participation and growing international food trade contributed to changes in food consumption and purchase. Dietary patterns have modified over time and an increased demand for processed foods; higher-value products, such as meat, fruit and vegetables; and food consumed away from home (such as in restaurants) and food prepared away from home delivered at home has been observed (Meemken et al. 2022).

Focusing on the recent popularity of home deliveries, the households that access food via digital channels have different purposes. Some consumers seek to obtain the versatility and variety of restaurants in the comfort and convenience of their homes and offices by using meal delivery services (Lau and Ng 2019). Others seek to replace trips to stores with grocery deliveries. In general terms, the consumer's perspective focuses on convenience; access to a wider range of food products, time savings, travel reduction and more recently, being the safer option to reduce the risk of COVID-19 infection.

Before the pandemic, shopping online for food was more prevalent among young, urban, affluent families seeking the convenience of delivery to their home (Bjørgen et al. 2019). In 2020, larger numbers of consumers tested home deliveries, such as in France, where during the lockdown a 24% increase in restaurant delivery users compared to pre-pandemic times was recorded (Statista 2022). This trend continued after the restrictions were lifted and, in Europe in 2021, deliveries from restaurants, fast-food chains and catering services accounted for 31% of households shopping online, compared to 29% in 2020 (EC 2022 -Eurostat: isoc_ec_ibuy).

Behaviour and expectations are continuously changing, since customers are getting used to high-standard services such as unlimited deliveries included in customer loyalty programmes, expanded delivery hours and offers for a wide selection of items with no minimum order size (see DoorDash for example). From the retailers' view, the offer of these services is part of their marketing strategy to win and retain consumers in order to consolidate the base and generate scale efficiencies (Simmons et al. 2022).

COVID-19 shifted part of the demand for food consumed away from home to food prepared away from home. Although unclear, the potential for personal trips to the restaurants or to the supermarkets to be replaced or substituted with home deliveries with commercial vehicles and bicycles, it is evident that the adoption of digital tools for accessing groceries and meals contributes to an evolution in the way food circulates in cities. This subsequently impacts the level of traffic and air quality. Little is known about home deliveries and the resulting environmental cost of transport. Most likely higher delivery frequencies of smaller orders, typical for online shoppers, generate negative impacts on traffic flows, road safety, loading factors and air quality.

Additional questions are raised such as how the consumer can influence the urban food distribution system and how passenger travel for food shopping contributes to poor air quality in urban areas (see Mattioli and Anable 2017). Raising awareness with respect to optimising frequency, volumes of purchases, or the choice of the most responsible carriers are examples of the potential actions of households to shape a more sustainable urban food transport system.

Among the stakeholders of the urban food transport system, households constitute a key new player in the food logistics chain and their preferences shape the organisation of the *last food mile*, having an impact on urban traffic and fleet composition. For example, consumers can influence the emergence of specific delivery services, such as electric cargo bike deliveries (see Chapter 5) or self-driving delivery robots, through their purchasing preferences.

Food Transport

Last Food Miles

The food logistics sector in an urban environment is an important yet problematic aspect of the supply chain, due to the high number of receivers and the resulting lack of efficiency in transport operations (Morganti and Gonzalez Feliu 2015). The last-mile deliveries from local warehouses, distribution centres, suppliers and farmers to urban food outlets and households are often characterised by small volumes, high frequency, non-homogeneous transport units (pallets, parcels and boxes) and a wide range of commercial vehicles, such as vans, small trucks and more recently cargo bikes (ibid.). The receivers, both businesses and households, set increasingly high-performance standards that must be met, including shorter time windows, no minimum order amount and higher frequency of deliveries. Empty runs and long dwell times at loading and unloading points are frequent and they can represent a significant waste of resources. Other constraints, such as distinct handling procedures and temperature-controlled transport, further affect the efficiency of the supply chain. Inefficient food transport operations generate a larger amount of waste in terms of food that is lost during the loading and unloading activities, transit and delivery. Food losses are highest for fruit and vegetables where on average 4–15% of all the production is lost during the distribution phase (Gustavsson et al. 2011), generating additional costs usually reflected in the price paid by consumers.

To reduce food losses during the last-mile deliveries, several factors need to be taken into account: temperature, humidity and water loss, atmospheric composition, physical injury and mixed load (Vigneault et al. 2009). Many trucks and vans deliver several types of produce in a single journey. Although last-mile deliveries are usually short trips (from local warehouses to city outlets), the quality of the load can be compromised if some produce is mixed with products with different storage requirements (ibid).

Due to the sophisticated logistics and little added value of the transport operations, this industry offers very low margins. Subcontracting is a common practice in the last-mile sector, both traditional couriers and digital platforms delegate driving and delivery to third-party groups and drivers. Usually, this business model allows these large companies to reduce employee benefits and overall costs while maintaining effective control over goods' movements. Large companies such as Deliveroo and Uber Eat are requested to offer greater transparency regarding the impact of algorithmic management with respect to terms and conditions of employment (Arasanz et al. 2021).

Refrigerated Vans

Trucks, lorries and vans are the most common way to move food within a country. On a domestic scale, perishable foods need to be transported in refrigerated commercial vehicles, stored in refrigerated warehouses and displayed in refrigerated cases. Logistics for the food sector demand high levels of food safety and traceability, such as short-lead time and distinct handling procedures.

In case of fresh, frozen and prepared food, temperature-controlled technology is required together with just-in-time deliveries and dedicated facilities and vehicles (Mahajan et al. 2017). Fresh food in general has a short shelf life and its value declines as appearance declines (Shewfelt 2017). The added costs associated with fresh foods, that non-perishable processed products do not have to consider, directly affect the availability of fruit and vegetables, meat and dairy products in stores and ultimately the food choice for the consumers.

Little is known about the transport operations for perishable food in urban areas and in particular in terms of the use of refrigerated light commercial vehicles (Yang et al. 2021). Refrigerated vans, not only used to deliver to food stores but an increasing number of households, are attracting attention as they become more and more popular; however limited data are available on the existing fleet and their contribution to greenhouse gas (CO_2) and nitrogen oxides (NO_x) emissions in urban areas.

Braithwaite (2017) suggested there were 15,000 refrigerated vans used for grocery home delivery in the United Kingdom in 2016 and the annual distance travelled by refrigerated vans is at least twice the average (DfT 2020). These vans are typically 3.5-tonne gross weight vehicles equipped with temperature-controlled units called Transport Refrigeration Units

(TRUs), which are usually powered via the vehicles' engine. It is obvious that vehicles with added weight of TRUs consume more fuel and emit more NO_x, let alone the vehicles' diesel engines are also powering the refrigeration units, which further elevates the emissions.

For the first time, Yang et al (2021) developed an estimation of real-world CO_2 and NO_x emission factors for refrigerated vans that have been developed using PHEM, and assessed that vans with TRUs generate ≈15% more CO_2 emissions and ≈18% more NO_x emissions than standard vans.

Cities

Developing more sustainable urban food transport depends on increased knowledge and co-operation between authorities, private business households and public society (Bjerkan et al. 2014). The urban food system resulting from recent events presents serious social-economic and public health issues, including access to affordable and nutritious food, digital divide, working conditions for delivery workers and dietary changes linked to eating restaurant food instead of eating home-cooked meals. Environmental challenges include food transport and waste, single-use packaging which cause air and water pollution as well as CO_2 emissions. These ongoing transformations require urgent attention from local policy-makers and administrators (Meemken et al. 2022).

Local authorities can influence both when and how urban distribution is performed. However, local authorities consist of a range of departments with different and potentially conflicting goals, rationalities and motivations. Public administrations can, among others, include food safety authorities, labour inspection agencies, agencies for planning and building services, police and parking agencies as well as local, regional and federal maintenance departments (ibid). This makes the governance of the last food miles more difficult to design and complex to implement.

In a growing number of cities worldwide, however, local governments have drafted and promoted food policy councils and food partnerships, including city officials from different departments, producer and consumer organisations, processing companies, retail and science partners (Moragues et al. 2013). From Belo Horizonte to Pisa, from Detroit to Nairobi, cities have encouraged strategies to increase the sustainability of the local food system, focusing on various goals such as access to affordable food, enhancement of regional and urban production and, in certain cases, transition to cleaner food transport, such as in Paris (Mairie de Paris 2015).

Local administrations usually conduct a preliminary evaluation of how a city is fed, looking for necessary data and information to start developing strategies, and then they begin a transversal conversation about priorities and actions. Managing links among the urban food transport stakeholders, distribution companies including digital platforms, transport operators and households is a key task for city governments. They play a crucial role in defining a new urban food-system plan in synergy with policies for clean air zones and poverty reduction, for example.

Conclusions

This chapter has explored the recent transformation of the urban food transport system through the analysis of the four main stakeholders, such as the food distribution sector, the households, the urban food transport industry and the city government.

In cities worldwide, besides the offer of 'brick and mortar' retailers, restaurants and cafes, online food shopping has become increasingly popular, especially during the lockdown of the COVID-19 pandemic. To a certain extent, these trends reversed, however the share of the market for online food shopping is constantly growing.

Within the urban food distribution channels, digital platforms are new leading players, offering the choice to order and pay online for meals and groceries on the one hand, and to connect restaurants and retailers with delivery drivers and riders on the other. They constitute an institutional innovation in the urban food transport system able to mobilise data, people and goods. New partnerships between platforms and traditional distributors are built and they generate new services in the last food mile system, including dark kitchens, dark stores and super apps.

The role of households has also evolved within the urban food transport system due to the increased demand for convenience and rapid deliveries, with homes becoming the final destination of commercial trips. In their purchasing behaviour and dietary choices, consumers are key to sustainability (Poore and Nemenecek 2018).

Urban food transport is the least efficient part of the supply chain, due to the high number of receivers and to their increasingly high-standard requirements. In the case of fresh food, distinct handling procedures and temperature-controlled transport represent additional constraints to the last-mile deliveries. In this context, more attention is needed to understand the specific contribution of domestic and urban food transport, as for example the additional GHG emissions generated by refrigerated vans.

Cities are becoming increasingly influential economic hubs on the global stage; however their capacity to improve environmental sustainability is still limited and there is the urgency to identify practical strategies to improve urban food transport operations. Food is rising up the urban agenda and stakeholders at the local level – from the public, private, and civil society sectors – are reasserting responsibility for food policy.

In the process of improving the access to healthy and affordable food while promoting a more sustainable food distribution system, transport and logistics operations have become a key element that requires more attention. Inefficiencies in food logistics have an impact on the competitiveness of distribution channels which in turn influences the access to affordable nutritious food. As a result, the *last food mile* has important implications for air quality and healthy diets. This chapter has presented some of the small but growing body of scientific evidence in this area and highlighted research gaps that are relevant for future studies.

References

Arasanz, J., Bazzani, T., and Sanz de Miguel, P. (2021). The definition of worker in the platform economy: Exploring workers' risks and regulatory solutions. Study for the European Economic and Social Committee, Brussels, European Union.

Aull, B., Perkins, A., Kohli, S., and Marohn, E. (2021) The state of grocery in North America https://www.mckinsey.com/industries/retail/our-insights/the-state-of-grocery-in-north-america (Accessed 11/11/2022).

Béné, C. (2020) Resilience of local food systems and links to food security – A review of some important concepts in the context of COVID-19 and other shocks, *Food Security*, 12, 805–822. https://doi.org/10.1007/s12571-020-01076-1

Bloomberg Second Measure (2022) Which company is winning the restaurant food delivery war? https://secondmeasure.com/datapoints/food-delivery-services-grubhub-uber-eats-doordash-postmates/ (Accessed 21/11/2022).

Braithwaite, A. (2017) *The implications of internet shopping growth on the van fleet and traffic activity. RAC Foundation*, London.

Bjerkan, K.Y., Sund, A.B., and Nordtømme, M.E. (2014). Stakeholder responses to measures green and efficient urban freight, *Research in. Transportation Business and Management,* 11, 32–42.

Bjørgen, A., Bjerkan, K., and Hjelkrem, O. (2019) E-groceries: Sustainable last mile distribution in city planning, *Research in Transportation Economics* https://doi.org/10.1016/j.retrec.2019.100805

Chew, Z. (2022) The future of food: How software feeds your stomach at: https://www.venturescale.to/post/the-future-of-food-how-software-feeds-your-stomach (Accessed 18/11/2022).

Dablanc, L., Morganti, E., Arvidsson, N., Woxenius, J., Browne, M., and Saidi, N. (2017) The rise of on-demand 'Instant Deliveries' in European cities, *Supply Chain Forum An International Journal*, 18(4), 203–217.

Das, S., and Ghose, D. (2019) Influence of online food delivery apps on the operations of the restaurant business, *International Journal of Scientific and Technology Research*, 8(12), 1372–1377.

Deloitte (2019). Delivering growth: The impact of third-party platform ordering on restaurants, https://www2.deloitte.com/uk/en/pages/financial-advisory/articles/delivering-growth.html

DfT Department for Transport (2020) Road traffic forecasts 2019 https://www.gov.uk/government/publications/road-traffic-forecasts-2019 (Accessed 15/7/2021).

Door Dash (2021) https://help.doordash.com/dashers/s/article/Dasher-How-does-DoorDash-work?language=en_US#:~:text=Description,made%20possible%20by%20independent%20contractors. (Accessed 18/12/2021).

Ecker, Y., and Strüver, A. (2022) Towards alternative platform futures in post-pandemic cities? A case study on platformization and changing socio-spatial relations in on-demand food delivery, *Digital Geography and Society*, 3, 100032, https://doi.org/10.1016/j.diggeo.2022.100032

European Commission EC (2022) E-commerce statistics for individuals https://ec.europa.eu/eurostat/statistics-explained/index.php?title=E-commerce_statistics_for_individuals (Accessed 09/11/2022).

Gawer, A. (2014) Bridging differing perspectives on technological platforms: Toward an integrative framework, *Research Policy*, 43, 7, 1239–1249, ISSN 0048-7333, https://doi.org/10.1016/j.respol.2014.03.006

Gustavsson, J., Cederberg, C., Sonesson, U., Otterdijk, Rv., and Meybeck, A. (2011) Global food losses and food waste: Extent, causes and prevention. In Interpack. Rome, Italy: Food and Agriculture Organization of the United Nations.

Haas, S., Kuehl, E., Moran, J., and Venkataraman, K., (2020) How restaurants can thrive in the next normal https://www.mckinsey.com/industries/retail/our-insights/how-restaurants-can-thrive-in-the-next-normal (Accessed 21/11/2022).

Hussey, A. (2021) The global state of foodservice delivery, available at: https://kerry.com/insights/kerrydigest/2020/global-foodservice-delivery (Accessed 01/11/2022).

Lau, T., and Ng, D. (2019) Online food delivery services: Making food delivery the new normal, *Journal of Marketing Advances and Practices*, 1, 62–77.

Lehdonvirta, V., Park, S., Krell, T., and Friederici, N. (2020) Platformization in Europe: Global and local digital intermediaries in the retail, taxi and food delivery industries. Oxford Internet Institute.

Li, M., Jia, N., Lenzen, M., Arunima, A., Wei, L., Jin, Y., and Raubenheimer, D. (2022) Global food-miles account for nearly 20% of total food-systems emissions, *Nature Food*, 3, 445–453.

Lindholm, M. (2012) How local authority decision makers address freight transport in the urban area. Procedia— *Social and Behavioral Sciences*, 39, 134–145.

Mahajan, R., Garg, S., and Sharma, P.B. (2017) Processed food supply chain: A framework for literature review, *Journal of Advances in Management Research*, 14(1), 91–109. http://dx.doi.org/10.1108/JAMR-05-2016-0035

Mairie de Paris (2015) Plan alimentation durable 2015–2020 https://cdn.paris.fr/paris/2019/07/24/e9152ce370f7eb9c36cc72ce873aa1a7.pdf (Accessed 29/11/2022).

Mattioli, G., and Anable, J. (2017) Gross polluters for food shopping travel: An activity-based typology, *Travel Behaviour and Society*, 6, 19–31.

Meemken, E.-M., Bellemare, M.F., Reardon, T., and Vargas, C. (2022) Research and policy for the food-delivery revolution, *Science*, 377, 810–813.

Moragues, A., Morgan, K., Moschitz, H., Neimane, I., Nilsson, H., Pinto, M., Rohracher, H., Ruiz, R., Thuswald, M., Tisenkopfs, T., and Halliday, J. (2013) Urban food strategies: The rough guide to sustainable food systems. Document developed in the framework of the FP7 project FOODLINKS (GA No. 265287).

Morganti, E., and Gonzalez-Feliu, J. (2015) City logistics for perishable products. The case of Parma's Food Hub, *Case Studies in Transport Policy*, 3(2), 120–128.

Poore, J., and Nemecek, T. (2018) Reducing food's environmental impacts through producers and consumers, *Science*, 360, 987–992.

Retail Gazette Grocery on-demand: What do the big supermarkets offer? May 16, 2022 https://www.retailgazette.co.uk/blog/2022/05/grocery-on-demand-what-do-the-big-supermarkets-offer/ (Accessed 18/08/2022).

Shewfelt, R.L. (2017) Why can't we find more locally produced and fresher food in our supermarkets and restaurants?. In: *In Defense of Processed Food*. Copernicus, Cham. https://doi.org/10.1007/978-3-319-45394-1_3

Simmons, V., Spielvogel, J., Björn, T., and Tjon Pian Gi, M. (2022) The next S-curve of growth: Online grocery to 2030 https://www.mckinsey.com/industries/retail/our-insights/the-next-s-curve-of-growth-online-grocery-to-2030 (Accessed 21/09/2022).

Statista (2021) eServices Report 2021 Online Food Delivery https://www.statista.com/study/40457/food-delivery (Accessed 5/10/2022).

Statista (2022) Increase in restaurant delivery users during the coronavirus (COVID-19) pandemic in selected European countries in 2020 https://www.statista.com/statistics/1176841/restaurant-delivery-user-growth-during-covid-in-europe-by-country/

Vigneault, C., Thompson, J., We, S., Hui, C., LeBlanc, D. (2009) Transportation of fresh horticultural produce, chapter 1 from *Postharvest Technologies For Horticultural Crops*, 2, 1–24. ISBN: 978-81-308-0356-2 Editor: Noureddine Benkeblia.

Wells, J. (July 2021) Instacart teams with Fabric on automated fulfilment service https://www.grocerydive.com/news/instacart-teams-with-fabric-on-automated-fulfillment-service/603744/

Yang, Z., Tate, J., Morganti, E., and Shepherd, S. (2021) Real-World CO_2 and NOX Emissions from Refrigerated vans, *Science of the Total Environment*, 763, 142974.

12
HEALTHCARE AND URBAN LOGISTICS

Liz Breen, Sarah Schiffling and Ying Xie

Introduction

Access to healthcare is a basic human right and therefore every effort should be made to ensure it is available. Providing services in densely populated urban areas improves coverage in health delivery but also provides greater traction with respect to population health agendas. However, locating healthcare services in urban areas is not without its challenges. This chapter will focus on developments in the health sector with specific consideration of the challenges urban location presents to health logistics and proposes possible solutions.

Health Provision Is a Global Agenda

The importance of healthcare provision is reinforced in the United Nations Sustainable Development Goals (SDGs) (United Nations, 2022a) when delivering to the SDG mission, relating to SDG 3, Good Health and Wellbeing – ensuring healthy lives and promoting wellbeing for all at all ages. Whilst all 17 SDGs promoted by the United Nations are critical to the sustainability and continuity of our societies, several of them directly impact on or are affected by healthcare logistics. These are captured in Figure 12.1.

Sustainable transport as a concept is threaded across several SDGs and targets, especially those related to food security, health, energy, economic growth, infrastructure, cities, and human settlements (United Nations, 2022b). The healthcare supply chain is complex (Bentahar, 2018), as it needs to source, procure, and deliver a wide variety of medical supplies to satisfy patients' needs, including pharmaceutical products, medical equipment, devices, and consumables. In the United Kingdom, the NHS (National Health Service) Supply Chain manages more than 8 million orders per year across 94,000 order points and 17,465 locations (NHS Supply Chain, 2022). Over 28 million lines of goods are sourced and consolidated from over 930 suppliers and delivered to the NHS annually (NHS Supply Chain, 2022).

The healthcare sector is the largest employer in many countries, including England (NHS England, 2022a) and the United States (United States Census Bureau, 2021). It serves the diverse needs of populations and is continuing to face many challenges ranging from the COVID-19 pandemic and growing mental health issues to rapid technological change (Deloitte, 2022). Research focusing on the development of greater resilience in the healthcare

Figure 12.1 Sustainability development goals and healthcare logistics

supply chain is abundant (Breen, 2021; Scala and Lindsay, 2021; Umer et al., 2021; Van Hoek, 2020; Yaroson et al., 2021). To deliver health services to global populations, supply chains have had to adapt and grow, responding to the challenges and opportunities presented.

Responsive Healthcare Logistics

Whilst some healthcare provision is pre-planned, much of it is in response to urgent and often unpredictable events, such as road traffic accidents. Therefore, health logistics systems must be agile to respond to fluctuations in demand from patients. Within any country, the main concentration of health provision is in city locations and access routes should be planned for these. Primary healthcare providers including dentists, pharmacists, and general practitioners, are often the first point of call for patients. In a setting like the community pharmacy, healthcare providers have to manage logistics alongside their service provision to a wide range of patients and many see support with logistics functions as important (Westerling et al., 2010). Secondary care, often called hospital and community care, is involved in both scheduled and emergency care (NHS Providers, 2022). For logistics operations, this creates highly predictable demand whilst other items need to be kept in stock ready to be deployed if the need arises. There has to be access to the supplies necessary for timely and effective care for every patient, whilst valuable hospital space and staff time should not be taken up by managing excess inventory (Neve and Schmidt, 2022). Staff skills (underpinned by dedicated information technologies) are essential in managing inventory and restocking for perishable and lifesaving supplies such as blood (Stanger et al., 2012). Inbound pharmaceutical stock is managed via logistics service providers (LSPs, such as pharmaceutical wholesalers) and direct distribution from manufacturers and suppliers. Tertiary care refers to highly specialised services – neurosurgery or secure forensic mental health services (NHS Providers, 2022). A narrower spectrum of services offered to this sector can simplify logistics, but often tertiary care is provided in co-location with other healthcare services that already necessitate a wide range of items, e.g., acute hospital settings.

As populations age and age-related health concerns increase in cities around the world, healthcare logistics is presented with a changing pattern of distribution locations. In the United Kingdom, the NHS Long Term Plan (2019) focussed on ensuring patient choice and control, empowering patients to become much more involved in their healthcare and services were designed to support this. The move to healthcare closer to home has led to developments in health logistics in the community and has prompted higher levels of responsiveness and community health supply chain resilience. This was evident during the COVID-19 pandemic with the provision of deliveries from community pharmacies to patients' homes via volunteers and other agencies (NHS England, 2021). Home healthcare necessitates a distribution of limited supplies to an increasing number of locations around any city (Taniguchi et al., 2014). Given that many healthcare products must be stored under certain conditions, such as temperature-controlled environments, distribution to locations that are not hospitals or other established healthcare facilities can be challenging.

Challenges Raised by City Locating of Healthcare Services

Urban areas are often the site of significant concentrations of healthcare infrastructure with most large hospitals and specialist services being offered in cities, but they also often contain areas of considerable health deprivation (Ademiluyi and Aluko-Arowolo, 2009; Doan et al., 2014). The logistics of providing healthcare in urban areas is complex. The scale of stock deliveries and other logistical activity can cause subsequent congestion and pollution issues. Solutions that can address and alleviate some of this impact should be considered, e.g., the use of last-mile logistics providers (Allen et al., 2021; Martinez Sykora et al., 2020); the adoption of consolidation centres (Cherrett et al., 2017; Triantafyllou et al., 2014; Savelsbergh and Van Woensel, 2016) or the consolidation of urban flows of goods without consolidation centres (Verlinde et al., 2012). Logistics research has shown that delivery consolidation has many benefits for manufacturers and customers. Within a healthcare setting multiple small deliveries can be consolidated into a reduced number of full loads. This reduces congestion at hospital Receipt and Distribution bays and works with staff operational activity, scheduling delivery times that suit them. It can promote optimal use of stockholding space and support greater hospital responsiveness to patient treatment. Agreements for consolidated services must be advantageous by both manufacturers using this service, e.g., a logistics services provider (LSP) and customers receiving stock. The acceptability of a consolidation service for medicines deliveries for a large teaching hospital in the North-West of England was explored by Breen (2004) who advocated for a greater role of pharmaceutical LSPs in providing consolidation services, something they did not provide at that time. Breen cautioned that the introduction of this service would rely on successful initial implementation and the co-operation of pharmaceutical suppliers (2004, p. 36). Within the United Kingdom, discussions are underway regarding changes in medicines dispensing and associated logistics. The Department of Health and Social Care in 2022 started a consultation on proposed changes to UK legislation that would enable wider use of hub-and-spoke dispensing (the supply of medicines would involve part of the dispensing process taking place at premises – the hub – other than the supplying pharmacy – the spoke) (Fiore, 2022). The benefits of the adoption of the hub-and-spoke model would be order consolidation, more upstream activity at the hub and less impact on the downstream workforce (the spoke) freeing up their time for value-add patient-facing activity.

Urban logistical challenges as outlined above are well known and research and practice continue to address these. A study conducted by Bailey et al. (2015) examined the implementation of innovative logistics solutions such as unattended electronic locker banks to reduce deliveries into Great Ormond St Children's Hospital in London. Other more recent innovative thinking can be seen through medicines deliveries via drones (Oakey et al., 2022; Smith et al., 2022, Chapter 6 of this book). Logistics activities themselves have a significant impact on the health of the residents in urban areas and the creation of innovative solution to reduce the frequency of deliveries into health settings and the reduction of traffic congestion is a constant area of focus (Grote et al., 2021). AI-enhanced medical drone application in healthcare supply chain contributes significantly to the reduction of mortality rates and the reduction of carbon emission (Damoah et al., 2021). Other studies also assert that not enough is done to drive innovation to improve logistical practice in health eco-systems. Velasco et al. (2018) completed a cross-case analysis with seven Colombian healthcare settings, four public hospitals and three private clinics. Their findings demonstrated that poor planning, little recognition from top management and a lack of personnel with specialist skills, undermined the ability to introduce innovative practice to improve logistical activities, particularly in public hospitals.

Digitalisation of Healthcare Supply Chains

Digitalisation can have a disruptive influence on healthcare supply chains, whilst improving their operational efficiency and cost effectiveness through the timely reporting and sharing of information which improves product creation and distribution. Due to the complex nature of urban logistics a truly data-driven approach facilitates prediction, advanced planning/scheduling and informed decision-making leading to better resource deployment and utilisation, and potential cost savings.

Crucial medical supplies, such as gloves, gowns, syringes, and so on, constitute key product groups in healthcare supply chains. A healthcare facility, such as a hospital trust, generally consumes up to 8000–9000 different stock-keeping units of medical supplies (Beaulieu et al., 2018), although a wide variety of medical supplies (with different stock-keeping units) can satisfy the same needs. The choice of medical supplies is heavily influenced by healthcare professionals (e.g., doctors and nurses) who take an autonomous approach to personalised patient-focussed care. This approach is different from other supply chains which focus on product standardisation, supply chain efficiency, and cost savings (Meijboom et al., 2011). This difference can result in a misalignment between clinical and logistics teams operational objectives, with clinical teams prioritising patients' needs (and subsequent costs) whereas the logistics team may aim to achieve process efficiency, cost, standardisation, etc. Such organisational tension may impede the pace and scale of digitalising the healthcare supply chain (Landry et al., 2016). To improve the performance of the healthcare supply chain, Beaulieu and Bentahar (2021) set out a roadmap for digitalisation initiatives in the healthcare supply chain (SC) that could generate significant benefits for this sector. The initiatives include developing demand predictors, making external distribution routes more dynamic, operating schedule more dynamic, internal flow more integrated, and improving the dynamics of inventory policies.

All of these initiatives require concerted effort to: (1) achieve better connection between two clinical and logistics information systems; (2) realise the potential of big data analytics and make data-informed decision-making; (3) upskill digital technology literacy of healthcare professionals and encourage them to take ownership of technology; and (4) foster greater collaboration and information sharing with stakeholders, and ultimately to improve end-end supply chain visibility (Beaulieu and Bentahar, 2021).

The greater use of digital technologies in healthcare supply chains brings multiple benefits to their stakeholders. Advanced technologies such as the Internet of Things (IoT), Cloud Computing and Augmented Reality have been developed to advance logistics planning and control. Cutting-edge technologies, such as blockchain and digital twins, are being implemented to improve the end-to-end supply chain visibility and to drive the capabilities of timely and consistent analysis of factors affecting demand forecasts, procurement, inventory management, and fulfilment. The digitalisation of healthcare supply chains enables the coordination and integration of supply chain activities, which subsequently improves operational efficiency and effectiveness.

Automating Information and Product Access

Poor visibility of a product along a supply chain could result in over-ordering, waste, overconsumption, delay in receiving the product, and possible counterfeiting. Counterfeiting of pharmaceuticals is a serious concern in the healthcare supply chain; it not only costs the industry in financial terms but also puts patients' lives at risk. For example, the World Health Organisation suggests the cost of counterfeiting is over $30 billion per annum (Green, 2018)

Digital technologies can help address counterfeiting by continuously tracking and tracing products along the supply chain. Blockchain technology, as a revolution in visibility, privacy, and security, makes it easy to track the life history of medical supplies, including seller information and when it enters the supply chain. The centralised digital records of medical supplies cannot be altered, making it easier to guarantee quality and authenticity. Blockchain technology shares information on medical supplies across all nodes through standardised documents, but visibility is limited to permitted stakeholders only (Sylim et al., 2018). The effective planning of urban-based logistics into healthcare sites requires the input of many stakeholders and blockchain technologies can effectively support such deliberations whilst also leveraging smart contracts and protecting related intellectual property rights for exclusive drugs (Dutta et al., 2020).

From 2010 onwards, the IoT started being widely applied to enable the digital transformation in different industries. The IoT connects devices and network systems through the internet and shares information from different locations in real time (Song et al., 2017). In the healthcare supply chain, the IoT proved to be a feasible and economical solution in managing healthcare equipment, e.g., it can predict equipment maintenance time and action (Peng et al., 2017). In relation to patient care, the hybrid Cloud and IoT information system has the potential to address the need for a real-time healthcare monitoring of patents, and to take proactive actions to avoid preventable deaths (Hossain and Muhammad, 2016).

Deliveries to city centre healthcare service providers can be via consolidation centres through specialist operations. Due to the scale of such operations, innovative technological solutions are commonplace. Robotics are a well-established feature in manufacturing plants and warehouses which can reduce production, packaging and picking times, and increase accuracy, offering significant economic and administrative advantages (Ramdani et al., 2019). Amazon's heavy investment in robotic automation within its fulfilment centres proved worthwhile during the COVID-19 lockdown period because it successfully maintained robust shipment of crucial medical supplies to hospitals and households when people were asked to stay indoors (Ackerman, 2019).

Data Management in Health Logistics

Big data, in the form of structured and unstructured data, and data analytics have become important tools and techniques to make data-driven supply chain decisions (Govindan et al., 2018). Structured data is highly organised and formatted, consisting of numbers and values, whereas unstructured data has no predefined format, making it more challenging to process and analyse, such as text files, audio, images, and video files. Business intelligence supported by data mining and analytics enables organisations to predict challenges and seize opportunities in the rapidly changing environment (Choi et al., 2017). Big data analytics play very important roles in risk analysis for logistics and supply chain systems, and this stream of work has expanded rapidly in the last decade (Choi et al., 2018).

Since 2015, a growing trend in the application of big data analytics in logistics planning, production planning, and scheduling has been observed (Ban and Rudin, 2018; Toole et al., 2015; Zhong et al., 2016). In response to the COVID-19 pandemic, Nikolopoulos et al. (2020) developed statistical epidemiological machine-learning models to forecast COVID-19 growth rates and excess demand for products and services. Ren et al. (2020) applied big data analytics to directly optimise the e-commerce system with respect to over-reservation and under-reservation risks for logistics capacity. Such technologies can also support decision-making in critical times especially in the healthcare sector (Zhong et al., 2016) and in humanitarian supply chains (Prasad et al., 2018). Big data analytics are required to develop preventative care plans to improve population health, to reduce healthcare cost, and to improve the quality and effectiveness of healthcare systems (Tiwari et al., 2018).

Artificial intelligence has brought new opportunities to the healthcare sector improving processes and enabling real-time responses to changing situations, optimised resource use, prompt, effective medical treatment, and cost savings (Nilashi et al., 2016). Empirical studies demonstrate that big data could also support societal development and environmental sustainability (Song et al., 2017). An empirical study conducted in French hospitals (public and private) showed that big data analytics and artificial intelligence have a significant effect on environmental process integration and green supply chain collaboration (Benzidia et al., 2021).

Supply Chain digitalisation opens many possibilities for healthcare organisations to improve data flow and analytics, connection with stakeholders, asset tracking, and patient care. However, many major challenges still exist when implementing digitalisation. Despite the development of a global strategy on digital health (World Health Organisation, 2021b) influencing the creation of regional and national digital healthcare strategies (Department of Health and Social Care, 2018; Topol Review Health Education England, 2019), there is still much that needs to be done to successfully move this agenda forward. Within the healthcare sector, the fast growth of digital primary care providers poses a major challenge to regulatory and policymakers, who need to respond to the developments to ensure high quality of care standards are met. Upscaling the use of information technology requires training as well as a good centrally executed plan across the healthcare sector, but there is limited evidence about the digital literacy of the NHS staff and the impact of digitalisation on their working lives. A further challenge is the issue of digital inclusion, i.e., the efforts to build access and capability among individuals and communities to ensure that everyone can benefit from health technologies.

Vaccine Logistics

Vaccines are crucial public health initiatives that target over 20 life-threatening diseases and prevent between two and three million deaths annually from diseases including measles, tetanus, and influenza (WHO, 2021a). Due to their ability to extend lives and improve quality of life, vaccination campaigns are some of the most cost-effective public health interventions (Taychakhoonavudh, 2020). The COVID-19 pandemic highlighted the importance of vaccination, but also highlighted existing inequalities between nations, and severe problems with logistics, especially beyond rich nations (Burki, 2021). Inequity in the access to vaccines is not solely down to logistics, but logistics is a significant contributor to it, which makes vaccines an important topic in healthcare logistics.

Vaccine supply chains have seen significant investment even prior to the COVID-19 pandemic (Rao et al., 2017), but many issues remain in bringing vaccines from manufacturers to patients. Duijzer et al. (2018) highlight the four areas of key decisions in improving vaccine logistics as selecting the right product to be used, setting an appropriate production schedule, prioritising those to be vaccinated, and reaching all potential recipients. All four tie into fundamental decision-making and operationalisation concerns in the logistics of vaccination campaigns as they affect the choice of the right product, as well as the right time and the right place to provide it. Identifying urban centres for vaccine delivery was a key contributor to the COVID-19 vaccine logistics success around the world.

Both demand uncertainty and a changeable supply impact how well vaccine logistics can be planned (Begen et al., 2016). Different vaccines have different criteria for their optimal storage and transport conditions that affect distribution, especially in low- and middle-income countries where infrastructure such as reliable cold storage may be a concern (Kristensen et al., 2016). Given the strict conditions necessary for the transport of vaccine, storage, and usage, vaccine waste is high, sometimes as much as 50% of the total volume (World Health Organisation, 2005). This amount of wastage results in a loss of money, but also in a loss of potentially lifesaving products. It is therefore desirable to minimise waste in this supply chain (Schiffling and Breen, 2021).

Whilst supplies are the obvious limiting factor for allocation, the logistics of reaching people also play a major role (Breen and Schiffling, 2020). Current vaccination strategies have in the main followed a set precedent focusing on people by age group, underlying health conditions, or occupation (Joint Commission on Vaccination and Immunisation, 2021). However, it can be prudent to consider the accessibility of certain populations, particularly when faced with the short shelf life and perishability of vaccines.

Within urban areas established distribution networks eased the passage of vaccines directly from manufacturers to the point of use, therefore eliminating any need for cross-docking and breaking up shipments (DHL, 2021). This is possible as long as each point of use has suitable storage facilities sufficient for an entire shipment, which is often the case for hospitals or other large healthcare centres in urban areas. Within the UK, this was the preferred mode of distribution for the early Pfizer/BioNTech vaccine rollout. However, to ensure a broad coverage, many smaller points were also utilised. In these cases, cities can set up a central hub for vaccine distribution that meets all the criteria for safe storage. In the United Kingdom, large teaching hospitals with the necessary logistical infrastructure and staff resources were the first hubs for COVID-19 vaccine delivery. Additional experience in delivery then facilitated the logistics moving closer to the patient, the government advocating that all patients should live within a ten-mile radius of a vaccination centre (Department of Health and Social Care, 2021). During the COVID-19 vaccine rollout, countries including Rwanda utilised central storage and distribution hubs to cater to all shipments arriving in the country before onward distribution (Andersen and Agnew, 2021).

Vaccine logistics will always have to be integrated with logistics for other essential products such as syringes or gloves. If these supply chains are misaligned, vaccines cannot be given to patients (Beaumont, 2021). Where there are challenges with assuring the continuity of all these supplies simultaneously, kits of items may be shipped together, thus cutting down on complexity (Kovács and Falagara Sigala, 2021) leading potentially to reduced but fuller delivery loads and the reduction in pollution and congestion and social disturbance in built-up urban areas.

While the infrastructure for vaccine logistics is often better in urban areas and it can be easier to serve sufficient patients to avoid wasting vaccines, it can be challenging to reach all relevant populations, particularly where certain groups are facing disadvantages and exclusion. Taychakhoonavudh (2020) highlights the importance of addressing the 3Cs – confidence, complacency, and convenience to manage the demand side of vaccine distribution. Successful urban vaccine logistics requires a consistent message and two-way communication to really understand the reasons behind any hesitancy (Goldstein et al., 2015). Confidence can be fostered by ensuring that vaccines are transported and stored appropriately, and wastage is avoided wherever possible (Schiffling and Breen, 2021). Convenience of location plays a pivotal role in people choosing to be vaccinated or not and influences the distribution network design. Meeting people where they are as part of their normal routines is the most desirable option (Arifin and Anas, 2021). However, this needs to be balanced with the feasibility of setting up a distribution system in such a way that it can operate efficiently.

Humanitarian Logistics in Urban Spaces

As the number of people affected by both natural and human-induced disasters around the world grows, the need for relief is growing as well and with it the demand for humanitarian logistics. Humanitarian logistics is a system concerned with "*planning, implementing and controlling the effective, cost-efficient flow and storage of goods and materials as well as related information, from the point of origin to the point of consumption for the purpose of meeting the end beneficiary's requirements*" (Thomas and Mizushima, 2005, p. 60). Humanitarian operations are complex, involve many different players, and have a significant financial value. Supply chain and logistics activities are approximated to account for as much as 60–80% of the total cost of humanitarian operations (Blecken, 2010; Van Wassenhove, 2006). Therefore, efficient and effective humanitarian logistics is vital from an economic standpoint, in addition to the moral imperative that is underlying humanitarian operations.

Humanitarian logistics is a growing concern in urban logistics (Taniguchi and Thompson, 2014). Urban centres are frequently affected by disasters and can have a devastating effect on healthcare provision and logistics infrastructure, for example when earthquakes destroy roads, bridges, and hospitals (Garrido et al., 2021). It is predicted that urban disasters will need more frequent responses in the future as urbanisation continues and vulnerabilities grow (Earle, 2017). With the population density of cities, the number of people affected is substantial and healthcare provision is urgently needed, making healthcare logistics one of the key focus areas of humanitarian relief. Logistics activities may include the relocation of healthcare facilities to match the needs of the affected population and the destruction brought by the disaster (Garrido et al., 2021).

Disasters and relief effort can themselves contribute to urbanisation when responses are focussed on urban areas, giving those in rural locations fewer opportunities for recovery and thus attracting them to cities (Wood and Frazier, 2019). Refugees and internally displaced people often flock to cities for support and international aid efforts often focus on urban areas that are more easily accessible. Apart from the evident needs of greater populations, this can also be attributed to simplified logistics, particularly where time-sensitive products in the healthcare supply chain are concerned. Whilst a more decentralised humanitarian aid delivery is therefore desirable, the current model still often focuses on urban areas (Wood and Frazier, 2019). Apart from the evident needs of greater populations, this can also be attributed to simplified logistics, particularly where time-sensitive products in the healthcare supply chain are concerned.

Driving the Sustainability Agenda

COVID-19 has highlighted the need for pharmaceutical supply chains to be resilient and flexible. Building them to be agile and adaptive mitigates risk from sudden changes in supply and demand. Simultaneously, other critical agendas such as designing and delivering responsible supply chains which reduce harm to our society have to be met. In striving towards a net zero future, the application of action (aligned with our SDGs) must be just, inclusive, and equitable. The Triple Bottom Line of Sustainability (Cioruta et al., 2018) advocates that operations should aim to be increasingly conscious of their responsibility and contribution to environmental, social, and economic sustainability. Developments in logistics within the healthcare sector are being pursued to respond to this. One such agenda is the global focus on climate change and the reduction of energy-related global greenhouse gas emissions and the role of transportation.

The UK's NHS's contribution to this is via the Greener NHS initiative. In October 2020 the NHS became the world's first health service to commit to reaching carbon net zero based on well-evidenced threats posed by climate change. Working with its personnel, suppliers, and partners, within one year the NHS has reported emissions reduction equivalent to powering 1.1. million homes annually (NHS England, 2022b). Carbon footprint assessment is ongoing within healthcare systems (Malik et al., 2018; Tennison et al., 2021; Wu, 2019;) to better appreciate the cause and scale of greenhouse gas (GHG) emissions. The pharmaceutical supply chain makes a notable contribution to healthcare systems' carbon footprints, with hospitals, pharmaceuticals, and transport reported as having a significant percentage of GHG emissions (Booth, 2022). Given the potential impact of urban logistics on our carbon footprint urgent steps to address this are needed.

Pharmaceutical products for patient care have to be available in the right quantity at the right time. In 2019, around $1.25 trillion USD had been spent on medicines globally, up from only $887 billion in 2010 and the spending on medicines is anticipated to increase to $1.59 billion by 2024 (Statista, 2020). Healthcare providers need to reduce their pharmaceutical spend through efforts such as effective waste management and associated costs and improving service quality (Altug and Sahin, 2019; Breen and Xie, 2015; Papalexi et al., 2020). Supply chain management and related variables are noted to be principal contributors to the generation of pharmaceutical waste. Inadequate storage conditions, the absence of specific stocking plans, and poor inventory management systems/practices can lead to significant medication spoilage and higher waste levels (Gebremariam et al., 2019).

The adoption of Circular Economy (CE) principles in healthcare logistics also aim to optimally utilise medicines in health settings. Kirchherr et al. (2017) asserted that the CE is the combination of reduce, reuse and recycle activities that we engage in to ensure systematic change. The application of the 9Rs of Circular Economy can be factored into 'Green Design' where the potential reuse, recycling or repurposing of whole products or components is possible. The 9R model is the optimal application of CE incorporating Refuse, Rethink, Reduce, Reuse, Repair, Refurbish, Remanufacture, Repurpose, Recycle, and Recover (Manavalan and Jayakrishna, 2019).

Whilst there has been a targeted focus on medicine reuse within its lifecycle, less consideration has been given to the use of integral components. Circular Economy practices advocate that a product, and its parts, can be repurposed. Research has indicated that the active pharmaceutical ingredients in medicines can be safely extracted from their host product and recycled for the same medicine or another product or stored for future use (Alshemari et al., 2020). Reverse logistics, the return of products to source for repair, reuse, resale and safe waste disposal has risen in popularity in recent years, heavily encouraged by the increase in online sales (and more recently the intensive online activity during the COVID-19 pandemic) and the disposal of COVID-19 healthcare waste (WHO, 2022). Whilst legislation is in place to legally reinforce the return and safe disposal of some products, e.g., white goods and batteries, no such legislation exists for the return of medication/pharmaceuticals (Xie and Breen, 2014). Product stewardship, whilst honourable in intent, is not active with respect to these products so the return and safe disposal of medicines is based on the social/ecoconsciousness of consumers/patients (de Brito et al., 2004).

Talent Management in Healthcare Logistics

In recent years, the increasing professionalisation of the logistics activities underpinning healthcare operations has been evident as providers strive to meet growing and changing demands in the most efficient ways possible, monitoring and optimising the flow of information, patients, and goods (Ageron et al., 2018). It is a well-recognised phenomenon that globally healthcare resources are stretched and this challenges the provision of healthcare services. Largescale shortages of staffing were caused by the COVID-19 pandemic, and temporary solutions were sought to address this (Okpala, 2021; Rasmussen et al., 2020). However, other persistent factors have led to the escalation of existing staffing issues in health services: changes in staffing requirements, reimbursement of services, aging staff, professional training and career route planning, and working conditions (Winter et al., 2020), climate change (Pendrey et al., 2021) and the demanding nature of the role, level of responsibility, career risk, remuneration and isolation within roles (Cabral et al., 2019). The situation is such that we now find that the sustainability of service provision is threatened if we do not address the issue of staffing shortages and the factors which influence the introduction of new talent into health supply chains. Given the rising importance of logistics within our health services, there are growing concerns as to shortages of staff and a skilled workforce to carry out these roles. This issue rose in significance when exacerbated by the COVID-19 pandemic and the lack of pharmaceutical manufacturer processing staff and drivers (Fiore and Lewis, 2021).

The concept of talent management, whilst well established in the private sector is in its infancy in public sector management (Kravariti and Johnston, 2020). Talent Management has been defined as the process of attraction, development, and retention of employees in order to improve capabilities, skills, and knowledge (Mitosis et al., 2021). Kravariti and Johnson (2020, p. 81) drawing on research in this field define public sector talent management as:

> The implementation of key procedures to ensure public sector employees possess the competencies, knowledge and core values in order to address complex contemporary challenges and fulfil public sector strategic objectives for the common good.

Within healthcare sectors, service provision is heavily reliant on the balance of human and technical resources. Staff are a key input and therefore attracting staff into key roles to ensure business continuity is of critical importance.

With an increased focus on improving resource utilisation, enhancing skills in logistics within the healthcare sector is paramount (Zhang et al., 2018). Moving towards a simpler, modular approach of providing healthcare logistics can improve processes and increases possibilities to consider external logistics service providers (Pohjosenperä et al., 2019). The use of specialised logistics providers is common in the healthcare sector (Ageron et al., 2018). However, due to the sensitive nature of this particular industry and the potentially significant impact on patient safety and continuity of service, thorough risk management is essential when choosing logistics providers and designing logistical pathways (Mokrini and Aouam, 2020).

Designing Resilient Healthcare Supply Chains for the Future

As demonstrated in the discussion above, health supply chains are critical for society to maintain healthy lives, living longer and living better. A large proportion of healthcare is delivered in cities, where logistics can be more complicated and patient treatment impeded if deliveries cannot be made in a timely fashion. The COVID-19 pandemic has shown the world that healthcare supply chains can adapt, can be innovative, and can quickly respond to major challenges. There is great potential in using emerging technologies to further enhance healthcare logistics systems to enable them to better meet future challenges in the face of increasing cost and staffing pressures. Driving innovation in product design, and logistical practice is key to health systems, and this should be underpinned by research, education and investment in the logistics profession. Removal of inefficiencies and weak practice should be a priority coupled with raising aspirations for innovation in practice within the pharmaceutical supply chain (Papalexi et al., 2021) plus technological and educational developments. Well-planned and designed logistics systems facilitate the timely delivery of inputs into urban healthcare settings, be it medicines, surgical items, food, or stationery. If key inputs are missing, then services cannot be offered, patients' health can be adversely affected, and business continuity jeopardised.

References

Ackerman, E. (2019). Amazon uses 800 robots to run this warehouse. https://spectrum.ieee.org/automaton/robotics/industrial-robots/amazon-introduces-two-new-warehouse-robots Accessed 16th February 2022.

Ademiluyi, I. A., and Aluko-Arowolo, S. O. (2009). Infrastructural distribution of healthcare services in Nigeria: An overview. *Journal of Geography and Regional Planning*, 2(5), 104–110.

Ageron, B., Benzidia, S., and Bourlakis, M. (2018). Healthcare logistics and supply chain–issues and future challenges. *Supply Chain Forum: An International Journal,* 19(1), 1–3.

Allen, J., Piecyk, M., Cherrett, T., Mcleod, F., Oakey, A., Piotrowska, M., Bates, O., Bektas, T., Wise, S., Cheliotis, K., and Friday, A. (2021). Combining on-foot porters with vans for last-mile parcel deliveries: Results of a study in central London. *World Review of Intermodal Transportation Research*, 10(1), 65–85.

Alshemari, A., Breen, L., Quinn, G., and Sivarajah, U. (2020). Can we create a Circular Pharmaceutical Supply Chain (CPSC) to reduce medicines waste? *Pharmacy*, 8(4), 221.

Altug, M.S. and Sahin, O. (2019). Impact of parallel imports on pricing and product launch decisions in pharmaceutical industry. *Production and Operations Management*, 28(2), 258–275.

Andersen, H. and Agnew, A. (2021). Vaccinating Africa: What governments can learn from Rwanda's effective rollout. Institute for Global Change. https://institute.global/sites/default/files/articles/Vaccinating-Africa-What-Governments-Can-Learn-From-Rwanda-s-Effective-Rollout.pdf Accessed 12th March 2022.

Arifin, B. and Anas, T. (2021). Lessons learned from COVID-19 vaccination in Indonesia: Experiences, challenges, and opportunities. *Human Vaccines and Immunotherapeutics*, 1–9. https://www.ncbi.nlm.nih.gov/pmc/articles/PMC8828161/

Bailey, G., Cherrett, T., Waterson, B., Breen, L., and Long, R. (2015). Boxed up and locked up, safe and tight! Making the case for unattended electronic locker bank logistics for an innovative logistics solution for NHS hospital supplies (UK). *International Journal of Procurement Management*, 8(1/2), 104–125.

Ban, G. Y. and Rudin, C. (2018). The big data newsvendor: Practical insights from machine learning. *Operations Research*, 67(1), 90–108.

Beaumont, P. (2021) How are the Covid vaccines produced and why have there been delays? *The Guardian*. https://www.theguardian.com/society/2021/mar/19/how-are-covid-vaccines-produced-and-why-have-there-been-delays

Beaulieu, M. and Bentahar O. (2021). Digitalisation of the healthcare supply chain: A roadmap to generate benefits and effectively support healthcare delivery. *Technological Forecasting and Social Change*, 167, 120717.

Beaulieu, M., Roy, J., and Landry, S. (2018). Logistics outsourcing in the healthcare sector: Lessons from a Canadian experience. *Canadian Journal of Administrative Sciences/Revue Canadienne des Sciences de l'Administration*, 35(4), 635–648.

Begen, M. A., Pun, H., and Yan, X. (2016). Supply and demand uncertainty reduction efforts and cost comparison. *International Journal of Production Economics*, 180, 125–134.

Bentahar, O. (2018). Key success factors for implementing purchasing groups in the healthcare sector. *Supply Chain Forum: An International Journal*, 19(1), 90–100.

Benzidia, S., Makaoui, N., and Bentahar, O. (2021). The impact of big data analytics and artificial intelligence on green supply chain process integration and hospital environmental performance. *Technological Forecasting and Social Change*, 165, 120557.

Blecken, A. (2010). Supply chain process modelling for humanitarian organisations. *International Journal of Physical Distribution and Logistics Management*, 40(8–9), 675–692.

Booth, A. (2022). Carbon footprint modelling of national health systems: Opportunities, challenges and recommendations. *International Journal of Health Planning and Management,* 37(4), 1885–1893.

Breen, L. (2004) Is there a place for third party logistics providers in the NHS pharmaceutical supply chain in hospital pharmacy? – the case of Central Manchester and Manchester Children's University Hospitals NHS Trust (CMMC). *Hospital Pharmacist*, 11, 33–36.

Breen, L. (2021). Learning from COVID: How to improve future supplies of medical equipment and vaccines. *The Conversation*. https://theconversation.com/learning-from-covid-how-to-improve-future-supplies-of-medical-equipment-and-vaccines-161054 Accessed 18th March 2022.

Breen, L. and Schiffling, S. (2020). Vaccines are here, but how will we get them to billions of people? *The Conversation*. https://theconversation.com/vaccines-are-here-but-how-will-we-get-them-to-billions-of-people-151132 Accessed 12th March 2022.

Breen, L. and Xie, Y. (2015). Waste not, want not. What are the drivers of sustainable medicines recycling in national health service hospital pharmacies (UK)? *International Journal of Procurement Management*, 8(1/2), 82–103.

Burki, T. (2021). Global COVID-19 vaccine inequity. *The Lancet Infectious Diseases*, 21(7), 922–923.

Cabral, A., Oram, C., and Allum, S. (2019). Developing nursing leadership talent—Views from the NHS nursing leadership for south-east England. *Journal of Nursing Management*, 27, 75–83.

Cherrett, T., Dickinson, J., McLeod, F., Sit, J., Bailey, G., and Whittle, G. (2017). Logistics impacts of student online shopping – Evaluating delivery consolidation to halls of residence. *Transportation Research Part C: Emerging Technologies*, 78, 111–128.

Choi, T. M., Chan H. K., and Yue X. H. (2017). Advances in forecasting-mediated operations management in big data era preface. *Asia-Pacific Journal of Operational Research*, 34(1), 1702001.

Choi, T. M., Wallace, S. W., and Wang, Y. (2018). Big data analytics in operations management. *Production and Operations Management*, 27(10), 1868–1883.

Cioruta, B., Coman, M., and Lauran, A. (2018). From Human-Environment Interaction to Environmental Informatics (II): The Sustainability evolution as requirement of Knowledge-based Society. *Hidraulica*, 2, 33–40.

Damoah, I. S., Ayakwah, A., and Tingbani, I. (2021). Artificial intelligence (AI)-enhanced medical drones in the healthcare supply chain (HSC) for sustainability development: A case study. *Journal of Cleaner Production*, 328, 129598, ISSN 0959-6526.

De Brito, M. P. and Dekker, R. (2004). A framework for reverse logistics, in Dekker, R., Fleischmann, M., Inderfurth, K. and van Wassenhove, L.N. (Ed.), *Reverse logistics, quantitative models for closed-loop supply chains*, Springer, Berlin, 3–28.

Deloitte (2022). 2022 Global health care outlook. https://www2.deloitte.com/global/en/pages/life-sciences-and-healthcare/articles/global-health-care-sector-outlook.html Accessed 13th March 2022.

Department of Health and Social Care (2018). The future of healthcare: Our vision for digital, data and technology in health and care. https://www.gov.uk/government/publications/the-future-of-healthcare-our-vision-for-digital-data-and-technology-in-health-and-care/the-future-of-healthcare-our-vision-for-digital-data-and-technology-in-health-and-care Accessed 5th March 2022.

Department of Health and Social Care (2021). UK COVID-19 vaccines delivery plan. https://www.gov.uk/government/publications/uk-covid-19-vaccines-delivery-plan/uk-covid-19-vaccines-delivery-plan Accessed 27th March 2022.

DHL (2021). Revisiting pandemic resilience. White paper. https://www.dhl.com/content/dam/dhl/global/csi/documents/pdf/Revisiting-Pandemic-Resilience-White-Paper-(English).pdf Accessed 12th March 2022.

Doan, T., Gibson, J., and Holmes, M. (2014). Impact of household credit on education and healthcare spending by the poor in peri-urban areas, Vietnam. *Journal of Southeast Asian Economies*, 31(1), 87–103.

Duijzer, L. E., van Jaarsveld, W., and Dekker, R. (2018). Literature review: The vaccine supply chain. *European Journal of Operational Research*, 268(1), 174–192.

Dutta, P., Choi, T. M., Somani, S., and Butala, R. (2020). Blockchain technology in supply chain operations: Applications, challenges and research opportunities. *Transportation Research Part E: Logistics and Transportation Review*, 142, 102067.

Earle, L. (2017). Addressing urban crises: Bridging the humanitarian–development divide. *International Review of the Red Cross*, 98(901), 1–10.

Fiore, V. (2022) Hub and spoke: NPA says DH's £4k set-up cost per pharmacy is 'very low estimate'. Chemist and Druggist. https://www.chemistanddruggist.co.uk/CD135988/Hub-and-spoke-NPA-says-DHs-4k-set-up-cost-per-pharmacy-is-very-low-estimate?utm_medium=email&utm_source=sfmc&utm_campaign=2022_03_21_CDDaily&utm_id=4273810&sfmc_id=88991113 Accessed 27th March 2022.

Fiore, V. and Lewis, G. (2021). Phoenix pauses OTC orders and trident delays deliveries due to staff shortages. Chemist and Druggist. https://www.chemistanddruggist.co.uk/CD135491/Phoenix-pauses-OTC-orders-and-Trident-delays-deliveries-due-to-staff-shortages Accessed 19th March 2022.

Garrido, A., Pongutá, F., and Buitrago, O. Y. (2022). Relocation of public healthcare network of a large city in the event of a major earthquake: A combined methodological analysis. *Journal of Humanitarian Logistics and Supply Chain Management*, 12(2), 220–248.

Gebremariam, E. T., Gebregeorgise, D. T., and Fenta, T. G. (2019). Factors contributing to medicines wastage in public health facilities of South West Shoa Zone, Oromia Regional State, Ethiopia: A qualitative study. *Journal of Pharmaceutical Policy and Practice*, 12, 1–7.

Goldstein, S., MacDonald, N. E., and Guirguis, S. (2015). Health communication and vaccine hesitancy. *Vaccine*, 33(34), 4212–4214.

Govindan, K., Cheng, T. C. E., Mishra, N., and Shukla, N. (2018). Big data analytics and application for logistics and supply chain management. *Transportation Research Part E: Logistics and Transportation Review*, 114, 343–349.

Green, C. (2018). Blockchain to cut fraud in healthcare supply chains. https://charitydigital.org.uk/topics/topics/blockchain-to-cut-fraud-in-healthcare-supply-chains-5072 Accessed 17th February 2022.

Grote, M., Cherrett, T., Whittle, G., and Tuck, N. (2023). Environmental benefits from shared-fleet logistics: Lessons from a public-private sector collaboration. *International Journal of Logistics Research and Applications*, 26(2), 128–154.

Health Education England (2019). The topol review. Preparing the healthcare workforce to deliver the digital future. https://topol.hee.nhs.uk/ Accessed 3rd March 2022.

Hossain, M. S. and Muhammad, G. (2016). Cloud-assisted industrial internet of things (iiot)–enabled framework for health monitoring. *Computer Networks*, 101, 192–202.

Joint Commission on Vaccination and Immunisation (2021). Advice on priority groups for COVID-19 vaccination. https://www.gov.uk/government/publications/priority-groups-for-coronavirus-covid-19-vaccination-advice-from-the-jcvi-30-december-2020/joint-committee-on-vaccination-and-immunisation-advice-on-priority-groups-for-covid-19-vaccination-30-december-2020 Accessed 16th March 2022.

Kirchherr, J., Reike, D., and Hekkert, M. (2017). Conceptualizing the circular economy: An analysis of 114 definitions. *Resources, Conservation and Recycling*, 127, 221–232.

Kovács, G. and Falagara Sigala, I. (2021). Lessons learned from humanitarian logistics to manage supply chain disruptions. *Journal of Supply Chain Management*, 57(1), 41–49.

Kravariti, F. and Johnston, K. (2020). Talent management: A critical literature review and research agenda for public sector human resource management. *Public Management Review*, 22(1), 75–95.

Kristensen, D. D., Lorenson, T., Bartholomew, K., and Villadiego, S. (2016). Can thermostable vaccines help address cold-chain challenges? Results from stakeholder interviews in six low-and middle-income countries. *Vaccine*, 34(7), 899–904.

Landry, S., Beaulieu, M., and Roy J. (2016). Strategy deployment in healthcare services: A case study. *Technological Forecasting and Social Change*, 113 (Part B), 429–437.

Malik, A., Lenzen, M., McAlister, S., and McGain, F. (2018). The carbon footprint of Australian health care. *The Lancet Planetary Health*, 2(2), 27–35.

Manavalan, E. and Jayakrishna, K. (2019). An analysis on sustainable supply chain for circular economy. *Procedia Manufacturing*, 33, 477–484.

Martinez Sykora, A., Mcleod, F., Lamas Fernandez, C., Bektas, T., Cherrett, T., and Allen, J. (2020). Optimised solutions to the last-mile delivery problem in London using a combination of walking and driving. *Annals of Operations Research*, 295(2), 645–693.

Meijboom, B., Schmidt-Bakx, S., and Westert, G. (2011). Supply chain management practices for improving patient-oriented care. *Supply Chain Management: An International Journal*, 16, 166–175.

Mitosis, K. D., Lamnisos, D., and Talias, M. A. (2021) Talent management in healthcare: A systematic qualitative review. *Sustainability*, 13, 4469. https://doi.org/10.3390/su13084469

Mokrini, A. E. and Aouam, T. (2020). A fuzzy multi-criteria decision analysis approach for risk evaluation in healthcare logistics outsourcing: Case of Morocco. *Health Services Management Research*, 33(3), 143–155.

Neve, B. V., and Schmidt, C. P. (2022). Point-of-use hospital inventory management with inaccurate usage capture. *Health Care Management Science*, 25(1), 126–145.

NHS (UK) 2019 The NHS Long Term Plan. https://www.longtermplan.nhs.uk/publication/nhs-long-term-plan/ Accessed 18th March 2022.

NHS England (2021) Home delivery of medicines and appliances during the COVID-19 outbreak: service specifications and guidance. https://www.england.nhs.uk/coronavirus/wp-content/uploads/sites/52/2020/03/C1198_Home-delivery-during-the-COVID19-outbreak-Service-Spec-and-guidanceV7.pdf Access 18th March 2022.

NHS England (2022a). Working for us. https://www.england.nhs.uk/about/working-for/ Accessed 16th March 2022.

NHS England (2022b) Greener NHS. Available at: https://www.england.nhs.uk/greenernhs/. Accessed 12th March 2022.

NHS Providers (2022). The NHS Provider sector. https://nhsproviders.org/topics/delivery-and-performance/the-nhs-provider-sector Accessed 16th March 2022.

NHS Supply Chain (2022). About NHS supply chain. https://www.supplychain.nhs.uk/about-us/. Accessed 16th February 2022.

Nikolopoulos, K., Punia, S., Schäfers, A., Tsinopoulos, C., and Vasilakis, C. (2020). Forecasting and planning during a pandemic: COVID-19 growth rates, supply chain disruptions, and governmental decisions. *European Journal of Operational Research*, 290(1), 99–115.

Nilashi M., Ahmadi, H., Ahani, A., Ravangard, R., and bin Ibrahim, O. (2016). Determining the importance of hospital information system adoption factors using fuzzy analytic network process (ANP). *Technological Forecasting and Social Change*, 111, 244–264.

Oakey, A., Grote, M., Royall, P. G., and Cherrett, T. (2022). Enabling safe and sustainable medical deliveries by connected autonomous freight vehicles operating within dangerous goods regulations. *Sustainability*, 14(2), 930.

Okpala, P. (2022). Using technology to ameliorate the effects of healthcare staff shortages during pandemics. *International Journal of Healthcare Management*, 15(3), 261–266.

Papalexi, M., Bamford, D., and Breen, L. (2020). Key sources of operational inefficiency in the pharmaceutical supply chain. *Supply Chain Management: An International Journal*, 25(6), 617–635.

Papalexi, M., Bamford, D., Nikitas, A., Breen, L., and Tipi, N. (2021). Pharmaceutical supply chains and management innovation? *Supply Chain Management: An International Journal*, 27(4), 485–508.

Pendrey, C. G., Quilty, S., Gruen, R. L., Weeramanthri, T., and Lucas, R. M. (2021). Is climate change exacerbating health-care workforce shortages for underserved populations? *The Lancet Planetary Health*, 5(4), e183–e184.

Peng, S., Su, G., Chen, J., and Du, P. (2017). Design of an IoT-BIM-GIS based risk management system for hospital basic operation, Service-oriented system engineering. *2017 IEEE symposium*, IEEE (2017), 69–74.

Pohjosenperä, T., Kekkonen, P., Pekkarinen, S., and Juga, J. (2019). Service modularity in managing healthcare logistics. *The International Journal of Logistics Management*, 30(1), 174–194.

Prasad, S., Zakaria, R., and Altay, N. (2018). Big data in humanitarian supply chain networks: A resource dependence perspective. *Annals of Operations Research*, 270(1), 383–413.

Ramdani, N., Panayides, A., Karamousadakis, M., Mellado, M., Lopez, R., Christophorou, C., Rebiai, M., Blouin, M., Vellidou, E., and Koutsouris, D. (2019). A safe, efficient and integrated indoor robotic fleet for logistic applications in healthcare and commercial spaces: The endorse concept. In *2019 20th IEEE International Conference on Mobile Data Management*, 425–430.

Rao, R., Schreiber, B., and Lee, B. Y. (2017). Immunization supply chains: Why they matter and how they are changing. *Vaccine*, 35(17), 2103–2104.

Rasmussen, S., Sperling, P., Såby Poulsen, M., Emmersen, J., and Andersenet, S. (2020). Medical students for health-care staff shortages during the COVID-19 pandemic. *The Lancet*, 395(10234), e79–e80.

Ren, S., Choi, T. M. Lee, K. M., and Lin, L. (2020). Intelligent service capacity allocation for cross-border-e-commerce related third-party-forwarding logistics operations: A deep learning approach. *Transportation Research Part E: Logistics and Transportation Review*, 134, 101834.

Savelsbergh, M. and Van Woensel, T. (2016) 50th anniversary invited article – City logistics: Challenges and opportunities. *Transportation Science*, 50(2), 579–559.

Scala, B. and Lindsay, C. F. (2021), Supply chain resilience during pandemic disruption: Evidence from healthcare. *Supply Chain Management*, 26(6), 672–688.

Schiffling, S. and Breen, L. (2021). COVID vaccine: Some waste is normal – but here's how it is being kept to a minimum. The Conversation. https://theconversation.com/covid-vaccine-some-waste-is-normal-but-heres-how-it-is-being-kept-to-a-minimum-152772 Accessed 12th March 2022.

Smith, A., Dickinson, J., Marsden, G., Cherrett, T., Oakey, A., and Grote, M. (2022). Public acceptance of the use of drones for logistics: The state of play and moving towards more informed debate. *Technology in Society*, 68, 101883.

Song, T., Li, R., Mei, B., Yu, J., Xing, X., and Cheng, X. (2017). A privacy preserving communication protocol for IoT applications in smart homes. *IEEE Internet of Things Journal*, 4(6), 1844–1852.

Stanger, S. H., Yates, N., Wilding, R., and Cotton, S. (2012). Blood inventory management: Hospital best practice. *Transfusion Medicine Reviews*, 26(2), 153–163.

Statista (2020) Global spending on medicines 2024 forecast. https://www.statista.com/statistics/280572/medicine-spending-worldwide/ Accessed 18th March 2022.

Sylim. P., Liu, F., Marcelo, A., and Fontelo, P. (2018). Blockchain technology for detecting falsified and substandard drugs in distribution: Pharmaceutical supply chain intervention. *Journal of Medical Internet Research*, 7 (9), e10163.

Taniguchi, E. and Thompson, R. G. (2014). *City logistics: Mapping the future*. CRC Press, Boca Raton.

Taniguchi, E., Thompson, R. G., and Yamada, T. (2014). Recent trends and innovations in modelling city logistics. *Procedia-Social and Behavioral Sciences*, 125, 4–14.

Taychakhoonavudh, S. (2020). Access to vaccines and immunisation programme in global pharmaceutical policy, book chapter. Edited by Babar, Z. Palgrave Macmillan, Singapore.

Tennison, I., Roschnik, S., Ashby, B., Boyd, R., Hamilton, I., and Oreszcyn, T. (2021). Health care's response to climate change: A carbon footprint assessment of the NHS in England. *The Lancet Planetary Health*, 5(2), 84–92.

Thomas, A. and Mizushima, M. (2005). Logistics training: Necessity or luxury? *Forced Migration Review*, 22, 60–61.

Tiwari, S., Wee, H. M., and Daryanto, Y. (2018). Big data analytics in supply chain management between 2010 and 2016: Insights to industries. *Computers and Industrial Engineering*, 115, 319–330.

Toole, J. L., Colak, S., Sturt, B., Alexander, L. P., Evsukoff, A., and González, M. C. (2015). The path most travelled: Travel demand estimation using big data resources. *Transportation Research Part C: Emerging Technologies*, 58, 162–177.

Triantafyllou, M. K., Cherrett, T. J., and Browne, M. (2014). Urban freight consolidation centers: Case study in the UK retail sector. *Transportation Research Record*, 2411(1), 34–44.

Umer, H. M., Iqbal, H. J., Webb, M., and Harrison, W. J. (2021). Applying changes made during the COVID-19 pandemic to the future: Trauma and orthopaedics. *British Journal of Healthcare Management*, 27(4), 1–7.

United Nations (2022a) The 17 Goals. Available at: https://sdgs.un.org/goals Accessed 12th March 2022.

United Nations (2022b) Sustainable transport. https://sdgs.un.org/topics/sustainable-transport Accessed 12th March 2022.

United States Census Bureau (2021). County business patterns 2019. https://www.census.gov/newsroom/press-releases/2021/county-business-patterns.html Accessed 16th March 2022.

Van Hoek, R. (2020). Research opportunities for a more resilient post-COVID-19 supply chain – closing the gap between research findings and industry practice. *International Journal of Operations and Production Management*, 40(4), 341–355.

Van Wassenhove, L. N. (2006). Blackett Memorial Lecture Humanitarian aid logistics: Supply chain management in high gear. *Journal of the Operational Research Society*, 57(5), 475–489.

Velasco, N., Moreno, J. P., and Rebolledo, C. (2018). Logistics practices in healthcare organizations in Bogota. *Academia Revista Latinoamericana de Administración*, 31(3), 519–533.

Verlinde, S., Macharis, C., and Witlox, F. (2012) How to consolidate urban flows of goods without setting up an urban consolidation centre? *Procedia Social and Behavioral Science*, 39, 687–701.

Westerling, A. M., Haikala, V. E., Bell, J. S., and Airaksinen, M. S. (2010). Logistics or patient care: Which features do independent Finnish pharmacy owners prioritize in a strategic plan for future information technology systems? *Journal of the American Pharmacists Association*, 50(1), 24–33.

Winter, V., Schreyögg, J., and Thiel, A. (2020). Hospital staff shortages: Environmental and organizational determinants and implications for patient satisfaction. *Health Policy*, 124(4), 380–388.

Wood, E. X. and Frazier, T. (2019). Decentralized humanitarian aid deployment: Reimagining the delivery of aid. *Journal of Humanitarian Logistics and Supply Chain Management*, 10(1), 1–20.

World Health Organisation (2005). Monitoring wastage at country level. https://apps.who.int/iris/bitstream/handle/10665/68463/WHO_VB_03.18.Rev.1_eng.pdf?sequence=1&isAllowed=y Accessed 12th March 2022.

World Health Organisation (2021a). Vaccines and immunization. https://www.who.int/health-topics/vaccines-and-immunization#tab=tab_1 Accessed 12th March 2022.

World Health Organisation (2021b). Global strategy on digital health 2020-2025. https://www.who.int/publications/i/item/9789240020924 Accessed 5th March 2022.

World Health Organisation (2022). Tonnes of COVID-19 health care waste expose urgent need to improve waste management systems. https://www.who.int/news/item/01-02-2022-tonnes-of-covid-19-health-care-waste-expose-urgent-need-to-improve-waste-management-systems Accessed 19th March 2022.

Wu, R. (2019). The carbon footprint of the Chinese health-care system: An environmentally extended input-output and structural path analysis study. *Lancet Planet Health*, 3(10), e413–e9.

Xie, Y. and Breen, L. (2014). Who cares wins? A comparative analysis of household waste medicines and batteries reverse logistics systems. *Supply Chain Management: An International Journal*, 19(4), 455–474.

Yaroson, E. V., Breen, L., Hou, J., and Sowter, J. (2021). Advancing the understanding of pharmaceutical supply chain resilience using complex adaptive system (CAS) theory. *Supply Chain Management*, 26(3), 323–340.

Zhang, C., Grandits, T., Härenstam, K. P., Hauge, J. B., and Meijer, S. (2018). A systematic literature review of simulation models for non-technical skill training in healthcare logistics. *Advances in Simulation*, 3(1), 1–16.

Zhong, R. Y., Newman, S. T., Huang, G. Q., and Lan, S. (2016). Big data for supply chain management in the service and manufacturing sectors: Challenges, opportunities, and future perspectives. *Computers & Industrial Engineering*, 101, 572–591.

13
CONSTRUCTION AND URBAN LOGISTICS

Russell G. Thompson, Oleksandra Osypchuk and Stanisław Iwan

Introduction

Construction of new buildings and infrastructure and the refurbishment of existing ones is vital for the development and renewal of cities. However, delivery of building materials, and removal of waste from urban construction sites can have a significant effect on traffic congestion, air pollution, noise and accidents. There are substantial challenges in improving the sustainability of urban construction logistics due to rapid urbanisation.

Although construction projects typically only have a short or medium-term duration, they can have a significant impact on road users and residents in urban areas. This is due to the intensity of freight movements attracted and generated as well as the diverse range of materials and equipment that often require large and heavy specialised vehicles.

Construction sites commonly operate within already urban congested networks with limited capacity. Additional freight transport to and from construction sites can add to congestion levels and disrupt urban traffic networks due to additional loading and unloading zones being required as well as temporary road closures. Queueing vehicles waiting to enter construction sites can cause increased emissions, noise and delays for other road users. Extended working hours can also be intrusive for residents.

There are a number of major trends in urban construction practices that are having a substantial effect on urban construction logistics. Lean construction methods can be used to reduce overall financial costs of construction as well as shorten the duration of construction projects but they can lead to more frequent and smaller deliveries (Vrijhoef, 2020). Financially, transport costs can be reduced by acquiring higher quantities of materials but this increases storage costs. Reliability of receiving materials at sites from external suppliers is an important factor especially in times where disruption is causing delays.

There is a recent trend towards modular construction practices that are based on prefabrication methods, with a large proportion of construction activity taking place in factory environments that use time-critical logistics systems. Modular construction can reduce traffic-related impacts and delays at the final construction site but require inventory management practices based on just-in-time distribution of material and components.

Construction supply chain management (CSCM) can improve performance at a firm and interfirm level. Advanced construction logistics including collaborative transport and consolidation centres and can increase efficiency and improve sustainability. Sustainable construction practice considers sustainable development principles. This involves implementing initiatives for mitigating the negative impacts of construction activities on the environment and social impacts on the community.

The construction industry is one of the industries that are particularly challenging for sustainable urban freight transport (Berden et al., 2019). Construction works entail the need for deliveries to be made to construction sites that may be located in city centres and no-traffic zones. Additional hindrances ensue from the specific nature of the construction industry, involving numerous subcontractors, various project sizes or contractors' priorities (Lundesjo, 2015). Deliveries made to construction sites often involve high-tonnage vehicles, they are fragmented rather than optimised, and there are often empty or "less-than-truckload" runs.

It is important to take measures so that construction site deliveries become more effective and efficient to significantly reduce the negative impacts on the urban transport system. Such measures may include the selection of a procurement type that suits the particular conditions and the application of telematics solutions (Browne et al., 2011; Papadonikolaki, 2020; Whitlock et al. 2018), as well as the appropriate organisation of processes (Allen et al., 2012; Bosona, 2020; Hamzeh et al., 2007). The construction procurement type is of particular importance, as it is decisive for the way deliveries are organised. Selection of a centralised, dispersed, or mixed procurement type, or deciding the procurement should be carried out by logistic organisational units, and must be based on the construction project implementation conditions. Each of the variants has its advantages and disadvantages (Osypchuk and Iwan, 2019), and it determines whether the transport of construction supplies will be more or less sustainable.

This chapter describes how city logistics solutions such as consolidation centres, construction delivery plans, night deliveries and inland waterways can be implemented to reduce the impacts of construction activities in cities. Methods for incorporating the interests of multiple stakeholders as well as social costs into evaluation methods are outlined. Opportunities for improving the sustainability of urban construction logistics using advancements in information and communication technology are also presented.

New Approaches

City Logistics

Construction-related transport can produce significant negative social, economic and environmental impacts. Freight traffic attracted to construction projects can produce safety issues as well as harmful emissions and excessive noise levels leading to health issues in local communities. There can also be substantial economic impacts for constructors from inefficient deliveries as well as to businesses from changes to the traffic network and parking supply near construction sites. It is common for substantial environmental impacts from vehicle emissions travelling to and from construction sites as well as queueing near sites.

City Logistics considers a broad set of benefits and costs associated with urban freight systems to evaluate initiatives for improving sustainability and efficiency (Taniguchi and Thompson, 2015). The impacts on key stakeholders such as shippers, carriers, receivers, residents and administrators are typically assessed. City Logistics solutions such as consolidation centres and collaborative freight systems can be implemented in urban construction logistics to improve sustainability and efficiency.

Multi-Actor Multi-Criteria Analysis (MAMCA)

Evaluating urban freight initiatives involves identifying problems, setting goals and objectives, defining criteria and predicting or measuring performance (Thompson, 2015). However, it is difficult to incorporate the objectives and criteria of numerous stakeholders. Multi-Actor Multi-Criteria Analysis (MAMCA) has been developed allowing for the assessment of different alternatives (i.e. projects, solutions, or initiatives) for objectives of key stakeholders (Macharis, 2007). MAMCA consists of several steps, determining a set of alternatives or initiatives for the problem of concern, identifying stakeholder groups that can impact or be impacted by the alternatives identified, defining criteria for each stakeholder, assessing the performance of each initiative for criteria for each stakeholder, determining a ranking of initiatives based on combining the performance of initiatives across all stakeholders and undertaking sensitivity analysis of the relative importance of each stakeholder (Macharis et al., 2009).

MAMCA was applied to evaluate alternatives such as night deliveries and the establishment of a bundling hub with electric vehicles or waterway transport compared with business as usual (standard practice) for constructing a new University campus in Amsterdam (Macharis et al., 2016). This involved five stakeholder groups, logistics service provider, supplier, building contractor, citizens and the municipality. For each stakeholder group, a small set (four or five) of criteria were defined. The relative importance of each criteria was determined by each group. Ratings of how the alternatives would achieve each criterion were determined for each group. This allowed the performance of alternatives to be assessed for each stakeholder group. MAMCA clearly showed the BAU alternative as the least-performing alternative for most stakeholders. The bundling hub with water transport was shown to perform best for a majority of stakeholders.

A construction logistics stakeholder framework was adapted from MAMCA for evaluating innovative schemes for the City Campus construction site in the Brussels-Capital Region (Brusselaers et al., 2021). The performance of four construction logistics schemes: Construction planning and JIT, Construction Consolidation Centre, use of preferred road network set by Brussels Mobility and EVs towards a zero-emission city were compared. Four stakeholder groups: construction site, construction logistics, Construction Federation & Research Institutes and Local or Regional (Urban Mobility) Authority & Urban Planning were considered. For each stakeholder group a set of economic, environmental and societal criteria were defined and their relative importance estimated. The framework allows stakeholders' interests to be considered in the planning stage. This allowed barriers to be identified and the role of local government to be determined that can facilitate implementation of novel construction logistics solutions.

Social Cost–Benefit Analysis (SCBA)

Recently links between personal health and vehicle noise and emissions have been determined, with studies estimating the costs of freight vehicles in cities (Den Boer et al., 2011; Gibson et al., 2014). SBCA methods that incorporate externalities from freight vehicles are becoming more common in the evaluation of urban freight projects (DfT, 2010; Kin and Macharis, 2015). SCBA involves monetising negative externalities such as noise and emissions. Financial rates for the amount of distance travelled by different-sized trucks have been determined for air pollution, climate change, noise, accidents, congestion and infrastructure.

These can be used to evaluate new initiatives such as alternative fuels and vehicle consolidation schemes.

Urban construction sites typically generate a high number of freight vehicle movements that produce a significant amount of emissions. Diesel-fuelled trucks and vans produce particulate matter (PM) and small particles such as PM2.5 (particulate matter less than 2.5 μm) are a major health risk more so than larger particles since they are more likely to be deposited deep into the lungs. Ambient air pollution in urban areas has been found to be a major factor in stroke, ischaemic heart disease, lung cancer, chronic obstructive pulmonary disease as well as acute respiratory infection (WHO, 2016). Noise from trucks in urban areas has also been shown to contribute to negative health outcomes, including cardiovascular disease, cognitive impairment in children, sleep disturbance, tinnitus and annoyance (WHO, 2011).

Initiatives

Consolidation Centres

Construction consolidation centres (CCCs) are logistics facilities for classifying, consolidating and delivering building materials to construction sites. CCCs make it possible to optimise deliveries, and reduce traffic intensity, energy consumption and emissions. They are aimed at reducing the number of deliveries, and increasing transport effectiveness and efficiency. CCCs are often built in the vicinity of major roads and railway stations to streamline the operation. They can serve one construction project and be liquidated on its completion, or they can operate on a permanent basis and serve more projects. CCCs can also offer their customers services that create added value, e.g. warehousing services, quality inspections, order picking, reverse logistics (Lundesjo, 2015; Muerza and Guerlain, 2021; Robbins, 2015). They can significantly reduce the negative impacts of construction projects in cities via transshipping materials from high-tonnage vehicles to smaller ones. Consolidated cargo helps limit the number of less-than-truckload (LTL) runs, while assuring more cost-effective vehicle runs. CCCs provide a facility for building materials to be dropped off to enable consolidated deliveries to construction sites, reducing the number of deliveries and, therefore, increasing the efficiency and effectiveness of logistics processes. CCCs can increase transport efficiency as well as reduce the number of trucks, distances travelled and emissions associated with deliveries to construction sites. Reduced disruptions at construction sites and higher degrees of reliability of deliveries are experienced.

Setting up CCCs is becoming a more common practice when large construction projects are implemented in cities. Between 1970 and 2010, 114 urban consolidation centres were identified in 17 countries. Out of them, only 7 were dedicated to construction projects. These were located in Great Britain, Germany and Sweden (Allen et al., 2012). Currently, the number of CCCs is growing, and their positive impact on logistics process implementation is to be found in most European countries. The rationale for establishing a CCCs was also examined in the SUCCESS project. A SWOT analysis was carried out, which showed that the strengths of the solution include: reducing the phenomenon of congestion, reducing the level of damaged and stolen materials, greater flexibility of deliveries and others. The weaknesses include: the fact that some materials are not suitable for storage, it is difficult to obtain short-term profits, the solution requires large investments. The opportunities include: development of ICT tools, the possibility of just-in-time work, positive experience of other industries. And the threats were: the weakening of the construction industry after the economic crisis and the lack of large projects (VPF, 2017). This has been confirmed by operational results of selected CCCs, e.g. those located in London and Stockholm.

In Stockholm, two construction consolidation centres were established to serve large investment projects, namely the Hammarby Sjöstad Logistics Centre and the Royal Seaport Construction Consolidation Centre. One of the goals of the city of Stockholm is to reduce the environmental impact of transport. For this purpose, opportunities were created for the organisation of CCC. This allowed, among other things, to reduce the flow of transport, increase the load on vehicles, use hybrid vehicles, and improve waste management (https://www.norradjurgardsstaden2030.se).

The Hammarby Sjöstad Logistics Centre was set up to serve a residential project and it operated between 2001 and 2010. Initially, the CCC was financed 95% by the city authorities, however, towards the end of its functioning the city contribution was reduced to 40%. The city took steps to disseminate knowledge about the benefits of using CCC, in addition, they were noticeable in practice. This led to increasing interest among businesses. Fees and allowances have been introduced, which allowed for reductions in public participation in costs. CCC was located directly adjacent to the construction site. Due to the geographic location and the district residents, deliveries of the construction site supplies could have been onerous, had it not been for the coordination done by the CCC. The CCC offered three services: goods consolidation, temporary storage of materials, and intelligent traffic control system. The Hammarby Sjöstad Logistics Centre helped achieve a 90% reduction in energy consumption and CO_2, NO_x, and PM emissions for deliveries from the CCC to the construction site. Additionally, the noise level was reduced, the vehicle stopping time was shortened from 60 to 6 minutes, and the vehicle cargo space utilisation rose from 50% to 85% (LIST & ITL, 2017).

The Royal Seaport Construction Consolidation Centre was established in 2011 in order to help construct residential and office buildings. The scheduled completion year is 2030 (http://www.stockholmroyalseaport.com). The CCC was set up and maintained by the city authorities and the contractors involved in the construction project were required to use the CCC. The CCC enabled a 75% reduction in the number of HGVs delivering the supplies directly to the construction site. Nevertheless, the clients of the centre complained about the need to order materials in advance and that an extra day was necessary for a delivery to be made.

In London, CCCs are widely used in the implementation of construction projects. In 2016 there were as many as 12 such centres (https://www.clocs.org.uk). The first London CCC pilot project was carried out in the years 2005–2007. It originated within the framework of a Public Private Partnership (PPP) and supplied four construction projects, enabling a 60–70% reduction in the number of freight fleet, in addition to that the delivery time was shortened by 2 hours. The delivery reliability rate reached 97% (which means that 97% of the materials were delivered correctly). Where no consolidation centre was used, the mean reliability rate was 39%. Also, a considerable reduction in negative environmental impacts of the deliveries was observed. It was not possible to estimate the achieved waste reduction, but there was a smaller number of damaged or stolen goods or those ordered in excess. Additionally, the quantity of recyclable packaging was increased, which helped reduce the waste transport (Transport for London, 2008). The results of the pilot project made it possible to widely use CCC in business practice.

Construction Logistics Plans

Construction Logistics Plans (CLPs) are documents detailing a logistics strategy for a construction project. CLP provides a framework to better manage different types of freight vehicle movements to and from construction sites (Transport for London, 2008). In the construction industry, logistics is often planned on a short-term basis, the process participants hardly cooperate, and the control level is not adequate for such a fragmented supply chain. Procurement focuses on the volumes purchased rather than the method of production, warehousing or delivery. This leads to various irregularities that exacerbate the negative environmental impacts of the project implementation. Drawing up a CLP makes it possible to organise the logistics of the construction project via identifying the key elements such as access management and journey planning, deliveries and materials management, demand for transport, construction machinery fleet, unloading, local roads works and temporary situations, consolidation (Browne, 2015; Robbins 2015).

Night Deliveries

Organising night deliveries by suppliers makes it possible to shorten the transport time and to increase effectiveness. In addition, this is one of the ways to reduce congestion and CO_2 emissions. A good practice applied in some countries in the area of construction supplies is consolidation of deliveries (Allen et al., 2012; Hamzeh et al., 2007). This concept is nothing new, still, it is effective in reducing the number of deliveries being made. However, it requires a centralised procurement system, procurement managed by logistic organisational units, or a mixed procurement system. Only these types of supplies allow for the consolidation of deliveries, which naturally reduces the amount of transport carried out and translates into noise emissions.

Cyclists

Good practice emanating from Great Britain is CLOCS (*Construction Logistics and Cyclist Safety*). In response to the results of the analysis regarding accidents involving vehicles delivering materials to construction sites, an industry programme was initiated, which later became the national standard that required all the stakeholders in the construction industry to take responsibility for people's health and safety. This contributed to taking joint efforts in order to prevent fatal or major collisions involving vehicles engaged in construction projects and unprotected road users (pedestrians, cyclists and motorcyclists), as well as to improve air quality and reduce the emissions and the number of vehicle runs. An important part of CLOCS is drawing up a CLP as a management tool for construction project planners, developers and contractors. CLOCS offers training in CLP development, as well as evaluation of all construction stages and details of vehicle routing, traffic control and social issues management (https://www.clocs.org.uk).

Permanent Unloading Areas

Another good practice is the establishment of permanent unloading areas, as it enables a reduction in congestion during deliveries. This is not a universal solution, since not every construction site has adequate space for that. Another advantage of unloading areas is a decreased risk of road accidents and cargo damage. Figure 13.1 presents permanent unloading areas set up in order to facilitate the Eiffel Tower painting in Paris, and the construction of the Sagrada Familia in Barcelona.

Permanent unloading areas are often set up via (partial) encroachment of the right-of-way, which may lead to exacerbating the problems related to transport congestion. On the

Construction and Urban Logistics

Figure 13.1 (a) Permanent unloading area next to the Eiffel Tower in Paris. (b) Permanent unloading area next to the Sagrada Familia in Barcelona

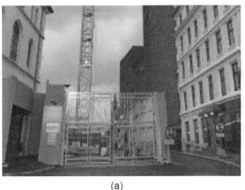

Figure 13.2 (a, b) Permanent unloading area in Oslo

other hand, it has a positive effect on the safety of unprotected road traffic participants. Figure 13.2 illustrates the permanent unloading areas next to construction sites in Oslo. An interesting solution is to provide a construction site with several entry gates located in different parts, which makes it possible to better utilise the space available and to supply cargo to the closest possible place of storage or use.

Alternative Storage Areas

In the course of the implementation of construction projects, it is necessary to keep stocks of materials directly at the construction site. However, in cities, this is often hindered due to limited space. A good solution in that respect is to establish alternative storage areas for materials. An example of this solution may be floating storage platforms placed on canals. This practice is often used in Amsterdam and Stockholm. An example is presented in Figure 13.3.

Figure 13.3 Construction materials storage on a canal in Stockholm

Multi-Modal Transport Networks

Inland waterways and railways in many cities have good potential for transporting building materials for construction projects to improve efficiently and sustainability. Compared to trucks, barges and trains have a vast capacity for transporting bulk materials. Trucks contribute to congestion and have substantially higher fuel consumption and emission rates. Barge and rail freight also have considerably less costs relating to infrastructure maintenance, operations, reliability, externalities and safety.

A special logistics office was established to develop Potsdamer Platz in Berlin (Maier, 1997). To ensure a high level of safety, efficiency and environmental outcomes this office was responsible for ensuring that the transport of all goods and materials to this site was undertaken by rail and water routes. The logistics system also ensured smooth and fast construction operations.

The benefits of using inland waterways to transport palletised building materials in Belgium have been investigated (Mommens and Macharis, 2014). This system involves the establishment of a network of hubs for transhipping goods to enable palletised building materials to be bundled onto barges. Using cost models and Geographic Information Systems (GIS) the optimal location of hubs was determined and the financial costs of changing modes as well as the reduction of CO_2 emissions were estimated. It was shown that the shift to inland waters has the potential for reducing financial costs as well as environmental and congestion costs.

The Amsterdam Vaart! project has been established in Amsterdam to shift transport to construction sites from roads to waterways. The project stimulates construction projects to shift their transport of construction equipment and materials from suppliers and distribution centres (DCs) to the city centre to barges using canals. So far, the effects have been significant with 37% less CO_2 emissions, 1,600 fewer truck trips in the city, and a reduction of 19,700 trips outside the city (Brauner et al., 2021)

The Brussels Construction Consolidation Centre (BCCC) operates on the Scheldt river receiving building materials on barges from DCs in Ghent, Wielsbeke and Burcht. It aims to increase economic and social attractiveness of the city of Brussels. Trucks are used for the last-mile transport to construction sites within the city.

In Paris, on the river Seine, transportation of various construction materials including cement and concrete blocks is conducted from a facility to Point P stores (a distributor of construction materials) which are often situated on the quayside. A special self-unloading vessel equipped with a crane is used to transport material. This system has led to a reduction in over 2000 truck movements per year (Janjevic and Ndiaye, 2014).

Sustainability Ratings

Construction activities are beginning to be incorporated into the environmental rating of buildings. For example, the Green Building Council of Australia has recognised that emissions from construction sites include transport of construction machinery and materials as well as the transport of waste (*Green Building Council of Australia*). The site-specific sustainability checklist contains transport initiatives that can be used as the basis for meeting the minimum requirement for the Carbon Neutral Construction Service Innovation Challenge. One such initiative involves fleet vehicles meeting Euro 4 emission standards or better. Another involves implementing measures to improve fuel use efficiency by implementing efficient driving operation. This is intended to encourage initiatives that reduce fuel use for construction activity such as implementing efficient driving practices during the long haul for earthworks, reducing idle times and maintaining tyre pressures.

Future Directions

The digital revolution provides great opportunities to integrate a range of data to coordinate activities for improving efficiency and sustainability of urban construction logistics. Telematics solutions that affect sustainable urban freight transport connected with construction site supplies can be divided into those related to procurement planning and those connected directly with transport. The solutions that enable more rational planning, which translates into decreasing the transport volume, include, e.g. Building Information Modelling (BIM) and Enterprise Resource Planning (ERP) systems.

BIM is software used in production and construction data management, which enables virtual generation of intelligent processes based on 3D models, making it possible for architects, engineers and construction workers to plan, design, construct and manage the buildings and infrastructure more effectively. BIM enables construction of a structure first in the virtual space, which makes it possible to solve any potential problems prior to commencing the actual works. Moreover, BIM supports effective management and handling of the space available for moving and storing the building materials, as well as coordination of works. Making use of the solution enables planning of the demand for materials as well as preparing schedules for orders and deliveries, thus providing more possibilities for consolidation (Whitlock et al., 2018).

ERP systems, in turn, are used in various industries and make it possible for users to better integrate diverse business functions such as accounting, finance, human resources, production or distribution. Due to the specific nature of the construction industry, ERP implementation may be hindered, nevertheless, it makes it possible for users to optimise the processes, provides better possibilities of control and greater organisational flexibility, facilitates decision-making processes, communicating the information to individual participants of the construction process, and supplies management, helps shorten project implementation time and reduce costs (Chung et al., 2009; Yang et al., 2007). Both BIM and ERP systems support materials flow in the course of the product life cycle, before they are delivered to the construction site. Combining them with RFID, GPS or bar codes makes it possible to control transport, distribution to the construction site or optimisation of warehousing (Papadonikolaki, 2020).

Telematics solutions connected directly with transport also include the use of alternative fuel vehicles (Browne et al., 2011), fleet and freight management support systems, mapping and visualising software, automated vehicle access control systems, automated toll collection (Oskarbski and Kaszubowski, 2016), driver assistance systems (e.g. predictive cruise control, front assist, and blind spot monitor) (Barth et al., 2015). Making use of alternative fuel vehicles is in line with measures taken by city authorities in order to establish low- and zero-emission zones. This leads to a reduction in negative environmental impacts of urban freight transport. Taking advantage of other solutions contributes to more rational delivery planning, increased road safety, shorter journey time, which in turn translates into reduced impacts of transport connected with construction site supplies in cities.

Conclusion

While construction projects in urban areas are vital for the development of cities, they can generate a significant amount of negative impacts that can be harmful to health and the environment. A range of city logistics initiatives such as consolidation centres, constructions delivery plans and multi-modal freight systems provide opportunities for improving sustainability and efficiency of urban construction logistics.

Multi-stakeholder evaluation methods provide a practical means of identifying options that have the potential for achieving the objectives of several stakeholders. Social cost–benefit analysis allows health and environmental costs to be incorporated into evaluation methods. Building information systems can improve the coordination of material flows to construction sites. Intelligent transport systems have the potential for improving the safety and efficiency of vehicle movements.

References

Allen, J., Browne, M., Woodburn, A., and Leonardi, J. (2012). The role of urban consolidation centres in sustainable freight transport. *Transport Reviews*, 32(4), 473–490.

Barth, M. J., Wu, G., and Boriboonsomsin, K. (2015). Intelligent transportation systems and greenhouse gas reductions. *Current Sustainable/Renewable Energy Reports*, 2(3), 90–97.

Berden, M., Morel, M., van Amstel, W. P., and Balm, S. (2019) Governance models for sustainable Urban construction logistics: Barriers for collaboration.

Bosona, T. (2020). Urban freight last mile logistics—challenges and opportunities to improve sustainability: A literature review. *Sustainability*, 12(21), 8769.

Brauner, T., Kahle, M., and Pauwels, T. (2021). Market review on city freight distribution using inland waterways, AVATAR, INTERREG.

Browne, M. (2015). The challenge of construction logistics. Chapter 1 in: G. Lundesjo (ed.), *Supply Chain Management and Logistics in Construction*, London: Kogan Page, 9–24.

Browne, M., Allen, J., and Leonardi, J. (2011). Evaluating the use of an urban consolidation centre and electric vehicles in central London. *IATSS Research*, 35(1), 1–6.

Brusselaers, N., Mommens, K., and Macharis, C. (2021). Building bridges: A participatory stakeholder framework for sustainable urban construction logistics. *Sustainability*, 13, 2678.

Chung, B., Skibniewski, M. J., and Kwak, Y. H. (2009). Developing ERP systems success model for the construction industry. *Journal of Construction Engineering and Management*, 135(3), 207–216.

CLOCS, (2023). Construction Logistics Plans, Construction Logistics and Community Safety, clocs.org.uk.

Den Boer, E., Otten, M., and van Essen, H. (2011). *STREAM International Freight 2011. Comparison of various transport modes on an EU scale with the STREAM database*, Delft.

DfT (2010). Freight consolidation centre study main report, prepared for department for transport by TTR & TRL, London.

Hamzeh, F. R., Tommelein, I. D., Ballard, G., and Kaminsky, P. (2007). Logistics centers to support project-based production in the construction industry. Proceedings of the 15th annual conference of the International Group for Lean Construction (IGLC 15).

Janjevic, M., and Ndiaye, A. B. (2014). Inland waterways transport for city logistics: A review of experiences and the role of local public authorities, *Urban Transport XX, WIT Transactions on The Built Environment*, 138, 279–290.

Kin, B., and Macharis, C. (2015). Social cost-benefit analysis of a private urban consolidation centre in Antwerp. *Steunpunt Goederenstromen*.

LIST, ITL (2017). Report on good practices in the EU and USA in construction logistics in urban area.

Lundesjo, G. (Ed.). (2015). *Supply Chain Management and Logistics in Construction: Delivering Tomorrow's Built Environment*. London: Kogan Page Publishers.

Macharis, C. (2007). Multi-criteria analysis as a tool to include stakeholders in project evaluation: The MAMCA method. In: E. Haezendonck (ed.), *Transport Project Evaluation, Extending the Social Cost–Benefit Approach*, Edward Elgar: Cheltenham, 115–131.

Macharis, C., De Witte, A., and Ampe, J., (2009). The multi-actor, multi-criteria analysis methodology (MAMCA) for the evaluation of transport projects: Theory and practice. *Journal of Advanced Transportation*, 43(2), 183–202.

Macharis, C., Kin, B., Balm, S., and van Amstel, W. P. (2016). Multiactor participatory decision making in urban construction logistics. *Transportation Research Record*, 2547, 83–90.

Maier, W. (1997). Construction logistics for potsdamer platz. *Structural Engineering International*, 7(4), 233–235.

Mommens, K., and Macharis, C. (2014). Location analysis for the modal shift of palletized building materials. *Journal of Transport Geography*, 34, 44–53.

Muerza, V., and Guerlain, C. (2021). Sustainable construction logistics in urban areas: A framework for assessing the suitability of the implementation of construction consolidation centres. *Sustainability*, 13(13), 7349.

Oskarbski, J., and Kaszubowski, D. (2016). Potential for ITS/ICT solutions in urban freight management. *Transportation Research Procedia*, 16, 433–448.

Osypchuk, O., and Iwan, S. (2019). Construction site deliveries in urban areas, based on the example of Szczecin. *Transportation Research Procedia*, 39, 389–397.

Papadonikolaki, E. (2020). The digital supply chain: Mobilising supply chain management philosophy to reconceptualise digital technologies and building information modelling (BIM). In: S. Pryke (ed.), *Successful Construction Supply Chain Management: Concepts and Case Studies*, Hoboken: John Wiley & Sons.

Robbins, S. (2015). Effective management of a construction project supply chain. Chapter 4 in: G. Lundesjo (ed.), *Supply Chain Management and Logistics in Construction*. London: Kogan Page, 62–76.

Taniguchi, E., and Thompson, R. G. (2015). *City Logistics – Mapping the Future*. Boca Raton: CRC Press.

Thompson, R. G. (2015). Evaluating city logistics schemes, Chapter 7. In: E. Taniguchi and R. G. Thompson (eds.), *City Logistics: Mapping the Future*, CRC Press, Boca Raton, 101–114.

Transport for London, (2008). *London Construction Consolidation Centre. Final Report*. Available from: https://www.ndslogistik.se/files/reports/1425975813_9.pdf.

United Nations. Available from: www.un.org.

VPF (2017). Business models for construction logistics optimisation and CCC introduction report.

Vrijhoef, R. (2020). Extended roles of construction supply chain management for improved logistics and environmental performance. In: *Lean Construction: Core Concepts and New Frontiers*, Abingdon, Oxon: Routledge, Taylor and Francis.

Whitlock, K., Abanda, F. H., Manjia, M. B., Pettang, C., and Nkeng, G. E. (2018). BIM for construction site logistics management. *Journal of Engineering, Project, and Production Management*, 8(1), 47–55.

WHO (2011). *Burden of Disease from Environmental Noise, Quantification of Healthy Life Years Lost in Europe*. Geneva, World Health Organisation.
WHO (2016). *Preventing Disease through Healthy Environments, a Global Assessment of the Burden of Disease from Environmental Risks*, (A. Prüss-Ustün, J. Wolf, C. Corvalán, R. Bos and M. Neira). Geneva, World Health Organisation.
Yang, J. B., Wu, C. T., and Tsai, C. H. (2007). Selection of an ERP system for a construction firm in Taiwan: A case study. *Automation in Construction*, 16(6), 787–796.

PART C
Technical Analysis

14
FACILITY LOCATIONS IN URBAN LOGISTICS

Takanori Sakai, Adrien Beziat and Adeline Heitz

Introduction

Logistics is one of the essential activities in the urban ecosystem that requires physical space and interacts with other urban activities. Compared with other land-use types in cities, which are the destinations of trips undertaken for specific purposes, such as home, work, school, and leisure, logistics land use has unique characteristics. Due to logistics being a network-based activity, the areas used for logistics facilities are intermediate points for commodity flows. While these facilities are usually in the realm of private business, logistics facilities function as nodes to facilitate "flows" in common with many public transportation hubs such as airports, seaports, and railway terminals.

In the last few decades, the key features of logistics land-use/facility locations in cities have been studied on account of: (1) the location dynamics triggered by logistics and supply chain innovations (e.g., pull-logistics, the rise of 3rd Party Logistics (3PL), and e-commerce), (2) the strong connection to retailing and consumer experiences, which became more relevant due to the rise of e-commerce, and (3) the local and global externalities caused by the associated freight. It is important to note that the mechanism for logistics facility locations cannot be separated from the associated supply chain, distribution system, transportation mode, and local and global negative impacts (carbon emissions, environmental damage, congestion, infrastructure damage, traffic accidents). Regarding (1) above, it is also important to note that the innovations in Information and Communication Technologies (ICTs) and globalization prompted "pull-logistics", in which supply chain management is driven by demand (i.e., how much of various products is being purchased), replacing traditional supplier-driven "push-logistics" (Hesse and Rodrigue, 2004). The evolution in logistics systems, which has occurred in the second half of the 20th century, has significantly lowered logistics costs through the reduction of inventory costs (Hesse and Rodrigue, 2004; Hall et al., 2006; McKinnon, 2009; Allen et al., 2012). It, furthermore, contributed to the urban logistics systems restructuring. The function of logistics facilities became more for goods handling than storage (Rodrigue, 2020a). Due to the above-mentioned situation, modern logistics facilities have different characteristics and location mechanisms from the conventional facilities, which, together with parallel changes in urban environments (i.e., external factors for location choice such as urban densification and expansion), causes unique dynamism in facility locations. The COVID-19 pandemic and the associated changes in the supply chain and consumption also have impacted this dynamism.

As for land-use policy, catering to the demand for land for logistics activities is critical. Demand for large-scale logistics facilities has been increasing and its growth is further predicted. The rapid growth in the e-commerce market contributes to such a trend in demand. For example, in the United States, Amazon has increased its total footprint from around 20 million square feet in 2008, to around 170 million square feet in 2019 (Rodrigue, 2020b). In the Greater Tokyo Area (seven prefectures including Tokyo), Japan, large-scale multi-tenant facilities have increased by 2.6 million square meters in 2020 alone (Japan Logistics Field Institute, Inc., 2020) and around 20–30% of them are used by e-commerce vendors. Furthermore, the demand for relatively small 'delivery centers' for last-mile deliveries has increased as well. The importance and urgency of securing the space for logistics activities are now recognized by researchers and practitioners.

This chapter describes the findings and implications on logistics facility locations from many studies that analyze different cities. Many of them focus on Europe (especially, France), Japan, and the United States, due to the richness of data and/or the high level of interest. There are differences among the studies in terms of the methodology and the data availability, quality, and format so that results of the studies are not directly comparable. However, the aim of this chapter is not the introduction of the studies independently; rather, to present generalizable insights on the phenomena which occur where the global dynamics in logistics interacts with the local urban contexts. While the locality exists, the similar locational phenomena occur in distant locations, which makes valuable policy insights commonly to different cities. Therefore, we provide the overview of the dynamism in the locational distribution of logistics facilities and the underlining mechanism as well as their implications for cities.

The rest of this chapter is organized as follows; the next section briefly summarizes the issues and discussions about typology and location factors of logistics facilities as well as the externality associated with logistics facility locations. This is followed by introducing several key dynamics of logistics facility locations observed in the last few decades with their implications; and the last section concludes the chapter, referring to the importance of this subject and the future challenges.

Typology, Location Factors and Externality

Typology

Logistics facilities, which we discuss in this chapter, are physical facilities for cross-docking, consolidation, fulfillment, delivery, storage, and/or associated value-added services. Despite their diversity in function, a typology of logistics facilities is usually lacking in government data. In the statistics of business establishment's, the categories used for logistics facilities are often too broad to describe the heterogeneity in logistics activities. This leads to a lack of publicly available data with details, which is a critical bottleneck impacting the study of logistics land use. For example, a North American Industry Classification System (NAICS) code that describes logistics facilities is chiefly NAICS 493 (*Warehousing*) and the four subcategories of NAICS 492 (Couriers and Messengers): *General Warehousing and Storage* (493110), *Refrigerated Warehousing and Storage* (493120), *Farm Product Warehousing and Storage* (493130), and *Other Warehousing and Storage* (4931290). However, the contemporary logistics activities include much more than simply warehousing and storage (see Figure 14.1). Furthermore,

Figure 14.1 Logistics facilities in Japan (left: a multi-story facility in a suburban area, mainly for cross-docking; right: a parcel delivery center in an urban area)

Source: Authors

the use of industrial category as the proxy of facility type is not appropriate because even an industry which extensively engaged in logistics service has both offices and logistics facilities of various kinds. Logistics facilities are heterogenous and their characteristics, such as function, operator, and goods type handled, are important. Without an understanding of such heterogeneity, policy discussions on logistics land use could become spurious.

Aiming to overcome such problems, past studies proposed typologies (Strale, 2013; Heitz et al., 2017, 2019; Notteboom et al., 2017; Onstein et al., 2021). The typology proposed by Heitz et al. (2019), who uses data from the Paris Region (the Ile-de-France), identifies 20 categories for logistics facilities based on four criteria: *function, operator, type of goods*, and *destination of goods*. Figure 14.2 is a simplified representation of the categories (refer to Heitz et al. (2019) for the definition of each class). It is obvious from the typology that the location factor also varies. Sakai et al. (2020) use this typology for the analysis of the heterogeneity of location factors by category. Onstein et al. (2021) proposed another typology based on the data from the Netherlands using six functional criteria which are relevant to facility size: *activity type, product type, product range and speed, network structure, market service area*, and *services days*. The proposed typology includes (1) *parcel lockers and pickup points*, (2) *city hubs*, (3) *parcel and postal sorting facilities*, (4) *regional food wholesale and retail facilities*, (5) *national retail and e-commerce facilities*, (6) *manufacture distribution center (DC) facilities*, (7) *bulk facilities*, and (8) *global agricultural auctions*, in the order of small to large.

With the increasing relevance of e-commerce in commodity flows, Rodrigue (2020b) introduces a typology for e-commerce, focusing on Amazon. The seven roles/functions that Rodrigue identified include: (1) *inbound cross dock* (unloading goods out of international containers; handling deliveries from local suppliers; serving e-fulfillment centers), (2) *e-fulfillment center* (assembling and shipping out online orders), (3) *air hub* (transferring parcels to and from air cargo services with regional fulfillment and sortation centers), (4) *sortation*

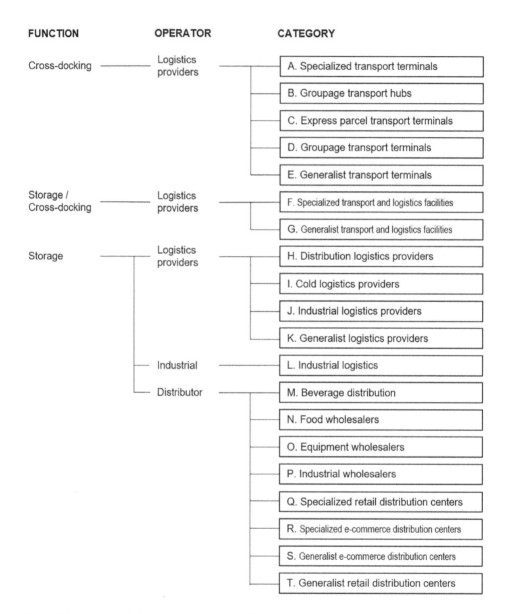

Figure 14.2 Logistics facility typologies proposed by Heitz et al. (2017, 2019)

center (arranging shipments by regional/local destinations), (5) *parcel delivery station* (sorting parcels for local delivery routes), (6) *local freight station* (serving as a pickup location), and (7) *fast delivery hub* (serving for fast deliveries with an inventory of limited items).

These typologies not only underline the heterogeneity but also imply the differences between each category in terms of its role in logistics and the urban ecosystem, as well as its environmental implications. Knowing the type of logistics facilities concerned is critical for discussing and addressing issues relevant to logistics facilities, and thus, the improvement of data collection practices for logistics facilities needs to be put forward.

Location Factors

The study of the business location mechanism dates back to Alfred Weber's classical industrial location theory of the 1920s in which cost minimization was the principal factor for location selection (Weber and Friedrich, 1929). Cost minimization is a powerful tool but often not practical as actual location selections for logistics facilities are not that simple, not least in terms of the assumption of perfect information. In the real world, there are many constraints and uncertainties. For policy development aiming at sustainable logistics land use, understanding the locational preference for logistics facilities is critically important.

Location factors with respect to logistics facilities include land price, accessibility to demand (or population, businesses, highway interchanges, and transportation hubs, e.g., railway terminals, seaports, and airports), accessibility to a workforce, local environment (e.g., local road conditions, congestion, land use, and density), public policies (e.g., incentives to attract jobs) and regulations. Logistics facilities also tend to cluster (Van den Heuvel et al., 2013; Kang, 2020), potentially due to economies of scale. Also, as a main constraint, land availability is a key factor that influences where facilities are located (especially for large-scale facilities) since cities are getting denser and larger. The relative importance of location factors differs by function (Heitz et al., 2019; Sakai et al., 2020a), the type of goods handled (Sakai et al., 2018), and the origins/destinations of goods (Sakai et al., 2020b). Furthermore, facilities developed at different points in time show different location preferences (Sakai et al., 2017; Kang, 2020). Due to the lack of data relating to logistics facilities and a robust typology (as mentioned earlier), existing knowledge is still limited with respect to locational preference. The findings from a study in the Tokyo Metropolitan Area (Sakai et al., 2020b) indicates:

- Accessibility to demand (shipment origins/destinations) is the most important factor, supporting the theory of Alfred Weber. It should be noted, however, that this may not be apparent or might not hold true for another city. Research by Sakai et al. (2020a), for example, indicates that the impact of zoning regulations (and limited land availability for logistics) overshadows the influence of demand accessibility in the Paris Region.
- Facilities that serve local, intra-regional demand are more sensitive to the accessibility to demand, land price, and population density than those serving inter-regional shipping. In other words, the selection of local facility locations needs to consider the complex trade-off among different factors more severely than that of non-local, inter-regional facilities.
- The locations of inter-regional facilities tend to be sub-optimal, often constrained by land availability. Historical industrial zones and the places close to expressway networks are often preferred.

It is important to emphasize that logistics facilities function in an integrated network system and location choice is connected to the facility's position in the system. Taking the example of Amazon, U.S., e-fulfillment centers, these locations are strategically selected considering population coverage (as delivery speed of e-commerce is highly dependent to the proximity of the fulfillment centers to the consumers) and inter-regional transportation connectivity. On the other hand, Amazon's delivery stations and the facilities of parcel delivery service for last-mile deliveries are in the places with the closest proximity to consumer location, ending up as a more uniform distribution pattern.

Externality

The externalities caused by shipments associated with logistics facilities are a key concern to planners considering the spatial distribution of logistics facilities. Externalities include traffic congestion, traffic accidents, road damage, noise, vibration, local pollution, and CO_2 emissions. The role of freight with respect to the negative impacts created by the urban transport system is significant. In the Paris Region, it is estimated that 36% of emissions from road traffic are due to goods vehicles (Coulombel et al., 2018). Logistics facilities, especially large facilities, have clear local negative impacts as the generator of goods vehicle traffic and they reduce the attractiveness of a neighborhood. While some cities welcome logistics facilities as job generators, others do not since the logistics activities prevent them from attracting residents and/or office buildings (which create jobs with higher income) (Dablanc and Rose, 2012). In contrast, the relationship between the spatial distribution of logistics facilities and the level of externality is not always clear at the city level. Analysis using the Urban Logistics Land-use and Traffic Simulator (ULLTRA-SIM) indicates that both centralization and de-concentration of logistics facilities could increase vehicle-travel distance if they are not aligned correctly with demand (Sakai et al., 2019). The following section discusses further the externality implications of different spatial distribution of logistics facilities (see also Chapters 23 and 24).

Trends in Spatial Distribution

This section introduces five types of spatial dynamics for logistics facilities: logistics metropolitan concentration, logistics sprawl, logistics clusterization, the growth in proximity logistics, and spatial hysteresis (see Figure 14.3). Each spatial dynamic implies a reorganization of cities' urban fabric and carries its own economic, environmental, and social implications.

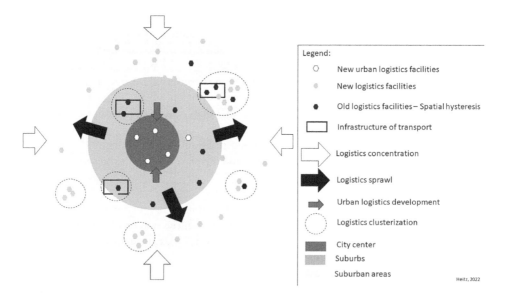

Figure 14.3 Trends in spatial distribution of logistics facilities

Logistics Metropolitan Concentration

Logistics facilities are mainly located in large cities and metropolitan areas (Hesse, 2008). In France, for example, Guerrero and Proulhac (2016) show that 75% of new warehouses were built in urban areas in the period between 1985 and 2009 (see Box 14.1). This concentration in urban areas was caused by several factors. First, logistics activities, particularly those in the distribution sector, need to be close to consumers, as they deliver goods to shops and residents. Furthermore, these activities can benefit from the proximity of a large labor pool. Although mechanization and automation are developing, logistics facilities continue to employ a large number of workers. The location of warehouses in large urban areas can also be explained by the concentration of transportation infrastructure that connects these areas at various scales, from local to national. These include ports, airports, highways, railroads and waterways. Hub functions increase the attractiveness of metropolitan areas for logistics activities. Furthermore, real estate developers, international private investors or funds who own logistics facilities seek safe and profitable investments. Real estate development in the logistics sector follows the same logic as any other real estate market. This profitability is linked to their potential use (rental) by logisticians and transporters. They will therefore give preference to metropolitan areas that are a focus for diversified potential customers. In the event of a crisis in a sector, they will be able to find tenants more easily, limiting the vacancy of their property. This refers to the "insurance value" of metropolises (Veltz, 2014). The real estate crises of 2008, 2012 and 2020 due to COVID-19, have shown the strength of the logistics real estate market in metropolitan areas (Dablanc et al., 2022).

However, as a result of this concentration in metropolitan areas, logistics facilities have to compete with other urban and metropolitan activities. Activities with higher productivity per square meter tend to be located in the center, while those with lower productivity per square meter – such as logistics activities – tend to be located in the periphery or in suburban areas where land prices are typically lower, and more land is available.

Box 14.1 Case Study: Metropolitan Concentration of Logistics Activities in France

The location of logistics activities in France illustrates the concentration of facilities in metropolitan areas. France's urban structure is heavily monocentric, with the Ile-de-France (the administrative region of Paris) accounting for 18% of the national population and the same proportion in terms of logistics' facilities' building surface area (Figure 14.4). Furthermore, many other logistics facilities are located in other regions immediately adjacent to the Paris Region.

Other secondary metropolitan areas include Lille in the North, Nancy and Strasbourg in the North East, Lyon in the East, Marseille and Aix-en-Provence in the South-East, Toulouse and Bordeaux in the South-West, Nantes in the West, Orléans and Tours in the Center, as well as Le Havre and Rouen in the North West. For each metropolitan area, there is a corresponding concentration of logistics facilities. Of course, other factors also help explain facility locations (e.g., borders with neighboring European countries and corridor effects between gateways and large metropolitan areas). However, the effects of the concentration of logistics activities in metropolitan areas are clear (Guerrero and Proulhac, 2016).

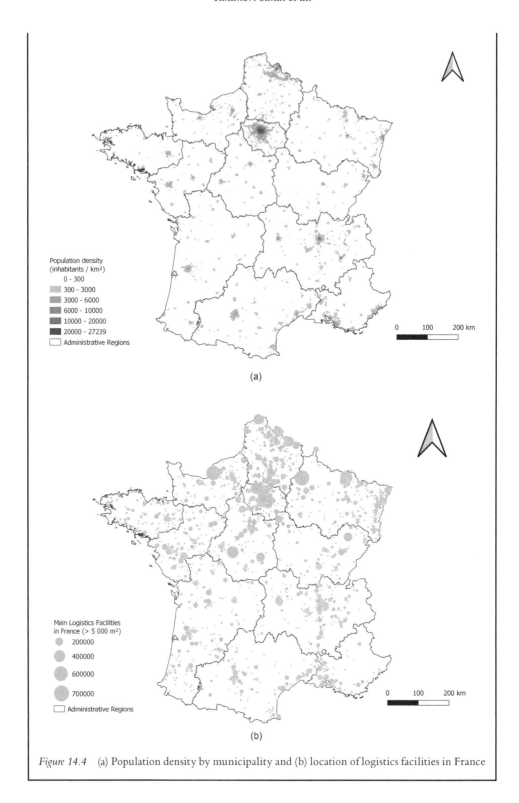

Figure 14.4 (a) Population density by municipality and (b) location of logistics facilities in France

Logistics Sprawl

At the local level, the concentration of logistics activities in metropolitan areas results in the location of facilities in the suburbs and outskirts. As a result of competition with other, more productive activities, logistics facilities gradually relocate to suburban areas: this process is usually referred to as logistics sprawl. We have been witnessing a phenomenon of logistical sprawl in many urban regions on a global scale over the last 30 years (Dablanc and Browne, 2020). Case studies are numerous in North America – Chicago (Cidell, 2011), San Francisco (Hesse, 2008), Atlanta (Dablanc and Ross, 2012), Los Angeles (Dablanc, 2014), Toronto, Vancouver, and Calgary (Woudsma et al., 2016) – as well as in Europe – Paris (Raimbault and Bahoken, 2014), The Randstad (Heitz et al., 2017), and Gothenburg (Heitz et al., 2020). A growing body of work also reports logistical sprawl in Latin America – Belo Horizonte (Guerin et al., 2021) – and East Asia – Tokyo (Sakai et al., 2015), Shanghai and the Yangtze River Delta (He et al., 2019), Wuhan (Yuan and Zhu, 2019) and Delhi (Gupta, 2017). This sprawl is also documented within emerging countries' metropolitan areas, including Casablanca (Mareï and Savy, 2021). The research work on logistics sprawl has alerted public authorities to this phenomenon and its consequences for the environment and the urban system. The introduction of sustainable objectives in urban planning documents in the 2000s, pushed public authorities to address urban sprawl and promote a more "compact" city.

Although logistics sprawl has been well-documented, its effect on carriers' operations has been a long-standing question, specifically whether the sprawl results in an increase of kilometers traveled per quantity of cargo moved. Early analyses indicated that logistics sprawl would have a negative impact, as it causes an increase in vehicle-kilometers traveled (VKT) (Dablanc and Rakotonarivo, 2010). On the other hand, a growing body of research underlines the importance of the relative distribution between logistics facilities and their catchment areas. Kang (2020), Sakai et al. (2019) and Gardrat (2021) also suggest that mismatch between logistics facilities' location and demand is a more relevant perspective and the estimation of the impact of logistics sprawl based only on the average distance between logistics facilities and the city center cannot reflect the real impacts. Sakai et al. (2017) corroborate that, in the case of the Tokyo Metropolitan Area (see Box 14.2), an increase in average load has counterbalanced longer distance trips related to logistics sprawl, which resulted in a decrease of VKT per quantity of cargo. This indicates that the optimization of urban logistics system, which proceeded along with logistics sprawl, improved efficiency. Guerrero et al. (2022) show that facilities located on the periphery of large metropolitan areas often serve non-local destinations, underlining the need to consider individual facilities' catchment areas. Robichet and Niérat (2021) confirm that when accounting for real-life demand data at the carrier level, optimal location for freight terminals (serving both the city's core and the periphery) is found outside of the city center even in a monocentric agglomeration. The study also found that carriers' current organization is close to the optimal situation (to reduce traveled VKT), given the location of freight demand.

While the relationship between logistics sprawl and efficiency is not obvious, there are other implications of logistics sprawl, which should not be neglected. Its impact in terms of land consumption is often-overlooked (McKinnon, 2009). Contemporary logistics facilities require a great amount of space. With logistics sprawl, development often takes place in rural and semi-rural areas, where land take leads to habitat loss and reduction in biodiversity (also, logistics facilities often require dedicated road infrastructure to connect to the existing network, which intensifies the impact). This problem is exacerbated when development occurs in an unorganized manner. Logistics sprawl can also have social implications. It could contribute to the increasing spatial mismatch between logistics workplaces and blue-collar workers' residential areas (Raimbault, 2019), increasing daily commute times for logistics workers. Yuan (2019) pointed to the existence of social justice issues as logistics facilities tend to concentrate in minority neighborhoods in the Los Angeles Metropolitan Region. Since logistics facilities require a lot of land and are usually single-story buildings, they tend to locate in less expensive areas. The disproportionate distribution of equipment generates negative externalities that can negatively impact quality of life in disadvantaged neighborhoods, contributing to economic, sociopolitical, and racial inequalities.

Box 14.2 Case Study: Logistics Sprawl in the Tokyo Metropolitan Area

In the Tokyo Metropolitan Area, many small logistics facilities in the center were replaced by large facilities in the suburbs during the period 2003–2013. This resulted in a significant increase in the average floor area (median floor area changed from 583 m² in 2003 to 1077 m² in 2013) and a 26% increase in the distance from the center. On the other hand, despite the associated longer truck travel distance, per-weight truck-km decreased by 4% during the same period due to the increase in the average load per travel (Sakai et al., 2017).

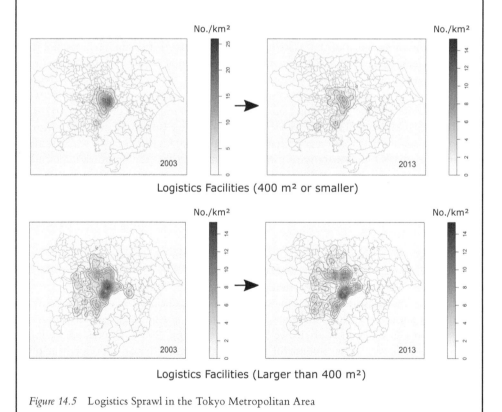

Figure 14.5 Logistics Sprawl in the Tokyo Metropolitan Area

Logistics Clusterization

Logistics clusterization is the spatial concentration of logistics and transportation firms. This phenomenon has been observed and documented extensively in various contexts, at various scales. For example, at the national scale, Rivera et al. (2014) identify over 60 logistics clusters in the United States, 2008, and report that these clusters are expanding and concentrating a larger share of logistics activities compared to 1998. At the regional scale, van den Heuvel et al. (2013) showed that between 1996 and 2009, in the Dutch province of North Brabant, the number of logistics facilities located within a cluster grew by 20% while the number of facilities in the rest of the region remained stable (+1%). This dynamic is also observed concomitantly with the sprawl of activities in the periphery of agglomerations. Cidell (2010), in the case of the United States, shows that logistics facilities are relocating further away from cities' core areas, but at the same time are forming denser clusters. Traditional economic theory posits that industrial clusters occur because they improve firms' productivity, due to economies of agglomeration. These positive externalities, in the case of intra- or inter-sectoral co-location of firms, materialize as a consequence of several factors: knowledge spillovers, the complementarity of specialized suppliers, the development of a skilled workforce, the integration of resources, and the sharing of infrastructure. Logistics agglomeration could lead to consolidation and pooling of transport flows, thus lowering transport costs, which would then lead to more clusterization, thus triggering a virtuous cycle.

Public stakeholders have tried to bring about these positive externalities through policies that encourage logistics clusterization via regulation, fiscal policies, subsidies, or zoning. These clusters have many names: freight villages (see Figure 14.6, as an example), logistics centers, logistics parks, logistics platforms, and transport centers (Baydar et al., 2017). The goal of freight villages is to encourage synergies and commercial cooperation, to provide a framework for the development of quality and up-to-standard logistics and transportation solutions and facilitate intermodal freight handling when possible.

Figure 14.6 Chanteloup Prologis 2 freight village in Moissy-Cramayel, France, 2022
Source: geoportail.gouv.fr

However, the expected positive impacts of logistics agglomeration on firms' productivity have been difficult to measure, and most analyses rely on surveys or qualitative approaches. Surveys of logistics establishments' managers show that synergies can arise through co-location (see Box 14.3 for example): combining transport capacity, availability of drivers, repair and maintenance facilities, and others (van den Heuvel et al., 2013; Rivera et al., 2016). Hylton and Ross (2017) show that clusterization has a positive impact on logistics clusters' growth, but the authors themselves admit that this indicator only offers indirect evidence. Sun et al. (2018) show a positive effect of logistics clusterization on logistics wages, which is again an indirect measure of productivity. On the other hand, using data on companies' turnover, Bounie and Blanquart (2016) show no effect of logistics clusterization on workforce productivity. This is consistent with other studies conducted in France, which show that the effects of agglomeration economies on logistics operations are very low (Masson and Petiot, 2015). This could be due to the emergence of agglomeration diseconomies, as concentration can also be a source of congestion and other externalities negatively impacting transport operations. Bounie and Blanquart (2017) also posit that physical proximity is not as relevant for logistics firms as it is for other industrial sectors (Figure 14.7).

Box 14.3 Case Study: Example of a Successful Cluster of Logistics Activities in the Paris Region

The Rungis International Market is a good example of a functional logistics cluster. Located in the southern suburbs of the Paris Region, about 10 km away from the city center, it is the largest wholesale food market in the world. It covers about 2.5 square kilometers, and processes over 2.8 million tons of food products per year. It holds around 1,200 businesses, mainly wholesalers, but also transport and logistics operators, brokers, and producers. Its logistics function is mainly local, but it also serves as a transit platform: 65% of the products are consumed in the Paris Region, 25% are shipped to other parts of France, and about 10% are shipped abroad. The International Market plays a very important role in the consolidation of flows in Ile-de-France. About 35% of annual incoming food products in region transit through Rungis (Institut Paris Region, 2015).

Facility Locations in Urban Logistics

Figure 14.7 The Rungis wholesale market
Source: geoportail.gouv.fr

A Trend for the Last-Mile Deliveries – Proximity Logistics

The development of proximity logistics is generally thought to be the opposite of logistics sprawl and a "return to the city center" for logistics (Taniguchi et al., 1999; Diziain et al., 2012; Buldeo Rai et al., 2022). Proximity logistics relies on the development of urban warehouses mostly dedicated to parcel delivery. They can be multi-story urban consolidation centers (UCC) from where cargo-cycles or electric vehicles perform the deliveries, or logistics hostels which integrate logistics activities in buildings where they coexist with other activities (housing, offices, retail), resulting in a functional mix within the building (see Box 14.4). A third type of urban logistics facilities would be urban warehouses dedicated to storing goods that need to be delivered rapidly. Linked to the "quick commerce" (a branch of e-commerce), instant deliveries and digital platform (Dablanc, 2018; Giuliano and Kang, 2018), these facilities rely on demand for small or medium facilities located in densely populated metropolitan areas. The rise of e-commerce and especially "quick commerce" have changed the logistics real estate market. Now, real estate developers look for facilities or space in dense areas to build urban facilities. Those buildings, designed to fit the urban fabric and adapt to the existing environment, can be new or the result of renovation.

Box 14.4 Case Study: Logistics Facilities for E-commerce in the Center of the Tokyo Metropolitan Area

In the Tokyo Metropolitan Area (TMA), Japan, a large share of multi-story for-lease facilities is used by e-commerce vendors for fulfillment. Based on an interview with one of the major logistics real estate developers in early 2022, roughly 30% of their tenants are e-commerce vendors. Furthermore, transportation service providers, who account for about 50% of the floor demand, are known to be handling an increasing share of e-commerce deliveries. In this situation, it is required to secure spaces close to the high-demand area in the TMA. The renovation of the coastal area (next to the urban center) occurred in the last two decades and old warehouses and factories were replaced by new facilities (Figure 14.8 left photograph). On the other hand, small facilities for the last mile (often called as delivery centers) of major service providers are densely located in the central business district, occupying the first floors of office buildings, from where deliveries are conducted by cargo bikes and trolleys (Figure 14.8 right photograph).

Figure 14.8 A modern multi-story logistics facility in the coastal area (left) and a delivery center in the central business district (right)

Source: Authors

Because real estate prices are so high in the city center, the cost–benefit balance for proximity logistics is hard to achieve and depends on at least two factors. It requires economies of scale (in terms of quantity of cargo handled) to reach profitability, which means that it requires a high density of receivers so that transport operations can be optimized (Allen et al., 2014). It also depends on funding, which can be public or private. Given these factors, it is not surprising that most urban logistics facilities are operated by e-commerce firms or large parcel delivery companies. These organizations can often achieve economies of scale due to their size, and they have a very high density of receivers. Furthermore, in the case of e-commerce, they can be operated at a loss (i.e., subsidized albeit by private entities) as part of aggressive business and commercial strategies aimed at disrupting existing retail ecosystems, as is the case for some e-groceries for example (Fornari et al., 2018).

Urban contexts, however, are evolving rapidly. Local authorities are increasingly restraining road traffic in city centers in favor of other modes of transportation. Urban and national policy-makers are introducing more and more stringent policies to address climate change and air pollution, restricting access to old and polluting vehicles. This could shift the cost–benefit arbitration against business-as-usual delivery schemes (i.e., delivery from XXL peripheral distribution centers) in favor of proximity logistics for more stakeholders beyond pure e-commerce players, as it could be operated with environmentally friendly transportation modes. Many sustainable last-mile innovations (Ranieri et al., 2018) – such as cargo bikes, e-vehicles, river or rail transportation, and crowd-shipping – will require space for consolidation, pooling, and unbundling of freight flows, which will necessitate urban logistics facilities. At the same time, some municipalities, such as the municipality of Paris or municipalities in the Paris' suburbs (Plaine Commune), secure space to preserve logistics facilities or foster the development of new ones by innovating in urban planning and land-use regulations (Box 14.5).

Box 14.5 Case Study: Logistics and Land-use Regulations in the City of Paris

The City of Paris, since 2013, has created a category in their land-use regulation dedicated to urban services including logistics facilities (Raimbault et al., 2018). All the black spaces (called "Urban Service Areas") on the local urban plan are areas where urban services such as logistics facilities are favored (see Figure 14.9 below). The UGA mainly concerns land used for (1) transport (passengers and goods), mainly rail transport; (2) urban ports installed on the banks of the Seine or canals; and (3) large areas already used for such services.

Figure 14.9 Zoning plan, extracted from the Paris urban local plan, 2013

Logistics Facilities and Spatial Hysteresis

While transport and logistics operators and public authorities are currently working on the development of urban logistics in dense areas, particularly in city centers, there are logistics facilities located in the suburbs, called intermediate logistics (Heitz, 2021). These facilities have remained in the dense part of the metropolitan areas. The spatial hysteresis designates the permanence of these facilities which have retained a fabric of logistics activities that continue to offer low-skilled jobs in former industrial suburbs affected by deindustrialization (Heitz and Beziat, 2016). These include old warehouses in the industrial or wholesale sector, often held by small business owners (Hesse, 2008; Strale, 2020).

Based on the case study focused on Paris, intermediate logistics facilities are located in a high-value area close to Paris, which is undergoing major urban development, subject to gentrification and where the competition for the land with other sectors (housing, offices) is not favorable to logistics. However, given the recent increase in demand for urban warehouses, the dominant logistics real estate developers have started to consider intermediate logistics as a potential resource to recycle the buildings or the land to develop the urban logistics dedicated to e-commerce. Intermediate logistics, poorly assessed by public policies, constitutes a significant land and real estate reservoir for logistics in a context of developing the "compact city" and limiting sprawl. The fact that they may disappear to the benefit of urban logistics facilities reinforces the idea of a "dualization". Suburban and urban logistics constitute the main part of the developing logistics real estate market. With declining intermediate logistics, those two forms could prevail in the metropolitan logistics landscape. Despite this decline, we observed a certain spatial permanence of these activities at the core of the agglomeration.

Also, a part of the parcel industry has been maintained in the dense area, thus serving as a stepping-stone for the development of a logistics dedicated to e-commerce. This *spatial hysteresis* is also the result of the concentration of logistics establishments inside the dense area, around several important nodal infrastructures.

Conclusion

This chapter introduced the key aspects in the analysis of logistics facility locations in cities and their dynamics observed in the last few decades. With the evolution of logistics systems, the spatial distributions of logistics facilities have been changing rapidly (even before the rise of the e-commerce market) which has many implications for the urban environment. However, details of the relationship between logistics land-use patterns and externalities are not fully understood. In fact, analysis of logistics land use itself is challenging due to a lack of data. As a result, even though more urban planners are aware of the necessity of public policies for logistics facility locations, many challenges remain to the design and implementation of suitable policies. Nonetheless, with the rise of e-commerce, the advent of novel goods transportation modes, and the continuing evolution of urban logistics systems, planning logistics facility locations is crucially important for the development of future sustainable urban logistics systems.

References

Allen, J., Browne, M., and Cherrett, T., (2012). Investigating relationships between road freight transport, facility location, logistics management and urban form. *Journal of Transport Geography*, 24, 45–57.

Allen, J., Browne, M., Woodburn, A., and Leonardi, J. (2014). A review of urban consolidation centres in the supply chain based on a case study approach. *Supply-Chain Forum: An International Journal*, 15–4, 100–112.

Baydar, A. M., Süral, H., and Çelik, M. (2017). Freight villages: A literature review from the sustainability and societal equity perspective. *Journal of Cleaner Production*, 167, 1208–1221.

Bounie, N., and Blanquart, C. (2016). Logistics centers and agglomeration economies: Logistics clusters or co-located logistics activities? The French case, World Conference on Transport Research 2016, 1–16.

Bounie, N., and Blanquart, C. (2017). Les zones d'activité logistique: clusters logistiques ou co-localisation d'activités logistiques? *Logistique & Management*, 25(3), 152–167.

Buldeo Rai, H., Dablanc, L., Kang, S., Sakai, T., Tejada, C., Yuan, Q., and Conway, A. (2022). "Proximity logistics": Characterizing the development of logistics facilities in dense mixed-use urban areas around the world. The 9th International urban freight conference, Long Beach, California, May 25–27, 2022.

Cidell, J. (2010). Concentration and decentralization: The new geography of freight distribution in US metropolitan areas. *Journal of Transport Geography*, 18(3), 363–371.

Cidell, J. (2011). Distribution centers among the rooftops: The global logistics network meets the suburban spatial imaginary. *International Journal of Urban and Regional Research*, 35(4), 832–851.

Coulombel, N., Dablanc, L., Gardrat, M., and Koning, M., (2018). The environmental social cost of urban road freight: Evidence from the Paris region. *Transportation Research Part D: Transport and Environment*, 63, 514–532.

Dablanc, L., and Rakotonarivo D., (2010). The impacts of logistics sprawl: How does the location of parcel transport terminals affect the energy efficiency of goods' movements in Paris and what can we do about it? *Procedia – Social and Behavioral Sciences*, 2–3, 6087–6096.

Dablanc, L., and Ross, C. (2012). Atlanta: A mega logistics center in the Piedmont Atlantic Megaregion (PAM). *Journal of Transport Geography*, 24, 432–442.

Dablanc, L. (2014). Logistics sprawl and urban freight planning issues in a major gateway city. In *Sustainable urban logistics: Concepts, methods and information systems*. Springer, Berlin, Heidelberg, pp. 49–69.

Dablanc, L. (2018). E-commerce trends and implications for urban logistics. In M. Browne, S. Berhends, J. Holguin-Veras, G. Giuliano and J. Woxenius (Eds.), *Urban logistics, management policy and innovation in rapidly changing environment*. London, Kogan Page.

Dablanc, L., and Browne, M., (2020). Introduction to special section on logistics sprawl. *Journal of Transport Geography*, 88. https://www.sciencedirect.com/science/article/pii/S0966692319300158

Dablanc, L., Heitz, A., Buldeo Rai, H., and Diziain, D. (2022) Response to COVID-19 lockdowns from urban freight stakeholders: An analysis from three surveys in France and policy implications. *Transport Policy*, 122, 85–94.

Diziain, D., Dablanc, L., and Ripert, C. (2012). How can we bring logistics back into cities? The case of Paris metropolitan area. *Procedia – Social and Behavioral Sciences*, 39, 267–281.

Fornari, E., Grandi, S., and Fornari, D. (2018). Retailing 4.0: The new Era of e-commerce in fast moving consumer goods. *Symphonia*, 2, 77–90.

Gardrat, M. (2021). Urban growth and freight transport: From sprawl to distension. *Journal of Transport Geography*, 91, 102979.

Giuliano, G., and Kang, S. (2018). Spatial dynamics of the logistics industry: Evidence from California. *Journal of Transport Geography*, 66, 248–258. January 2018.

Guerrero, D., and Proulhac, L. (2016). The spatial dynamic of logistics activities in the French urban areas. *Cybergeo: European Journal of Geography*, Espace, Société, Territoire, 773, URL: http://journals.openedition.org/cybergeo/27517.

Guerrero, D., Hubert, J.-P., Koning, M., and Roelandt, N. (2022). On the spatial scope of warehouse activity: An exploratory study in France. *Journal of Transport Geography*, 99, 103300.

Guerin, L., Vieira, J. G. V., de Oliveira, R. L. M., de Oliveira, L. K., de Miranda Vieira, H. E., and Dablanc, L. (2021). The geography of warehouses in the São Paulo metropolitan region and contributing factors to this spatial distribution. *Journal of Transport Geography*, 91, 102976.

Gupta, S. (2017). Logistics sprawl in timber markets and its impact on freight distribution patterns in metropolitan city of Delhi. India. *Transportation Research Procedia*, 25, 965–977.

Hall, P., Hesse, M., and Jean-Paul, M. (2006). Reexploring the interface between economic and transport geography. *Environment and Planning A*, 38(8), 1401–1408.

He, M., Zeng, L., Wu, X., and Luo, J. (2019). The spatial and temporal evolution of logistics enterprises in the Yangtze, River Delta. *Sustainability*, 11, 5318.

Heitz, A., and Beziat, A. (2016). The parcel industry in the spatial organization of logistics activities in the Paris Region: Inherited spatial patterns and innovations in urban logistics systems. *Transportation Research Procedia*, 12, 812–824.

Heitz, A., Launay, P., and Beziat, A. (2017). Rethinking data collection on logistics facilities: New approach for determining the number and spatial distribution of warehouses and terminals in metropolitan areas. *Transportation Research Record*, *2609*(1), 67–76.

Heitz, A., Launay, P., and Beziat, A. (2019). Heterogeneity of logistics facilities: an issue for a better understanding and planning of the location of logistics facilities. *European Transport Research Review*, *11*(1), 1–20.

Heitz, A., Dablanc, L., Olsson, J., Sanchez-Diaz, I., and Woxenius, J. (2020). Spatial patterns of logistics facilities in Gothenburg, Sweden. *Journal of Transport Geography*, *88*, 102191.

Heitz A., (2021). The logistics dualization in question: Evidence from the Paris metropolitan area. *Cities*, *119*(3), 103407.

Hesse, M., and Rodrigue, J. P. (2004). The transport geography of logistics and freight distribution. *Journal of Transport Geography*, *12*(3), 171–184.

Hesse, M. (2008). *The city as terminal. In Logistics and freight distribution in an urban context*. Aldershot, Ashgate Publishing.

Hylton, P. J., and Ross, C. L. (2017). Agglomeration economies' influence on logistics clusters' growth and competitiveness. *Regional Studies*, *52–3*, 350–361.

Institut Paris Region (2015). Les filières courtes de proximité au sein du système alimentaire francilien, Focus sur la logistique et les flux de transport, Rapport Institut Paris Region, p. 47.

Japan Logistics Field Institute, Inc. (2020). The trend in the logistics real estate market and the future outlook. http://www.logifield.com/public_files/letter_20201030.pdf

Kang, S. (2020). Relative logistics sprawl: Measuring changes in the relative distribution from warehouses to logistics businesses and the general population. *Journal of Transport Geography*, *83*, 102636.

Masson, S., and Petiot, R. (2015). Spatial dynamics in warehousing activities and agglomeration economies: Lessons from the French case, Working paper ARTDev, Research report, P. 33.

Mareï, N., and Savy, M. (2021). Global South countries: The dark side of city logistics. Dualisation vs Bipolarisation. *Transport Policy*, *100*, 150–160.

McKinnon, A. (2009). The present and future land requirements of logistical activities. *Land Use Policy*, *26*, S293–S301.

Notteboom, T., Parola, F., Satta, G., and Risitano, M. (2017). A taxonomy of logistics centres: Overcoming conceptual ambiguity. *Transport Reviews*, *37*(3), 276–299.

Onstein, A. T., Bharadwaj, I., Tavasszy, L. A., van Damme, D. A., and el Makhloufi, A. (2021). From XXS to XXL: Towards a typology of distribution centre facilities. *Journal of Transport Geography*, *94*, 103128.

Raimbault, N. and Bahoken, F. (2014). Quelles places pour les activités logistiques dans la métropole parisienne? *Territoire en mouvement Revue de géographie et aménagement* (*Territory in Movement Journal of Geography and Planning*) 23–24(3), 53–74.

Raimbault N., Heitz A., and Dablanc L. (2018). Urban planning policies for logistics facilities: a comparison between US metropolitan areas and the Paris region. In M. Browne, S. Berhends, J. Holguin-Veras, G. Giuliano, and J. Woxenius (Eds.), *Urban logistics, management policy and innovation in rapidly changing environment*. London, Kogan Page, 82–87.

Raimbault, N. (2019). Multiplication of logistics parks and invisibilisation of blue-collar workplaces in post-industrial metropolises. *Lo Squaderno*, *51*, 65–69.

Ranieri, L., Digiesi, S., Silvestri B., and Roccotelli, M. (2018). A review of last mile logistics innovations in an externalities cost reduction vision. *Sustainability*, *10–3*, 782.

Rivera, L., Sheffi, Y., and Welsch, R. (2014). Logistics agglomeration in the US. *Transportation Research Part A: Policy and Practice*, *59*, 222–238.

Rivera, L., Sheffi, Y., and Knoppen, D. (2016). Logistics clusters: The impact of further agglomeration, training and firm size on collaboration and value added services. *International Journal of Production Economics*, *179*, 285–294.

Robichet, A., and Nierat, P. (2021). Consequences of logistics sprawl: Order or chaos? - the case of a parcel service company in Paris metropolitan area. *Journal of Transport Geography*, *90*, 102900.

Rodrigue, J. P. (2020a). *The geography of transport systems*. Abingdon, Routledge.

Rodrigue, J. P. (2020b). The distribution network of Amazon and the footprint of freight digitalization. *Journal of Transport Geography*, *88*, 102825.

Sakai, T., Kawamura, K., and Hyodo, T. (2015). Locational dynamics of logistics facilities: Evidence from Tokyo. *Journal of Transport Geography*, *46*, 10–19.

Sakai, T., Kawamura, K., and Hyodo, T. (2017). Spatial reorganization of urban logistics system and its impacts: Case of Tokyo. *Journal of Transport Geography*, *60*, 110–118.

Sakai, T., Kawamura, K., and Hyodo, T. (2018). The relationship between commodity types, spatial characteristics, and distance optimality of logistics facilities. *Journal of Transport and Land Use*, *11*(1), 575–591.

Sakai, T., Kawamura, K., and Hyodo T. (2019). Evaluation of the spatial pattern of logistics facilities using urban logistics land-use and traffic simulator. *Journal of Transport Geography*, *74*, 145–160.

Sakai, T., Beziat, A., and Heitz, A. (2020a). Location factors for logistics facilities: Location choice modeling considering activity categories. *Journal of Transport Geography*, *85*, 102710.

Sakai, T., Kawamura, K., and Hyodo, T. (2020b). Logistics facilities for intra and inter-regional shipping: Spatial distributions, location choice factors, and externality. *Journal of Transport Geography*, *86*, 102783.

Strale, M. (2013). An empirical typology of logistics platforms and activities. *Revue d'économie régionale et urbaine*, *2013*(01), 139–162.

Strale, M. (2020). Logistics sprawl in the Brussels metropolitan area: Toward a socio-geographic typology. *Journal of Transport Geography*, *88*, 102372.

Sun, B., Li, H., and Zhao, Q. (2018). Logistics agglomeration and logistics productivity in the USA. *The Annals of Regional Science*, *61*, 273–293.

Taniguchi, E., Thompson, R., and Yamada, T. (1999). Modelling city logistics. In E. Taniguchi and R. G. Thompson (Eds.), City logistics i, 1st international conference on city Logistics. Institute of Systems Science Research.

van den Heuvel, F. P., De Langen, P. W., van Donselaar, K. H., and Fransoo, J. C. (2013). Spatial concentration and location dynamics in logistics: the case of a Dutch province. *Journal of Transport Geography*, *28*, 39–48.

Veltz, P. (2014). *Mondialisation, villes et territoires. L'économie d'archipel*. Presses Universitaires de France, Quadrige.

Weber, A., and Friedrich, C. J. (1929). *Alfred weber's theory of the location of industries*. Chicago, University of Chicago Press.

Woudsma, C., Jakubicek, P., and Dablanc, L. (2016). Logistics sprawl in North America: methodological issues and a case study in Toronto. *Transportation Research Procedia*, *12*, 474–488.

Yuan, Q. (2019). Does context matter in environmental justice patterns? Evidence on warehousing location from four metro areas in California. *Land Use Policy*, *82*, 328–338.

Yuan, Q., and Zhu, J. (2019). Logistics sprawl in Chinese metropolises: Evidence from Wuhan. *Journal of Transport Geography*, *74*, 242–252.

15
MULTI-ECHELON URBAN DISTRIBUTION NETWORKS
Models, Challenges and Perspectives

Imen Ben Mohamed, Olivier Labarthe, Yann Bouchery,
Walid Klibi and Gautier Stauffer

Introduction

The rapid expansion of e-commerce coupled with the increased attention to sustainability in urban logistics and the evolution of logistics assets capability have unquestionably changed the logistics landscape. The COVID-19 pandemic further accelerated this trend and opened the door for more urban innovations. According to the U.S. Census Bureau (Goldberg, 2022), online sales in the United States have shown a yearly increase of 14% in 2021, and a 50% increase compared to 2019. Similarly, Europe e-sales grew 30% from 2019 to 2021 (Retailing, 2021). Besides, online customers are more service conscious and have significantly increased their expectations regarding delivery times in the last decade: they now expect to receive their orders within hours rather than days (Invesp, 2017; Marty, 2022). This brings additional changes in the way companies are reaching urban consumers to meet expectations: ship-to-locations (SL) now include stores, lockers, relay points, drives, and collection stores in addition to home delivery (Gao and Su, 2017). These trends affect the distribution scheme and routing operations of retailers, logistics service providers and parcel delivery companies that used to regulate the volume and speed of deliveries when seeking cost containment.

In such a context, several global B-to-C players, and especially companies operating in the retail sector, such as Walmart, Carrefour, Amazon and jd.com, have reengineered their distribution networks. Historically, the ideal location of warehouse platforms (WP) was driven by sourcing considerations, centralization, and risk-pooling incentives and financial constraints. These considerations have resulted in distribution networks dominated by single-echelon structures, in which the network topology includes, essentially, a layer of warehouse platforms where the inventory is held, and a layer of customers' ship-to locations. Products are shipped from WPs directly to SLs via large trucks that possibly visit multiple SLs (Nagy and Salhi, 2007; Hemmelmayr et al., 2012). An example of one-echelon distribution network is illustrated in Figure 15.1(a). In recent years, several retailers have realized that their distribution networks were not optimized to provide next-day and/or same-day deliveries, or to efficiently operate fulfillment and urban shipment services. Indeed one-echelon networks usually limit the companies' ability to provide fast delivery services, and reduce opportunities to capture online orders, as WPs can be outside the urban area and thus far

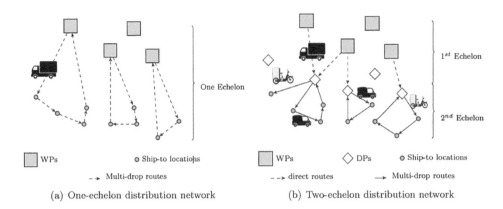

Figure 15.1 Typical distribution networks
Source: Adapted from Ben Mohamed et al. (2022)

from SLs. Major actors are now considering the proximity to their key customers in the reengineering of their network. This leads to a reconsideration of the interplay between network location and routing.

In the same vein, parcel delivery has played a key role in the development of the economy for many years, as it is an essential enabler of e-commerce. Global urbanization, which is expected to reach 68% by 2050 (United Nations, 2018), and the rapid growth of e-commerce, are contributing to an ever-increasing demand for parcel logistics services, motivating the search for sustainable innovations in urban logistics. According to the European Commission (Directorate General for Internal Market, Industry, Entrepreneurship and SMEs, European Commission, 2022), in 2020 the number of parcels handled by all operators at the European level represented 8.23 billion, an increase of 18.1% compared to 2019. This trend accelerated during the COVID-19 pandemic, forcing operators to increase their last-mile delivery capacity in the face of the transition to online channels (Wade and Bjerkan, 2020). Accordingly, urban parcels delivery is undoubtedly the most significant and challenging example of a shift from a one-echelon to a two-echelon urban distribution network setting (Crainic et al., 2016; Janjevic et al., 2019; Rudolph et al., 2022). Traditionally organized in multi-tier urban distribution systems in a tree-like schema (from international/national to local), such systems have been recently challenged to become more interconnected at the urban layer for better performance (Crainic and Montreuil, 2016). Besides, the big players such as UPS, DHL, and La Poste Groupe, many start-ups, including Flexe.com and Darkstore, have recently launched warehousing and delivery services to support ultra-fast delivery.

To address this challenge, attention has been turned toward multi-echelon distribution structures with additional distribution platforms that can be dynamically adjusted to changing business needs over time (Janjevic and Ndiaye, 2014). A typical predisposition, claimed now by practitioners, is the two-echelon distribution network as illustrated in Figure 15.1(b). The network topology includes an intermediate echelon of warehousing/fulfillment platforms located between the WPs and the ship-to locations. For instance, Walmart turned several Sam's Club stores into e-commerce fulfillment centers to support their rapid e-commerce growth (Weinswig, 2018). Another example is La Poste Groupe which recently engaged in the design of a new layer of micro-hubs in urban areas to support the growth of their parcel deliveries (Leveque, 2023).

Furthermore, this trend to increase the number of echelons in urban areas is amplified by increasing congestion and new environmental regulations that impose new modes of transportation, such as small and eco-friendly vehicles (electric vans and cargo bikes), for last-mile deliveries (Winkenbach et al., 2016; Janjevic and Winkenbach, 2020). Such a trend clearly calls for more micro-consolidation in the city and thus the introduction of new micro-hubs or urban fulfillment hubs at the heart of the city. Figure 15.1(b) illustrates a typical two-echelon distribution network supported by cargo bikes. Each echelon has its own assignment-transportation scheme that must be adapted in response to the dynamics shaping the business operations. The above discussion underlined the importance of location and routing decisions within typical model-based decision-making approaches. Location and routing models have been investigated for decades already in the operations research literature. A key question for an urban logistics analyst is the adequacy of existing models with the new challenges offered by the urban landscape. To this end, this chapter will focus on two-echelon models that consider location and/or routing decisions and then will discuss their characteristics and solvability.

The chapter is structured as follows. In the following section, two-echelon location and routing models are presented and their characteristics and solvability are discussed. Then new paradigms in urban logistics and their challenges are described. Finally, the chapter concludes with a discussion of the emerging challenges related to governance, green logistics, smart cities, and hyperconnected logistics.

Two-Echelon Location and Routing Models

As underlined in the early-stage comprehensive review of Nagy and Salhi (2007), the phrase "location-routing problem" is misleading, as location-routing is not a single well-defined problem like the Weber problem. In this chapter, we attempt to divide the literature into two different streams when it comes to design distribution networks where location and routing decisions are considered jointly. One stream of research regards location decisions as strategic and routing decisions as more tactical/operational decisions (see Klibi et al., 2010; Snoeck et al., 2018; Ben Mohamed et al., 2020), while the other stream considers that these decisions are taken simultaneously (see Laporte, 1988).

Depending on the distribution context, the type of models to build can certainly fit with one of these streams. For instance, large postal companies operating historically in city centers usually own real estate that they now consider a primary asset for urban parcel delivery (Leveque, 2023). Besides, oftentimes routing is externalized to subcontractors and there is no control over the corresponding route choices and costs, and thus they have to be estimated (Leveque, 2023). In contrast, due to the introduction of new actors, such as flexe, that offer on-demand warehousing, new actors in the parcel delivery business and omnichannel retailers have now the possibility to build and re-engineer their network on a much more regular basis. When the timing and time granularity of the location and routing decisions starts to align, this calls for models that consider location and routing simultaneously. There are many settings in which this may happen. For instance, there are pilots where mobile hubs such as containers (see Faugère et al., 2020), or autonomous vehicles (see Carreta, 2022) are deployed on a daily basis over the city and delivery tours are organized from these hubs. In such context, it makes perfect sense to optimize the location of the hubs and the tours simultaneously. Other examples include ship-from-stores (Hübner et al., 2022) where stores can be used as micro-hubs upon needs and the decision on which stores to use could be reconsidered daily, truck-and-drone delivery (Moshref-Javadi et al., 2021) where the hubs (trucks) are in permanent motion, and mobile parcel lockers (Schwerdfeger et al., 2020; Li et al., 2021).

We now review the standard approaches for 2-echelon location and routing models for both streams. We focus here on cost-effective and/or profit-driven distribution models as this constitutes the main focus of the existing literature.

Hierarchical Location and Routing Approaches

When location decisions have to be taken at a different *timing and* with a different time granularity to routing decisions, one natural approach consists of solving separate problems. Firstly, location decisions are taken by estimating routing costs as finished products flow toward end-customers and then routing optimization is done in a second step after the locations have been fixed. However, the literature has agreed that these are two interrelated decisions and that integrating them in the same model-based decision-making approach is worthy of consideration. When the integration of location and routing decisions is made in a hierarchical manner, the main concern is to decide on the location where the routing is an anticipation mechanism to evaluate the quality of the location decisions. The review of Nagy and Salhi (2007), considers that such an approach pertains to the class of location-routing problems dedicated to modeling and solving locational problems.

The point of departure here is that the corresponding locational models lead to an extension of the classic facility location problem (FLP) to the two-echelon FLP (2E-FLP). This latter could be enriched at both echelons by alternative modeling of the routing feature such as flow decisions, all or subset of routes design, transportation capacity allocation, route length estimation, or a combination of them.

In the first echelon, where large quantities move toward intermediate hubs via fully loaded vehicles, it is standard to approximate routing as network flows while in the second echelon such an approximation is inappropriate usually if customers are considered individually. The standard approach then consists of aggregating the customers into groups or zones and to consider the flows from the intermediate hubs to the groups (see Simchi-Levi et al., 2007). The corresponding models lead to the two-echelon FLP (2E-FLP), and have been studied extensively (see Correia et al., 2013; Georgiadis et al., 2011). The aggregation of flows is often considered for large demand zones with high volumes, which initially lead to the study of flows of fully loaded vehicles (as for the first echelon) rather than daily explicit routes (Klibi et al., 2010). For instance, Ben Mohamed et al. (2020) considered a hierarchical 2-Echelon distribution network design problem that is formulated as a stochastic multi-period location-capacity allocation model.

However, more recent works by Winkenbach et al. (2016), Merchán and Winkenbach (2018) and Janjevic et al. (2019) considered more realistic estimations of the routing cost in the corresponding zones. The idea is to use asymptotic results on the length of an optimal tour in a uniformly distributed unit square: the optimal tour length of n customers uniformly distributed in a unit square tends to $k \times \sqrt{n}$ as n tends to infinity, for some constant k (Beardwood et al., 1959). Daganzo (1984) exploited this idea to estimate the (average) routing length and costs, for several vehicles with identical capacity departing from a single depot, by splitting the delivery cost estimation into the long-haul costs (to reach the zone) and the on-site costs estimated by adjusting the asymptotic formula to take into account the typical detour in the zone (with respect to bird distance). The initial approximation was later extended to consider different vehicle capacities and other more realistic assumptions on the topology of the cities by several authors (Winkenbach et al., 2016; Merchán and Winkenbach, 2018; Janjevic et al., 2019; Leveque, 2023).

Some models (Klibi et al., 2010; Ben Mohamed et al., 2022) consider that the hierarchy between location and routing decisions is due to the time lag between these decisions and decide upon the location of the hubs using a more advanced two-stage stochastic optimization framework (location decisions are modeled as a first stage decision while routing decisions are second stage ones). For instance, the work of Ben Mohamed et al. (2022) considered a hierarchical setting to define the two-echelon stochastic multi-period capacitated location-routing problem (2E-SM-CLRP), with the aim to integrate a more precise anticipation of the routing costs at the design level. Such approaches allow to integrate more scenarios of future demand, customer distribution and routing aspects and are certainly desirable but they are also much more challenging computationally (for a discussion on the trade-off between modeling precision and computational challenge, see Klibi et al., 2016).

Once location decisions are fixed, the problem reduces to a two-echelon vehicle routing problem (2E-VRP) with a much-refined time granularity than when it is approximated at the network design level. The 2E-VRP is formally introduced by Crainic et al. (2009a), where the authors study a rich variant of a 2E-VRP problem with multiple products and depots, time dependencies, and vehicle synchronization. Perboli et al. (2011) formalized the 2E-VRP and introduced a mathematical model for the 2E-VRP with a single depot. In the 2E-VRP, first-echelon vehicles transport goods from warehouses to intermediate distribution platforms located at the border between the echelons. At the intermediate distribution platforms, goods are unloaded from the first-echelon vehicles and loaded into smaller second-echelon vehicles that satisfy the second-echelon requirements. Next, the second-echelon vehicles perform the freight deliveries from the intermediate distribution platforms to the customers. Several models and exact methods (Perboli and Tadei, 2010; Perboli et al., 2011; Baldacci et al., 2013) and heuristics (Crainic et al., 2011; Hemmelmayr et al., 2012; Breunig et al., 2016; Wang et al., 2017) have been developed in the literature. Recent reviews on the 2E-VRPs can be found in Cuda et al. (2015) and Sluijk et al. (2023).

Simultaneous Location-Routing Approaches

The first contributions to simultaneous two-echelon location-routing were from Jacobsen and Madsen (1980) and Madsen (1983) who introduced the two-echelon LRP (2E-LRP) in the context of newspaper distribution. The model determines the location of the second-echelon platforms at no cost and without capacity limitations. In recent years with the high growth of e-commerce, 2E-LRPs have gained increasing attention, and models consider platform costs and capacity limitations. Sterle (2010) formally introduces the two-echelon Capacitated LRP (2E-CLRP) in an urban context and proposes three mixed-integer programming formulations. The same model is studied by Boccia et al. (2010); Contardo et al. (2012) and Schwengerer et al. (2012) who focus on the development of exact and heuristic solution methods. Nguyen et al. (2012a, 2012b) examine a 2E-CLRP including a single warehouse in the first echelon already located with unlimited capacity. A few recent works by Mirhedayatian et al. (2019) and Farham et al. (2020) study a variant of the 2E-CLRP with time windows. In Mirhedayatian et al. (2019), delivery and pick-up operations are also incorporated. Finally, Darvish et al. (2019) consider also flexibility in due dates.

The literature on 2E-LRP is still scarce, however, and considers mostly a deterministic-static setting (Prodhon and Prins, 2014; Cuda et al., 2015). It is not surprising as the problem generalizes two hard combinatorial optimization problems that have been the subject of intensive research efforts but that are still challenging computationally: facility location problems and vehicle routing problems. For additional references on the problem and solution approaches, see Section 3.1 in Prodhon and Prins (2014).

Beyond Pure Mathematical Programming Approaches

Designing distribution networks has critical impacts for city logistics stakeholders on cost, revenue and service levels to the city citizens. Using mathematical models to design the optimal distribution network is particularly constrained by the characterization of the operating environment and multiple factors such as demand, product portfolio, inventory levels, response time and returnability. Complementing analyses associated with optimal solutions with simulation approaches for evaluating transportation systems enables the development of more efficient and robust distribution networks (Bektas et al., 2017). Numerous publications present results of case studies that exploit simulation models to assess the environmental and economic impact of last-mile distribution networks and urban freight distribution (Allen et al., 2014; Karakikes and Nathanail, 2017; Giampoldaki et al., 2021).

The following four selected publications illustrate the complementarity between simulation and optimization for distribution network design and routing in urban logistics. To solve a two-echelon location-routing problem (2E-LRP), Gruler et al. (2017) integrate a Monte Carlo simulation to represent the demand in order to find the location of urban consolidation centers (UCCs) and estimate the total routing cost (sum of deterministic and stochastic costs). Uncertainty concerning the demand of 342 final customers in Athens (Greece) is considered during the simulation phases to estimate the expected penalization costs of returning to the UCC in case of route failures. According to this research, consolidating last-mile deliveries by opening two UCCs suggests potential savings of 38%. To solve a Dynamic and Stochastic VRP with Time Window problems (DS-VRPTWs), the Monte Carlo simulations enable the generation of multiple instances of operational days for parcel deliveries in an urban context (Perboli et al., 2018). The results associated with the case study based on the city of Turin (Italy) demonstrate the positive impacts associated with the introduction of cargo bikes and lockers by the reduction of kilometers traveled, the operating costs (-37%) and environmental costs (-40%). More recently, the strategic design of last-mile distribution networks with continuous response and tight delivery deadlines is presented in Snoeck and Winkenbach (2022). The authors proposed a metamodel simulation-optimization solution approach where the simulation model is used to evaluate different KPIs related to strategic network cost and operational cost for a scenario of traffic and demand. Kim et al. (2021) designed a decision and system architecture of a hyperconnected urban system within an optimization-supported agent-based simulation platform. The aim of this work is to investigate the potential of the transformation toward hyperconnected fulfillment and last-mile delivery, considering multiple retailers, in a two-tier urban area. Finally, we consider the simulation-based optimization framework proposed by Osorio and Bierlaire (2013) that enables the efficient use of complex stochastic urban traffic simulators to address various transportation problems.

New Paradigms in Urban Logistics

The models described in the previous section can be applied in principle to address network design and routing problems in urban logistics. However, new paradigms are emerging that challenge the corresponding models. As underlined in the introduction, a recent trend for urban delivery is the development of new modes of transportation and new types of facilities in complex urban areas. While cities have always been laboratories for logistics, freight accessibility to city centers is more difficult nowadays due to congestion and access restrictions. This challenging environment is also specific to each and every city and this makes it difficult to develop one-size-fits-all solutions. This led to innovative transportation projects to assess the efficiency of different alternatives to trucks and vans such as the use of public transportation (tramway, metro, buses), on-foot delivery, and the use of cargo bikes. Each of these options has its specific advantages and challenges. The subsections below will discuss these new paradigms, the way they can be incorporated into traditional models and the novel questions they raise.

Cargo Bikes

This section focuses on the routing approaches dedicated to cargo bikes as this one is among the fastest-growing delivery modes in urban areas (see Chapter 5; see Figure 15.2).

An electric cargo bike can be viewed as a special vehicle with carrying capacity of around 1 cubic meter on average and a limited catchment area due to a lack of efficiency if traveling long distances. However, cargo bikes are less sensitive to congestion, and parking is much easier than for trucks or vans. Therefore, they are very efficient for the last miles/feet of delivery in city centers. These features are confirmed in a study based on trials and simulation

(a) La Poste, France, 2022
(J. Leveque – CC BY-SA)

(b) UPS, Germany, 2019
(JoachimKohlerBremen – CC BY-SA 4.0)

(c) PostNL, The Netherlands, 2022
(D. Trung Quoc Don – CC BY-SA 4.0)

(d) DHL, Austria, 2021
(Tischbeinahe – CC BY-SA 4.0)

Figure 15.2 Examples of cyclo-logistics solutions

from Sheth et al. (2019), who show that cargo bikes are more cost effective than trucks for delivering in dense areas with small delivery volumes per stop in close proximity to the distribution center. Melo and Baptista (2017) perform an evaluation of cargo-bike-delivery features in Porto (Portugal) and they conclude that 10% of the deliveries made by vans could be made more efficiently by cargo bikes and Elbert and Friedrich (2020) demonstrate through a simulation study that cargo bikes are a suitable addition to urban consolidation centers. Gonzalez-Calderon et al. (2022) also discuss in detail the use and interest of cargo bikes in Medellin (Colombia). Cargo bikes are also relevant from an environmental point of view (Fraselle et al., 2021). Therefore, cargo-bike deliveries are likely to expand further in the near future in city centers.

While the cargo bike is a new mode of transportation for urban logistics, network design and routing models have long been able to include several modes of transportation that have specific features. However, we believe that the emergence of cargo-bike deliveries in urban areas leads to new challenges in terms of routing estimation and optimization but also to new opportunities in terms of design. We identify three main features: First, cargo bikes are much more sensitive to the load factor and route gradient as compared to other modes of transportation, which might heavily influence travel speed. This leads Fontaine (2022) to develop a new VRP with load-dependent travel times. The author shows that the new model developed can achieve a 22% reduction in travel time as compared to traditional VRP with time windows. Second, the network available is usually assumed to be known for VRP problems. However, there is no clear knowledge of the exact network usable by cargo bikes as they do not have standard dimensions. This makes some streets unusable for some cargo bikes but not for others. Therefore, the network available needs to be discovered through practice and this calls for new simulation-optimization techniques (Frifita et al., 2022). Third, cargo bikes have a limited carrying capacity, but they usually drive multiple tours by reloading new cargo at the depot during their working day. This practice opens up new recourse options in case of disruption or uncertainty. Martins-Turner and Nagel (2019) show that the ability to make multiple tours within a delivery day leads to a reduction of vehicles required and therefore this reduces distribution costs.

In addition, using cargo bikes in combination with urban depots may open up new businesses and thus generate a need for new models. For instance, local pick-up and delivery can be made on the same day by different vehicles if they both pass by the same urban depot. This practice would also enable dynamic re-optimization of routing and cargo re-balancing between vehicles during the working day. This additional flexibility could be a game changer for improving customer service levels. Besides, this would positively affect the performance of routing and this calls for taking these new routing approaches into account while designing the distribution network.

Omnichannel Logistics

A special emerging problem that challenges urban distribution and fits into the two-echelon setting is omnichannel retailing (see Chapter 10). The rise of e-commerce represents about 19% of total retail sales, with a projected growth of over 50% over the next few years (Statista, 2022). Accordingly, several retailers have engaged in developing their online sales channels and moving to an omnichannel retailing strategy. The omnichannel operations research stream is still in its infancy (Chopra, 2018). The recent review of Melacini et al. (2018) identified the most promising research streams for omnichannel: the distribution network design with the evolution in the number and types of logistics facilities, the inventory management for different channels, and how to efficiently use stores to reduce logistics costs, improve service levels and compete with online retailers. In the same way, Ishfaq et al. (2016) found that the stores become more and more critical in the physical distribution process, where many retailers are willing to use the stores as forwarding fulfillment centers to fill online orders, provide last-mile delivery service and handle returns from online customers, which call for multi-tier urban distribution networks.

Recently, several retailers considered the implementation of ship-from-store (SFS) policy through the online channel to ensure a competitive response time. SFS takes advantage of the existing physical network by turning certain store locations to ship-from points for online sales. Recent contributions on network design (Guerrero-Lorente et al., 2020; Arslan et al., 2021) and fulfillment (Bayram and Cesaret, 2021) showed the benefit of using SFS channels, especially to increase the service level perceived by customers. For instance, Arslan et al. (2021) studied the design of omnichannel networks with the implementation of SFS option, which incurs the selection of the store to ship-from at the second echelon based on a two-stage stochastic location-allocation model under uncertain online orders, store sales and capacities. Despite these recent works, one should notice that only a few quantitative fulfillment/delivery models were proposed in the omnichannel distribution (see also Agatz et al., 2008; Hübner et al., 2016). Future models toward omnichannel distribution must better capture the multi-echelon structure of the network and characterize the specific routing requirements.

Multi-modality

The design and deployment of distribution and mobility networks in peri-urban and urban areas represent major challenges (freight in urban traffic, road occupancy, and vehicle access regulations). Designing cost-effective and sustainable first- and last-mile operations is an important line of research that relies on the positioning of small distribution centers/warehouses in relation to the density and size of demand areas, as illustrated in Figure 15.3 (a).

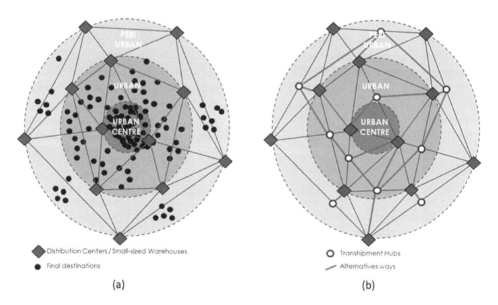

Figure 15.3 Example of web distribution in urban zones
Source: Klibi et al. (2014)

In order to enable efficient use of all existing transportation means and thus to meet environmental and societal goals, one should facilitate multimodal distribution in particular (see Fatnassi et al., 2015; Oliveira et al., 2017; Faugère et al., 2020). For this purpose, it is critical that storage and transshipment points are introduced to provide alternative route and vehicle choices (energy modes and capacities) as illustrated in Figure 15.3(b).

The introduction of such new hubs and transportation means creates additional connections in the traditional tree-like distribution structures and triggers a shift to more web-like networks. The major challenge for cities and operators lies in the positioning of the transshipment and the resulting logistics organization: upstream for their supply, and downstream for delivery to customers. Dealing with the underlying route and vehicle choice issues, the synchronization of the different modes of transportation and calibrating the size/capacity of the storing points brings new challenges to the models in term of design and routing. On the other hand, it offers the opportunity to integrate better pick-up and delivery and to offer in particular new fast delivery services: transshipment points can also be used as pick-up points in particular and the web structure allows for fast intra-mural pick-up and delivery (Leveque, 2023).

At the technological level, a common element to all multimodal urban logistics projects is the development of modular and standardized logistics units that guarantee better interoperability between the different systems and modes of transport. This subject is at the heart of the ETP-Alice vision in the implementation of the Physical Internet concept.

The rapid development of new modes of last-mile delivery in the urban landscape leads to an interest in the opportunities arising from connected or even hyperconnected city logistics, but also to question the approaches to synchronizing multi-modes of goods in multi-platform networks (mobile and shared with passengers). The work of Kechir et al. (2023) discusses the benefit of building on synergies between freight logistics and passenger mobility in urban systems and the ability of ensuring an adequate delivery service using public transportation instead of dedicated on-demand vehicles, while reducing the parcel's time-space footprint within the urban area (see also Chapter 7).

Emerging Challenges

To conclude this chapter, several emerging challenges are discussed. To keep the discussion practice-driven, we begin the section with several innovative examples. The KoMoDo project (KoMoDo, 2018) in Germany exploits a stationary micro-depot made available by the city of Berlin to enable collaboration between several operators: it serves as a collaborative cross-docking station. In France, the cities of Paris and Strasbourg are experimenting with the temporary parking of mobile micro-depots with the provision of public space. The micro-depots arrive loaded, serve as a deposit point and can leave the parking space with freight collected during the day. They can be managed by one or more operators, and they are parked at a dedicated location for a given period of time, generally one day or half a day. In all cases, parcels are usually transferred to e-cargo bikes or small e-vehicles that make several trips on the same day (recharging equipment is usually available). The discussion below paves the way toward novel modeling approaches to the realization of innovative practices.

Governance

From the city's point of view, logistics activity generates a set of negative externalities such as traffic congestion, air, and noise pollution. City decision-makers are finding it difficult to contain these externalities and to foresee the actions of operators, but above all to have adequate decision-support tools to help them make robust decisions. From the operators' point of view, last-mile delivery in urban areas represents a significant part of the costs of parcel distribution, considered as the least efficient transport segment. The concept of "Freight Traffic Control" proposed by Allen et al. (2017) aims to develop collaborative relationships between multi-carriers (sharing fleets of vehicles and warehousing capacity) based on data exchange and cooperative game theory. Trust is fundamental for such initiatives to take off. This will come through the introduction of appropriate fair cost/profit sharing mechanisms and with the protection of the sensitive company data in particular. Models that take these aspects into account in network design and routing in urban logistics are crucial. Guajardo and Rönnqvist (2016) review the literature on the cost allocation mechanisms for horizontal collaboration in transportation, while Pan et al. (2019) review some of the core implementation issues. Sharing a micro-depot is a first step in collaboration and some cities invest in such equipment to avoid complicated cost-sharing mechanisms between different operators and thus facilitate collaboration. The introduction of mobile micro-depots is a way to short-cut large investments in real estate in urban cities. Besides, they can change location during the day to provide more flexibility to the network and allow more accessibility to parcels (Verlinde et al., 2014). Mobile micro-depots (Lan et al., 2022) can take the form of a container temporarily positioned near a distribution area or an ephemeral transshipment area.

Recent research (Ben Mohamed et al., 2020) promotes the importance of challenging the existing two-echelon network design and routing models to integrate such mobile structures. This will certainly bring new interesting mathematical models and computational challenges. These multiple challenges of urban logistics on economic, ecological, and societal facets are notably stated in Savelsbergh and Van Woensel (2016). The scaling up of these organizational innovations must be aligned with the goals of a sustainable city. In a dual way, cities are receiving more and more requests for the provision of micro-consolidation spaces, but in a disjointed manner and without clear visibility on the master plan to be deployed. From a modeling perspective, a great deal remains to be done to bring existing 2-Echelons models to the stage of collaborative/mutualized networks and pooling/shared routes.

Fast and Green

Urban freight delivery is also deeply time-constrained. Indeed, e-commerce players have started a race toward the reduction of click-to-possession following the on-demand economy paradigm. While we discussed above some of the key options to tackle this challenge, fast shipping is often correlated with higher environmental impact as it limits the ability to bundle shipments (Muñoz-Villamizar et al., 2021). While customers have increasing expectations of fast delivery, they are also becoming more and more sensitive to the environmental impacts of last-mile delivery. Muñoz-Villamizar et al. (2022) recently showed through a case study that carbon emissions can be reduced from up to 56% by having up to 4 days for deliveries. This result proves that extending delivery slots can be required to offer greener delivery services. This calls for a better segmentation of the demand as not all customers would require the same shipment delivery for each and every order. Managing the demand side of urban delivery can be achieved in many ways and is among the most promising development area of last-mile logistics. Waßmuth et al. (2023) provide one of the first overviews of how this new paradigm can change operational, tactical, and strategic decisions. From a modeling perspective, the demand management side of urban logistics induces drastic changes in routing decision models by considering some constraints as decision variables.

Hyperconnected Logistics

Clearly, Information and Communication Technology present in smart cities initiatives offers further opportunities as described in the conceptual framework of Smart City Logistics presented by Pan et al. (2021). As stated by Taniguchi et al. (2020), city logistics is evolving through the adoption of new modes of transport and innovative information-based technologies. The availability of information constitutes one of the innovations that can provide anticipatory capabilities to the real urban freight distribution system. Exploiting real-time data on vehicle location and traffic congestion in particular provides new opportunities to improve logistics processes such as booking delivery space and assigning delivery route points (Comi et al., 2018). Given the complexity of the corresponding dynamic systems, data-driven approaches require the definition of new optimization and simulation models. There are already interesting developments. For instance, digital representations of the physical and functional properties through digital twins allow analysts to replicate and predict the dynamics of logistics activities to connect different transport modes (Tavasszy, 2020). The literature review presented in Büközkan and Ilıcak (2022) provides a detailed overview of the integration of innovative logistics solutions associated with the deployment of new technologies in smart cities. Smart cities enable in particular more collaboration between actors and the use of more dynamic solutions for the management of the distribution network/web.

To conclude, we aim to refer to the concept of hyperconnected city logistics (HCL; Crainic and Montreuil, 2016, Crainic et al., 2023), which is at the intersection of the established concept of city logistics (CL; Crainic et al., 2009b; Taniguchi, 2014) and the emerging concept of the Physical Internet (PI) and its enabled hyperconnected logistics (HL; Montreuil, 2011; Ballot et al., 2014), so as to allow for order-of-magnitude improvements in the efficiency, capability, resiliency, and sustainability of urban transport and logistics systems. Inspired by the HCL concept, several novel modeling approaches have been recently proposed: a two-tier urban hyperconnected system with fulfillment and delivery decisions (Kim et al., 2021); a two-tier HCL system for tactical planning of a service network design, including the coalition of carriers and logistic operators, sharing their fleets of vehicles and warehousing capacity (Crainic et al., 2020).

Conclusion

As underlined in this chapter, the new logistics landscape offers several interesting research opportunities in the field. A special focus is given here to integrated and multi-echelon distribution models that we believe are more suitable for the current and future urban context. Primarily, the chapter discussed how these models could be designed given the importance of location decisions, their link to routing decisions, and the inherent challenge of their adequacy and solvability. It also recalls the complexity faced by large-scale optimization models and invites the readers to recent contributions in advanced solution methods, simulation-optimization approaches, and continuous approximation-based reformulations. Secondly, the chapter underlines the difficulty to develop one-size-fits-all solutions and thus calls for the integration of several customized urban innovations. Nowadays, new opportunities offered by the usage of technologies, the expansion of cargo bikes, the predisposition of multi-modality, the synergies with public transportation, and the omnichannel offer, are key to consider in future distribution models.

Finally, the chapter puts light on the emerging paradigms grouped under three umbrellas: governance, fast and green, and hyperconnected logistics. It discusses major organizational initiatives impacting the future urban context such as mutualization, green deliveries, and hyperconnected networks. The latter calls for a new generation of distribution models as well as solution approaches combining optimization, simulation, statistics and machine learning, and game theory frameworks. Much remains to be done from a modeling perspective and implementation to close the gap with urban' decision-maker needs.

References

Agatz, N., Fleischmann, M. and Van Nunen, J. A. (2008) E-fulfillment and multi-channel distribution–a review, *European Journal of Operational Research*, **187**, 339–356.

Allen, J., Bektas, T., Cherrett, T., Friday, A., Mcleod, F., Piecyk, M., Piotrowska, M. and Austwick, M. (2017) Enabling the freight traffic controller for collaborative multi-drop urban logistics: Practical and theoretical challenges, in *Transportation Research Board 96th Annual Meeting*.

Allen, J., Browne, M., Woodburn, A. and Leonardi, J. (2014) A review of urban consolidation centres in the supply chain based on a case study approach, *Supply Chain Forum: An Inter-National Journal*, **15**, 100–112.

Arslan, A., Klibi, W. and Montreuil, B. (2021) Distribution network deployment for omnichannel retailing, *European Journal of Operational Research*, **294**, 1042–1058.

Baldacci, R., Mingozzi, A., Roberti, R. and Calvo, R. W. (2013) An exact algorithm for the two-echelon capacitated vehicle routing problem, *Operations Research*, **61**, 298–314.

Ballot, E., Montreuil, B. and Meller, R. D. (2014) *The Physical Internet*, La Documentation Française.

Bayram, A. and Cesaret, B. (2021) Order fulfillment policies for ship-from-store implementation in omni-channel retailing, *European Journal of Operational Research*, **294**, 987–1002.

Beardwood, J., Halton, J. and Hammersley, J. (1959) The shortest path through many points, *Mathematical Proceedings of the Cambridge Philosophical Society*, **55**, 299–327.

Bektas, T., Crainic, T. G. and Woensel, T. V. (2017) From managing urban freight to smart city logistics networks, In *Network Design and Optimization for Smart Cities* (Eds.) K. Gakis and P. Pardalos, World Scientific, 143–188.

Ben Mohamed, I., Klibi, W., Sadykov, R., Şen, H. and Vanderbeck, F. (2022) The two-echelon stochastic multi-period capacitated location-routing problem, *European Journal of Operational Research*, 306(2), 645–667.

Ben Mohamed, I., Klibi, W. and Vanderbeck, F. (2020) Designing a two-echelon distribution network under demand uncertainty, *European Journal of Operational Research*, **280**, 102–123.

Boccia, M., Crainic, T. G., Sforza, A. and Sterle, C. (2010) A metaheuristic for a two echelon location-routing problem. In *Experimental Algorithms. SEA 2010. Lecture Notes in Computer Science*, vol. 6049 (Ed.) P. Festa, Springer, Berlin, Heidelberg. https://doi.org/10.1007/978-3-642-13193-6_25

Breunig, U., Schmid, V., F, R. F. H. and Vidal, T. (2016) A large neighbourhood based heuristic for two-echelon routing problems, *Computers & Operations Research*, **76**, 208–225.

Büközkan, G. and Ilıcak, O. (2022) Smart urban logistics: Literature review and future directions, *Socio-Economic Planning Sciences*, **81**, 101197.

Carreta. (2022). Carreta Project at La Poste, https://www.lapostegroupe.com/fr/actualite/des-premiers-tests-reussis-pour-carreta-le-vehicule-autonome-daide-au-facteur, accessed: 2022-10-26

Chopra, S. (2018) The evolution of omni-channel retailing and its impact on supply chains, *Transportation Research Procedia*, **30**, 4–13.

Comi, A., Schiraldi, M. M. and Buttarazzi, B. (2018) Smart urban freight transport: Tools for planning and optimizing delivery operations, *Simulation Modelling Practice and Theory*, **88**, 48–61.

Contardo, C., Hemmelmayr, V. and Crainic, T. G. (2012) Lower and upper bounds for the two-echelon capacitated location-routing problem, *Computers & Operations Research*, **39**, 3185–3199.

Correia, I., Melo, T. and Saldanha-da Gama, F. (2013) Comparing classical performance measures for a multi-period, two-echelon supply chain network design problem with sizing decisions, *Computers & Industrial Engineering*, **64**, 366–380.

Crainic, T. G., Errico, F., Rei, W. and Ricciardi, N. (2016) Modeling demand uncertainty in two-tier city logistics tactical planning, *Transportation Science*, **50**, 559–578.

Crainic, T. G., Gendreau, M. and Jemai, L. (2020) Planning hyperconnected, urban logistics systems, *Transportation Research Procedia*, **47**, 35–42.

Crainic, T. G., Klibi, W. and Montreuil, B. (2023) Hyperconnected city logistics: A conceptual framework. In *Handbook on City Logistics and Urban Freight*, Cheltenham, Edward Elgar Publishing. https://www.e-elgar.com/shop/gbp/handbook-on-city-logistics-and-urban-freight-9781800370166.html

Crainic, T. G., Mancini, S., Perboli, G. and Tadei, R. (2011) Multi-start heuristics for the two-echelon vehicle routing problem, in *European Conference on Evolutionary Computation in Combinatorial Optimization (EvoCOP)*, **6622**, 179–190.

Crainic, T. G. and Montreuil, B. (2016) Physical Internet enabled hyperconnected city logistics, *Transportation Research Procedia*, **12**, 383–398.

Crainic, T., Ricciardi, N. and Storchi, G. (2009a) Models for evaluating and planning city logistics systems, *Transportation Science*, **43**, 432–454.

Crainic, T. G., Ricciardi, N. and Storchi, G. (2009b) Models for evaluating and planning city logistics systems, *Transportation Science*, **43**, 432–454.

Cuda, R., Guastaroba, G. and Speranza, M. G. (2015) A survey on two-echelon routing problems, *Computers & Operations Research*, **55**, 185–199.

Daganzo, C. (1984) The distance traveled to visit n points with a maximum of c stops per vehicle: An analytic model and an application, *Transportation Science*, **18**, 331–350.

Darvish, M., Archetti, C., Coelho, L. C. and Speranza, M. G. (2019). Flexible two-echelon location routing problem, *European Journal of Operational Research*, **277**(3), 1124–1136.

Elbert, R. and Friedrich, C. (2020) Urban consolidation and cargo bikes: a simulation study, *Transportation Research Procedia*, **48**, 439–451.

European-Commission (2022) Growth internal market, industry, entrepreneurship and smes, https://webgate.ec.europa.eu/grow/redisstat/databrowser/view/, accessed: 2022-08-31.

Farham, M. S., Iyigun, C. and Süral, H. (2020) The two-echelon location-routing problem with time windows: Formulation, branch-and-price, and clustering, e-print available at http://www.optimization-online.org/DB_HTML/2020/03/7658.html.

Fatnassi, E., Chaouachi, J. and Klibi, W. (2015) Planning and operating a shared goods and passengers on-demand rapid transit system for sustainable city-logistics, *Transportation Research Part B: Methodological*, **81**, 440–460.

Faugère, L., White, C. and Montreuil, B. (2020) Mobile access hub deployment for urban parcel logistics, *Sustainability*, **12**(17), 7213.

Fontaine, P. (2022) The vehicle routing problem with load-dependent travel times for cargo bicycles, *European Journal of Operational Research*, **300**, 1005–1016.

Fraselle, J., Limbourg, S. L. and Vidal, L. (2021) Cost and environmental impacts of a mixed fleet of vehicles, *Sustainability*, **13**, 9413.

Frifita, S., Bouchery, Y., Klibi, W. and Labarthe, O. (2022) Data-driven cargo bikes routing in last-mile delivery, In *23ème congrès annuel de la Société Française de Recherche Opérationnelle et d'Aide à la Décision*.

Gao, F. and Su, X. (2017) Omnichannel retail operations with buy-online-and-pick-up-in-store, *Management Science*, **63**, 2478–2492.

Georgiadis, M. C., Tsiakis, P., Longinidis, P. and Sofioglou, M. K. (2011) Optimal design of supply chain networks under uncertain transient demand variations, *Omega*, **39**, 254–272.

Giampoldaki, E., Madas, M., Zeimpekis, V. and Vlachopoulou, M. (2021) A state-of-practice review of urban consolidation centres: Practical insights and future challenges, *International Journal of Logistics Research and Applications*, 1–32. DOI: 10.1080/13675567.2021.1972950

Goldberg, J. (2022) E-commerce sales grew 50% to $870 billion during the pandemic, https://www.forbes.com/sites/jasongoldberg/2022/02/18/e-commerce-sales-grew-50-to-870-billion-during-the-pandemic/?sh=138ef1c24e83, accessed: 2022-05-31.

Gonzalez-Calderon, C. A., Posada-Henao, J. J., Granada-Muñoz, C. A., Moreno-Palacio, D. P. and Arcila-Mena, G. (2022) Cargo bicycles as an alternative to make sustainable last-mile deliveries in Medellin, Colombia, *Case Studies on Transport Policy*, **10**(2), 1172–1187.

Gruler, A., Juan, A. A., Klüter, A. and Rabe, M. (2017) A simulation-optimization approach for the two-echelon location routing problem arising in the creation of urban consolidation centres, In *Simulation in Produktion und Logistik*, 129–138.

Guajardo, M. and Rönnqvist, M. (2016) A review on cost allocation methods in collaborative transportation, *International Transactions in Operational Research*, **23**, 371–392.

Guerrero-Lorente, J., Gabor, A. F. and Ponce-Cueto, E. (2020) Omnichannel logistics network design with integrated customer preference for deliveries and returns, *Computers & Industrial Engineering*, **144**, 106433.

Hemmelmayr, V. C., Cordeau, J.-F. and Crainic, T. G. (2012) An adaptive large neighborhood search heuristic for two-echelon vehicle routing problems arising in city logistics, *Computers & Operations Research*, **39**, 3215–3228.

Hübner, A., Hense, J. and Dethlefs, C. (2022). The revival of retail stores via omnichannel operations: A literature review and research framework, *European Journal of Operational Research*, **302**(3), 799–818.

Hübner, A., Holzapfel, A. and Kuhn, H. (2016) Distribution systems in omni-channel retailing, *Business Research*, **9**, 255–296.

Invesp (2017) The importance of same day delivery – statistics and trends, https://www.Invespcro.com/blog/same-day-delivery/, accessed: 2021-03-10.

Ishfaq, R., Defee, C., Gibson, B. and Raja, U. (2016) Realignment of the physical distribution process in omni-channel fulfillment, *International Journal of Physical Distribution & Logistics Management*, **46**(6/7), 543–561.

Jacobsen, S. and Madsen, O. (1980) A comparative study of heuristics for a two-level location-routing problem, *European Journal of Operational Research*, **6**, 378–387.

Janjevic, M. and Ndiaye, A. (2014) Development and application of a transferability framework for micro-consolidation schemes in urban freight transport, *Procedia-Social and Behavioral Sciences*, **125**, 284–296.

Janjevic, M. and Winkenbach, M. (2020) Characterizing urban last-mile distribution strategies in mature and emerging e-commerce markets, *Transportation Research Part A: Policy and Practice*, **133**, 164–196.

Janjevic, M., Winkenbach, M. and Merchán, D. (2019) Integrating collection-and-delivery points in the strategic design of urban last-mile e-commerce distribution networks, *Transportation Research Part E: Logistics and Transportation Review*, **131**, 37–67.

Karakikes, I. and Nathanail, E. (2017) Simulation techniques for evaluating smart logistics solutions for sustainable urban distribution, *Procedia Engineering*, **178**, 569–578.

Kechir, M., Clautiaux, F., Labarthe, O. and Klibi, W. (2023). An integrated two-layer network design model for an Interconnected Public and Freight Transportation System, in ROADEF 2023, Rennes, France. https://roadef2023.sciencesconf.org/436618/document. Accessed: 2023-03-03.

Kim, N., Montreuil, B., Klibi, W. and Kholgade, N. (2021) Hyperconnected urban fulfillment and delivery, *Transportation Research Part E: Logistics and Transportation Review*, **145**, 102104.

Klibi, W., Labarthe, O., Deschamps, J.-C. and Babai, Z. (2014) The role of peri-urban networks in building efficient and sustainable distribution systems, in *Proceedings of 1st International Physical Internet Conference*.

Klibi, W., Lasalle, F., Martel, A. and Ichoua, S. (2010) The stochastic multiperiod location transportation problem, *Transportation Science*, **44**, 221–237.

Klibi, W., Martel, A. and Guitouni, A. (2016) The impact of operations anticipations on the quality of stochastic location-allocation models, *Omega*, **62**, 19–33.

KoMoDo (2018) Komodo project in berlin, https://https://www.komodo.berlin/, accessed: 2022-09-20.

Lan, Y.-L., Liu, F.-G., Huang, Z., Ng, W. W. Y. and Zhong, J. (2022) Two-echelon dispatching problem with mobile satellites in city logistics, *IEEE Transactions on Intelligent Transportation Systems*, **23**, 84–96.

Laporte, G. (1988) Location-routing problems, In *Vehicle Routing: Methods and Studies* (Eds.) B. L. Golden and A. A. Assad, North-Holland, Amsterdam, 163–198.

Leveque, J. (2023) *Conception de Réseaux de Distribution Urbains Mutualisés en Mode Doux*, Ph.D. thesis, University of Bordeaux.

Li, J., Ensafian, H., Bell, M. G. and Geers, D. G. (2021). Deploying autonomous mobile lockers in a two-echelon parcel operation. *Transportation Research Part C: Emerging Technologies*, **128**, 103–155.

Madsen, O. (1983) Methods for solving combined two level location-routing problems of realistic dimensions, *European Journal of Operational Research*, **12**, 295–301.

Martins-Turner, K. and Nagel, K. (2019) How driving multiple tours affects the results of last mile delivery vehicle routing problems, *Procedia Computer Science*, **151**, 840–845.

Marty, J. (2022) Consumer/user/customer integration in supply chain management: A review and bibliometric analysis, *Supply Chain Forum: An International Journal*, **23**, 181–196.

Melacini, M., Perotti, S., Rasini, M. and Tappia, E. (2018) E-fulfilment and distribution in omni-channel retailing: a systematic literature review, *International Journal of Physical Distribution & Logistics Management*, **48**, 391–414.

Melo, S. and Baptista, P. (2017) Evaluating the impacts of using cargo cycles on urban logistics: Integrating traffic, environmental and operational boundaries, *European Transport Research Review*, **9**, 1–10.

Merchán, D. and Winkenbach, M. (2018) High-resolution last-mile network design, In *City Logistics 3: Towards Sustainable and Liveable Cities* (Eds.) E. Taniguchi and R. G. Thompson, New York, Wiley Online Library, 201–214.

Mirhedayatian, S. M., Crainic, T. G., Guajardo, M. and Wallace, S. W. (2019) A two-echelon location-routing problem with synchronisation, *Journal of the Operational Research Society*, **72**(1), 1–16.

Montreuil, B. (2011) Toward a physical internet: Meeting the global logistics sustainability grand challenge, *Logistics Research*, **3**, 71–87.

Moshref-Javadi, M., Hemmati, A. and Winkenbach, M. (2021). A comparative analysis of synchronized truck-and-drone delivery models. *Computers & Industrial Engineering*, **162**, 107648.

Muñoz-Villamizar, A., Velázquez-Martínez, J. C., Haro, P., Ferrer, A. and Mariño, R. (2021) The environmental impact of fast shipping ecommerce in inbound logistics operations: A case study in Mexico, *Journal of Cleaner Production*, **283**, 125400.

Muñoz-Villamizar, A., Velázquez-Martínez, J. C., Mejía-Argueta, C. and Gámez-Pérez, K. (2022) The impact of shipment consolidation strategies for green home delivery: A case study in a Mexican retail company, *International Journal of Production Research*, **60**, 2443–2460.

Nagy, G. and Salhi, S. (2007) Location-routing: Issues, models and methods, *European Journal of Operational Research*, **177**, 649–672.

Nguyen, V. P., Prins, C. and Prodhon, C. (2012a) Solving the two-echelon location routing problem by a grasp reinforced by a learning process and path relinking, *European Journal of Operational Research*, **216**, 113–126.

Nguyen, V. P., Prins, C. and Prodhon, C. (2012b) A multi-start iterated local search with tabu list and path relinking for the two-echelon location-routing problem, *Engineering Applications of Artificial Intelligence*, **25**, 56–71.

Oliveira, C. M. d., Albergaria De Mello Bandeira, R., Vasconcelos Goes, G., Schmitz Gonçalves, D. N. and D'Agosto, M. D. A. (2017) Sustainable vehicles-based alternatives in last mile distribution of urban freight transport: A systematic literature review, *Sustainability*, **9**, 13–24.

Osorio, C. and Bierlaire, M. (2013) A simulation-based optimization framework for urban transportation problems, *Operations Research*, **61**, 1333–1345.

Pan, S., Trentesaux, D., Ballot, E. and Huang, G. Q. (2019) Horizontal collaborative transport: survey of solutions and practical implementation issues, *International Journal of Production Research*, **57**, 5340–5361.

Pan, S., Zhou, W., Piramuthu, S., Giannikas, V. and Chen, C. (2021) Smart city for sustainable urban freight logistics, *International Journal of Production Research*, **59**, 2079–2089.

Perboli, G., Rosano, M., Saint-Guillain, M. and Rizzo, P. (2018) Simulation–optimisation framework for city logistics: An application on multimodal last-mile delivery, *IET Intelligent Transport Systems*, **12**, 262–269.

Perboli, G. and Tadei, R. (2010) New families of valid inequalities for the two-echelon vehicle routing problem, *Electronic notes in discrete mathematics*, **36**, 639–646.

Perboli, G., Tadei, R. and Vigo, D. (2011) The two-echelon capacitated vehicle routing problem: models and math-based heuristics, *Transportation Science*, **45**, 364–380.

Prodhon, C. and Prins, C. (2014) A survey of recent research on location-routing problems, *European Journal of Operational Research*, **238**, 1–17.

Retailing, I. (2021) European eCommerce revenues jump 30% to US$465bn in 2021, Internet Retailing, available from https://internetretailing.net/rxgeu/rxgeu/ european-ecommerce-revenues-jump-30-to-us465bn-in-2021.

Rudolph, C., Nsamzinshuti, A., Bonsu, S., Ndiaye, A. and Rigo, N. (2022) Localization of relevant urban micro-consolidation centers for last-mile cargo bike delivery based on real demand data and city characteristics, *Transportation Research Record*, **2676**, 365–375.

Savelsbergh, M. and Van Woensel, T. (2016) 50th anniversary invited article—city logistics: Challenges and opportunities, *Transportation Science*, **50**, 579–590.

Schwengerer, M., Pirkwieser, S. and Raidl, G. R. (2012) A variable neighborhood search approach for the two-echelon location-routing problem, in *European Conference on Evolutionary Computation in Combinatorial Optimization*, Springer, 13–24.

Schwerdfeger, S. and Boysen, N. (2020). Optimizing the changing locations of mobile parcel lockers in last-mile distribution. *European Journal of Operational Research*, **285**(3), 1077–1094.

Sheth, M., Butrina, P., Goodchild, A. and McCormack, E. (2019) Measuring delivery route cost trade-offs between electric-assist cargo bicycles and delivery trucks in dense urban areas, *European Transport Research Review*, **11**, 1–12.

Simchi-Levi, D., Kaminsky, P. and Simchi-Levi, E. (2007) *Designing and Managing the Supply Chain: Concepts, Strategies, and Case Studies*, McGraw-Hill Professional.

Sluijk, N., Florio, A., Kinable, J., Dellaert, N. and Van Woensel, T. (2023) Two-echelon vehicle routing problems: A literature review, *European Journal of Operational Research,* **304**(3), 865–886.

Snoeck, A. and Winkenbach, M. (2022) A discrete simulation-based optimization algorithm for the design of highly responsive last-mile distribution networks, *Transportation Science*, **56**, 201–222.

Snoeck, A., Winkenbach, M. and Mascarino, E. (2018) Establishing a robust urban logistics net- work at FEMSA through stochastic multi-echelon location routing, In *Logistics 2: Modeling and Planning Initiatives* (Eds.) E. Taniguchi and R. G. Thompson, New York, Wiley online library, 59–78.

Statista. (2022). Retail e-commerce sales worldwide from 2014 to 2026. https://www.statista.com/statistics/379046/worldwide-retail-e-commerce-sales/. Accessed: 2023-03-06.

Sterle, C. (2010) *Location-Routing models and methods for Freight Distribution and Infomobility in City Logistics*, Ph.D. thesis, Università degli Studi di Napoli "Federico II".

Taniguchi, E. (2014) Concepts of city logistics for sustainable and liveable cities, *Procedia-social and behavioral sciences*, **151**, 310–317.

Taniguchi, E., Thompson, R. G. and Qureshi, A. G. (2020) Modelling city logistics using recent innovative technologies, *Transportation Research Procedia*, **46**, 3–12, the 11th International Conference on City Logistics, Dubrovnik, Croatia, 12th - 14th June 2019.

Tavasszy, L. A. (2020) Predicting the effects of logistics innovations on freight systems: Directions for research, *Transport Policy*, **86**, A1–A6.

United-Nations (2018) 2018 revision of world urbanization prospects.

Verlinde, S., Macharis, C., Milan, L. and Kin, B. (2014) Does a mobile depot make urban deliveries faster, more sustainable and more economically viable: Results of a pilot test in Brussels, *Transportation Research Procedia*, **4**, 361–373.

Waßmuth, K., Köhler, C., Agatz, N. and Fleischmann, M. (2023) Demand management for attended home delivery–a literature review, *European Journal of Operational Research*, In press. https://doi.org/10.1016/j.ejor.2023.01.056

Wade, M. and Bjerkan, H. (2020) Three proactive response strategies to COVID-19 business challenges, *MIT Sloan Management Review*. https://sloanreview.mit.edu/article/three-proactive-response-strategies-to-covid-19-business-challenges/, accessed: 2023-03-03

Wang, K., Shao, Y. and Zhou, W. (2017) Metaheuristic for a two-echelon capacitated vehicle routing problem with environmental considerations in city logistics service, *Transportation Research Part D: Transport and Environment*, **57**, 262–276.

Weinswig, D. (2018) Sam's club is closing one-tenth of its stores and converting 12 to e-commerce hubs: Proof that store closures have become respectable? https://www.linkedin.com/ pulse/sams-club-closing-one-tenth-its-stores-converting-12-hubs-weinswig/, accessed: 2018-03-05.

Winkenbach, M., Kleindorfer, P. R. and Spinler, S. (2016). Enabling urban logistics services at la poste through multi-echelon location-routing, *Transportation Science*, **50**, 520–540.

16
COMPUTING TECHNOLOGY AND ITS APPLICATIONS IN URBAN LOGISTICS

Lóránt Tavasszy and Hans Quak

Introduction

Urban logistics is growing in complexity. While consumers still buy the majority of their goods in brick-and-mortar retail outlets, online shopping is becoming more and more popular. E-commerce allows consumers to order at home and choose between many delivery options. Automated logistics management systems assist in the planning and execution of deliveries, with sophisticated online marketing and service systems that instantly adapt to changing customer needs. These e-commerce platforms process large amounts of data and have an increasing degree of autonomy in logistics decision-making, be it about which products are sold to whom or which way they are shipped. All this data also allows improved strategic intelligence for business and government, to make decisions about operations, investments and even public policies. As the pressure on urban logistics is increasing to become environmentally friendly and socially equitable, new management approaches are needed to cope with the burgeoning of platforms and continuous launching of new online services. Companies apply data analytics to develop consumer profiles and calibrate their omni-channel service offerings to their customers' needs. By leveraging rich data sources about citizen and business activities, city governments are also increasingly capable of recognising problems and quickly responding to them through new regulation. Digitalisation has not only created new ways to earn money, but it has also empowered politicians and their constituents, the citizens, to act in informed ways. In short, computing technology and its applications are revolutionising urban logistics.

Interestingly, digitalisation and automation have been developing since the 1960s, it seems that only since the turn of the century, after the mass deployment of internet connections and the smartphone, the digital industry has tapped into the vast resource of consumer needs and powers. Still, however, in many ways, the digitalised world of logistics is old-fashioned. Most private and public computer systems are centralised, many global logistics standards are not harmonised or adjust badly to changing practices, most of the data exchanged is paper-based, and the service industry is still fragmented. As part of the digitalisation revolution, these practices still have to change. When they have, data will flow even more easily and larger systems can be coordinated or optimised, creating another step change in efficiency and effectiveness of logistics systems.

Figure 16.1 Conceptual framework for this chapter

The aim of this chapter is to systematically explore this development, by means of an inventory of relevant computing technologies and an analysis of their role in urban logistics, and provide an evaluation of their expected impacts. The conceptual model above is followed, which builds from individual computing technologies, to purpose-built logistics innovations, to future urban logistics systems into which these innovations converge (Figure 16.1).

The chapter is built up along these lines. The following section briefly introduces the main innovations in computing technology that affect logistics systems. This is followed by an exploration of how these technologies individually or collectively seep into system innovations, creating increased logistics value. An identification of the three concurrent development pathways for future urban freight systems, that build on these innovations is provided and finally, the chapter is summarised and closed in the conclusions.

Innovations in Computing Technology

Without the ambition to give a comprehensive account of the new opportunities of the ICT revolution, this section reiterates the main technological innovations that have found application in urban logistics, or which are being considered. Recent reviews (Büyüközkan and Göçer, 2018; Ferrari et al, 2022, Iddris, 2018) have detailed these technologies and discussed their generic impact on logistics systems. Four broad areas of innovation are distinguished in which computing technology developments can be characterised: hardware, software, data and networked applications.

Ubiquitous hardware: Following a continued trend of decades, computers are becoming smaller and more powerful, to an extent that they will be less obtrusive making them portable and wearable, integrated into everyday apparel and clothing. Satellites and embedded software allow all-to-all communication between objects. After the smartphone and smartwatch, tracking of objects and sensing of their states at low prices, and virtual and augmented reality gear are the next practical steps.

Big data storage and processing: The digitalisation of administrative systems is now moving from the early stages of governmental spheres, to single and multi-company proprietary systems. In places where these spheres meet (e.g. digital bills of lading) that innovations in logistics affect entire communities. It also allows an increase in data availability within these communities, and automation of data processing facilities, eventually including automated decision-making. The development raises new concerns about data ownership, exchange and use. Not only are new data markets developing but also the governance of these markets is in its early stages.

Decision support software: The increased availability of data, especially of streaming data from operational processes has opened new possibilities for data analytics. The data analytics pipeline includes capture, processing, storage, analysis and usage of data for various purposes, including monitoring and evaluation of processes, diagnosis of problems, prediction of activities and predictive purposes, to optimise and manage processes. Our ability to reproduce the working of a system with software has strongly improved, leading to the advent of digital twins of systems. Eventually, decision support software could evolve into automated decision-making, where humans are no longer critical. This move towards artificial intelligence (AI)-based operations is problematic where demands on explainability (Taj and Zaman, 2022) are high, or moral decisions are at stake. Current applications of AI are still modest, therefore, focusing on pattern recognition from data to ease interpretation of large amounts of data.

Networked applications: The miniaturisation of electronics has spurred the development of decentralised and distributed (cloud and fog) computing, where computing power is shared and divided amongst different objects. If these objects happen to be parcels or containers, shipments are ready to become intelligent, opening the door towards completely decentralised decision-making in logistics. It requires distributed software, supported by IoT (internet of things) connectivity and new platform technologies to aggregate signals, for such distributed systems to work. Platform-based markets that connect supply and demand for services and collaborative, or cross-chain control towers are concrete examples.

Collective impact: One can look at individual technologies, but also at how these work together to create new opportunities to manage the urban freight transport system, and how they cooperate with humans. This idea of technology convergence or human-machine convergence is important in studies of the future of larger social-technological systems. Futuristic visions that include notions of convergence and are relevant for urban logistics include Cyber-Physical Systems (also called Industry 4.0) and the Physical Internet. We argue that it is important to take such visions as a starting point. Not only does it help to sketch a realistic image of how technologies would be co-existing, but it also allows us to see their roles and functions in the system, and the way in which together they determine the future performance of the system. Such new configurations of new technologies are capable of forming entirely new services (e.g. e-commerce through a smart combination of digital trading, logistics and banking) or opportunities to control the urban logistics system in different, more productive ways than before (e.g. smart cities through digital twins and control towers). Tang and Veelenturf (2019) even argue that logistics has a strategic role in the Industry 4.0 era and that, together, these technologies and services can also create environmental and social value. In the following section, three different ways are discussed in which these technologies together can create new added value in the logistics services sector.

Impact Pathways of Computing Technology into Logistics Systems

The expected benefits of digitalisation of logistics systems are enormous. The World Economic Forum estimates that improved coordination will provide 3.4 trillion USD in new business value for the logistics services industry, which is in the order of magnitude of 10% of the current logistics services market (Snabe and Weinelt, 2016). But how will this new business value materialise? This section first looks at the principles of value creation from digitalisation, compared to a formerly physical world. The promising innovative implementations in urban logistics are discussed both it in existing services and in new ones.

Value creation by digitalisation involves a marriage between physical and digital systems, in a way that new customer value is generated. Hofmann and Ruesch (2017) provide an introduction to the way in which digital technologies can add value to logistics systems. Their conceptual model is used as inspiration and a simplified version of this is taken as a starting point (Figure 16.2).

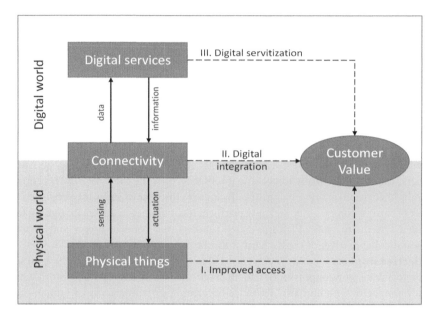

Figure 16.2 New business value of physical-digital integration in logistics

The Figure shows that there is a physical world (lower half of the figure) to which the new digital world (upper half) is adding value, by improving access, providing additional services or reducing physical needs with digital services. The interface between the two worlds is arranged through a connectivity layer, exchanging data and information and physically connecting them via sensors and actuators. Sensors include traffic detectors in roads, cameras and air monitoring devices. Actuation in the physical world happens through logistics management decisions of humans and their decision support systems but also of automated control devices. One can distinguish different management decisions here, for different actors and time cycles. For example, the classical infrastructure policy loop is a long-term, public management cycle, responding to the reporting of accessibility problems, suggestions for solutions, votes in governmental arenas and policy implementation – altogether, it can take decades before an infrastructure policy cycle is completed. Shorter time cycles involve investment decisions in real estate and fleets by service providers, of changes in transport service offerings, of daily planning of delivery trips and their execution, with drivers making decisions by the minute, and traffic lights responding within seconds. It is widely expected that these decisions will benefit from digitalisation.

Indeed, the addition and completion of a layer of digitalised services (the "digital world" in Figure 16.2) will allow these decisions to respond more quickly, accurately and comprehensively to information from sensors. They will be quicker, as digital information doesn't rely on paper-based exchange through multiple layers of organisations. They will be more accurate as data are recorded digitally, allowing them to be shared, improved and analysed easily, so that evidence-based decision-making becomes easier. Also, they will be comprehensive as lower costs of communication mean that decisions can be coordinated to be consistent and mutually reinforcing. Altogether, digitalisation is expected to increase the customer value of all existing services in the physical logistics world. In terms of customer value, this means an increased value of the availability of goods.

In addition to this new value of availability, a new series of digitalised services will develop and, with these, new physical services will emerge that can only exist with digital support – these are shown as value of digital servitisation and value of digital integration as shown in Figure 16.2. New digital services can be manifold. The simplest form of service is the digital delivery of previously paper-based information (e.g. a digital invoice, customs declarations); here services have become digital, and physical services have become replaced or enhanced by digital services – servitisation. New information during the shipping process will become available, like status information or delivery time predictions. Also, digital information upstream (from consumer to service provider) will be possible, allowing changes in delivery when needed. This can invoke a delay or acceleration of shipments or even a transfer of ownership, if re-routing, temporary storage or return arrangements are made. Finally, also completely new forms of physical delivery (e.g. crowd-shipping or instant delivery) will become possible, which can only exist when all information systems are digitalised and new digital platforms are created allowing fast access and communications. This servitisation is exemplified by the growth of the platform economy, where the ICT sector also competes with incumbent, less digitalised logistics services through digital integration services (see Müller and Knitschky, 2021).

Table 16.1 lists the most frequently named digitalised innovations in urban logistics. Each innovation includes a brief description and is classified according to (1) the leading technology as discussed in the previous section (hardware, data, software or networked applications) and (2) the type of service improvement: value in (physical) availability of goods, value in digital servitisation and value in digital integration.

The above-listed technologies are not independent. They can interact in the transport chain (e.g. lockers and autonomous delivery vehicles) causing complications in the delivery of goods. They can depend on each other or reinforce each other (e.g. RFID and transport process information) and could even compete (e.g. IoT and platforms). These interdependencies are important to understand and manage, as they determine the speed at which technologies are adopted and, eventually, the speed at which their joint deployment can create synergies to realise the expected total benefits for the logistics system. This joint deployment is the subject of the next section. Our focus will be on the long-term vision concerning this convergent use of technologies. The section does not detail short-term interdependencies and interconnections between technologies (e.g. TMS and WMS integration issues). Nor does it attempt to predict whether or when individual technologies will see a breakthrough (e.g. blockchain applications). Instead, the question addressed is by which logic these technologies are likely to converge in the urban system: what will drive their joint deployment, what will be their expected collective impact, and how can one describe the resulting strategic change at the level of the urban logistics system? The following discusses three ways in which individual technologies are converging into the urban logistics systems of the future.

Convergence into the Urban Logistics System: 3 Pathways

To understand the future functioning of applications of computing technologies, in relation to each other and within the entire system, they are positioned in light of the vision of the Physical Internet (Montreuil, 2011). The Physical Internet (PI) is a long-term vision for the global logistics system where due to far-reaching digitalisation and automation of all processes, physical distribution systems around the world can be optimised across large, multi-company networks. This optimisation affects all decisions in logistics, from daily routing, vehicle and mode choice, to distribution and even ownership of goods. The current

Table 16.1 Digitalised innovations in urban logistics

Innovation	Key proposition	Typical application	Key tech (H/D/S/N)[a]	Value (A/S/I)[b]
Drones	Fast access to goods for difficult (built/remote) areas	Urgent and rescue logistics	S	A
Robotized warehouses	High capacity, flexible handling and sorting	Complex cross-docking and warehouse ops	H/S	A
Blockchain	Access to a distributed transaction ledger	Smart contracts	D	S
Product and service sales platforms	Shop from home, service optimisation	E-commerce websites, crowd logistics, collaboration, auctions	N	A S
Advanced data analytics	Insights and predictions from big data	Forecasting, business intelligence (BI)	D	I
Electric vehicles	Environment-friendly delivery	Zero-emission zones	H	S
Autonomous vehicles	Lower transport costs, DIY (un)load	Niches (humanitary, restaurants)	S	S
Coded parcel lockers	Flexibility in pick-up and delivery	Alternative for home delivery	S	A
Barcodes and RFID	Information embedded in shipment	Supply chain digitalisation	H	I
VR/AR applications	Personal and situational information	Shopping experience, warehousing	H	S (consumer) I (services)
Transport and shipment process information	Track- and traceability, forecasting	Communication within supply and transport chain	D	S (consumer) I (services)
Digital twins of hubs, chains, cities	Enhanced business intelligence (BI), control and autonomy	Niches (military, production)	S	S (BI) I (control)
Internet of Things	Objects exchange information autonomously	Wearable tech, object tracking, inventory management	H	I
3D printing (additive manufacturing)	Production of objects at home, customizability	Specialised small products (niches)	H	A S

a Hardware, data, software or networked applications
b Value in (physical) availability of goods, servitisation and integration

roadmaps for the Physical Internet to be completed reach until the 2040s (ALICE, 2020) while experts believe that this timeline is too short (Fahim et al., 2021). While, over the course of a decade, an extensive body of literature has developed about the PI, the topic of urban logistics has not been treated in much detail. Based on the limited literature that operationalises the PI for urban logistics, i.e. hyperconnected urban logistics (e.g. the conceptual and quantitative models in (Crainic and Montreuil, 2016) and (Kim et al., 2021) respectively, there is no reason to believe that ICT will be deployed in a different way in urban logistics than in the wider, global system. This chapter develops this reasoning for deployment of specific technologies and of their convergence, into the PI system.

In the context of urban logistics, an important and underdeveloped part of the PI literature, is its governance. While the PI roadmaps do mention that the PI needs some form of public governance, this need has not been operationalised in much detail. At least two characteristics of the PI make it necessary to pay special attention to its governance in an urban freight setting. Firstly, the main promise of the PI vision is the expected quantum leap in logistics efficiency and effectiveness. Although this probably will have significant impacts on emissions and safety risks of the system, these impacts remain externalities, meaning that incentives for their containment are not built-in. Secondly, the PI will be optimised at the system level, meaning that there will be distributive effects, concerning both the internal, logistic KPIs as well as the external impacts. As, also here, the basic definition of the system lacks incentives to steer the distribution of effects (and rather steer on optimising the aggregate), one cannot tell beforehand whether the resulting distribution will be socially acceptable. Therefore, some form of control mechanism must be developed that keeps the PI in the urban area within bounds, supported by the same advanced levels of ICT.

Instrumental for both developments above will be decision support tooling. Although one can expect that many decisions at a tactical or operational level (such as dynamic planning of shipments) will be automated, especially strategic or long-term decisions (such as investments in innovations) will be human-driven and subject to a process of alignment between public and private stakeholders. New computing technologies also provide important opportunities to support these alignment and decision-making processes. Although digital twins are already mentioned in Table 16.1 as one of the individual innovations, we argue that they are a convergent technology also, as more and more features of cities accumulate. Moreover, their development and use in the urban environment depend on the successful deployment of the other technologies. These are discussed in the last part of this section.

Pathway 1: The Physical Internet

Montreuil (2011) and subsequent work on the foundations of the Physical Internet (PI) defined a number of key building blocks for the PI:

- **Unified set of standard modular logistics containers, containerised logistics equipment and technology** promote the shared use of assets, reducing fixed costs and improving utilisation levels, while in the longer term also reducing the global pool of transportation assets. This standardisation is aided by **standard logistics services and operation protocols** which allows asset sharing through interoperability.
- **Certified open logistics facilities and open logistics service providers** allow to specify service offerings that are transparent towards a broad base of potential clients, support easy entry and exit of service providers and switching of clients between service providers.
- **Information systems** that include global logistics monitoring; smart data-driven analytics and logistics decisional and transactional platforms. Clearly automated and cross-system decision-making requires large-scale continuous information exchange. These systems should evolve to an extent that PI operations can be run reliably. Automated decision-making implies that sensing information, analytics and actuation (execution of decisions) can all function in very short timeframes (say, seconds).

Table 16.2 Role of advanced computing technology in the PI

Innovation	Role in the PI
Blockchain	Supports smart contracts and decentralised sensing of events
Product and service sales platforms	Digital entry for consumers to all PI services
Advanced data analytics	Allows AI-based real-time decision-making
Autonomous delivery vehicles	Strong reduction of transport costs
Coded parcel lockers	Allows sharing of locker space
Barcodes and RFID	Required for decentral data and automated processing
Transport and shipment information	Required for track- and traceability, forecasting, certification
Internet of Things	Allows distributed information carriage and sharing
Digital twins of hubs, chains, cities	Lower-level DTs can be embedded in a city DT
3D printing	Ultimate postponement of manufacturing

Several of these are dependent on step changes in our digital systems, while the last building block clearly shows the dependence of the PI on the establishment of a control loop, from monitoring to analytics to action. This could extend in several directions. Pan et al. (2017) add three requirements to this for these components to function as a self-organising system: openness, intelligence and decentralised control. This will eventually lead to a so-called "hyperconnected" transportation system, where all transportation options are possible, interoperable and available to choose the best alternative that the circumstances require. The degree to which such an advanced state of the freight logistics system can be achieved heavily depends on the availability and performance of computing technology. Table 16.2 sketches the role of the relevant computing technologies in the PI. Different technologies have different roles, while some are not indispensable within the PI vision. This underscores the idea that the PI is a convergent innovation for various computing technologies, as they will all work within the same system.

Pathway 2: Control in the Smart City

The focus of this section is on applications that oversee the functioning of the urban logistics system within its social and environmental context. Next, it also examines how computing technologies are converging into a control mechanism that keeps freight activities in the urban environment within acceptable limits.

Why is control necessary, and how is it exercised now? Despite its sheer necessity, urban freight transport also has adverse effects that cannot be repaired by private markets and justify government intervention. In order to protect their living environments, local and national governments are setting ambitious goals, such as halving the use of "conventionally-fuelled" vehicles in urban transport by 2030, and to phase them out in cities by 2050. Recently, the EU set a specific goal of achieving "essentially CO_2-free urban logistics" in major urban centres by 2030. The measures being taken can be summarised as *access management* and include low emission zones, time windows, axle-weight and/or length limitations. These practices are usually quite generic in their regulatory approach, and locally limited in their applicability. Applying the same regulations everywhere usually does not address specific challenges of specific cities nor does it always confront the relevant actors (e.g. heavy duty vehicles delivering to shops during the morning or the many "white vans"). The fragmented national landscapes of regulations cause difficulties to transport companies that operate in several cities as they have to cope with a variety of rules and regulations. Also, access management typically has static regulations, i.e. fixed in time, and cannot adjust to temporary changes in the state of a city. In short, the current system of fragmented and static access management can be counterproductive and even cause detours, illegal parking and unnecessary emissions (Quak, 2015).

Digital innovations in urban logistics services could potentially contribute to more tailored and intelligent access schemes for cities. Cities that use digitalised services accessible to all are now using the label *Smart City*; logistics systems can be a part of this concept. The potential for identification of vehicles and their location as well as communication with the urban environment enables new forms of access management and enforcement of regulations. Geofencing is a technology based on telematics and satellite positioning which allows to remotely monitor a geographic area surrounded by a virtual fence (geofence) and automatically to detect when tracked vehicles enter or exit these (urban) areas. Sensors are needed on the vehicles for communication with satellite systems delimiting specific urban zones. The long-term vision would be that each city is divided into geofenced zones and that is possible to change access requirements for specific urban freight vehicles to these zones in real time, adapting to the current needs of urban areas. Applied to logistics, this technology provides a possibility to enable intelligent access management for the specific zones, including an automated data collection and monitoring process, by means of:

- Dynamic regulation of pedestrian zones, low-/zero-emission zones;
- Parking, kerb-side loading/unloading;
- Use of public transport lanes;
- Dynamic time windows of deliveries;
- Use of digital permit systems including payment and auctioning;
- Monitoring of drivetrain use (e.g. in case of hybrid vehicle: electric or diesel);
- Digital enforcement of regulations;
- Communication between traffic lights and heavy vehicles to optimise traffic flow.

Table 16.3 shows the relevance of computing technologies for the Smart City. Clearly, one can see that transport data generation, analytics and communication are central in this proposition.

Table 16.3 Role of advanced computing technology in control of urban logistics in the city

Innovation	Role in smart city control
Blockchain	Allows distributed control of shared space
Product and service sales platforms	Allows auctioning of permits
Advanced data analytics	Insights and predictions from big data on city performance
Electric delivery vehicles	Locally environment-friendly delivery
Barcodes and RFID	Support geolocation and access control
Transport and shipment information	Support geolocation and access control
VR/AR applications	Improved visibility of processes and impacts
Digital twins of hubs, chains, cities	Improved visibility, control and autonomy

These applications all use the opportunities offered by advanced computing technology and can result in more evidence-based and fair policy measures in urban logistics. The key advantages are: (a) the flexibility, which is created by combining a common framework for various levels of regulation (in geofenced zones) with local implementation at the levels required; (b) a common framework that can be applied to any urban area, thus respecting national and municipal regulations while providing intelligent access restrictions to specific urban areas/neighbourhoods. Otte and Meisen (2021) conceptually sketch how such a control mechanism can develop based on computing technologies, allowing city governments to more dynamically manage urban logistics. This approach can make it easier and more attractive for cities to implement regulations and ensure that the implemented technologies and regulation frameworks are harmonised across cities. A shared standard needs to be achieved to create the scale required for low-cost implementation.

Specific groups of stakeholders would enjoy additional benefits:

- Policy-makers get opportunities to address actual problems of specific areas, thus obtaining a higher impact from their policy actions on congestion, noise, emissions and safety. The system easily allows for shifts in priorities of the local authorities. Intelligent access management systems provide a way to better data collection on urban commercial transport and make digital enforcement possible, thus increasing efficiency of enforcement measures.
- Transport companies have to deal with only one system nationwide, which automatically introduces measures relevant to the specific area. Vehicle navigation systems could be connected to automatically (re-)calculate routes and provide up-to-date information loading and unloading spaces.
- Ultimately, citizens would benefit from less congestion, less pollution and noise and increased safety. Also, the amount of information available would allow them to experience new levels of transparency about the city's processes and priorities.

Pathway 3: Digital Twins for Collaborative Innovation

The above-sketched developments of, on the one hand, a largely autonomous Physical Internet and, on the other, urban governments trying to establish some form of control over it, raise the compelling question as to how this confrontation could be managed. More precisely, in the specific context of this chapter: is there a role for computing technology to guide these opposing forces? Besides increasing efficiency and allowing means for control, the technologies above also allow advanced decision support, to both the logistics sector and governments. This development is known as *digital twins* and part of the *smart city* paradigm. A digital twin (DT) of a city entails a computerised representation, or simulation, of all the objects and activities inside the city at the same levels of geographical and temporal resolution as in real life. It digitally visualises the city and reproduces its behaviour, both autonomously as in response to external influences (Kaur et al., 2020; Raes et al, 2021) (see Table 16.4).

Digital twins are expected to have a profound impact on decision-making about urban freight systems, both from the public and the private side. Currently, conventional decision-making processes on both sides rely on rather slow cycles of information gathering, generation of alternative solutions, evaluation of solutions, decision taking, implementation and learning. The number of cycles per unit of time, or frequency of decision-making, is determined by the duration of each stage and the quality of connections. Typical frequencies

Table 16.4 Role of advanced computing technology in digital twins

Innovation	Role in a DT
Product and service sales platforms	Digital representation of markets
Advanced data analytics	Processes sensing data and helps to predict behaviour
Barcodes and RFID	Sensors to inform a DT
VR/AR applications	Supports communication of city visualisations
Transport and shipment information	Input to DT of real flows
Internet of Things	Sensors to inform a DT

differ between decision problems, roughly between once daily for trip planning to once in four years for infrastructure planning. An important effect of DTs is that they speed up each individual stage of the decision-making cycle and also connect them digitally. The ultimate impact could be a fully automated, fast and responsive decision-making process. Before this state is achieved however, the main change is that decision-making processes will be based on more transparent information and move from the current low-frequency processes to higher-frequency ones (Batty, 2018; Otte and Meisen, 2021).

Due to the detailed level of visibility provided by urban logistics processes, DTs not only impact the frequency of decision-making of actors, but also how these actors collaborate. Whereas traditionally models considered long-term processes and zonal level flows, today's models use detailed, micro-level simulations of individual parcels, including their strategic alignment in supply chains, business ecosystems and social networks (De Bok and Tavasszy, 2018; Stinson and Mohammadian, 2022). As our modelling capabilities allow emulating real-life processes in more and more detail, models are evolving from stylised representations towards full digital twins of real urban systems. A major advantage of this is increasing transparency about the everyday processes that decision makers are familiar with. Whereas in the past, managers and civil servants had to grapple with abstractions of cities invented by modelling specialists (with typical notions such as traffic analysis zones, discrete choice models, and network optimisation), they can now follow the daily functioning of the system, with a much higher level of face validity than ever before. Also, while models used to be targeted towards either public governments (focusing on fields of public interest like traffic congestion and emissions) or private companies (focusing on optimisation opportunities for their individual supply chain), current data-driven models are comprehensive agent-agnostic: as a result, all are looking at the same processes that can easily be observed in real life and will therefore be trusted more quickly by both sides. This is particularly relevant for innovation processes, where decision-making is traditionally problematic, especially in complex social-technological systems like urban logistics. A DT that is connected to sensors in the city allows a continuous measurement and evaluation of the impacts of innovations. Cities can act as living laboratories where innovations are introduced incrementally and experimentally (Marcucci et al., 2020; Quak et al., 2016; Thomke, 2020).

Conclusions

The digital revolution has accelerated the way in which logistics operations are planned and executed in the urban environment. It has also changed the landscape of urban logistics, in the sense that multiple technologies have allowed entirely new services to appear.

The long-term outlook is that urban logistics will become vastly more efficient and effective, through full visibility and automated coordination, in a system that is now labelled Physical Internet. From the public government perspective, cities are becoming smarter, which provides new capabilities for sensing the state of the city, be it concerning congestion, emissions or citizen satisfaction. Smart cities are also developing new approaches for control over activities by advanced forms of access control and traffic management. While the Physical Internet and Smart Cities, both spurred by digitalisation, could develop as opposing forces, the increasing visibility of urban logistics processes and their impacts could be beneficial for their alignment. Both will be reliant on digital twins of the real system, to manage their own decisions (dominantly private and public, respectively). Although perspectives from which these digital twins would develop differ, they will both make use of the same data, related to real-world logistics processes. In a setting of collaborative innovation, it would be logical to allow digital twins to merge, to arrive at major decisions on urban logistics together. If urban logistics is the place where the Physical Internet and the Smart City will meet, a shared digital twin could be the virtual arena where battles are fought out and constructive scenarios forward are designed.

References

ALICE (2020) Physical Internet Roadmap, etp-logistics.eu, accessed 1 March 2023.

Batty, M. (2018) Digital twins. *Environment and Planning B: Urban Analytics and City Science*, 45(5), 817–820.

Büyüközkan, G., and Göçer, F. (2018) Digital supply chain: Literature review and a proposed framework for future research. *Computers in Industry*, 97, 157–-177.

Crainic, T. G., and Montreuil, B. (2016) Physical internet enabled hyperconnected city logistics. *Transportation Research Procedia*, 12, 383–398.

de Bok, M., and Tavasszy, L. (2018) An empirical agent-based simulation system for urban goods transport (MASS-GT). *Procedia computer science*, 130, 126–133.

Fahim, P. B., Rezaei, J., van Binsbergen, A., Nijdam, M., and Tavasszy, L. (2021) On the evolution of maritime ports towards the Physical Internet. *Futures*, 134, 102834.

Ferrari, A., Mangano, G., Cagliano, A.C., and De Marco, A. (2022) 4.0 technologies in city logistics: An empirical investigation of contextual factors. *Operations Management Research*, 1–18. https://link.springer.com/article/10.1007/s12063-022-00304-5#citeas

Hofmann, E., and Rüsch, M. (2017) Industry 4.0 and the current status as well as future prospects on logistics. *Computers in industry*, 89, 23–34.

Iddris, F. (2018) Digital supply chain: Survey of the literature. *International Journal of Business Research and Management*, 9(1), 47–61.

Kaur, M.J., Mishra, V.P., and Maheshwari, P. (2020) The convergence of digital twin, IoT, and machine learning: Transforming data into action. In M.J. Kaur, V.P. Mishra, P. Maheshwari (eds.), *Digital Twin Technologies and Smart Cities*. Springer, 3–17.

Kim, N., Montreuil, B., Klibi, W., and Kholgade, N. (2021) Hyperconnected urban fulfillment and delivery. *Transportation Research Part E: Logistics and Transportation Review*, 145, 102–104.

Marcucci, E., Gatta, V., Le Pira, M., Hansson, L., and Bråthen, S. (2020) Digital twins: A critical discussion on their potential for supporting policy-making and planning in urban logistics. *Sustainability 12*, 10623.

Montreuil, B. (2011) Toward a physical internet: Meeting the global logistics sustainability grand challenge. *Logistics Research*, 3(2), 71–87.

Müller, S., and Knitschky, G. (2021) Platform economics in logistics-Servitization of a service sector? *Revue Européenne d'Économie et Management des Services*, 12, 17–34.

Otte, T., and Meisen, T. (2021) A reference framework for the performance-based decision support of city authorities in urban freight transport. In: *2021 International Conference on ICT for Smart Society (ICISS)*. IEEE, 1–7.

Pan, S., Trentesaux, D., and Sallez, Y. (2017) Specifying self-organising logistics system: Openness, intelligence, and decentralised control. In T. Borangiu et al. (eds.), *Service Orientation in Holonic and Multi-Agent Manufacturing, Studies in Computational Intelligence 694*. Springer, 93–102. https://link.springer.com/book/10.1007/978-3-030-27477-1

Quak, H. (2015). Access restrictions and local authorities' city logistics regulation in urban areas. In E. Taniguchi and R.G. Thomson (eds.), *City Logistics Mapping the Future*, CRC Press, 177–199. https://www.taylorfrancis.com/books/mono/10.1201/b17715/city-logistics-russell-thompson-eiichi-taniguchi

Quak, H., Lindholm, M., Tavasszy, L. and Browne, M. (2016) From freight partnerships to urban logistics living labs–Giving meaning to the elusive concept of living labs. *Transportation Research Procedia 12*, 461–473.

Raes, L., Michiels, P., Adolphi, T., Tampere, C., Dalianis, T., Mcaleer, S., and Kogut, P. (2021). Duet: A framework for building secure and trusted digital twins of smart cities. *IEEE Internet Computing 26*(3), 43–50.

Snabe, J.H., and Weinelt, B. (2016). Digital transformation of industries: Logistics industry. In: *Geneva: World Economic Forum*.

Stinson, M., and Mohammadian, A.K. (2022). Introducing CRISTAL: A model of collaborative, informed, strategic trade agents with logistics. *Transportation Research Interdisciplinary Perspectives, 13*, 100539.

Taj, I., and Zaman, N. (2022). Towards industrial revolution 5.0 and explainable artificial intelligence: Challenges and opportunities. *International Journal of Computing and Digital Systems, 12*(1), 295–320.

Tang, C., and Veelenturf, L. (2019). The strategic role of logistics in the industry 4.0. *Transportation Research Part E, 129*, 1–11.

Thomke, S.H. (2020). *Experimentation Works: The Surprising Power of Business Experiments*. Harvard Business Press.

17
SMALL CONTAINERS FOR EVOLVING LOGISTICS IN CHANGING CITIES

Michael G. H. Bell, Veronica Schulz and Shengda Zhu

Introduction

The aim of this chapter is to review the changing nature of city logistics and the emerging case for a new form of intermodality involving a small city container. The pandemic, and consequent lockdowns and social distancing, has provided an opportunity for change in city logistics. Through 2020 and 2021 extensive working from home, more online shopping, increased use of private and active transport, along with the abandonment of city centre workplaces and businesses, accelerated a shift in the pattern of city logistics that was already underway before the pandemic (Greater Sydney Commission, 2020). These changes included the integration of e-commerce and conventional retail, the growth of on-demand and same-day delivery, and the transition to battery electric pickup and delivery vehicles.

The pandemic also accelerated changes to the city streetscape. The process of reallocating road space in favour of active transport was well underway in many cities prior to the pandemic. The pandemic, however, increased the popularity of active transport (Greater Sydney Commission, 2020) and hastened the rollout of bike lanes (City of Sydney, 2020) in time to accommodate the increase in the number of e-bikes used for pickup and delivery in the gig economy. The result has been city streets that not only accommodate more bikes and pedestrians but also offer more space, as well as cleaner and quieter environments for social activities.

The changing streetscape, together with the increasing number of small shipments in circulation, has strengthened the case for a city container to facilitate intermodality in the final and intermediate mile. DHL (van Amstel, 2018a) has been developing its CityHub concept around a container with the footprint of the Europallet (80 cm wide by 120 m long) and 100 cm tall, giving a volume of around one cubic meter. These containers, referred to as meter cube boxes, are lightweight and can be carried by a quadricycle, like the Armadillo (Velove, 2022), as well as by truck. As they have caster wheels they can be easily pushed on and off trucks using ramps. The DHL CityHub concept involves the truck acting as a mobile hub transferring city containers to and from quadricycles in standard parking spaces or loading zones, with meter cube boxes offering intermodality in the same way as much larger and heavier shipping containers.

The potential for public transport networks to support city logistics, referred to as co-modality, has long been appreciated but to date, schemes have mostly not outlasted the field trial stage. The experience with co-modality is reviewed and the reasons for lack of long-term success to date analysed. Key reasons include the absence of a sustainable business model as well as the absence of a city container to facilitate the swift and efficient transfer of cargo between modes, in particular on and off public transport.

A recent feasibility study (Schulz et al., 2022) looked at the potential for transporting meter cube boxes by Sydney Ferries. As the gangways are 1 m wide and the containers have caster wheels, they can be pushed on and off the ferries after passengers have boarded and alighted. As a key to success will be the ability to load and unload the meter cube boxes with minimum disruption to passenger services, it is suggested that freight should be limited to off-peak times.

This chapter begins by reviewing recent changes in retail behaviour, the growth of e-commerce, and the evolution of omni-channel retail as e-commerce and conventional retail merge. The implications for supply chain configuration of the growth of on-demand and same-day delivery is covered next followed by a brief review of the role of automation in facilitating faster delivery. The shift to electric vehicles and micro-logistics, in particular cargo e-bikes, along with the reallocation of road space to favour 'place' over 'link', is discussed, leading to the case for a city container with the footprint of the Europallet to facilitate the carriage of cargo by both micro-logistics and public transport. The chapter culminates with a review of the feasibility of transporting cargo on Sydney's passenger ferries using city containers.

Changing Retail Behaviour

The inception of the World Wide Web in 1991 saw the exponential growth of e-commerce, with one development leading inexorably to the next. In 1994, Netscape launched its Navigator browser, facilitating online marketplaces like Amazon, founded in 1994, and eBay, founded in 1995. In 1998, PayPal was founded, leading to greater trust in online payment. In 2003 Apple launched iTunes, heralding the arrival of digital stores and services. In 2006, Facebook began selling advertisements, marking the entry of social media into e-commerce.

E-commerce originally developed in parallel to conventional retail (see, e.g. Rodrigue, Slack and Comtois, 2017), with order fulfilment centres, sometimes referred to as dark stores, in place of the distribution centres of conventional retail and home delivery executed by third-party logistics providers. Conventional retailers, however, rapidly realised that e-commerce was a sector they could not afford to ignore, but were concerned about cannibalising their existing market share, leading to their initial hesitancy. Gradually the synergies offered by integrating the conventional and e-commerce channels led to the evolution of omni-channel retail (see Chapter 12). In particular, customer data harvested by e-commerce proved to be of great value to conventional retail and supplemented data yielded by customer loyalty schemes.

One manifestation of the integration of e-commerce and conventional retail is 'click & collect' services offered by most major grocery chains. Customers order online, order picking is performed in the conventional store, and the shopping is collected from the collection counter at the store, from a locker, or is delivered to the home or workplace. Although this is more costly than centralised order picking in a dark store, labour intensive and sometimes unpopular with shoppers, conventional stores are often located closer to the customers, reducing delivery times when shoppers request home delivery. As a consequence, some grocery chains are closing their dark stores in favour of in-store order picking (Nott, 2021).

The dark store concept (see Chapter 10), however, is not dead. Rapid grocery dark stores have been proliferating, with about 200 such stores in the United Kingdom in 2022, operated by rapid grocery players such as Getir, Gorillas, Gopuff, Zapp and Jiffy (Nott, 2022). They are establishing themselves on high streets, where vacant stores are readily available and from where customers can be rapidly reached. However, this development is not without controversy. Rotterdam and Amsterdam halted new dark stores of this type due to complaints from residents about reckless delivery riders, noise and congestion (Nott, 2022).

Underperforming conventional stores can be transformed into dark stores, where their locations offer shorter home delivery or customer pickup times. Kmart in Australia is turning three underperforming stores into dark stores (Fitz-Walter, 2020) and Walmart in the United States has repurposed a Dallas store to click & collect only (Mahoney, 2021).

Retail behaviour has been changing to match the evolution of omni-channel retail, given impetus by the pandemic. The IBM Institute for Business Value surveyed 19,103 consumers across 28 countries towards the end of 2021 and found that 42% of respondents learnt about products or brands online while 32% cited social media as a shopping resource. While 65% said they still shop in store, 50% did so via mobile apps and 42% through websites (Straight, 2022a).

On-Demand and Same-Day Delivery

Supply chains are reorganising themselves to accommodate the increasing demand for on-demand and same-day delivery. This involves holding inventory and order picking close to the consumer. Often this entails repurposing local, convenience or high-street stores. Amazon has been pioneering same-day delivery on a variety of items, and third-party delivery services have been partnering with restaurants and other retailers to meet the growing demand for same-day delivery (Putzger, 2020). 7-Eleven in the United States has been testing on-demand ordering for both delivery and in-store pickup at selected convenience stores with its 7NOW app (Mastroberte, 2018). German startup Kiefkaufhaus is an online shop that only features local stores and offers same-day delivery by cargo bike (Peters, 2015). Kiefkaufhaus is a cooperative joined by local stores, each owning equal shares of the online platform. The cooperative earns 10% on sales to cover its costs.

Groceries are perceived as a promising sector for same-day delivery. Aldi in the United Kingdom has extended its rapid grocery delivery service London-wide after a trial with Deliveroo from eight stores (Ascentialedge, 2020). Customers in Camden, London, living within 3 km of an Aldi store can select products from a range of 200 essential items for home delivery within thirty minutes. Aldi staff pick and pack the orders in-store, which are then delivered by Deliveroo. Australian inner-city residents can get groceries delivered in ten minutes through services like Milkrun (Butler, 2022). However, competitors Send in Melbourne and Quicko in Sydney have collapsed, leaving Voly in Sydney and Milkrun in both Sydney and Melbourne. Obstacles to this kind of grocery retail are labour and warehouse costs, as well as the dispersed nature of Australian cities. Home delivery margins are small, even for large supermarkets not offering a same-day service.

While there is clearly demand for on-demand and same-day delivery, this is likely to remain a niche market dominated by meals delivered by global operators like Deliveroo or Uber Eats and groceries delivered by logistics providers from local stores. However, the on-demand and same-day delivery market is offering new opportunities for centrally located stores on high streets once suffering from competition from edge-of-town supermarkets and e-commerce (WEF, 2016).

A challenge for on-demand delivery is in-coming legislation in a number of countries to curb the inequities of the gig economy (see Chapter 27), whereby typically drivers are treated as independent contractors who are not eligible for statutory leave, health cover and other entitlements received by those who are employed (see Chapter 29). This is widely regarded as exploitative and unfair for those who are in fact working full or part time for their employer. In 2016, two Uber drivers in the United Kingdom successfully argued before an employment tribunal that Uber was wrong to treat them as independent contractors. The tribunal ruled they were 'workers' under British employment law, with rights to entitlements including a minimum wage and holiday pay (Veen, Barrat and Goods, 2021). After a series of unsuccessful appeals, Uber in the United Kingdom eventually conceded and now pays their drivers hourly while they work rather than per delivery and provide some entitlements like holiday pay, a retirement contribution and sick leave. Similar developments are anticipated in other countries leading to changing business models for home delivery and inevitably cost increases for the use of delivery drivers and riders.

Automation in Retail

Another emerging trend in retail is automation, particularly for order picking and packing (Volovich, 2020). JD.com, a leading supply chain technology and service provider, recently opened two robotic shops in the Netherlands, where robots pick goods ordered online and prepare parcels for either pickup in store or home delivery (Yang, 2022). After the shopper's QR code is scanned at the check-out, the order arrives by conveyer belt.

Automation is not limited to picking and packing. Startup Ottonomy is rolling out its electric, autonomous robots for retail and restaurant deliveries within geofenced properties (Fisher, 2022). The Ottobots, which resemble autonomous shopping trollies, are reported to be making deliveries at Cincinnati International Airport, Kentucky, where they deliver food and beverage orders from restaurants to travellers waiting at the gates. One could envisage Ottobots delivering goods ordered online to parked cars.

Automated last-mile delivery has long been a theme in urban logistics. FedEx announced it will work with retailers such as Lowe's, Pizza Hut, Target, Walgreens and Walmart in the United States to help fulfil same-day deliveries with an autonomous mobile locker using the sidewalk, joining the likes of Amazon, Starship Technologies and Australia Post, who have also experimented with such robots (Bennett, 2019). However, sidewalk robots face obstacles like steps and garden gates, particularly in suburban areas, and are banned from sidewalks in San Francisco.

A more promising use of autonomous mobile lockers is mobile vending machines. US startup Robomart revealed a prototype self-driving convenience store in Las Vegas 2018 (van Rompaey, 2018). It has cooled shelves for about 50–100 different fresh food items, like vegetables, fruit, dairy and meat. The vehicle can reach 25 kph and a range of about 130 km. The startup wants to lease its technology to retailers, arguing that a self-driving convenience store is cheaper than a physical store and retailers retain customer data. Another promising use of autonomous mobile lockers is as mobile hubs to support couriers picking up and delivering parcels (Li et al., 2021). They would allow depots to extend their coverage while couriers retain human contact with customers.

Electric Commercial Vehicles

Concern with urban air quality and climate change is driving a transition to electric pickup and delivery vehicles in many countries. Battery electric vehicles (BEVs) are proving to be suitable for city logistics tasks as they are quiet and generate zero emissions at the point of use. BEVs have limited range before needing to charge (of the order of 150 km) and then take some time to charge. Hydrogen electric vehicles (HEVs), which store electricity as compressed hydrogen rather than in batteries, have around twice the range and can be refilled rapidly. However, the energy efficiency of HEVs is only about half that of BEVs, largely because of the energy consumed in producing hydrogen by electrolysis. HEVs are more likely to be adopted for long-distance trips with large trucks rather than for city logistics.

The limited range of BEVs is impacting the design of city logistics networks. For example, the parcel company DPD has introduced satellite consolidation centres in London leading to a two-echelon parcel pickup and delivery operation. In the case of the Westminster satellite, 7.5-tonne eCanters with 82 kWh batteries capable of travelling up to 135 km between charges are used to trunk parcels between Westminster and the London City depot on the periphery of the city. From the satellite, smaller Nissan eNV200s and Paxsters are used for parcel pickup and delivery (Pink, 2018). In London, BEVs are exempt from the central area congestion charge and meet the requirements of the Ultra-Low Emission Zone.

The limited range of BEVs does not, however, imply a limit on their size or capacity. Construction traffic is a major cause of noise, vibration and emissions at construction sites in part because of the size and weight of the vehicles involved. Volvo produces an e-truck capable of carrying a payload of 12,400 kg, which is largely silent and emission-free at the point of use. With air suspension and a steered tag axle, it is ideal for city refuse collection, construction and other urban applications (Pink, 2019).

Bike Lanes and the Meter Cube Box

Growing concern for the urban environment and climate change is having a transformative impact on the urban streetscape. Priority in design is shifting from motor vehicles to pedestrians, cyclists, other vulnerable road users, as well as public transport. The dual function of streets as both locations for activities (the 'place' function) and conduits for traffic (the 'link' function) have been widely recognised (see, e.g., NSW, 2020), with prominence increasingly given to the place function in more central locations. In some central locations, this has involved the exclusion of motor vehicles completely or at certain times, while in more suburban locations, road space has been reallocated to pedestrian precincts or bike lanes. Figure 17.1 shows a recent scheme to reallocate road space to bike lanes in suburban Sydney, Australia, exemplifying many such schemes now found around the world.

During the pandemic, many cities used the opportunity offered by reduced vehicle traffic to extend bike lanes (Nikitas et al., 2021). The City of Sydney (2020) permitted pop-up cycleways without the normal planning approval to protect the health, safety and welfare of the public.

It is within this rapidly evolving road infrastructure that city logistics must take place. Delivery riders on electric bikes (e-bikes) have been able to make use of the proliferating bike lanes and pedestrian precincts to pick up and deliver small shipments. For larger shipments, quadricycles like the Armadillo (Velove, 2022) are finding favour in Europe. DHL have based their CityHub concept, referred to earlier, around the Armadillo and a lightweight container with caster wheels (Erlandsson, 2017, van Amstel, 2018b). With a width of 80 cm, the container is suitable for use in standard bike lanes with a lane width of 150 cm. A similar solution has emerged in the United States where Urb-E builds e-bikes with trailers designed to carry a similarly sized foldable, roll-on, roll-off container (Straight, 2022b).

While the Europallet is a convenient footprint for a city container, being narrow enough (80 cm) for bike lanes yet not too long (120 cm) for cargo bikes, it could come in a range of

(a) (b)

Figure 17.1 Reallocation of road space to a bike lane in suburban Sydney
Source: Authors

heights. Assmann and Behrendt (2017) investigated the optimal height for a city container taking into account the typical dimensions of a van. The issue arises because the optimal height for a cargo bike, at about 150m, wastes space in a van. Conversely, the height that would best use van capacity, when the containers are double-stacked, would be about 120 cm. On this basis, the container height chosen by DHL is sub-optimal for both van and cargo bike. However, as with shipping containers, intermodality only requires standardisation of the width as variations in length and height can be accommodated.

Co-modality

Co-modality, the term given to the use of public transport networks and services for transporting cargo, has a long history. Where transport infrastructure is scarce, as it frequently is in urban areas, any spare public transport capacity could theoretically be valuable for freight, provided passengers are not inconvenienced. In addition, this could help reduce traffic congestion, noise and emissions in city centres. Historically, co-modality was commonplace on tram networks. However, many recent co-modality projects in urban areas have failed for a range of reasons.

In suburban or regional settings, co-modality has proved successful. In the case of buses, an example is the KombiBus scheme of the Uckermärkische Verkehrsgesellschaft in Germany, which not only carries passengers but also packages and frozen food (KombiBus, 2019). As 'combination buses', they serve all the stops in the local public transport network and deliver goods to shops, restaurants and companies several times a day, and return bicycles to the shops where they were rented. In the case of rail, an example is Swift Express Freight in the United Kingdom (Railway Gazette, 2021a). Electric multiple-units are converted to carry roll cages for a fast, cost-effective and low-carbon alternative to lorries and vans for the replenishment of shops.

In an urban setting, there have been a number of noteworthy co-modality projects involving trams, mostly discontinued. De Lange et al. (2019) provide a useful review and cost analysis of tram-based co-modality, distinguishing between schemes involving dedicated freight trams, freight trailers for passenger trams, and freight carried alongside passengers inside trams. From March 2007, CityCargo in Amsterdam held a pilot project using two cargo trams to distribute goods in the centre of Amsterdam (De Lange, 2019). The project sought to demonstrate that the use of trams to deliver goods in the inner city is viable, but was abandoned in 2009 due to lack of public funds.

In Frankfurt am Main cargo trams were tested in combination with e-cargo bikes (van Amstel, 2018c). Most of the downtown tram lines now run underground, with the remaining surface track in the inner city seeing no more than one tram in four minutes on average, even in peak hours. The cargo trams are older trams, run without passengers at quiet times on the network. The tram is used for line haul between micro-hubs, while e-bikes are used for the first- and last-mile pickup and delivery (Meldner, 2018). The meter cube box, referred to earlier, is used together with a rack to stack the boxes. This rack can be pushed on and off a tram trailer. The bike trailer can add or remove a box from the rack without the need for the rider to lift it. This field trial is also believed to have ended (van Amstel, 2020).

The failure of many co-modality projects appears to be due to the difficulty in finding a sustainable business model. The challenge is to offer a service for which cargo owners are willing to pay enough to cover the costs. To improve the quality of service, public transport IT specialist INIT is developing a booking, transport management, payment and shipment tracking system for the RegioKArgo freight tram project in Karlsruhe, Germany (Railway Gazette, 2021b). The project will assess the feasibility of urban deliveries by trams off-peak in compartments that could be used by passengers in the peak. Parcels delivered to logistic sites are loaded onto a tram for transport to city centre hubs and then delivered from there by cargo bike or e-van.

Two projects of note that involved freight-only trams sharing the tram infrastructure with passenger trams are Tramfret in France and CarGoTram in Germany. Tramfret in Saint-Étienne, central France, uses old trams to move produce from a warehouse on the outskirts of the town to downtown stores owned by Casino (Forrest, 2017). While the trams could be loaded with roll cages at the depot fairly easily, they had to be unloaded on street by a number of staff as roll cages are difficult to control on street. At least in one case, the stop was in the middle of the street and separated from the store by a lane of traffic. Eventually, Casino decided that store replenishment by truck was simpler and more cost-effective. The CarGoTram freight tram service in Dresden carried automotive parts from a logistics centre on one side of the city to a Volkswagen factory on the other using freight trams specially designed for the purpose (Railway Gazette, 2021c). Loading and unloading were off-street, so free of the complications faced by Tramfret. Nonetheless, this has ended too. The trams were costly to maintain and breakdowns were increasingly regularly.

The only established and successful European urban freight tram service is to be found in Zürich (Tramways & Urban Transit, 2021). Introduced in 2003, the service offered a car-free alternative to Zürich residents to dispose of their bulky waste. In 2006 Zürich introduced a similar service for the removal of electrical and electronic waste. Today, cargo trams make about 18 round trips every month and the service is available free of charge to residents.

Lessons that can be learnt from failed urban co-modality projects are that:

1 Loading and unloading cargo from public transport vehicles swiftly, efficiently and safely is challenging, and on-street loading and unloading should be avoided where possible.
2 There needs to be an efficient and cost-effective means of first- and last-mile transport between the origin or destination of the cargo and the tram, metro or bus stop.
3 A competitive service needs to be accompanied by an efficient booking, transport management, payment and shipment tracking system.
4 Cargo should be carried in standard containers, like the meter cube boxes, that are easy to carry by and transfer between public transport, cargo bikes and vans.

Meter Cube Boxes on Ferries

In harbour or river cities, such as Sydney, there is potential to use spare capacity in the ferry system to move cargo and thereby decongest the road networks and improve air quality. A recent feasibility study identified the DHL meter cube box as a suitable 'unit load device' (ULD) for moving cargo by passenger ferries (Schulz et al., 2022). This container offers flexibility as it can be carried by cargo bike (Figure 17.2a shows the Armadillo quadricycle), truck or ferry. The gangway used by Sydney Ferries (Figure 17.2b) is just wide enough at 1 m to allow the meter cube box, 80 cm wide, to be pushed on- and off-board.

The scenario studied by Schulz et al. (2022) is where each ferry designates an area on the main deck for storing the containers located close to the point where the gangway connects to the ferry. In subsequent work, a model has been developed which assigns full and empty containers to ferry routes to minimise expected shipping time including waiting time at ferry stations. Some ferry stations will send more containers than they receive. Empty containers are repositioned from surplus ferry stations (those receiving more containers than they send) to deficit ferry stations (those sending more containers than they receive) to minimise expected shipping and waiting time.

(a) (b)

Figure 17.2 (a) The metre cube box. (b) Ferry berthing and gangway in foreground
Source: (a) DHL (2019) Copyright © DHL International GmbH. All Rights Reserved., (b) authors

Schulz et al. (2022) also looked at types of cargo that could benefit from this service (the contestable market) and different business models. The business models included a 'container load service', where customers are provided with empty containers by the logistics service provider but pack and unpack the containers themselves, and a 'less than container load service', where the logistics service provider collects the cargo and consolidates it in containers at depots operated by the logistics service provider.

With respect to the lessons learnt from past co-modality projects:

1 Loading and unloading are not on street. Ferry stations with good road access were identified, so that meter cube boxes could be readily picked up or delivered by van or cargo bike. Loading and unloading cargo from the ferries involves pushing the boxes across the gangway. To avoid disruption to passengers, it is suggested that this be done during off-peak times. Lashing and unlashing the boxes on board could be performed while the ferry is unberthing or berthing respectively, so as not to delay services more than necessary.
2 First- and last-mile pickup and delivery could be accomplished by van or cargo bike, which we envisage as being battery-powered.
3 As mentioned, two forms of service were studied, namely a container load service and a less than container load service. In either case, there will need to be an efficient booking, transport management, payment and shipment tracking system. The requirements for container tagging, tracking and tracing were identified.
4 The DHL meter cube boxes are a convenient size for cargo bike, van and ferry. They should be lightweight and have caster wheels, which can be locked when the boxes are stationary. As with the much larger shipping containers, there will need to be a weight limit to prevent damage to the boxes, vehicles, gangways or the staff moving the boxes.

While this study benefits from the lessons learnt from past failed co-modality projects, discussed earlier, it did not include a field trial to establish technical feasibility and provide data to estimate the contestable market for such a service more accurately.

Discussion

This chapter has reviewed recent changes in city logistics, pointing to the growth of omni-channel retail, the increasing use of BEVs and changes to the streetscape, leading to more small shipments on the transport network. The pandemic has accelerated these changes. The potential benefits for traffic congestion, noise and vibration of using spare capacity on public transport networks to carry cargo, referred to as co-modality, has long been talked about but projects to realise the concept in urban areas have mostly failed. The chequered history of such schemes is reviewed highlighting the need for cost-effective first- and last-mile pickup and delivery, good IT systems, efficient transfer of cargo between modes of transport, and robust business models.

Key to transporting the increasing volume of small shipments is a standard city container that can be carried by cargo bike, truck and public transport. With the footprint of the Europallet (120 cm long by 80 cm wide), the DHL meter cube box offers intermodality at the city level as it is compatible with all the relevant modes of transport and can make use of standard bike lanes. Variations in height, and indeed length, can be accommodated provided there is no variation in the width. It took twenty years from its invention for the much larger shipping container to begin revolutionising global logistics. It remains to be seen whether it will take a similar period for a standard city container to eventually transform city logistics, and if it does so, what the long-term impact on land use and supply chains will be.

References

Ascentialedge (2020) Aldi UK partners with 'delivery intermediary' Deliveroo in London, https://www.ascentialedge.com/insights/ecommerce-blog/grocery/aldi-uk-trials-demand-delivery-Deliveroo, viewed 22/8/22.

Assmann, T., and Behrendt, F. (2017) Determining optimal container heights for cargo-bike crossdocking schemes in urban areas, *ResearchGate*, https://www.researchgate.net/publication/317617634_Determining_optimal_container_heights_for_cargobike_crossdocking_schemes_in_urban_areas, viewed 7/6/22.

Bennett, T. (2019) Autonomous last mile delivery robots are gaining traction, slowly, https://which-50.com/autonomous-last-mile-delivery-robots-are-gaining-traction/, viewed 22/8/22.

Butler, B. (2022) Australian grocery delivery startups face funding difficulties as venture capital checks out, *The Guardian*, https://www.theguardian.com/business/2022/jun/06/australian-grocery-delivery-startups-face-funding-difficulties-as-venture-capital-checks-out, viewed 6/6/22.

City of Sydney (2020) Creating pop-up cycleways in Sydney, https://www.cityofsydney.nsw.gov.au/building-new-infrastructure/creating-pop-up-cycleways-in-sydney, viewed 6/6/22.

De Lange, K., Meersman, H., Sys, C., Van de Voorde, E., and Vanelslander, T. (2019) How to make urban freight transport by tram successful? *Journal of Shipping and Trade*, https://doi.org/10.1186/s41072-019-0055-4, viewed 25/8/22.

DHL (2019) *First Cubicycle to Electrify DHL Express's Green Fleet in Taiwan*, image, DHL, https://www.dhl.com/tw-en/home/press/press-archive/2019/first-cubicycle-to-electrify-dhl-express-green-fleet-in-taiwan.html, viewed 22/8/22.

Erlandsson, J. (2017) More city containers in new pilot with DHL express in Frankfurt and Utrecht, *Velove*, https://www.velove.se/news/city-containers-new-pilot-dhl-express-frankfurt-utrecht, viewed 25/8/22.

Fisher, J. (2022) Last-mile delivery workers that never need a break: Meet the Ottobots, https://www.fleetowner.com/technology/article/21213588/lastmile-delivery-workers-that-never-need-a-break-meet-the-ottobots, viewed 12/1/22.

Fitz-Walter, T. (2020) Transforming retail stores into online micro fulfilment centres is not a simple fix, *DCN*, https://www.thedcn.com.au/opinion-transforming-retail-stores-into-online-micro-fulfilment-centres-is-not-a-simple-fix/, viewed 27/7/20.

Forrest, A. (2017) The electric trams shuttling car parts and groceries around European cities, *The Guardian*, https://www.theguardian.com/sustainable-business/2017/jul/21/electric-trams-cities-groceries-europe-edinburgh-dresden, viewed 22/8/22.

Greater Sydney Commission (2020) City-shaping impacts of COVID-19, https://greatercities.au/thought-leadership/city-shaping-impacts-of-covid-19, viewed 8/6/22.

KombiBus (2019) KombiBus – transport service for Uckermark: https://land-der-ideen.de/en/project/kombibus-transport-service-for-uckermark-526, viewed 22/8/22.

Li, J., Ensafian, H., Bell, M. G. H., and Geers, D. G. (2021) Deploying autonomous mobile lockers in a two-echelon parcel operation, *Transportation Research C*, **128**, 103155.

Mahoney, N. (2021) Walmart retools Dallas store into fulfillment center, *Modern Shipper*, https://www.freightwaves.com/news/walmart-retools-dallas-store-into-fulfillment-center, viewed 30/12/21.

Mastroberte, T. (2018) Should convenience stores dive into same-day delivery?, *Convenience Store News*, https://csnews.com/should-c-stores-dive-delivery, viewed 22/8/22.

Meldner, R. (2018) Frankfurt testing public trams for package deliveries, https://esellercafe.com/frankfurt-testing-public-transit-trams-for-package-deliveries/, viewed 28/5/20.

Nikitas, A., Tsigdinos, S., Karolemeas, C., Kourmpa, E., and Bakogiannis, E. (2021) Cycling in the Era of COVID-19: Lessons learnt and best practice policy recommendations for a more bike-centric future, *Sustainability*, https://doi.org/10.3390/su13094620, viewed 6/6/22.

Nott, G. (2021) Why are supermarkets scrapping their dark stores? *The Grocer*, https://www.thegrocer.co.uk/online/why-are-supermarkets-scrapping-their-dark-stores/653886.article, viewed 22/8/22.

Nott, G. (2022) Rapid grocery dark stores in UK set to number 1,500 by 2030, *The Grocer*, https://www.thegrocer.co.uk/technology-and-supply-chain/rapid-grocery-dark-stores-in-uk-set-to-number-1500-by-2030/664831.article, viewed 1/3/22.

NSW (2020) *Practitioner's Guide to Movement and Place*, https://www.governmentarchitect.nsw.gov.au/resources/ga/media/files/ga/manuals-and-guides/practitioners-guide-to-movement-and-place-2020-06-04.pdf, viewed 22/8/22.

Peters, A. (2015) Who needs Amazon? Support local businesses and get same-day delivery by cargo bike, *Fast Company*, https://www.fastcompany.com/3045525/who-needs-amazon-support-local-businesses-and-then-get-same-day-delivery-by-bike, viewed 22/8/22.

Pink, H. (2018) DPD UK opens an all-electric last-mile delivery operation 2018, *Motor Transport*, https://motortransport.co.uk/blog/2018/10/17/dpd-opens-its-first-all-electric-last-mile-delivery-site/, viewed 22/8/22.

Pink, H. (2019) Volvo trucks offers its new FE-Electric range for construction, https://motortransport.co.uk/blog/2019/10/29/volvo-to-showcase-fe-electric-6x2-hook-lift-rigid-at-freight-in-the-city-expo-on-6-november/, viewed 22/8/22.

Putzger, I. (2020) Amazon launches new assault on retail sector: Suburban mini-fulfilment, *The Loadstar*, https://theloadstar.com/amazon-launches-new-assault-on-retail-sector-suburban-mini-fulfilment/, viewed 22/8/22.

Railway Gazette (2021a) Swift express freight EMU conversions agreed, https://www.railwaygazette.com/uk/swift-express-freight-emu-conversions-agreed/60372.article, viewed 27/1/22.

Railway Gazette (2021b) Parcel tram software under development, https://www.railwaygazette.com/technology-data-and-business/parcel-tram-software-under-development/59490.article, viewed 27/1/22.

Railway Gazette (2021c) CarGoTram freight tram service comes to an end, https://www.railwaygazette.com/light-rail-and-tram/cargotram-freight-tram-service-comes-to-an-end/58270.article, viewed 27/1/22.

Rodrigue, J. P., Slack, B., and Comtois, C. (2017) *The Geography of Transport Systems, 5th edition*, Routledge, Abingdon, Oxon.

Schulz, V., Bell, M. G. H., Zhu, S., Geers, G., and Bhattacharjya, J. (2022) *Co-modality for Sydney's ferries*, https://ses.library.usyd.edu.au/handle/2123/28682, viewed 8/6/22.

Straight, B. (2022a) Shifting behaviours: Hybrid shopping, purpose-driven consumers change retail's outlook, *Modern Shipper*, https://www.freightwaves.com/news/shifting-behaviors-hybrid-shopping-purpose-driven-consumers-change-retails-outlook, viewed 15/1/22.

Straight, B. (2022b) Expansion to LA (from NY) sets up big year for Urb-E, *FreightWaves*, https://www.freightwaves.com/news/expansion-to-la-sets-up-potentially-big-year-for-urb-e, viewed 22/1/22.

Tramways & Urban Transit (2021) Zurich's cargo tram, http://www.tautonline.com/zurichs-cargo-tram/, viewed 29/8/22.

van Amstel, W. P. (2018a) DHL Express opens CityHub in Groningen, *CityLogistics*, http://www.citylogistics.info/business/dhl-express-opens-cityhub-in-groningen-nl/, viewed 22/8/22.

van Amstel, W. P. (2018b) DHL express taking the next step in city logistics containerisation, *CityLogistics*, http://www.citylogistics.info/business/dhl-express-taking-the-next-step-in-city-logistics-containerisation/, viewed 8/6/22.

van Amstel, W. P. (2018c) Frankfurt is testing cargo tram for parcels, *CityLogistics*, http://www.citylogistics.info/projects/frankfurt-d-is-testing-cargo-tram-for-parcels/#more-1570, viewed 22/8/22.

van Amstel, W. P. (2020) Using trams for parcels in Frankfurt (D): The lessons learned, *CityLogistics*, http://www.citylogistics.info/projects/using-trams-for-parcels-in-frankfurt-d-the-lessons-learned/, viewed 29/8/22.

van Rompaey, S. (2018) This self-driving convenience store brings fresh food to your door step, https://www.retaildetail.eu/en/news/food/self-driving-convenience-store-brings-fresh-food-your-door-step, viewed 22/8/22.

Veen, A., Barrat, T., and Goods, C. (2021) New deal for Uber drivers in UK, but Australia's gig workers must wait, https://www.sydney.edu.au/news-opinion/news/2021/03/30/deal-for-uber-drivers-in-uk-but-australias-gig-workers-must-wait.html, viewed 28/7/22.

Velove (2022) We use the Number 1 electric cargo bike in the world, https://www.velove.se/electric-cargo-bike, viewed 24/8/22.

Volovich, V. (2020) Solving economics of last mile through micro-fulfillment centers (MFCs), https://www.ascentialedge.com/insights/ecommerce-blog/omnichannel/solving-economics-last-mile-through-micro-fulfillment-centers, viewed 22/8/22.

WEF (2016) Adapting to an omni-channel consumer world, https://reports.weforum.org/digital-transformation/adapting-to-an-omni-channel-world/, 8/6/22.

Yang, V. (2022) JD.com launches robotic shops 'ochama' in the Netherlands, https://jdcorporateblog.com/jd-com-launches-robotic-shops-ochama-in-the-netherlands/, viewed 12/1/22.

PART D
Policy

18
POLICY AND PLANNING FOR URBAN LOGISTICS

Laetitia Dablanc

Introduction: What Is a Policy for Urban Logistics?

Urban logistics can be defined as the set of service provisions contributing to efficiently managing the movements of goods in cities and providing innovative responses to customer demands (Dablanc, 2019). This chapter looks at policies, mostly at the local level, that target, directly or indirectly, urban logistics in order to reduce its negative impact: pollution, energy consumption, congestion, accidents; and increase its positive impacts: provision of urban jobs, promotion of the economic vitality of cities, service innovation. Urban logistics meets societal demands and therefore policies. Urban freight emits 52% of transportation-related NOx in Paris (Coulombel et al., 2018) and the stakes of air pollution are also economic, since it damages the image of major cities. Urban freight is also responsible for 20–30% of urban transportation-related CO_2 emissions and contributes to climate change. This share is currently growing. Protection against risks, from extreme weather events to terrorism and pandemics, is a priority for local action, and among the targets that need protection are warehouses close to cities, especially those storing hazardous materials. The organization of the distribution of goods is at the forefront of plans to prepare cities for exceptional events, such as demonstrated by the COVID-19 pandemic. On a more common occurrence, technological developments and new forms of consumption have made freight issues visible for residents and policy-makers. Self-employed couriers on bicycles or motorbikes in the streets of cities worldwide pose road safety problems and their situation challenges labor law (Dablanc et al., 2017). These on-demand "instant" delivery platforms also bring thousands of job opportunities to young people and migrants, re-introducing low-skilled jobs into urban centers.

Faced with these new challenges, urban logistics policies are taking shape. According to Letnik et al. (2019), out of 129 medium and large European cities, 15 had adopted a "freight plan" and 84 included logistics measures in their urban mobility plans at the time of the authors' survey. Involvement in urban freight for the public sector can be manifold and at various levels. Municipalities are in charge of the urban road network, which is heavily impacted by commercial vehicle traffic. Cities are also interested in local economic development, and therefore have to make sure that the provision of goods and logistics services is adequate. Cities control land use, including the land necessary for logistics activities (warehouses and terminals), and are in charge of local traffic and parking regulations, including all regulations that relate to delivery vehicles. Finally, cities deal with environmental and social issues, which are strongly associated with urban freight activities. Metropolitan-wide agencies in charge of transportation infrastructure and master plans are also involved in freight issues. Higher levels – regional, national, co-national (e.g. the European Union) – promote policies related to air quality, climate change, job creation, and economic development. They set legislation such as air quality standards, organize data collection frameworks, and promote research programs that may have a direct impact on urban freight. This is also true at an international level, with an increasing number of organizations publishing reports and guidelines on urban freight (SPIM-Taryet, 2019, ICLEI, 2021). Major events such as the organization of the Olympic Games provide opportunities to instigate a change in urban freight operations citywide. The City of Paris together with the freight and logistics industry is developing a freight strategy for the Olympics in 2024, following the example set by Greater London (Browne et al., 2014). In many other cities, major infrastructure projects such as the implementation of a subway system can also play that role. However, despite many drivers and mandates, actual strategies of local public authorities regarding freight and logistics remain modest. Many local governments continue to design their urban freight policy around routine truck traffic and parking management. They view commercial traffic as something that should be banned or at least strictly regulated, and not as a service they should help organize. Local policies are often parochial and can be conflicting, one municipality acting in contradiction with surrounding municipalities on truck bans or warehousing park development for example.

To discuss these issues and indicate directions for progress, the chapter is organized around nine "best practices" in urban logistics policies, each (more or less) represented by a city. These initiatives were chosen (by the author) because they have an interesting cost/benefit balance. They include freight consultation forums, low- and zero-emission zones, the promotion of clean delivery vehicles, road pricing, off-hour deliveries, curbside management, urban planning, support for innovative start-ups, and new methods for freight data collection. For each of the described initiatives, when possible, the specific case of urban logistics policies in cities of developing countries is presented, drawing from recent research results.

In the conclusion, recommendations to cities for a more efficient urban logistics policy are proposed.

Nine Best Practices in Logistics Policies

Best practices in urban logistics policies can be identified (Allen and Browne, 2016) and the choice in this chapter, for illustrative purposes, is to characterize best practices within specific cities. This list of initiatives results from a personal choice by the author. Each of these initiatives has demonstrated that it provides at least partially significant results, without requiring an exceptional level of public or private financial involvement, or too much technical expertise from the municipal staff. Typically, the list does not include sophisticated pilots or experiments that have very good environmental results but could not be deployed at a macro scale due to their cost or because of other challenges common in cities, such as lack of enforcement tools for example.

The selected initiatives include freight consultation forums, low-emission zones and zero-emission zones, the promotion of clean delivery vehicles, road pricing for freight, support for off-hour deliveries, curbside management, logistics spatial urban planning, support for innovative logistics start-ups, and new methods for urban freight data collection. The cities that have carried out these policies are: Barcelona, London, New York City, Paris, Rotterdam, Shenzhen, and Singapore.

Consulting with Freight Stakeholders: The Basis of an Urban Logistics Policy

Many cities around the world, and especially in Europe, have set up freight partnerships, which are instances of consultation between stakeholders. They are forums for consultation, and in some cases negotiation, about freight and logistics problems, and policy and industry solutions. "Freight Forums," "Freight Quality Partnerships," and "urban logistics charters" have become part of cities' vocabulary. These engagement processes include delivery companies and their organizations, retailers and retailers' groups, shippers' associations, infrastructure managers (such as port authorities), local governments, and – but more rarely – neighborhood groups and community leaders as well as local academic institutions. The design and implementation of a consultation process do not represent any major technical, political, or financial difficulty, although it is not always easy to make sure that all stakeholders are involved (Le Pira et al., 2017). These forums provide opportunities for collaboration between private companies and local administrations that otherwise are not willing to work together.

Interesting examples of freight forums are the Charter for Sustainable Urban Logistics in Paris signed by 80 carriers' and shippers' associations in 2013, and updated in 2021–2022. The Freight Quality Partnerships of the various boroughs of London are also a classic example (Allen et al., 2010). The process of "Living Labs," bodies for consultation, design, and implementation that go along an urban project, often has a variation for urban logistics (CITYLAB, 2019). The Multi-Actor Multi-Criteria Analysis (MAMCA) is proposed by Macharis et al. (2019) as a tool to better involve urban logistics stakeholders. It uses stakeholder objectives as evaluation criteria for the different solutions that are considered. More focused on research and experiments, the "Urban Freight Lab" of Seattle in the United States brings together the municipality, the University of Washington (which runs the laboratory) and logistics, transportation, and real estate companies. When these bodies have reached a certain longevity, they act as a forum for *negotiating* measures such as setting an urban pricing scheme or setting up a labeling system for carriers, like the Fleet Operator Recognition Scheme (FORS) in London, which awards medals (bronze, silver, gold) to delivery companies on the basis of their environmental and social performance. Certification provides operators with a competitive advantage when bidding for contracts. It gives companies access to data, benchmark information, and training programs for their drivers.

Discussion forums between cities exist also at a trans-national level, such as within POLIS, a network of European cities and regions dedicated to transportation policies that leads numerous actions on freight transportation, or the Alliance for Logistics Innovation through Collaboration in Europe (ALICE), one of whose committees is dedicated to urban freight. C40 Cities, a network of mayors of global cities, now has a freight group. Platforms such as ALICE provide networks promoting the exchange of best practices as well as representation of the interests of urban freight within the broader transportation and planning issues.

Low-Emission Zones and Zero-Emission Zones: An Opportunity to Reinvent Urban Trucking

Low-emission zones (LEZ) are areas where old vehicles are banned, and zero-emission zones (ZEZ) are areas to which only zero-emission vehicles have access. LEZ targets are local emissions from traffic such as nitrogen oxides and particulate matters. Rules generally do not encompass CO_2 emissions although carbon emissions are *de facto* also reduced when a LEZ or a ZEZ is applied. The rules that apply are often based on vehicle manufacturing standards such as the "Euro standards" in the EU[1]. Low-emission zones are deployed in many European cities today, but with various levels of intensity. A study by Belliard (2021) ranks European countries for the efficiency of their low-emission zones toward urban freight. They use four criteria (see Table 18.1). Denmark in 2021 was the "best" and Greece the "worst" country in Europe in implementing efficient low-emission zones for logistics. This ranking will change as more countries, such as France, are now engaged in a comprehensive LEZ deployment policy.

The London low-emission zone is the best-known LEZ in the world. It has existed since 2008, it covers both heavy goods vehicles and vans, whereas many LEZ only include trucks, potentially generating substitution effects (operators using multiple vans instead of one truck to deliver into a city). The London LEZ corresponds to the entire metropolitan area (Greater London) and not just a small portion of the city center, like many other LEZ. The Euro 6 standard has been applied to the whole area since 2021 for commercial vehicles, making it one of the strictest LEZ in Europe. As a further ingredient of success, enforcement has always been carried out by ANPR (Automated Number Plate Recognition) cameras. London now plans to implement three zero-emission zones by 2025. Other cities have announced plans for ZEZ: Dutch cities, Oslo in Norway for example. From 2024 (Paris) until 2028 (Strasbourg), several French municipalities have committed to implementing "non-diesel" zones, a French particularity. In New York City, the municipal fleet including that of the city's 50 agencies will be 100% electric by 2040 (Executive Order no. 53, 2020).

Table 18.1 Ranking of EU countries for the efficiency of low-emission zones for urban logistics

Country	Number of LEZ/ number of large cities in the country	Average of the Euro standards selected for diesel vans and for trucks	Type of support framework	Type of enforcement (ANPR = automated number plate recognition cameras)	Final rank (weighted average of the four criteria)
Denmark	1	5 and 5	National	ANPR and manual	3.8
Sweden	2	5 and 5	National	Manual	3.3
The Netherlands	0.77	4 and 4.2	National	ANPR and manual	3.15
Norway	0.66	6 and 5	National	Manual	3
Italy	4.17	4.07 and 4.07	Regional	ANPR and manual	3
Germany	1.58	4.06 and 4.06	National	ANPR and manual	2.95
Belgium	0.80	4.5 and 4.5	Regional	ANPR and manual	2.9
France	0.20	4.25 and 4	National	Manual	2.15
Austria	1.25	0 and 3.4	Regional	Manual	2.15
Spain	0.04	4 and 4	National	Manual	2
Finland	0.16	0 and 5	Local	Manual	1.5
Portugal	0.25	4 and 4	Local	Manual	1.15
Czech Republic	0.25	0 and 4	Local	Manual	0.95
Greece	0.20	2 and 2	Local	Manual	0.9

Low-emission zones are useful tools for an efficient city logistics policy for two reasons. One is obvious: LEZ accelerates the greening of urban delivery operators' vehicles, reducing emissions from the logistics sector. This is especially important for NOx, whose emissions come in a large part from freight transportation because of its important use of diesel. Another benefit is less known but may be as or even more important: low-emission zones lead to the restructuring of the freight transport sector, by "forcing" modernization, optimization, and the acquisition of more recent vehicles or alternative vehicles: electric vans, cargo cycles, or electric mopeds (see the section below). Very small companies challenged by the introduction of a LEZ have to become more efficient, or they may have to leave the market. This effect was evidenced in the cases of London, Berlin, and Gothenburg (Dablanc and Montenon, 2015).

Facilitating the Use of Clean Delivery Trucks and Vans

Clean delivery vehicles are varied and include zero-emission trucks and vans, electric mopeds, cargo cycles, but also pedestrian deliveries, and delivery robots or robot-assisted deliveries. While there has been a lot of attention provided to cycle-logistics (Verlinghieri et al., 2021), the positive impacts of a fast transition of truck and van fleets to zero-emission are potentially much higher than the increase in the use of cargo bikes, because of the important share of trucks and vans into delivery fleets. Thanks to the relatively low cost of electricity (at least before the energy crisis of 2022) and the low cost of vehicle maintenance, total cost of ownership (TCO) of electric vans is close to the TCO of vans with internal combustion engines. However, only 4% of newly registered vans in France in June 2022 were electric (as compared with 13% of private cars), and this disappointing figure has not received the attention it required. Large delivery operators and third-party logistics providers (e.g. DHL, Amazon) are advertising their increasing uptake of clean delivery vehicles in city centers but these efforts have not yet translated into a significant increase in the average number of zero-emission delivery vehicles in urban areas. The lack of charging stations, for electricity as well as natural gas, is one of the factors explaining the low uptake of cleaner freight vehicles.

In that regard, Shenzhen in China provides an interesting example of voluntary policy. As documented by Crow et al. (2020), there were 70,000 electric delivery vehicles, a world record, in Shenzhen by 2019. Multi-dimensional municipal support for the development of electric delivery vehicles seems to explain the high rate of "electric logistics vehicles" as they are identified officially. This support includes: financial subsidies given according to vehicle use (subsidies increase with the distance traveled by vehicles), massive deployment of recharging stations, and the provision of clear regulatory advantages for electric vans' users (Crow et al., 2020).

Urban Pricing for Freight Vehicles Is Barely Emerging Despite Its Benefits

Urban tolls represent an opportunity to "fine-tune" freight transportation patterns: tolling makes it possible to price differently when circulating at specific hours (off-hours versus peak hours) or on specific days, or when using specific vehicles (clean vehicles). However, there are few practical cases of road freight pricing in urban areas. The most famous city charge is the Singapore Electronic Road Pricing system (ERP), in place since 1998. Trucks pay 1.5 times what passenger cars pay. The London congestion charging system, implemented in 2003, is much smaller as it only covers parts of the city center. Commercial vehicles pay the same amounts as private vehicles, due to a two-year negotiation that took place before the implementation of the congestion pricing scheme. Carriers' organizations argued that trucks and vans should not pay at all as there is no alternative to using a road vehicle, and the position of Transport for London was that freight vehicles should pay more than cars as they contribute more to pollution and they inflict more important damages to roads. Both parties compromised in the middle: trucks now pay the same amount as cars. The scheme "Area C" in Milan, Italy, serves both as a low-emission zone and a pricing system. There are also truck tolls in Scandinavia (Stockholm and Gothenburg in Sweden for example) as well as in Brussels, Belgium. Truck toll rates in New York City, which are applied when passing a bridge or a tunnel, are now significant, from $11 dollars for small trucks to up to $30 for 5-axle trucks (fees applied in 2021). See Chapter 23.

An interesting example is the Heavy Vehicle Fee (HVF) in Switzerland. It is a national truck pricing scheme based on distance traveled and differentiating trucks according to their age and size. What makes Switzerland a specific case is that all roads and streets, including urban streets, are included in the scheme, making the fee a *de facto* urban truck toll. The HVF has seen positive results, as it has reduced the number of trucks and increased its load factor (Initiative des Alpes, 2021). However, no specific evaluation of the scheme on urban trucking has been made. The pricing system in Brussels, Belgium, is also kilometer-based. In France, due to protests from regional farmers and local freight carriers, a comprehensive scheme for truck tolling on the main roads of the country (apart from private highways, which are already priced) was abandoned in 2014. Although not an official urban toll, it was targeting ring-roads around Paris as well as the urban highways in and out of the main cities in France, acting therefore as a metropolitan toll for trucks. The failure of the French project illustrates that it is important to take into account public acceptance of tolls. However, if political caution is justified in some cases, it should however not be used as a presumption that nothing can be done.

The Promotion of Off-Hour Deliveries: An Overlooked Policy

Night deliveries, or rather deliveries late in the evening or early in the morning, are an important way of optimizing logistics and decreasing its impact on cities (Savadogo and Beziat, 2021). Tests have shown that companies delivering at night can save up to 30% in delivery cost and 25% in diesel consumption (Holguin-Veras, 2008). Logistics operators are generally in favor of off-hour operations, but goods receivers such as shops or restaurants are more reluctant, as they prefer to be on the premises during deliveries. In megacities in developing countries, with extremely severe traffic congestion levels during day time and specific challenges to logistics operations (Castillo et al., 2019), benefits of off-hour deliveries are very important (Dias et al., 2019). However, at night, security issues (thefts) arise in some neighborhoods. Early morning deliveries are more secure although less accepted by residents because of noise.

The promotion of off-peak hour deliveries, and in parallel the reduction of noise caused by deliveries, are new targets of municipal policies. Some cities stand out in the care they take in promoting them. New York City gives direct financial subsidies to encourage businesses to organize unattended deliveries. The PIEK program in the Netherlands, a national initiative, covers all aspects of research, development, support, and regulation to reduce noise from night deliveries, including vehicles, rolling stock, handling equipment, and driving practices. Noise emissions in Dutch cities must be kept below 65dB for night deliveries. Building trust between delivery operators and receivers is an important part of the role that local governments can play to promote off-peak-hour deliveries. Memorandums of understandings and partnership charters can help convince reluctant receivers in accepting to be delivered in depots or buffer areas when staff is not in attendance.

Curbside Management and Deliveries

Freight-focused curbside management needs a complete overhaul. Curbside management needs to accommodate freight and logistics operations (Diehl et al., 2021), although few cities in the world systematically include logistics concerns when managing the curb. Freight parking on traditional loading/unloading bays is increasingly inadequate (Malik et al., 2017). Freight operators need good access to dedicated on-street loading and unloading areas in areas where off-street parking is not available. As Abel et al. (2021) point out, deliveries on the curb have increased and diversified with the increase in on-demand deliveries and e-commerce, generating "increased pressure" to better manage and monitor the use of loading zones at the curb. The lack of a sufficient number of delivery areas transfers delivery operations on traffic lanes (double-parking) or sidewalks, and leads to congestion and traffic accidents. In busy urban areas and city centers, the use of on-street loading and unloading must be better controlled. Specific attention must be provided to the coordination of freight and cycling (Pitera et al., 2017). In megacities of developing countries, with even more severe "competition for space" (Cruz-Daravina et al., 2021) between public transportation, private passenger transportation, and freight, the need for a better management of the street space is even higher.

Cities implement very local solutions, without common operating procedures emerging nor innovative design. Municipalities have a rather case-by-case response. The first national technical guideline on the subject in France was only published in 2013, much later than guidelines for bus-stop or bike-lane design for example. The City of Paris has organized its own procedures for the implementation of loading bays. A minimum of one loading zone every 100 meters in the city streets is required, and a loading bay cannot be less than ten meters long to allow drivers to use a tailgate lift. Some municipalities have organized curbside and loading zones more innovatively. On-street delivery areas in Barcelona, Spain are now managed digitally. Delivery drivers must register on a smartphone application (AreaDUM) with their vehicle registration number. Once they arrive at a delivery bay, the application identifies their location, to which they must confirm. A 30-minute window then opens to carry out the delivery operation. In Seattle, USA, the Urban Freight Lab, a partnership between the city, the University of Washington and delivery operators, experiments with innovative set-ups for loading and unloading on-street facilities. The focus is on the "final 50 feet" of freight activities in cities, testing solutions such as new design for loading bays or common carrier delivery lockers (Urban Freight Lab, 2018). Some municipalities in Europe organize parking permits for trucks or trailers serving as a temporary depot from which cargo bikes make delivery rounds in the neighborhood. Time-sharing is another way to improve street parking capacity for deliveries. On Barcelona's main boulevards, the two lateral lanes are dedicated to traffic during peak hours, deliveries during off-peak hours, and residential parking during the night. The urban planning concept of "complete streets" (FHA, 2022) increasingly includes freight and delivery activities, although timidly. Conway et al. (2019) provides the first comprehensive guidelines for a better integration of truck parking and loading infrastructure in street design and management. The equivalent guidelines are still needed for cargo cycles and delivery of two wheelers.

Spatial Planning and Zoning: A New Field of Policy Intervention

Long ignored by urban planning and development policies (Sanchez-Diaz and Browne, 2018), the spatial organization of freight facilities has primarily responded to real estate market forces. The absence of a regional overview of logistics land use has given way to logistics development on the edge of cities, the result of negotiation between isolated municipalities and a dynamic real estate industry integrated into international financial markets (Raimbault, 2022). The evolution of the location of logistics facilities is in contradiction with two current objectives of public authorities: reducing urban sprawl and reducing land artificialization (OECD, 2018). Far-away logistics facilities tend to generate more truck-miles as delivery trucks need to cover longer distances to reach urban destinations (Dablanc and Rakotonarivo, 2010). This situation favors logistics sprawl, i.e. the spatial decentralization of logistics buildings over time from dense areas to distant suburbs (Dablanc and Ross, 2012), increasing traffic emissions, noise, and congestion. The consumption of land (or land artificialization) around cities has also been identified as a problem, especially in European countries where legislation is now considered so as to minimize the total number of new developments, whether residential or commercial, including logistics. A new trend in the logistics real estate market sees the development of warehouses in more central urban areas. This is the result of the demand from e-commerce retailers and parcel express operators in need of facilities close to consumer markets to serve rapidly increasing online orders. Amazon added a total of nine warehouses in 2020 in New York City itself, in addition to the five already existing (Haag and Hu, 2021). While peripheral logistics facilities are large, standardized one-story buildings (multi-story buildings have recently made an apparition) mostly intended for logistics service providers, mass retail, or industry (Heitz et al., 2019), urban logistics facilities are "tailor-made" buildings that are subject to special attention to facilitate their urban integration. They are aimed at logistics markets such as parcel delivery, e-commerce or instant deliveries, and quick commerce. This urban market of warehouses includes vertical buildings. Underground development is also becoming common, in former car park facilities for example.

The concomitant development of large logistics facilities at the edge of metropolitan areas and urban warehouses within central areas require new types of land use planning and construction policies: regional spatial logistics planning on the one hand; and urban zoning promoting environment-friendly urban warehouses on the other hand. So far, few regional master plans have set out guidelines for logistics land use. As a positive example, the Chicago Metropolitan Agency for Planning sets provisions for better-accommodating freight land uses in the communities and providing more efficient freight infrastructure (CMAP, 2018). Some issues are often left unresolved such as public transportation access to logistics developments. An Amazon giant warehouse near Amiens in France opened in 2017 without anyone having thought of changing bus itineraries to site a bus stop near the warehouse (interviews from the author).

Paris stands out from other large cities because of its long-term policy of logistics spatial planning. The municipality has been looking for solutions to accommodate logistics facilities within the city boundaries since the 2000s. The objective is to facilitate freight consolidation and the reduction in distances traveled for last-mile deliveries. The 2016 zoning plan (Figure 18.1) organizes the "zone of major urban services" as an anchor for large logistics terminals. The objective of the zone is to improve "the reception, distribution, and removal of goods of all kinds by reducing pollution due to their transport through the use, in particular, of rail or waterways and all alternative modes of transport." The city also promotes the implementation of smaller logistics facilities in all neighborhoods. 61 land parcels have been identified as "logistics perimeters": a developer that has a project on any of the targeted land parcels is obliged to integrate a logistics hub into the programming of the project. The municipality of Paris has also launched several bids for tenders for innovative use of spaces

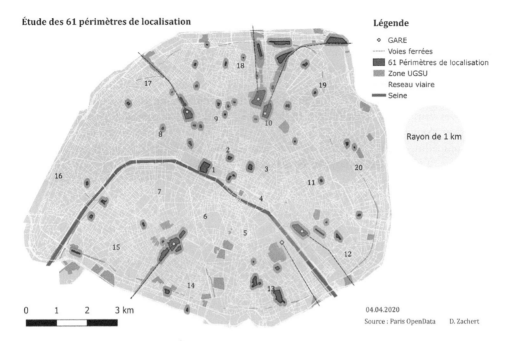

Figure 18.1 "Logistics perimeters" in the Paris 2016 zoning ordinance
Source: Zachert (2020), from data from the City of Paris
Source: Belliard (2021)
Source: City of Rotterdam, data presented in Adoue (2022)

such as unused gas stations or brown-fields to logistics operators that propose sustainable city logistics. Gas stations and car parks have been converted into logistics facilities. Other cities have seen interesting developments. In London, the Cross-river partnership identifies potentially available "urban logistics hubs" and "micro logistics hubs" across central London for logistics operators. The logistics developer Prologis routinely builds ten-story logistics terminals in central Tokyo and opened the first three-story warehouse in Seattle in 2017. The acceptance of urban warehouses is increasingly conditioned to environmental criteria and to a careful attention to the integration of buildings into the urban esthetics. Some cities accept or even promote the development of mixed (multi-activity) buildings, with logistics on underground or street levels and other activities on the upper levels. One example is the Chapelle "logistics hotel" that opened in Paris in 2018. Built on four levels, it combines an intermodal rail-road freight facility, a large underground warehouse, offices, a gym, a data center, as well as public sports facilities and a farm on the rooftop (Dablanc, 2023).

Support for Innovation and Urban Logistics Start-Ups

Support for innovation can be twofold. Some experts see it as a necessary path for local government toward sustainable urban logistics (Pani, 2021). It can also fail in providing large-scale results, as will be discussed at the end of this section. In effect, several local governments are promoting innovation in urban logistics with efficiency and/or environmental mitigation as objectives. Some cities such as Paris, France, and Barcelona, Spain have set up innovation agencies with a focus on urban logistics. Paris implemented an incubator for urban logistics start-ups. The "London Freight Lab" started in 2021 with an Innovation Challenge bringing together hundreds of start-ups and SMEs in urban freight tech. Electrically assisted cargo bikes have been popular with municipalities, especially in Europe. A world cargo-bike festival took place in Groningen in the Netherlands in 2019 and another one is scheduled for October 2022 in Amsterdam, supported by local governments. Local administrations open bus and bike lanes to cargo bikes, which gives a considerable competitive advantage to cargo bikes over vans and delivery trucks. In 2019, New York City authorized pedal assist cargo bikes from Amazon, DHL, and UPS to operate in the city, using some of the municipal on-street unloading/loading zones at no fee. Several local and national governments are also supporters of unmanned automated vehicles (UAVs) for deliveries, from drones to droids to automated trucks. The city of Rejkjavik, Iceland, has authorized Flytrex and retail distributor Aha to organize a regular drone delivery line over one of the city's bays. Swiss Post operates the drone delivery of pharmaceutical products in partnership with the municipalities of Zurich and Lugano in Switzerland. At the State and Federal levels in the United States, authorizations are provided to delivery companies to test and operate drone delivery lines, such as UPS on campuses, and FedEx and Walgreens in association with Wing. The municipality of Santa Monica, in the United States, is associated with the experimental deployment of "coco" robots for food deliveries.

These innovation policies can fail, however. Much of the innovation support is provided through projects that focus mainly on high-cost demonstrators whose mass development remains limited. More fundamentally, cities are seeing the fast train of e-commerce innovations and deliveries pass by without a coordinated response, with each municipality identifying for example its own policy to manage data sharing, or to regulate digital delivery platforms, or to organize the implementation of automated delivery lockers in public spaces. Few coordinated public policy initiatives are engaged, in areas where market and business strategies are increasingly global. It should also be noted that technologies for the management of urban logistics using public-private cooperation are still surprisingly limited. Delivery route optimization software rarely takes into account, for example, access rules or delivery schedules, nor lane closures related to road works. Similarly, municipalities do not have access to company data on urban freight (see the section below). Taniguchi et al. (2018) proposed ways to develop public-private partnerships through an integrated platform for innovative city logistics using big data from private companies and public agencies.

Innovative Urban Freight Data Collection Methods

Current urban freight statistics and data on urban logistics' impacts are of poor quality. Precisely why should the local government need data and indicators on logistics? What business is it of theirs when it is a private activity whose optimization needs already make logistics operators users of their own data? Good data enable diagnoses to be made, which then make it possible to adopt appropriate policies. Regularly updated information on logistics activities allows policy-makers to accomplish several things: to help with traffic management and infrastructure planning through better modeling or simulation of the impacts of measures, to evaluate the effects of a sustainable logistics policy, to facilitate the decarbonization of freight by establishing carbon footprint assessments. This enables cost-benefit analyses of public policies such as the implementation of low-emission zones and their positive and negative impacts on freight companies. It provides information to transport operators so that they can situate themselves in relation to average indicators for the sector, such as the share of clean vehicles in delivery vehicle fleets, for example.

Traditional urban freight surveys (such as the ones made in France, see Toilier et al., 2018) are comprehensive and provide excellent information but they are expensive and local governments are reluctant to pay for them. They cannot be done frequently, and it is therefore difficult to use them for historical comparisons nor up-to-date information. New ways of collecting data represent therefore a potential area of progress for urban logistics policies. Several new methods for freight data collection can be identified:

- Use of GPS data from telecom operators.
- Use of data from logistics operators, e-retailers, delivery apps.
- Use of data from municipal agencies such as for example Automatic Number Plate Recognition – ANPR – enforcement cameras.

These methods represent opportunities but also huge technical, strategic or regulatory challenges. As an example, a consultant study in 2020 (Roland Berger and Kisio, 2020) using vehicle location data from Orange, a telecom operator, led to misinterpretation due to the difficulty in identifying trucks in the dataset. Efforts to unveil "freight behaviors" in global mobility data by artificial intelligence are underway but there is not yet a clear solution (Nguyen et al., 2021). Freight patterns may be easier to identify in open-access data such as bike-sharing public services. Bike-sharing schemes are routinely used by delivery riders working for instant delivery platforms such as UberEATS, and their mobility patterns (trip routes, places of pickup and delivery, total volume of activity) are specific and could be singled out from bike-sharing mobility data. ANPR camera data could provide regular and robust indicators of urban freight activity. However, they meet with technical and regulatory challenges. Privacy issues prevent the use of a lot of (or of "live") data. The European GDRP[2] regulation has tightened conditions for cities and research centers to use mobility data. In Sweden, the use of ANPR data for research has not yet been authorized and "it is really a pity to not be able to use data that is actually there" (representative of the City of Gothenburg DOT, webinar, March 23, 2021). France has only recently authorized ANPR cameras for enforcement of low-emission zones but under very strict conditions, one of them being that all data must be destroyed immediately and no data can be kept for later use, even if anonymized. Partnerships and data sharing with logistics operators, e-retailers, and delivery apps could be a good way forward for local authorities to retrieve regular information. At the moment, research teams interested in operators' data go operator per operator (non-disclosure agreements and memorandums of understanding need to be carefully crafted), which makes the process very slow. Caution is necessary as companies are reluctant to provide their data, key to their business models.

Two examples provide interesting directions for progress. In Barcelona, Spain, the municipal application AreaDUM (see above) allows the municipality to retrieve real-time information, that can also be used by scholars for the analysis of urban freight mobility (Kolbay et al., 2018). The available data, anonymized, are the following: delivery zone, type of vehicle, type of activity, day, and time. Barcelona is thus one of the few cities in Europe that, at the time of the first lockdown during the COVID-19 pandemic, had accurate information on the real-time impacts of the pandemic on the logistics system. In the Netherlands, freight operators' data sharing has been accelerated by a national provision: by 2025, Dutch cities must implement zero-emission zones that include freight, and the process includes plans for a shared data model with potential benefits for companies sharing data such as prioritized access. In Rotterdam, the Ecostars labeling system (awarding one, two, or three stars to logistics providers according to their environmental performance) includes the mandatory

Table 18.2 Example of use of ANPR cameras' data in Rotterdam, the Netherlands

		Total number of vehicles	Number of emission-free vehicles	Percentage of emission-free vehicles
Delivery vans	Business registration	12,260	173	1.41%
	Self-employed and private individuals	10,932	11	0.10%
	Total	23,192	184	0.79%
Lorries	Business registration	3590	7	0.19%
	Self-employed and private individuals	373	0	0.00%
	Total	3863	7	0.18%

sharing of a list of indicators by all transport companies who want to be labeled. Charters ("covenants") have been set up with operators, although an initial assessment showed that only five companies out of 69 signatories to the charter had begun to organize the sharing of data with the municipality (Adoue, 2022). ANPR camera data (see Table 18.2) have been quite extensively used by Dutch research (Bok et al., 2022), consultants, and local governments to increase knowledge on freight mobility, providing the country with an expertise that few other cities in the world have yet. Data available are: types of vehicles, the Euro standard, the brand, the size of the vehicles, and the category (van, truck). What are missing are information on foreign vehicles, and information on itineraries and time of exit of the zones (Dablanc, 2023).

Key Recommendations for an Urban Logistics Policy

Since the COVID pandemic, urban logistics has been made more visible to the media and public opinion as well as to politicians. Policy-makers and local managers need to use this as an opportunity to include urban logistics in their policy agenda and develop new methods for urban logistics policies. This chapter has looked at several ways to do so, identifying "best practices" around the world. Freight stakeholders' forums are a first step to discuss issues with retailers' associations, transportation companies, and all other stakeholders involved in urban logistics. To go further, cities need to implement low- and zero-emission zones, promote clean delivery vehicles, promote off-hour deliveries, support "urban freight tech" innovations, experiment truck pricing, and implement spatial planning and zoning toward logistics land uses. One of the most important bases to develop efficient measures is to collect better data on freight mobility. Cities should use models for assessing and monitoring freight mobility, with a specific focus on local emissions from urban logistics. Delivery motorcycles and mopeds in particular are often underestimated in traffic counts. New methods for data collection need to be developed, by using municipal data (such as provided by enforcement technologies) and by convincing logistics operators to provide indicators. Data sharing with freight stakeholders is an increasingly important topic. Retailers and delivery companies must provide data to municipalities, while municipalities need to feed companies involved in urban logistics with municipal information on local regulations on traffic, parking, delivery areas, delivery time windows, or the forecasting of road works and street or lane closures.

There is an important need for urban warehouses in the urban logistics industry. New formats such as micro-hubs and logistics hotels improve the reception, distribution, and removal of goods of all kinds. Municipalities should promote the protection of existing logistics facilities as well as the development of new urban warehouses and logistics clusters, using innovative zoning, design, planning, and architecture concepts wherever possible.

Freight and logistics are a key economic sector for the future of cities and local and national stakeholders may find it useful to develop or reinforce educational and training programs for the diverse jobs that urban logistics represents. The objective is to increase the attractivity of careers in the sector. One specific focus of attention is gig delivery workers involved in "quick commerce" and "instant deliveries." Demonstrations and litigation are increasing and cities can help negotiate a better organization of labor between gig workers' representatives and on-demand delivery platforms (see Chapter 27).

In cities from developing countries, specific policies can be designed. Local universities and research centers in Latin America, Africa, South-East Asia need to come forward and promote data collection and local design of urban logistics. They can take advantage of a growing interest for urban logistics from international agencies, groups, and networks such as the World Bank, and include local inputs into these international discussions. Focusing part of the data collection effort and design of strategy on informal sectors and their logistics (supply and waste removal of open markets, supplies to local workshops, to street vendors, to local convenience stores) can provide important benefits. Optimizing nanostores' logistics (IT, suppliers network optimization, payment methods) is a key element of an urban logistics strategy in cities from developing countries (Blanco and Fransoo, 2015). Also, road infrastructure improvement in neighborhoods with a high rate of delivery generation is very important for the development of modern urban logistics.

Urban logistics policy strategies can be defined in planning documents such as Sustainable Urban Logistics Plans (SULP), using several topical guidelines that exist today (Aifandopoulou and Xenou, 2019). Local governments in both developed and emerging countries are increasingly interested in defining an action plan on urban logistics and have the means, sometimes unsuspected, to do so.

Notes

1 The Euro standards are vehicle emission standards for pollution from the use of new motor vehicles (including vans and trucks) sold in the European Union. The current Euro standard is Euro 6, and expected new standards should be announced before the end of 2022.
2 General Data Protection Regulation.

References

Abel, S., Ballard, M., Davis, S., Mitman, M., Stangl, K., Wasserman, D. (2021) Curbside inventory report. Institute of transportation engineers, federal highway administration, report FHWA-HEP-21-028. Retrieved from: https://rosap.ntl.bts.gov/view/dot/58181 (accessed on September 14, 2022).

Adoue, F. (2022) *Nouvelles méthodes de collecte de données sur la logistique urbaine, exemple de Rotterdam* (new methods to collect urban logistics data, case study Rotterdam, The Netherlands – in French). Report for the logistics city chair, University Gustave Eiffel, Paris. Retrieved from: https://www.lvmt.fr/wp-content/uploads/2022/09/Collecte-de-donnees-sur-la-logistique-urbaine-a-Rotterdam-Pays-Bas-rapport-dexpertise-Francois-Adoue-pour-la-chaire-Logistics-City-.pdf (accessed on September 16, 2022).

Aifandopoulou, G., and Xenou, E. (2019) *Sustainable Urban Logistics Planning*. European Commission. Retrieved from: https://www.eltis.org/sites/default/files/sustainable_urban_logistics_planning_0.pdf (accessed on September 14, 2022).

Allen, J., and Browne, M. (2016) *Success Factors of Past Initiatives and the Role of Public-Private Cooperation*. Deliverable 2.3, CITYLAB project, H2020, CIVITAS, European Commission. Retrieved from: https://www.citylab.soton.ac.uk/deliverables/D2_3.pdf (accessed on September 15, 2022).

Allen, J., Browne, M., Piotrowska, M., and Woodburn, A.G. (2010) Freight quality partnerships in the UK: An analysis of their work and achievements. Project report. Green logistics report, University of Westminster, UK. Retrieved from: https://westminsterresearch.westminster.ac.uk/item/9045v/freight-quality-partnerships-in-the-uk-an-analysis-of-their-work-and-achievements (accessed on September 14, 2022).

Belliard, L. (2021) Low emission zones in France and Europe. Master's thesis, Sorbonne Université, Paris. English summary and full report (in French) available from: https://www.lvmt.fr/wp-content/uploads/2021/10/2021-Brief-EN-Lucas-Belliard.pdf (accessed on September 14, 2022).

Blanco, E.E., and Fransoo, J.C. (2015). *Reaching 50 Million Nanostores: Retail Distribution in Emerging Megacities.* (BETA Working Paper Series; Vol. 404). Technische Universiteit Eindhoven.

Bok, M.de, Tavasszy, L., and Toen, S. (2022) Application of an empirical multi-agent model for urban goods transport to analyze impacts of zero emission zones in The Netherlands. *Transport Policy,* 124, 119–127.

Browne, M., Allen, J., Wainwright, I., Palmer, A., and Williams, I. (2014) London 2012. Changing delivery patterns in response to the impact of the games on traffic flows. *International Journal of Urban Sciences.* 18(2), 244–261.

Castillo, J.C., Goicochea, E., Chong, M., and Rodriguez, M. (2019) Inmegacity characterization: Trends and realities. *Management Research: Journal of the Iberoamerican Academy of Management,* 17(2). https://www.emerald.com/insight/content/doi/10.1108/MRJIAM-05-2018-0835/full/html

Chicago Metropolitan Agency for Planning (CMAP) (2018) "Mobility" chapter in On To 2050 Plan. Retrieved from: https://www.cmap.illinois.gov/2050/mobility/freight (accessed on September 15, 2022).

Conway, A. et al. (2019) *Complete Streets Considerations for Freight and Emergency Vehicle Operations.* Albany, NY: New York State Energy Research Development Authority, United States. Available from: https://metrans.org/news/new-metrofreight-publication-a-guidebook-for-considering-freight-in-complete-street-design- (accessed on September 14, 2022).

Coulombel, N., Dablanc, L., Gardrat, M., and Koning, M. (2018) The environmental social cost of urban road freight: Evidence from the Paris region. *Transportation Research Part D,* 63, 514–532.

Crow, A., Mullaney, D., Liu, Y., and Wang, Z. (2020) *A New EV Horizon, Insights from Shenzhen's Path to Global Leadership in Electric Logistics Vehicles.* Rocky Mountain Institute report. Retrieved from: https://rmi.org/insight/a-new-ev-horizon/ (accessed on September 15, 2022).

Cruz-Daravina, P. Sánchez-Díaz, I., and Bocarejo, J.P. (2021) Bus Rapid Transit (BRT) and Urban Freight—Competition for space in densely populated cities. *Sustainability.* 13(12), 6611.

Dablanc, L. (2019) City Logistics. *International Encyclopedia of Geography: People, the Earth, Environment and Technology.* Wiley Online Library. Available from: https://doi.org/10.1002/9781118786352.wbieg0137.pub2

Dablanc, L. (2023) Land use planning for a more sustainable urban freight. Chapter 3.1 in Marcucci, E., Gatta, V., and Le Pira, M. (Eds.), *Handbook on City Logistics and Urban Freight.* Edward Elgar, forthcoming.

Dablanc, L., and Montenon, A. (2015) Impacts of environmental access restrictions on freight delivery activities, the example of Low Emission Zones in Europe. *Transportation Research Record: Journal of the Transportation Research Board,* 2478, 12–18.

Dablanc, L. Morganti, E., Arvidsson, N., Woxenius, J., Browne, M., and Saidi, N. (2017) The rise of on-demand "Instant Deliveries" in European cities. *Supply Chain Forum – An International Journal,* 18(4), 203–217.

Dablanc, L., and Rakotonarivo, D. (2010) The impacts of logistic sprawl: How does the location of parcel transport terminals affect the energy efficiency of goods' movements in Paris and what can we do about it? Procedia – Social and behavioral sciences, the sixth international conference on city logistics, Edited by E. Tanguchi and R. G. Thompson, Volume 2, Issue 3, 6087–6096.

Dablanc, L., and Ross, C. (2012) Atlanta: A mega logistics center in the Piedmont Atlantic Megaregion (PAM). *Journal of Transport Geography,* 24, 432–442.

Dias, P., Yoshizaki, H., Favero, P., and Vidal Veira, J. (2019) Daytime or overnight deliveries? Perceptions of drivers and retailers in São Paulo City. *Sustainability,* 11, 6316.

Diehl, C., Ranjbari, A., and Goodchild, A. (2021) Curbspace management challenges and opportunities from public and private sector perspectives. *Transportation Research Record: Journal of the Transportation Research Board,* 2675, 11.

Federal Highway Administration (FHA) (2022) *Moving to a Complete Streets Design Model: A Report to Congress on Opportunities and Challenges.* Retrieved from: https://highways.dot.gov/sites/fhwa.dot.gov/files/2022-03/Complete%20Streets%20Report%20to%20Congress.pdf (accessed on September 15, 2022).

Haag, M., and Hu, W. (2021) As online shopping surged, amazon planned its New York takeover. *New York Times*, March 4.

Heitz, A., Launay, P., and Beziat, A. (2019) Heterogeneity of logistics facilities: An issue for a better understanding and planning of the location of logistics facilities. *European Transport Research Review*, 11(1), 1–20

Holguin-Veras, J. (2008) Necessary conditions for off-hour deliveries and the effectiveness of urban freight road pricing and alternative financial policies in competitive markets. *Transportation Research Part A: Policy and Practice*, 42(2), 392–413.

ICLEI-Local Governments for Sustainability (2021) *EcoLogistics Low Carbon Action Plan for Urban Freight (LCAP-UF) – A Guide to Developing An LCAP-UF.* Bonn, Germany. Retrieved from: https://sustainablemobility.iclei.org/wpdm-package/ecologistics-lcap-uf-guidebook/?wpdmdl=71315 (accessed on September 15, 2022).

Initiative des Alpes (2021) *Les 20 ans de la RPLP : une réussite dans la politique du transport suisse* (Twenty years of success for HVF: A positive achievement for Swiss transport policy – in French). Retrieved from: https://www.alpeninitiative.ch/fr/20-ans-de-la-rplp/ (accessed on September 16, 2022).

Kolbay, B., Mrazovic, P., and Larriba-Pey, J.L. (2018). Analyzing Last Mile Delivery Operations in Barcelona's Urban Freight Transport Network. In: Cloud Infrastructures, Services, and IoT Systems for Smart Cities. IISSC CN4IoT 2017 2017. Lecture Notes of the Institute for Computer Sciences, Social Informatics and Telecommunications Engineering, vol 189. Springer, Cham. https://doi.org/10.1007/978-3-319-67636-4_2

Le Pira, M., Marcucci, E., Gatta, V., Ignaccolo, M., Inturri, G., and Pluchino, A. (2017) Towards a decision-support procedure to foster stakeholder involvement and acceptability of urban freight transport policies. *European Transport Research Review*, 9(54). https://etrr.springeropen.com/articles/10.1007/s12544-017-0268-2#citeas

Letnik, T., Marksel, M., Luppino, G., and Bardi, A. (2019) Urban freight transport policies and measures implemented in strategic documents of European cities, a review. *European Review of Regional Logistics*, 2, 11–15.

Macharis, C., Kin, B., and Lebeau, P., (2019) Multi-actor multi-criteria analysis as a tool to involve urban logistics stakeholders. Chapter 13 in Browne, M., Behrends, S., Woxenius, J., Giuliano, G., and Holguin-Veras, J. (Eds.), *Urban Logistics. Management, Policy and Innovation in a Rapidly Changing Environment*. Kogan Page, London, 274–292.

Malik, L., Sanchez-Dias, I., Tiwari, G., and Woxenius, J. (2017) Urban freight-parking practices: The cases of Gothenburg (Sweden) and Delhi (India). *Research in Transportation Business & Management*, 24, 37–48.

Nguyen, A., Lamouri, S., Pellerin, S., and Tamayo, S. (2021) Data analytics in pharmaceutical supply chains: State of the art, opportunities, and challenges. *International Journal of Production Research*. DOI:10.1080/00207543.2021.1950937

OECD (2018) *Rethinking Urban Sprawl, Moving Towards Sustainable Cities.* Report, 168 pages, https://doi.org/10.1787/9789264189881-en 9789264297951 (EPUB) 9789264189881 (PDF)

Pani, A. (2021) An essential shift to sustainable freight transport in the aftermath of the COVID-19 pandemic: Autonomous robots, crowdshipping and cargo bikes. LEDS global partnership report. Retrieved from: https://slocat.net/wp-content/uploads/2021/07/LEDS-GP_An-Essential-Shift-to-Sustainable-Freight-Transport-in-the-Aftermath-of-the-COVID-19-Pandemic.pdf (accessed on September 16, 2022).

Pitera, K., Pokorny, P., Kristensen, T., and Bjørgen, A. (2017) The complexity of planning for goods delivery in a shared urban space: A case study involving cyclists and trucks. *European Transport Research Review*, 9(46). https://etrr.springeropen.com/articles/10.1007/s12544-017-0262-8#citeas

Raimbault, N. (2022) Outer-suburban politics and the financialisation of the logistics real estate industry: The emergence of financialised coalitions in the Paris region. *Urban Studies*, 59(7), 1481–1498.

Roland Berger and Kisio (2020) Mobilité: donner une nouvelle "voix" à l'Ile-de-France (*Mobility: provide a new "voice" to the Paris region*). Roland Berger report, 28 pages. Retrieved from: file:///C:/Users/laetitia.dablanc/Downloads/MKT_Publi_2020_005_Kisio_Blue_V4%20(1).pdf (accessed on September 16, 2022).

Sanchez-Diaz, I., and Browne, M. (Ed.) (2018) Topical collection on accommodating urban freight in city planning. European Transport Research Review, 10(55). DOI: 10.1186/s12544-018-0327-3

Savadogo, I., and Beziat, A. (2021) Evaluating the potential environmental impacts of a large-scale shift to off-hour deliveries. *Transportation Research Part D*, 90, 102649.

SPIM - Taryet (2019) Estrategia CAF en Logística Urbana Sostenible y Segura, CAF Ediciones, 250p. (in Spanish). Retrieved from: https://scioteca.caf.com/handle/123456789/1510 (accessed on September 15, 2022).

Taniguchi, E., Dupas, R., Deschamps, J-C., and Qurecshi, A.G. (2018) Concepts of an integrated platform for innovative city logistics with urban consolidation centers and transshipment points. in Taniguchi, E. and Thompson, R.G. (Eds.), *City Logistics 3: Towards Sustainable and Liveable Cities*. ISTE, Wiley, London, 129–146.

Toilier, F., Gardrat, M., Routhier, J.L., and Bonnafous, A. (2018) Freight transport modelling in urban areas: The French case of the FRETURB model. *Case Studies on Transport Policy*, 6(4), 753–764.

Urban Freight Lab (2018) *The Final 50 Feet – Urban Goods Delivery System, Research Scan and Data Collection Project*. Final report, Seattle department of transportation, 176p. Retrieved from: https://depts.washington.edu/sctlctr/sites/default/files/SCTL_Final_50_full_report.pdf (accessed on September 15, 2022).

Verlinghieri, E., Itova, I., Collignon, N., and Aldred, R. (2021) The promise of low-carbon freight benefits of cargo bikes in London. Research report for Possible, 37 pages. Retrieved from: https://www.wearepossible.org/our-reports-1/the-promise-of-low-carbon-freight (accessed on September 18, 2022).

Verlinghieri et al: Zachert, D. (2020) *La logistique dans le PLU de Paris* (logistics in Paris PLU). M1 Master's Thesis, University of Strasbourg.

19
POLICY ACCEPTABILITY AND IMPLEMENTATION IN URBAN LOGISTICS

Edoardo Marcucci, Valerio Gatta and Ila Maltese

Introduction

Urban logistics is a key driver for the competitiveness of a city and its markets. It contributes to the efficiency of freight transport systems (Taniguchi et al., 2014) and to the well-being of its inhabitants (Chatziioannou et al., 2020), since it enables normal daily production and consumption activities (i.e., urban life as a whole), making a city attractive for both citizens and companies (Dolati Neghabadi et al., 2019). Yet, freight distribution is a central element in the complexity of mobility and accessibility planning (Axinte et al., 2022; Strale, 2019; Zenezini and De Marco, 2016) because of the several and strong interdependencies with all other economic and social activities (Macário et al., 2008).

At the same time, urban logistics can have a negative impact on the quality of life, especially in large cities and when it is not planned and managed in a systematic way (Sharma and Singh, 2022). Indeed, it affects every dimension of sustainability (Russo and Comi, 2020; Janjevic et al., 2019), in terms of: congestion (economic); pollution – both air and acoustic – and visual intrusion (environmental); road safety, accessibility, public space (Ville et al., 2013; Browne et al., 2012; Anderson et al., 2005) and, more recently, working conditions (social) (Pan et al., 2021). Moreover, from a more dynamic point of view, the recent growth of e-commerce – also due to the outbreak of the worldwide COVID-19 pandemic and its related lockdown measures that strongly restricted passenger mobility in the last few years (Migliaccio et al., 2021; Roland Berger – FM Logistic, 2020; Sernicola et al., 2020) – raises many concerns about the aggravation of the external effects of urban distribution of goods (Lozzi et al., 2022; Patier and Routhier, 2020; Lagorio et al., 2016; Taniguchi et al., 2016). It should be noted, in fact, that the tendency of citizens to request what they have ordered in the shortest possible time implies, in the absence of regulation, a real challenge to sustainability in the urban distribution of goods, multiplying the number of trips, at any time, and everywhere on the territory (Gatta et al., 2021; Keough et al., 2021). This calls for political intervention to minimize negative impacts (Paddeu et al., 2018); indeed, local and national policymakers have begun to take an interest in the issue of urban logistics (Dablanc, 2021), which has become the subject of various public policies and urban planning.

However, since the public decision maker is involved in a segment of transport that is *de facto* exclusively managed by the private sector (Rosales and Haarstad, 2022; EU COMM,

2017a, b; Macharis and Kin, 2017), policies for urban logistics need to be carefully designed and must also consider their acceptability. In fact, as if this were not enough to what has been perceived for years as undue interference by the public sector in the private sector (Browne and Goodchild, 2023; Janjevic et al., 2019; Lindholm and Behrends, 2012), two additional critical aspects emerge.

The first difficulty is the coexistence of many different stakeholders – defined as individuals and organizations that hold a particular interest in a specific area (city) and field (urban logistics), without necessarily being formally invested in a decision-making role (Cascetta et al., 2015) – that are involved in urban logistics. It is based on horizontal competition between couriers and vertical cooperation between logistics and transport operators, retailers, and citizens (Marcucci et al., 2013), thus involving a wide audience of highly interrelated stakeholder groups from both public and private domains (Browne et al., 2021), whose interests, aims and behaviours may not always align (Ballantyne et al., 2013; MDS Transmodal, 2012). This is evident, for example, between different users of the same infrastructures (think of the competition for public land – roads and parking areas – between residents and city users, on the one hand, and freight transport operators on the other) and, more generally, whenever external costs are generated by the movement of passengers and goods in urban areas. With different stakeholders' utility functions (Stathopoulos et al., 2012) that prelude different and potentially conflicting impacts of the measure to be adopted, the heterogeneity of preferences becomes even more relevant and significant for the decision-making process (Marcucci et al., 2012). This induces the search for a policy mix that maximizes the acceptability of the policy – which is an attitudinal construct, changes from individual to individual, even over the individual's lifetime (Mitsopoulos-Rubens and Regan, 2017), and indicates the degree to which an intervention is appreciated and agreed upon – among different stakeholders.

The second critical aspect relates to the difficulty for citizens to be aware of their own role in the urban logistics distribution chain. They are customers of logistics services and thus ultimately the drivers of demand; in particular, they are either customers of the shops where the goods are delivered, or, with the recent increasingly prevalent advent of e-commerce, end users of the supply chain, receiving at their home or place of work the item requested online. At the same time, they are also, and above all, third parties who suffer the negative effects of intensive urban logistics, such as, for example, the problems of unavailable parking space and high pollution, and an excessive number of vehicles circulating on the road for deliveries. Yet, citizens themselves do not seem to be very skilled with respect to logistics elements (Marcucci et al., 2019b), nor aware of their own responsibilities in generating freight distribution trips and related negative consequences (Marcucci et al., 2013; Lindholm and Behrends, 2012). Nevertheless, urban logistics impact on the quality of life is attracting attention also among the citizenry, whose involvement and requests are future challenges to address (Maltese et al., 2023; Amaya et al., 2020).

Last but not least, in addition to its very complex and fast-changing nature, urban logistics is currently facing new challenges as well as opportunities, such as, for instance, the possibility to employ digital-based technologies for tracking parcels (thus increasing the efficiency of the service) or alternative fuelled vehicles (for minimizing the negative impact on the environment). Not only the private sector has invested in new technologies and solutions since 2000 (Benjelloun and Crainic, 2008), but also EU encourages the use of new technologies (EU Comm, 2017a, b), Furthermore, sharing economy including co-modality and the Physical Internet also helps to reduce the number of circulating freight vehicles (Jaller et al., 2020; Taniguchi et al., 2018, 2020, 2016) and consequently also the congestion and danger on the roads (i.e., the social impact of urban logistics).

How urban freight policy planning is performed is relevant to the results it can or cannot achieve. In fact, focusing on *ex-ante* policy acceptability is fundamental for decision makers to assess and identify the most prominent and sustainable interventions. To this aim, this chapter provides an overview of current knowledge on policy acceptability and implementation in urban logistics discussing three key elements, namely: stakeholders' engagement, stakeholders' preferences, and process replicability.

The structure of the chapter includes, after this introduction, a second section describing the importance of the *ex-ante* acceptability of urban logistics policies. The third section discusses how to perform stakeholders' engagement within the policy-making process. Section four focuses on the methodologies enabling the elicitation of stakeholders' preferences to be considered for policy-making. The fifth section is devoted to the most recent, standardized, and transferable ways of designing and implementing urban logistics policies, aimed at guaranteeing a high level of process replicability. The chapter ends with some concluding reflections.

Policy Acceptability

Due to current and significant changes in both socio-economic dynamics and political and institutional context, public policies have become complex to implement. At the same time, due to often widespread mistrust of those who govern, on the one hand, and the "technological" transparency to which they are subjected, on the other, public policies are constantly under scrutiny by the local community (Marcucci et al., 2019a). Consequently, within the *policy-making* cycle, the analysis and evaluation of the decisions taken in the name and on behalf of citizens have become an essential tool for evaluating their effectiveness, i.e., the achievement of the expected results, and efficiency, in terms of the best possible allocation of the (public) resources employed. In particular, as for the first phase of policy design (identification of critical issues; formulation of solution alternatives; final decision), the *ex-ante* evaluation purpose is to establish the "convenience", in a broad sense, of undertaking a given intervention, i.e., whether the benefits expected from the *manoeuvre* are greater than the measured and estimated costs, also including any delays due to contrasts and conflicts between the involved stakeholders. This is especially true for urban logistics policies, whose nature is complex and fast-changing and whose issues can be the most diverse: from infrastructure to technology to pollution abatement (De Marco et al., 2018); not surprisingly, several policies for urban logistics have failed or produced limited effects due to a lack of stakeholder engagement (Zenezini et al., 2018; Kiba-Janiak, 2017; Allen et al., 2012; Anand et al., 2012). For example, Vahrenkamp (2016) and Vural and Aktepe (2021) discuss failures with respect to Urban Consolidation Center and Collection-Delivery Points, while Van Duin and Quak (2007) with respect to infrastructural, operational, and regulatory ones. Since it is not difficult to understand the correlation between the success of a decision-making process and the consensus given to its promoters, the acceptability level of a policy becomes particularly relevant for minimizing the time and cost of its implementation (Loures and Crawford, 2008) as well as potential conflicts. Moreover, it should be referred to the preferences of all the categories of interested parties (de Oliveira et al., 2019; Macharis et al., 2014). Thanks to clearly identified stakeholders and their needs, it is in fact possible to measure the acceptability of the proposal in advance, thus reducing time and costs of the decision-making process and minimizing potential conflicts during its implementation; this increases the chance of success of the measure, at the same time increasing the reliability of the decision maker (Marcucci et al., 2019a; Ruesch et al., 2012). The *ex-ante* evaluation, therefore, would become a process in which operators and stakeholders take part, with the aim of knowing in advance the effects of the decision to be taken. Indeed, the lack of awareness can both make sustainable goals difficult to achieve and provoke an unmanageable heterogeneity in policy acceptability (Gonzalez-Feliu et al., 2014).

Urban logistics policy acceptability requires, not only, the collection of a large amount of, potentially sensitive, data (Janjevic et al., 2019; Marcucci et al., 2012), but also accurate analyses and methodologically correct estimates/predictions (Le Pira et al., 2017). These are mostly carried out through interviews, focus groups, and/or administering questionnaires (Adell et al., 2014). Focus groups are organized in the early stages of policy design when more qualitative data are needed, so it is not essential that there is a representative sample. If there are several categories of stakeholders, however, it is good to ensure that they are all represented, possibly even in different focus groups (Stathopoulos et al., 2011). The size of the group should be quite limited (6–10 people) with a moderator who is well aware of and able to manage the different positions and bring out different attitudes as well as possible barriers to acceptability. From the methodological point of view, it is necessary to start with a general question about the area of interest and then begin the discussion and try to get all the necessary information for which the group was created (*ibidem*). Questionnaires are used when the researchers adopt a quantitative approach. This typically applies when there is a clear idea of the characteristics of the measures proposed allowing the definition of reliable scenarios. In this case, more specific questions can be asked, possibly partly differentiated by category of stakeholders, related to the consequences of the policy (Gatta and Marcucci, 2016). Answers allow for the building of a database which is then used to develop models useful for the *ex-ante* evaluation of scenarios and future stakeholders' behaviour (Taniguchi and Thompson, 2014).

Stakeholder Engagement

The acceptability of a policy is greatly enhanced by adequate stakeholder engagement, understood as the participation of various interested parties (producers and shippers, freight transport and logistics operators, recipients, residents, local public authorities, and others) in the decision-making process (EU COMM, 2017a, b). It is nowadays considered as an integral step in policy design and implementation (Crainic et al., 2009), since it allows for the identification of controversial issues and it makes the policy-making process more representative and transparent, creating a sense of ownership of decisions and measures, and favouring the acquaintance among stakeholders. Stakeholder engagement helps involving people and creating awareness with respect to the relevant topics discussed.

The participation of the recipients of public policy enriches the decision-making process (Formez, 2006) as it is an opportunity for dissemination, comparison, learning, and rational support to decision makers (Quick, 2014). However, despite its widely acknowledged importance, this process can be difficult and lengthy. Stakeholder participation in urban (freight) mobility decision-making processes is often very low (Marcucci et al., 2017a, b) or limited to the early stages of consultation, which does not always translate into a constant and ongoing commitment over time.

Among the most predictable reasons, it is the difficulty in identifying all the necessary stakeholders. Although stakeholders' preferences and behaviour are expected to be carefully mapped and considered by decision makers for developing the right solutions for city logistics (Gatta and Marcucci, 2016; 2014; Holguín-Veras et al., 2015), according to Dablanc (2008) one can fail in including all types of stakeholders needed, thus leading to the wrong or unaccepted solution. Therefore, she suggests setting up a dedicated consultation process, to cover a metropolitan area or region and to choose a responsible institution with sufficient legal and political influence (Dablanc, 2011). In the same vein, the lack of communication, so to speak "structural", i.e., dependent not on a precise will or inability, but on the objective lack or unavailability of data, can be considered an obstacle to participation.

The exchange of data, which is crucial for individual and collective evaluation, at every stage (*ex-ante, in-itinere, ex-post*) of the assessment process (Marcucci et al., 2019a) can transform the *ex-ante* evaluation in a co-participated and transferable process for discovering in advance the effects of the decision to be made (LEAD, 2020). Cooperation is based on communication and dissemination of outcomes, knowledge sharing, and information exchange between stakeholders and decision makers (*ibidem*) for whom data availability and access are crucial (Ruesch et al., 2020). In this respect, one must recall that another obstacle could be the lack of cooperation. An interesting paper by Lindawati et al. (2014) explores the stakeholders' willingness to participate in urban logistics collaboration initiatives in Singapore in terms of motivations and barriers. While suggesting the need to share information among stakeholders, it emphasizes how complicated it could be to convince a stakeholder to share information on its operational strategies with its direct competitors. In addition, Hofenk (2012) links the willingness to improve urban logistics to the stakeholders' perceived need for change as well as to their trust in the initiative, while Bjørgen et al. (2021) identify a low level of the public institution authority, which does not enjoy the trust of the private sector, as a motivation for low stakeholder participation. Within this context, transparency of the process, and both the reliability and credibility of the decision makers, can be of paramount importance; credible objectives and strategies must be clearly identified as well, for better assessing *ex-ante* effects (Nuzzolo and Comi, 2014).

Yet according to De Souza et al. (2014), the solution for synchronizing the last mile of delivery, which is crucial but challenging to implement, since it requires cooperation among all stakeholders, could be that of encouraging participation in co-creating solutions. Therefore, specific mechanisms to discuss freight issues among Local Authorities, private sector (operators and customers) and communities (receivers) must be established to have an effective stakeholder participation and commitment. This also allows identifying potential solutions and the role of the various actors, as well as to secure commitments to a strategy of improvements (Holguín-Veras et al., 2015).

Complex tools for participation that can be useful for evaluating policies for urban logistics have been gaining ground in recent years, also thanks to the spread of communication technologies available to individuals with great ease of use and affordability. The Freight Quality Partnership is one of the most important examples for setting up a formal working environment (COESUF, 2021; Lindholm, 2014; Lindholm and Browne, 2013) that helps stakeholders' cooperation with clear roles and responsibilities (LEAD, 2021). It is supposed to be a basic, informal, repeatable, and multilateral relationship among representatives from both public and private sector aimed at working together, discussing issues, and identifying concrete actions to improve freight planning and operations (Lozzi, 2018). It enhances mutual understanding and shared knowledge to identify solutions, also improving public-private cooperation and obviously it implies that the most relevant stakeholders related to specific interests and objectives in a specific area are identified and included in a manageable number (De Souza et al. 2014). Another example comes from Paddeu and Aditjandra (2020) who used a participatory approach to allow stakeholders to identify the problem and co-design a set of solutions by sharing their different visions of urban logistics. Interestingly, they considered the importance of an "engaging" and "easy-to-use" process for supporting decision makers to design and implement consistent urban logistics policies. Finally, Golini et al.

(2018) used a visual tool to foster stakeholder engagement providing easy-to-understand information aimed at assessing potential solutions.

Stakeholder Preferences

Investigating the acceptability of policies for urban logistics is a widely used practice in the literature, through combined surveys of focus groups and questionnaires, which are often used sequentially to capture respondents' preferences. The collected observations allow, using Discrete-Choice Models (DCMs), to investigate potentially effective and efficient policies for urban logistics. Among the tools available to carry out an *ex-ante* evaluation, Stated Preference (henceforth SP) surveys are one of the most promising ones[1]. They allow for the assessment of hypothetical scenarios and the estimation of the willingness to pay on the basis of a robust theoretical reference paradigm (Marcucci et al., 2015). From a methodological point of view, Stated Choice Experiments are to be preferred, which consist of several options from which the respondents can choose according to their preferences. Each choice task presents a series of alternatives described by different characteristics/attributes. In this way, through econometric analysis, it is possible to study the relative influence of a single independent variable (the attribute) on a given observed phenomenon (the choice).

For example, Marcucci et al. (2007) estimate private operators' willingness to pay for using an Urban Distribution Center, through SP and DCMs, identifying different propensity levels according to the commodity category of the supply chain. Stathopoulos et al. (2011, 2012) develop a ranking experiment aimed at assessing agent-specific preferences for freight policy measures – specifically a (freight) Limited Traffic Zone (LTZ) issued in Rome – illustrating how to carry out the various complex stages required to study freight agent behaviour. Suksri and Raicu (2012) apply the multi-agent system approach for analysing the behaviour of several stakeholders and their interactions to prioritize urban freight distribution strategic policies, while Marcucci and Gatta (2013) analysed alternative policy scenarios inherent to urban freight transport in the LTZ in Rome. Stressing that the success of such innovative measures mostly depends on the competence and awareness of decision makers (Lindholm and Blinge, 2014), the authors test, from the policymaker's point of view, what are the implications arising from the presence of heterogeneity among different agents and within the same category. To this end, great attention is given to stakeholders' behaviour, which is often little considered in more traditional decision-making approaches, demonstrating its importance in the design phase to produce efficient and effective measures. Gatta and Marcucci (2014) analyse and discuss useful tools to assess the *ex-ante* acceptability of policies by different stakeholders (retailers, own account carriers, and third-party carriers); the aim is to identify packages of measures (economic, operational, and infrastructural) that, taking into account the heterogeneity of agents' preferences, can balance the effects in terms of utility/disutility. Interestingly, the results show that there was no single policy that was at the same time acceptable for all the three categories of stakeholders, thus implicitly highlighting a trade-off in terms of utility and forcing to seek a policy mix that maximizes policy acceptability of the different stakeholders. This is also in line with Gonzalez-Feliu and Salanova (2012) and Paddeu et al. (2018) who analysed the potential benefits of the stakeholders' cooperation.

From a purely methodological point of view, the integration of DCMs and Agent-Based Models (ABMs) is also proposed to support a participatory decision-making process. For instance, multilayer network and opinion dynamics models were applied to the case of the freight LTZ in Rome (Gatta et al. 2017; Le Pira et al. 2017). In this way, the two approaches intend to explore the heterogeneity of stakeholders' preferences and predict behavioural choices in terms of acceptability (Valeri et al. 2016) so as to reproduce, through the impact on utility functions of different stakeholders, the opinion dynamics formulation. This approach allows analysing the interaction between stakeholders and overcoming, through simulation processes, the potential problem of different attitudes, capacity, and strength of opinion expression by stakeholders, without building complex weighting systems. The application refers to a short-period scenario in which the measure is predetermined and well known to the stakeholders in terms of its consequences. In this way, the aim is to reduce the conflict between different stakeholder interests in order to structure an effective policy, maximizing consensus, but at the same time understanding the mechanisms of a participatory decision-making process between stakeholders.

Le Pira et al. (2017) proposed a similar model that takes into account the co-presence of several stakeholders. By combining the two methodologies (DCM and ABM) – thereby overcoming their weaknesses and corroborating their strengths – they manage to test the potential acceptability of the proposed solution. This integrated model, which can be used to support policy-making decisions for freight transport, proves to be a good way to handle the complexity of such measures. Its aim is to stimulate an effective participatory process to lead to consensus building between the different stakeholders.

Even more recently, SP has been used to establish the acceptability of innovative solutions for urban logistics in the city of Rome, such as, for example, the acceptability of operators towards off-hour deliveries (Gatta et al., 2019a ; Marcucci and Gatta, 2017), and, widening the audience to citizens, the installation of automatic parcel lockers (Iannaccone et al., 2021) or the propensity to join a crowd-shipping service based on urban public transport both as users and carriers (Gatta et al., 2019b, 2018,).

Process Replicability

The most effective response to the European Union's ambitious goal of achieving carbon-neutral urban freight distribution by 2050 is the Sustainable Urban Logistics Plan (SULP), a replicable policy-support tool for modelling urban logistics (Matusiewicz, 2019), aimed at ensuring efficient and sustainable freight mobility within urban areas (Fossheim and Andersen, 2017). Whether independent or included in the larger Sustainable Urban Mobility Plan (SUMP), whose primary focus tends to be passenger sustainable mobility (Letnik et al., 2018) achieved throughout participation – as widely recommended by the EU (Wefering et al., 2014) – it adopts a long-term strategic perspective for participatory approach and engagement (Gatta et al., 2021; Maltese et al., 2021), starting with the analysis of the needs of users, the requirements of operators and urban objectives. It consists of a strategically selected set of diverse policy measures, indicating that the transition towards sustainable urban logistics includes multiple policy domains at multiple scales (Janjevic et al, 2019) and, according to the European Guidelines (Eltis, 2019) should follow a comprehensive and efficient procedure. For example, it could make use of a multi-criteria decision analysis tool called the Logistics Sustainability Index for the scenario assessment and comparison, including the different stakeholder perspectives (Comi et al., 2020). In particular, it should assume the current urban logistics system characteristics, involve relevant stakeholders from the earlier stages of the process on shared understandings of the problems and potential solutions set up systematic and continuous monitoring and learning activities to check for effectiveness and possible adaptation needs, thus representing a policy innovation going beyond business-based solutions (Rosales and Hardstaat, 2022). However, since the interaction between, and cooperation of, all involved actors with the city authorities to discuss and develop concrete actions is often limited, another tool has been implemented.

The Living Lab (LL) is a structured and replicable approach that can be useful for SULP. It is a permanent working group where stakeholders discuss policy proposals, share their own opinions and needs while gaining insight into those of others, and actively participate in the implementation of the solutions (Nesterova and Quak, 2016; Quak et al., 2018). The main aim of the LL is, in fact, to make stakeholders work together towards common goals (Tanda and De Marco, 2021) and co-create, both designing and implementing, policies (Gatta et al., 2017). In fact, co-created solutions prove to be more effective, as they are built on the synthesis of logistics and behavioural studies (Wang et al., 2021, 2019,). A logistic LL must include the following steps: 1. Practical, "real life" setting, with implementation in the field; 2. Multiple stakeholders (public authorities, logistics service providers, research institutes, and the public); 3. Co-creation of innovative solutions and end-user involvement; and 4. Iterative learning and development in the context of city logistics (CITYLAB, 2015). Moreover, according to Tolentino-Zondervan et al. (2021), a LL can be set up more easily when the logistic objectives are clearly stated in the plan. A permanent group – also as a virtual platform for communication and interaction – should be established among stakeholders in order to exploit the "learning by doing" approach. In addition, freight transport data and information must be collected and shared (Dablanc, 2021), especially because the sparse knowledge of city logistics, also due to multiple distribution actors, and the predominance of small companies, is one of the challenges LL must cope with (CITYLAB, 2018). Additionally, LL is intended to be a generic decision-making framework for interaction among stakeholders (Ballantyne et al., 2013; CITYLAB, 2015; Eriksson et al., 2005), and it can ensure a coherent and complementary relationship between bottom-up and top-down approaches, which can be useful within the realm of urban logistics planning, and sheds light on the power relations among stakeholders (Gardrat, 2018). Within this context, Gatta et al. (2017) proposed LL as an additional integrated approach for making decisions inherent to urban freight transport that is also transferable to different urban realities. This approach includes city logistics measures, instances of stakeholders and all behavioural, technical, operational, organizational, and financial aspects. It involves three steps: (1) desk research of data; (2) a LL approach to stimulate co-creation among stakeholders; and (3) model building to assess the acceptability of policies and their eventual mixes. In this way, decision makers' knowledge and awareness of the context are increased, freight transport policies are integrated with other planning aspects through participatory processes, a valid and robust *ex-ante* assessment of policies in terms of acceptability is carried out through behavioural analysis. Gatta et al. (2018) describe the LL approach carried out in the Horizon 2020 CITYLAB project, which involved seven European cities,[2] for the co-creation of innovative measures in freight transport by public and private actors, able to produce positive effects in terms of economic, environmental, and social sustainability. They propose both *ex-ante* and *ex-post* behavioural analyses. The former allows us to adapt the policy as it goes along and to discover, through the appropriate identification of barriers and enablers, how to adjust innovative solutions. The latter, which takes into account context specifications, also in terms of the social and territorial peculiarities (as recommended by Reda et al., 2020; Rose et al., 2017, Alho and e Silva; 2015; Macário, 2013; Muñuzuri et al., 2005), tests the outcome, the replicability, and the transferability of the identified solutions.

Conclusions

Despite its crucial role as a key element in the complex realm of mobility and accessibility planning, urban logistics has often been neglected in formal urban policy-making. However, with the current unprecedented spread of e-commerce and new technologies, it can no longer be left on the sidelines of sustainable mobility strategies and must be addressed as an urban governance challenge. Moreover, various environmental, social, and economic challenges may arise among private and public actors, thus fostering conflicting interests towards sustainability issues. In some cases, private stakeholders are independently improving the sustainability of their logistics, by sharing the current public orientations set on a path towards decarbonization and modal shift within the scope of their corporate social responsibility.

Urban logistics must then be reframed as a public governance topic to prioritize, where policy acceptability and implementation become fundamental. Stakeholder engagement, stakeholder preferences, and process replicability represent the most relevant aspects to be addressed. Specifically, as the primary goal of urban logistics policies is to enhance accessibility and quality of life of the city without impacting its economic development, stakeholder engagement initiatives can then accelerate this transition. Therefore, in order to ensure maximum efficiency and effectiveness of policy implementation, the acceptability of the policy itself should be tested among the numerous and heterogeneous (in terms of preference) stakeholders, fostering participation and sharing and the co-creation of urban logistics solutions, for instance, within a LL. This discussion group, in fact, not only provides valuable information to the policymaker on stakeholder preferences, but also fosters dialogue – sharing their success/failures and discussing measures – and ultimately the co-creation of solutions to the critical issues represented by the new challenges of urban logistics. Such an approach also favours replicability not only from a territorial point of view, but also in terms of content. In addition, in the case of urban logistics, it is an undoubted support, given the great heterogeneity of preferences inherent in this segment of urban transport.

Recently, the attention paid to public policies has stimulated the development of innovative methods to investigate and evaluate the link between costs and expected effectiveness of different policy alternatives, as well as their redistributive impact. These methodologies are often based on behavioural studies starting from economic experiments which, under the simple hypothesis of utility/profit maximization and depending on the part of the market considered, are able to predict the behaviour of the economic stakeholders; this makes it possible to design effective and efficient policies by evaluating their *ex-ante* acceptability. Recognizing, moreover, the presence of heterogeneity of preferences among stakeholders, ultimately means acquiring awareness of the fact that there is unlikely to be a single strategy valid for all; instead, a mix of measures should be constructed which is as equal as possible and shared in terms of impact. This implies that individual decisions should be carefully analysed considering the categories of the actors involved (institutional, market, and external) and their preferences, attitudes and behavioural choices. This focus should be maintained in the analysis of the transferability of results.

In this way, especially in complex contexts such as freight transport in urban areas, where agents interact strongly and present heterogeneous preferences, it is good to explicitly consider their utilities and involve them in the decision-making process since the moment of the definition of the policies themselves in the planning phase. Also, for this reason, the belief that the decision-making process should be participatory, involving all identified stakeholders, in a shared LL perspective is reinforced. This also implies a greater guarantee of replicability and scalability of the policy for urban logistics.

Notes

1 There are other examples of *ex-ante* analysis tools used for urban logistics policies. For instance, the Multi-Actor Multi-Criteria Analysis includes weighted qualitative as well as quantitative criteria

defined by the various stakeholders, for facilitating the decision-making process (Macharis et al., 2014) or the Complex Adaptive System perspective adopted to better understand the urban logistics stakeholder behaviours and predict the effects of different policies (Janjevic et al., 2019). More focused on the decision structure rather than on the notion of decision preferences, Knoppen et al. (2021) provides empirical evidence of a stakeholder participation approach based on Analytic Hierarchy Process and pursuing cognitive consensus to develop and prioritize urban logistics policies.

2 Namely: Amsterdam, Brussels, London, Oslo, Paris, Rome, Southampton.

References

Adell, E., Nilsson, L., and Várhelyi, A. (2014). How is acceptance measured? Overview of measurement issues, methods and tools, in Regan M. A., Horberry T., Stevens A. (eds.), *Driver Acceptance of New Technology. Theory, Measurement and Optimisation*. Burlington, Ashgate, 73–89.

Alho, A. R., and e Silva, J. D. A. (2015). Utilizing urban form characteristics in urban logistics analysis: A case study in Lisbon, Portugal. *Journal of Transport Geography*, *42*, 57–71.

Allen, J., Browne, M., Woodburn, A., and Leonardi, J. (2012). The role of urban consolidation centres in sustainable freight transport. *Transport Reviews*, *32*(4), 473–490.

Amaya, J., Arellana, J., and Delgado-Lindeman, M. (2020). Stakeholders perceptions to sustainable urban freight policies in emerging markets. *Transportation Research Part A: Policy and Practice*, *132*, 329–348.

Anand, N., Quak, H., van Duin, R., and Tavasszy, L. (2012). City logistics modeling efforts: Trends and gaps-A review. *Procedia-Social and Behavioral Sciences*, *39*, 101–115.

Anderson, S., Allen, J., and Browne, M. (2005). Urban logistics—how can it meet policy makers' sustainability objectives? *Journal of Transport Geography*, *13*(1), 71–81.

Axinte L., Bohler S, Huaylla K., and Fenton P. (2022). The current status & experience of SULP in Europe, ULaaDS webinar presentation, February 10th, 2022.

Ballantyne, E. E. F., Lindholm, M., and Whiteing, A. (2013). A comparative study of urban freight transport planning: Addressing stakeholder needs. *Journal of Transport Geography*, *32*, 93–101.

Benjelloun, A., and Crainic, T. G. (2008). Trends, challenges, and perspectives in city logistics. *Transportation and Land Use Interaction, Proceedings TRANSLU*, *8*, 269–284.

Bjørgen, A., Fossheim, K., and Macharis, C. (2021). How to build stakeholder participation in collaborative urban freight planning. *Cities*, *112*, 103149.

Browne, M., and Goodchild A. (2023). Overview on stakeholder engagement, in Marcucci E., Gatta V., Le Pira M. (eds.), *Handbook of City Logistics and Urban Freight*. Edward Elgar, *forthcoming*.

Browne, M., Holguin-Veras, J., and Allen J. (2021). Urban logistics and freight transport, in Vickerman, R. (eds.), *International Encyclopedia of Transportation*, *3*, 178–183.

Browne, M., Allen, J., Nemoto, T., Patier, D., and Visser, J. (2012). Reducing social and environmental impacts of urban freight transport: A review of some major cities. *Procedia-Social and Behavioral Sciences*, *39*, 19–33.

Cascetta, E., Cartenì, A., Pagliara, F., and Montanino, M. (2015). A new look at planning and designing transportation systems: A decision-making model based on cognitive rationality, stakeholder engagement and quantitative methods. *Transport Policy*, *38*, 27–39.

Chatziioannou, I., Alvarez-Icaza, L., Bakogiannis, E., Kyriakidis, C., and Chias-Becerril, L. (2020). A structural analysis for the categorization of the negative externalities of transport and the hierarchical organization of sustainable mobility's strategies. *Sustainability*, 12(15), 6011.

CITYLAB (2018). CITYLAB handbook for city logistics living laboratories, Deliverable 3.4, Horizon 2020 Programme, European Commission.

CITYLAB (2015). Lessons and experiences with living laboratories. Deliverable 3.3, Horizon 2020 Programme, European Commission.

COESUF (2021). Available online: https://www.sipotra.it/wp-content/uploads/2018/04/Study-on-urban-logistics.pdf (accessed https://coe-sufs.org/wordpress/ncfrp33/psi/stakeholder/ https://www.sipotra.it/wp-content/uploads/2018/04/Study-on-urban-logistics.pdf (accessed on 27th March 2022)

Comi, A., Persia, L., Polimeni, A., Campagna, A., and Mezzavilla, L. (2020). A methodology to design and assess scenarios within SULPS: the case of Bologna. *Transportation Research Procedia*, *46*, 269–276.

Crainic, T. G., Ricciardi, N., and Storchi, G. (2009). Models for evaluating and planning city logistics systems. *Transportation Science*, 43(4), 432–454.

Dablanc, L. (2021) Urban freight policy, in Vickerman, R. (eds.), *International Encyclopedia of Transportation*. Vol. 6, UK, Elsevier Ltd, 278–285.

Dablanc, L. (2011). City distribution, a key element of the urban economy: Guidelines for practitioners, in Macharis, C. and Melo, S. (eds.), *City Distribution and Urban Freight Transport*. UK, Edward Elgar Publishing Ltd, 13–36.

Dablanc, L. (2008). Urban goods movement and air quality policy and regulations issues in European cities. *Journal of Environmental Law*, 20, 245–267.

De Marco, A., Mangano, G., and Zenezini, G. (2018). Classification and benchmark of city logistics measures: An empirical analysis. *International Journal of Logistics Research and Applications*, 21(1), 1–19.

de Oliveira, L. K., Leite Nascimento, C. D. O., de Sousa, P. R., de Resende, P. T. V., and Ferreira da Silva, F. G. (2019). Transport service provider perception of barriers and urban freight policies in Brazil. *Sustainability*, 11(24), 6890.

De Souza, R., Goh, M., Lau, H. C., Ng, W. S., and Tan, P. S. (2014). Collaborative urban logistics–synchronizing the last mile a Singapore research perspective. *Procedia-Social and Behavioral Sciences*, 125, 422–431.

Dolati Neghabadi, P., Evrard Samuel, K., and Espinouse, M. L. (2019). Systematic literature review on city logistics: Overview, classification and analysis. *International Journal of Production Research*, 57(3), 865–887.

Eltis. (2019). *Guidelines for Developing and Implementing a Sustainable Urban Mobility Plan* (2nd ed.) available at: https://www.eltis.org/sites/default/files/sump_guidelines_20 19_interactive_document_1.pdf. (accessed on 27 July 2022)

Eriksson, M., Niitamo, V. P., and Kulkki, S. (2005). State-of-the-art in utilizing living labs approach to user-centric ICT innovation. CDT, Luleå University of Technology, Sweden.

EU COMM - DG Mobility and Transport (2017a). Study on urban logistics. The integrated perspective, Final report of the EU Commission, Available online: https://www.sipotra.it/wp-content/uploads/2018/04/Study-on-urban-logistics.pdf (accessed on 27th March 2022)

EU COMM - DG Mobility and Transport (2017b), Engagement of stakeholderswhen implementing urban freight logistics policies, Final report of the EU Commission. Available online: https://www.opwegnaarzes.nl/application/files/9516/1227/2790/Engagement-of-stakeholders-when-implementing-urban-freight-logistics-policies.pdf (accessed on 27 March 2022)

Formez (2006). *Valutare gli effetti delle politiche pubbliche/Metodi e applicazioni al caso italiano*, Edizioni Formez, Napoli. http://costopa.formez.it/sites/all/files/Valutare%20gli%20effetti%20dellle%20politiche%20pubbliche.pdf

Fossheim, K., and Andersen, J. (2017). Plan for sustainable urban logistics–comparing between Scandinavian and UK practices. *European Transport Research Review*, 9(4), 1–13.

Gardrat, M. (2018). Observing Interactions between urban freight transport actors: Studying the construction of public policies. *City Logistics 1: New Opportunities and Challenges*, 265–285.

Gatta V., Maltese I., and Marcucci E. (2021). I PUMS *e le politiche d'intervento nel settore della distribuzione urbana delle merci nelle città: il caso di Roma*, in Marcucci E., Magazzino C., Intorno alla Politica Economica – Saggi in Onore di GianCesare Romagnoli, FrancoAngeli, Milano, 217–231.

Gatta, V., Marcucci, E., Delle Site, P., Le Pira, M., and Carrocci, C. S. (2019a). Planning with stakeholders: Analysing alternative off-hour delivery solutions via an interactive multi-criteria approach. *Research in Transportation Economics*, 73, 53–62.

Gatta, V., Marcucci, E., Nigro, M., and Serafini, S. (2019b). Sustainable urban freight transport adopting public transport-based crowdshipping for B2C deliveries. *European Transport Research Review*, 11(1), 1–14.

Gatta, V., Marcucci, E., Nigro, M., Patella, S. M., and Serafini, S. (2018). Public transport-based crowdshipping for sustainable city logistics: Assessing economic and environmental impacts. *Sustainability*, 11(1), 145.

Gatta, V., Marcucci, E., and Le Pira, M. (2017). Smart urban freight planning process: integrating desk, living lab and modelling approaches in decision-making. *European Transport Research Review*, 9(3), 32.

Gatta, V., and Marcucci, E. (2016). Stakeholder-specific data acquisition and urban freight policy evaluation: Evidence, implications and new suggestions. *Transport Reviews*, 36(5), 585–609.

Gatta, V., and Marcucci, E. (2014). Urban freight transport and policy changes: Improving decision makers' awareness via an agent-specific approach. *Transport Policy*, 36, 248–252.

Golini, R., Guerlain, C., Lagorio, A., and Pinto, R. (2018). An assessment framework to support collective decision making on urban freight transport. *Transport, 33*(4), 890–901.

Gonzalez-Feliu, J., Semet, F., and Routhier, J. L. (Eds.). (2014). *Sustainable Urban Logistics: Concepts, Methods and Information Systems,* 113–143. Berlin, Heidelberg, Springer Berlin Heidelberg.

Gonzalez-Feliu, J., and Salanova, J. M. (2012). Defining and evaluating collaborative urban freight transportation systems. *Procedia-Social and Behavioral Sciences, 39,* 172–183.

Hofenk, D. (2012). Making a better world – Carrier, retailer, and consumer support for sustainable initiatives in the context of urban distribution and retailing, PhD thesis, Open University of the Netherlands, The Netherlands.

Holguín-Veras, J., Amaya-Leal, J., Wojtowicz, J., Jaller, M., González-Calderón, C., Sánchez-Díaz, I., Wang, X., Haake, D.G., Rhodes, S.S., Frazier, R.J., Nick, M.K., Dack, J., Casinelli, L., and Browne, M. (2015). Improving freight system performance in metropolitan areas: A planning guide (No. Project NCFRP-38), retrieved at https://coe-sufs.org/wordpress/ncfrp33/ (last accessed on January, 27th, 2022)

Iannaccone, G., Marcucci, E., and Gatta, V. (2021). What young e-consumers want? Forecasting parcel lockers choice in Rome. *Logistics, 5*(3), 57.

Jaller, M., Otero-Palencia, C., and Pahwa, A. (2020). Automation, electrification, and shared mobility in urban freight: Opportunities and challenges. *Transportation Research Procedia, 46,* 13–20.

Janjevic, M., Knoppen, D., and Winkenbach, M. (2019). Integrated decision-making framework for urban freight logistics policy-making. *Transportation Research Part D: Transport and Environment, 72,* 333–357.

Keough, B., Goodchild, A., and Dalla Chiara, G. (2021). Urban Freight Innovation: Leading-edge strategies for smart cities. *Coast Guard Journal of Safety & Security at Sea, Proceedings of the Marine Safety & Security Council, 78*(2), 44–49.

Kiba-Janiak, M. (2017). Opportunities and threats for city logistics development from a local authority perspective. *Journal of Economics & Management, 28,* 23–39.

Knoppen, D., Janjevic, M., and Winkenbach, M. (2021). Prioritizing urban freight logistics policies: Pursuing cognitive consensus across multiple stakeholders. *Environmental Science & Policy, 125,* 231–240.

Lagorio, A., Pinto, R., and Golini, R. (2016). Research in urban logistics: A systematic literature review. *International Journal of Physical Distribution & Logistics Management, 46*(10), 908–931.

LEAD (2021). Innovative business models, governance and public-private partnerships. Knowledge for innovative actions, measures and business models. Deliverable 1.3. H2020 research project LEAD. Available online: https://www.leadproject.eu/wp-content/uploads/2021/12/LEAD-D1.3.pdf (accessed on 27 March 2022)

LEAD (2020). City Logistics landscape in the era of on-demand economy Main challenges, trends and factors influencing city logistics. Deliverable 1.1. H2020 research project LEAD. Available online: https://www.leadproject.eu/wp-content/uploads/2021/02/LEAD_D1.1_City-Logistics-landscape-in-the-era-of-on-demand-economy-1.pdf (accessed on 27 March 2022)

Le Pira, M., Marcucci, E., Gatta, V., Ignaccolo, M., Inturri, G., and Pluchino, A. (2017). Towards a decision-support procedure to foster stakeholder involvement and acceptability of urban freight transport policies. *European Transport Research Review 9*(4), 54. https://doi.org/10.1007/s12544-017-0268-2

Letnik, T., Marksel, M., Luppino, G., Bardi, A., and Božičnik, S. (2018). Review of policies and measures for sustainable and energy efficient urban transport. *Energy, 163,* 245–257.

Lindawati, van Schagen, J., Goh, M., and de Souza, R. (2014). Collaboration in urban logistics: Motivations and barriers. *International Journal of Urban Sciences, 18*(2), 278–290.

Lindholm, M. (2014). Successes and failings of an urban freight quality partnership–The story of the Gothenburg local freight network. *Procedia-Social and Behavioral Sciences, 125,* 125–135.

Lindholm, M. E., and Blinge, M. (2014). Assessing knowledge and awareness of the sustainable urban freight transport among Swedish local authority policy planners. *Transport Policy, 32,* 124–131.

Lindholm, M., and Behrends, S. (2012). Challenges in urban freight transport planning–a review in the Baltic sea region. *Journal of Transport Geography, 22,* 129–136.

Lozzi, G., Iannaccone, G., Maltese, I., Gatta, V., Marcucci, E., and Lozzi, R. (2022). On-demand logistics: Solutions, barriers, and enablers. *Sustainability, 14*(15), 9465.

Lozzi, G. (2018). *In varietate concordia*: A cooperative model to gently improve freight goods distribution in European cities: The case of Rome. PhD thesis Available online: https://arcadia.sba.

uniroma3.it/handle/2307/55/simple-search?location=2307%2F55&query=lozzi (accessed on 27th March 2022).

Loures, L., and Crawford, P. (2008). Democracy in progress: Using public participation in post-industrial landscape (re)-development. *WSEAS Transactions on Environment and Development*, 4(9), 794–803.

Macário, R. (2013). Modeling for public policies inducement of urban freight business development, in Ben Akiva, M., Meersman, H., and van de Voorde, E. (eds.), *Freight Transport Modelling*. Emerald Group Publishing Limited (Chapter 20), 405–432.

Macário, R., Galelo, A., and Martins, P. M. (2008). Business models in urban logistics. *Ingeniería y Desarrollo*, 24, 77–96.

Macharis, C., and Kin, B. (2017). The 4 A's of sustainable city distribution: Innovative solutions and challenges ahead. *International Journal of Sustainable Transportation*, 11(2), 59–71.

Macharis, C., Milan, L., and Verlinde, S. (2014). A stakeholder-based multicriteria evaluation framework for city distribution. *Research in Transportation Business and Management*, 11, 75–84.

Maltese I., Sciullo A., Marcucci E., Gatta V., and Rye T. (2023). Citizen participation and sustainable urban logistics planning: The case of Rome, capitolo in revisione per Public participation in transport in times of change, curato da Hansson L., Rye T., Sørensen C.H., Emerald (*forthcoming*).

Maltese, I., Gatta, V., and Marcucci, E. (2021). Active travel in sustainable urban mobility plans. An Italian overview. *Research in Transportation Business and Management*, 40, 100621.

Marcucci E., Gatta V., and Maltese I. (2019a). Accettabilità delle politiche pubbliche a sostegno del processo decisionale: alcuni metodi d'analisi, in G.Cesare Romagnoli, "Le frontiere della politica economica" Franco Angeli, 83–95.

Marcucci, E., Maltese, I., Gatta, V., and Surace, M. (2019b). *Piano Urbano della Mobilità Sostenibile a Roma: il Piano della Logistica Urbana*, report per il Comune di Roma Capitale, 210–228, https://romamobilita.it/sites/default/files/PUMS%20ROMA%20vol%202.pdf

Marcucci, E., Le Pira, M., Gatta, V., Inturri, G., Ignaccolo, M., and Pluchino, A. (2017a). Simulating participatory urban freight transport policy-making: Accounting for heterogeneous stakeholders' preferences and interaction effects. *Transportation Research Part E: Logistics and Transportation Review*, 103, 69–86.

Marcucci, E., Gatta, V., Marciani, M., and Cossu, P. (2017b). Measuring the effects of an urban freight policy package defined via a collaborative governance model. *Research in Transportation Economics*, 65, 3–9.

Marcucci, E., and Gatta, V. (2017). Investigating the potential for off-hour deliveries in the city of Rome: Retailers' perceptions and stated reactions. *Transportation Research Part A: Policy and Practice*, 102, 142–156.

Marcucci, E., Gatta, V., and Scaccia, L. (2015). Urban freight, parking and pricing policies: An evaluation from a transport providers' perspective. *Transportation Research Part A: Policy and Practice*, 74, 239–249.

Marcucci, E., Gatta, V., Valeri, E., and Stathopoulos, A. (2013). *Urban Freight Transport Modelling: An Agent-Specific Approach*, FrancoAngeli, Milan.

Marcucci, E., Gatta, V., and Marcucci, G. (2013). Intra-agent heterogeneity in urban freight distribution: The case of own-account operators. *Intra-Agent Heterogeneity in Urban Freight Distribution: The Case of Own-Account Operators*, 267–286.

Marcucci, E., Stathopoulos, A., Gatta, V., and Valeri, E. (2012). A stated ranking experiment to study policy acceptance: The case of freight operators in Rome's LTZ. *Italian Journal of Regional Science*, 11(3), 11–30.

Marcucci, E., Danielis, R., Paglione, G., and Gatta, V. (2007). Centri urbani di distribuzione delle merci e politiche del traffico: una valutazione empirica tramite le preferenze dichiarate. In *Atti del 7 congresso CIRIAF*, 373–378.

Matusiewicz, M. (2019). SULP (Sustainable Urban Logistics Plan) as a tool for shaping sustainable urban logistics: A review of European projects supporting the creation of sulp. *Transport Economics and Logistics*, 84, 71–78.

MDS Transmodal Limited, Centro per il Trasporto e la Logistica (2012). DG MOVE European commission: Study on urban freight transport. Final Report, MDS Transmodal Limited, Chester, UK.

Migliaccio M., Buono A., Maltese I., and Migliaccio M., (2021). The 2020 Italian spring lockdown: A multi-disciplinary analysis over Milan urban area. *World*, 2(3), 391–414; https://doi.org/10.3390/world2030025

Mitsopoulos-Rubens E., and Regan, M. A. (2017). Measuring acceptability through questionnaires and focus groups, in Horberry, T. and Regan M. A. (eds.), *Driver Acceptance of New Technology*. CRC Press, Boca Raton, Florida, 89–104.

Muñuzuri, J., Larrañeta, J., Onieva, L., and Cortés, P. (2005). Solutions applicable by local administrations for urban logistics improvement. *Cities, 22*(1), 15–28.

Nesterova, N., and Quak, H. (2016). A city logistics living lab: A methodological approach. *Transportation Research Procedia, 16*, 403–417.

Nuzzolo, A., and Comi, A. (2014). City logistics planning: demand modelling requirements for direct effect forecasting. *Procedia-Social and Behavioral Sciences, 125*, 239–250.

Paddeu, D., and Aditjandra, P. (2020). Shaping urban freight systems via a participatory approach to inform policy-making. *Sustainability, 12*(1), 441.

Paddeu, D., Parkhurst, G., Fancello, G., Fadda, P., and Ricci, M. (2018). Multi-stakeholder collaboration in urban freight consolidation schemes: Drivers and barriers to implementation. *Transport, 33*(4), 913–929.

Pan, S., Zhou, W., Piramuthu, S., Giannikas, V., and Chen, C. (2021). Smart city for sustainable urban freight logistics. *International Journal of Production Research, 59*(7), 2079–2089.

Patier, D., and Routhier, J.-L. (2020). Urban logistics in the light of sustainable development: Still a long way to go. *Transportation Research Procedia, 46*, 93–100. https://doi.org/10.1016/j.sbspro.2010.04.033

Quak, H., Kok, R., and den Boer, E. (2018). The future of city logistics–Trends and developments leading toward a smart and zero-emission system. *City Logistics 1: New Opportunities and Challenges*, 125–146.

Quick, K. S. (2014). Public participation in transportation planning, in Garrett M. (ed.), *Encyclopedia of Transportation: Social Science and Policy*. Sage Publications, Thousand Oaks, CA, 1132–1137.

Reda, A. K., Gebresenbet, G., Tavasszy, L., and Ljungberg, D. (2020). Identification of the regional and economic contexts of sustainable urban logistics policies. *Sustainability, 12*(20), 8322.

Roland Berger - FM Logistic (2020). *Urban logistics faced with economic and environmental challenges*, Roland Berger GMBH.

Rosales, R., and Haarstad, H. (2022). Governance challenges for urban logistics: Lessons from three Norwegian cities. *Environmental Policy and Governance*. 1–11. https://doi.org/10.1002/eet.2015

Rose, W. J., Bell, J. E., Autry, C. W., and Cherry, C. R. (2017). Urban logistics: Establishing key concepts and building a conceptual framework for future research. *Transportation Journal, 56*(4), 357–394.

Ruesch, M., Todesco, P., and Hegi, P. (2020). A positive planning approach to secure logistics facilities in urban areas. *Transportation Research Procedia, 46*, 69–76.

Ruesch, M., Hegi, P., Haefeli, U., Matti, D., Schultz, B., and Rütsche, P. (2012). Sustainable goods supply and transport in conurbations: Freight strategies and guidelines. *Procedia-Social and Behavioral Sciences, 39*, 116–133.

Russo, F., and Comi, A. (2020). Investigating the effects of city logistics measures on the economy of the city. *Sustainability, 12*(4), 1439.

Sernicola, F., Maltese, I., Gatta, V., Iannaccone, G., and Marcucci, E. (2020). Impatto del lockdown sulla spesa degli italiani: quale futuro per l'e-grocery?. *REPoT-Rivista di Economia e Politica dei Trasporti*, n.3, art.4, pp.1–13 Available at: https://www.openstarts.units.it/handle/10077/32169 (accessed on 27th March 2022)

Sharma, S. K., and Singh, A. P. (2022). Urban logistics stakeholder priority assessment to improve urban planning policy. *International Journal of Construction Management*, 1–10. https://www.tandfonline.com/doi/full/10.1080/15623599.2022.2106042

Stathopoulos, A., Valeri, E., and Marcucci, E. (2012). Stakeholder reactions to urban freight policy innovation. *Journal of Transport Geography, 22*, 34–45.

Stathopoulos, A., Valeri, E., Marcucci, E., Gatta V., and Nuzzolo, A. (2011). Urban freight policy innovation for Rome's LTZ: A stakeholder perspective, in *City Distribution and Urban Freight Transport*. Edward Elgar Publishing. https://www.e-elgar.com/shop/gbp/city-distribution-and-urban-freight-transport-9780857932747.html

Strale, M. (2019). Sustainable urban logistics: What are we talking about? *Transportation Research Part A: Policy and Practice, 130*, 745–751.

Suksri, J., and Raicu, R. (2012). Developing a conceptual framework for the evaluation of urban freight distribution initiatives. *Procedia-Social and Behavioral Sciences, 39*, 321–332.

Tanda, A., and De Marco, A. (2021). A review of an urban living lab initiative. *Review of Policy Research, 38*(3), 370–390.

Taniguchi, E., Thompson, R. G., and Qureshi, A. G. (2020). Modelling city logistics using recent innovative technologies. *Transportation Research Procedia, 46*, 3–12.

Taniguchi, E., Thompson, R. G., and Qureshi, A. G. (2018). Recent developments and prospects for modeling city logistics. *City Logistics 1: New Opportunities and Challenges*, 1–27. https://www.wiley.com/en-ie/City+Logistics+1:+New+Opportunities+and+Challenges-p-9781119527756

Taniguchi, E., Thompson, R. G., and Yamada, T. (2016). New opportunities and challenges for city logistics. *Transportation Research Procedia, 12*, 5–13.

Taniguchi, E., and Thompson, R. G. (Eds.). (2014). *City Logistics: Mapping the Future.* CRC Press.

Taniguchi, E., Thompson, R. G., and Yamada, T. (2014). Recent trends and innovations in modelling city logistics. *Procedia-Social and Behavioral Sciences, 125*, 4–14.

Tolentino-Zondervan, F., Bogers, E., and van de Sande, L. (2021). A managerial and behavioral approach in aligning stakeholder goals in sustainable last mile logistics: A case study in the Netherlands. *Sustainability, 13*(8), 4434.

Vahrenkamp, R. (2016). 25 Years City Logistic: Why failed the urban consolidation centres?. *European Transport\Transporti Europei, 60*(4), 6.

Valeri, E., Gatta, V., Teobaldelli, D., Polidori, P., Barratt, B., Fuzzi, S., Kazepov, Y., Sergi, V., Williams, M., and Maione, M. (2016). Modelling individual preferences for environmental policy drivers: Empirical evidence of Italian lifestyle changes using a latent class approach. *Environmental Science & Policy, 65*, 65–74.

Van Duin, J. H. R., and Quak, H. J. (2007). City logistics: A chaos between research and policy making? A review. *WIT Transactions on the Built Environment, 96*, 135–146.

Ville, S., Gonzalez-Feliu, J., and Dablanc, L. (2013). The limits of public policy intervention in urban logistics: Lessons from Vicenza (Italy). *European Planning Studies, 21*(10), 1528–1541.

Vural, C. A., and Aktepe, Ç. (2022). Why do some sustainable urban logistics innovations fail? The case of collection and delivery points. *Research in Transportation Business & Management, 45*, 100690.

Wang, X., Wong, Y. D., Li, K. X., and Yuen, K. F. (2021). A critical assessment of co-creating self-collection services in last-mile logistics. *The International Journal of Logistics Management, 32*(3), 846–871. https://doi.org/10.1108/IJLM-09-2020-0359

Wang, X., Yuen, K. F., Wong, Y. D., and Teo, C. C. (2019). Consumer participation in last-mile logistics service: An investigation on cognitions and affects. *International Journal of Physical Distribution & Logistics Management, 49*(2), 217–238. https://doi.org/10.1108/IJPDLM-12-2017-0372

Wefering, F., Rupprecht, S., Bührmann, S., and Böhler-Baedeker, S. (2014). Guidelines. In Developing and Implementing a Sustainable Urban Mobility Plan. Rupprecht Consult – Forschung und Beratung GmbH.

Zenezini, G., van Duin, J. H. R., Tavasszy, L., and De Marco, A. (2018). Stakeholders' roles for business modeling in a city logistics ecosystem: Towards a conceptual model. *City Logistics, 2*, 39–58.

Zenezini, G., and De Marco, A. (2016). A review of methodologies to assess urban freight initiatives. *IFAC-PapersOnLine, 49*(12), 1359–1364.

20
THE ROLE OF ROAD PRICING AND INCENTIVES IN URBAN LOGISTICS MANAGEMENT

Oriana Calderón, José Holguín-Veras and Stephen Ison

Introduction

Urban logistics are essential for the economic development of cities allowing for the connection of supply chain links, from the production to the consumption of goods. However, the logistical activities also produce negative impacts that require addressing. According to the United States Environmental Protection Agency (2021), the transportation sector accounted for 29% of the total U.S. Greenhouse Gas Emissions in 2019. This situation has been exacerbated by the rise of e-commerce, which has led to an unprecedented increase in urban deliveries, resulting in an increase in congestion, emissions, and other externalities produced by logistical activities. In an era where climate change is an important concern worldwide, undoubtedly, the transportation sector plays a critical role. Hence, the need to design mechanisms to promote efficient logistical operations that are also aligned with governmental goals of promoting sustainable cities.

This chapter aims to provide an overview of the role of road pricing and incentives initiatives—programs, policies, and projects—relating to urban logistics management, and the role of potential pricing and incentive measures that not only make the urban activity more efficient but also contribute to sustainable cities. This chapter seeks to summarize the economics of road pricing, discuss its advantages and disadvantages, analyze the current freight road pricing measures, discuss the use of incentives as an alternative to road pricing, and examine the lessons learned from implementations that have taken place. This chapter also suggests potential freight road pricing measures that allocate the externalities to the agent causing them, and discusses considerations for the design or reforming of freight road pricing schemes in an era of technological and climate change.

Road Pricing

The notion of pricing, as it relates to roads, dates back to Pigou (1920), who argued that the marginal private cost and the marginal social cost could differ due to externalities produced by agents. In these situations, public intervention can be seen as necessary using taxes, a Pigouvian tax, to compensate for the welfare loss that externalities cause.

Since then, there has been a great deal of research relating to road pricing, be it the underpinning economic, political, or technological aspects (Foster, 1974; Holguín-Veras et al.,

2003; Blythe, 2005). Based on the work of Pigou, Walters (1961) suggested that imposing a charge equal to the difference between the private cost and the social cost would reduce traffic levels on congested urban roads. Implementation of road pricing first materialized in 1975 with the Area Licensing Scheme (ALS) in Singapore, which consisted of license fees on a restricted congested zone at peak hours by vehicle type (Menon et al., 1993). The ALS initiative resulted in a reduction of congestion during peak hours. In the original pricing scheme, freight vehicles were exempt from the measure. Although the car traffic reduced after the pricing measure was imposed, freight traffic increased, especially trucks passing through. The issue was addressed in a revised ALS, where freight vehicles were also charged. As a result of the measure, truck traffic during rush hour was reduced by more than 50% (Menon et al., 1993). The Singapore experience evidences the crucial role of road pricing as a measure to control traffic demand. Since then, several road pricing initiatives have been implemented worldwide, for example, the Port Authority of New York and New Jersey's Time-of-Day pricing (Holguín-Veras et al., 2006), the Central London Congestion Charge (Transport for London, 2007), and the Stockholm scheme (Börjesson et al., 2012).

The theoretical underpinning of road pricing consists of evaluating the tradeoff between the generalized cost, namely the cost of fuel, the wear and tear on the vehicle, and monetary cost of the time taken; and the traffic flow, essentially vehicles per hour per lane. In normal conditions, freight operators (if they were the only vehicles on the road) only consider their own private cost and not the externalities caused by the traffic flow, imposed on other road users and third parties. Hence, a charge is needed, equal to the difference between the private and social costs (a Pigouvian tax), to make freight agents internalize the externalities they produce, e.g., extra delay, congestion, and pollution. Imposing a charge, the traffic flow would reduce, and the optimal level of traffic would be achieved.

There is evidence that, in the case of passenger cars, road pricing is effective as a demand management measure. The main reason is that the decision-maker, namely the driver, is directly affected by the charge. However, there are limitations in achieving a reduction of externalities when it relates to freight traffic. In general, road pricing policies assume that the charge signal will impact the decision-maker, mistakenly believed always to be the road users, which in terms of freight are the carriers. In other words, imposing a charge will effectively induce carriers to use alternative highways, transportation modes, time-of-travel, or other behavior changes. Past experiences have shown that this is not borne out in practice; imposing a charge oriented to freight drivers does not necessarily translate into a reduction in freight congestion (Holguín-Veras, 2011). In the case of time-of-day charges, as explained later in this chapter, pricing does not succeed in shifting truck traffic from regular hours to off-hours. One of the reasons is that the decision of delivery times falls on the receivers, not the carriers. Road pricing for urban deliveries will be effective *if* and *only if* the agent with the power to change the decision relating to the time-of-day, vehicle utilization, or the technology used is charged (Jacobi, 1973). Hence, it is essential to identify the agents interacting in supply chains that have the power to make logistical decisions.

Three key agents participating in supply chains are: *shippers*, the agents who manufacture and ship the supplies; *carriers*, the agents that transport the supplies; and *receivers*, the agents that receive and use the supplies. The interaction between these agents results in logistical decisions, which ultimately influence the urban freight system. The influence of one agent over another is conditioned by their level of power and the nature of the market. For instance, in competitive markets, receivers have a higher degree of power over the carriers and shippers, and shippers over carriers. Carriers are the weakest, in terms of freight decisions, since the ease of entry into the trucking industry has created an oversupply of trucks

(Holguín-Veras et al., 2015). The trucking industry is being seen, to a certain extent, as a contestable market. In essence, due to the highly competitive market, receivers can replace the carriers, if they do not meet their needs.

Generally speaking, the decision of the delivery time is made by the receivers, who prefer regular hours (6 am to 7 pm), since their labor force is already there. In contrast, carriers prefer to deliver during off-hours (7 pm to 6 am) because their productivity transporting goods is higher (Holguín-Veras et al., 2015). Since receivers have a higher degree of power, the delivery time is usually done during regular hours. The main implication is that road pricing policies for urban deliveries directed to the weakest supply chain agent will be less effective in reducing the externalities produced by freight activity. In contrast, policies focusing on the agent with the highest decision-making power will be more effective.

In general, road pricing is useful as a means of managing travel demand, i.e., to have a desirable mix of traffic by area and time-of-day. It helps to improve the efficiency in the use of a network by relieving congestion, which results in lower travel times, and a reduction in air pollution. The revenue collected from the charge can be used for transportation improvements, cover the maintenance costs of the urban infrastructure, and finance other transportation programs.

Nevertheless, road pricing for urban logistics has a deeper functionality. The main goal of pricing in freight is to reduce the externalities produced by logistic activities. Road pricing mechanisms for urban deliveries are powerful in inducing behavioral changes in supply chain agents to mitigate the negative effects produced by their logistic decisions. Road pricing also encourages companies to be more efficient from an economic point of view. That is to say, more efficient logistics operations lead to higher productivity and a reduction in logistical costs. Road pricing for urban deliveries also promotes sustainable supply chains, improving overall urban sustainability.

The magnitude of the benefits of road pricing depends on the pricing scheme, charge value, to whom it is oriented, enforcement level, and alternatives to using the charged facility, if any (Holguín-Veras et al., 2012a). For charges to be effective, they must be oriented to the right decision-makers. One of the most effective policies to improve the efficiency of urban goods movement is off-hour deliveries (OHD). Policies inducing receivers—the decision-makers of the delivery times—to switch the deliveries from regular hours to off-hours will reduce travel times, which translates into less-operational costs, less congestion, and less truck pollution. Moreover, switching to off-hours will lead to lower truck idling and reduce fuel consumption.

Notwithstanding the benefits of road pricing for urban deliveries, there are challenges that depend on the type of charging scheme implemented. For example, in the case of road charges, the traffic on untolled roads, if any, and if carriers have the possibility to change routes, could increase due to trucks looking to avoid the toll cost. This is important because some roads are not designed to support heavy trucks and can result in pavement damage (Atkinson, 2019); ultimately, it adds more externalities. Moreover, since the value of travel time of carriers is high, if the charge is small, the effect of switching the truck traffic to off-hours is small too. In essence, small tolls will not change the logistic decisions of carriers. As for fuel taxes, even though this measure considers the distance traveled, the toll rate compared to the fuel cost is not large enough to induce an efficient use of roads.

Acceptance is a general issue in the implementation of pricing policies. In the trucking industry, the agents who oppose charging depend on the pricing scheme and who will be affected. For example, carriers oppose cordon time-of-day schemes (see below) because they absorb toll costs, while receivers will not be affected by the measure. In contrast, in time-distance schemes (see below), carriers can pass the toll costs to the receivers, and thus, it is more likely that receivers will be opposed to time-distance pricing measures (Holguín-Veras, 2011).

Freight Road Pricing Schemes

This section distinguishes three types of freight road pricing measures according to what is regulated: freight road charging, freight parking pricing, and freight vehicle taxation.

Freight Road Charging

There are several freight road charging schemes. Some regimes depend on the distance traveled, such as Germany's distance-based road pricing for heavy goods vehicles of 7.5 tons or above (Department for Transport, 2017); others are time-varying, with higher tolls at more congested times, and lower tolls at less congested times; and others vary according to the vehicle type.

Two road charging schemes that have been studied in great detail for urban deliveries are time-of-day cordon/area, and time-distance tolls. Time-of-day *cordon/area* is one of the most common road pricing schemes to mitigate traffic congestion. In this scheme, a toll surcharge is imposed during regular hours in a closed-loop cordon around congested areas (Yang and Huang, 2005). Time-of-day cordon/area has been widely implemented; for example, in Singapore (Phang and Toh, 2004), London (Transport for London, 2007), and New York City (Port Authority of New York and New Jersey, 2020). This road pricing measure has limitations as a freight demand management tool because it fails in switching truck traffic from regular hours to off-hours. The reason is that in competitive markets, carriers have to absorb the toll cost because they cannot transfer it to the receiver, the agents with the decision power of the delivery time (Holguín-Veras, 2011). In essence, the toll signal will not reach the receiver. Also, for a carrier to move to off-hours, all the receivers must switch their deliveries to off-hours, which is very unlikely; otherwise, it is not profitable (Holguín-Veras, 2011).

In *Time-distance tolls*, the road charge depends on the time and the distance traveled in a tolled area (Holguín-Veras, 2011). Unlike the time-of-day cordon/area regimes, time-distance tolls can be transferred to the receivers since the toll is part of the marginal cost. In time-distance tolls, the price signal reaches the receiver of supplies, and the carrier will not be affected by the toll. However, the magnitude of the impact of this regime in changing the delivery time of receivers is very low. For a time-distance road pricing to be effective, the toll amount should be high enough to induce the receivers to accept off-hours. But such a high toll is politically unfeasible. Thus, it is recommended to complement time-distance schemes with other initiatives that foster participation in off-hour deliveries.

Freight Parking Pricing

While freight road charging aims to allocate externalities for the use of roads to vehicles in movement, parking pricing focuses on the use of infrastructure designated as a temporary stop. Parking pricing is related to allocating curb space among users (Holguín-Veras et al., 2020b). An adequate number and location of parking spaces for freight vehicles are essential for the efficient operation of logistical activities.

Parking pricing aims to improve traffic conditions and increase the efficiency of the use of curb space through improved turnover (Holguín-Veras et al., 2013). Parking pricing also allows for collecting revenue that could be used for transportation infrastructure improvements, such as the construction of parking lots. The larger rotation resulting from a parking measure, will also reduce the likelihood of double parking, freight vehicles cruising, and parking fines. It also contributes to protecting historical areas and improving the charged area's environmental conditions. This is the case of a parking policy implemented in the historical area of Copenhagen, Denmark (City Ports, 2005). The measure intended to improve the environmental condition of the area due to the loading and unloading operations of freight vehicles. To this effect, the parking charge aimed to increase the loading factor of trucks, and switch to smaller and more environmentally friendly vehicles (City Ports, 2005). In Parma, Italy, a pay parking zone was designated in the historic center, where freight vehicles can load and unload cargo during specific time windows and a maximum time of 30 minutes (City Ports, 2005). In New York City, the Commercial Parking/Congestion Pricing program uses parking charges to increase turnover and improve the efficiency of the curb space (Holguín-Veras et al., 2020b).

The implementation cost of a parking pricing policy is low, generally accepted, and benefits from existing technology (City Ports, 2005). Parking charges should be large enough to induce shorter parking time, and should be larger in areas with large freight attraction and limited parking areas. While increased costs due to parking charges cannot always be passed to receivers, carriers will still benefit from parking pricing measures. Carriers will have more parking availability, and reduce parking fines (Holguín-Veras et al., 2005).

Freight Vehicle Taxation

Freight vehicle taxation is related to the ownership and use of trucks. Two taxation policies for freight vehicles most used are fuel charges and vehicle taxes. Fuel charges require drivers to pay a broad average cost of the distance traveled. This measure partially charges for the costs that vehicles impose on society. The charge varies with the type of fuel, i.e., petrol or diesel. The fuel tax is an efficient and transparent pricing method, in the sense that: it is easy to collect, it roughly values the cost of distances traveled, and it is a clear statement of the additional cost that the trucking industry is imposing on the system (National Academy of Sciences, 2010). Fuel charges could be passed to the receivers as part of their shipping rates, and could have an effect on modifying the delivery patterns. However, fuel charges do not consider the location (Buchanan et al., 2017) or time of travel, namely spatial and temporal issues (Atkinson, 2019), making it an inefficient way to represent the externalities produced. If fuel charges are high, it could induce changes to more fuel-saving technologies and fuel-efficient operations (National Academy of Sciences, 2010). In contrast, if the tax is low as a proportion of the fuel cost, the signal does not induce changes in the agents making travel decisions, resulting in an ineffective measure.

Another pricing measure is vehicle taxes, which are charges associated with the ownership of vehicles. An example is the Vehicle Excise Duty (VED) imposed in the United Kingdom to use public roads. VED is an annual fixed tax that vehicle owners pay according to the vehicle type, vehicle age, and the pollution associated with the vehicle. Vehicle owners with fuel-efficient trucks pay less than those who do not, and zero-emission vehicles are exempt from paying the tax (Association for Consultancy and Engineering, 2018). Like fuel charges, these measures roughly allocate the externalities to the vehicle owners.

Incentives

An alternative to road pricing measures is the use of incentives to achieve more efficient supply chains, while reducing the externalities produced by freight activity. Incentive programs seek to encourage supply chain agents to foster sustainable practices (Holguín-Veras et al., 2020b). Incentives could be monetary or non-monetary and include recognition programs, certification programs, and incentives for electric/low-emission vehicles (Holguín-Veras et al., 2020a; Holguín-Veras et al., 2020b). Recognition programs use the public acknowledgment to recognize exceptional achievements, motivating others to follow good practices. In essence, the tenet of incentives is that good behavior fosters good behavior. There is a dearth of literature analyzing how effective a recognition program is. Still, one of them is the Off Hour Delivery OHD project in New York City, where behavioral micro-simulation shows that public recognition increases the likelihood of participating in unassisted OHD programs (Holguín-Veras and Aros-Vera, 2014). Certification programs acknowledge participants who meet a minimum performance standard and follow a well-defined certification path. Certification programs are designed to address specific business operation needs, including driver skills, vehicle maintenance, and logistic operations (Transport for London, 2013; Holguín-Veras et al., 2020b). Other certification programs aim to diminish environmental impacts, or foster safety. Meeting the requirements of different levels of certification programs is sometimes recognized using distinctive colors or signs, such us bronze, silver, and gold.

Incentives can also be provided to foster the use of electric/low-emission vehicles. Switching fuel trucks to environmentally friendly vehicles is an important solution to reduce the externalities produced by freight activity. The use of electric trucks or alternative fuels benefits society since it helps reduce emissions, while it also benefits supply chain agents due to the reduction or elimination of fuel costs. Electric trucks are especially beneficial to making urban deliveries since the average range of driving distance currently technologically supported is 100 miles. However, one of the challenges for businesses to change their fleet to electric trucks is the high upfront cost. Hence, using monetary incentives to induce changes in the fleet or the technology used in existing trucks is essential.

Incentives to induce the adoption of electric trucks could be in the form of (i) funding incentives, tax credits, or rebates to purchase freight vehicles, and (ii) operational incentives such as truck charging at reasonable electric costs (Union of Concerned Scientists, 2019). Operational incentives also include providing preferential access to restricted areas for environmentally friendly vehicles (BESTUFS, 2007) or designating green loading zones for electric trucks (New York State Department of Transportation, 2014).

Two successful implementations of incentive programs to foster the adoption of electric trucks has occurred in California, U.S. One is the Hybrid and Zero-Emission Truck and Bus Voucher Incentive Project (HVIP), launched in 2009 and led by the California Air Resource Board, which intends to make clean commercial vehicles affordable in the state. The HVIP is a first-come first-served incentive scheme that has served as a good strategy for early market penetration of commercial vehicles (California HVIP, 2022a). In its freight component, the HVIP offers incentives ranging between $60,000 and $120,000, depending on the vehicle characteristics to purchase electric trucks (California HVIP, 2022b). The second program is the Low Carbon Fuel Standard (LCFS) which seeks to achieve air quality by reducing the use of carbon fuel (State of California, 2022). Companies using green technologies in their vehicle fleet can generate credits and sell them in the credit market.

New York has the Truck Voucher Incentive Program (NYTVIP), which provides vouchers or discounts to purchase or lease commercial vehicles that use clean technology, such as electric trucks (New York State Energy Research and Development Authority, 2022). The voucher value considers the difference between the cost of a zero-emission truck and a diesel vehicle (up to a cap), and differs according to the vehicle characteristics and location. Incentive programs in New York City include the Hunts Point Clean Trucks Program (HPCTP), which secures funding to transition from diesel to cleaner technologies in the trucking industry (NYC Clean Trucks Program, 2022). In Europe, incentives to purchase commercial zero-emission vehicles have also been provided in Germany, Spain, Italy, and France (International Energy Agency, 2021). Examples of operational incentives include lower costs or free parking. For example, some cities in China offer free first two hours, first hour, 50% or 100% off of parking (International Energy Agency, 2021).

In general, monetary, and non-monetary incentives could be provided to all agents participating in the supply chains that seek to foster sustainable practices for the good of society.

Vignettes

This section discusses three vignettes detailing freight road pricing and incentive schemes, one in the United Kingdom and two in the United States.

Heavy Goods Vehicle Road User Levy in UK

The Heavy Goods Vehicle (HGV) User Levy was implemented on 1 April 2014 in the United Kingdom (UK) (Department for Transport, 2018a). The levy is a time-based charge that can be paid daily, weekly, monthly, or yearly. The road pricing measure applies to vehicles weighing 12 tons or more, and varies with the maximum weight and axle configuration. The primary purpose of the measure is that HGV operators, UK or non-UK registered HGVs, using the UK road network contribute to their use. The rationale behind this measure is that because heavier vehicles have a higher impact on road damage, HGVs should pay more than other vehicles to cover road maintenance costs. The measure is also intended to make the UK truck industry fairer, since British HGV drivers had to pay for the use of EU roads but not the other way around (The Parliament Magazine, 2016).

Even though the pricing strategy collects revenue to maintain the roads, the measure is not effective in reducing congestion, emissions, collisions, or optimizing the use of the network. Studies have found that HGVs only pay approximately a third of the social cost they produce (Campaign for Better Transport, 2018). To achieve environmental objectives of reducing emissions and improving air quality, the levy was reformed in 2019. To this effect, the revised levy rate also varies according to the Euro emission standard of the vehicle (GOV.UK, 2021).

Port Authority of New York and New Jersey's Time-of-Day Pricing

In January 2001, the Port Authority of New York and New Jersey (PANYNJ) introduced a time-of-day pricing initiative for its six tunnels and bridges. The freight component consisted of increasing the truck tolls to reduce the level of congestion during peak hours. During peak periods, truck toll rates increased between 50% and 67%, depending on the payment technology (Holguín-Veras et al., 2006). The strategy intended that the toll would induce truck drivers to deliver during off-hours, consolidate orders, or other behavior changes that reduce truck traffic during the day. However, the decision on the delivery time, and frequency of orders are made by the receivers of supplies in competitive markets (Holguín-Veras et al.,

2015). Receivers have higher market power over the carriers. In essence, carriers adjust their operational decisions based on the requirements of the receivers. As a result, the time-of-day initiative was ineffective since most carriers (91%) were not able to pass the toll cost on to the receivers (Holguín-Veras et al., 2006). Due to the cordon area of the toll, carriers could not modify their delivery routes. Many carriers had to absorb the toll cost and reacted by improving their productivity in order to compensate for the cost increase while meeting the needs of receivers.

The key lesson of the time-of-day pricing, the largest road pricing program in the United States, is that initiatives targeting the weakest agent are of little effectiveness in changing behavior, i.e., switching the freight traffic from regular hours to off-hours. In the PANYNJ case, the toll increase did not reach the decision-makers, the receivers; carriers cannot force the receivers to accept off-hour deliveries. The net effect was an increase in the costs for carriers. Hence, this program was only effective for revenue-collecting purposes.

Off-Hour Deliveries in New York City

The OHD initiative was implemented as a pilot in New York City in 2010 involving a small number of companies. The goal of the program was to switch the deliveries from regular hours (from 6 am to 7 pm) to off-hours (from 7 pm to 6 am) to reduce congestion during the day. The receivers were provided with a financial incentive of $2,000 to participate in the program. The pilot results revealed that participating receivers were satisfied with the program (Holguín-Veras et al., 2012b). The carriers were also pleased since they naturally prefer to make deliveries during non-peak hours for higher productivity and less stress when driving.

Consequently, the OHD program was included in the sustainable plan of the city of New York (City of New York, 2011). Also, the Federal Highway Administration (FHWA), in partnership with the Environmental Protection Agency (EPA), promoted a project to expand the OHD program to other urban areas of the United States (Federal Highway Administration, 2012). The impact of full implementation of an OHD program could be enormous; it could decrease travel time by about 11%, 5% of reduction in CO_2 (Savadogo and Beziat, 2021), plus a decrease in truck congestion, fewer parking fines, and an overall increase in the productivity of the freight activity (Holguín-Veras et al., 2011).

The rationale behind the success of the OHD program is that unlike the PANYNJ initiative—which was oriented on carriers—the OHD program was directed to the key decision-maker of delivery times, the receivers of supplies. The OHD program in New York City also demonstrated that the use of incentives effectively induces changes in the decision of the receivers about the delivery times.

Potential Freight Road Pricing and Incentive Measures

This section discusses potential road pricing and incentive measures to manage urban deliveries considering all supply chain agents that create externalities, technological innovations, and environmental concerns.

Allocation of Externalities among Supply Chain Agents

At first glance, it seems that carriers—the agents transporting the goods—are responsible for creating all the externalities. Thus, policymakers are keen to design policies centered on carriers to improve the traffic conditions of urban areas. As shown in the PANYNJ road pricing initiative, programs focusing on carriers are of little effectiveness in reducing congestion. Although, due to the operational activity that carriers perform, some externalities are produced—which is demonstrated during night deliveries where carriers create externalities—the truth is that there is a possibility that decisions made by other supply chain agents could contribute to these externalities. There is, therefore, a need to identify the agents that contribute to the externalities generated in urban areas and allocate the corresponding externality cost. By so doing, it is easier to propose effective policies oriented to achieve sustainable practices. This rationale is consistent with the tenet proposed by Pigou (1920) that the generator of externalities must pay for them, "the polluter pays principle."

The role of pricing in urban deliveries is to reduce the externalities produced by freight activity, and enhance a more sustainable transportation market. Since the transportation of goods is only a portion of the supply chain, it is necessary to consider the rest of the supply chain agents. For example, the agents hiring the carriers could have a role in creating externalities by putting pressure on carriers to meet certain requirements. Carriers, as cost minimizer agents, want efficient logistic operations. However, they are constrained by the market conditions. Carriers prefer to deliver at night when externalities are fewer, but supply chains decide to work during daytime hours, where more externalities occur. They only provide the transportation service because they do not have the economic strength to oppose the customers' requirements.

Freight agents do not work unilaterally, and the externalities are a consequence of the decisions resulting from the interactions of the economic agents involved in supply chains. Understanding who and how the logistical decisions are made, sheds light on the design of initiatives centered on the agents producing the externalities. For example, offering incentives to receivers to induce changes in their delivery times is effective, as shown in the OHD program implemented in New York City. Another example, considering that receivers decide the ordering patterns of supplies, is charging receivers for the externalities they created to induce them to reduce the number of deliveries needed (Holguín-Veras and Sánchez-Díaz, 2016). In essence, fewer delivery trips translate into less congestion and emissions produced by freight operations. The effect of pricing policies can be boosted if they are combined. For instance, "carrier-receiver" policies combine carrier-centered approaches such as road charges, with policies focused on the receivers (Holguín-Veras, 2011).

To this effect, it is necessary to develop methods that allocate the externalities to each responsible agent in a practical manner. Even though in an ideal scenario, each agent should pay for the externalities produced, in reality, it is a complex task. However, policymakers should guarantee the design of strategies to allocate the largest externality costs to the agent responsible for creating them. Formulating this type of initiative will allow the agents to pay for the externalities produced and/or induce behavioral changes to mitigate them.

New Technologies and Road Pricing and Incentives

In an era of new technologies and climate change, switching the truck fleet to cleaner vehicles is essential to reducing emissions. The transition to zero-emission vehicles is becoming a reality; for example, the ban on commercializing new fuel or diesel vehicles, and a pathway to zero-emission vehicles in the United Kingdom effectively by 2040 (Department for Transport, 2018b). The environmental goals, to a large extent, influence freight road pricing and incentives policies. In particular, because of the fuel carbon dependence, fuel charges and VEDs will be ineffective in managing the traffic demand or raising revenues in the near future.

The reduction in revenues, as a proportion of the Gross Domestic Product (GDP), will produce a deficit in the funding to maintain the road infrastructure (Association for Consultancy and Engineering, 2018). Additionally, the increase in electric vehicles will create a need for more charging infrastructure and other technologies, e.g., on-road charging, that allows an efficient transportation system. This is especially important for trucks, which usually travel long distances. Funding is also important if we consider the introduction of connected and autonomous vehicles (CAVs), which need additional technological solutions so that CAVs can perceive the road space and the driving environment accurately (Buchanan et al., 2017). To this effect, more funds are needed to maintain the road network. Considering these new technologies and their requirements, and recent regulations that exempt, for instance, electric vehicles from fuel taxes and VEDs, there is a need for new funding sources.

Moreover, even though the upfront cost of electric vehicles is high, there are significant fuel cost savings. This could induce an increase in electric vehicles leading to more congestion. Even though cleaner vehicles could reduce emissions, congestion issues will persist. Hence, the need to rethink freight road pricing policies and design incentive programs in an era of technological changes and environmental goals to have new funding sources and manage the traffic demand. Overall, careful consideration must be given when imposing charges on electric vehicles so that the charge will not have a negative effect, such as inducing a decline in the adoption of electric vehicles (Atkinson, 2019).

Furthermore, a pricing structure is needed that charges the agents that are producing externalities in a more realistic and fair way, as well as increasing the efficiency of the use of the road networks. To this effect, technological tools such as global positioning systems (GPS) devices could help record the distance traveled by trucks and monitor the location where the trucks make the deliveries. The information gathered can be used to compute, in real-time, the externalities produced and allocate them to the corresponding agent. Modern technology can also be used to handle toll-collection methods, especially those related to dynamic fees based on time-of-day (Holguín-Veras et al., 2012a).

Conclusions

This chapter has discussed two different approaches to managing urban deliveries: road pricing and incentives. It is important to consider both because there are cases in which incentives might be the most effective approach, and it is not likely to produce conflicts, as shown in the OHD initiative in New York City. Among the pricing schemes, we discussed freight road charges, freight parking pricing, and freight vehicle taxation. In the case of freight road charges, the discussion in this chapter established that time-of-day pricing is not a good idea because carriers are the agents paying the toll (not the receivers); thus, it does not have an effect on switching the truck traffic to off-hours. In contrast, road pricing schemes that reach receivers, such as time-distance tolls, are more successful in making supply chains more efficient while reducing the externalities produced by urban deliveries. Freight parking pricing helps manage curbside areas for logistical operations. Adequate parking spaces result in efficient unloading and loading activities, and reduce the likelihood of vehicles cruising or double parking, resulting in better traffic conditions. Freight vehicle taxation charges a vague estimate of the use of freight vehicles, such as fuel taxes, and the ownership of these vehicles, such as vehicle excise duty. If the charge is small, the effect of the freight vehicle tax will likely be low too.

In the case of incentives, the chapter considers monetary and non-monetary mechanisms. Incentives can be in the form of recognition programs, certification programs, and incentives for electric/low-emission vehicles. The use of incentives such as the financial incentives provided to receivers to change their delivery hours in OHD programs is effective in changing the behavior of supply chain agents. Moreover, monetary and non-monetary incentives for electric/low-emission vehicles, such as funding incentives and preferential access to restricted zones, foster the adoption of clean technologies.

Central to this chapter is the principle that freight road pricing and incentives should reach the appropriate decision-maker. For instance, in competitive markets, the receivers of supplies decide the ordering patterns, such as the delivery time. Similarly, other supply chain agents could contribute to the creation of externalities produced in urban deliveries. Freight road pricing and incentives should be designed to reach the key agent.

The discussion carried out in this chapter also invites readers to reflect on the redesign of freight road pricing and incentive measures in an era of technological changes. The arrival of electric vehicles, connected and autonomous vehicles, and other technological advances challenge current freight road pricing and incentive measures. Even though the use of clean technologies is undoubtedly helpful in reducing emissions, congestion and other externalities caused by urban deliveries will persist.

References

Association for Consultancy and Engineering (2018). Funding Roads for the Future. Creating a More Productive and Sustainable Road Network in England. https://www.acenet.co.uk/media/1139/funding-roads-for-the-future.pdf.

Atkinson, R. D. (2019). A Policymaker's Guide to Road User Charges. Information Technology & Innovation Foundation. https://itif.org/publications/2019/04/22/policymakers-guide-road-user-charges.

BESTUFS (2007). Good Practice Guide on Urban Freight Transport. University of Westminster. BESTUFS http://www.bestufs.net/.

Blythe, P. T. (2005). "Congestion Charging: Technical Options for the Delivery of Future UK Policy." *Transportation Research Part A* **39**(7-9): 571–587. 10.1016/j.tra.2005.02.012

Börjesson, M., J. Eliasson, M. B. Hugosson and K. Brundell-Freij (2012). "The Stockholm Congestion Charges—5 Years on. Effects, Acceptability and Lessons Learnt." *Transport Policy* **20**: 1–12.

Buchanan, P., K. Arter, L. Dean, G. Matthews, J. Siraut, S. Rodoulis and S. Cohen (2017). *Pricing for Prosperity*. 2017 Wolfson Economics Prize, London, UK.

California HVIP (2022a). "About HVIP." Posted: Retrieved 13 April 2022, from https://californiahvip.org/about/.

California HVIP (2022b). "Vehicles and Eligible Technologies." Posted: Retrieved 13 April 2022, from https://californiahvip.org.

Campaign for Better Transport (2018). Department for Transport Call for Evidence: Reforming the HGV Road User Levy. https://bettertransport.org.uk/sites/default/files/research-files/Reforming%20the%20HGV%20road%20user%20levy%20Jan%202018.pdf.

City of New York (2011). "PlaNYC: A Greener, Greater New York: Update 2011." Posted: Retrieved 1 May 2011, from http://www.nyc.gov/html/planyc/downloads/pdf/publications/planyc_2011_planyc_full_report.pdf.

City Ports (2005). City Ports Project Interim Report. European Project City Ports Interreg Programme III B CADSES. **Interim Report**

Department for Transport (2018a). HGV Levy Driver/Operator Supplementary Guidance. https://assets.publishing.service.gov.uk/government/uploads/system/uploads/attachment_data/file/937112/hgv-levy-supplementary-guidance-driver-operator.pdf.

Department for Transport (2018b). The Road to Zero. https://assets.publishing.service.gov.uk/government/uploads/system/uploads/attachment_data/file/739460/road-to-zero.pdf.

Department for Transport (2017). Reforming the HGV Road User Levy: Call for Evidence. https://assets.publishing.service.gov.uk/government/uploads/system/uploads/attachment_data/file/661814/reforming-hgv-road-user-levy.pdf.

Federal Highway Administration (2012). "Federal Grant Opportunity Request for Applications (RFA): Off Hours Freight Delivery Pilot Project." Posted: Retrieved July 1, 2012, from http://apply07.grants.gov/apply/opportunities/instructions/oppDTFH61-12-RA-00016-cfda20.200-cidDTFH61-12-RA-00016-instructions.pdf.

Foster, C. D. (1974). "The Regressiveness of Road Pricing." *International Journal of Transport Economics* **1**: 186–188.

GOV.UK (2021). "HGV Road User Levy." Posted, 9 December 2021, Retrieved 31 March 2022, from https://www.gov.uk/government/collections/hgv-road-user-levy.

Holguín-Veras, J. (2011). "Urban Delivery Industry Response to Cordon Pricing, Time-Distance Pricing, and Carrier-Receiver Policies in Competitive Markets." *Transportation Research Part A* 45: 802–824.

Holguín-Veras, J., J. Amaya Leal, I. Sanchez-Diaz, M. Browne and J. Wojtowicz (2020a). "State of the Art and Practice of Urban Freight Management Part II: Financial Approaches, Logistics, and Demand Management." *Transportation Research Part A: Policy and Practice* 137: 383–410. 10.1016/j.tra.2018.10.036

Holguín-Veras, J. and F. Aros-Vera (2014). "Self-Supported Freight Demand Management: Pricing and Incentives." *EURO Journal on Transportation and Logistics* 3(1): 1–24. 10.1007/s13676-013-0041-1

Holguín-Veras, J., F. Aros-Vera and M. Browne (2015). "Agent Interactions and the Response of Supply Chains to Pricing and Incentives." *Economics of Transportation*. http://dx.doi.org/10.1016/j.ecotra.2015.04.002

Holguín-Veras, J., C. Jones, B. Miller and R. Barone (2012a). Study of Goods Movement through I-278 NYC and NJ. University Transportation Research Center. U. T. R. Center. http://www.utrc2.org/publications/study-of-goods-movement-through-I-278.

Holguín-Veras, J., K. Ozbay, A. Kornhauser, S. Ukkusuri, M. A. Brom, S. Iyer, W. F. Yushimito, B. Allen and M. A. Silas (2012b). *Overall Impacts of Off-Hour Delivery Programs in the New York City Metropolitan Area: Lessons for European Cities*. European Transport Conference 2012.

Holguín-Veras, J., K. Ozbay, A. L. Kornhauser, M. Brom, S. Iyer, W. Yushimito, S. Ukkusuri, B. Allen and M. Silas (2011). "Overall Impacts of Off-Hour Delivery Programs in the New York City Metropolitan Area." *Transportation Research Record* 2238: 68–76.

Holguín-Veras, J., J. Polimeni, B. Cruz, N. Xu, G. List, J. Nordstrom and J. Haddock (2005). "Off-Peak Freight Deliveries: Challenges and Stakeholders' Perceptions." *Transportation Research Record* 1906: 42–48.

Holguín-Veras, J., D. Sackey, S. Hussain and V. Ochieng (2003). "Economic and Financial Feasibility of Truck Toll Lanes." *Transportation Research Record* 1833: 66–72. http://dx.doi.org/10.3141/1833-09

Holguín-Veras, J. and I. Sánchez-Díaz (2016). "Freight Demand Management and the Potential of Receiver-Led Consolidation Programs." *Transportation Research Part A* 84: 109–130. 10.1016/j.tra.2015.06.013

International Energy Agency (2021). Global EV Outlook 2021. https://www.iea.org/reports/global-ev-outlook-2021.

Jacobi, S. N. (1973). The Use of Economic Incentives to Relieve Urban Traffic Congestion. *45th Congress Australian and New Zealand Association for the Advancement of Science*. Perth, Australia.

Menon, A. P. G., S. H. Lam and H. S. L. Fan (1993). "Singapore's Road Pricing System: Its Past, Present and Future." *ITE Journal* **63**(12): 44–48.

National Academy of Sciences (2010). *Technologies and Approaches to Reducing the Fuel Consumption of Medium- and Heavy-Duty Vehicles*, The National Academies Press.

New York State Department of Transportation (2014). New York City Green Loading Zones Study-Final Report. New York State Energy Research and Development Authority (NYSERDA), and New York State Department of Transportation (NYSDOT), Albany, NY. **C-13-52** https://energyplan.ny.gov/-/media/Files/Publications/Research/Transportation/New-York-City-Green-Loading-Zones-Study.pdf.

New York State Energy Research and Development Authority (2022). "New York Truck Voucher Incentive Program." Posted: Retrieved 13 April 2022, from https://www.nyserda.ny.gov/All-Programs/Truck-Voucher-Program.

NYC Clean Trucks Program (2022). "NYC Clean Trucks Program." Posted: Retrieved 13 April 2022, from https://www.nycctp.com/.

Phang, S. Y. and R. S. Toh (2004). "Road Congestion Pricing in Singapore: 1975 to 2003." *Transportation Journal* **43**(2): 16–25.

Pigou, A. C. (1920). *The Economics of Welfare*. London, MacMillian and Co., Ltd.
Port Authority of New York and New Jersey (2020). "Toll Rates for All Port Authority Bridges & Tunnels." Posted: Retrieved May 15, 2021, from https://www.panynj.gov/bridges-tunnels/en/tolls.html.
Savadogo, I. and A. Beziat (2021). "Evaluating the Potential Environmental Impacts of a Large Scale Shift to Off-hour Deliveries." *Transportation Research Part D: Transport and Environment* **90**. 10.1016/j.trd.2020.102649
State of California (2022). "Low Carbon Fuel Standard." Posted: Retrieved 15 April 2022, from https://ww2.arb.ca.gov/our-work/programs/low-carbon-fuel-standard/about.
The Parliament Magazine (2016). "Commission Warns UK Against New Road Charge." Posted, 12 May 2016, Retrieved 28 February 2022, from https://www.theparliamentmagazine.eu/news/article/commission-warns-uk-against-new-road-charge.
Transport for London (2013). "Fleet Operator Recognition Scheme." Posted: Retrieved January 24th, 2013, 2013, from http://www.fors-online.org.uk/.
Transport for London (2007). Central London Congestion Charging Impacts Monitoring Fifth Annual Report. http://www.tfl.gov.uk/assets/downloads/fifth-annual-impacts-monitoring-report-2007-07-07.pdf.
Union of Concerned Scientists (2019). Ready for Work. www.ucsusa.org/resources/ready-work.
Walters, A. A. (1961). "The Theory and Measurement of Private and Social Cost of Highway Congestion." *Econometrica* **29**(4): 676–699.
Yang, H. and H. J. Huang (2005). *Mathematical and Economic Theory of Road Pricing*, Elsevier.

21
URBAN CONSOLIDATION CENTRES

Emine Zehra Akgün and Jason Monios

Introduction

While freight vehicles make up a smaller share of total urban traffic than passenger vehicles, they nevertheless also cause their own share of negative externalities, such as air pollution, congestion and accidents (Nordtømme et al., 2015; Paddeu, 2017). In order to face these challenges, local authorities are increasingly taking direct policy action (see Chapter 18). Some of these policy interventions affect all road users (e.g. low-emission zones, congestion charging – see Chapter 20 – and pedestrianisation), while others are specifically targeted at freight vehicles (e.g. time windows for deliveries and urban consolidation centres) (Stathopoulos et al., 2012; Kiba-Janiak, 2017). Various cities (e.g. London, UK; Gothenburg, Sweden) have been implementing low-emission zones and congestion charging schemes for many years now (Ellison et al., 2013; Akgün et al. 2019). Urban consolidation centres (UCCs) are logistics facilities located at the edge of city centres that consolidate deliveries into fewer vehicles, preferably low or zero-emission vehicles such as cargo bikes (see Chapter 5). While UCCS are most commonly developed initially by local authorities (Allen et al., 2014; Giampoldaki et al., 2021), if they are to be successful it is inevitable that a range of stakeholders will need to work closely together. The primary stakeholders are local authorities, logistics service providers (LSPs) and retailers, each having their own priorities (Harrington et al., 2016). While UCCs can potentially contribute to public priorities of reducing congestion and improving air quality in the city centre by consolidating traffic and using zero-emission vehicles for deliveries, private freight operators and retailers are reluctant to disrupt their existing supply chains by switching to the use of UCCs. The result is that UCCs frequently are not able to attract enough users to achieve financial viability. Previous research shows that the majority of UCCs are not able to continue operation without public subsidy, and many do not even proceed beyond an initial feasibility study (Allen et al., 2012; Kin et al., 2016; Johansson and Björklund, 2017; Paddeu, 2017). For example, the consolidation trial in Oslo (Nordtømme et al., 2015), SamCity pilot study in Malmö (Katsela and Pålsson, 2021), and a UCC study in Perth, Scotland (Akgün et al., 2020) were all discontinued due to a lack of necessary resources.

This chapter first presents a definition of UCCs and an overview of their activities and service offerings. A case study of a successful UCC in Gothenburg, Sweden is then described,

DOI: 10.4324/9781003241478-26

followed by a reflection on the challenges of setting up a UCC. Efforts by local authorities to provide supporting policies to assist successful UCC developments are then discussed, before conclusions are drawn regarding some of the key challenges and enabling factors for successful UCCs in the future, mostly revolving around the need to build a partnership with logistics service providers rather than putting them in competition with a new UCC development.

Types of Urban Consolidation Centres and Their Service Offerings

Allen et al. (2012) reviewed 114 UCC schemes and categorised three different types of UCCs. The first two are those serving urban areas and those serving specific single locations such as an airport or shopping centre. Both of these types of UCCs handle retail products, office products and food supplies. The third type is more specialised, serving construction sites and handling building materials. While the second and third types of UCCs are located at shopping malls or building sites where there are few issues in terms of space, the first type, serving urban centres, often has to deal with locations having narrow streets and historic layouts which often necessitate traffic restrictions and difficulty in creating sufficient loading and unloading bays.

As types two and three are directly linked to existing business developments, they are established by those commercial actors. By contrast, the first type of UCCs is often initiated by local authorities seeking to improve the environmental impact and reduce congestion in the urban centre, hence they may be publicly supported in a variety of ways. While they are usually initiated by the local authorities, later they are either subcontracted to a third-party logistics provider or a trade association. The public ownership (in most cases) is transferred to other parties at some point; however, they may still be supported through additional funding and/or policies. The Bristol & Bath Freight Consolidation Centre and Stadsleveransen in Gothenburg, Sweden are two UCC projects that are still operational to this date (Björklund et al., 2017; Paddeu, 2017; Akgün et al., 2020). Both UCCs have been initiated and financially supported by the cities' municipal authorities. Bristol's centre is subcontracted to DHL Supply Chain and Stadsleveransen is subcontracted to a small logistics service provider called Paket Logistik AB. Public support may relate to favourable regulations relating to road access or direct financial support via a public subsidy during the start-up phase (Allen et al. 2014; Lebeau et al. 2017). This chapter focuses on this first kind of UCC, serving all or part of an urban area and usually specialising in retail products. The review by Allen et al. (2012) showed that these are by far the dominant type.

The distribution model for UCCs is that, instead of LSPs transporting goods through the city centre directly to retailers, they will drop off their deliveries at the UCC which will be located at the edge of the urban area being served. Thus, the LSPs can use a larger truck to bring all the deliveries together, and will not need to enter the congested urban area. The UCC will then perform the deliveries to the retailers, usually using low- or zero-emission vans or cargo bikes. As well as lowering or eliminating emissions, such smaller vehicles can better navigate the urban area.

The location of one or more UCCs in a city in relation to the city's spatial layout and position in the supply chain is depicted in Figure 21.1. Large distribution centres (DCs) are located on the outskirts of the city, usually next to motorway/freeway junctions. Goods arrive by heavy goods vehicles (HGVs) from around the country to stock the DCs. LSPs then serve retailers from these DCs with a variety of heavy or light goods vehicles. Within the larger city area, there may be more than one congested or sensitive urban area. These are often historic centres with narrow streets and old buildings but may also be popular shopping areas that are increasingly pedestrianised. A UCC may be located on the edge of such areas, and the LSP will then send their deliveries from the DC to the UCC instead of serving the stores directly. The UCC will undertake to make the final delivery.

Given that the goods for many receivers are passing through the UCC, it is possible to offer a variety of services to these retailers (Table 21.1). These services include the provision of off-site storage space, pre-retailing tasks, e-commerce services, information systems that enable tracking and tracing, recycling, waste management and customised delivery times (Browne et al., 2005; Björklund et al., 2017; Paddeu, 2017; Johansson and Björklund, 2017; Akgün et al., 2020). Key to a viable UCC business model is to generate sufficient revenue, which is often linked to the ability to provide attractive services (Björklund et al., 2017) that are competitive with existing provision in the area (Paddeu, 2021). The challenge is that this business model needs to find a balance of costs and revenue that is acceptable to each stakeholder (Johansson and Björklund, 2017), so that the UCC does not capture revenue streams to the disadvantage of LSPs currently serving the retailers.

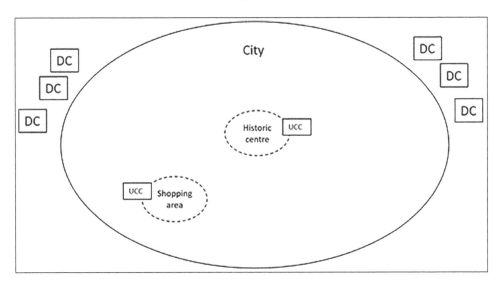

Figure 21.1 Diagrammatic representation of the location of UCCs in relation to the city and surrounding distribution centres

Source: Authors

Table 21.1 Services that may be offered at a UCC

Service type	Service
Stock and material management	Additional stockholding
	Pre-retailing services (e.g. repacking, labelling, security tags, creating promotional displays and stands)
	Waste management and recycling
Information systems	E-commerce support
	Information system enabling tracking & tracing
Delivery management	Customised delivery date and time
	Delivery by low-emission vehicles (e.g. cargo bike, electric van)

One of the key early studies on UCCs by Browne et al. (2005) pointed out that UCCs can offer an attractive package to retailers by providing storage space at the UCC thus saving the need to dedicate space for storage at the retail premises where rents are higher and space is at a premium, and in addition, the UCC can provide pre-retailing services. These services enable shop owners to increase space and reduce time dedicated to unpacking and waste handling (Johansson and Björklund, 2017). This increased flexibility can enable retailers to extend their product range and spend more time with customers (Browne et al., 2005; Allen et al., 2014; Paddeu, 2017). As UCCs prioritise electric vans and cargo bikes for deliveries, receiving their deliveries from UCCs rather than LSPs can provide retailers with the option to reduce their environmental impact (Browne et al., 2005; Allen et al., 2014; Paddeu, 2017). The benefits of using UCCs are not only restricted to retailers. LSPs can obtain savings by sending their deliveries via UCCs in historic town centres and streets with strict traffic regulations, if the vehicles of the UCC are exempted from these restrictions (Akgün et al., 2020).

Case Study of a Successful UCC in Gothenburg, Sweden[1]

The Gothenburg UCC was part of two funded research projects. The first was the Sendsmart project, financed by the national funding body Vinnova and running from 2012 to 2014. This project focused on freight transport provision in the city of Gothenburg, and had the intention to improve the overall level of sustainability. With particular relevance to UCCs, part of the project focused on the consolidation of freight flows in order to reduce empty running, increase fill rates, both of which could reduce overall freight trips leading to a reduction in congestion and emissions (Lindholm, 2014). The second project was the SMARTSET project which ran from 2013 to 2016 and was partially funded by the Intelligent Energy – Europe II Programme. This project had a specific focus on increasing the consolidation of freight transport in Gothenburg, with a broader aim to establish a UCC business model that would be financially viable as well as potentially replicable in other cities across Europe (Ablasser et al., 2016).

The Gothenburg UCC project has a number of aims common to most UCC projects. The overall aim was to consolidate deliveries hence reduce total freight traffic, specifically at peak hours when demand for road space was at its highest. At the same time, a reduction in large delivery vehicles was intended to keep the city centre safer for other road users such as pedestrians and cyclists. The UCC is not owned by the public authority, but by the Gothenburg association of real estate owners and shops (Innerstaden) and it is operated by a locally-based courier company. The business model is based on an agreement between the UCC and two logistics companies that would consent to committing a certain proportion of their parcels to the UCC to deliver to the final receivers in the city centre. The ability to obtain commitment at the start from two large logistics companies followed the logic of many successful startups by establishing a core demand base rather than having to rely on individual businesses with lower and fragmented volumes. The UCC serves the Domkyrkoplan shopping district and the establishment of the UCC is located in the inner city of Gothenburg, 3.5 km away from the shopping district. The UCC's building is located in a business complex with other logistics and distribution companies. The building was used by another logistics service provider previously and then inherited by the UCC as the two companies started to collaborate in the UCC project.

The UCC uses its own vehicles to deliver to the retailers in the city centre area, focusing on those with less complex transport and handling needs, meaning those specialising in products such as clothing and footwear rather than food and perishable goods. The UCC processes 500 incoming and outgoing packages in total per day, serving approximately 200 shops. All deliveries are executed by zero-carbon transport modes, sharing the deliveries between two electric cargo bikes and three electric cars (with trailers). These vehicles are all exempt from most of the transport restrictions currently in place in the city, such as time window restrictions, weight restrictions and pedestrianised areas.

As reported by Akgün et al. (2020), the UCC development evolved through three phases. The first phase was the concept phase (2012–2013), funded by the local authority, the UCC owner Innerstaden and the Sendsmart project. During this time a pilot study took place involving a small number of local stores. The second phase was the development phase (2014–2016). During this time, the focus was on increasing the number of users of the UCC and beginning to consider the provision of value-added services. They were able to increase usage of the UCC by signing up both an international LSP as well as the national mail service, both of whom committed a portion of their deliveries to the UCC. The UCC also developed a new revenue stream by selling advertising on the sides of their vehicles. By the time this stage ended, the UCC was already doing well, having reduced the needed public subsidy to only 20% of total revenue. The final phase was the establishment phase, which started in 2017. The aim of the UCC is to become a fully commercial business and to expand its network of users across the city area.

Challenges Faced by UCC Developments

Despite the large body of research that has been published on UCCs over almost two decades (see Björklund and Johansson, 2018, for a review of the entire field of literature), the fundamental challenge of financial viability remains difficult to resolve. While Browne et al. (2011) showed that increasing the consolidation of goods flows can produce many advantages for society, particularly improving air quality by reducing the number of trips performed by conventional vehicles, the level of inertia in the industry remains high. LSPs already plan their own distribution networks and are usually reluctant to change this existing arrangement. Adding a UCC as an additional link may increase costs without obtaining any benefits (Browne et al. 2005). Indeed, transferring these deliveries to a UCC may lead to a loss of revenue for the LSP. However, Janjevic and Ndiaye (2017) contend that a UCC could obtain improvements in delivery times due to their shorter delivery distances which can ultimately lower the costs of delivery. The ability to do so, however, also depends to some degree on the conditions in the particular urban area being served, whether these be existing restrictions in traffic, congestion levels or spatial constraints (Kin et al., 2016; Aljohani and Thompson, 2021).

If improvements cannot be made in the delivery time and cost, the main avenue to attract users is to offer relevant services, as noted earlier. Yet such offerings can also be challenged by the need to develop a business model that requires modifications to the LSP's existing processes, which can mean they lose direct contact with both customers and suppliers (Browne et al., 2005: Allen et al., 2012). In order to address this problem, Aljohani and Thompson (2021) recommended that UCCs should adopt marketing strategies that will enable long-term relationships with both existing and potential stakeholders. The UCC business model will need to consist of various components such as financial models, operational dynamics and models of collaboration and cooperation among stakeholders (Nordtømme et al., 2015; Björklund et al., 2017). Akgun et al. (2020) also found an issue with regard to the use of IT systems by LSPs to track their deliveries and enable downstream customers to view their incoming deliveries. It is not uncommon that different LSPs use different systems, so if the

UCC is going to provide tracking data to each LSP, they would need a single unified system that can interact seamlessly with the different systems used by each one.

Recent studies have put considerable effort into building models that aim to produce solutions for the current financial challenges of UCCs. Common features of these models include identifying potential costs for each stakeholder, as well as modelling how the inclusion of external costs can bridge the gap between the operational costs of a system with and without a UCC. Anand et al. (2021) argued that a successful UCC project can be supported by developing a consistent subsidy or tax scheme such as carbon credit points, which aims to incorporate the negative external effects of the conventional distribution network in the total cost of operations. The authors emphasised, however, that the success of any such policy depends on the involvement of a multi-stakeholder perspective, as also highlighted by previous studies. Katsela et al. (2021) also stress the necessity of including the cost of externalities in the evaluation of urban distribution networks. The authors calculated the amount of externalities and their cost implications for different combinations of UCCs and microhubs. They concluded that absorbing the increased cost of adding extra nodes in the distribution network is a challenge in UCC projects.

Apart from highlighting the financial struggles of UCCs, other studies have investigated and revealed various operational challenges. A review by Lagorio et al. (2016) highlighted several operational causes of UCC failure, such as long delivery distances and the inability to provide tracking and tracing, lack of confidence in the security of their goods, all of which potentially weaken their ability to control and maintain their expected levels of customer service. Ultimately, LSPs are reluctant to relinquish their direct control and oversight of the customer relationship and ability to take active decisions in the management and execution of deliveries.

Paddeu (2021) identified that there is a lack of performance measurement systems in place for ex-ante and ex-post analyses, which would quantify the performance dimensions and enable conclusions to be drawn regarding what extent project objectives are reached and policy goals are achieved. The author proposed a model to evaluate the efficiency of a UCC with respect to particular performance attributes such as cost, time, quality, productivity and the environment.

Use of Supporting Policies for UCC Developments

Table 21.2 presents a list of related UFT policies that local authorities may adopt either directly or indirectly to support a UCC project. In particular, allowing exemptions for UCC users to existing UFT policies such as a congestion charging zone can be used as an incentive to switch deliveries to a UCC. The review by Panero et al. (2011) of 39 UCCs identified the importance of existing restrictions such as low-emission zones, which can be waived for the UCC vehicles. A later study by Lebeau et al. (2017) of 61 UCCs divided the potential policies into three types. The first category was financial support (start-up, structural and indirect), the second was direct regulatory support (e.g. one compulsory UCC, favourable measures to UCC operator) and, finally, indirect regulatory support (e.g. time windows, size restrictions, vehicle age and engine type, urban toll).

Several case studies have been published in which particular supportive policies have been trialled. Marcucci and Danielis (2008) tested the use of subsidies against fee exemption, comparing a full public subsidy, increasing access fees to limited traffic zones and a mix of both, and calculated that the share of traffic that switches to the UCC can be increased by as much as 29%, 27% and 78%, respectively. Ville et al. (2013) analysed a UCC in Italy in

Table 21.2 Supportive policies that may incentivise use of a UCC

Policy type	Policies
Financial	Start-up funding for the UCC
	Ongoing operational subsidy until the UCC becomes financially viable
Parking and loading	Parking restrictions (exempt if using the UCC)
	Loading/unloading restrictions (exempt if using the UCC)
	Time window restrictions (exempt if using the UCC)
	Increased availability of dedicated loading and unloading bays for UCC vehicles
Emissions and congestion	Low-emission zones (exempt if using the UCC)
	Congestion charge (exempt if using the UCC)
Other	Delivery and servicing plans for UCC customers
	Pedestrianisation (exempt if using the UCC)
	Permission for off-peak deliveries

which the local authority attempted to encourage or almost force the use of the UCC by implementing traffic restrictions in the area. This policy was deeply unpopular and even led to a legal dispute based on the position that such restrictions represented an unfair limitation on the ability of operators to conduct their business. Such a response indicates the importance of treading carefully and developing a positive rather than antagonistic relationship between the public and private actors. It is likely to be more welcome if supportive policies can act more as incentives rather than directives, for example the case of a UCC in Bristol reported by Allen et al. (2014), whereby the local authority agreed to a trial period in which they granted access for the UCC vehicles to bus lanes, so that their vehicles would flow more freely and lead to savings in delivery times. A similar type of exemption approach was used in another case in Italy, where entry fees to a restricted city area were lifted for the UCC users (Björklund et al., 2017). Another policy that has been covered in the literature is the use of off-hour deliveries (OHD). Marcucci and Gatta (2017) analysed this strategy in Rome and found that the most popular combination of those operators surveyed was to combine OHD with the use of a UCC. The work of Akgün et al. (2020) concurred with the findings of previous authors regarding the successful use of supportive policies, but they warned that such policies are unlikely to be sufficient on their own. A subsidy for starting up and even over the medium term would still remain essential in most cases, aligned with a good relationship between the public and private actors over a long time period. Thus policy measures should not be considered simply as tools to support the UCC or force operators to use them, but as part of an ongoing process of stakeholder engagement.

Conclusion

Developing a UCC requires that both public and private actors navigate a series of complicated relationships over a sustained time period. This means that the local authority promoting the development needs to bring together the UCC with the LSPs and retailers and coordinate their individual objectives (Harrington et al., 2016; Björklund and Johansson, 2018). An initial market research study and dedicated start-up funding may enable public authorities to analyse the economic context and operational requirements of the potential stakeholders and establish an appropriate business model tailored to the local situation (Wagner et al., 2021). Moreover, the earlier in the process that each of these stakeholders can commence their involvement, the better for building trust and developing joint plans and the higher the likelihood of eventual success. Potential barriers should be identified early and attention paid both to leveraging large players as well as empowering smaller actors (Van Duin et al., 2018).

Retailers are not generally in favour of using UCCs because it represents a disruption of their current distribution networks. Yet it is not in fact the retailers who are most affected by restrictive UFT policies, but the LSP making the deliveries. The problem is that if retailers switch their deliveries to the UCC, not only will the LSP potentially lose some delivery revenue but they might also lose revenue from the provision of additional services if the retailer is also convinced to switch these services to the UCC. The successful UCC project in Gothenburg involved two large LSPs in the project from the beginning and the local authority supported the project by exempting the electric trucks and cargo bikes of the UCC from the existing mobility restrictions in the urban shopping area. Many studies agree that the lengthy time period needed to build up a successful UCC and develop a business model with attractive service provision means that very few will survive without a long period of public subsidy.

Future research is needed on the LSP perspective and how it can be aligned with the use of UCCs so that neither stakeholder is disadvantaged. It is clear that, for a UCC project to succeed, the UCC operator will need to work well with both the retailers and the LSPs. The role of the local authority is therefore not only to support the start-up phase of the UCC with funding, but to create such a coalition of stakeholders.

Note

1 A detailed study of this UCC was published by Akgün et al. (2020); a summarised version is presented here.

References

Ablasser, G., Berlini, S., Coldrey, M., Dotter, F., Dunder, H., Frigato, F., Mattisson, P. H., König, P., Lundgren, M., Menge, J., Michalk, P., Nussio, F., Ravaioli, F., Siciliano, G., Slobodova, O., Surace, M., Widegren, C., Widenfalk, T., Wolfswinkel, F., and Zunder. A. (2016). SMARTSET final report: Experiences of a European project for cleaner, safer and more efficient freight transport. Available at: http://smartset-project.eu/downloads

Akgün, E. Z., Monios, J., Rye, T., and Fonzone, A. (2019). Influences on urban freight transport policy choice by local authorities. *Transport Policy*. 75: 88–98.

Akgün, E. Z., Monios, J., and Fonzone, A. (2020). Supporting urban consolidation centres with urban freight transport policies: A comparative study of Scotland and Sweden. *International Journal of Logistics: Research & Applications*. 23 (3): 291–310.

Aljohani, K., and Thompson, R. G. (2021). Profitability of freight consolidation facilities: A detailed cost analysis based on theoretical modelling. *Research in Transportation Economics*. 90: 101122.

Allen, J., Browne, M., Woodburn, A., and Leonardi, J. (2012). The role of urban consolidation centres in sustainable freight transport. *Transport Reviews*. 32 (4): 473–490.

Allen, J., Browne, M., Woodburn, A., and Leonardi, J. (2014). A review of urban consolidation centres in the supply chain based on a case study approach. *Supply Chain Forum: An International Journal*. 15 (4): 100–112.

Anand, N., van Duin, R., and Tavasszy, L. (2021). Carbon credits and urban freight consolidation: An experiment using agent based simulation. *Research in Transportation Economics*. 85: 100797.

Björklund, M., Abrahamsson, M., and Johansson, H. (2017). Critical factors for viable business models for urban consolidation centres. *Research in Transportation Economics*. 64: 36–47.

Björklund, M., and Johansson, H. (2018). Urban consolidation centre – a literature review, categorisation, and a future research agenda. *International Journal of Physical Distribution & Logistics Management*. 48 (8): 745–764.

Browne, M., Allen, J., and Leonardi, J. (2011). Evaluating the use of an urban consolidation centre and electric vehicles in Central London. *IATSS Research*. 35 (1): 1–6.

Browne, M., Sweet, M., Woodburn, A., and Allen, J. (2005). *Urban freight consolidation centres final report*. Transport Studies Group, University of Westminster.

Ellison, R. B., Greaves, S. P., and Hensher, D. A. (2013). Five years of London's low emission zone: Effects on vehicle fleet composition and air quality. *Transportation Research Part D: Transport and Environment*, 23: 25–33.

Giampoldaki, E., Madas, M., Zeimpekis, V., and Vlachopoulou, M. (2021). A state-of-practice review of urban consolidation centres: Practical insights and future challenges. *International Journal of Logistics Research and Applications*, 2021: 1–32.

Harrington, T. S., Srai, J. S., Kumar, M., and Wohlrab, J. (2016). Identifying design criteria for urban system 'Last-Mile' solutions – A multi-stakeholder perspective. *Production Planning & Control*. 27 (6): 456–476.

Janjevic, M., and Ndiaye, A. (2017). Investigating the theoretical cost-relationships of urban consolidation centres for their users. *Transportation Research Part A: Policy and Practice*. 102: 98–118.

Johansson, H., and Björklund, M. (2017). Urban consolidation centres: retail stores' demands for UCC services. *International Journal of Physical Distribution & Logistics Management*. 47 (7): 646–662.

Katsela, K., and Pålsson, H. (2021). Viable business models for city logistics: Exploring the cost structure and the economy of scale in a Swedish initiative. *Research in Transportation Economics*. 90: 100857.

Katsela, K., Pålsson, H., and Ivernå, J. (2021). Environmental impact and costs of externalities of using urban consolidation centres: A 24-hour observation study with modelling in four scenarios. *International Journal of Logistics: Research and Applications*. In press.

Kiba-Janiak, M. (2017). Urban freight transport in city strategic planning. *Research in Transportation Business & Management*. 24: 4–16.

Kin, B., Verlinde, S., van Lier, T., and Macharis, C. (2016). Is there life after subsidy for an urban consolidation centre? An investigation of the total costs and benefits of a privately-initiated concept. *Transportation Research Procedia*. 12: 357–369.

Lagorio, A., Pinto, R., and Golini, R. (2016). Research in urban logistics: A systematic literature review. *International Journal of Physical Distribution & Logistics Management*. 46 (10): 908–931.

Lebeau, P., Verlinde, S., Macharis, C., and Van Mierlo, J. (2017). How can authorities support urban consolidation centres? A review of the accompanying measures. *Journal of Urbanism: International Research on Placemaking and Urban Sustainability*. 10 (4): 468–486.

Lindholm, M. (2014). Slutrapport-sendsmart. Available at: https://closer.lindholmen.se/sites/default/files/content/resource/files/slutrapport_sendsmart_slutlig.pdf

Marcucci, E., and Danielis, R. (2008). The potential demand for an urban freight consolidation centre. *Transportation*. 35 (2): 269–284.

Marcucci, E., and Gatta, V. (2017). Investigating the potential for off-hour deliveries in the city of Rome: Retailers' perceptions and stated reactions. *Transportation Research Part A: Policy and Practice*. 102: 142–156.

Nordtømme, M. E., Bjerkan, K. Y., and Sund, A. B. (2015). Barriers to urban freight policy implementation: The case of urban consolidation center in Oslo. *Transport Policy*. 44: 179–186.

Paddeu, D. (2017). The Bristol-Bath urban freight Consolidation Centre from the perspective of its users. *Case Studies on Transport Policy*. 5 (3): 483–491.

Paddeu, D. (2021). The Five Attribute Performance Assessment (FAPA) model to evaluate the performance of an urban consolidation centre. *Research in Transportation Economics*. 90:101065.

Panero, M. A., Shin, H-S., and Lopez, D. P. (2011). *Urban distribution centers: A means to reducing freight vehicle miles travelled*. The NYU Rudin Center For Transportation Policy and Management: New York, NY. https://www.dot.ny.gov/divisions/engineering/technical-services/trans-r-and-d-repository/C-08-23_0.pdf

Stathopoulos, A., Valeri, E., and Marcucci, E. (2012). Stakeholder reactions to urban freight policy innovation. *Journal of Transport Geography*. 22: 34–45.

Van Duin, R., Slabbekoorn, M., Tavasszy, L., and Quak, H. (2018). Identifying dominant stakeholder perspectives on urban freight policies: A Q-analysis on urban consolidation centres in the Netherlands. *Transport*. 33 (4): 867–880.

Ville, S., Gonzalez-Feliu, J., and Dablanc, L. (2013). The limits of public policy intervention in urban logistics: Lessons from Vicenza (Italy). *European Planning Studies*. 21 (10): 1528–1541.

Wagner, N., Iwan, S., and Kijewska, K. (2021). The assumptions, conditions and barriers of the development of the Urban Consolidation Centre for Municipal Entities (UCC-ME). *European Research Studies*. 24 (1): 806–821.

22
SUCCESS FACTORS FOR URBAN LOGISTICS PILOT STUDIES

Andisheh Ranjbari, Anne Goodchild and Elizabeth Guzy

Introduction

The last mile of delivery is undergoing major changes, experiencing new demand and new challenges. The rise in urban deliveries amid the societal impacts of the COVID-19 pandemic has dramatically affected urban logistics. Since lockdown in March 2020, online sales increased by over 30% in the United States (U.S. Census Bureau, 2021), and the World Economic Forum has predicted a 78% worldwide increase in urban last-mile deliveries between 2020 and 2030 (WEF, 2020). So, there is a need for new transportation options and novel technologies to meet this ever-increasing demand. When testing new strategies or technologies, empirical research and pilot tests are an important addition to theoretical and simulation research, as they provide a realistic setting. In the pilot environments, unforeseen obstacles are encountered, risk appetites tested and economic motivations revealed. However, pilot tests are time-consuming, costly and strategically-intensive.

The level of understanding is increasing as cities and companies pilot strategies that pave the way for efficient urban freight practices. Parcel lockers, for instance, have been shown to reduce delivery dwell times with such success that Denmark increased its pilot program of 2,000 lockers to 10,000 over the past two years (Apex Insight, 2019). The authors' own experiment with parcel lockers found the introduction of a parcel locker at a multi-story residential condominium reduced delivery time inside the building by 50% and delivery vehicle dwell times at the curb by 30% (Ranjbari et al., 2022). Another series of pilot projects have shown that incentivizing businesses to receive deliveries outside of traditional business and peak-congestion hours, namely at night or early morning, can also reduce city-wide congestion. Pilot results from a wide spread of cities, from New York City (USA) to Stockholm (Sweden), São Paulo (Brazil) and Addis Ababa (Ethiopia), have revealed how shifting deliveries to off-hours improves delivery speed and efficiency while reducing emissions and vehicle-miles traveled (Kebede and Gebresenbet, 2017; Fu and Jenelius, 2018; Holguín-Veras et al., 2018). Furthermore, cities, such as Santa Monica and Los Angeles in California, USA, have been piloting zero-emission delivery zones (LACI, 2020), aiming to provide a blueprint and best practice for cities and carriers to adopt and promote zero-emission delivery, while providing immediate benefits to the local community, such as reduced air pollution, greenhouse gas emissions and traffic congestion, as well as improved safety and economic opportunity to small businesses. Whether by rethinking street design to consider the needs and prevalence of urban freight operations, or through reconfiguring how we think about policy and technology to create safer and cleaner urban environments, there are several approaches that cities and companies are testing and implementing worldwide. The authors have carried out a number of urban logistics pilots in Seattle, Washington, USA over the period 2019–2021, including installing parcel lockers, deploying street parking sensors, setting up and operating a multi-service microhub, and collaborating in a cargo e-bike implementation.

This chapter focuses on challenges faced during those pilots from technical, managerial and operational perspectives, and offers examples and lessons learned for those who are planning to design and/or run future pilot tests. It should be noted that the challenges mentioned in this chapter are from pilots in the United States, and while most of them are generalizable to any location around the world, some nuances may not apply to other countries. The aim of this chapter is to aid others (a) articulate research and implementation plans involving pilot tests better and more realistically, and (b) save time and resources by avoiding some of the challenges and obstacles that the authors faced. The challenges can be grouped into five overall categories namely *Identifying the Right Location, Securing Required Permits and Agreements, Collaboration between Involved Parties, Engaging Local Agencies and Community Associations in Marketing and Advertising Efforts,* and *Missing Regulations and Processes for New Strategies/Technologies,* as detailed in the following sections.

Identifying the Right Location

Finding the right location is one of the most important aspects of a pilot. It affects the pilot feasibility, traction received from the community, public agencies' involvement, drivers' and operators' participation, and the process to secure agreements between parties. In the following, we discuss the process and obstacles faced when seeking locations for deploying a microhub and parcel lockers. Generally, for a successful pilot implementation, the needs and constraints of three groups should be considered, namely *operators, users* and the *community*.

Example: Microhub

A microhub, also known as an urban consolidation center, is a logistics facility inside the urban area boundaries, where goods are sorted and consolidated. It serves a certain spatial range, allowing a mode shift to low-emission and/or soft transportation modes, such as cargo bikes, for last-mile deliveries. Microhubs are a new concept in the United States, but they have been implemented in several cities in Europe, such as London (UK), Paris (France), Brussels (Belgium) and Nijmegen (Netherlands) (Van Rooijen and Quak, 2010; Diziain, Ripert, and Dablanc, 2012; Verlinde et al., 2014; Clarke and Leonardi, 2017). Microhubs typically serve urban areas where delivery activities are difficult to perform, because of limited curb space for parking large vehicles, limited street access and restricted traffic conditions, and are usually implemented in high-demand, high-density and high-real estate value areas. Therefore, finding the right location is imperative for a successful operation. Browne et al. (2005), Urban Freight Lab (2020), Katsela et al. (2022) discuss microhubs' application, implementation and effectiveness, and provide examples.

When establishing a novel pilot project such as a microhub, which also involves various partners serving as operators, it is essential to make every effort to accommodate all location needs and requirements of different partners in order to maximize buy-in and project success. Interviewing involved partners as to their needs and requirements for the location is a necessary step in better understanding the parameters to work within. These interviews can then inform the development of surveys, which are a useful tool in helping involved parties rank order requirements for their involvement. Results from these surveys help prioritize the group's requirements of a location and should be used as parameters for evaluating the candidate locations. Results of the survey and identification of locations that meet some or all of these requirements should be presented for discussion among the project partners. It may be unlikely to find a location that meets all needs and requirements of all the partners, but collaborative discussion about necessary trade-offs will result in identifying the best possible location.

Through the use of interviews and surveys, the Seattle microhub project partners prioritized: access to power and wi-fi, walkability, truck access and proximity to the downtown area as location requirements. Ultimately, a surface parking lot with access to power and ability to install necessary technical hardware, with both street and alleyway access for cars and trucks in close proximity to the iconic Seattle's Space Needle and was chosen as the location for the microhub (Figure 22.1). This location met the requirements of most partners and proved to be ideal for the project operation, although some trade-offs, such as proximity to highways, had to be made.

We encourage those working on identifying the right location for a pilot which involves various partners to spend time communicating with partners about their location requirements and work to help the group prioritize these requirements with the understanding that some trade-offs are unavoidable. In the end, partners are more likely to accept trade-offs if they feel they have been heard and involved in the location selection process.

When identifying the right location, it is also important to consider the perspective of the users from the surrounding community and what elements would be most appealing to them. Distributing a community survey is a good way to solicit input on requirements that are deemed critical in choosing a location, such as walkability, hours of operation and safety. Moreover, surveying potential users early in the project, when evaluating candidate locations, can help build awareness of the pilot among the community.

Figure 22.1 Seattle microhub location
Source: Urban Freight Lab at University of Washington

Example: Parcel Lockers

Parcel lockers are automated multi-compartment storage systems that enable temporary storing of parcel deliveries in a secure space until picked-up by the consumer. Delivery couriers deposit packages in an available compartment, and upon delivery, consumers receive an electronic notification and a unique access code that allows them to open the compartment (through the locker digital keypad) and retrieve their packages at a convenient time. By providing a safe and reliable place for consumers to conveniently retrieve packages, parcel lockers eliminate failed delivery attempts and the need for an additional trip. They also help consolidate deliveries and reduce vehicle dwell times for carriers.

Studies in the Netherlands, Italy and Poland reveal that parcel lockers generate a considerable reduction in vehicle-miles traveled and carbon emissions (Iwan, Kijewska, and Lemke, 2016; Behnke, 2019; Van Duin et al., 2020). A cost-benefit analysis of a prospective parcel locker project for a residential complex in South Korea stated a benefit-cost ratio of 4.89 over a 10-year time horizon (Pham and Lee, 2019), with primary benefits stemming from travel time savings, along with vehicle cost and emissions reductions. A 2019 study of a 62-story office building in downtown Seattle, WA reported a 78% reduction in delivery times inside the building and zero failed delivery attempts to the building, after installing a parcel locker system in the building lobby (Goodchild et al., 2019). A more recent study in the same area showed that installing a parcel locker in a multi-story residential building reduced the average time delivery couriers spent inside the building by 50%, and the average delivery vehicle dwell time at the curb by 33% (Ranjbari et al., 2022).

Parcel lockers may be placed in residential buildings, stores, transit stations or neighborhood hubs, serving different groups of consumers. In our parcel locker pilot in Seattle, we explored diverse locations for parcel lockers: a multi-story residential building, a commercial building garage and a surface parking lot.

In the following, we share what can be learnt from these various locations and provide suggestions for successful parcel locker implementation considering the needs of the operator, users and community.

From the *operator*'s perspective, the locker location needs to have a level base, electrical power and stable internet connection, be in a secure location, have on-site management, be easily accessible for carriers, and have a postal address.

The former three, **level base, electrical power** and **stable internet connection**, are from the installation perspective, and they are usually less challenging and less expensive for private properties. Figure 22.2 shows three installations of parcel lockers in a residential condominium, a commercial building and a surface parking lot respectively. The residential condominium installation was the easiest of the three, where the ground was level and electrical power and wi-fi were available in the building. The commercial building locker was installed in the parking garage underneath the building, wherein there was power but it took a while to obtain internet connection, due to problems with amplifying the wi-fi signal in a concrete parking garage. The base was also quite sloped, and the operation team had to construct a level concrete pad to properly place the locker on. For the parking lot locker, power had to be provided from a nearby building, which although not technically difficult, required permission and agreement over utility payment. The parking lot locker also experienced several power outages due to storms and vandalism of the power outlet, proving consistent power provision to the locker to be very challenging. All three of the aforementioned factors, however, required significantly more time and resources for a

Success Factors for Urban Logistics Pilot Studies

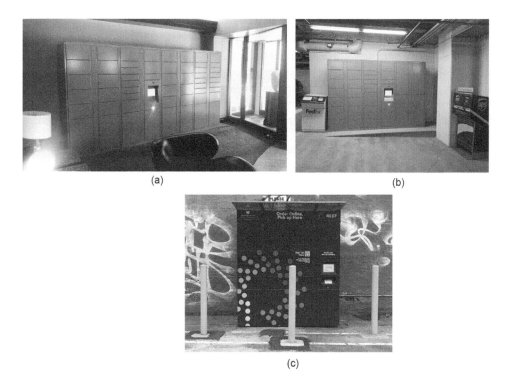

Figure 22.2 Three installations of parcel lockers in (a) a residential condominium, (b) a commercial building and (c) a surface parking lot

Source: Urban Freight Lab at University of Washington

public property locker installation. The authors had planned to install a parcel locker on a sidewalk. Due to the hilly streets of Seattle, almost any potential location for the locker required building a platform on the sidewalk pavement to accommodate a level base. However, the most difficult issues in that case were obtaining power and wi-fi from adjacent properties, which proved almost impossible due to the inaccessibility, privacy concerns and construction costs.

The fourth factor, the **secure location**, is to protect the locker from vandalism or unintentional damages, such as a vehicle hitting the locker in a parking lot. To alleviate the latter, safety poles can be installed in front of the locker (such as those in Figure 22.2c). Most lockers have a camera, and one strategy to prevent vandalism is to highlight that. On the parking lot locker shown in Figure 22.2c, a friendly message was used ("Smile! You are in front of the camera!") to do so.

On-site management proved to be critical for locker operations. Similar to any new deployment, it takes time for the operation to become stable, and no matter how well you plan and execute your pilot, something will invariably go wrong. In the first couple of weeks of installing the residential building locker, there were some technical issues with the locker digital keypad. Moreover, some of the couriers delivering to the building did not know how to work with the locker and would therefore leave packages in the lobby.

Since the building management monitored the locker regularly and quickly reported these issues to the locker provider company's customer service team, there was never a disruption in locker operations, and after a month, all issues were resolved – the locker kept working smoothly and carriers delivering to the locker, except for some occasional weekend deliveries. In the case of the public locker (in the parking lot) though, there were two instances that created major operation disruptions, one where the locker lost power and the digital keypad became inactive, and another where the locker was graffitied overnight. We found having an on-site manager who is able to address or report issues imminently is essential for success.

The final two factors namely, **accessibility for carriers** and **having a postal address**, ensure that carriers are able to find the locker location, secure a convenient nearby parking space, get past security points and easily navigate through the horizontal or vertical space to reach the locker. Parcel locker providers have a carrier relationship team who will reach out to the carriers and provide them with a digital access code and instructions on how to deliver a package to the locker, yet the locker needs to have a postal address associated with it and be in an accessible location.

From the *users' perspective,* the main location criteria are **safety** and **accessibility**. A locker needs to be in a safe and well-lit location so that users feel safe retrieving their package(s). For outdoor locations, being within transit terminals or next to stores or coffee shops/restaurants, which have pedestrian traffic even during evenings, are deemed as good locations. A 24/7 access and enabling people to pick up their packages at any time is also another factor that needs to be considered when selecting a location for a locker. Lockers that are located inside retail stores or parking garages which have certain operating hours would be less appealing to users. When planning for a locker installation, it is also important to consider the local climate, such as providing an awning that will shield users from the rain. From our survey of the neighborhood wherein the public locker was located, we ascertained that many users praised the convenience of the locker, but requested that the time window to pick up packages be extended to three weeks or more, and also offer refrigerated options for perishable food deliveries

While not everyone will use lockers, the entire community (building, block or neighborhood) in which a locker is being installed will be impacted by the new technology. To ensure success of a pilot (and a long-term deployment), needs and concerns of the community have to be considered. Lockers will attract a lot of pedestrian traffic, and while some property owners (such as retailers) might see this as a benefit and welcome having a locker in or next to their property, others (residential and commercial building managers) might not like that. We heard concerns from a few building managers that a locker could provide a corner for unsolicited gathering. We made an extensive outreach to private property owners in Seattle (including residential and commercial buildings and parking lots), and it took us 49 emails, 19 phone calls, 7 in-person meetings and 7 site visits to get the first approval for hosting a locker. Lockers also take up space and managers of the residential/commercial buildings that we worked with reported some resistance from the tenants about installing a locker in common areas of the building (such as the lobby) because of that.

Securing Required Permits and Agreements

Working with local governments and private sector partners in deploying a pilot can require formal agreements and permits, which clarify the terms of the project, ensure regulations are followed and maintain transparency for all involved parties. However, when working to establish pilot projects that have never been done before, securing these necessary documents and approvals requires additional time spent on researching and identifying appropriate processes. We provide examples and suggestions on how best to approach this challenge below.

Example: Permit Application for Lockers on Public Property

In addition to the technical and behavioral challenges associated with installing a locker on public property, which were explained above, this process requires securing permits. In case of installing a locker on a sidewalk, we had to apply for a private infrastructure/public amenity permit with the Street Use division within the City of Seattle's Department of Transportation (DOT). The permit process required a detailed aerial site plan and an elevation plan, and investigated lateral clearance and distance from intersections and bus stops, to make sure installing a locker on the sidewalk would not have disturbed pedestrian accessibility and flow. Figures 22.3 and 22.4 show samples of the site plan and elevation plan developed for the sidewalk locker permit application. This process took quite a long time (5.5 months) as the Street Use division also needed to consider other pending permit applications (including private infrastructure deployment, construction and use of sidewalks for outdoor dining) submitted for locations near our proposed site for the locker, and in some cases, they deemed another proposed use more urgent/beneficial to the area, and selected that over ours. By the time we finally received the permit for a proposed location on a sidewalk, we had moved forward with another private property location and could not take advantage of the issued permit. As such, we encourage those who are looking to install a locker on public property to set aside sufficient time in their planning process for obtaining permits.

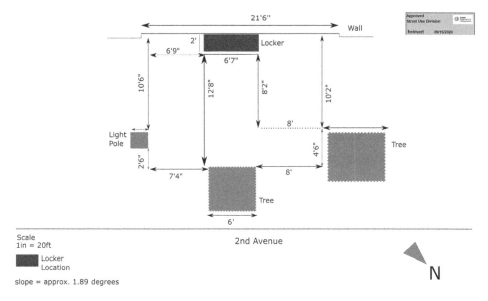

Figure 22.3 Sample site plan developed for the street use permit application for the sidewalk locker installation

Source: Urban Freight Lab at University of Washington

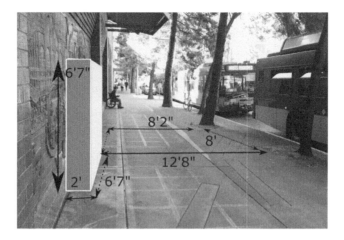

Figure 22.4 Sample elevation plan developed for the street use permit application for the sidewalk locker installation
Source: Urban Freight Lab at University of Washington

Example: Microhub Partner Agreements

There is no roadmap to managing novel projects such as a microhub, so it is important to establish agreements to address all responsibilities and liabilities of the project. The development of these agreements between partners can be time-intensive and might involve more parties than expected, including legal teams, risk analysts and other unforeseen administrative approvals. Transparency and consistent communication with involved parties in securing these agreements are essential. The partner agreement development process for the Seattle microhub project proved successful due to motivated partners who helped facilitate all necessary steps and unforeseen challenges of securing the agreements. Quick daily check-ins with these motivated partners during the agreement development phase helped identify roadblocks more quickly and expedited the entire process. When pioneering new project models, we recommend identifying motivated partners at the beginning of the agreement process and checking in with them regularly to help streamline the complex process.

Collaboration between Involved Parties

Conducting a pilot requires collaboration and agreement between numerous parties, each of which may have different goals, expectations and risks. Sometimes different divisions within the same institution do not communicate with each other, and sometimes two different institutions work collaboratively as one unit. In the following, we present examples of inter- and intra-institution coordination and lessons learned on how to reach agreements faster and more effectively.

Example: Cargo e-bike and Microhub Partners

The goal in conducting collaborative pilot projects is to ensure diverse partners understand the project goals, remain motivated throughout the project and participate in transparent communication. The best way to achieve this goal is by setting the clear expectation that all partners attend weekly check-in meetings throughout the duration of the project. The weekly check-ins should be held in an easily accessible format for all partners, such as videoconference. Setting the expectation that attendance is mandatory at these meetings creates continuity in communication. Problems can be identified and decisions can be made in real time, saving valuable time and keeping project timelines on target. The weekly meetings for our Seattle cargo e-bike project proved essential in real-time problem-solving when unforeseen issues arose, such as the delivery routes provided being uphill and not suitable for a cargo bike (see Chapter 5). The feedback the logistics team received from the bike operator helped identify an important issue that the delivery routing application was designed solely for cars, and improvements were immediately made for the remaining cargo-bike deliveries. Moreover, the project team was able to coordinate the on-site installation of necessary technologies like AI-trained cameras, analyze locker delivery data and troubleshoot electrical power issues to the microhub locker, all in real time during the team's weekly check-ins. Providing consistent communication opportunities, where project goals are reiterated and problem-solving is encouraged is essential to successful collaboration between partners in pilot projects.

Example: Installation of Parking Sensors

In another pilot, we built a parking information and prediction application for commercial vehicles, which collected real-time data from parking sensors. The parking sensors deployment and app development was another example of a pilot project with multiple partners involved, including academic researchers (at a university), researchers and software programmers (at a national laboratory), a sensor provider company, a curb technology provider company and city DOT staff. Unlike the microhub pilot, we started this project by having separate meetings with individual project partners: a monthly meeting with the city DOT, a biweekly meeting with the national lab and on-demand meetings with the two private companies. Moreover, the city DOT and the sensor provider company had separate meetings together, and so did the two private companies. While the separate meetings were set to respect partners' times and to avoid unnecessary meetings, the lost/mis-communication between partners made the coordination very challenging, and created additional work for us as the project management unit, requiring countless emails, calls and meetings throughout the three years of the project. Also, from time to time, partners would divert from the main goal of the project, or aspire to achieve parallel objectives, all of which required reminding them of the set project goals and tight timeline and bringing them back on track.

Moreover, in this pilot, the university, the national lab and the city DOT were initial project partners (i.e. from the start of the project), and the two private companies were later hired and contracted by the city through a vendor solicitation process. This structure created some confusion for the two private companies (and consequently for the entire project team) as to whom they should report to or ask questions of (e.g. the university as the project manager, or the city as their direct sponsor) and whose goals needed to be met.

As mentioned above for the microhub pilot, having regular check-ins with all project partners and ensuring there is a mutual understanding of the project goals could have saved a lot of time in managing that project and accelerated implementing the pilot.

Engaging Local Agencies and Community Associations in Marketing and Advertising Efforts

For pilot projects where participation from users is needed (e.g. parcel lockers), marketing plays an important role and might require spending substantial project resources. Marketing should be done early and consistently. Engaging local agencies and community associations also proved to be immensely helpful.

Example: Marketing Campaigns for Parcel Lockers

The diverse locations of the Seattle parcel lockers required strong marketing campaigns tailored to the adjacent communities. Local organizations and community associations became essential partners in developing the marketing campaigns, as they had extensive connections in the communities. For example, reaching the community organizations' social media audiences was extremely helpful in building awareness of the nearby lockers. However, those organizations had limited staff and bandwidth to devote to this marketing effort. To help streamline the communication process and maximize engagement with them, requests needed to be simple and as clear as possible. Examples of these requests included, providing

(a)

(b)   (c)

Figure 22.5 Examples of marketing materials developed for the parcel lockers with assistance from local organizations: (a) flyers, (b) sandwich boards and (c) postcards

Source: Urban Freight Lab at University of Washington

content ready for distribution to the organization's social media accounts with a detailed posting schedule.

Utilizing existing relationships with the local public transportation agencies also proved invaluable in the marketing efforts for pilots. We worked with a local transit agency for the parcel lockers marketing campaign. Marketing experts at the agency advised the campaign and provided access to in-house design of a website, postcards, flyers and sandwich boards (Figure 22.5). The agency also helped disseminate these materials using their established outreach methods. We would not have been able to reach the number of residents and business owners we did without the assistance of that transit agency.

One of the Seattle parcel lockers was located in the parking garage of a commercial building, and required the assistance of the building management in raising awareness about the locker amenity. The building management utilized their existing e-newsletter which was sent to a building-wide listserv to inform tenants of the locker and to encourage sign-ups. The building management also allowed the placement of promotional materials developed by the project team in the building common areas and helped answer tenants' questions about the locker. We recommend, when preparing for pilot projects, significant time be devoted to developing relationships with local agencies and community associations to assist with the marketing efforts. Doing marketing early in the project and consistently will ensure receiving traction and reaching a large group of potential users.

Missing Regulations and Processes for New Strategies/Technologies

Regardless of how experienced the project team is, when a strategy/technology is being tested for the first time, it will suffer from the lack of relevant regulations and processes, requiring additional time and resources. Examples of this include applying for a permit for a locker on public property when such an infrastructure is not defined in any street use guidelines, figuring out if a cargo bike is classified as a bike or as a commercial delivery vehicle, or finding bike riders who are willing and experienced enough to operate a cargo bike in a hilly neighborhood.

Example: Sidewalk Locker

Since parcel lockers are a new technology, in the permit application form for the sidewalk locker, there was no defined use code for such an infrastructure. After discussion with the city staff, the "public amenity" use code under the "private structure" category seemed like the best fit. That private structure category included public amenity uses (e.g. public seating, parklets, planters, artwork), business uses (e.g. signs, cafes, merchandise display), property uses (e.g. fences, walls, balconies, areaways, private utilities), underwater street uses (e.g. moorage, floating structures) and other miscellaneous long-term uses.

However, some sections of the permit application form were irrelevant to lockers, and at the same time, some concerns were raised around having a locker on a sidewalk which were not captured by the criteria listed in the permit application, and required additional scrutiny and at times discussion with other departments within the DOT or even other agencies (e.g. transit agencies). Two of the aforementioned concerns were lateral clearance and proximity to bus stops. In the former case, it was unclear whether the depth of the locker alone should be considered for clearance, or the space taken when a person stands in front of a locker and opens a compartment to deliver/pick up a package should also be considered. In the latter case, transit agencies were concerned as to whether placing a locker next to a transit stop could result in delivery vehicles stopping at the bus stop and blocking buses.

Moreover, the street use team was unsure if a construction use permit, which is usually required for long-term use in the private structure category, was also required for the locker. Figuring out all of these answers took more time than expected and significantly delayed the issuance of a permit for the sidewalk locker.

Cities are encouraged to revise their regulation accordingly to be able to accommodate timely installation of new urban logistics infrastructures and technologies.

Example: Microhub

A major challenge in implementing pilots is determining whether the pilot is following regulations when this type of project has never been undertaken before. Often there is limited understanding as to how to approach novel projects, but spending time researching what related policies and regulations exist will help ensure questions asked of regulatory agencies are productive. When working with regulatory agencies, it is helpful to proceed with the understanding that the pilot is a learning process and can help inform future regulations and processes for similar projects. This approach proved effective with the microhub project, wherein both private and public sector partners were extremely interested in exploring the outcomes. Research of land use regulations revealed that running this novel operation would be very different if located on public versus private property. Hosting the microhub on public property would require abiding by existing regulations such as city permit requirements, being explicit about restrictions and accepting limited hours of operation. Ultimately, the project partners chose to operate the microhub on private property due to fewer regulations, but acquired some valuable insights for consideration in future projects. One insight, which should be considered for future projects was that, although no current regulations exist regarding limiting truck traffic to/from a microhub in a residential area, this is a growing community concern around that. We encourage working with public agencies and community organizations in the pursuit of novel pilot projects as all parties will benefit from the findings in shaping future projects.

Example: Cargo e-Bike

The traditional standards for regulating e-bikes divide them into three classes: those with pedal assist and a maximum speed of 20 mph, those with a throttle and maximum speed of 20 mph and those with a throttle and maximum speed of 25mph (NYCDOT, 2020). For e-bikes operating above these thresholds, various additional requirements are put in place including driver's license and vehicle registration. Cargo bikes, which are often electric to assist with carrying large/heavy loads, would also fall under these categories requiring additional regulations/permits. There is an abundance of studies on cargo-bike/e-bike pilots worldwide; however, challenges like regulations, cycling infrastructure and winter weather remain to be addressed as these delivery modes become more widespread (Rudolph and Gruber, 2017; Verlinghieri et al., 2021; Dybdalen and Ryeng, 2022).

Operating a cargo e-bike delivery pilot on Seattle streets proved to be a learning process given the unknown regulatory category of cargo bikes. Figure 22.6 showcases the cargo e-bike and trailer used in the Seattle pilot. Many cities are presently grappling with how best to regulate commercial cargo-bike operations, especially electric cargo bikes that can run at higher speeds while carrying large loads, while still promoting them as an efficient, safe and sustainable model for urban deliveries.

Working with the Seattle DOT officials helped clarify that a commercial cargo bike would be categorized as a bike (rather than a commercial vehicle) and identify the allowable parts of

Figure 22.6 The cargo e-bike and trailer (EP1 smart pallet) used in the Seattle pilot
Source: Urban Freight Lab at University of Washington

the street and curb for riding and parking it. Seattle city staff were eager to advise the cargo-bike operations as it would help inform the development of guidelines for their forthcoming "Green & Healthy Streets", a part of C40 "Fossil Fuel Free Streets" declaration (Seattle's Clean Transportation Electrification Blueprint, 2021). The city encouraged the cargo-bike operator to ride in the bike lanes and park the bike near existing bike corrals. However, the cargo-bike operator experienced difficulty using the bike lane (compared to using the sidewalk) for routes with clustered stops (where they had to exit and re-enter the bike lane in short intervals to make deliveries), or in places where the bike lane was not fully protected from fast-moving traffic. The operator reported feeling safer riding on sidewalks, and that parking the bike close to building entrances significantly improved their accessibility and efficiency (Urban Freight Lab, 2021). We shared this information with the city staff, who found this feedback helpful in understanding how different bike riders are using the city infrastructure and considering the requirements of future cargo-bike operators in larger commercial operations settings.

Further understanding from the Seattle cargo-bike pilot was the difficulty in applying existing routing/navigation technologies and finding a workforce tailored for vehicle-based deliveries to cargo-bike delivery operations. Trucks/Vans and bikes operate very differently, especially in a city like Seattle where there are many hills, one-way streets and cobblestone areas. As a result, it was very challenging to find a skilled workforce for bike delivery. The cargo-bike operator experienced lots of difficulty with the routing application, which did not take into account the aforementioned geographical complexities for cyclists. Even with the assistance of the electric motor, the operator had difficulty completing routes that required the bike to go up and down hills all day. Given this initial feedback, the technology company that had programmed the routing application was able to apply relevant modifications for a broader cargo-bike operation, as well as a few immediate improvements, such as enabling the operator to see more than just the next forthcoming delivery on the tour to identify and plan for any geographical challenges. We encourage those piloting novel processes and technologies to work closely with involved local agencies and technology providers in providing consistent feedback, so that questions can be answered and improvements made more efficiently.

Conclusions

Summary of Major Findings and Lessons Learned

The lessons learned from the aforementioned urban logistics pilots can be summarized as follows:

- **Motivation and support required from key stakeholders.** Organizing and implementing a pilot requires effort and action from a number of different players. Before starting a pilot, ensure that you have the right resources from the right people. There will be unforeseen challenges, and a commitment to the outcome will carry you through challenging times;
- **Identify the right location.** Finding the appropriate location is a critical step in a pilot. It affects the pilot feasibility, traction received from the community, involvement of public agencies, driver/operator participation and the process to secure agreements between parties. In order to achieve a successful pilot, the needs and constraints of users, operators and community should be considered when choosing the location;
- **Have on-site management.** No matter how well you plan and execute your pilot, something will invariably go wrong. Having an on-site manager who is able to address or report issues in a timely manner is essential for the success of the project;
- **Apply for permits and agreements early on.** Obtaining required permits and agreements could take a long time. Identify the required permits and agreements for the pilot early in the project and apply for them as soon as possible;
- **Have an established point of contact per organization and regular check-ins with all involved parties.** Ensure there is a mutual understanding of the project goals, and have regular check-ins with all involved parties to share progress updates and solve problems in real time;
- **Do marketing/advertising early and consistently and, if possible, engage local agencies and community associations in those efforts**. For pilot tests where participation from users is needed (e.g. parcel lockers), marketing plays an important role and could require substantial resources. Marketing should be done early and consistently. Engaging local agencies and community associations also proved to be very helpful in tailoring the advertisements to the community needs and accessing local platforms for posting them;
- **Work with cities and local authorities to revise their regulations accordingly for new infrastructures/technologies.** Regardless of how experienced your team is, when a strategy/technology is being tested for the first time, it will be impacted from the lack of relevant regulations and processes, requiring additional time and resources.

Cities are encouraged to revise their regulations accordingly to be able to accommodate timely installation of new infrastructures/technologies;
- **Ensure sufficient budget to accommodate unexpected charges.** In all of our pilot projects, we faced unexpected charges which resulted in additional costs. For example, the cost of removing graffiti from a locker, the cost of providing electric power and wi-fi to a locker, and an unexpected change of location due to selling of private land on which the pilot was supposed to take place. Anticipate extra costs and build your budget considering those.

Strategies for Moving Forward

While this chapter highlighted the challenges of carrying out pilots, such projects are necessary to generate improvements in urban logistics. Without pilots, we cannot understand and address the practical and economic challenges associated with the adoption of new solutions that seem good in theory or simulation. Moving forward, we encourage cities, private companies and third parties to push for testing solutions on the ground in pilots, and to scale pilots and pave the way for adoption. Cities can provide space, permits and incentives for companies to experiment with new strategies and technologies. Companies can deploy tests to learn and improve; ultimately having more success in their market. Third parties, such as the academic institutions and non-profit organizations, can seek grant funding to ease the cost burden, help initiate experimentation and perform the evaluation and analysis.

The material covered in this chapter could reduce the cost of pilot tests, and encourage further experimentation, leading to a wider variety of solutions being tested, useful revisions in those solutions and getting refined solutions to market more quickly. The more pilot tests being implemented, the more lessons being learned and disseminated, and the less the cost burden associated with empirical research.

References

Apex Insight (2019). SwipBox and PostNord Launch Danish Parcel Locker Network. Available from: https://apex-insight.com/swipbox-and-postnord-launch-danish-parcel-locker-network/ [accessed May 2022]

Behnke, M. (2019) Recent Trends in Last Mile Delivery: Impacts of Fast Fulfillment, Parcel Lockers, Electric or Autonomous Vehicles, and More. *Logistics Management*, 141–156. https://doi.org/10.1007/978-3-030-29821-0_10.

Browne, M., Sweet, M., Woodburn, A.G. and Allen, J. (2005). *Urban Freight Consolidation Centres: Final Report*. University of Westminster, Transport Studies Group. https://ukerc.rl.ac.uk/pdf/RR3_Urban_Freight_Consolidation_Centre_Report.pdf [accessed October 2022].

Clarke, S. and Leonardi, J. (2017). *Parcel Deliveries with Electric Vehicles in Central London - Category 3: Single Carrier Consolidation Centre Targeting Poor Air Quality Zones Enabling Manual Delivery Methods. Data Report*. Greater London Authority. University of Westminster. Available from: https://westminsterresearch.westminster.ac.uk/download/c85e71d2c0a2f04f6de57ee874b6f72adeccabce82d20e6d2bf5bf9ef82d1645/4896435/GLA-Agile3-DataReport-4May2017.pdf [accessed October 2022].

Diziain, D., Ripert, C. and Dablanc, L. (2012). How Can We Bring Logistics Back into Cities? The Case of Paris Metropolitan Area. *Procedia – Social and Behavioral Sciences*, 39, 267–281. https://doi.org/10.1016/j.sbspro.2012.03.107.

Dybdalen, Å. and Ryeng, E.O. (2022). Understanding How to Ensure Efficient Operation of Cargo Bikes On Winter Roads. *Research in Transportation Business & Management*, 44, p.100652. https://doi.org/10.1016/j.rtbm.2021.100652.

Fu, J., and Jenelius, E. (2018). Transport Efficiency of Off-Peak Urban Goods Deliveries: A Stockholm Pilot Study. *Case Studies on Transport Policy*, 6(1), 156–166. https://doi.org/10.1016/j.cstp.2018.01.001.

Goodchild, A., Kim, H., and Ivanov, B. (2019). *Final 50 Feet of the Urban Goods Delivery System: Pilot Test of an Innovative Improvement Strategy*. University of Washington. http://hdl.handle.net/1773/44473.

Holguín-Veras, J., Encarnación, T., González-Calderón, C. A., Winebrake, J., Wang, C., Kyle, S., Herazo-Padilla, N., Kalahasthi, L., Adarme, W., Cantillo, V., Yoshizaki, H., and Garrido, R. (2018). Direct Impacts of Off-Hour Deliveries on Urban Freight Emissions. *Transportation Research. Part D: Transport and Environment*, 61, 84–103. https://doi.org/10.1016/j.trd.2016.10.013.

Iwan, S. Kijewska, K. and Lemke, J. (2016) Analysis of Parcel Lockers' Efficiency as the Last Mile Delivery Solution – The Results of the Research in Poland. *Transportation Research Procedia*, 12, 644–655. https://doi.org/10.1016/j.trpro.2016.02.018.

Katsela, K., Güneş, Ş., Fried, T., Goodchild, A. and Browne, M. (2022). Defining Urban Freight Microhubs: A Case Study Analysis. *Sustainability*, 14(1), 532.

Kebede, A. and Gebresenbet, G. (2017). Mapping out Goods Flow to Addis Ababa City, Ethiopia, and Its Impact on the Environment. *Transportation Research Procedia*, 25, 1008–1020. https://doi.org/10.1016/j.trpro.2017.05.475.

LACI (2020). Santa Monica Zero Emissions Delivery Zone Pilot. Available from: https://laincubator.org/zedz/ [accessed June 2022].

New York City DOT. (2020) *Electric Bicycles & More*. Available from https://www1.nyc.gov/html/dot/html/bicyclists/ebikes.shtml [accessed October 2022].

Pham, H.T. and Lee, H. (2019) Analyzing the Costs and Benefits of Installing Unmanned Parcel Lockers: Focusing on Residential Complexes in Korea. *Journal of International Logistics and Trade*, 17, 43–54. https://doi.org/10.24006/jilt.2019.17.2.002.

Ranjbari, A., Diehl, C., Dalla Chiara, G., Goodchild, A. (2022). Improving Delivery Efficiency and Understanding User Behavior through Common Carrier Parcel Lockers. 9th Metrans International Urban Freight conference, May 25–27, Long Beach, CA. Available from: https://depts.washington.edu/sctlctr/sites/default/files/research_slides/andisheh_ranjbari-0.pdf [accessed May 2022].

Rudolph, C. and Gruber, J. (2017). Cargo Cycles in Commercial Transport: Potentials, Constraints, and Recommendations. *Research in Transportation Business & Management*, 24, 26–36.

Seattle's Clean Transportation Electrification Blueprint – Electrifying Our Transportation System (2021). *Seattle Department of Transportation*. Available from: https://www.seattle.gov/documents/Departments/OSE/ClimateDocs/TE/TE%20Blueprint%20-%20March%202021.pdf [accessed May 2022].

Urban Freight Lab. (2020) *Common MicroHub Research Project: Research Scan*. University of Washington, Supply Chain Transportation and Logistics Center. Available from: https://depts.washington.edu/sctlctr/sites/default/files/research_pub_files/SCTL-Microhub-Research-Scan.pdf [accessed October 2022].

Urban Freight Lab. (2021). *The Seattle Neighborhood Delivery Hub Pilot Project: An Evaluation of the Operational Impacts of a Neighborhood Delivery Hub Model on Last-Mile Delivery*. University of Washington, Supply Chain Transportation and Logistics Center. Available from: https://depts.washington.edu/sctlctr/sites/default/files/research_pub_files/UFL-Sea-Neighborhood-Delivery-Hub_Final-Report.pdf [accessed March 2022].

U.S. Census Bureau. (2021). *Quarterly Retail E-Commerce Sales*; 2021.

Van Duin, J.H.R., Wiegmans, B.W., van Arem, B., and van Amstel, Y. (2020). From Home Delivery to Parcel Lockers: A Case Study in Amsterdam. *Transportation Research Procedia*, 46, 37–44. https://doi.org/10.1016/j.trpro.2020.03.161.

Van Rooijen, T. and Quak, H. (2010). Local Impacts of a New Urban Consolidation Centre – the Case of Binnenstadservice.nl. *Procedia – Social and Behavioral Sciences*, 2(3), 5967–5979. https://doi.org/10.1016/j.sbspro.2010.04.011.

Verlinde, S., Macharis, C., Milan, L. and Kin, B. (2014) Does a Mobile Depot Make Urban Deliveries Faster, More Sustainable and More Economically Viable: Results of a Pilot Test in Brussels. *Transportation Research Procedia*, 4, 361–373. https://doi.org/10.1016/j.trpro.2014.11.027.

Verlinghieri, E. Itova, I., Collignon, N., and Aldred, R. (2021) *The Promise of Low-Carbon Freight – Benefits of Cargo Bikes in London*. Possible. Available from: https://static1.squarespace.com/static/5d30896202a18c0001b49180/t/61091edc3acfda2f4af7d97f/1627987694676/The+Promise+of+Low-Carbon+Freight.pdf [accessed October 2022].

World Economic Forum (2020). *The Future of the Last-Mile Ecosystem*. Available from: https://www.weforum.org/reports/the-future-of-the-last-mile-ecosystem [accessed June 2022].

PART E

Sustainability

23
CLIMATE CHANGE AND URBAN LOGISTICS

Maria Attard

Introduction

It has become necessary to contextualize all human activities and the carbon emissions that are generated within the debate about climate change. Urban logistics, within the greater context of freight transport, is no exception. The increase in activity and impact match the growing global population, economic growth and consumption. Climate change is defined as long-term shifts in temperatures and weather patterns. These shifts are influenced by natural events, such as variations in the solar cycle; however, since the 1800s, the major force to drive climate change has been the burning of fossil fuels to support human activities (IPCC, 2021). According to the Intergovernmental Panel on Climate Change, many of the changes observed so far have been unprecedented in thousands of years and some of them, such as the rise in sea level, will be difficult to reverse over hundreds to thousands of years in the future (IPCC, 2021).

Increasing consumption and demand for goods and services as a result of economic growth, including the recovery from the current COVID-19 pandemic (see Chapter 29), global population increase and the increased digitalization of activities and services have the potential to increase further carbon emissions. These could well counterbalance any climate change mitigation gains that would be achieved as a result of technology and innovation in energy generation, product development and most importantly in transport and distribution of people and goods. The IPCC Sixth Assessment Report (AR6) is clear in (i) attributing the widespread and rapid changes we are experiencing in the atmosphere, ocean, cryosphere and biosphere to human influence; (ii) describing the scale of recent changes across the climate system as unprecedented over many centuries to many thousands of years; and (iii) providing the evidence of observed changes in weather and climate extremes in every region of the globe with heatwaves, heavy precipitation, droughts and tropical cyclones, all attributed to human influence (IPCC, 2021).

The changes to the weather and climate go beyond the rise in global temperatures, as climate change is having different effects in all regions of the world (UCAR, 2022). A number of changes can now be observed including the intensification of the water cycle, bringing more intense rainfall and flooding, as well as drought in many regions of the world. Coastal areas will experience a rise in sea level, increasing the frequency of coastal flooding and coastal erosion. Islands in the Pacific Ocean already report losses of land to sea level rise with the potential for them disappearing increasingly becoming a reality. Much of Kiribati in the South Pacific, for example, is at serious risk of inundation by 2100 (Cauchi et al., 2021; Sabūnas et al., 2021). Evidence points to the loss of Arctic sea ice (see NSIDC, 2022), as well as the melting of glaciers and ice sheets. Alongside the thawing of the permafrost, these can further accelerate global warming. The changing temperatures will undoubtedly affect the oceans with more frequent heatwaves and ocean warming, acidification and potential reduced oxygen levels to support marine life. And finally, it is also evident that climate change effects will be greater in cities where heatwaves will be hotter, longer and heavy precipitation will flood cities more often, especially those already struggling with sea level rise.

In summer of 2021, the United Nations Chief António Guterres dubbed the IPCC AR6 scientific report as a "code red for humanity" (UN, 2021). The IPCC scientists warn of global warming of 2°C being exceeded during the 21st century and that unless a rapid and deep reduction in CO_2 and other greenhouse gas emissions occur, achieving the goals of the 2015 Paris agreement, of limiting the increase in global temperature to 1.5°C, will be impossible. The report continues to state that net anthropogenic greenhouse gas emissions have increased since 2010 across all major sectors globally, with an increasing share of emissions attributed to urban areas.

Climate Science and What It Is Telling Us

Following the publication of scientific assessment reports by the Intergovernmental Panel on Climate Change (IPCC), up to the sixth published in 2021, there has been mounting evidence that the warming of the climate system is unequivocal (IPCC, 2021) and that it is due to human activity and influence (IPCC, 2021). The problem arises from (i) the extraction and burning of vast amounts of fossil fuel (coal, oil and gas) at a fast pace year on year; (ii) the deforestation of much of the earth's land surface, releasing CO_2 from vegetation and removing the opportunity for forests to absorb CO_2; and (iii) due to all of this, the accumulation of CO_2 in the atmosphere in a relatively short period of time. The Keeling Curve is the daily record of global atmospheric CO_2 concentrations, maintained by the Scripps Institution of Oceanography at University of California San Diego which shows the steep rise from 250 ppm in 1850 to 421.26 ppm on 30 May 2022, time of writing of this chapter. When this is put into the planetary context, over thousands of years, it becomes evident that we have shifted critically away from the natural cycles of the earth (Figure 23.1).

CO_2 is very effective at trapping heat in the atmosphere and the greenhouse gas effect demonstrated by John Tyndall in the 1860s describes the connection between CO_2 concentrations in the air mass and its temperature. However, it is not only CO_2 that warms the earth's atmosphere. Other gases with global warming potential (GWP) include methane (CH_4), nitrous oxide (N_2O) and a variety of hydrofluorocarbons (HFCs) reinforcing the effects of CO_2 to varying degrees. The potential of these gases depends on the energy they absorb and the length of time in the atmosphere with some, having a much greater impact than CO_2 over 100 years. CH_4 is 21 times, N_2O is 310 times and HFC123 is 11,700 times greater (UNFCCC, 2022). These pollutants are emitted in lower volumes than CO_2 however as the earth's atmosphere warms up the potential of releasing the frozen methane currently trapped in the tundra and under the sea bed might impact greatly the natural cycles of climate change.

A number of these tipping elements were initially defined by Lenton et al. (2008) as being large-scale components of the Earth system and having a significant impact on

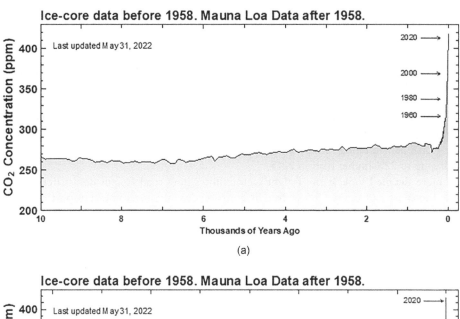

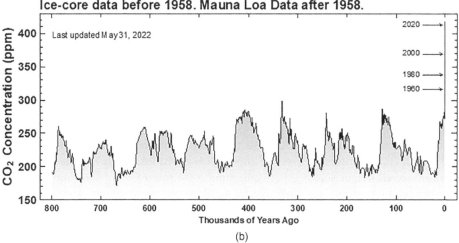

Figure 23.1 CO$_2$ concentrations (a) over 10,000 years and (b) over 800 thousand years

Source: Scripps Institution of Oceanography (2022); Keeling et al. (2001); MacFarling Meure et al. (2006); Lüthi et al. (2008). https://keelingcurve.ucsd.edu/permissions-and-data-sources/

climate change. Their evaluation included an assessment of their tipping point – the threshold at which a tiny perturbation can qualitatively alter the state or development of a system. These included components such as the Amazon Forest, the Indian Monsoon, the Boreal Forest and others. Changes to any of these elements, such as the dieback of the world's forests, have been identified as "tipping points" able to trigger a cycle of climatic change and causing irreversible damage, and in turn, posing a major environmental threat to humans (Lenton et al, 2008; Schellnhuber, 2009). For most tipping elements, changes and their impacts have started already being observed and measured (see, e.g., Price et al., 2013 for impacts on boreal forests; Boulton et al., 2022 for impacts on the Amazon rainforest).

Climate Change and Freight Transport

Fifteen per cent of the total global emissions for 2019 were attributed to passenger and freight transport, with CO_2 accounting for 96% of all greenhouse gas emissions from transport operations alone (IPCC, 2022). The International Energy Agency (IEA) (2018) attribute 8% of global greenhouse gas emissions to freight transport, whilst the International Transport Forum (ITF) (2019) estimates this total to go up to 11% when warehouses and ports are included. Freight was responsible for 42% of all transport emissions in 2019 and it continued to rise to 50% in 2020 because of the sharp fall in passenger transport due to COVID-19. In addition, growing economies, like those in Asia, Africa and Latin America are expected to triple global demand for goods by 2050 which will increase twofold the emissions from this activity, up to 22% higher than in 2015.

A more detailed look at the freight sector shows how road freight dominates surface goods transport and emits 65% of freight emissions, whilst maritime transport accounts for around 20% of the CO_2 emissions from freight transport (ITF, 2021). Transport by rail and inland waterways emit the least CO_2 emissions but they only accounted for 30% of the global surface transport in 2015. According to ITF (2021), freight transport by rail experienced a decline in the OECD countries, the EU and the United States in 2019. A stable outlook was maintained with respect to air cargo which is by far the most carbon-intensive freight mode, and caters for high-value and lightweight goods. Air freight remained stable for the first half of this decade but started to increase in the second half (ICAO, 2018 in ITF, 2021).

There is indeed a country and regional specificity to the amounts of emissions released by freight transport, as this is dependent on a number of factors including age and technology of the fleets. The transport sector in the United States, for example, accounts for nearly 60% of NOx (Nitrogen Oxides) and 22% of VOC (Volatile Organic Compounds; Giuliano, 2019). Twenty-three per cent of all greenhouse gas emissions from road transport comes from freight movements. From 1990 to 2017, the total GHG emissions from transport increased by 22% with truck emissions increasing almost 90% (US EPA, 2019). This is due to the growth in overall freight volumes, the continuing trend toward using faster modes, rising congestion, and the technology challenges of developing cleaner medium and heavy-duty vehicles (Giuliano, 2019).

In Europe, the total demand for inland freight transport by road, rail, inland waterways and pipelines, increased by 22% between 2000 and 2019. In 2019 alone, 2,411 billion tonne-kilometre were transported in the EU. The share of road transport in this demand grew from 68% in 2000 to 73% in 2019 (EEA, 2022). The European Union is the world's third-largest emitter of greenhouse gases and has therefore a crucial role in reaching climate change targets. Since 1990 transport emissions in this region have grown by 33%. And whilst passenger cars and vans are the greatest contributors, heavy-duty vehicles carrying primarily goods are the second-greatest contributor to greenhouse gas emissions (15% and 5%, respectively, in 2018; Buysse and Miller, 2021).

Contribution of Urban Logistics to Climate Change

The UN estimates that already 55% of the global population is urban and this figure will continue to increase to 68% by 2050 (UN DESA, 2018). Cities will continue to grow as activity hubs and centres of consumption. They will also be sources of greenhouse gas emissions and be impacted heavily by climate change effects. The need for managing holistically the urban domain will grow in importance, as will the need to manage and reduce the environmental burden of urban deliveries as they increase with growing population densities and contribute to the increasing congestion in cities (Wygonik et al., 2015).

Urban delivery trips are by definition short, numerous and carry small loads. The increase in urban logistics brought about by changing consumer patterns has implications on the freight transport system and last-mile services, especially with the growing concern for home deliveries which are carried out with little to no route optimization, in a fragmented manner, and delivering smaller and smaller goods. Indeed, home deliveries often include repeated or failed deliveries, returns and significant waste throughout the supply chain (Wygonik and Goodchild, 2018). Indeed, Chakravarty (2014) estimated that nearly 30% of products bought online are returned for some reason or another (see Chapter 11 on Retail). Such urban delivery trips represent only 3% of the total freight activity but account for around 20% of all freight emissions. Indeed as global freight activity fell by 4% in 2020 due to the COVID-19 pandemic restrictions, emissions from the sector dropped only by 1% due to an increase in high-emitting urban deliveries (ITF, 2021).

Urban freight occurs at a local or regional scale from terminals to final destinations and end consumers, and it is also the main user of urban space and is central to the complexity of cities and the way they function. The increase in urban freight of 7% registered between 2019 and 2020 was primarily driven by the pandemic and the increase in e-commerce and home deliveries. There is still uncertainty as to how this will continue developing in a post-pandemic world. E-commerce and home deliveries have also shifted the activity space from retail and shopping centres to homes and more sensitive residential areas (Visser et al., 2014). Urban freight contributes highly to carbon emissions amongst all transport modes, except aviation (ITF, 2021). As such the European Union's goal to achieve carbon-neutral city logistics by 2030 (European Commission, 2013) will require bold actions, some of which are quite restrictive to control the emissions from the movement of goods in the urban areas.

It is also evident from the literature that with increasing attention being paid to sustainability and climate change, the focus on urban freight has increased within the wider discussions on urban mobility. Many local authorities however still ignore freight and logistics in their urban planning (Cui et al., 2015; Bjørgen et al., 2019). At the same time, climate policies are including more efficient and environmentally friendly technology and solutions that bring together various actors within the wider social and technological systems. Perhaps a realization that one solution, for example, shifting vehicles fleets to electric drive, will not be enough and that different actors working at different levels will be required to align policies, regulations and practices (Geels, 2012; Dijk et al., 2019).

Climate Change Impacts in Urban Logistics – Policy and Actions

The urgency to cut emissions from all sectors, including urban logistics is clear and is mandated in a number of documents that predict a growth in the freight sector, but at the same time set very high ambitions of cutting greenhouse gas emissions to mitigate climate change. As stated earlier, the European Commission has set the goal of achieving CO_2-free city logistics by 2030 (European Commission, 2013) and this will reflect in a number of policy and planning approaches to deliver goods in an efficient and clean manner. But governments are not all expected to reduce the same amount of emissions, as global efforts are dictated by what is termed as the principle of "Common but Differentiated Responsibilities". This was a key decision of the 1992 UN Conference on Environment and Development in Rio de

Janeiro where countries shared the responsibility for the environmental problems however their contributions should reflect the different stages of economic development (McKinnon, 2018).

Over the years, as the challenges of urban logistics unfolded (Cherrett et al., 2012; Macharis and Kin, 2017), increasing urban freight volumes have continued to contribute to greenhouse gas emissions, congestion and challenging (urban) logistics. Bjørgen and Ryghaug (2022) report on how the Norwegian cities of Oslo, Trondheim and Bodø all struggle with increases in urban freight and deliveries, affecting their ability to achieve climate goals.

According to the IPCC AR6 Working Group III report, digital technologies have an important contribution to make to mitigating climate change in a number of sectors (IPCC, 2022). Technologies such as sensors, drones, robotics and 3-D printing all play a role in changing structures of production and distribution in our cities (see, e.g., Melo, 2022). Birtchnell and Urry (2013), for example, discuss the future of manufacturing and transport of goods in light of the developments in 3-D printing and the impact this might have on global supply chains. All these technologies allow for the adoption of low-emission technologies also in urban contexts.

The promise of further cuts in urban emissions from the electrification of transport systems in urban areas is certainly receiving a lot of attention both at the supranational and national levels. The European Union is increasing its efforts to end the importation of internal combustion engine vehicles (termed more colloquially, the end of ICE), and with the publication of the EU Green Deal and Fit for 55 package – the EU's plan for a green transition, there is considerable emphasis on electrification. Indeed, many reported a strong presence and focus on electrification even at the Glasgow Committee of Parties (COP) meeting in 2021, with possibly too little attention given to non-polluting, non-motorized forms of transport (see Wilson, 2021), also indicated by some as being ideal and truly green transport options for urban deliveries (Schliwa et al., 2015; Comi and Savchenko, 2021; Jaller et al., 2021). At national levels, governments are tirelessly promoting electrification through fiscal incentives to support a shift to electric mobility, investment in public charging infrastructures and regulations. In 2019, the United Kingdom published its strategy for Electric Vehicle Charging in Residential and Non-Residential Buildings, pushing further the electrification agenda (Department for Transport, 2018). Similarly the EU with its proposal for the revision of the Energy Performance in Building regulations which are set to include requirements for extensive electric vehicle charging infrastructure to be provided in parking areas in new build or renovations (European Commission, 2021).

The projections made by the International Energy Agency (2021) show how electrification and technology improvements will enable average heavy trucks to be almost three times more efficient in 2050. In their Net Zero Scenario, the sales of battery-electric and fuel-cell trucks rise above 50% of the overall truck market by 2030 and in parallel, the efficiency of conventional heavy trucks also improve by one-third by 2030. By 2050 battery-electric and fuel-cell trucks dominate the global fleet IEA (2021). This is a highly ambitious target considering the low uptake of electric vehicles in general, even in highly developed economic regions such as Europe (see Figure 23.2).

The impact of change in the sector of urban logistics could be considerable. And literature shows how, in principle, some of the emerging practices of online shopping and home deliveries reduce personal travel demand and thus reduce car trips for shopping (Cairns, 2005; Wygonik and Goodchild, 2018). It is also evident however that innovations must be significant to be effective (Siikavirta et al., 2008; Melo et al., 2014). In addition, further research

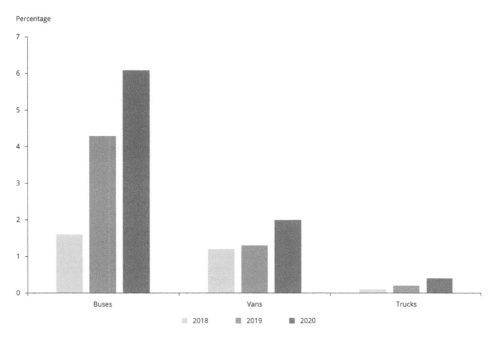

Figure 23.2 Share of electrically chargeable vans, buses and trucks in new vehicle sales in the EU-27, 2018–2020

Source: European Automobile Manufacturers' Association (ACEA) in EEA (2022)

is needed into the complexities that embody shopping, trip chaining and overall patterns of consumption and delivery to better capture and substantiate the emission reduction and climate change impacts.

Conclusions

The evidence about the risks associated with climate change in urban areas is clear and stronger than ever. Many cities globally have already experienced effects related to global warming and climate change in the form of heatwaves, flooding or drought, and sea level rise. There is indeed an urgency to limit the emissions and shift to green consumption. Urban logistics are a critical infrastructure within cities and to date, they function primarily on fossil fuels and contribute significantly to the detrimental quality of the urban environment and challenge the ambitions for emission reductions. The literature in this field is growing; however the world is also changing, and fast. The COVID-19 pandemic has accelerated growth and changes in urban logistics, first through the health restrictions put in place in most countries limiting the mobility of people, and secondly through the rise in e-commerce and home deliveries.

Research in the field has been for some time pointing towards the need for better management, coordination and the implementation of innovative technologies to handle complexities and increase efficiency. There is however the need to better understand the post-pandemic reality for many cities both in the developed and developing world. Much of this chapter has focused on the Global North where indeed much innovation is happening. The need for transfer of knowledge, technology and practices to the Global South will be critical to achieve the ambitious climate change targets (see Chapter 25). As was discussed earlier, achieving "global" change will be necessary to curtail emissions effectively.

Much of the future research agenda will be dictated by the climate emergency. Evidence to support decision-making and policy will be required to ensure effective deployment and replicability at a relatively fast pace to achieve the 2030 and 2050 targets. There is indeed scope for much research into the environmental impacts of supply chains, new consumption patterns, distributional effects, freight transport geographies, individual behaviour patterns and ultimately logistics to support the ever-growing challenge of climate change.

References

Birtchnell, T. and Urry, J. (2013). Fabricating futures and the movement of objects. *Mobilities*, 8, 388–405.
Bjørgen, A. and Ryghaug, M. (2022). Integration of urban freight transport in city planning: Lesson learned. *Transportation Research Part D: Transport and Environment*, 107, 103310.
Bjørgen, A., Seter, H., Kristiansen, T. and Pitera, K. (2019). The potential for coordinated logistics planning at the local level: A Norwegian in-depth study of public and private stakeholders. *Journal of Transport Geography*, 76(4), 34–41.
Boulton, C.A., Lenton, T.M. and Boers, N. (2022). Pronounced loss of Amazon rainforest resilience since the early 2000s. *Nature Climate Change*, 12, 271–278.
Buysse, C. and Miller, J. (2021). *Transport Could Burn Up the EU's Entire Carbon Budget*. The International Council on Clean Transport. Available at https://theicct.org/transport-could-burn-up-the-eus-entire-carbon-budget/ [Accessed 16 June 2022].
Cairns, S. (2005). Delivering supermarket shopping: More or less traffic? *Transport Reviews*, 25(1), 51–84.
Cauchi, J.P., Moncada, S., Bambrick, H. and Correa-Velez, I. (2021). Coping with environmental hazards and shocks in Kiribati: Experiences of climate change by atoll communities in the Equatorial Pacific. *Environmental Development*, 37, 100549.
Chakravarty, A.K. (2014). *Supply Chain Transformation: Evolving with Emerging Business Paradigms*. Springer. London.
Cherrett, T., Allen, J., McLeod, F., Maynard, S., Hickford, A. and Browne, M. (2012). Understanding urban freight activity – key issues for freight planning. *Journal of Transport Geography*, 24C, 22–32.
Comi, A. and Savchenko, L. (2021). Last mile delivering: Analysis of environment-friendly transport. *Sustainable Cities and Society*, 74, 103213.
Cui, J., Dodson, J. and Hall, P.V. (2015). Planning for urban freight transport: An overview. *Transport Reviews*, 35(5), 583–598.
Department for Transport (2018). *Electric Vehicle Charging in Residential and Non-Residential Buildings*. HM Government, UK. Available at https://assets.publishing.service.gov.uk/government/uploads/system/uploads/attachment_data/file/818810/electric-vehicle-charging-in-residential-and-non-residential-buildings.pdf [Accessed 16 June 2022].
Dijk, M., Backhaus, J., Wieser, H. and Kemp, R. (2019). Policies tackling the 'web of constraints' on resource efficient practices: The case of mobility. *Sustainability: Science, Practice, and Policy*, 15(1), 62–81.
EEA (2022). *Transport and Environment Report 2021 | Decarbonising Road Transport - The Role of Vehicles, Fuels and Transport Demand*. Report (02/2022). European Environment Agency. Available at https://www.eea.europa.eu/publications/transport-and-environment-report-2021 [Accessed 16 June 2022].
European Commission (2013). A call to action on urban Logistics. Available at https://smartcities.at/wp-content/uploads/sites/3/A-call-to-action-on-urban-logistics.pdf [Accessed 16 May 2022].
European Commission (2021). Proposal for a Directive of the European Parliament and of the Council on the energy performance of buildings (recast). COM(2021) 802 final, 2021/0426(COD). Available at https://eur-lex.europa.eu/legal-content/EN/TXT/?uri=CELEX%3A52021PC0802&qid=1641802763889 [Accessed 16 May 2022].
Geels, F.W. (2012). A socio-technical analysis of low-carbon transitions: Introducing the multi-level perspective into transport studies. *Journal of Transport Geography*, 24, 471–482.

Giuliano, G. (2019). Freight flows in cities. *International Encyclopedia of Transportation*, Vol. 3. Elsevier. Oxford, 168–177.
ICAO (2018). *ICAO Annual Report of the Council, 2017*. International Civil Aviation Organization. Available at https://www.icao.int/annual-report-2017/Documents/Forms/AllItems.aspx [Accessed 16 June 2022].
IEA (2018). *CO2 Emissions from Fuel Combustion 2018*. International Energy Agency. Available at https://doi.org/10.1787/co2_fuel-2018-en [Accessed 16 June 2022].
IEA (2021). *Net Zero by 2050 Hinges on a Global Push to Increase Energy Efficiency*. International Energy Agency. Available at https://www.iea.org/articles/net-zero-by-2050-hinges-on-a-global-push-to-increase-energy-efficiency [Accessed 16 June 2022].
IPCC (2021). Working Group I Contribution to the Sixth Assessment Report: Summary for policy makers. Intergovernmental Panel on Climate Change. Available at https://www.ipcc.ch/assessment-report/ar6/ [Accessed 16 May 2022].
IPCC (2022). Working Group III contribution to the Sixth Assessment Report: Summary for policy makers. Intergovernmental Panel on Climate Change. Available at https://www.ipcc.ch/assessment-report/ar6/ [Accessed 16 May 2022].
ITF (2019). *International Transport Forum Transport Outlook 2019*. International Transport Forum, OECD. Available at https://doi.org/10.1787/transp_outlook-en-2019-en [Accessed 16 June 2022].
ITF (2021). *International Transport Forum Transport Outlook 2021*. International Transport Forum, OECD. Available at https://doi.org/10.1787/16826a30-en [Accessed 16 June 2022].
Jaller, M., Pineda, L., Ambrose, H. and Kendall, A. (2021). Empirical analysis of the role of incentives in zero-emission last-mile deliveries in California. *Journal of Cleaner Production*. 317, 128353.
Keeling, C.D., Piper, S.C., Bacastow, R.B., Wahlen, M., Whorf, T.P., Heimann, M. and Meijer, H.A. (2001). Exchanges of atmospheric CO_2 and $13CO_2$ with the terrestrial biosphere and oceans from 1978 to 2000. I. Global aspects, SIO Reference Series, 01–06, Scripps Institution of Oceanography, San Diego.
Lenton, T.M., Held, H., Kriegler, E., Hall, J.W., Lucht, W., Rahmstorf, S. and Schellnhuber, H.J. (2008). Tipping elements in the Earth's climate system. *Proceedings of the National Academy of Sciences*, 105, 1786–1793.
Lüthi, D., Le Floch, M., Bereiter, B., Blunier, T., Barnola, J.-M., Siegenthaler, U., Raynaud, D., Jouzel, J., Fischer, H., Kawamura, K. and Stocker, T.F. (2008). High-resolution carbon dioxide concentration record 650,000-800,000 years before present. *Nature*, 453, 379–382.
MacFarling Meure, C., Etheridge, D., Trudinger, C., Steele, P., Langenfelds, R., van Ommen, T., Smith, A. and Elkins, J. (2006). The Law Dome CO2, CH4 and N2O ice core records extended to 2000 years BP. *Geophysical Research Letters*, 33, 14, L14810 10.1029/2006GL026152.
Macharis, C. and Kin, B. (2017). The 4A's of sustainable city distribution: Innovative solutions and challenges ahead. *International Journal of Sustainable Transportation*, 11(2), 59–71.
McKinnon, A. (2018). *Decarbonising Logistics. Distributing Goods in a Low-Carbon World*. Kogan Page. London.
Melo, S., Baptista, P. and Costa, A. (2014). The cost and effectiveness of sustainable city logistics policies using small electric vehicles. Chapter 12. In Macharis, C., Melo, S., Woxenius, J. & van Lier, R. (eds.) *Sustainable Logistics*. Transport and Sustainability Volume 6. Emerald Publishing. Bingley, 295–314.
Melo, S. and de Jesus Ferreira, L. (2022). Pandemic lasting effects on freight networks: Challenges and directions from cities and industry. Chapter 14. In Attard, M. and Mulley, C. (eds.) *Transport and Pandemic Experiences*. Transport and Sustainability Volume 17. Emerald Publishing. Bingley, 257–269.
NSIDC (2022). Artic Sea Ice News and Analysis. National Snow & Ice Data Centre. Available at http://nsidc.org/arcticseaicenews/ [Accessed 16 May 2022].
Price, D.T., Alfaro, R.I., Brown, K.J., Flannigan, M.D., Fleming, R.A., Hogg, E.H., Girardin, M.P., Lakusta, T., Johnston, M., McKenney, D.W., Pedlar, J.H., Stratton, T., Sturrock, R.N., Thompson, I.D., Trofymow, J.A. and Venier, L.A. (2013). Anticipating the consequences of climate change for Canada's boreal forest ecosystems. *Environmental Reviews*, 21(4), 322–365.
Sabūnas, A., Miyashita, T., Fukui, N., Shimura, T. and Mori, N. (2021). Impact assessment of storm surge and climate change-enhanced sea level rise on atoll nations: A case study of the Tarawa Atoll, Kiribati. *Frontiers in Built Environment*, 7. Available at https://www.frontiersin.org/article/10.3389/fbuil.2021.752599 [Accessed 16 May 2022].

Schellnhuber, H.J. (2009). Tipping elements in the Earth System. *Proceedings of the National Academy of Sciences*, 106, 20561–20563.

Schliwa, G., Armitage, R., Aziz, S., Evans, J. and Rhoades, J. (2015). Sustainable city logistics - Making cargo cycles viable for urban freight transport. *Research in Transportation Business and Management*, 15(1), 50–57.

Scripps Institution of Oceanography (2022). The keeling curve. Available at https://keelingcurve.ucsd.edu/ [Accessed 16 May 2022].

Siikavirta, H., Punakivi, M., Kärkkäinen, M. and Linnanen, L. (2008). Effects of E-commerce on greenhouse gas emissions: A case study of grocery home delivery in Finland. *Journal of Industrial Ecology*, 6(2), 83–97.

UCAR (2022). Climate change: Regional impacts. University Corporation for Atmospheric Research. Available at https://scied.ucar.edu/learning-zone/climate-change-impacts/regional [Accessed 10 August 2022].

UN (2021). Secretary-general calls latest IPCC Climate Report 'Code Red for Humanity', Stressing 'Irrefutable' evidence of human influence. United Nations Press Release Available at https://www.un.org/press/en/2021/sgsm20847.doc.htm [Accessed 16 June 2022].

UNFCCC (2022). Global warming potentials. United Nations Framework Convention on Climate Change. Available at https://unfccc.int/process/transparency-and-reporting/greenhouse-gas-data/greenhouse-gas-data-unfccc/global-warming-potentials [Accessed 16 May 2022].

UN DESA (2018). 2018 Revision of the world urbanization prospects. Population Division, United Nations Department for Economic and Social Affairs. Available at https://www.un.org/development/desa/en/news/population/2018-revision-of-world-urbanization-prospects.html [Accessed 16 June 2022].

US EPA (2019). Fast facts: US transportation sector greenhouse gas emissions, 1990–2017. US Environmental Protection Agency, Office of Transportation and Air Quality. Available at https://nepis.epa.gov/Exe/ZyPDF.cgi?Dockey=P100WUHR.pdf [Accessed 16 May 2022].

Visser, J., Nemoto, T. and Browne, M. (2014). Home delivery and the impacts on urban freight transport: A review. *Procedia Social and Behavioural Sciences*, 125, 15–27.

Wilson, K. (2021). COP26 'Transport Day' ignores everything but eVs. Streetsblog USA. Available at https://usa.streetsblog.org/2021/11/10/cop26-transport-day-ignores-everything-but-evs/ [Accessed 16 June 2022].

Wygonik, E. and Goodchild, A.V. (2018). Urban form and last-mile goods movement: Factors affecting vehicle miles travelled and emissions. *Transportation Research Part D: Transport and Environment*, 61, 217–229.

Wygonik, E., Bassok, A., Goodchild, A., McCormack, E. and Carlson, D. (2015). Smart growth and goods movement: Emerging research agendas. *Journal of Urbanism: International Research on Placemaking and Urban Sustainability*, 8(2), 115–132.

24
DECARBONIZING ROAD FREIGHT AND ALTERNATIVE FUELS FOR URBAN LOGISTICS

Genevieve Giuliano and Sue Dexter

Introduction

Road freight is a significant and growing source of greenhouse gas (GHG) emissions worldwide. Globally the transport sector accounts for about 15% of all GHGs; the share is higher in high-income countries. For example, the transport share in the US accounts for 27% of all GHGs, with medium and heavy-duty trucks accounting for about one-quarter of transport sector emissions. Emissions from trucks will have to be reduced to achieve GHG reduction goals. This chapter examines the decarbonization of medium and heavy-duty trucks. Our basic premise is that goods movement is essential for both people and the economy, and demand for goods movement will continue to grow. A broad range of technology and policy solutions is considered, with a particular focus on alternative fuels as the strategy with both the greatest potential and greatest risks.

Growth of Urban Freight

Trucks are the workhorse of surface goods movement; they transport two-thirds of all goods by weight in the United States and account for nearly all urban last-mile deliveries (U.S. Department of Transportation Bureau of Transportation Statistics, 2022a). Short-haul (regional, city-wide) and long-haul (interregional, interstate) trucking are increasing and are expected to grow 31% by 2045 in the United States (U.S. Department of Transportation Bureau of Transportation Statistics, 2019, 2022b). Globally, road freight (ton-kilometers) is expected to increase by 300% from 2015 to 2050, with non-OECD countries having the most significant impact due to rapid population growth and often unplanned urbanization (International Transport Forum, 2019). Dar es Salaam, Tanzania, presents one example of the potential growth of a city in the Global South and its implications for truck demand. See the textbox.

Highlight on Dar es Salaam: Major African Seaport and Transportation Center

By 2050, the urbanized population is expected to increase by 2.5 billion people, with 88% of the increase anticipated in emerging markets of Africa and Asia. Dar es Salaam, United Republic of Tanzania, is one of these cities, growing at previously unseen rates (see Figure 24.1). Over the past 12 years, the urban population has almost doubled to 7.4 million and is expected to double again by 2035 (Rosen, 2019). Unprecedented growth in predominantly informal settlements has led to congestion, land scarcity, and uncontrolled sprawl. Transportation infrastructure is constantly playing catch up. Urban development is concentrated along "finger" transportation corridors, but limited connectivity, poor roads, and crowded spaces with limited parking restrict commerce activity. Trucks and vans are the preferred methods of freight movement in the city and nationally, but vehicles are older and more polluting than models used in the Global North. Freight operations are, on average, highly inefficient. Focusing decarbonization efforts on fast-growing megacities like Dar es Salaam should be a priority to limit global GHGs and other climate change toxins; however, financing is a significant barrier to implementation (United Nations Climate Change, 2022).

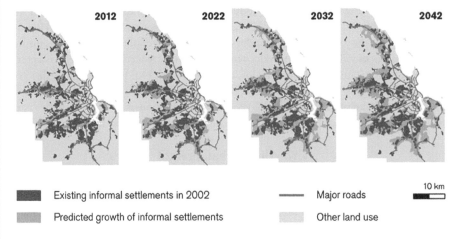

Figure 24.1 Dar es Salaam projected growth of informal settlements if past trends continue
Source: Abebe, F.K., Modelling Informal Settlement Growth in Dar es Salaam (MSc thesis). Used with permission (Abebe, 2011)

Trucking demand is increasing worldwide due to increased consumer demand (a result of increased per capita income), continued demand for velocity in the supply chain, and more complex and time-dependent distribution systems associated with e-commerce. Home deliveries fueled by e-commerce and online shopping have exploded worldwide since the COVID-19 pandemic, and they are here to stay. For a select group of countries (including the US), the UN estimated e-commerce rose to 19% of all retail sales in 2020 (United Nations News, 2021).

The rise in direct consumer deliveries has changed the urban delivery landscape. First, the number of delivery vehicles has increased, adding to already congested city streets and generating more demand for scarce curb space. New York provides one example. The New York Times said e-commerce brings "chaos to N.Y. streets" from increased pedestrian safety risk and traffic flow. Parking, which has always been a problem, has become near impossible as delivery vehicles park illegally (New York Times, 2019). Given the demands of delivery vehicles, ride-hailing services, transit, bike share, and parking, how to manage curb space has become a major urban planning problem.

Second, the demand for in-city warehouse and distribution space has increased. As cities grew and land became more expensive in the core, warehouse distribution moved outwards to the periphery. However, this distribution model does not work for same-day or "instant" (2-hour) deliveries. Major online retailers require distribution hubs located closer to the population to be served. New models of service delivery have also emerged. "Quick commerce" which provides ultra-fast deliveries of food items and consumer goods, has rapidly developed since 2020. To make these fast deliveries possible, firms have opened small urban warehouses called "dark stores" close to demand while retaining their larger, more distant facilities (Dablanc, 2022).

Environmental Impacts

Whether freight originates from a city factory, distribution center, seaport, or inland rail terminal, medium and large trucks transport goods around and through the city center emitting carcinogenic air toxins in urban areas. Truck airborne gases, ground-level ozone, and particulate matter from nitrogen oxide, sulfur oxide, and unburned carbon particles have been linked to lung disease and other significant health impacts (Krivoshto et al., 2008). Emissions are also a recognized environmental justice problem because lower-income, minority populations tend to be exposed disproportionately. Figure 24.2 shows the global breakdown in transportation CO_2 emissions by mode as of 2018. Medium and heavy-duty trucks account for almost 30% of the total. As other sectors become less carbon-intensive, the transport share will increase. With the expected growth in goods movement by truck and the threat of climate change, alternative fuel trucks are necessary to reduce carbon emissions from goods movement.

Recognition of health impacts and the climate crisis motivates efforts to reduce emissions from the transport sector. Several countries have announced targets to end the sale of internal combustion passenger vehicles, and high-income countries are investing heavily

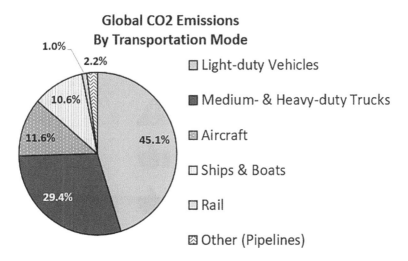

Figure 24.2 Global transportation CO_2 emissions
Source: International Energy Agency (Teter et al., 2020)

in alternative fuel technologies. All levels of government are using subsidies and other incentives to accelerate the adoption of zero-emission vehicles. Notable cases like Norway (where 65% of new 2021 car sales are zero emission) show what can be done via public policy (Norway Today, 2021). Progress has been much slower for medium and heavy-duty vehicles because these vehicles are dependent on high-energy-intensity fuels.

The remainder of this chapter includes options for decarbonization, some measurement issues, an in-depth discussion of alternative fuels, and a review of related policy strategies.

Options for Decarbonizing Urban Freight

What can be done to reduce freight GHG and toxic emissions? Figure 24.3 outlines the possibilities using the ASIF rule (Schipper et al., 2000). GHG emissions are a function of energy consumption. The ASIF rule lays out the options for reducing energy consumption: reducing goods movement, shifting to more energy-efficient modes, improving truck energy efficiency, and switching to low or zero-carbon fuels. As previously mentioned, urban freight demand is increasing and is forecast to continue to increase. Economies need efficient goods movement to thrive; limiting freight would raise prices and reduce access to consumer goods. Shifting to more energy-efficient modes has proven difficult because these modes (rail and water) are slower. Slower shipments add to holding costs and require longer delivery times. This is particularly true at the metropolitan level, where trip distances are relatively short. As a practical matter, if cities chose to heavily subsidize rail or water, they would need to build the infrastructure, which would be prohibitively costly. Trucks are the most efficient delivery mechanism because of their speed, flexibility, and use of roads and highways already built.

Increasing Efficiency

For these reasons, transport decarbonization strategies focus on increasing efficiency and using lower or zero-carbon fuels. Increasing efficiency often leads to eco-efficiencies: trucking benefits from reduced costs while society benefits from reduced GHG emissions. Eco-efficiency strategies are extensive and include more efficient routing and scheduling, load consolidation, pickup and delivery time windows, more fuel-efficient engines, designing trucks using new and lighter materials or tires with less friction, and many other strategies.

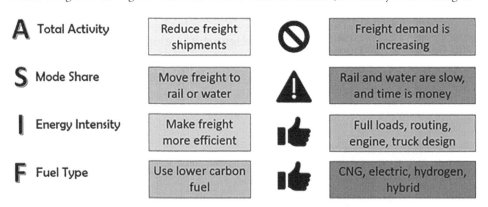

Figure 24.3 Alternatives for decarbonizing urban freight
Source: Adapted from Schipper et al. (2000)

Public policy plays a significant role in promoting efficiencies. Countries worldwide have established fuel efficiency standards for trucks as part of CO_2 reduction strategies, starting with Japan in 2006. China issued standards in 2012, India in 2017, and the EU in 2018 (Delgado and Gonzalez, 2018). US Federal Corporate Average Fuel Economy standards were applied to medium and heavy-duty vehicles starting in the 2014 model year. Estimates of increased fuel efficiency by 2018 range between 6% and 23% (TransportPolicy.net, 2021).

When benefits are not obvious to shippers or carriers, the public sector often serves as a facilitator when additional costs may be imposed on participants. For example, several demonstrations of off-peak deliveries were publicly funded to understand under what circumstances off-peak deliveries are feasible. A major barrier was the unwillingness of receivers to accept night deliveries because of the added labor costs. Strategies to address the problem included subsidies to receivers and digital security methods to allow deliveries when warehouses were closed (Holguín-Veras et al., 2014).

Alternative Fuel Vehicles

Although efficiency strategies can lead to significant energy and GHG savings, dependence on fossil fuel (primarily diesel) limits potential savings. Moving from fossil fuels is a challenge. As noted above, trucks require high-energy-intensity fuels to carry heavy loads along with the fuel. Currently, there is no alternative fuel technology that delivers both performance and price comparable to diesel. Consequently, the public sector is deeply involved in funding the science for creating alternative fuels, funding demonstrations, providing subsidies, establishing technology-forcing standards, and developing regulations that incentivize using zero or near-zero-emission vehicles. Because policies to reduce or eliminate diesel trucks have become a crucial part of climate mitigation targets, we examine these strategies in detail.

Evaluating Alternative Fuel Decarbonization Strategies

Careful evaluation of decarbonization strategies requires thoroughly examining outcomes and unintended consequences, as well as clearly stating what is to be measured.

What to Measure

Identifying the most effective decarbonization strategies depends on what is measured. It is often the case that motor vehicle policies focus on fuel consumption. For example, electric vehicles may be deemed zero emission in operation, but the source of electricity may not be. A full assessment of decarbonization strategies requires measuring emissions from the production of inputs to their ultimate disposal. A life cycle analysis (LCA) collects data about resource and energy use and their resulting by-products from the harvesting and transformation of raw materials into a finished good (or service). LCA also includes all interactions during the use of the product/service through disposal or recycling. "Cradle to grave" or "well to wheels" for transportation-related products are standard terms to describe the analysis.

The LCA approach is vital because "zero-emission technology vehicles" is misleading at best and a downright lie at worst. No vehicle is emission-free. Only recently have policymakers seen past the tailpipe. Electric cars are not clean unless the grid that powers them is clean. Hydrogen fuel is not clean when the hydrogen is produced from natural gas. Studies have shown that a midsized electric car powered from a fossil fuel grid is more polluting (from a lifecycle perspective) than an internal combustion car (Sobol and Dyjakon, 2020).

Operational Considerations

As this chapter is written, alternative fuel trucks (AFTs) include natural gas, battery electric, hydrogen fuel cell, hybrid, and biofuel. Each is in different stages of technology development, has different purchase prices and operating costs, and has unique performance characteristics. There are numerous considerations for replacing an internal combustion engine (ICE) truck with an AFT. For example, using a battery electric truck (BET) means a reduction in daily mileage and weight carried. The reduced capacity and range of BETs may require fleets to replace an existing diesel truck with more than one BET.

For businesses, the impact of this one-to-one-plus conversion is costly in terms of vehicles and drivers for those additional trucks, and it imposes constraints on routing of daily trips/tours. Yards may need to be reconfigured for charging equipment. Additional trucks on the road increase vehicle miles traveled (VMT) and contribute to congestion. Extra trucks also mean using more raw materials for manufacturing. Hydrogen, electric, or biofuels will require new fueling infrastructure and adequate supplies of fuel. For example, converting truck fleets to electric will generate a large increase in energy demand. In times when demand is near capacity with the potential for rolling blackouts, firms could be without energy to charge their vehicles. The resiliency of power grids must be guaranteed for operators to be confident in adopting BETs. Vehicle replacement before normal retirement may create tremendous waste by scrapping vehicles with significant useful lives. However, it is also possible that older trucks in the Global North will be exported to other economies to replace even older versions that are much more polluting.

Availability

Among the five types of alternative fuel vehicles currently available or under development, natural gas (LNG or CNG) is the most widely available. Natural gas, hybrid, and biodiesel trucks have similar operating characteristics to diesel. Natural gas and hybrids require different engine technology. Biodiesel is typically used as up to 20% blend fuel in conventional diesel trucks (U.S. Department of Energy, 2017). Using these fuels reduces particulate and hydrocarbon emissions. However, it does not eliminate GHG emissions in the use phase. BETs and hydrogen fuel cells do not generate GHGs in the use phase and therefore are viewed as "zero-emission" vehicles.

The availability of BETs is increasing. Major truck OEMs like Peterbilt, Kenworth, Volvo, Freightliner, and newer companies like Xos, Lion, and Nikola have released BET models (CALSTART Drive to Zero, 2022). Medium-duty BETs are in operation as part of many cities' short-haul fleets. Heavy-duty BETs are in demonstrations in short-haul markets. Hydrogen fuel cell trucks are still in development, with only a few in demonstration in the

Table 24.1 Summary of alternative fuel trucks, compared to conventional diesel

	Biodiesel blended	Natural gas	Hybrid	Battery electric	Hydrogen fuel cell
Available for purchase	Yes	Yes	Yes	Yes	No
Purchase price	Same	Slightly more	Slightly more	Two to four times more	Two to four times more
Infrastructure	Available	Available	Available	Need charging infrastructure	Need fueling infrastructure
Performance	Same	Same	Similar	Less range, more fueling	Similar
Maintenance and fuel costs	Same	Slightly more	Slightly more	Lower	Higher
Tailpipe emissions	Lower	Lower	Lower	None	None
Life cycle emissions	Lower	Lower	Lower	Lower	Lower or higher[a]

Source: Adapted from Cunanan et al., 2021 (U.S. Department of Energy, 2022a)
a Depends on energy source

United States, EU countries, and South Korea. Table 24.1 summarizes the state of the market for five alternative fuel trucks.

Medium-Duty Trucks

Medium and heavy-duty trucks have different duty cycles depending on their use. Heavy-duty (HD) trucks can carry liquid chemicals, shipping containers, or refrigerated groceries to a customer, while medium-duty (MD) trucks may deliver packages or goods to numerous customers on a single tour. According to the US Federal Highway Administration, MD trucks are defined as classes 3–6 (26,000 lbs. or less gross vehicle weight rating), while HD trucks are classes 7–8 (over 26,001 lbs.) (U.S. Department of Energy, 2011). The medium and heavy-duty zero-emission truck (ZET) market is forecasted at an 8% compound annual growth rate from 2022 to 2027, with Asia having the most significant share (Mordor Intelligence, 2022).

MD alternative fuel trucks and cargo vans are far less reliant on energy-intensive fuels than their HD counterparts because they carry lighter loads and have less demanding duty cycles. MD truck mileage is 100–200 miles/day, with numerous delivery destinations that return to base at the end of the day. HD trucks in the urban market tend to have longer daily tours and trips, though still in the short-haul range of less than 500 miles. (Long-haul HD operations are beyond the scope of this chapter.) MD home and commercial delivery BET trucks are in use across the globe and increasing. Companies like Coca-Cola, Frito-Lay, Amazon, and FedEx have purchased large fleets of these vehicles. In the MD market, the higher upfront capital cost is offset by savings in maintenance and fueling. Nevertheless, MD BETs are not yet fully substitutable with their diesel counterparts. Table 24.2 shows when MD BETs are expected to reach parity on various performance dimensions. For most, parity will be achieved by 2030, except for public charging stations. Time for charging will continue to be more than filling the tank with diesel fuel well into the future.

Table 24.2 Medium-duty truck/van (classes 3–6) parity between electric and diesel powertrains

Medium-duty Electric Truck vs. Diesel		2020	2025	2030	2035+
Weight	Average				
	Max		Parity		
Cost	Initial			Parity	
	Operating				
	Residual value			Parity	
Maintenance	Service Center availability			Parity	
	Remote diagnostics				
Vehicle life	10-years				
Range	Average				
	max			Parity	
Electric availability	Yard				
	Truck stop				Parity
	Recharge time				
General	Technology maturity				Parity
	Safety				
Comparison to diesel:		Worse	Parity	Better	

Source: North American Council for Freight Efficiency (2018)

Heavy-Duty Trucks

Battery electric or hydrogen fuel cell (FC) heavy-duty trucks face significant obstacles to implementation. The first is weight restrictions for BETs. In the US maximum gross vehicle weight is 80,000 pounds.[1] An incredible amount of energy is required to pull a full load of 40,000–50,000 pounds. To provide the energy, BETs require large and heavy batteries of 5,000 pounds or more, which reduces load capacity (Smith et al., 2019). Carriers transporting loads near the maximum would have to add extra trips to satisfy the same demand (Giuliano et al., 2021). The United States has recognized the impact of battery weight and adjusted maximum permissible weights for these trucks (the United States added 2000 lbs., which is not enough to solve the problem for HD trucks) (U.S. Department of Transportation Federal Highway Administration, 2019). Additional challenges for BETs are limited range and long fueling times. A shorter range means that long tours cannot be performed, and with charging facilities only at the home base, BETs must return to base for refueling. Refueling takes hours, reducing the time the vehicle can be in service.

A second challenge is acquisition cost. BETs and FCs currently cost double or more than conventional diesel. For BETs, fleets must also bear the cost and yard space for installing costly charging infrastructure at their "home" base. Those leasing space may be hesitant to improve property that is not their own. For short-haul urban operators, zero or near-zero-emission HD trucks must be able to travel 300 miles between a charge, or operations may be significantly impacted. In 2022, battery electric trucks with full loads average between 100 and 135 miles per charge and less in cold weather. However, range is quickly improving (Giuliano, et al., 2020); 200 miles is expected within the next few years. Range anxiety will remain a top concern until convenient public charging stations are available for mid-day in-route charging. Likewise, fuel cell trucks also require community fueling stations.

Given the limited range and hours-long charging times, BETs are most promising for specialized short-haul markets such as the drayage industry, where running one or two shifts with short trips/daily tours is a common duty cycle. Fleets operating their trucks around the clock will be hard-pressed to find the opportunity to charge them. As batteries become more efficient and faster to charge, more firms will be able to reduce emissions by using these products (Figure 24.4).

In the near term, hybrid diesel or natural gas trucks are a viable option with comparable ranges to conventional diesel trucks. These hybrids can accommodate the weight and similar duty cycle. The substitution of vehicles is one-to-one, substantially reducing capital costs relative to BET. Until range can be improved, fleet operators in the drayage space prefer NG hybrids to ZETs (Giuliano et al., 2020). Using hybrid trucks in the battery-only mode in limited target areas to reduce hyper-local air toxins in communities is one possibility for reducing exposure without having to wait until BETs are more competitive.

A third challenge is the lack of FC vehicles on the market. Only two manufacturers, Hyundai and Hyzon, have had heavy-duty fuel cell trucks in mass production since early 2022; others are still being proven (FuelCellWorks, 2021). One such demonstration is a joint venture between Kenworth and Toyota with ten fuel cell vehicle (FCV) HD truck prototypes hauling freight from the Port of Los Angeles and Long Beach within the Los Angeles region. A vital component of this test is the implementation of two truck filling stations at the port complex and Inland Empire. Firms using these vehicles regularly are pleased with the performance and range but note that the hydrogen supply chain is "fragile" (California Air Resources Board, 2021). FC fueling time is comparable to diesel, and the range is higher. Within the next few years, numerous FC trucks from established and new OEMs should be in the market.

There are additional challenges associated with ownership and use. There are uncertainties regarding the life span of the batteries, residual values, and fuel/electricity prices. Maintenance

Figure 24.4 Volvo VNR regional class 8 heavy-duty electric truck
Photo courtesy of Volvo Truck North America; used with permission

Table 24.3 Cost comparison of different powertrains for class 8 truck (day cab) based on 2021 prices

Class 8-day cab heavy-duty truck	New vehicle cost ($000)					Total cost of ownership ($000)				
	2020	2025	2030	2035	2050	2020	2025	2030	2035	2050
Diesel	93.3	98.7	101.8	104.9	109.5	600.9	567	562.7	560.0	567.4
BEV	409.1	189.4	140.4	120.0	113.4	1036.6	606.2	516.3	472.4	447.3
FCEV	238.6	151.8	114.9	106.3	100.2	1454.9	832.1	658.1	614.5	564.9

Source: Argonne National Laboratory's 2021 report on cost comparisons for different powertrains (Burnham et al., 2021)
Note: Does not include charging infrastructure capital costs. TCO includes purchase price, financing, taxes, fuel, and maintenance.

of these vehicles comes with a new set of concerns, including adequately trained mechanics, plus an increasing electricity demand from vehicle charging on current grid capacity. Adding to this, manufacturers may face challenges accessing rare minerals for production. To address risks and the higher price tag of alternative fuel vehicles, governments offer incentives in the form of grants, vouchers, subsidies, and tax breaks to encourage purchasing decisions.

Over time these subsidies will decrease as the technology matures and prices come down. Table 24.3 compares various powertrain costs for class 8 trucks from 2020 to 2050. New fuel cell trucks are projected to be similar in cost to diesel by 2035, while the total cost of ownership is more favorable for BET over diesel starting in 2030. Hydrogen trucks are significantly less costly to acquire than comparable electric vehicles through 2030. Note that these comparisons are one-to-one and hence do not account for the need for additional vehicles to perform the same work.

While costs are expected to go down, performance is expected to improve. For BETs, range is expected to be competitive after 2030. A critical issue is developing and funding the charging infrastructure to support an electric truck fleet. Strategically placed charging stations will be necessary for operators to be comfortable running BETs. One example is the string of five charging stations that will connect northern and southern California by 2024 (Truckinginfo, 2022). The construction of charging stations (as well as hydrogen production/fueling stations) will be costly, and governments will be called upon to subsidize efforts in the short term to promote these technologies.

Finally, conversion of the fleet also depends on the useful life of the existing truck fleet. Heavy-duty trucks last an average of about 15 years. Absent aggressive regulations that force early turnover of the existing fleet, significant numbers of alternative fuel trucks are not expected to be on the road before 2030.

Lifecycle Analysis

LCA gives the best information on the relative advantages and disadvantages of ZET alternatives. We present an LCA comparison of BE and FC HD trucks to illustrate. The first step is constructing a material flow with inputs and outputs. A sample system flow is shown in Figure 25.5. In this diagram, five distinct phases are identified. Starting from the left, raw materials like iron, rubber, and minerals for batteries are extracted from the earth. Energy is required for extraction (like mining) and water; emissions/toxic pollutants are an unintended output. The manufacturing phase includes refining the raw materials for component

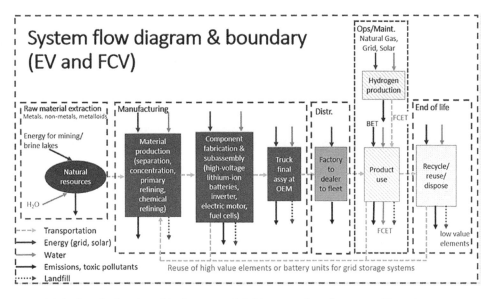

Figure 24.5 Sample electric and hydrogen truck LCA system flow diagram and boundary
Source: Dexter, S., Cradle-to-grave life cycle assessment and operational impact analysis of zero-emission heavy-duty trucks (Ph.D. thesis) (Dexter, 2022)

fabrication and, ultimately, the final truck assembly. Between these two phases, energy is expended for transporting materials. For example, minerals are taken from the four corners of the globe.

The subsequent two phases are getting the final product to the customer and using the product. The operations/maintenance phase includes all activities to keep the vehicle running, like parts replacement and service. For purposes of analysis, the functional unit is one truck mile. The fuel cycle is included in the operations/maintenance phase. It consists of the extraction and processing of crude oil into diesel fuel and distribution for diesel vehicles. Electric vehicles include all activities to manufacture electricity based on grid feedstocks.

Hydrogen must be manufactured for FCVs. Hydrogen can be made in numerous ways; the most common is steam methane reforming (called SMR) and electrolysis, which uses electricity for production (Muradov, 2015). For this analysis, green hydrogen is assumed to be powered by solar energy. The infrastructure to support the various fuel production processes (electric plants/hydrogen plants/solar panels) is excluded. The decision to exclude fueling infrastructure eliminated a positive bias toward diesel since the infrastructure already exists. The final phase is the end-of-life. Of course, the preferred end game is recycling or reusing as much of the truck as possible. It must be noted that the recycling of components like large batteries or fuel cells is abysmal at present, so activity in this phase is low.

Two prototype heavy-duty electric and hydrogen trucks are compared with a comparable diesel powertrain to answer the questions: which truck is best for the environment? Which produces the least emissions? We use Argonne National Laboratory's Alternative Fuel Life Cycle Environmental and Economic Transportation (AFLEET) and Greenhouse Gases, Regulated Emissions, and Energy use in Technologies (GREET) tools for this analysis (Argonne National Library, 2017; Argonne National Laboratory, 2021). GHG emissions are measured in carbon dioxide equivalent units (CO_2e).

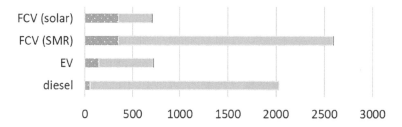

Figure 24.6 Results of LCA comparing HD truck powertrains on CO_2e
Note: The functional unit (FU) is one mile. Source: Dexter, S., Cradle-to-grave life cycle assessment and operational impact analysis of zero-emission heavy-duty trucks (Ph.D. dissertation) (Dexter, 2022)

Figure 25.6 gives results for CO_2e. FC trucks using SMR-produced hydrogen emit more CO_2e than comparable battery electric or diesel trucks per mile, but FC trucks using "green" hydrogen are similar to BETs. Renewable energy hydrogen plants are coming online globally; recent counts show 100 such plants in progress in the United States, EU, Australia, China, Saudi Arabia, and South America. Likewise, using renewable grids for electricity generation could drastically change BET results for the better. Figure 25.6 is based on the best available current data. There are many opportunities to further reduce GHGs, including improving the end-of-life phase, especially for expensive batteries in BETs and FC trucks, and recycling rare minerals. For example, the US Department of Energy's Argonne Labs is funding startups investigating ways to extract and reuse precious metals in EV batteries. Norway's Hydrovolt recycling plant aims to recycle 300,000 tons of batteries/year by 2030 and allow for "up to 95% of materials to be recovered from batteries, including plastics, copper, aluminum and black mass (a compound containing nickel, manganese, cobalt, and lithium)" (Kane, 2022).

Public Policy

This chapter closes with a discussion of public policy and decarbonization of the vehicle fleet. Market forces are insufficient to achieve widespread implementation of alternative fuel trucks in the foreseeable future. No technology is competitive yet with conventional diesel with respect to price and performance. And the required infrastructure to support an alternative fuel fleet does not yet exist. Ambitious public policy interventions will be necessary. Policy interventions take place at all levels, from the international global agreements to set and meet GHG reduction targets to local governments regulating truck access in city cores. This section provides an overview of truck decarbonization policies.

The discussion is organized around two general policy types: market-based and rules-based. Market-based policies use incentives (or disincentives) to influence firm and individual behavior. Carbon cap and trade programs are one example. The stock of carbon emission credits is bought and sold among firms, leaving the firm to decide whether to purchase more credits or invest in carbon-reduction strategies. Rules-based policies set targets that all firms must achieve, for example, fuel efficiency targets. These policy types have contrasting advantages and disadvantages; see Giuliano and Hanson (2017) for a discussion. Rules-based policies are far more common than market-based policies.

National Policy

Table 24.4 summarizes some of the most common national and US state policies being implemented. In the United States, some states have the authority to impose emissions standards that are more stringent than federal standards. As a result, some states, especially California, have emerged as international leaders in vehicle decarbonization policy. The reliance on rules-based policies is evident. Apart from cap and trade (which applies beyond

Table 24.4 National/US state truck decarbonization policies

Policy	Target	Purpose	Examples
Cap and trade	Energy producers, OEMs	Economically efficient method to reduce carbon emissions	Western Climate Initiative (California and Québec), Regional Greenhouse Gas Initiative (11 US states), EU Emissions Trading System, China
Fuel economy standards and targets	OEMs, vehicle purchasers	Force technology development to achieve targets	US, EU, Japan, India, China
Zero-emission vehicle sales targets	OEMs, vehicle purchasers	Force technology development, accelerate market penetration	California Advanced Clean Truck Regulation (plus 14 other US states), India, China, Japan, EU, US, New Zealand
Low carbon fuel standard (LCFS)	Energy producers, OEMs	Reduce carbon intensity of fossil fuels	California, British Columbia
Charging and fueling infrastructure	Highways, energy providers	Facilitate market penetration	California, EU, UK, Canada, Sweden
Carbon tax	Energy consumers	Economically efficient method to reduce carbon emissions	None
Vehicle purchase subsidies	Vehicle purchasers and operators	Offset higher purchase cost of ZE vehicles	California, UK
Demonstrations	Vehicle purchasers and operators	Facilitate learning for future ZE users	California, Germany/Netherlands/Belgium/France (H2-Share), UK (ZERF), Alberta (AZETEC)

Sources: Taylor (2018); California Air Resources Board (2020a,b); Fuel Cells Bulletin (2020); International Energy Agency (2021); Center for Climate and Energy Solutions (2021); Giuliano et al. (2021); Emissions Reductions Alberta (2022); U.S. Department of Energy (2022b); International Energy Agency (2022); Buckley (2022).

the freight sector) and subsidies, most policy efforts are regulatory. Except for California and the EU, cap and trade programs are restricted to certain markets and generous with the cap, limiting their impact. Historically fuel and energy efficiency improvements have been accomplished via regulation, for example, the CAFÉ standards of the United States. Fuel efficiency standards are relatively easy to enforce and track. Therefore, it is not surprising that fuel efficiency targets are common and growing worldwide. Success will depend on other supportive policies, including funding and providing the necessary infrastructure and subsidizing vehicle purchases until prices reach parity with conventional fuel vehicles; cap and trade funds can provide a resource for funding investment and subsidy programs.

Local policies

Local policies also have a role to play. Table 24.5 provides examples of local policies. Local policies are aimed primarily at the local delivery market and have multiple objectives: to solve congestion and safety problems, reduce air toxic emissions, and reduce GHG emissions.

As experience with decarbonization policies has been gained, it has become evident that coordinated suites of policies are likely to have the most impact. California provides an example. Figure 24.7 shows how California has developed policies addressing each phase

Table 24.5 Local truck decarbonization policies

Policy	Target	Purpose	Examples
Low-emission zones	Local delivery services	Incentivize use of low or zero-emission trucks	Stockholm – first to implement in 1996 Madrid – entry to city core area only for hybrid, BET, FCV Paris – restrictions on diesel trucks in city core
Cordon pricing	All commercial vehicles	Reduce peak congestion, promote use of ZE vehicles	London – low-emission commercial vehicles exempt from cordon fee
Off-peak deliveries	Local delivery services, receivers	Reduce peak congestion	New York City, Sao Paulo, Paris, London
Charging and fueling infrastructure	AF truck fleets and operators	Facilitate market penetration	San Francisco to Los Angeles truck corridor public–private partnership
Low-emission loading zones	Local delivery services	Reduce local congestion, increase safety, promote use of ZE trucks	Paris, Pittsburg, Los Angeles/Santa Monica Bremen Germany
Warehouse indirect source regulation	Warehousing and distribution	Reduce localized air pollution, promote use of ZE trucks	Southern California

Sources: Holguín-Veras et al. (2014); Broaddus et al. (2015); Holman et al. (2015); Bernard et al. (2020); South Coast Air Quality Management District (2021); Zhai and Wolff (2021); Maxner et al. (2022)

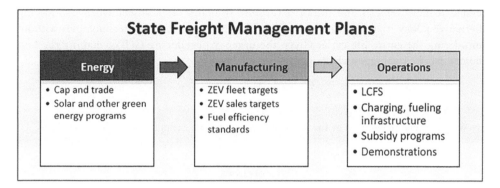

Figure 24.7 California's truck decarbonization policies
Source: Authors

of the truck life cycle. For simplification, we focus on energy production, manufacturing, and operations. California's energy mix now includes 48% of renewables (solar, wind, water), accomplished through green energy investments, targets for GHG reductions, and the cap and trade program (California Energy Commission, 2022). Targets for fuel efficiency, zero-emission truck share, and new truck sales requirements will increase the number ZETs. Another set of policies focuses on operations. All these policies are linked and coordinated via several state-level freight plans.

Challenges Ahead

Urban freight is undergoing a revolution, and local, state, and national governments are grappling with the changes. Freight is increasing along with pressures to reduce climate-changing emissions. Globally, plans and regulations are emerging to address these crucial issues. There is much progress in decarbonizing urban logistics helped by government programs across the globe. As freight volumes increase, technology is becoming more efficient and less expensive. Leaders in government and industry are analyzing their policies and supply chains to reduce waste, including understanding the lifecycle impacts of product development and use.

There are many challenges yet to be addressed. First, although it appears that BETs will serve much of the medium-duty market, this is not the case for the heavy-duty market. FCVs or biofuels may be more suitable for long distances and heavy loads. Multiple fuel production and distribution systems would generate high costs and practical problems, like how multiple fueling options can be located in dense urban areas. Second, the world's freight transport industry is built upon fossil fuels and its associated infrastructure of oil production, refining and distribution, and retail fueling systems that have grown and evolved over more than a century. Replicating such a system for BETs or FCVs – or both – is a massive undertaking and one that is just beginning to be addressed. The private market is unlikely to invest in the infrastructure until there is sufficient scale. If left to fleet owners and operators, the added costs will be a strong deterrent to using the new technologies. Third, policy discussions have not yet advanced much beyond operational considerations. There is a growing awareness that where the electricity comes from matters, but long-term implications of battery waste and disposal, mining of rare metals, and water demands associated with fuel production are not yet part of policy choices. The energy costs embedded in new vehicles and infrastructure are similarly often absent when considering alternative policy strategies There is a risk of investing in the wrong technologies without considering the entire life cycle. Given the urgency of reducing GHGs, making the best choices may be the biggest challenge.

Note

1 Weight limits are enforced by the states, and states can issue exemptions for overweight loads.

References

ABEBE, F.K. (2011) *Modelling Informal Settlement Growth in Dar es Salaam, Tanzania*. MSC thesis. Enschede: Universiteit Twente.

ARGONNE NATIONAL LABORATORY (2021) *AFLEET Tool*. [Online] Argonne National Laboratory. Available from: https://afleet-web.es.anl.gov/home/ [Accessed 17/04/21].

ARGONNE NATIONAL LIBRARY (2017) *Argonne GREET Model*. Available from: https://greet.es.anl.gov/index.php [Accessed 04/09/22].

BERNARD, Y. MILLER, J., WAPPELHORST, S. and BRAUN, C., (2020) *Impacts of the Paris Low-Emission Zone and Implications for Other Cities*. [Online] International Council on Clean Transportation. Available from: https://theicct.org/publication/impacts-of-the-paris-low-emission-zone-and-implications-for-other-cities/ [Accessed 10/08/22].

BROADDUS, A., BROWNE, M. and ALLEN, J. (2015) Sustainable Freight. *Transportation Research Record*, 2478(1), 1–11.

BUCKLEY, S. (2022) *Zero Emission Road Freight Demonstrations: Battery Electric and Hydrogen Fuel Cell Trucks*. [Online] Innovate UK KTN. Available from: https://ktn-uk.org/wp-content/uploads/2022/08/ZERFD_presentations.pdf [Accessed 04/09/22].

BURNHAM, A., GOHLKE, D., RUSH, L., STEPHENS, T., ZHOU, Y., DELUCCHI, M. A., BIRKY, A., HUNTER, C., LIN, Z., OU, S., XIE, F., PROCTOR, C., WIRYADINATA, S., LIU, N. and BOLOOR, M., (2021) *Comprehensive Total Cost of Ownership Quantification for Vehicles with Different Size Classes and Powertrains*. Argonne.

CALIFORNIA AIR RESOURCES BOARD (2021) *2021 Annual Evaluation of Fuel Cell Electric Vehicle Deployment and Hydrogen Fuel Station Network Development*. Sacramento.

CALIFORNIA AIR RESOURCES BOARD (2020a) *Advanced Clean Trucks*. Available from: https://ww2.arb.ca.gov/our-work/programs/advanced-clean-trucks [Accessed 18/10/22].

CALIFORNIA AIR RESOURCES BOARD (2020b) *Low Carbon Fuel Standard*. Available from: https://ww2.arb.ca.gov/our-work/programs/low-carbon-fuel-standard/about [Accessed 18/10/22].

CALIFORNIA ENERGY COMMISSION (2022) *New Data Indicates California Remains Ahead of Clean Electricity Goals*. Available from: https://www.energy.ca.gov/news/2022-02/new-data-indicates-california-remains-ahead-clean-electricity-goals [Accessed 04/09/22].

CALSTART DRIVE TO ZERO (2022) *Zero-Emission Technology Inventory Tool*. Available from: https://globaldrivetozero.org/tools/zeti/ [Accessed 27/08/22].

CENTER FOR CLIMATE AND ENERGY SOLUTIONS (2021) *Cap and Trade Basics*. [Online] Center for Climate and Energy Solutions. Available from: https://www.c2es.org/content/cap-and-trade-basics/ [Accessed 04/09/22].

CUNANAN, C., TRAN, M.K., LEE, Y., KWOK, S., LEUNG, V., and FOWLER, M. (2021) A Review of Heavy-Duty Vehicle Powertrain Technologies: Diesel Engine Vehicles, Battery Electric Vehicles, and Hydrogen Fuel Cell Electric Vehicles. *Clean Technologies*, 3(2), 474–489.

DABLANC, L. (2022) La logistique et la ville. Questions environnementales et territoriales de la logistique urbaine. *L'Information géographique*, 86(3), 49–77.

DELGADO, O. and GONZALEZ, F. (2018) CO_2 *Emissions and Fuel Consumption Standards for Heavy-Duty Vehicles in the European Union*. Washington, D.C.

DEXTER, S. (2022) *Cradle-To-Grave Life Cycle Assessment and Operational Impact Analysis of Zero-Emission Heavy-Duty Trucks*. Ph.D. Dissertation (unpublished). Los Angeles: University of Southern California.

EMISSIONS REDUCTIONS ALBERTA (2022) *Alberta Zero Emissions Truck Electrification Collaboration.* [Online] Emissions Reductions Alberta. Available from: https://www.eralberta.ca/projects/details/alberta-zero-emissions-truck-electrification-collaboration-azetec/ [Accessed 04/09/22].

FUEL CELLS BULLETIN (2020) H2-Share Starts Demo of Hydrogen Powered Truck in Netherlands. (5), [Online] Available from: doi.org/10.1016/S1464-2859(20)30184-X [Accessed 14/09/2022].

FUELCELLWORKS (2021) *The First Hydrogen Trucks Are Rolling in Europe.* Available from: https://fuelcellsworks.com/news/the-first-hydrogen-trucks-are-rolling-in-europe/ [Accessed 04/08/22].

GIULIANO, G., DESSOUKY, M., DEXTER, S., FANG, J., HU, S., STEIMETZ, S., O'BRIEN, T., MILLER, M., FULTON, L. (2020) *Developing Markets for Zero Emission Vehicles in Short Haul Goods Movement.* [Online] UC Davis: National Center for Sustainable Transportation. http://dx.doi.org/10.7922/G2DN43BT Retrieved from https://escholarship.org/uc/item/0nw4q530 [Accessed 11/11/22].

GIULIANO, G., DESSOUKY, M., Dexter, S., Fang, J., Hu, S. and Miller, M., (2021) Heavy-Duty Trucks: The Challenge of Getting to Zero. *Transportation Research Part D: Transport and Environment*, 93, 102742.

GIULIANO, G. and HANSON, S. (2017) Looking to the Future. In: GIULIANO, GENEVIEVE and HANSON, SUSAN (eds.) *The Geography of Urban Transportation.* New York: The Guilford Press, 359–388.

HOLGUÍN-VERAS, J., WANG, C., BROWNE, M., DARVILLE HODGE, S. and WOJTOWICZ, J., (2014) The New York City Off-Hour Delivery Project: Lessons for City Logistics. *Procedia - Social and Behavioral Sciences*, 125, 36–48.

HOLMAN, C., HARRISON, R. and QUEROL, X. (2015) Review of the Efficacy of Low Emission Zones to Improve Urban Air Quality in European Cities. *Atmospheric Environment*, 111, 161–169.

INTERNATIONAL ENERGY AGENCY (2022) *Global EV Policy Explorer.* [Online] International Energy Agency. Available from: https://www.iea.org/articles/global-ev-policy-explorer [Accessed 30/08/22].

INTERNATIONAL ENERGY AGENCY (2021) *Policies to Promote Electric Vehicle Deployment.* [Online] International Energy Agency. Available from: https://www.iea.org/reports/global-ev-outlook-2021/policies-to-promote-electric-vehicle-deployment [Accessed 29/08/22].

INTERNATIONAL TRANSPORT FORUM (2019) *ITF Transport Outlook 2019.* Paris: OECD.

KANE, M. (2022) *Hydrovolt Launches Europe's Largest EV Battery Recycling Plant.* [Online] InsideEVs. Available from: https://insideevs.com/news/586335/hydrovolt-europe-largest-ev-battery-recycling-plant/ [Accessed 06/08/22].

KRIVOSHTO, I.N., RICHARDS, J.R., ALBERTSON, T.E. and DERLET, R.W., (2008) The Toxicity of Diesel Exhaust: Implications for Primary Care. *Journal of the American Board of Family Medicine*, 21(1), 55–62.

MAXNER, T., GOULIANOU, N., RANJBARI, A. and GOODCHILD, A., (2022) Urban Delivery Company Needs and Preferences for Green Loading Zones Implementation: A Case Study of NYC. In: WEI, H. (ed.) *International Conference on Transportation and Development 2022: Transportation Planning and Workforce Development.* Seattle: American Society of Civil Engineers, 323–334.

MORDOR INTELLIGENCE (2022) *Medium and Heavy-Duty Commercial Vehicles Market (2022–27).* Available from: https://mordorintelligence.com/industry-reports/medium-and-heavy-duty-commercial-vehicles-market [Accessed 02/08/22].

MURADOV, N. (2015) Low-Carbon Production of Hydrogen from Fossil Fuels. In: SUBRAMANI, V., BASILE, A. and VEZIROĞLU, T.N. (eds.) *Compendium of Hydrogen Energy: Hydrogen Production and Purification.* Amsterdam: Woodhead Publishing, 489–522.

NEW YORK TIMES (2019) *1.5 Million Packages a Day: The Internet Brings Chaos to N.Y. Streets.* Available from: https://www.nytimes.com/2019/10/27/nyregion/nyc-amazon-delivery.html [Accessed 24/08/22].

NORTH AMERICAN COUNCIL FOR FREIGHT EFFICIENCY (2018) *Medium-Duty Electric Trucks: Cost of Ownership.* Available from: https://nacfe.org/emerging-technology/medium-duty-electric-trucks-cost-of-ownership/ [Accessed 02/08/22].

NORWAY TODAY (2021) *More Than 110,000 Electric Cars Have Been Sold in Norway in 2021.* Available from: https://norwaytoday.info/finance/more-than-110000-electric-cars-have-been-sold-in-norway-in-2021/ [Accessed 30/07/22].

ROSEN, J.W. (2019) *Dar es Salaam Is Growing Rapidly—And Its Planners Are Struggling to Keep Up.* [Online] National Geographic. Available from: https://www.nationalgeographic.com/environment/article/tanzanian-city-may-soon-be-one-of-the-worlds-most-populous [Accessed 02/08/22].

SCHIPPER, L., MARIE-LILLIU, C. and GORHAM, R. (2000) Flexing the Link between Transport and Greenhouse Gas Emissions – A Path for the World Bank. *International Energy Agency, Paris,*

[Online] Available from: http://www.iea.org/textbase/nppdf/free/2000/flex2000.pdf [Accessed 04/09/2022].

SMITH, D., GRAVES, R., OZPINECI, B., JONES, P.T., LUSTBADER, J., KELLY, K., WALKOWICZ, K., BIRKY, A., PAYNE, G., SIGLER, C., and MOSBACHER, J. (2019) *Medium- and Heavy-Duty Vehicle Electrification: An Assessment of Technology and Knowledge Gaps* (No. ORNL/SPR-2020/7). Oak Ridge National Laboratory (ORNL) and National Renewable Energy Laboratory (NREL), Oak Ridge, TN.

SOBOL, Ł. and DYJAKON, A. (2020) The Influence of Power Sources for Charging the Batteries of Electric Cars on CO_2 Emissions during Daily Driving: A Case Study from Poland. *Energies 2020*, 13(16), 4267.

SOUTH COAST AIR QUALITY MANAGEMENT DISTRICT (2021) *Warehouse Indirect Source Rule – Warehouse Action and Investments to Reduce Emissions (WAIRE) Program*. California.

TAYLOR, M. (2018) *Assessing California's Climate Policies-An Overview*. Sacramento.

TETER, J., TATTINI, J. and PETROPOULOS, A. (2020) *Tracking Transport 2020*. Paris.

TRANSPORTPOLICY.NET (2021) *US: Heavy-Duty: Fuel Consumption and GHG*. Available from: https://www.transportpolicy.net/standard/us-heavy-duty-fuel-consumption-and-ghg/ [Accessed 04/09/22].

TRUCKINGINFO (2022) *Volvo Trucks Building Electrified Charging Corridor in California*. Available from: https://www.truckinginfo.com/10176830/volvo-trucks-constructing-electrified-charging-corridor [Accessed 28/08/22].

UNITED NATIONS CLIMATE CHANGE (2022) *C40 Cities Finance Facility*. Available from: https://unfccc.int/climate-action/momentum-for-change/financing-for-climate-friendly-investment/c40 [Accessed 02/08/22].

UNITED NATIONS NEWS (2021) *Global e-commerce jumps to $26.7 trillion, fuelled by COVID-19*. Available from: https://news.un.org/en/story/2021/05/1091182 [Accessed 02/08/22].

U.S. DEPARTMENT OF ENERGY (2022a) *Alternative Fuels Data Center: Biodiesel Vehicle Emissions*. Available from: https://afdc.energy.gov/vehicles/diesels_emissions.html [Accessed 12/10/22].

U.S. DEPARTMENT OF ENERGY (2022b) *Alternative Fuels Data Center: Electricity Laws and Incentives in California*. [Online] U.S. Department of Energy. Available from: https://afdc.energy.gov/fuels/laws/ELEC?state=CA [Accessed 04/09/22].

U.S. DEPARTMENT OF ENERGY (2017) *Alternative Fuels Data Center: Biodiesel Basics*. Available from: https://afdc.energy.gov/files/u/publication/biodiesel_basics.pdf [Accessed 12/10/22].

U.S. DEPARTMENT OF ENERGY (2011) *Alternative Fuels Data Center: Maps and Data - Vehicle Weight Classes & Categories*. Available from: https://afdc.energy.gov/data/10380 [Accessed 27/08/22].

U.S. DEPARTMENT OF TRANSPORTATION BUREAU OF TRANSPORTATION STATISTICS (2022a) *Freight Facts and Figures*. Available from: https://www.bts.gov/product/freight-facts-and-figures [Accessed 14/10/22].

U.S. DEPARTMENT OF TRANSPORTATION BUREAU OF TRANSPORTATION STATISTICS (2022b) *Moving Goods in the United States*. Available from: https://data.bts.gov/stories/s/Moving-Goods-in-the-United-States/bcyt-rqmu [Accessed 14/06/22].

U.S. DEPARTMENT OF TRANSPORTATION BUREAU OF TRANSPORTATION STATISTICS (2019) *Freight Facts and Figures: Freight Transportation and the Economy*. Available from: https://data.bts.gov/stories/s/Freight-Transportation-the-Economy/6ix2-c8dn/ [Accessed 02/08/22].

U.S. DEPARTMENT OF TRANSPORTATION FEDERAL HIGHWAY ADMINISTRATION (2019) *The Consolidated Appropriations Act, 2019, Truck Size and Weight Provisions*.

ZHAI, M. and WOLFF, H. (2021) Air Pollution and Urban Road Transport: Evidence from the World's Largest Low-Emission Zone in London. *Environmental Economics and Policy Studies*, 23(4), 721–748.

25
URBAN LOGISTICS IN THE GLOBAL SOUTH

Nora Mareï

Introduction: Logistics as a Gateway into Urban Economies in the Global South[1]

Logistics[2] has become a key urban function in modern economies as well as an indicator of economic development and, guided by this idea, some governments have undertaken to give a high priority to this sector, presenting it as a lever for competitiveness and growth. In 2007, this awareness was further consolidated by the publication of the World Bank's Logistics Performance Index[3] (LPI), a benchmarking tool that considers logistics as one of the essential conditions for trade, productivity, and job creation (Hallward-Driemeier and Nayyar, 2018). Although such indicators can be debated, they contribute to disseminating ideas on the relationship between logistics, competitiveness, and economic development in the Global South. Under the influence of donors, multinationals and international institutions, logistics projects are presented by governments as policy choices that foster development (Nugent, 2018).

In this institutional context, it is relevant to analyze how logistics strategies are implemented in cities that are faced with strong demographic and spatial growth, but suffer from a lack of planning, organization, and compliance with development and urbanism standards. This chapter starts from the hypothesis that a logistics transition works alongside an urban transition, and with a modification of production and consumption systems. The key research question this chapter addresses is *How do these different processes intermingle, disrupt and complement each other in the making of urban logistics in the Global South?* An interesting example can be found in Morocco where, from 2010, the state deployed a national strategy to develop its competitiveness in the logistics sector. This case allows us to jointly analyze the growth of logistics on different scales and the territorial difficulties encountered in the process (Debrie and Mareï, 2019). As we will see, other countries are now also enacting similar strategies: examples include Mexico, Vietnam, India, Senegal, Egypt, and Ghana.

When examined in relation to other examples in developing and emerging countries, the Moroccan case highlights two different scales at which logistics issues can be studied. At a national scale, connections between cities and ports have become a fundamental factor affecting freight distribution. Worldwide, the organization of hinterlands has become the focus of increased attention in recent years with the development of inland ports and logistics zones whose reach is both international and urban (Notteboom and Rodrigue, 2007; Merk and Notteboom, 2015; Monios, 2011). Countries in the Global South have embraced this evolution, as shown by Nugent (2018) with respect to governance of large logistics infrastructure in Africa, or by studies on the location of dry ports in Asia (Nguyen and Nottebom, 2015; Ng and Cetin, 2012). Logistics platforms are typically created as part of national or regional development programs, with public-private partnerships associating intermodal operators with central or regional governments. This "platformization" plays a key part in the reorganization of logistics chains in the Global South, as in the Global North, and these platforms are a source of added value (via investment from large operators) and places from which the multi-scale logistics networks are controlled (Raimbault, 2019; Savy and Burnham, 2013).

While the last two decades have seen the development of an up-to-date and in-depth knowledge base on urban logistics in the Global North (see in particular Dablanc and Frémont, 2015; Taniguchi and Thompson, 2014; Dablanc et al, 2013; Hesse, 2002), in contrast, the issues affecting strictly urban logistics are far less understood by public authorities in the Global South, and less analyzed in the academic literature. However, recent publications show that a new research dynamic is underway: Kin et al. (2017) study urban goods transport in megacities in emerging markets; Malik et al. (2017) compare freight parking practices in Gothenburg and Delhi, showing that these practices pose a common problem despite the variety of local contexts; and Sekhani et al. (2019) explore the relationship between informal and formal aspects in the street vending logistics chain. Following on from these studies, Mareï and Savy (2021) show that logistics in cities of the Global South rely on systems that associate the foreign experience with local practices. Based on case studies, the authors characterize logistics issues in dense cities where urban planning is poorly developed and often anarchic. In terms of method and data, these studies are impeded by the heterogeneity of the data (type, dates), due to the lack or non-communication of official sector data in developing countries. While such gaps make it difficult to establish systematic comparisons, these studies all highlight a number of distinctive traits in urban logistics in emerging and developing countries: heavy congestion; the lack of space for loading and unloading; the occupation of public or even domestic space for storage; the absence, inadequacy or poor enforcement of municipal legislation; the essential role of proximity and small operators in last mile logistics.

The combination of these two scales of transformation makes logistics a major aspect of the urban transition in cities of the Global South, which are among the densest in the world. The theme of transition is gaining importance in territorial analyses in the humanities and social sciences, in the dual context of the accelerating contemporary globalization and its crisis (Rosa, 2013). The concept of transition first of all implies a visible change that proceeds in stages, with a sector shifting from one situation to another: e.g. demographic, urban, or energy changes are generally studied by scholars as transitions. In this sense, this conceptual framework is used to analyze evolutions and qualify them according to known patterns. The urban transition is intensely discussed around the world, as the growth of cities is bringing about different crises and accelerations (Ghorra-Gobin and Azuelos, 2015; Steck, 2006; Daniels, 2004). Contemporary globalization is also marked by an unprecedented growth in exchanges at all scales, for which transport and logistics provide necessary and indispensable channels. In this perspective, by studying the theme of urban logistics jointly alongside that of urban transition, we can position the cities of the Global South on a logistical trajectory in relation to other cities around the world. This chapter, which follows on from earlier research and field studies (particularly in the Maghreb (Morocco) and West

Africa (Mauritania)), draws on secondary data from academic and institutional literature to provide a review of current knowledge on logistics in the Global South, and to identify the issues and trends impacting this key aspect of urban development.

The Logistics Transition on a National Scale

The Emergence of Logistics Issues on Political Agendas

Political decision makers around the world are showing a newfound awareness of the importance of the logistics function, which is apparent through their statements on emergence, development, and competitiveness. Logistics is now presented by state authorities as a key aspect of their national policies, with the implementation of sector-specific programs and logistics observatories, and/or the publication of annual reports on this topic.

Morocco and Vietnam are two examples of developing countries where the targeting and implementation of a national logistics policy is relatively advanced. Comparisons between logistics policies in Morocco (Debrie and Mareï, 2019; AMDL, 2016) and Vietnam (Ministry of Industry and Trade, 2020; Vu, 2019; Nguyen and Notteboom, 2016) point to the institutionalization of logistics as a priority sector. In both cases, the authorities' interest in logistics is relatively recent, and directly related to World Bank Reports describing how inefficient logistics systems hinder export growth and competitiveness. Interest in this sector is justified by the issue posed by the significant weight of logistics in GDP: both countries report logistics costs amounting to more than 20% or even 25% of their GDP, and ambition to bring them below 15%, in line with the average rates of developed countries (between 8% and 15% according to the World Bank and the OECD) (Rantasila and Ojala, 2012; Shepherd, 2011).

On the African continent, the modernization of transport and logistics systems is presented by many countries as one of the key challenges targeted by their respective emergence programs by 2030/2050.[4] Strategies including the "Emerging Senegal Plan" (2014), Ghana's "Medium-Term Development Policy Framework" (MTDF 2018–2021), and the 2019 law voted by Egypt's Ministry of Transport to establish seven logistics cities (OECD, 2020) all feature at least one project involving the creation of an integrated and multimodal urban logistics hub. The modernization of logistics systems is presented as a pathway to economic development and emergence. Advertising such ambitious logistics policies also gives these countries access to aid from international donors, who invest in infrastructure projects and initiatives to professionalize the sector as a means of tackling the informal economy (Ohnsorge and Yu, 2021; Kumar et al., 2021). For example, in Egypt, the dry port project adjacent to the 6th of October City (one of the country's first new cities) has secured the support of the European Investment Bank, the European Bank for Reconstruction and Development and the African Development Bank. A consortium led by the German company DB Schenker has been selected for the contract to operate this first dry port, whose governance is based on a public-private partnership.[5]

These different examples reflect a complex logistics agenda, both from a political and a functional perspective, whose ambitions are clearly linked to national economic competitiveness. The strategy is set through sector-specific plans (industry, trade, and agriculture) in which logistics is a transversal lever for action. The consideration of logistical aspects relies on the evolving relationship between governments, national transport and logistics operators, international or regional donors, and the international private sector, which is the main beneficiary of the upgrading of infrastructure.

Finally, it should be noted that the issue of logistics is also present in local development projects, although their implementation is often hindered by their mainly top-down approach, and by the complexity of the interplay between the public sector and private interests. For example, in Vietnam, although large logistics infrastructure projects are being developed around Ho Chi Minh City, the ministries of transport, finance, planning, and investment are involved in this sector which results in a regulatory environment that is difficult to grasp (Banomyong et al., 2015). In Morocco, the national strategy for the development of logistics competitiveness was initially drafted by the Ministry of Planning from 2005 to 2006, and then by the Ministry of Equipment and Transport from 2010. Its local implementation is proving difficult, and raising associated funding, particularly for the development of logistics platforms, is a slow process. Over ten years after the launch of the strategy, the Moroccan press still reports delays in signing the implementation contracts. These delays are in turn blocking the implementation of the contractual framework between the Ministries of Finance and Equipment, the agency dedicated to logistics (created in 2012), and the local stakeholders (regions, municipalities). Field observations and interviews conducted in Casablanca and Tangier between 2017 and 2019 show that a gap persists between the scale of this program (a national strategy with its specific governance via a dedicated agency) and the consideration of logistical factors in local land-use planning documents – even though these two cities benefit the most from the national strategy (Debrie and Mareï, 2019).

Logistics Areas, Platforms, and Dry Ports: Hubs as Spatially Structuring Figures

Seaports and airports are often the largest logistics facilities in the Global South. It is around these facilities that domestic and urban logistics activities are generally enacted. Road transport is then deployed from these gateways. This mode of transport is more expensive than in the North, due to the time lost in heavily congested ports and urban traffic jams, but also to the additional cost of prolonged goods storage, and to the poor management of supply chains, not to mention the cost of delivery trucks often returning empty (World Bank, 2008).

In this context, port cities are the first to benefit from strategies that favor the logistics sector. The modernization of port infrastructure and environments will boost international logistics and the integration of Southern countries into global value chains (see Box 25.1). Such efforts generally contribute to improving the countries' ranking in international databases where connectivity indicators play an important role. They also lead to the construction of dry ports or inland platforms that facilitate connections with large urban markets, as described above in the case of Egypt, Vietnam, and Morocco. N'Djamena, the capital of Chad, a landlocked African country, provides an interesting example. The country has no seaport but it has access to a freight corridor emanating from Cameroon. Munoz (2021) explains the very beginnings of metropolitan logistics from the Ngueli platform, some 20 km from the capital. This key node, a dry port on the Douala-N'Djamena corridor, is now becoming a multi-service logistics zone. It is interesting to note that connections to the city are deployed under restrictive municipal legislation: as trucks are prohibited from driving through the city center during the day, rotations between the platform on the outskirts and the city take place between 10:00 pm and 6:00 am.

Box 25.1 International vs Metropolitan Logistics in Tangier and Casablanca (Morocco)

The *Tanger-Med* project was the largest transport and logistics project undertaken in Morocco in the 2000s. It has impacted the country's national competitiveness and territorial organization, with the creation in the north of the country of a structuring industrial port zone with a national and international reach. Adjacent to the port, the *Medhub* logistics free-trade zone operates as a bonded warehouse, in compliance with the latest international standards. It hosts about fifty companies and its objective is to facilitate value-added logistics operations: storage, grouping, repackaging, and labeling before the goods are dispatched – mainly on a macro-regional scale (Euro-Mediterranean area and Africa), but also to other free-trade zones in the Tangier-Tetouan region. Retailers such as Decathlon and Inditex also use it to supply the Moroccan domestic market on a just-in-time basis.

Casablanca, a metropolis of 7 million inhabitants, is now Morocco's main economic hub. The city is directly impacted by various logistics projects, ranging from completely private initiatives to the priority areas drawn up by the national logistics policy in 2005. The creation of standardized logistics platforms and areas dedicated to logistics is now clearly visible in the urban landscape, both around the port (Mita logistics area) and along the main national axis connecting Casablanca, Mohammedia and Rabat (Zenata logistics area). These new warehouses are for the most part managed by state operators (transport operators, railway networks such as ONCF) who fully benefit from logistics planning, particularly because they own land, often in dense areas, and long-established infrastructure in strategic locations. This modern form of logistics, deployed from ports through to remote peripheries, creates a sprawling, standardized metropolis – not very different from certain cities in the Global North – which appears as the hub of an economic and multi-scalar system.

Tanger-Med has become an extra-urban industrial and logistics hub (40 km from the city of Tangier), or even an "extra-territorial" hub: many local transporters and logisticians operate completely outside of this framework, which they do not see as relevant to them; others struggle to adapt to it, complaining about the high cost of services designed to meet European standards, or about the heavy administrative and customs procedures and their lack of relevance to local and national needs. Moreover, the connections between *Tanger-Med* and Tangier-City have been mostly left unaddressed by the project, as have the urban logistics of this metropolis that continues to attract workers and tourists. In Casablanca, a port city where economic activities are closely interwoven on diverse scales, urban logistics is more directly impacted by large-scale national projects, but it remains complex to manage, especially at the finest scales. For example, the municipality plans to identify and register light vehicles that transport goods. Three-wheelers have proliferated in recent years because of a gap in legislation, as they have the same status as two-wheelers. The municipality aims to better manage small-scale urban transport, without having to replace it with another system to service the dense city center. However, vehicle registration requires control: deploying this project will be a challenge in an economic sector where informality still prevails.

Sources: Field observations and interviews conducted by the author between 2016 and 2019. For more on this case study, see Debrie and Mareï (2019); on the implementation of Morocco's logistics policy, see Mareï et al. (2019), AMDL (2016)

In many cities of the Global South, the modernization of ports, or gateways in general, has created favorable conditions for the development of integrated logistics schemes between cities and ports, in particular thanks to the development of inland platforms on the outskirts of large cities. The aim of this development is to make port-city logistics more efficient, by redeploying the main freight activities outside the city to address problems posed by congestion and security. Inland sites with multimodal access tend to become larger logistics areas, serving the urban markets of major metropolises. These inland hubs are expected to deliver a significant number of traditional freight handling functions and services, and to attract a wide range of urban logistics services, including trucking companies, distribution centers, packaging, and packing plants. Studies on the location of dry ports in Asia (Nguyen and Notteboom, 2016; Ng and Cetin, 2012) show that they were developed with the initial aim of improving the efficiency of inland logistics and serving export-focused industrial zones, which have grown across the continent since the 1980s. However, due to the dependence of developing countries, including those in Asia, on supplies of all types, the main purpose of dry ports is now one of the hubs for both inbound and outbound flows, and therefore to be integrated into import and export logistics chains. Logistics areas, dry ports, and new warehouses are thus created as part of economic development policies involving the upgrading of transport infrastructure to international standards, and the establishment of public-private partnerships. These facilities generally serve both urban functions (facilitating the supply of increasingly dense urban markets) and international functions (facilitating international container flows). A form of geography of hubs, already studied in the Global North (see Debrie 2010; Rodrigue et al., 2010), is taking shape in the South, thus contributing to the production of a multi-scalar logistics space – urban, national, and international. These platforms host both logistics facilities and economic activity, sometimes in the form of free-trade zones. They are powerful tools for bringing logistics up to standard: on the one hand, they contribute to modernizing logistics landscapes in the Global South; on the other, they help disseminate international models for the governance of logistics sites. However, this spectrum of international standardization and logistics transition in the Global South experiences the difficulty of penetrating urban systems that are generally poorly planned and therefore suffer from a lack of compliance with standards.

The Behind-the-Scenes Logistics of Southern Metropolises

On-Street Logistics and So-Called Informal Practices

In many cities in the Global South, logistics is generally a visible activity in the everyday urban landscape. Obvious phenomena include the anarchic and often illegal long-term parking of heavy and light goods vehicles, unloading on the public highway, and the overflow of commercial activities onto the sidewalks. In addition, there is competition for the roadway between delivery trucks of all sizes, three-wheelers, carts pulled by animals or humans, public transport, private cars, and pedestrians who are sometimes pushed off the sidewalks. Storage in vehicles, on the ground floor of apartment buildings or even at home, is also widespread. The occupation of public space by logistics activities, but also by distribution and services, is thus a notable difference between urban practices and landscapes in the Global North and South (see Box 25.2). Ultimately, the performance of logistics operations in non-dedicated spaces can pose various problems of safety and cause conflict between users in densely populated cities with defective infrastructure (Dimitriou, 2006).

> **Box 25.2 The Emergence of Urban Logistics in Nouakchott (Mauritania)**
>
> In Nouakchott, the country's political and economic capital with a population of about one million, the central urban area's three markets – "Capitale," "Socim," and "Socogim/Mosquée Marocaine" – and its extension to the BMD crossroads form a lively trading area, packed with attractive activities (historical meat and coal markets, fruit and vegetable markets from Morocco (90% of the volume of fresh produce found in the area), diverse grocery stores, fabric markets and miscellaneous products from China). The daily operation of this area, targeting wholesale, semi-wholesale, and private customers, involves the access, parking, and unloading of delivery vehicles, from carts to semi-trailers. In addition, the area also attracts customers on foot, in private vehicles, in cabs, or on buses. The streets must therefore accommodate the traffic of goods vehicles together with pedestrians, street vendors, and products displayed for sale. The saturation of the traffic is such in this area that at certain times of the day, the district's crossroads and main roads become inaccessible. In this context of a large central urban market, all the residential houses around the market have been turned into warehouses by the retailers, thereby expanding the market area.
>
> It should be noted, however, that logistics is considered in the city's local land-use and urban planning strategies (PLU and SDAU): dedicated land has been allocated to logistics infrastructure and equipment, and some reflection went into determining the location of wholesale and semi-wholesale markets. In this context, in 2020, the trucks bound for the "Mosquée marocaine" market were "transferred" to another site in the north of the city, on a private logistics area on the road of the new airport inaugurated in 2016. However, this situation did not last: by 2021, the trucks loaded with fruit and vegetables from Morocco (about 15 to 20 per week) returned to unloading around the "Mosquée marocaine" market. Our hypothesis is that a lack of insights into the urban logistics chain and of manpower has hindered the separation between trading activities and fresh produce supply logistics, in relation to additional costs for transporters and retailers. The relocation of the wholesale fruit and vegetables market outside the city is now under study, to relieve congestion in the city center.
>
> Sources: field observations and interviews conducted between
January 2020, and June 2022, JICA (2018)

Many of the practices described above are regarded as informal – i.e., not subject to a declaration of activity, and therefore undetected by statistics, taxation, or national accounting. Portes (1983) points out that the distinction between the formal and informal sectors did not exist in 19th-century capitalism, but that the organizations that are now referred to as informal existed before the recent formal organization of the economy. By analogy with the work of Godard (2002) on urban passenger transport in African cities, we could describe informal urban logistics practices as artisanal, or even independent and controlled by small players. These activities are in fact governed by rules of use and organizations, and they are generally subject to local taxes and restrictions, for example to temporarily occupy a particular space. In addition, operations (vehicles, storage facilities) may be governed by professional organizations, or even unions, overseeing collective bargaining agreements and individual responsibilities. In this context, all the categories and hierarchies of formal activities are present: owners, operators, subcontractors, intermediaries – but with cheap labor and

Figure 25.1 Photographs of the surroundings of the "Mosquée marocaine" market, January 2020
Source: Author

a much more atomized structure, which leads to a fragmented distribution structure, due to the multiplication of intermediaries within logistic chains. The consequence is a multiplication of journeys between wholesalers, semi-wholesalers, and stores, often with low stocks. In their North-South comparative study, Malik et al. (2017) observed 97 trips per day in a shopping district of Gothenburg (Sweden), against 140 in the Indian case study considered as equivalent, i.e., 44% more. They also found that 76% of the flows were carried by light vehicles (less than 7.5 t.) in Delhi, while 80% were carried by heavy vehicles in Gothenburg (7–26 t.). This more fragmented organization does increase the number of parties involved in the distribution chain, but it is particularly suited to dense city centers. The last mile, relying on clean, electric, animal or human-powered vehicles, is also relatively environmentally friendly. Due to these cities' urban and cultural characteristics, the last mile is typical of the Global South. In this context, the structure of trade plays a large part in the atomization of urban distribution (Figure 25.1).

Trade Structure and Urban Logistics: Context, Evolution, and Resistance

The logistics of distribution is a textbook case for explaining the organizational characteristics of cities in the Global South. Long-established forms of retail, based on small neighborhood stores,[6] are deeply rooted in everyday practices. Such shops are the norm in trading; proximity plays a key role in their operation, in a context where households remain poorly motorized.[7] These small shops are ubiquitous, and can be found on almost every street corner in working-class neighborhoods. They sell small quantities of everyday products (dry groceries, fresh products, cleaning products). They often receive deliveries several times a day, sometimes directly from a distributor's warehouse, as is the case for the distribution of cold drinks in individual packages, and with an efficient reverse logistics system. These forms of distribution are generally complemented by street vending and open-air markets, which play an important role in household purchases and contribute to the visibility of so-called informal trading and logistical activities in the public space (Sekhani et al., 2019).

Mass retail and its modern logistics have developed in the cities of the Global South for the last 20 years (Sonntag and Kulke, 2021). As in the North, mass retail (owned by national capital or international joint ventures) was first developed in urban peripheries on very large sites, following the shopping mall model. The emergence of large retailers did not fundamentally change the structure of commerce in the Global South, since these mainly catered for the upper middle class. The creation of these new stores did not therefore significantly impact small street corner businesses. However, over the last decade, large-scale retailers have moved into city centers and residential neighborhoods, offering smaller stores and more adapted products (smaller formats, sale by the unit to reach lower-income households). The low level of household motorization and the difficulty of reaching the outskirts by public transport have determined the model of the suburban shopping center, which is adapted to the suburbs of developed countries, rather inoperative in the South. Due to this urban penetration of mass retail, modern organization models tend to become more widespread in the Global South, but there is reluctance from the part of potential users (retailers, transporters). "Pen and paper" accounting, to quote the logistics operators interviewed in 2018 in Tangier, is often preferred over digital tracing, which would allow the authorities to control their activities. Modernization and mass retail practices therefore only have a limited influence in logistics in the Global South. In Morocco, 15% of goods flows (retail sector) transit through the new warehouses built in dedicated areas in the periphery (Debrie and Mareï, 2019). In India, only 7–10% of trade transits through mass retail. Small grocery stores, or *kiranas*, remain predominant. Their supplies are delivered several times a day through a local platform, whose function is not solely dedicated to logistics. These small retailers maximize their assets to resist the offensive of mass retail throughout the country: their ability to sell very small quantities, the provision of credit, proximity, and even home delivery. In reaction to the resistance of small shop owners, of which there are about 15 million in India, the state is creating many obstacles to the establishment of foreign capital (Franz and Müller, 2015).

Ultimately, modern and artisanal supply chains transit through different channels and are increasingly competing in the cities of the Global South. This is what we call the dualization of logistics (Debrie and Mareï, 2019; Mareï et al., 2019; Mareï and Savy, 2021): the coexistence of, on the one hand, standardized and modernized practices implemented by large international operators and distributors, and on the other hand persisting, and often predominant, informal or artisanal practices. Geographically, there is a distinction between the center and the periphery, with fine, fragmented logistics that are very well adapted to dense city centers, and new logistics that require space and set up their warehouses in the periphery. It is likely that these two forms of urban logistics will evolve side by side, with little prospect of hybridization, even if e-commerce is likely to mix some of these flows.

Finally, small-scale logistics – relying on carts, trolleys, and three-wheelers – keeps the price of last mile services low, but partly hinders the development of logistics in line with international standards of safety and quality. Small traders depend on a supply chain that does not comply with international standards in terms of vehicles, storage, and handling. The hidden economic and social costs of these practices are difficult to assess, but issues include the lack of insurance in case of problems, the frequency of road accidents, and the large disparities in wages. Despite these dysfunctions, this commercial and logistical environment is the source of many jobs of all types, maintaining essential connections in the social and economic structures of developing countries (Mareï and Savy, 2021). These small actors also have a remarkable capacity to adapt: some of them now use WhatsApp to take orders from their customers and deliver them, and they are also able to obtain supplies at low prices on the internet, thus adapting their practices while remaining rooted in the local community. In this context, changes in the urban distribution sector are contributing to the strengthening of a service economy. The latter has benefited from the development of IT (notably access to a phone line and the internet), the increased availability of second-hand three-wheelers, and the Covid-19 pandemic that has helped promote urban delivery in the Global South countries.

Conclusion and Discussion: Transitions and Diversification in Urban Logistics

Logistics provides a framework for analyzing ongoing changes in the world's cities, including those of the Global South, from a territorial, multi-scalar, and forward-looking perspective. Some trends are accelerating in the Global South, including the standardization and internationalization of flows: these trends are consolidated by the influence of globalized discourses, practices, and standards, most of which are devised in other parts of the world. In contrast, the Global North is seeing a significant rise in local dynamics and proximity logistics, often backed by militant discourses on short supply chains. In the Global North, last miles logistics is also becoming increasingly fragmented and relying on job insecurity. Cities in developing and emerging countries are thus evolving in reverse from cities in developed countries (Mareï and Savy, 2021). However, the evolution of the sector may not be summarized by this oscillation between standardization and fragmentation: the key characteristic resides above all in the wide variety of logistics systems according to the urban, economic, and political context. The logistics transition is therefore multiform. While this concept is not yet established in the academic literature, it is interesting to consider it to explain the ongoing, visible, and probably profound changes at work in logistics systems, which also affect the cities of the Global South.

These observations present similarities with reflections on the diverse forms of capitalism and their regulation: scholars are now moving away from the idea of a global convergence toward uniform, institutionalized, and standardized operations, and discussing the role of small actors and more "informal" or even hybrid models that respond to local specificities and are also less costly (Amable, 2009; Hall and Soskice, 2002; Portes, 1983). The diversity of jobs provided by the informal sector (Daniels, 2004), together with the social stability that it generates, make its eradication unlikely in developing countries. Nevertheless, the risks associated with precarious and low-performing urban logistics by the standards of developed countries are real. In particular, the impact of distribution costs on the prices of everyday consumer goods is high, despite a last mile that benefits from cheap labor. Paradoxically, in the Global South, the price of transport weighs on the population's purchasing power even more than in the Global North. Some practices are also dangerous: uncontrolled storage, unsafe and overloaded vehicles, conflicting uses, and modes of transport on the public highway due to a lack of planning. The regulation of traffic, parking, and storage poses major issues in urban planning policies, which are becoming increasingly necessary. However, in the cities of the Global South, moving people remains a priority over transporting goods. Urban passenger transport has undergone major changes with, for example, the introduction of dedicated transport corridors (tramways, bus rapid transit). It should be noted that these transformations have not eliminated small-scale passenger transport. Goods transport is only beginning to be considered in urban master plans, after being initially relegated to the outskirts (creation of warehouses and dry ports), and therefore remains a marginal consideration on the agendas of municipal authorities.

This Global South perspective prompts us to reflect on the notion of logistical transition in the world's major metropolises, as well as on the circulation of urban distribution models between the North and South, and vice-versa. The mobility of people and goods does not only rely on conventional travel systems (mass transport and storage); it is also increasingly dependent on alternative modes, such as the three-wheelers that have become popular in the Global South (Tastevin, 2012), or non-motorized modes that have long been used in these countries to respond to the need of local retail and to the cities' sometimes impracticable density. If we consider that we are currently witnessing a logistical transition, this change should lead to the coexistence of diversified practices, both in the Global South and North.

Notes

1. For a complete definition of Global South, see https://globalsouthstudies.as.virginia.edu/what-is-global-south. Two elements from this definition should be highlighted. First, Global South has traditionally been used as post-cold war alternative to Third World and is now often preferred to developing countries by many scholars. Second, on recent years and within a variety of fields, it is used to indicate that there are economic "Souths" in the geographic North and "Norths" in the geographic South. This second approach is very useful in geography because it allows comparisons between countries of the geographical North and South.
2. Logistics can be defined as the sum of activities and operations that enable the transport of goods within and between urban areas. Urban areas can refer to urban or metropolitan areas, where constraints can be strong (population density, urban sprawl). These aspects are even more manifest in Southern cities. Urban logistics is a specific and important segment of logistics, which is strongly influenced by the local political and spatial framework.
3. Other indices exist, such as private group Agility's "Emerging markets logistics index," based on domestic and international economic indicators for a series of countries regarded as emerging.
4. Out of 54 African countries, 37 have launched a medium-term "emergence" plan. *The Conversation*, 2021: https://theconversation.com/ce-qui-emerge-dans-lemergence-de-lafrique-99165
5. Egypt's logistics projects progress, EUI, 2021: http://country.eiu.com/article.aspx?articleid=840601067&Country=Egypt&topic=Economy&subtopic=Forecast&subsubtopic=Economic+growth
6. Nicknamed "nanostores" (Blanco and Fransoo, 2013).
7. For example, in sub-Saharan Africa, Diaz Olvera et al. (2020) indicate that in spite of a strong rise of household car ownership, the sub-continent that was home to 13% of the world's population in 2015 only accounted for 2% of car ownership (including over a third in South Africa).

References

Agence japonaise de coopération internationale (JICA) (2018). *Le Projet d'Élaboration du Schéma Directeur d'Aménagement et d'Urbanisme de la Ville de Nouakchott en République Islamique de Mauritanie*. Rapport final, RECS International Inc., CTI Engineering International Co., Ltd., PACET Corporation, PASCO Corporation.

Agence Marocaine du Développement de la logistique (AMDL) (2016). *Guide national de la logistique urbaine. Comment structurer la logistique urbaine au sein des villes marocaines*. Agence marocaine pour le développement de la logistique, sd.

Amable, B. (2009). Capitalisme et mondialisation: une convergence des modèles ? *Cahiers français*. 349, 57–62.

Banomyong, R., Thai, V. V., and Yuen, K. F. (2015). Assessing the national logistics system of Vietnam. *The Asian Journal of Shipping and Logistics*. 31(1), 21–58.

Dablanc, L., and Frémont, A. (eds.) (2015). *La métropole logistique, le transport de marchandises et le territoire des grandes villes*, Paris, Armand Colin.

Dablanc, L., Giuliano, G., Holliday, K., and O'Brien, T. (2013). Best practices in urban freight management: lessons from an international survey. *Transportation Research Record*. 2379(1), 29–38.

Daniels, P. W. (2004). Urban challenges: the formal and informal economies in mega-cities. *Cities*. 21(6), 501–511.

Debrie, J. (2010). *Contribution à une géographie de l'action publique: le transport entre réseaux et territoires*. Habilitation à Diriger des Recherches, Tome 3, Université Paris 1 Panthéon-Sorbonne.

Debrie, J., and Mareï, N. (2019). The evolution of State action in development and planning policies in Morocco: the case of logistics. *L'Espace Politique*. 36 | 2018-03, Varia 2019.

Dimitriou, H. T. (2006). Towards a generic sustainable urban transport strategy for middle-sized cities in Asia: Lessons from Ningbo, Kanpur and Solo. *Habitat International*. 30(4), 1082–1099.

Franz, M., and Müller, P. (2015). *Foreign direct investment in Agri-food networks in India and Sub-Saharan Africa*. Bischöfliches Hilfswerk MISEREOR e.V., Mendelova Univerzita in Brno, Caritas Czech Republic. Aachen, Praha.

Ghorra-Gobin, C., and Azuelos, M. (2015). Capitalism in the global age: Beyond national specificities? *Revue LISA/LISA e-journal. Littératures, Histoire des Idées, Images, Sociétés du Monde Anglophone – Literature, History of Ideas, Images and Societies of the English-speaking World*. 13(2). https://doi.org/10.4000/lisa.8189

Godard, X. (eds.) (2002). *Les transports et la ville en Afrique au sud du Sahara: Le temps de la débrouille et du désordre inventif*. Karthala/INRETS, Paris.

Hall, P. A., and Soskice, D. (2002). Les variétés du capitalisme. *L'Année de la regulation*. 6, 47–124.

Hallward-Driemeier, M., Nayyar, G. (2018). *Trouble in the making? The future of manufacturing-led development*. World Bank, Washington, DC.

Hesse, M. (2002). Shipping news: the implications of electronic commerce for logistics and freight transport. *Resources, Conservation and Recycling*. 36(3), 211–240.

Kin, B., Verlinde, S., and Macharis, C. (2017). Sustainable urban freight transport in megacities in emerging markets. *Sustainable Cities and Society*. 32, 31–41.

Kumar, A., Zimmerman, S., Arroyo Arroyo, F., SSATP (2021). *Myths and Realities of Informal Public Transport in Developing Countries: Approaches for Improving the Sector - Discussion Paper*. World Bank, Washington, DC.

Malik, L., Sanchez-Díaz, I., Tiwari, G., and Woxenius, J. (2017). Urban freight-parking practices: the cases of Gothenburg (Sweden) and Delhi (India). *Research in Transportation Business & Management*. 24, 37–48.

Mareï N., Debrie J. and et Lombard J. (2019). Sur la route des métropoles logistiques du Sud. L'exemple de Casablanca. *Urbanités*. #11 / Bouger en ville.

Mareï, N., and Savy, M. (2021). Global South countries: The dark side of city logistics. Dualisation vs Bipolarisation. *Transport Policy*. 100, 150–160.

Merk, O., and Notteboom, T. (2015). *Port hinterland connectivity*. Discussion paper, no. 2015/13, IFT / OECD.

Ministry of Industry and Trade (2020). *Vietnam logistics report 2020. Reduce logistics costs*. Industry and Trade Publishing House, Hanoï.

Monios, J. (2011). The role of inland terminal development in the hinterland access strategies of Spanish ports. *Research in Transportation Economics*. 33(1), 59–66.

Munoz, J-M (2021). A truck driver's-eye view of N'Djamena's shifting logistics. *APAD 2021 International conference: circulations in the global south: ethnographic explorations of globalized exchanges*, Lomé, 29/11 – 3/12, 2021.

Ng, A. K., and Cetin, I. B. (2012). Locational characteristics of dry ports in developing economies: some lessons from Northern India. *Regional Studies*. 46(6), 757–773.

Nguyen, L. C., and Notteboom, T. (2016). A multi-criteria approach to dry port location in developing economies with application to Vietnam. *The Asian Journal of Shipping and Logistics*. 32(1), 23–32.

Notteboom, T., and Rodrigue, J. P. (2007). Re-assessing port-hinterland relationships in the context of global supply chains. In Wang, J., Notteboom, T., Olivier, D. and Slack, B. (eds), *Ports, Cities, and Global Supply Chains*. Aldershot, Ashgate, 51–68.

Nugent, P. (2018). Africa's re-enchantment with big infrastructure: White elephants dancing in virtuous circles? In Schubert, J., Engel, U., and Macamo, E. (eds), *Extractive industries and changing state dynamics in Africa*. Routledge, Abingdon, 22–40.

OECD (2020). *OECD investment policy reviews: Egypt 2020*. OECD Investment Policy Reviews. OECD Publishing, Paris.

Ohnsorge, F., and Yu, S. (eds) (2021). *The long shadow of informality, challenges and policies*. World Bank Group, Washington, DC.

Portes, A. (1983). The informal sector: Definition, controversy, and relation to national development. *Review (Fernand Braudel Center)*. 7(1), 151–174.

Raimbault, N. (2019). From regional planning to port regionalization and urban logistics. The inland port and the governance of logistics development in the Paris region. *Journal of Transport Geography*. 78, 205–213.

Rantasila, K., and Ojala, L. (2012). *Measurement of national level logistics costs and perfomance*. Discussion Paper 2012-4, OECD/ITF.

Rodrigue, J. P., Debrie, J., Fremont, A., and Gouvernal, E. (2010). Functions and actors of inland ports: European and North American dynamics. *Journal of Transport Geography*. 18(4), 519–529.

Rosa, H. (2013). *Social acceleration – A new theory of modernity*. Columbia University Press, New York.

Savy, M., and Burnham, J. (2013). *Freight transport and the modern economy*. Routledge, Abingdon.

Sekhani, R., Mohan, D., and Medipally, S. (2019). Street vending in urban 'informal' markets: Reflections from case-studies of street vendors in Delhi (India) and Phnom Penh City (Cambodia). *Cities*. 89, 120–129.

Shepherd, B. (2011). *Logistics costs and competitiveness: measurement and trade policy applications*. World Bank, Washington, DC.

Sonntag, C., and Kulke, E. (2021). The expansion of supermarkets and the establishment of delivery systems and intermediaries for fresh fruit and vegetables in the Global South–the case of Kenya and Tanzania. *DIE ERDE – Journal of the Geographical Society of Berlin*. 152(3), 166–183.

Steck, J. F. (2006). La rue africaine, territoire de l'informel ? *Flux*. 4, 7386.

Taniguchi, E., and Thompson, R. (Eds.) (2014). *City logistics: mapping the future*. CRC Press, London.

Tastevin, Y. P. (2012). Autorickshaw (1948-2...). A success story. *Techniques & Culture. Revue semestrielle d'anthropologie des techniques*. 58, 264–277.

Vu, H. N. (2019). The strategic development in logistics in Vietnam. *European Journal of Engineering and Technology Research*. 4(6), 69–73.

World Bank (2008). *World development report 2009: reshaping economic geography*. The World Bank.

26
URBAN LOGISTICS IN MEGACITIES

Quan Yuan and Zhiwei Yang

Introduction

Urban logistics is an indispensable part of the economy and an important basis for social life. Its sustainable development is key to economic growth and social welfare improvement. The latest data from the United Nations shows that more than 4.2 billion people, 55% of the world's population live in cities and towns (World Bank, 2018). In order to provide such a large urban population with a wealth of goods and services, the demand for urban logistics has been growing rapidly since the beginning of the 21st century. In addition to supporting industrial and commercial activities, logistics demand for serving online shopping customers has roared in response to the rise of e-commerce in the past decade. These changes have brought about new challenges to the coordinated and sustainable development of urban logistics systems.

Given the multi-dimensional demand, there has been a dramatic increase in terms of urban logistics facilities, land uses, and activities in megacities around the world. For instance, between 2014 and 2018, the average annual growth rate of the square footage of logistics and storage facilities in the five cities of Shanghai, Suzhou, Wuxi, Hangzhou, and Jiaxing in the Yangtze River Delta region was as high as 26% (Equal Ocean Logistics, 2019). According to the Report, the three megacities of Shanghai, Suzhou, and Hangzhou have been driving such growth, given their economic importance in the region. In the megacities where people cluster in large numbers, logistics facilities, and related activities generate negative environmental impacts including air pollution, noise, land-use inefficiency, and fragmentation of urban texture across the urban space, in spite of their significant social benefits. These impacts pose a serious threat to the health of local residents and the sustainable development of urban space (Yuan, 2018a, 2021).

According to the trajectories of policy formulation in recent years, the environmental governance of urban logistics has become a key item on the agenda of local transportation departments, especially in megacities where land is more valuable while spatial conflicts are more severe. How can megacities make plans to accommodate diversified logistics demand from a large population without imposing a significant environmental burden? One of the prerequisites for formulating urban logistics plans in line with sustainable development goals is to fully understand the complex interactions between logistics activities and urban space.

Based on the literature review, especially empirical results in the past 20 years, this chapter, from a composite spatial-temporal perspective, examines how logistics activities are associated with changing urban form and structure, and closely linked to the environmental sustainability of megacities, given the various negative externalities generated during logistics movement. On this basis, suggestions are proposed on urban logistics planning practices to address such externalities in highly heterogeneous urban space.

Defining Megacities: Why Do They Differ in the Setting of Urban Logistics?

Cities differ in terms of population size, geographic area, and economic structure, so they play varying roles in the global and domestic logistics systems. Megacities such as New York, London, and Shanghai have enormous economic power, large populations, and considerable international influence. Those characteristics determine how megacities can reshape urban logistics in a different way from smaller cities.

First, megacities invest significantly more in technological innovation, industrial upgrade, and other macroeconomic measures than cities of a smaller size. Megacities play a leading role in the industrial and economic development of the regions where they are located. Second, megacities are home to a large population size. There are both advantages and disadvantages of having people clustered in a relatively small area of land. Dense population and diverse distribution patterns of population can not only create economies of scale and agglomeration effects, but also difficulties with respect to governance. Megacities usually develop around a strong urban core and are surrounded by multiple sub-centers (Dong and Yan, 2021). The core-periphery structure leads to dramatic differences in land values and development costs. The urban core, which has limited spatial scope and land space, is featured by extremely high development intensity. The suburbs, on the other hand, have large parcels of relatively cheap developable land. In addition, the urban core with a dense population may pay more attention to environmental impacts and have more incentives to resist environmentally unwanted land use than the periphery areas.

Interactions Between Logistics Industry and Urban Space

Over the past decade, the process of economic globalization has greatly facilitated the exchange of goods and services between different regions and stimulated the growth in the demand for logistics services. Logistics demand in urban areas has been rapidly expanding in terms of both scale and intensity. A great proportion of the logistics demand is concentrated in the world's major economies and important gateway cities. Statistics from the U.S. Bureau of Statistics showed that the logistics industry employment in California was significantly concentrated in the four major cities (Los Angeles, San Francisco, San Diego, and Sacramento), while the number of logistics industry employment in all other smaller cities and rural areas was only 13%.

The highly uneven distribution of logistics demand has profound impacts on the location choices of the logistics industry within urban areas. Research showed that where logistics establishments are located is strongly subject to characteristics of a city itself, such as international trade status, industrial distribution, and geographic morphology, as well as economic and social attributes of urban space (Giuliano, Kang and Yuan, 2016). Megacities usually stand out in terms of these characteristics and are therefore subject to the following trends. First, as megacities are spatial carriers of highly concentrated production and consumption activities, logistics demand is derived from those activities. Meanwhile, with the growing personalized needs of urban residents, urban logistics services are becoming increasingly diversified and responsive to the new demand. Finally, technological improvements, including containerization, just-in-time (JIT) technologies, and automated systems, have contributed to the emergence of various value-adding logistics services in megacities. The new-generation logistics services have extended from distribution and logistics to inventory management, commercial services such as materials handling and packaging, and information processing (Lean et al., 2014). To provide these services in a timely manner, many logistics operators and developers have to reconsider the spatial distribution of their activities in urban areas where spatial and temporal constraints are present.

On the other hand, the logistics industry has reshaped the urban form and structure in the megacities to a substantial degree. First, logistics has played a significant role in promoting urban agglomeration. As a key support for the modern manufacturing industry, the logistics industry helps improve the efficiency of resource utilization through enhancing specialization and scale economies. Specifically, the efficient operation of the logistics network can not only reduce transaction costs along the supply chains, but also facilitates the connections and communications between upstream and downstream players. With the support of an efficient logistics network, the exchange of production factors such as information, technology, and capital between the regions has been further strengthened, thus promoting the agglomeration of the city. Second, high land rent in the urban core of megacities poses great challenges to logistics developers who have become increasingly concerned about land availability and costs. To meet the growing demand for logistics services, those developers have made decisions with respect to reorganizing their activities within megacities. Suburbs have become popular choices for locating logistics land uses, which in turn has shaped the landscape of suburban areas. Finally, logistics creates incentives for urban expansion. To a certain extent, the spatial distribution of logistics establishments provides a reference for the location of enterprises that rely on logistics services. Rather than passively relocating to match local demand, logistics establishments have started to exert influences on the location of their customers. For instance, distribution and fulfillment centers of major online shopping platforms have become local magnets for suppliers, which can enjoy low costs and high reliability of logistics movement.

Logistics Restructuring in Megacities: Changes and Responses

According to the neoclassic location theory (Alonso, 1964; Isard, 1956; Losch, 1959), accessibility to the market, transportation, and other resources is important to industrial location. Like other industries, the logistics industry was historically influenced by similar factors, such as the proximity to the market, land cost, and transportation access (Cidell, 2010; Sakai et al., 2018). The location choice of logistics industry was largely based on the population factor so that the related activities mostly occurred in the central areas (McKinnon, 1983). For example, Yeh and Wu (1996) pointed out the central location of industrial sites in the pre-reform period of Guangzhou. In the 1980s and early 1990s, the logistics development sites were designated and planned in the urban core to support the urban growth and take advantage of the transportation infrastructure in the city.

Fully fledged urban transport network provides logistics establishments greater locational flexibility. Any city, regardless of its size, needs transportation infrastructure services, but the larger the city, the more complex the supply of transportation infrastructure. Especially in megacities, the larger population requires better transportation infrastructure support, which is a major challenge. For this reason, compared with other cities, each megacity has spent more on transport infrastructure including freeways, airports, seaports, and intermodal facilities over the last decades. The improved transport access throughout the megacities offers suburbs great conveniences. The technological advances in transportation such as autonomous driving can further increase the accessibility of suburbs in general. Urban cores therefore no longer have dominant advantages over the periphery, especially when considering the aggravated congestion in the urban cores (Giuliano, 2004). Transport costs become increasingly even across places in the same megacities, and such changes offer logistics developers more flexibility in location choices.

The differentiation of land values in megacities has accelerated in the recent two decades, and greatly affected the distribution of the logistics industry. The densified land development and the rapid urbanization have jointly contributed to the substantial appreciation of land in the urban core (Henderson, 1974). When the land was repriced in the market, the allocation of the land was more tightly associated with revenue generation of different land uses (Tian and Ma, 2009; Zhang, 2000). Compared with most industries, the economic profit per unit of land created by the logistics industry is limited, and the competitiveness of land with high economic value is also limited. Thus, the logistics industry is at a particular disadvantage in competing for land in the central areas (Cidell, 2011). Logistics land uses thus became less spatially matched with the increased land rent in central areas. Suburbs, on the other hand, become increasingly popular as they offer attractively priced large tracts of land in addition to many other amenities (Yuan, 2018b). In many metro areas, a number of large logistics centers have been developed along the transportation corridors in the suburbs.

While the market forces and changes in urban structure have incentivized the logistics industry to spatially shift from urban cores to the suburbs, land-use decisions can still be largely dependent on local zoning and land-use planning (Bolton and Wei, 2003; Tian, 2015). The role of institutions in planning and facilitating land-use development is highlighted in the context of many megacities (Tian et al., 2017; Zhu, 2002). The land-use plans and development policies drafted by the local governments have strong influences on logistics development. As the logistics industry usually has lower job densities than many other industry sectors (Cidell, 2011) and generates limited local tax revenue, many local governments have stayed neutral or even discouraged logistics development in their jurisdictions through developing land-use policies or making development plans (Yuan, 2019).

Overall, technological advances, urban structure changes, and institutional changes jointly lead to the logistics spatial restructuring. The large-scale restructuring would in turn contribute to increased concern over environmental impacts associated with logistics activities.

Environmental Impacts of Logistics in Megacities: A Temporal Perspective

The benefits of logistics activities in fueling the economy and bolstering social welfare are self-evident. However, logistics activities also generate many categories of environmental impacts that cannot be ignored (Yuan and Chen, 2021). The large-scale occupation of land by logistics facilities, the potential environmental hazards of stored goods, and the air pollution generated by trucks, to name a few, all belong to the list of environmental impacts associated with logistics activities. In megacities with high densities of population and economic activities, those environmental impacts pose threats to health and well-being of residents and workers. Public concern over the impacts is growing, making it necessary to closely examine and evaluate the environmental impacts of logistics activities.

Short-Term Environmental Impacts

Among the negative environmental impacts caused by logistics activities, typical short-term ones include noise, traffic safety threats, and air pollution. The generation and emission of these environmental impacts are relatively immediate and rapid. For example, air pollutants, noise, traffic congestion, and accidents all occur simultaneously or immediately with the operation and movement of logistics vehicles. Without considering secondary effects or further interactions with the natural and built environment, the duration of these impacts is relatively low. The duration of vehicle noise is usually within minutes (Davis, 2017), the basic cycle of the concentration and dissipation of air pollutants ranges from several hours to tens of hours (Boubel et al., 2013; Mayer,1999), and traffic congestion and accidents usually take no more than one day to resolve (Sun et al., 2016). What's corresponding to the immediacy of these environmental impacts is their easy-to-observe characteristic. Pollutants from trucks can be performed by air quality monitoring devices (United States Environmental Protection Agency, 2020). Similarly, the monitoring of noise sources and the handling of traffic accidents are also on the routine agendas of departments of environmental protection and traffic police.

Medium-Term Environmental Impacts

The medium-term environmental impacts caused by logistics activities, including urban heat island effects, land-use inefficiency, and ecosystem destruction, are commonly featured by a relatively longer formation process and generate non-intuitive effects (Strale, 2019; Yuan, 2018a). With the increasing demand for logistics automation in logistics facilities, the sizes of those facilities, in terms of floor space and built-up area, have increased significantly in recent years. Facilities with huge flat roofs (see Figure 26.1) have a much higher heat capacity and thermal conductivity as well as low reflectivity and high absorption of sunlight than most buildings, resulting in a high-temperature microenvironment (Li, Bou-Zeid, and Oppenheimer, 2014). The spatial agglomeration of logistics facilities further aggravates the heat island effects, which could greatly harm the physical and mental health of people (Heaviside, Macintyre, and Vardoulakis, 2017).

Figure 26.1 Typical examples of logistics facility clusters in the Shanghai Metropolitan Area
Source: Rivermap

Long-Term Environmental Impacts

Impacts related to urban land value and socioeconomic structure of population last even longer, but are more often ignored by urban transportation and environmental policy-makers. Due to the large number of vehicles loading and unloading, maintenance, and storage activities, parking lots attached to logistics facilities occupy large parcels of land. Large-scale facilities and lots jointly contribute to low-density development, which has not been carefully regulated by land-use plans and thus created profound impacts on the urban form of megacities. The so-called "logistics sprawl" phenomenon has been discovered in quite a few megacities around the world. Vacant land at low prices and flexible development policies have made the suburbs a hot spot for the development of low-density logistics land uses (Aljohani and Thompson, 2016; Dablanc and Rakotonarivo, 2010). Due to the interdependent relationship in land-use development, land uses in close vicinity of those logistics facilities would be significantly affected (Yuan, 2018b).

Therefore, the aforementioned short-term and medium-term negative environmental externalities may cause the depreciation of land values and the imbalance of socioeconomic structure in communities with clustered logistics land uses and beyond. To be specific, environmental pollution can reduce the quality of life of surrounding residents, leading to a decline in the demand for surrounding residential units. Simultaneously, changes in land-use patterns can reduce the demand for land-use types with a high added value per unit area (such as commercial land and office). These changes have caused the expected values of the land to constantly shrink, or even caused equity concerns. In the long run, logistics-related environmental impacts can be a critical factor that leads to differences in socioeconomic status and demographic characteristics across places in megacities.

On the one hand, strong economic power and abundant social resources provide megacities particular advantages in attracting high-income individuals and families. On the other hand, well-established manufacturing and service industries demand a large number of migrant workers with lower incomes. Consequently, the income gap within megacities is increasing and the pattern of housing segregation increasingly affects the way megacities are organized. In general, low-income population groups, with less socioeconomic resources, are more likely to be affected by negative logistics environmental externalities. Among the few empirical evidence studies, Yuan (2021) tested whether warehouses are disproportionately associated with minority and low-income neighborhoods using data from the Los Angeles region. A set of econometric models were developed and their results indicated that logistics location was significantly and positively associated with the minority concentration but its relationship with the household income level was mixed. Such findings were consistent with several important articles in the environmental justice literature (Mohai and Saha, 2007; Pastor et al., 2016). Minority neighborhoods as a whole bear higher logistics-related environmental hazards, but low-income minority ones do not suffer from particularly higher impacts than other minority communities. This is a clear indication of environmental inequity in logistics development.

Changes in the land-use development usually take place on an annual basis or even in a longer temporal cycle, so environmental impacts subsequent to those changes can be irreversible and influential in the long-term vision of megacities (Yuan and Chen, 2021).

Policy Interventions and Responses: A Spatial Perspective

The environmental impacts of urban logistics activities have attracted growing attention from the public sector in recent years. Although the environmental impacts are mainly generated by point features such as vehicles, facilities, and land-use parcels, the scope and the way of their influences are often subject to the socioeconomic processes at different spatial scales. Policy interventions cannot be effectively conducted without paying attention to the spatial dimensions. Megacities with a large spatial extent and complex urban structure may pose challenges as well as opportunities for policy interventions at both a regional and a local scale (Yuan and Chen, 2021).

Observation and Coordination at the Regional Scale

Much of the environmental impact of urban logistics is not limited to the community, but also expands and spreads to the whole region through socioeconomic and ecological processes. The "logistics sprawl" phenomenon mentioned above is widely seen in megacities in both developed and developing countries. The sprawling expansion of logistics land uses can damage the landscape and texture of the suburbs, challenging the balance and integrity of region-wide land-use patterns (Aljohani and Thompson, 2016; Yuan, 2018a). Affected by the concentrated logistics activities, land use density, floor area ratio, community activity, and commercial vitality of surrounding areas may all experience a significant decline. The regional landscape would become segregated and fragmented due to the socioeconomic process. In this sense, the environmental impact of these facilities not only affects local communities, but also extends to the regional scale.

Logistics linkages are driven by complex and highly localized supply chain requirements. Given the high activity density and serious congestion in urban central areas or at intermodal hubs, vehicle emission processes can vary widely across locations. Although the suburban areas have low overall traffic volume, the proportion of trucks among all vehicles is high, and so is the proportion of diesel combustion-related pollutants in all ground traffic air pollutants. Meanwhile, air pollutants produced by individual vehicles would diffuse through atmospheric processes and chemically react with other substances in the air, ultimately affecting the air quality of the entire region. According to Yuan (2021), the spatial distribution of PM10, an important cargo truck air pollutant, in the Los Angeles metropolitan area is highly correlated with logistics activities. Due to the complex process of atmospheric flow, the air quality of the entire metropolitan area is affected by the emissions of trucks across places. Accordingly, the way logistics vehicles contribute to air pollution varies across urban and suburban contexts, thus leading to the complexity and regionalization of environmental impacts.

Communicate and Act at the Community Scale

The community scale is the most intuitive and fundamental scale for understanding and analyzing the environmental impacts of urban logistics movement. All enterprises, businesses, and residents in the community are intimate stakeholders regarding the environmental impacts. The coordination and mitigation of conflicts of interest among the stakeholders would depend on the design of conflict management mechanisms at the community scale.

Let's take the noise caused by logistics activities as an example. Due to the characteristics of logistics demand, especially e-commerce logistics demand, a large number of logistics vehicles enter and exit logistics facilities and hubs 24/7. These vehicle activities result in considerable mechanical noise, which seriously affects the lives of surrounding residents and the operation of commercial facilities. In order to solve this problem, the community can reduce the noise impact to an acceptable level through means such as creating vegetation and structure buffers and setting time windows for vehicle use (Yuan, 2019). Therefore, a community-scale communication and coordination mechanism is the prerequisite for solving this problem. In contrast, higher-level administrative agencies often have a limited understanding of the scope and extent of the impacts, and it is also difficult to deeply involve them in the process of communication and coordination. In this case, those agencies cannot make fundamental contributions to the solution of the problem.

Road congestion, noise pollution, and hidden traffic safety hazards caused by logistics distribution have become chronic problems in many megacities. Therefore, some cities have implemented policies that use communities as the unit of action, such as the "Off-Hour Delivery Program" pilot project in New York City. This plan involves stakeholders in urban distribution activities at the community level. Developing a community interest complex consisting of receiving merchants, logistics vehicle drivers, shipping companies, and surrounding residents is the key to the success of the plan. The community complex collects the needs and costs of different parties, offers feedback through multi-party meetings and consultations, and seeks action plans that meet the interests of all parties while satisfying the city's sustainable development goals.

The importance of combining regional and community-level mechanisms in resolving logistics-related environmental externalities can be seen in a typical case of Carson City in the Los Angeles region, a typical polycentric megacity model. Carson, a medium-size city in the region, has been reconsidering its logistics development history and searching for policy options to mitigate negative environmental consequences. Ever since the city was incorporated in 1968, residents have been dealing with quite a few locally unwanted land uses, including garbage dumps and waste treatment plants. Many of these facilities were "not in my backyard" legacies from the early 20th century when Carson was an unincorporated area of the region and lacked the political clout to block their arrival. Despite many years of effort to replace those facilities, other contaminated industrial sites still act as a hurdle to new development (City of Carson, n.d.). In these circumstances, much of the land in Carson remained industrial, and logistics land uses had grown rapidly in recent decades. Local residents as well as regional agencies noticed the environmental threats from logistics activities. A specialist from the South Coast Air Quality Management District referred to a policy guidance letter regarding a logistics project in Carson, saying, "the project did not comply with our regulatory guidance for performing a mobile source health risk assessment. As you know, we have been monitoring the emissions from the heavy-duty diesel-fueled vehicles related to logistics projects in the region".

Therefore, city planners in Carson were faced with strong demand for logistics development and increasing conflicts between logistics and residential land uses, as well as limited information to resolve the conflicts. The city attempted to learn from other cities with intensive logistics development, but existing successful models were scarce in the region. Therefore, the city "decided to take a step back and do some research first". Carson adopted a 45-day temporary moratorium on truck yards, logistics facilities, hazardous materials, or waste facilities, container storage, and container parking in 2016 (City of Carson, 2017). According to the moratorium, new logistics development was temporarily banned during the period. The ban was extended to March 2018 so city leaders could have more time to work out "new, permanent ground rules to protect residents from heavy truck traffic and pollution" (Mazza, 2017). This temporary pause in logistics development was originally driven by the residents and actively pursued by the local government. The planner from Carson mentioned above talked about their plan:

> We are planning to update the regulations on logistics development, but it may take a few years and cost millions of dollars. Although it is not easy, we know this is something we need to figure out as soon as possible.
>
> *(Carson planner, personal communication, July 11, 2017)*

A resident interviewee supported the plan, saying, "This is a good start. We do not want to tolerate the air pollution and noise. Hope the city can figure out a long-term solution" (Carson resident, personal communication, July 12, 2017). Among all case study cities, Carson is, however, the only one that adopted designated restrictions on logistics development. The progress the city has made in regulating logistics-related externalities offers a valuable lesson to other logistics-intensive cities.

All in all, the growth and development of the logistics industry result from long-term collaboration and competition among a large number of enterprises and individuals. Its interactions with urban land-use systems and transportation network systems are complex and multi-dimensional (Giuliano, Kang, and Yuan, 2018). We should not only analyze the impacts of urban logistics activities on the environment from a static perspective, but also the dynamic characteristics of this process cannot be ignored. It is particularly important in megacities which usually have a long trajectory of urban development and sophisticated relationships between local governments. Therefore, public policy formulation and social governance related to logistics are complex. In addition, different types of environmental impacts vary in modes of action, scope, and mechanism, which are worthy of consideration and attention among urban transportation policy-makers (Yuan and Chen, 2021).

Conclusion

In the era of supply chain globalization and e-commerce, sustainable development of urban civilization is highly dependent on the coordination, symbiosis, and mutual support of urban systems and logistics systems. Only by fully understanding the social benefits and costs of urban logistics and evaluating the significance and feasibility of logistics planning and policies can we maximize the social values of logistics movement. This chapter proposes a spatiotemporal perspective for studying urban logistics and exploring its path toward long-term sustainability in the context of megacities.

The ultimate goal of developing sustainable urban logistics is to improve the quality of the environment and human life. Using the spatiotemporal perspective to measure the logistics-related environmental impacts will help more comprehensively understand the roles and needs of citizens in the urban logistics system. The operation and expansion of the logistics system have brought much convenience to citizens' daily life by offering time savings and providing opportunities for lifestyle evolution. However, the clustering of logistics activities in terms of both time and space, such as the noise by delivery vehicles at night, congestion around logistics facilities, and pollution emissions close to seaports all have imposed additional negative effects on certain communities. This imbalance of benefits and costs across places and time periods is deeply embedded in the process of social economy, urban development, and land use expansion. Before the effective intervention of public policies, it is usually difficult for the market to respond with an account of both efficiency and fairness.

The logistics industry is making a great contribution to the social and economic operations, so providing development space for the logistics industry is a necessary choice for urban development. The spatial exclusion of the logistics industry is not the realistic goal of environmental justice policy analysis. Therefore, adhering to the concept of people-oriented governance, the public sector might choose to regulate environmental impacts through strategic plans and policies. Policy-makers may consider the following points when making those policies. First, to increase the transparency of the environmental impact of logistics facilities and ensure the accuracy and timeliness of the environmental impact report. At the same time, it is important to improve community residents' understanding and awareness of the environmental impact and eliminate information asymmetry. Second, to improve the environmental protection requirements for the construction and usage of logistics facilities and minimize the environmental impact of logistics facilities and their activities on surrounding communities. Third, to promote the efficient use of land by logistics facilities and reduce the damage of facilities to the artificial environment of the community through architectural and landscape design innovation. Finally, to make full use of economic and administrative means to increase the cost of the unequal spatial distribution of logistics facilities, and effectively subsidize or support vulnerable groups and enhance their ability to get rid of the burden of an unequal environment.

Urban logistics in megacities is a highly complicated system. More attention is needed to evaluate its evolving mechanism and discover ways to achieve long-term sustainability in those urban contexts with rapid growth in demand, limited environmental space and resources, and multi-stakeholder gaming.

References

Aljohani, K., and Thompson, R. G. (2016). Impacts of logistics sprawl on the urban environment and logistics: taxonomy and review of literature. *Journal of Transport Geography*, 57, 255–263.

Alonso, W. (1964). *Location and land use*. Harvard University Press, Cambridge.

Bolton, M., and Wei, Y. (2003). Distribution and logistics in today's China. China *Business Review*, 30 (5), 8–17.

Boubel, R. W., Vallero, D., Fox, D. L., Turner, B., and Stern, A. C. (2013). *Fundamentals of air pollution*. Academic Press, Cambridge.

Cidell, J. (2010). Concentration and decentralization: the new geography of freight distribution in US metropolitan areas. *Journal of Transport Geography*, 18, 363–371.

Cidell, J. (2011). Distribution centers among the rooftops: the global logistics network meets the suburban spatial imaginary. *International Journal of Urban and Regional Research*, 35 (4), 832–851. DOI:10.1111/j.1468-2427.2010.00973.x.

City of Carson. (2017). Logistics facilities moratorium. Retrieved from http://ci.carson.ca.us/CommunityDevelopment/AdHocMoratorium.aspx

City of Carson. (n.d). Growing pains of a young city. Retrieved from http://ci.carson.ca.us/About-Carson/GrowingPains.aspx

Dablanc, L., and Rakotonarivo, D. (2010). The impacts of logistics sprawl: how does the location of parcel transport terminals affect the energy efficiency of goods' movements in Paris and what can we do about it? *Procedia-Social and Behavioral Sciences*, 2 (3), 6087–6096.

Davis, R. (2017). Long-term noise exposures: a brief review. *Hearing Research*, 349, 31–33.

Dong, R., and Yan F. (2021). Revealing characteristics of the spatial structure of megacities at multiple scales with jobs-housing big data: a case study of Tianjin, China. *Land*, 10, 1144. DOI:10.3390/LAND10111144.

Equal Ocean Logistics. (2019). The amount is comparable to that of New York and Los Angeles. Where is the difference of logistics in the Yangtze River Delta? https://www.iyiou.com/p/109007.html.

Giuliano, G. (2004). Land use impacts of transportation investments. *The Geography of Urban Transportation*, 3, 237–273.

Giuliano, G., Kang, S., and Yuan, Q. (2016). Spatial dynamics of the logistics industry and implications for freight flows. National Center for Sustainable Transportation Los Angeles: METRANS Center.

Giuliano, G., Kang, S., & Yuan, Q. (2018). Spatial dynamics of logistics facilities and implications for freight flows. Institute of Transportation Studies, UC Davis.

Heaviside, C., Macintyre, H., and Vardoulakis, S. (2017). The urban heat island: implications for health in a changing environment. *Current Environmental Health Reports*, 4 (3), 296–305.

Henderson, J. V. (1974). The sizes and types of cities. *The American Economic Review*, 64(4), 640–656.

Isard, W. (1956). *Location and the space economy*. MIT Press, Cambridge, MA.

Lean, H., Huang, W., and Hong, J. (2014). Logistics and economic development: experience from China. *Transport Policy*, 32, 96–104.

Li, D., Bou-Zeid, E., and Oppenheimer, M. (2014). The effectiveness of cool and green roofs as urban heat island mitigation strategies. *Environmental Research Letters*, 9(5), 055002.

Losch, A. (1959). *The economics of location*. Yale University Press, New Haven, CT.

Mayer, H. (1999). Air pollution in cities. *Atmospheric Environment*, 33, 4029–4037.

Mazza, S. (2017). Carson extends ban on industrial growth through 2018. https://www.dailybreeze.com/2017/05/03/carson-extends-ban-on-industrialgrowth-through-2018.

McKinnon, A. (1983). The development of logistics in England. *Geoforum*, 14 (4), 389–399.

Mohai, P., and Saha, R. (2007). Racial inequality in the distribution of hazardous waste: a national-level reassessment. *Social Problems*, 54 (3), 343–370.

Pastor, M., Sadd, J., and Hipp, J. (2016). Which came first? Toxic facilities, minority move-in, and environmental justice. *Journal of Urban Affairs*, 23 (1), 1–21.

Sakai, T., Beziat, A., Heitz, A., and Dablanc, L. (2018). Testing the "Freight Landscape" concept for Paris. *Transportation Research Record: Journal of the Transportation Research Board*, https://doi.org/10.1177/0361198118776783.

Strale, M. (2019). Sustainable urban logistics: what are we talking about? *Transportation Research Part A: Policy and Practice*, 130, 745–751.

Sun, C., Hao, J., Pei, X., Zhang, Z., and Zhang, Y. (2016). A data-driven approach for duration evaluation of accident impacts on urban intersection traffic flow. IEEE International Conference on Intelligent Transportation Systems. IEEE.

The World Bank. Urban Development (2018). https://data.worldbank.org/topic/urban-development.

Tian, L. (2015). Land use dynamics driven by rural industrialization and land finance in the peri-urban areas of China: "the examples of Jiangyin and Shunde." *Land Use Policy*, 45, 117–127.

Tian, L., Ge, B., and Li, Y. (2017). Impacts of state-led and bottom-up urbanization on land use change in the peri-urban areas of Shanghai: planned growth or uncontrolled sprawl? *Cities*, 60, 476–486.

Tian, L., and Ma, W. (2009). Government intervention in city development of China: a tool of land supply. *Land Use Policy*, 26, 599–609.

United States Environmental Protection Agency. (2020). Outdoor air quality data. https://www.epa.gov/outdoor-air-quality-data/about-air-data-reports.

Yeh, A. G. O., and Wu, F. (1996). The new land development process and urban development in Chinese cities. *International Journal of Urban and Regional Research*, 20 (2), 330–353.

Yuan, Q. (2018a). Environmental justice in logistics location: state of the art. *Journal of Planning Literature*, 33 (3), 287–298.

Yuan Q. (2018b). Mega Freight generators in my backyard: a longitudinal study of environmental justice in logistics location. *Land Use Policy,* 76, 130–143.

Yuan, Q. (2019). Planning matters: institutional perspectives on logistics development and mitigating its negative impacts. *Journal of the American Planning Association*, 85(4), 525–543.

Yuan Q. (2021). Location of warehouses and environmental justice. *Journal of Planning Education and Research*, 41(3), 282–293.

Yuan, Q. and Chen, X. (2021, March). Discussion on the environmental impacts of logistics in a spatiotemporal framework. *Urban Transport of China*, 19 (2), 29–36.

Zhang, T. (2000). Land market forces and government's role in sprawl. *Cities*, 17 (2), 123–135.

Zhu, J. (2002). Urban development under ambiguous property rights: a case of China's transition economy. *International Journal of Urban and Regional Research*, 26 (1), 41–57.

27
THE GIG ECONOMY AND URBAN LOGISTICS

Geraint Harvey, Naveena Prakasam and Refat Shakirzhanov

Introduction

Work in the gig economy (Woodcock and Graham, 2019) currently represents the means to remuneration for a sizeable and increasing proportion of the workforce who opt for this kind of work, resort to 'gigging' in the absence of alternatives or engage in 'side hustling' (Sessions et al., 2021) as a means of increasing income. In the United States, for example, around one-third of workers claimed to work in the gig economy in 2017 and it was anticipated that around half of the workforce would be operating as a freelancer by 2023 (Karra, 2021). In the United Kingdom, around 15% of the workforce get paid via digital platform apps, principally among them the urban logistics firms, Uber, Deliveroo and Amazon's delivery arm, Flex (Butler, 2021). In most locations, gig workers in the urban logistics sector are legally classified as self-employed or freelance, despite efforts by workers and trade unions to classify these workers as employees. The reclassification campaigns are driven by a desire to ensure that these workers receive a decent income for the work they perform: to provide some security in an otherwise hugely insecure context. Whereas the legal status of an employee would be beneficial to many, it would not be so for all engaged in gig economy work. There have been arguments made against employee status for gig economy workers because such a move might exclude a large proportion of the labour work engaged in the gig economy in many countries that are migrants and do not have a formal work permit (Ro, 2022).

The legal status of the urban logistics gig economy workforce is one that is being fought by workers and organisations across the globe. Our purpose in this chapter is to examine the nature of work at three urban logistics organisations: Uber, Deliveroo and Amazon Flex, explaining why the work is often considered to be false self-employment. We also explore whether this kind of work meets the characteristics of neo-villeiny (Harvey et al., 2017).

False Self-employment

'Self-employment' relates to a type of professional relationship where workers are expected to manage their own business, set their rates for work and be in control of their own time (Gov.uk, 2021). 'False self-employment', sometimes referred to as bogus, synthetic or ambiguous self-employment, on the other hand, is a type of 'subordinate employment relations which are disguised as autonomous work, usually for fiscal reasons, or in order to avoid the payment of social security contributions … reduce labour costs, or to circumvent labour legislation and protection' (Eurofound, 2013: n.p.). Newsome et al. (2018) extend this definition to include dependence of workers on a limited number of clients for sources of income.

False self-employment exists where 'normal activities of self-employment are limited or non-existent, such as tendering for different contracts, negotiating prices for services with clients or employing workers in addition to, or in place of, themselves' (Behling and Harvey, 2015: 970). The relationship between the organisation and the independent contractor represents false self-employment where there is a 'substantial continuity of engagement with a single employer over many contracts, lack of control over working times, not supplying plant or materials, or obeying instructions in everyday routines' (Ibid).

An alternative and more exploitative work relationship has been identified more recently. Labelled neo-villeiny, this relationship between worker and organisation has been observed in the work of the fitness industry self-employed personal trainer (SEPT), but several of its characteristics have since been identified in other industries such as the airline industry and in firms such as Ryanair (Harvey and Turnbull, 2020).

Neo-Villeiny

Neo-villeiny is a label first applied to work in the fitness industry to encapsulate a distinctive relationship between self-employed personal trainers (SEPT) and the gym where they operate. Neo-villeiny is distinctive from genuine self-employment and also false self-employment, and its characteristics resemble the core characteristics of the feudal relationship between the lord and tenant serfs.

There are four characteristics of neo-villeiny. The first of these is the absence of a guaranteed income. This is a common feature of self-employed work, however, it combines with a second characteristic: unpaid labour that benefits the organisation, to indicate a significant risk on the part of the worker. The SEPT must engage members of a gym in the hope that they become paying clients and only then will the SEPT generate an income. If the member does not hire the SEPT then the latter receives no income. There is a significant disincentive for gym members to solicit the services of the SEPT because of the associated cost. However, in attempting to attract the client, the SEPT engages in activities that are of benefit to the gym but are not financially rewarded. For example, the SEPT might provide the gym member with fitness advice or support them, while they exercise so that they create an opportunity through which to promote their services directly to a potential client. Other examples include basic maintenance of fitness equipment, resolving problems (with lockers) and cleaning. These activities would otherwise be undertaken by paid staff.

A third characteristic is the rent that a SEPT must pay to a gym in order to gain access to the members (potential clients) in a captive environment. The gym member attends the gym in order to work out (e.g., to get fit) and the SEPT is then able to promote their services (e.g., how to get fit) directly to someone who is more receptive to the service (as they are in the gym they have some interest in their health and wellbeing) than someone reached through cold calling, for example. It is for this reason that the fourth characteristic of neo-villeiny is bondage, not necessarily to one gym (as the serf was to a landlord) but to operating in a gym.

The often substantial rent is paid because SEPTs have access to a large number of potential clients, but also to expensive fitness equipment and a facility in which to train clients.

Work in urban logistics is different from work in the fitness industry, but urban logistics work is part of the broader service industry that is particularly fecund ground for the spread of neo-villeiny. We assess the nature of work at several organisations according to the characteristics of false self-employment and neo-villeiny starting with Uber.

Uber

Like other genericised trademarks such as Kleenex and Hoover before it, Uber has become the proprietary eponym for taxi service. In just over 10 years, the company has become the most 'valuable start up in the world' (Ojo, 2017) and the dominant force in urban transportation. The success of Uber's app-based model is thanks in no small part to its creative destruction (Schumpeter, 1942) in a sector that was previously highly regulated and so Uber has toppled the prevailing system of regulations that protect 'medallion holders' monopoly rents'[1] (Rogers, 2015: 87; see also Woodcock and Graham, 2019).

The social impacts of Uber's model have been hypothesised by some (Rogers, 2015) and tested by others. For instance, a case has been made for the positive impact of work for Uber presented as the benefits afforded by work flexibility. Chen et al. (2019) argue that the flexibility afforded by driving for Uber far exceeds the flexibility available in other comparable work. In contrast, a good deal of the analysis reveals a negative impact on wages among taxi drivers in the United States, for example, where data indicate a 10% decrease as a consequence of Uber's entry into the market (Berger et al., 2018). Others have argued that the asymmetry of risk and benefit is stacked too greatly in favour of Uber also. As one driver put it:

> It's not fair that they get 60–70% of the fare when we do everything. We risk our life, we pay for insurance, we pay for the car and maintenance, we pay for everything.
> *(Uber driver, quoted in Sainato, 2021)*

Uber has been the subject of a good deal of criticism for its surge pricing algorithm that allows the organisation to raise fares based on supply and demand. However, it is for its people management strategy that the organisation continues to draw ire from the public and political sphere. Uber has inspired the neologism of 'Uberization' that represents 'conversion of regular work into contingent, itinerant and insecure 'gigs' mediated by digital algorithms and controlled by large corporations' (Fleming et al., 2019).

The status of Uber drivers is a contested terrain that differs according to any particular jurisdiction. For example, Uber drivers have been classified as employees in New York. In California, the controversial Proposition 22 signed into law in 2020 meant that Uber was able to continue 'subcontracting' to 'independent workers' (i.e., drivers), despite the 2019 Assembly Bill 5 that required firms to recognise gig workers as employees.

In 2021, the UK Supreme Court upheld an earlier ruling that Uber drivers were employees (Russon, 2021). Among the factors taken into consideration by the supreme court were that Uber drivers were in a position of subordination to Uber that:

- set the fare (and consequently determined how much drivers could earn);
- determined the terms of the contract between the driver and Uber;

- penalised drivers if they did not conform to organisational mandates, for example, if they reject too many rides (in other words if they didn't obey instructions or follow routines); and
- monitored drivers' performance through the star rating and has the capacity to terminate the relationship.

A class action lawsuit is underway in Ontario, Canada where it is argued that Uber drivers meet the definition of employees under Ontario's Employment Standards Act and should be entitled to minimum wage, vacation pay and other protections (Deschamps, 2021). Legal counsel commented on Uber workers in Ontario that

> Uber has complete control over these drivers, when they work, how they work, what they get paid for the work that they do… there are so many examples of how Uber has this control over these drivers, yet the drivers don't have the benefits and the protections that employees would normally have in situations, where the employer is in control.
>
> *(Quoted in Deschamps, 2021)*

There are several aspects of work at Uber (as set out by Rosenblat, 2016) that align with what is commonly understood to be false self-employment. First, the driver is unable to negotiate prices for services with clients. Uber is responsible for setting and changing the fares passengers pay. It is possible for the driver to offer the passenger a lower fare, but the driver cannot increase the fare. Should the driver reduce the fare then any reduction is taken from their income for the ride because the driver has no way of changing the fare within the Uber driver app.

Second, the driver must obey instructions and adhere to organisational routines. For instance, Uber sets performance targets for drivers that include the 'driver's rating, how many rides the driver accepts, and how many times they cancel a ride' (ibid). Drivers can be excluded from work (or deactivation) if they drop below an acceptance rate of 80% and maintain a very low cancellation rate. Customer rating influences whether the driver is deactivated and drivers must maintain an extremely high score. Finally, Uber imposes a large degree of control over working times by 'nudging' 'offline drivers to work at certain times or in certain locations through various incentives and messaging' (ibid).

Finally, there is a substantial continuity of engagement with a single organisation over many contracts. Uber drivers are dependent workers in the sense that they are dependent upon the platform for clients. In this way, they are very similar to the archetypal neo-villeins – the self-employed personal trainers who rely on the gym both for the means of production (the equipment) and the membership of that gym for a client base. Thus, the Uber driver experiences bondage to the app and to the organisation, without which they would struggle to generate clients. The Uber driver also has no guaranteed income and is only paid for the rides they provide. There is, however, a difference between the Uber driver and the archetype of neo-villeiny here. Uber is dependent upon customers using the service (and paying the driver) and so there is a mutual although asymmetric benefit for both the driver and Uber, both of whom get paid only when customers use the service. In contrast, gym members pay their membership fees irrespective of whether a member uses the services of the SEPT. The gym has no such motivation to ensure that members become clients of personal trainers. *Whereas the work of the self-employed personal trainer is consequently more precarious, there is no guaranteed income for either worker.*

There are two characteristics of neo-villeiny that separate it from false self-employment more generally. The first of these is the rent required by an organisation in order for the worker to operate. Whereas the personal trainer pays a rent on a monthly basis, the driver pays a rent to Uber in the form of a fee per fare and a commission based on the total fare. Second, there is the unpaid labour, unrecognised and unrewarded by the organisation. For the self-employed personal trainer, this work can take many forms as discussed above. For the Uber driver, this might include the provision of perks, such as 'phone chargers or bottled water', for example, or by 'Go[ing] above and beyond to make the experience special, such as opening doors for riders when possible,' and 'Ask[ing] if the rider has a preferred route,' (Rosenblat, 2016). Most important of all, however, is the time spent waiting for a fare or travelling to collect a passenger.

Recent changes to the law in Canada at first appeared to offer digital workers some hope of better terms and conditions. The announcement of 'historic' new legislation in Ontario meant that gig workers would be included in minimum wage legislation. The Working for Workers Act that came into effect in June 2022 will guarantee gig workers a $15CAD per hour minimum wage.[2] However, the minimum wage applies only to active hours, which means that a large percentage of a gig worker's time, e.g., waiting for the next fare estimated to be around 40% of the worker's time, will not be covered by the legislation.

Amazon Flex

Amazon has become a key economic player in the Western hemisphere: an employer with more than 1.3 million employees worldwide (and the second largest employer in the United States, Glazer, 2021) and a ubiquitous part of everyday life of consumption (Altenried, 2019). While considerable attention has been paid to Amazon's less-than-stellar track record of work conditions within its 'fulfilment centres' (Delfanti, 2021; Richardson et al., 2020; Purkayastha and Tangirala, 2019; Briken and Taylor, 2018), the discussion around the nature of its 'crowdsourcing' work within the field of urban logistics remains relatively novel. Considering the expansive growth of Amazon over the period of the COVID-19 pandemic, adding hundreds of thousands of people to its workforce (Businesswire, 2021; Rapp and Harty, 2021; Weise, 2021), further discussions about the nature of its 'crowdsourcing' within urban logistics could not be any more relevant.

'Crowdsourcing' through digital platforms, or apps, is a type of logistics work within the 'last mile' – that extremely competitive stage of the supply chain that sees products delivered to the customer – predicated upon digital platforms that manage customer orders and workflows, providing individuals with an opportunity to 'book' work and be paid on a per-job basis (Asdecker and Zirkelbach, 2020; Fernie and McKinnon, 2009). Crowdsourcing is a rapidly changing labour domain emerging at the crossroads of a number of trends:

- the rise and accessibility of smartphone technology;
- the normalisation of 'non-traditional' work unbound from the 'conventional' work space;
- the growth of value chain intermediaries, propagation of self-employment and informal recruitment practices;
- the spread of 'nonstandard'[3] and 'bogus or ambiguous self-employment'; and
- an increase in unpaid labour in online work, blurring the distinction between work and private life (Huws et al., 2017: 317).

Work at Amazon Flex is precarious precisely due to the highly flexible and individualised character of digital platform work. Although urban crowdsourcing may be attractive to its workers for the illusory promise of employment autonomy (Asdecker and Zirkelbach, 2020), such flexibility disproportionately benefits the employer.

Amazon crowdsources private individuals to act as casual, self-employed delivery drivers – otherwise known as 'independent contractors' – to deliver some of the packages to customer doorsteps (Parliament UK, n.d.). Amazon Flex delivery work is algorithmically managed, i.e., managed entirely through a digital platform, an app, that allocates work, provides guidance to picking up and delivering parcels, collects and analyses the relevant performance and customer satisfaction metrics, and replaces direct oversight of managers over its workers (Altenried, 2019).

Although Amazon Flex drivers are defined by the organisation as self-employed, the nature of their contracts points to such work being false self-employment. Amazon workers find themselves in a situation of close digital scrutiny and route in-app control, or else risk arbitrary deactivations for 'breaching' Amazon Flex's terms of service, thus effacing any real semblance of the promised autonomy of self-employment (McGrath et al., 2021; Palmer, 2021; Soper, 2021; Semuels, 2018). The digital nature of work at Amazon Flex highlights its neo-Taylorist tendencies for totalising control of its workforce predicated upon 'a variety of forms and combinations of software and hardware ... for new modes of standardisation, decomposition, quantification and surveillance of labour' (Altenried, 2019: 122).

The UK website for Amazon Flex encourages workers to 'Adjust your work, not your life' and to 'Get paid, enjoy life, repeat' and promises to provide anyone in a possession of a smartphone and a driver's licence with an opportunity to sign up via a dedicated app and start delivering (Amazon Flex UK, 2021: n.p.). This opportunity comes at the cost of security.

Precarious employment of this kind represents an asymmetry of benefits weighted in favour of the 'employer'. Flexibility for the worker entails uncertainty, financial insecurity and work intensification (Underhill and Quinlan, 2011; Kalleberg, 2009). This process is by no means novel (see, e.g., Umney and Kretsos, 2014; Gill, 2007; Standing, 1997). However, what sets urban logistics platform work apart from other fields is the digital nature of management, control and surveillance (Altenried, 2019) that distances its self-employed workers from any traditional management oversight hierarchies.

Understanding the 'crowdsourcing' work at Amazon Flex through the lens of 'false self-employment' is only helpful in recognising some of the emerging issues of pervasive employment precariousness. The concept of 'neo-villeiny' may in fact provide a better analytical frame for understanding such work. First, workers are bonded – or dependent – upon the digital platform in order to provide work. Second, workers have no guaranteed income. With an extensive 'reserve army' (Bourdieu, 1998: 82) of workers at their disposal, Amazon Flex does not guarantee any work, or 'blocks', to their drivers, leaving them often at the mercy of non-transparent 'algorithmic' management and unfair dismissals. Third, workers pay rent indirectly in the form of vehicle maintenance, insurance and general subsistence, as well as covering any other costs related to smartphone purchasing and bills, in order to qualify to be a delivery driver – costs that would otherwise be the businesses to bear. Although these payments do not go directly to the 'lord of the land' – Amazon – such flexible arrangements directly benefit the employer by reducing the costs of running the business under the 'traditional' contractual obligations (Friedman, 2014). These costs lower the real income of these workers (McGrath et al., 2021; Semuels, 2018) and also lower business costs for Amazon. Finally, the work involves extensive unpaid labour that these workers are tacitly expected to do, such as waiting for assignments to arrive, attend training sessions, scan packages, or dealing with work-related injuries (Tims, 2019; Zaleski, 2018).

Coupled with pervasive financial insecurity, it is not difficult to imagine how Amazon Flex drivers have become exemplar subjects of 'neo-villeiny' at the forefront of contemporary urban logistics.

Deliveroo

Deliveroo, founded in 2013, is a UK-based online food delivery platform that offers distribution services from local restaurants (Briziarelli, 2019). Deliveroo workers carry out geographically tethered work (Woodcock and Graham, 2019), i.e., work tied to a particular geographic location. The provision of work is exclusively organised online. Deliveroo is a 'service providing intermediary digital platform organisation' (Duggan et al., 2020: 118) through which workers perform food delivery tasks. Duggan et al. (2020) explain this process as a multiparty working relationship which involves the supplier, the customer, the app and the worker. In the case of Deliveroo, the customer uses the Deliveroo app to order food from a participating restaurant (supplier), the app notifies the worker, who then collects the food from the restaurant and delivers it to the customer. Deliveroo displaces its business risk by outsourcing most of its assets, and the only item that Deliveroo owns is 'an (inter) mediation, i.e., an exclusive delivery service relationship between buyers – the customers ordering food delivery – and sellers, the restaurants' (Briziarelli, 2019: 824) in addition to the app and intellectual property. In other words, Deliveroo, like most platforms, tightly manages a large and invisible workforce by acting as an intermediary (Prassl, 2018).

Deliveroo workers are classified as 'self-employed contractors rather than employees of the company' (Gregory, 2021: 317). Such a legal designation has repeatedly been considered for legal scrutiny. For instance, Deliveroo successfully intervened in a case brought by the Independent Worker Union of Great Britain, to argue that Deliveroo workers should not have worker status which alleviates Deliveroo from any responsibilities towards workers should something go wrong (Woodcock and Graham, 2019). Deliveroo work has been referred to as 'sham self-employment' (Gregory, 2021: 317; Leighton, 2016). The employment conditions of these workers are characterised by the 'demutualisation of risk' (Gregory, 2021: 317; DeStefano, 2016). This means that the risks encountered during work are fully transferred to workers and none of it is borne by the employer. Such precarisation of work (see Alberti et al., 2018) is reflective of gig work at large, which are forms of work that are both precarious and fractured (Woodcock and Graham, 2019) because there is little possibility for career advancement. Gig work has become temporary and unstable due to the economic transformation that has taken place through the gig economy, which has led to workers spending less time at one job, undertaking more jobs and spending unpaid time searching for gigs. Even though Deliveroo allocates work to its workers through its in-built logistics using algorithms, there is a lack of transparency around the algorithm used to allocate work (Gregory, 2021).

The characteristics of neo-villeiny have been explained in the preceding sections of this chapter. These characteristics can be identified in Deliveroo. Two of the characteristics of neo-villeiny which include, absence of guaranteed income, and bondage, are linked to algorithmic management. Algorithmic management causes uncertainty and confusion amongst workers because they are designed in a way, which means that workers do not quite understand how it works (Gregory, 2021; Woodcock and Graham, 2019). Algorithmic management is a system of control where algorithms make key decisions that affect workers and labour. These algorithms don't just produce similar decisions consistently, but they also write themselves based on workers' performance (Duggan et al.,2020). Specifically, in the case of Deliveroo, the uncertainty around how the algorithm works relates to work allocation, and whether accepting more rides favours the workers in any way. Uncertainty over the availability of future work means that Deliveroo app-workers do not have a guaranteed level of income. Such a lack of guaranteed income is a key characteristic of neo-villeiny work.

In August 2016, a protest was staged by Deliveroo workers in London over an announced change in payment policy from an hourly wage to piecework payment. Approximately 150 moped drivers gathered outside Deliveroo's head office in London. These moped drivers were subsequently joined by cyclists. This protest was accompanied by an unofficial strike where workers logged out from the app, leading to the disruption of work. The protest and strike led to Deliveroo withdrawing the new payment policy at that time (Tassinari and Maccarrone, 2020). However, this has subsequently changed, and Deliveroo workers now get paid per delivery. As the per-delivery payment does not account for the travel and waiting time of a gig, Deliveroo workers often carry out unpaid work when travelling and waiting times are longer than expected. This unpaid labour is a characteristic of neo-villeiny.

Deliveroo workers encounter physical, financial and epistemic risks (Gregory, 2021). Physical risks could include the risk of bodily harm through road accidents or physical assaults. The impact of the risk is heightened due to the COVID-19 pandemic, as workers received little support if they contracted COVID-19 (Skelton, 2021). Financial risks involve the risk of being completely financially dependent on unguaranteed Deliveroo earnings. For instance, one rider fell off her bike and felt pressured to get back on her bike as soon as possible because she was financially dependent on Deliveroo (Gregory, 2021). This financial dependence on Deliveroo, results in a substantial continuity of engagement with a single employer. While Deliveroo workers are also able to work for other types of platforms at the same time, the fact they are dependent on platform work can be seen as bondage, another characteristic of neo-villeiny.

A connection between neo-villeiny and financial risk is the ongoing costs for equipment maintenance, such as Deliveroo workers having to maintain their own bikes. This can be seen as an example of workers paying rent to their employers. Additionally, if the Deliveroo box (provided by the company) were to break, then Deliveroo would charge the workers the money to make up for the costs, which can also be viewed as rent, a characteristic of neo-villeiny. The more the Deliveroo workers rely on the employer, the more financial risk they incur (Gregory, 2021). Finally, epistemic risk refers to the lack of transparency around algorithmic control. Accepting or rejecting orders contribute towards worker performance metrics, but it isn't clear how the algorithms work as discussed earlier in the preceding sections. The control over Deliveroo workers is largely facilitated via algorithmic management systems that have control over workers' schedules (Gregory, 2021).

In the absence of traditional HRM processes, app-work still carries out HRM-like activities including but not limited to processes such as assigning tasks and performance management. However, the way the working relationship is managed has raised concerns over power imbalances as well as worker wellbeing (Duggan et al., 2020; Healy et al., 2017). The algorithmic mechanisms contradict the supposed flexibility and autonomy offered by Deliveroo to create precarious workers. As neo-villeiny suggests, the distinction between self-employed workers and employed workers is blurred as self-employed workers carry out many activities carried out by employees, so too is the case with Deliveroo workers who undertake false self-employment.

Conclusion

Organisations such as Uber, Amazon Flex and Deliveroo maintain that the work documented herein is genuine self-employment, throwing huge sums of money into campaigning and legally defending challenges from workers. For example, Uber invested $205 million in order to get Proposition 22 passed (Hiltzik, 2020). Meanwhile, many (but not all) workers with a contract for services will argue that they are entitled to a contract of service and the attendant benefits. Irrespective of the legal status of these workers, it is clear from the discussion in this chapter that work for these organisations bears the hallmarks of neo-villeiny.

In the last 2 years, the COVID-19 pandemic had a profound and grave impact on many industries. Many gig workers either lost their source of income or faced a reduction in hours as a consequence of the crisis (Karra, 2021). However, the pandemic has had a positive impact on the urban logistics sector as consumerism was forced online consolidating the already dominant position of online retail (Charm et al., 2020) (see Chapter 29). At the same time, the pandemic has inspired what has become known in the United States as the Great Resignation to describe the unprecedented number of people leaving their jobs. More than 24 million people left their jobs in the United States between April and September 2021 (Sull et al., 2022). This phenomenon is not exclusive to the United States (Cook, 2021; Tharoor, 2021). It should be noted that the Great Resignation has been redubbed the Great Renegotiation (Rosalsky, 2022) as many of the departures reflect a move out of low-paid employment rather than a movement out of the labour market. As a consequence of the Great Resignation (or Great Renegotiation), there is an increased demand for urban logistics staff at a time when there is an increasingly tight labour market.

Then there is the Russian invasion of Ukraine that has led to the forced migration of more than 5.3 million[4] Ukrainian people many of whom will look to these organisations for work. Nonetheless, the crisis has also had a major impact on fuel costs as countries including the United Kingdom and the United States have banned the import of Russian oil – that comprises 10% of the global oil supply.[5] And so, while these organisations might exploit a desperate reserve labour force in the form of Ukrainian immigrants, the work itself is far less lucrative as a consequence of the costs associated with driving. These crises may well precipitate a change in the nature of work within urban logistics as the fully automated vehicle or delivery by drone are still some distance away.

Notes

1. Prior to Uber the taxi service in the United States was regulated such that a driver would be required to obtain a permit to act in this capacity, constraining the supply of cabs.
2. https://www.cbc.ca/news/canada/toronto/ontario-legislation-gig-workers-minimum-wage-1.6366844
3. To borrow on a term coined by Kalleberg (2009).
4. https://www.bbc.co.uk/news/world-60555472
5. https://www.nytimes.com/explain/2022/03/09/business/gas-oil-russia-ukraine

References

Alberti, G., Bessa, I., Hardy, K., Trappmann, V., and Umney, C. (2018). In, against and beyond precarity: Work in insecure times. *Work, Employment and Society, 32*(3), 447–457.

Altenried, M. (2019). On the last mile: Logistical urbanism and the transformation of labour. *Work Organisation, Labour & Globalisation, 13*(1), 114–129. https://doi.org/10.13169/workorgalaboglob.13.1.0114

Amazon Flex UK. (2021). Become an Amazon Flex Delivery Driver in the UK. https://flex.amazon.co.uk/

Asdecker, B., and Zirkelbach, F. (2020). What drives the drivers? A qualitative perspective on what motivates the crowd delivery workforce. *Hawaii International Conference on System Sciences 2020 (HICSS-53)*. https://aisel.aisnet.org/hicss-53/in/crowdsourcing/3

Behling, F., and Harvey, M. (2015). The evolution of false self-employment in the British construction industry: A neo-Polanyian account of labour market formation. *Work, Employment and Society, 29*(6), 969–988.

Berger, T., Chen, C., and Frey, C. B. (2018). Drivers of disruption? Estimating the Uber effect. *European Economic Review, 110*, 197–210.

Bourdieu, P. (1998). *Acts of resistance: Against the new myths of our time* (Reprint). Polity Press.

Briken, K., and Taylor, P. (2018). Fulfilling the 'British way': Beyond constrained choice—Amazon workers' lived experiences of workfare. *Industrial Relations Journal, 49*(5/6), 438–458. https://doi.org/10.1111/irj.12232

Briziarelli, M. (2019). Spatial politics in the digital realm: The logistics/precarity dialectics and Deliveroo's tertiary space struggles. *Cultural Studies, 33*(5), 823–840.

Businesswire (2021, April 29). Amazon.com announces first quarter results. https://www.businesswire.com/news/home/20210429006037/en/Amazon.com-Announces-First-Quarter-Results

Butler, S. (2021, November 5) Gig-working in England and Wales more than doubles in five years. *The Guardian*.

Charm, T., Coggins, B., Robinson, K., and Wilkie, J. (2020, August 4). The great consumer shift: Ten charts that show how US shopping behavior is changing. *McKinsey and Company*.

Chen, M. K., Rossi, P. E., Chevalier, J. A., and Oehlsen, E. (2019). The value of flexible work: Evidence from Uber drivers. *Journal of Political Economy, 127*(6), 2735–2794.

Cook, I. (2021, September 15). Who is driving the great resignation? *Harvard Business Review*.

Deschamps, T. (2021, August 13) Ontario court certifies class action against Uber that could see some workers recognized as employees. *cbc.ca*. https://www.cbc.ca/news/canada/toronto/Uber-class-action-toronto-employees-david-heller-1.6139825

Delfanti, A. (2021). Machinic dispossession and augmented despotism: Digital work in an Amazon warehouse. *New Media & Society, 23*(1), 39–55. https://doi.org/10.1177/1461444819891613

DeStefano V (2016) Introduction: crowdsourcing, the gig-economy and the law. *Comparative Labor Law & Policy Journal, 37*(3), 461–470.

Duggan, J., Sherman, U., Carbery, R., and McDonnell, A. (2020). Algorithmic management and app-work in the gig economy: A research agenda for employment relations and HRM. *Human Resource Management Journal, 30*(1), 114–132.

Eurofound. (2013). Self-employed or not self-employed? - Working conditions of 'economically dependent workers', 18.

Fernie, J., and McKinnon, A. (2009). Part 4. Emerging issues: Technology and environmental logistics - Chapter 10. The development of e-tail logistics. In *Logistics & Retail Management* (pp. 207–232). Kogan Page Ltd. https://www.proquest.com/docview/275965666/abstract/7A251222A5CB46BEPQ/1

Fleming, P., Rhodes, C., and Yu, K. H. (2019). On why Uber has not taken over the world. *Economy and Society, 48*(4), 488–509.

Friedman, G. (2014). Workers without employers: Shadow corporations and the rise of the gig economy. *Review of Keynesian Economics, 2*, 171–188. https://doi.org/10.4337/roke.2014.02.03

Gill, R. (2007). *Technobohemians or the new cybertariat? New media work in Amsterdam a decade after the web*. Institute of Network Cultures.

Glazer, A. (2021) Amazon now employs almost 1 million people in the U.S. — or 1 in every 169 workers. *NBCnews.com*, July 30th.

Gregory, K. (2021). 'my life is more valuable than this': Understanding risk among on-demand food couriers in Edinburgh. *Work, Employment and Society, 35*(2), 316–331.

Gov.uk. (2021). Working for yourself. *GOV.UK*. https://www.gov.uk/working-for-yourself

Harvey, G., Rhodes, C., Vachhani, S. J., and Williams, K. (2017). Neo-villeiny and the service sector: The case of hyper flexible and precarious work in fitness centres. *Work, Employment and Society, 31*(1), 19–35.

Harvey, G., and Turnbull, P. (2020). Ricardo flies Ryanair: Strategic human resource management and competitive advantage in a Single European Aviation Market. *Human Resource Management Journal, 30*(4), 553–565.

Healy, J., Nicholson, D., and Pekarek, A. (2017). Should we take the gig economy seriously? *Labour & Industry, 27*(3), 232–248.

Hiltzik, M. (2020, November 4) Column: With Prop. 22, Uber and Lyft used their wealth to reshape labor law in their sole interest. *Los Angeles Times*.

Huws, U., Spencer, N., Syrdal, D., and Holts, K. (2017). Work in the European Gig Economy: Research results from the UK, Sweden, Germany, Austria, The Netherlands, Switzerland and Italy. FEPS, UNI Europa, University of Hertfordshire. https://uhra.herts.ac.uk/bitstream/handle/2299/19922/Huws_U._Spencer_N.H._Syrdal_D.S._Holt_K._2017_.pdf

Kalleberg, A. L. (2009). Precarious work, insecure workers: Employment relations in transition. *American Sociological Review; Washington*, 74(1), 1–22. https://search.proquest.com/docview/218852964/abstract/AAA4F72B1FC4408CPQ/1

Karra, S. (2021, May 13) The gig or permanent worker: Who will dominate the post-pandemic workforce? *Forbes*.

Leighton, P. (2016). Professional self-employment, new power and the sharing economy: Some cautionary tales from Uber. *Journal of Management & Organization*, 22(6), 859–874.

McGrath, P., Smiley, M., and Chalmers, M. (2021, August 28). 'This is just no way to live': What it's like delivering parcels for Amazon. *ABC News*. https://www.abc.net.au/news/2021-08-29/amazon-flex-delivery-drivers-voice-safety-concerns/100404498

Newsome, K. J., Moore, S., and Ross, C. (2018). 'Supply chain capitalism': Exploring job quality for delivery workers in the UK. 22.

Ojo, S. (2017). The uber case: The future of an innovative and disruptive start-up firm. In *SAGE Business Cases*. SAGE Publications: SAGE Business Cases Originals.

Palmer, A. (2021, February 4). Amazon is using AI-equipped cameras in delivery vans and some drivers are concerned about privacy. *CNBC*. https://www.cnbc.com/2021/02/03/amazon-using-ai-equipped-cameras-in-delivery-vans.html

Parliament UK. (n.d.). Amazon Flex TOC. https://www.parliament.uk/globalassets/documents/commons-committees/work-and-pensions/Written_Evidence/Amazon-flex-contract.pdf

Prassl, J. (2018). *Humans as a service: The promise and perils of work in the gig economy*. Oxford: Oxford University Press.

Purkayastha, D., and Tangirala, V. K. (2019). Dark side case: Amazon.com, Inc. and the human cost of fast shipping. *Academy of Management Proceedings*, 2019(1), 11833. https://doi.org/10.5465/AMBPP.2019.11833abstract

Rapp, N., and Harty, D. (2021). Just how massive Amazon has grown during the pandemic, in 8 charts. *Fortune*. https://fortune.com/2021/10/18/amazon-massive-growth-covid-pandemic-8-charts/

Richardson, R. E., Gordey, L., and Hall, R. (2020). Amazon's fast delivery: The human cost. *Journal of Business Ethics Education*, 17, 251–254. https://doi.org/10.5840/jbee20201716

Ro, C. (2022, March 8) Why gig work is so hard to regulate. *BBC.com*. https://www.bbc.com/worklife/article/20220308-why-gig-work-is-so-hard-to-regulate

Rogers, B. (2015–2016). The social costs of Uber. *University of Chicago Law Review Dialogue*, 82, 85–102.

Rosalsky, G. (2022, January 25) The great resignation? More like the great renegotiation. *NPR.org*.

Rosenblat, A. (2016, April 6). The truth about how Uber's app manages drivers. *Harvard Business Review*. https://hbr.org/2016/04/the-truth-about-how-Ubers-app-manages-drivers

Russon, M-A. (2021) Uber drivers are workers not self-employed, Supreme Court rules. *BBC.com*, February 19th. https://www.bbc.com/news/business-56123668.

Sainato, M. (2021) 'A slap in the face': California Uber and Lyft drivers criticize pay cuts under Prop 22. *The Guardian*, May 16th.

Schumpeter, J. (1942) *Capitalism, socialism and democracy*. New York: Harper.

Semuels, A. (2018, June 25). I delivered packages for Amazon and it was a nightmare. *The Atlantic*. https://www.theatlantic.com/technology/archive/2018/06/amazon-flex-workers/563444/

Sessions, H., Nahrgang, J. D., Vaulont, M. J., Williams, R., and Bartels, A. L. (2021). Do the hustle! Empowerment from side-hustles and its effects on full-time work performance. *Academy of Management Journal*, 64(1), 235–264.

Skelton, S.K. (2021, April 7th) Deliveroo riders strike over pay and work conditions. https://www.computerweekly.com/news/252498995/Deliveroo-riders-strike-over-pay-and-work-conditions

Soper, S. (2021, July 3). Fired by bot at Amazon: 'It's you against the machine'. *The Seattle Times*. https://www.seattletimes.com/business/amazon/fired-by-bot-at-amazon-its-you-against-the-machine/

Standing, G. (1997). Globalization, labour flexibility and insecurity: The era of market regulation. *European Journal of Industrial Relations*, 3(1), 7–37. https://doi.org/10.1177/095968019731002

Sull, D., Sull, C., and Zweig, B. (2022). Toxic culture is driving the great resignation. *MIT Sloan Management Review, 63*(2), 1–9.

Tassinari, A., and Maccarrone, V. (2020). Riders on the storm: Workplace solidarity among gig economy couriers in Italy and the UK. *Work, Employment and Society, 34*(1), 35–54.

Tharoor, I (2021) The great resignation goes global. *The Washington Post*, October 18th.

Tims, A. (2019, April 14). Fines and a frantic life on the road – the lot of Amazon's harried staff. *The Observer.* https://www.theguardian.com/money/2019/apr/14/amazon-fines-depot-workers-driver

Umney, C., and Kretsos, L. (2014). Creative labour and collective interaction: The working lives of young jazz musicians in London. *Work, Employment and Society, 28*(4), 571–588. https://doi.org/10.1177/0950017013491452

Underhill, E., and Quinlan, M. (2011). How precarious employment affects health and safety at work: The case of temporary agency workers. *Relations Industrielles / Industrial Relations, 66*(3), 397–421. https://doi.org/10.7202/1006345ar

Weise, K. (2021). Amazon's profit soars 220 percent as pandemic drives shopping online. *The New York Times.* https://www.nytimes.com/2021/04/29/technology/amazons-profits-triple.html

Woodcock, J., and Graham, M. (2019). *The gig economy. A critical introduction.* Cambridge: Polity.

Woodcock, J. (2020). The algorithmic panopticon at Deliveroo: Measurement, precarity, and the illusion of control. *Ephemera, 20*(3), 67–95.

Zaleski, O. (2018, November 10). Drivers for Amazon Flex can wind up earning less than they realize. *The Seattle Times.* https://www.seattletimes.com/business/amazon/drivers-for-amazon-flex-can-wind-up-earning-less-than-they-realize/

28
GENDER DIVERSITY IN URBAN LOGISTICS

Anicia Jaegler, Salomée Ruel, Nadine Kafa and Lucy Budd

Introduction

A growing body of evidence from the International Labour Organization (ILO), the European Commission, national Government agencies, corporate groups and individual companies attest to the economic benefits and social importance of gender diversity and equality in the workforce. Employing women alongside men on an equal basis has repeatedly been shown to enhance business outcomes across a range of performance metrics and economic sectors (on which see Chang, 2019). These studies have collectively shown that gender diversity improves business outcomes and that inclusive corporate cultures, in which all workers are valued for their individual skills and contributions irrespective of their gender, ethnicity and other personal characteristics, outperform other enterprises on measures ranging from creativity to innovation to profit (Chang, 2019). Transportation, supply chains and the urban logistics sector are no exception.

However, despite this, and in common with other modes of transport (see Hamilton *et al.*, 2005; Wright *et al.*, 2022), the global urban logistics sector remains dominated by men. In 2017, it was estimated that only 2% of logistics workers worldwide were female and although this figure masks some significant regional differences (see the following section), the fact remains that despite recognition in some quarters of the financial and corporate benefits of having a more gender-diverse and gender-equal workforce and contemporary discourses concerning gender mainstreaming (see Banks, 2022), the urban logistics sector remains overwhelmingly male dominated.

This lack of diversity not only affects institutional governance and corporate culture but also potentially limits innovation, impacts a company's brand reputation and reduces its attractiveness to potential employees and investors. Research indicates that a lack of gender diversity also affects tangible financial performance indicators including sales, suppressing return on investment, limiting revenue potential and, ultimately, restricting potential profits (on which see Tidsdale, 2022). Although there is a growing body of work exploring gender in transportation (French and Strachan, 2009) and supply chains (Pavia *et al.*, 2020; Ruel and Jaegler, 2021), until recently, there has been relatively little academic research into the opportunities for, benefits of, and challenges to achieving, greater gender diversity in urban logistics.

The purpose of this chapter is thus threefold. First, it elucidates the key benefits of gender diversity in the workforce and applies this to urban logistics. Second, it highlights the challenges to achieving gender diversity and equality in the urban logistics workforce and, thirdly, offers practical recommendations as to how urban logistics can become more gender-equal and benefit from a more diverse talent pool.

To achieve this aim, the chapter is structured as follows: The following section reviews the current state of the sector pertaining to women's employment in logistics and the extent of the "gender gap" in urban logistics. This is followed by an exploration of the nature of the gender pay gap in logistics, with particular reference to the United Kingdom where all companies employing 250 or more personnel are legally required to submit annual data on pay by gender. This leads into a discussion in the next section on the gender leadership gap in logistics and identifies the importance of female recruitment, retention and progression to securing a diverse talent pipeline of future leaders. The penultimate section explores initiatives that commercial companies and legislators can take to make urban logistics a more attractive and inclusive employment destination for women. The chapter ends with a short conclusion that summarizes the key points and identifies areas for future research.

The Gender Gap in Urban Logistics

It is estimated that almost 90% of countries worldwide have some form of legal restriction on women working (ILOSTAT, 2022). In a small number of cases, women are legally prevented from engaging in any form of paid employment while other countries explicitly prohibit women from working in specified job roles (e.g. front-line combat positions in the military). Even in countries that have passed specific gender-equality legislation, the reality is that women typically shoulder a greater share of unpaid caring and domestic responsibilities than men (ILO, 2018a), earn less than men for doing equivalent jobs, are more likely to work part time and in insecure employment, and are less likely to be promoted to senior leadership positions than their male counterparts, despite their educational achievements and qualifications often being equal to, or (in some cases) superior than, those of men (see ILOSTAT, 2022).

At the international level, the United Nations embed gender equality in the 17 Sustainable Development Goals, with SDG 5 specifically seeking to "achieve gender equality and empower all women and girls" (United Nations, 2015). The ILO states that equal opportunities and equal treatment in the labour market are the core of "decent work" but recognizes women face multiple barriers to accessing equal employment and professional development opportunities on account of their gender (ILO, 2018a; ILOSTAT, 2022). Depending on geographic location and cultural context, specific occupations and certain types of work may pose additional challenges to female participation, often on account of cultural norms and historical value judgements framing what types of jobs were/are considered to constitute "appropriate" forms of work for women.

Such occupational job segregation by gender is particularly evident in the fields of transportation and logistics which, historically, required (or at least were perceived to require) relatively high levels of manual labour and physical strength for which women were considered physiologically unsuitable or unable to perform. Although increased digitization, automation and a greater emphasis on customer service and client communication have collectively transformed many aspects of logistics, gender segregation remains. For example, in the United Kingdom, it is estimated that fewer than 1.5% of heavy goods vehicle (HGV) drivers, 2.5% (approximately 1 in 40) of forklift truck drivers, 7% (1 in 14) of van drivers and 16% of warehouse operatives are women and only 16% of all staff employed at road transport companies were women (Tidsdale, 2021).

In Germany, a survey undertaken for the Federal Logistics Association (BVL) reported that the proportion of women in the logistics, transport and traffic industries in 2017 was 20.7%, a figure which increased to 28.7% if drivers were excluded (BVL, 2019). Where women were employed in the sector, the survey revealed that they still predominately held what are often seen as being traditionally "female" roles in human resources, procurement and purchasing. As tellingly, perhaps, according to the same source, women accounted for only 18.6% of board members of the top 100 German logistics companies (BVL, 2019). In the United Kingdom, the equivalent figure for managers and directors in all logistics companies has been reported to be 25% (under the UK average of 39%; Tidsdale, 2022).

Such findings confirm the fact that women are particularly scarce at middle and senior management levels (particularly at C-Suite and Director/Executive Board level) within transportation firms (see Amaugo, 2022; McLaughlin and Fearon, 2022) with the higher the level of corporate or operational responsibility the lower the number of women. The lack of progression from junior to senior roles and the subsequent relative absence of female talent at Board level has been described as the "leaky pipeline" and multiple policy initiatives and practical interventions at a range of levels have been proposed as a means to address it. This is an issue that is explored in more detail below. As well as a difference in the absolute number and promotion prospects of women employees in logistics, the difference in pay awarded to men and women working in the sector is another measurable indicator of potential inequality and it is to this issue that the chapter now turns.

The Gender Pay Gap in Urban Logistics

Although the pay gap between women and men has declined in some countries, it remains significant with global estimates in 2018 suggesting, overall, women's pay was at 22% of men's median monthly wages (ILO, 2018b). Notable variations in the gender pay gap between countries, by ethnicity and social status, and within individual economic sectors are also apparent.

Despite the ILO Equal Remuneration Convention of 1951 (No. 100) being one of the most widely ratified conventions by the ILO Member States, the principle of "equal remuneration for work of equal value" is highly complex and the comparison of equivalent work may not always be applied. In 2017, the ILO, in conjunction with the OECD and the United Nations Entity for Gender Equality and the Empowerment of Women, launched the Equal Pay International Coalition to support national governments, employers and workers' organizations to take positive action to reduce the gender pay gap. Some national governments have also introduced mandatory pay gap reporting in the expectation that placing this information in the public domain will encourage a conversation around the gender pay gap and a shift in employer behaviour.

The United Kingdom is one country that has adopted this regulatory approach. The UK Government defines the gender pay gap as being the difference between the average (mean or median) earnings of men and women across a workforce. It is calculated as the difference between average hourly earnings (excluding overtime) of men and women as a proportion of men's average hourly earnings (excluding overtime). It is important to note, however, that this is a measure across all jobs in the United Kingdom, not of the difference in pay between men and women for doing the same job (ONS, 2022).

From 2017, all UK employers with a headcount of 250 or more employees must comply with the gender pay gap reporting regulations. The resulting data and calculations are based on annual payroll information submitted by each firm on a specific reporting date each year. Employers may, if they wish, also submit a voluntary supporting narrative and action plan with their payroll data. The resulting information is available at https://gender-pay-gap.service.gov.uk/ and can be searched either by an individual company name or by using a Standard Industrial Classification (SIC) code which groups organizations according to their core areas of activity.

Pre-pandemic figures from 2018 to 2019 showed that, across the UK logistics sector, more than 75% of logistics companies paid men, on average, 9.7% more than women, a figure which hides significant gaps in some individual companies (Tidsdale, 2021). In April 2021, across the United Kingdom as a whole, the gender pay gap was 7.9%, down from 9.0% in April 2019. Although caution is needed given the impact of the pandemic, national lockdowns and furlough, the figures show considerable variation in pay between different regions of the United Kingdom and also notable differences in the gender pay gap between employees aged 40+ years and those aged under 40. Overall, there is a much larger difference in hourly pay between men and women in the higher pay bands than there is between those on lower hourly wages. The data also reveals differences within and between economic sectors.

Although there is no single SIC code for urban logistics, the most relevant are 49200 (Freight rail transport), 49410 (Freight road transport) and 49410 (Road transportation and storage). In the case of Freight rail transport, the seven companies that reported under this category in 2020/2021 had a mean hourly difference in pay between men and women between 7.5% and 26%. Women dominated the lower pay bands but only accounted for 4.1–13.9% of staff in the upper hourly pay quarter band (UK Government, 2022).

The UK Office for National Statistics (ONS) also publishes data on gender pay by occupation. Table 28.1 details the gender pay gap and average hourly pay for men and women in four occupation classifications relevant to urban logistics. In the case of managers and directors in transport and logistics, women earn an average of 15.2% less than men. The pay gap for road transport drivers (which has the highest hourly pay of the four categories considered here) is 11.3% while for other drivers and transport operatives, the difference is 0.5%. Interestingly, women working as managers and directors in transport and distribution earn 1.1% more than men.

Table 28.1 Gender pay gap in selected logistics occupations, UK, 2021

Occupation classification	Gender pay gap	Average hourly pay – Women	Average hourly pay – Men
Managers and Directors in transport and logistics	Women earn 15.2% less than men	£13.64	£16.08
Road transport drivers	Women earn 11.3% less than men	£10.06	£11.34
Other drivers and transport operatives	Women earn 0.5% less than men	£23.97	£24.09
Managers and Directors in transport and distribution	Women earn 1.1% more than men	£18.14	£17.97

Source: Data derived from ONS (2022)

The Gender Leadership Gap in Urban Logistics

In addition to there being a demonstrable gender pay gap in urban logistics, there is also evidence of a significant leadership gap with fewer women applying for, or being appointed to, executive boards and directorship positions. Studies in the United States have shown that gender-diverse boards outperform male-only ones on a range of key performance indicators including return on sales and capital and profitability (see Tidsdale, 2022) and there is a strong business case as well as a moral/ethical imperative to promote women into these positions. Work undertaken by Kolasińska-Morawska *et al.* (2019) investigated the role of women leadership and discussed the role of female contributions to the success of logistics companies. However, despite evidence of the commercial benefits of gender-diverse leadership teams, progress has been slow. The "glass ceiling" in logistics, above which women do not rise, and which Lynagh and colleagues identified in the late 1990s (Lynagh *et al.*, 1996, 1999), is arguably still relevant and one which many firms are seeking to actively address through a range of initiatives which aim to enhance female participation and promotion in urban logistics.

Enhancing Female Participation in Urban Logistics

The underrepresentation of women in all (but particular senior) roles is not, of course, an issue confined solely to urban logistics and the sector can actively learn from best practices adopted elsewhere. In terms of recruitment, a range of interventions including promoting logistics careers at school, ensuring images of the workforce on corporate publications feature a diverse range of colleagues, reviewing job titles and descriptions in job advertisements to ensure gender neutrality and avoid gender bias, and asking applicants to submit anonymous CVs to remove the potential for unconscious bias by shortlisting committees can be enacted.

A number of firms have recognized that the subject decisions taken at school are instrumental in shaping students' future careers and that a range of interventions can be made at a relatively young age to make students aware of the career opportunities in logistics and give them information to enable them to make informed choices about which subjects to study (Benson and Chau, 2017). Studies have shown that students form perceptions about the suitability (or otherwise) of future careers relatively early and that some careers are considered less attractive to women as they are deemed to be less compatible with family life (see Knemeyer *et al.*, 1999). An increased expectation from employees that companies will promote greater work-life balance and deploy flexible ways of working is one legacy of the COVID-19 pandemic but may not always be compatible with work that requires a physical presence on site.

When at the interview stage, it may be appropriate to ensure gender-diverse panels who appoint a person based on their competence, not confidence. Companies can also benchmark their wages, bonus criteria and roles to ensure greater transparency and senior managers can demonstrate their commitment to diversity.

Once employed, companies can help to ensure an inclusive culture. This can be through steps as seemingly simple as ensuring that shift patterns and uniforms/personal protective equipment (if required) are appropriate and (in the case of apparel) comfortably and safely fit different body sizes and shapes and that men and women have access to appropriate changing and sanitary facilities when at work (see Kuknor and Bhattacharya, 2021). Companies can also publish guidance on what is considered acceptable behaviour in the workplace and raise awareness of inclusivity.

Managers and Directors can also formalize mentoring arrangements which encourage and empower female employees to apply for promotion, pay increases and bonuses on an equal footing to men as well as clearly defining promotion and bonus criteria and applying them equally to all employees (Tidsdale, 2019). Of particular importance here is having women role models occupying senior positions to make female presence and contributions to the business visible to all employees and external customers and stakeholders. This is important, for as Zinn et al. (2018) have shown, lack of visible female role models can reduce the appeal of logistics to other women.

As well as providing support from within a company, there is also a role for external advocacy and support networks for women working in logistics. In 1981, women in logistics (WIL) was established in California. This non-profit organization provides a forum for networking, knowledge exchange and mentoring for women and men who work in transportation, supply chain and logistics. In the United Kingdom, a dedicated women in logistics forum was established in 2008. In 2018, it became incorporated into the Chartered Institute for Logistics and Transport (CILT UK) and has a vision to "Improve the lives of women in logistics in the UK and address gender imbalance, enabling the logistics industry to benefit from female talent". Both organizations seek to enhance networking opportunities, share best practice and enable women logistics professionals and businesses to benefit from more gender-equal working environments.

At a global level, in 2013, CILT International launched Women in Logistics and Transport (WiLAT) to promote the industry to female workers and encourage and support female career development through advocacy and empowerment. Dr Dorothy Chan, WiLAT Global Chairperson and Global Advisor, stated in June 2019 that *"we firmly hold the view that diversity and encouraging more female participation in our industry… will do the industry well"*. However, to achieve this, urban logistics companies need to address some of the historic structural inequalities and actual or perceived barriers to enable greater levels of female participation, integration and engagement in the sector.

Conclusion

Gender in urban logistics is an issue which, until recently, has been largely overlooked in the academic literature. The fact that women are still poorly represented in the urban logistics sector is likely not due to their qualifications or aspirations. It is rather more likely to be a legacy of a corporate culture that historically has been run by men, for men, and with arguably little consideration of the corporate and social benefits of a more diverse and inclusive workforce.

By reviewing the current state of the sector pertaining to women's employment in logistics and the extent of the "gender gap" in urban logistics, the chapter has shown that it is not just the absolute number and proportion of women employed in the sector which is significant but also the difference between roles wo/men perform and the wages/salaries they command. In addition to revealing often considerable differences in mean hourly pay, statistics from the United Kingdom also expose disparities in job roles, including the over-representation of women in lower-paid administrative and supporting roles and their underrepresentation in the higher pay bands, especially in C-Suite and Director level posts. The gender leadership gap in logistics is notable but one which can be addressed through targeted female recruitment, retention and progression. Commercial companies and legislators are already seeking to make urban logistics a more attractive and inclusive employment destination for all workers, including women.

Digitization, automation and a greater focus on communication, flexibility and customer service is rapidly transforming the public image of logistics from one of hard manual labour in which workers manoeuvred heavy roll cages in draughty warehouses towards a more service-based, digitized and people-focused work environment. Logistics companies are now representing themselves to potential workers in new ways and are seeking to become much more attractive employers through changes in working practices and contracts which allow for more flexibility and a better work-life balance.

References

Amaugo, A. (2022) *Examining the culture of women in aviation leadership: A case of UK airports* in Wright, T., Budd, L. and Ison, S. (Eds) *Women, work and transport* Bingley, Emerald; 189–206.

Banks, S. (2022) Logistics needs more women. *Logistics Management* 28/03/2022.

Benson, G. E., and Chau, N. N. (2017). The selection of a supply chain management major by female students. *Journal of Higher Education Theory and Practice*, 17(4), 24–39.

BVL (2019) *Man's world?! Opportunities for and with women in logistics.* Federal Logistics Association (BVL), Germany, conducted on behalf of transport logistic, 04/19. Available online at https://transportlogistic.de/en/trade-fair/industry-insights/women-in-logistics-professions/Accessed 17/06/22.

Chang, J-H. (2019) *Unpacking the business case for gender diversity* in Kuptsch, C. and Charest, É. (Eds) *The future of diversity* Geneva, ILO: 15–29.

French, E., and Strachan, G. (2009). Evaluating equal employment opportunity and its impact on the increased participation of men and women in the transport industry. *Transportation Research Part A: Policy and Practice*, 43(1), 78–89.

Hamilton, K., Jenkins, L., Hodgson, F., and Turner, J. (2005). *Promoting gender equality in transport* (Vol. 34). Equal Opportunities Commission, Manchester.

ILO (International Labour Organization). (2018a.) *Care work and care jobs for the future of decent work.* ILO, Geneva. Available online at https://www.ilo.org/global/publications/ books/WCMS_633135/lang--en/index.htm.

ILO (2018b) *Global Wage Report 2018/19: What lies behind gender pay gaps.* ILO, Geneva. Available online at https://www.ilo.org/global/publications/books/WCMS_650553/lang--en/index.htm.

ILOSTAT (2022) *International labour organisation labour force statistics.* Available online at https://ilostat.ilo.org/

Knemeyer, A. M., Murphy, P. R., and Poist, R. F. (1999). Opportunities for women in logistics: An analysis of student perspectives. *Transportation Journal*, 39(1), 34–41.

Kolasińska-Morawska, K., Sułkowski, Ł., and Brzozowska, M. (2019). Leadership and the role of women in the success of logistics companies. *Leadership*, 5(4), 93–107.

Kuknor, S., and Bhattacharya, S. (2021). Exploring organizational inclusion and inclusive leadership in Indian companies. *European Business Review*, 33(3), 450–464.

Lynagh, P. M., Murphy, P. R., and Poist, R. F. (1996). Career-related perspectives regarding women in logistics: A comparative analysis. *Transportation Journal*, 36(1), 35–42.

Lynagh, P. M., Murphy, P. R., and Poist, R. F. (1999). Career perspectives of women in distribution: congruency or contrast? *International Journal of Physical Distribution & Logistics Management*, 29(3), 192–207.

McLaughlin. H., and Fearon, C., (2022). *Closing the gender gap in the maritime industry: A career-decision approach* in Wright T, Budd L and Ison S (Eds) *Women, work and transport* Bingley, Emerald: 265–278.

ONS (2022) *Gender pay gap in the UK: 2021.* Available online at https://www.ons.gov.uk/employmentandlabourmarket/peopleinwork/earningsandworkinghours/bulletins/genderpaygapintheuk/2021 Last accessed 20/06/2022.

Pavia, E., Tonelli, M. J., Miguel, P., and Biazzin, C., (2020) *Supply chain management and gender: challenges for a changing world* in Choi, T. Y., Li, J. J., Rogers, D. S., Schoenherr, T. and Wagner S. M. *The Oxford handbook of supply chain management.* Oxford, Oxford University Press.

Ruel, S., and Jaegler, A. (2021). Impact of gender and expatriation choice on career paths in supply chain management: Evidence from master of science graduates. *Sustainability*, 13(12), 6907.

Tidsdale, K. (2019). *Inspiring change: The gender pay gap and why it matters.* CILT UK.

Tidsdale, K. (2021). *Why trends for women in logistics are important for your business.* 6/10/21. Available online at https://www.shdlogistics.com/women-logistics/why-trends-women-logistics-are-important-your-business.

Tidsdale, K. (2022). *Why diversity trends in logistics are important for your business.* SHD Logistics. Available online at https://cet.gcp.informamarkets.com/sites/cet.com/files/Diversity_Trend-Logistics_eBook.pdf. Accessed 29/06/2022.

UK Government (2022) *Gender pay gap reporting.* Available online at www.gov.uk/gender-pay. Last Accessed 20/07/22.

United Nations (2015) *The 17 United Nations sustainable development goals.* Available online at https://sdgs.un.org/goals.

Wright, T., Budd, L., and Ison, S. (2022). *Introduction* in Wright, T., Budd, L. and Ison, S. (Eds) *Women, Work and Transport* Bingley, Emerald: 1–10.

Zinn, W., Goldsby, T.J., and Cooper, M.C. (2018). Researching the opportunities and challenges for women in supply chain. *Journal of Business Logistics, 39*(2), 84–86.

29
POST-PANDEMIC IMPACTS OF COVID-19 ON URBAN LOGISTICS

John R. Bryson

Introduction

COVID-19 has been both a discontinuity and an inflection point (Bryson and Vanchan, 2020; Bryson et al., 2021; Andres et al., 2022). A discontinuity represents a lack of continuity or some form of interval, break, or gap; with discontinuities being disruptions of a current trend, and this trend might continue once the discontinuity has concluded. An inflection point is a significant event that changes the trajectory of some process, and this could involve a social-cultural inflection point resulting in major socio-economic changes. Inflection points represent a period of disruptive change and are much more significant than more incremental changes. A discontinuity, combined with a cultural inflection point, represents a period of unusual change which transforms the future.

COVID-19 challenged the existing trajectory of globalisation based on increased fragmentation of supply chains (Bryson and Vanchan, 2020). There were problems sourcing products and components linked to lockdowns that impacted factories as well as logistics. A series of incidents highlighted the dangers of over-dependency on global supply chains. In March 2021, the Ever Given container ship became wedged across the Suez Canal for six days. Around 12% of global trade travels along this canal and this blockage delayed 420 ships. It impacted global supply chains for approximately two months as the planned geography of freight traffic had been disrupted with container ships unable to meet their agreed schedules (Bryson, 2022). The Russian invasion of Ukraine which commenced on 24 February 2022 also highlighted the risks associated with over-dependency on global supply chains. For Russia, sanctions were imposed that severed Russia from global flows of components, products, raw materials, expertise and money. Over-dependence on Russian oil and gas resulted in major problems for countries like Germany, Bulgaria and Poland as Russia engaged in a game of 'energy poker' (Kumar, 2021). The outcome is an appreciation of the need to balance local supply with global supply chains to enhance economic security or sovereignty (Bryson et al., 2021). Economic sovereignty has moved up the political agenda as governments increasingly appreciate the need to maintain the continuity of supply of components, raw materials and products. One solution is the on-going emergence of a new form of globalisation based on a different blend of local versus global provision with important implications for logistics. An excellent example is the European Union's Digital Compass plan that was announced on 9 March 2021 (European Commission, 2021). This plan intends to double the manufacture of semi-conductor chips in Europe to represent 20% of the global market by 2030. This is a policy based on digital sovereignty which is intended to safeguard European citizens against supply chain disruptions and over-dependency on chip-making plants located in other national jurisdictions. This relates to enhancing the security of supply and reflects macro-scale adjustments that are rippling across the globe as governments and companies become increasingly concerned with supply chain contingency planning.

COVID-19 altered capitalism's trajectory in multiple ways. On the one hand, it accelerated the adoption of working from home, resulting in companies introducing a different balance between working in employer premises and home working. Multilocational work alters the geography of work but also has important implications for the geography of consumption (Andres et al., 2022). On the other hand, COVID-19 accelerated the transition from bricks and mortar retailing to e-commerce with important implications for urban logistics as retailers had to rapidly improvise solutions to alterations in the nature of demand (see Chapter 10). The shift towards e-commerce can be traced back over the last two decades and has been driven by alterations in supply and consumer behaviour (Bryson, 2021). Nevertheless, COVID-19 accelerated this process as retailers were forced to either adopt e-commence or to enhance existing provision. It is important to appreciate that 'working from home' does not necessarily involve working from home but might involve working close to home in a co-working space or third space in which people perform work away from employers' premises.

COVID-19 altered the geography of demand and supply for consumer goods in cities and this then has important implications for urban logistics. This includes an escalation in the adoption of e-commerce with a resulting increase in last-mile deliveries. In the United Kingdom, between July 2019 and 2020, there was a 5.2% increase in light commercial traffic vehicle miles and a −8.6% decline in vehicle miles by cars and taxis (Department for Transport, 2021a). Over the ten-year period ending June 2011, light commercial vehicle miles increased by 29.3% compared with a 10.4% decline in vehicle miles by cars and taxis (Department for Transport, 2021a). These shifts can be explored by focusing on pre-pandemic trends, during the pandemic impacts and post-pandemic implications. It is important to appreciate that the COVID-19 pandemic is transitioning into a virus that is endemic in the population. Vaccination programmes have reduced the health implications of catching COVID-19 as societies are learning to live with this virus (Andres et al., 2022). Some of the most important societal changes have resulted in alterations to work and the place in which work is enacted. A key point here is that the discontinuity and the inflection point that is associated with the pandemic also involves the acceleration of pre-pandemic trends. Thus, many of the alterations in urban living and livelihoods can be traced back to processes that predated the pandemic, but the pandemic led to an acceleration of these trends.

This chapter is divided into four sections. The following section explores urban logistics with a focus on pre-COVID trends with much of the analysis exploring vans and local delivery within urban areas. This is followed by a review of the impacts of the pandemic on urban logistics and then explores longer-term impacts and finally, a conclusion is provided.

Urban Logistics and Vans: Pre-COVID Trends

Logistics services rely on a complex array of interwoven transportation and communication networks. Each network reflects the activities of a set of companies, institutions and regulators involved in the delivery of a transport-enabled service comprising the movement of a product from one location to another. These infrastructure networks involve ports, airports, river transport, maritime transport, air freight systems, roads and communication networks, including satellites that track flows of people, parts, and products. It also includes specialist logistics providers and warehouse operators. On-going developments in e-commerce are reshaping the geography of retailing. Part of this reshaping shifts retailing from high streets to extremely large warehouses located in central locations and adjacent to key transportation routes (see Chapter 14). In addition, the application of just-in-time systems to manufacturing has altered supply chain logistics; a continual stream of lorries delivering components and products has replaced the need for large warehouses to be co-located with manufacturing plants. Just-in-time systems altered urban logistics. It is important not to confuse the escalation of business-to-business (B2B) urban freight logistics with the impacts that COVID-19 has had on business-to-consumer (B2C) logistics flows.

Urban logistics can be defined in two ways. On the one hand, the definition can focus on freight distribution in urban areas including an emphasis on enhancing efficiency, reducing costs and environmental externalities (see Chapter 2). This definition highlights the importance of treating urban logistics as an integrated infrastructure system that includes warehouse facilities providing storage and distribution hubs combined with appropriate delivery modes (cars, vans, trucks). On the other hand, a broader definition of urban logistics includes a focus on logistics linked to home delivery (see Chapter 8). Home delivery linked to the rapid growth of e-commerce is altering the urban logistics balance between delivery and collection from centralised nodes, or shops or designated collection points, and home delivery. COVID-19 accelerated the shift towards home delivery and increased the importance of enhancing the efficiency and reducing the negative externalities linked to the last-mile delivery of goods.

The increase in home delivery has involved a dramatic escalation in the frequency of deliveries to homes from stores and warehouses and, in many cases, these delivery vans are only partly full. This escalation in the frequency of urban delivery journeys has its origins before COVID-19. Between 1996 and 2016, vans were the fastest-growing vehicle type in the UK with the number of licensed vans increasing by 74%, from 2.2 to 3.8 million (Department for Transport, 2017). It is impossible to isolate the contribution that alterations in urban logistics have made to this increase. Nevertheless, between 2015 and 2016, van traffic grew more rapidly than any other vehicle type with an increase of 4.7% compared to 2% for car traffic. In 2016, vans accounted for 49.1 billion vehicle miles (bvm) across the United Kingdom with 26% of journeys involving the delivery or collection of goods and 53% the carriage of equipment (Department for Transport, 2017). By 2016, vans in the United Kingdom accounted for 15% of all motor vehicle traffic compared to 9% in 1986 (Department for Transport, 2017). In 2011, vans accounted for 13% of all motorised traffic in vehicle kilometres with approximately 3.8 billion van-kilometres driven annually and this was about four times that for HGVs (Transport for London, 2015: 2).

The growth in the number of vans has, according to the Department for Transport, 'followed changes in the economy closely' (Department for Transport, 2017: 12). This increase reflects the establishment of new firms, as well as growth of existing firms, as the UK van fleet follows these trends. Nevertheless, between 2012 and 2016 van traffic increased more rapidly than gross domestic product (GDP). Three reasons for this growth have been identified: growth in internet shopping and home deliveries, changes in company car taxation which might have encouraged people to switch to vans from cars and a reduction in regulations on driver training and driver hours (Department for Transport, 2017: 12). Much of this increase in van miles in the United Kingdom predates the growth in internet shopping linked to COVID-19 adjustments in the balance between bricks and mortar and online sales (Department for Transport, 2021b). One of the drivers has been the growth in self-employment with vans used to transport equipment related to the provision of services, for example services related to building and construction. Another important driver has been an escalation in the adoption of just-in-time rather than just-in-case inventory systems. This has been reflected in alterations in retailing as well as in offices. For retailing, there has been a shift to more frequent deliveries from centralised warehouses with each shop holding reduced stock levels. Offices have tended to replace holding large stocks of stationery and office materials with just-in-time ordering. The business case rests on the costs related to holding and managing stock, including storage costs. A just-in-time approach to managing inventory was adopted to overcome business inefficiencies related to just-in-case inventory systems. Nevertheless, there are implications that come from this shift. On the one hand, there has been a growth in the number of vans in urban areas and a related increase in employment and self-employment in urban logistics. In London, a 2015 Transport for London report noted that 56% of vans in London were privately owned with the rest being commercially owned and were part of company fleets (Transport for London, 2015: 4). On the other hand, just-in-time inventory related logistics results in major problems for providers including poor utilisation of vehicles, driver recruitment and fleet maintenance and renewal. Many vans are left idle for most of the day as they are used to transport worker(s) and their equipment to a site. An important point comes from a study of van use in London in 2014 that identified that 'the average load factor for vans in London is 38 per cent (about 300kg payload)' and that 'thirty-nine per cent of vans are less that one quarter full' (Transport for London, 2015: 5). This study also identified that only 14% of vans were full.

There are important implications related to the increase in van use for urban air quality and for the efficiency of urban logistics businesses. For air quality, it is important to appreciate that most of these vans are diesel-fuelled. As such, the 2014, London study identified that 92% of vans registered in London were diesel-fuelled. Diesel is associated with the emission of pollutants (soot or particulate matter (PM), oxides of nitrogen (NOx), hydrocarbons (HC), carbon monoxide (CO) and other hazardous air pollutants) that play an important role in localised air pollution and can cause heart and lung disease and other health effects. Urban logistics is a highly competitive industry with low margins. This is then reflected in van fleet composition. In 2019, only 0.3% of vans operating in Great Britain were classed as ultra-low emission vehicles (ULEV). More importantly, the 2019–2020 van survey in Great Britain identified that 'over a quarter (27%) of vans were 3 years old or less, 4 out of 10 (40%) were between 3 years and 10 years old, and a third were over 10 years old (33%)' (Department for Transport, 2021c: 7). Van age is closely related to ownership with 17% of vans owned by businesses being more than ten years old compared to 54% for vans driven by private keepers (Department for Transport, 2021c: 7). Older vehicles will be less efficient and will also produce more air pollutants. Higher carbon-emitting vans were more likely to be second-hand compared to ULEVs.

ULEVs are defined as vehicles that emit less than 75g of carbon dioxide (CO_2) from their tailpipes for every kilometre travelled. The term ULEV is usually applied to refer to battery electric, plug-in hybrid electric and fuel cell electric vehicles (Department for Transport, 2021c: 24). In Great Britain, the 2019–2020 van survey found that only 0.2% of the van fleet was classed as ULEVs, but the number of ULEV vans was increasing. There are some interesting trends related to the purchase and use of ULEV vans. Most were purchased new and owned outright rather than on hire purchase (Department for Transport, 2021c: 25). ULEV vans had an estimated annual mileage of 7,200 or 54.5% the annual mileage of non-ULEV vans (13,200 miles). On a typical day, 72% of ULEV vans remained in the local area defined as being within 15 miles of their base compared to 51% of non-ULEV vans.

There will be a gradual shift in the composition of the urban vehicle van fleet towards ULEVs, and this shift will accelerate as more charging points become available and as the cost of ULEV vans falls with an increase in supply and demand. The 2019–2020 Great Britain van survey explored the factors influencing ULEV van purchase (Department for Transport, 2021c). The most important factors were the purchase, or leasing price, followed by running/operating costs, performance including reliability and safety considerations. Environmental concerns were ranked as the seventh most important factor and low emissions/clear air zones as tenth (Department for Transport, 2021c: 29). The purchase price was considered the most important barrier to purchasing a ULEV van followed by the vehicle's suitability (size, range, capacity) and the availability of charging points (Department for Transport, 2021c: 29).

For urban logistics, the challenge is the development of an efficient and flexible system based on minimising costs and air pollutants. A key challenge is to enhance fleet utilisation and to reduce the number of partly loaded vans on the road. This requires increased digitalisation and co-operation between companies to reduce the number of van journeys by enhancing fleet utilisation. This could include consolidating deliveries and the development of a network of conveniently located click-and-collect centres.

The shift towards ULEV vans is part of the solution as long as this is combined with electricity generation that is pollution free. Nevertheless, the focus should be on enhancing the efficiency of urban vans to enhance fleet utilisation rather than on relying on a shift towards ULEVs to reduce air pollution. There are two challenges here. On the one hand, ULEV vans remove tailpipe pollutants, but still produce particulate pollution from brake and tyre wear and still create noise pollution. The number of particulates produced by a van is related to its weight and ULEV vans are heaver given the additional weight from the batteries. ULEV vans are only part of the solution towards reducing air pollution. On the other hand, increasing urban well-being requires developing a new balance between accessing goods and services, including urban infrastructure, and enhancing urban environmental quality. This includes enhancing air quality and reducing noise pollution.

New approaches to planning and managing cities are emerging and being tested that have important implications for urban logistics. This includes debates on the 15-minute city based on the development of decentralised urban areas in which residents could access their daily needs by a quarter-hour walk or cycle. Cities like Paris and Birmingham, UK, are exploring approaches to introducing decentralised urban living to minimise urban-related impacts on climate change and to enhance urban liveability (Andres et al., 2021). Sweden is experimenting with a very different approach to the 15-minute city based around the introduction of hyperlocal urban living or the one-minute city. These reflect two very different urban scales; the 15-minute city is based around blocks or zones whilst the one-minute city is focused on streets and on encouraging residents to become co-architects of their own streets. The 15-minute approach is based on decentralising urban logistics and enhancing walking and cycling as transport modes. The one-minute city is not about enabling access to products and services but is focused instead on transforming streets to ensure that every street is healthy and sustainable.

Urban Logistics Ecosystems: During and Post-COVID Trends

COVID-19 accelerated the shift towards e-commerce and lifestyles that are more orientated towards ordering online and home deliveries. There has also been a shift towards multilocational work, including working from home and this has led to an increase in e-commerce. One important impact of the pandemic was that it highlighted the role urban logistics plays as an essential public service enabling the supply of essential goods. On 20 March 2020 in the United Kingdom, urban logistics workers were recategorised as keyworkers. The UK keyworker list included those involved in transport who were involved in keeping air, water, road and rail passenger and freight transport modes operating during the pandemic and those involved in transport systems through which supply chains operate including food and goods and those involved in the sale, delivery and distribution of food. Elizabeth de Jong, the Freight Transport Association's policy director noted that 'logistics workers are the unsung heroes in today's economy, ensuring that shops, schools and hospitals, as well as manufacturing and our homes, have the products they need, when they need them' (Logistics UK, 2020).

During the pandemic, restaurants and retailers introduced delivery services as one way of adapting to the restrictions placed on consumer behaviour (Bryson, 2021). Companies had problems responding to the increase in e-commerce and deliveries and this included staffing and capacity problems. The pandemic was also associated with a shift towards contactless deliveries to reduce the possibilities of disease transmission. Companies were forced to introduce new digital solutions to underpin delivery transactions.

Homeworking and e-commerce have been on-going trends, but COVID-19 forced employers to apply homeworking to the delivery of tasks and demonstrated, for some firms, that homeworking was a viable alternative to office-based employment. In addition, COVID-19, forced consumers and retailers who were reluctant users of e-commerce to embrace this retail channel. This led to a step-change in the adoption of online retailing and it is estimated that this will result in permanent change as 'many apprehensive internet shoppers may emerge as full "online converts"' (Alvarez and Marsal, 2020: 11). These two impacts have important implications for urban logistics as they alter the geography of work and consumption. Home working or spending more time working from home and perhaps two days a week working from employer premises, enables employees to live further away from their employer's premises. This alteration in the place of work then shifts the geography of demand closer to residential districts and away from city centres.

For retail workers, COVID-19 accelerated the shift to e-commerce, and this includes the growth in e-commerce-related employment in more peripheral locations close to the motorway network and a reduction in retail employment in central locations. For bricks and mortar retailers and the hospitality industry COVID-19 has resulted in an enhanced focus on productivity and automation to reduce the cost of in-person service provision. There has been an acceleration in the introduction of less labour-intensive business models including takeout-only ghost or dark kitchens, or delivery-only restaurants, and dark stores, or retail distribution centres that only service online customers. During the pandemic, some retail outlets were converted to dark stores (Bryson, 2021). With the easing of pandemic restrictions, some retail outlets have developed a hybrid form with an outlet acting as a dark store as well as continuing to sell directly to customers (see Chapter 10).

During the period when pandemic restrictions reduced citizen mobility, e-commerce providers benefited from increased demand and urban deliveries experienced enhanced effectiveness given the reduction in congestion and easier access to parking. Nevertheless, the pandemic's impact on the acceleration of e-commerce adoption has had important implications for urban logistics. The increase in dark stores and ghost restaurants reflects the emergence of a new category of e-commerce termed quick commerce, or q-commerce, based on ultrafast delivery speeds of less than two hours. For some companies, this involves deliveries within minutes of products that are intended for immediate consumption. Delivery Hero, an online-food ordering service, was established in Sweden in 2008, but by 2022 operated in over 50 countries (Delivery Hero, 2021). Q-commerce companies have been growing rapidly. In 2020, Delivery Hero employed 29,552 people, but this had increased to 45,445 by 2021 (Delivery Hero, 2021: 6). This company has been investing in research and development (R&D) with 6.6% of employees involved in R&D in 2021, or 3,425 people, and 2,167 people were employed in R&D in 2020 (Delivery Hero, 2021: 6). Delivery Hero has established a local delivery platform based on an ecosystem of riders, restaurants, shops, and partners to deliver prepared meals, groceries, flowers, coffee, and medicine to customers. This includes a network of Dmarts, or delivery-only supermarkets, that are centrally located warehouses optimised for delivery that in some countries enable goods to be delivered in less than 15 minutes. With q-commerce, the key competitive differentiator is based on delivery speed, and this requires local stores or warehouses, two-wheeled vehicles rather than vans and limited product choice for consumers.

For urban logistics, a key question concerns the legacy of pandemic impacts on consumer and business behaviours. Three pandemic-related accelerations of existing trends can be identified that will continue to alter urban logistics: the shift towards e-commerce and on-demand service that has forced providers to introduce omnichannel retail provision; working from home and the shift to multilocational work; and shifts in transport modes with increased walking and cycling as well as the use of private vehicles. A key post-COVID-19 urban logistics and city-region management challenge is to develop strategies that will encourage enhanced efficiency in urban deliveries. Continued growth in e-commerce will result in an increase in the number of deliveries as well as increasing fragmentation of loads and trips. All this will add to urban congestion impacting delivery times and increasing the time spent travelling between deliveries. Any increase in both the quantity of delivery trips, and the time required for each delivery will have a negative impact on urban air and noise pollution.

The shift towards delivery-orientated lifestyles has major implications for urban planning and urban logistics. There are solutions that could be applied to reducing the negative impacts of the rise in home deliveries. An important challenge, for example, is to separate van movement linked to last-mile deliveries from the movement of the heaviest lorries. Heavy lorries and HGVs have greater negative environmental and societal impacts. London, for example, introduced the London Lorry Control Scheme (LLCS) in 1985 which restricts the movement of the heaviest lorries to a limited number of routes around central London at night and during weekends (Arup, 2021). The LLCS is a control intervention intended to manage the environmental impacts of HGV journeys in London with a focus on minimising noise pollution. Heavy vehicle drivers and their operators are issued with Penalty Charge Notes (PCNs) when they drive on non-permitted routes. Enhancing fleet utilisation of the heaviest vehicles is relatively simple as are policies intended to reduce journeys and to limit negative impacts.

Developing solutions to reducing the negative impacts of the last mile based on transporting products to local consumers from local providers, or by establishing logistics hubs or final distribution centres, is much more challenging (Deloison et al., 2020; Suguna et al., 2021). Companies have focused on developing solutions, and these include robots, or automated ground vehicles (AGVs) and drones (see Chapter 6). In Milton Keynes, Starship Technologies, an American company headquartered in San Francisco, has been testing the application of small, six-wheeled autonomous vehicles that travel along pavements to transport small deliveries to residents and workers. Residents can download an app to buy cooked food or small orders from supermarkets (Hern, 2020). FedEx, the US transportation, e-commerce, and services conglomerate, has been testing the application of autonomous trucks and flying drones to carry small numbers of packages as last-mile solutions (Arup, 2021). A key challenge is the reliability of the technology, battery life, and establishing supplier and consumer social acceptance.

Innovations in urban logistics include increased demand for q-commerce transactions combined with more conventional e-commerce. This escalation in last-mile deliveries has important implications for spatial planning and urban management. Cities, and urban logistics providers, have been re-evaluating the relationship between logistics infrastructure and communities to try to reduce negative environmental impacts including the emission of air pollutants, increased congestion and noise. For logistics providers, the emphasis must be on enhancing fleet utilisation and reducing negative impacts. Progressive town planning includes a focus on increasing or encouraging localism through mixed-use developments and balancing the tensions between enabling the establishment of an effective local urban logistics ecosystem and designing liveable neighbourhoods to promote well-being by encouraging active travel by walking, cycling and public transport.

E-commerce has many advantages including reduced staffing and capital costs compared to bricks and mortar retailing. There are, however, very different logistics and customer challenges. E-commerce clothing retailing is associated with high return rates resulting in wastage and costs related to checking returned goods and dealing with returned goods that cannot be sold including their disposal. One of the problems is that consumers surf the web and order different sizes of the same clothing item, and this creates a returns problem for the consumer and provider. This is also an urban reverse logistics problem given the additional costs of returning and checking returned products. To manage the returns problem retailers are identifying customers who are more likely to return items and then working to try to deter them from overordering that then results in every order being associated with a returns problem. Retailers are also shifting away from returns being free. Thus, Zara, the fashion retailer, introduced charges for returns in 2022 with customers having to pay £1.95 to return items. This additional cost is subtracted from the customer's refund, but items purchased online can still be returned for free in stores.

Climate change, and concerns with sustainability, have led to the application of circular economy (CE) approaches based on 'closed loop' systems that are intended to minimise waste with an emphasis on efficient resource use (Andersen, 2007). CE approaches include take-back programmes, product swaps, product libraries and repair services (Brydges, 2021). All these practices involve reverse logistics as the product must be returned to the producer or an intermediary involved in recycling and product repurposing including repairs. With climate change, there will be an acceleration in the adoption of CE approaches, and this will result in increased demand for localised reverse urban logistics, which will add to congestion and urban logistics-related pollution.

Urban logistics must innovate in response to technological, organisational and societal change that includes an increase in local delivery and returns combined with pressures to decarbonise logistics. Innovations in urban logistics that need to become common practice include:

i Adoption of ULEVs for last-mile deliveries based on electric vans and couriers using electric cargo (e-cargo) bikes.
ii Collection points located close to the final delivery point that can be accessed by customers, for example click-and-collect arrangements with local shops and the provision of proprietary lockers in retail stores, workplaces and other locations.

iii A shift towards the introduction of delivery microhubs or a logistics facility where goods are bundled together for individual customers. Microhubs should be distributed across urban areas to enable the last-mile delivery to be made by ULEVs or by soft transportation modes, for example walking or cycling (Ballare and Lin, 2020).
iv A microhub may be used by one carrier or many and may function as an urban consolidation centre (see Chapter 21). A microhub that is also engaged in order product consolidation between many different suppliers reduces the number of journeys required to transport products and increases fleet utilisation rates.
v Repurposing of inner-city sites to facilitate efficient and effective urban logistics including drop-off and pick-up points with officials involved in urban management identifying and facilitating the establishment of networks of microhubs.
vi Establishment of multi-brand parcel shops to reduce congestion and air pollution. This requires logistics companies to cooperate by establishing shared retail spaces and to integrate their supply chains.
vii The integration of public transport as a transport mode for urban logistics (see Chapter 7).

Crowdshipping, or crowdsourced delivery as an urban logistics mode, has emerged based on the peer delivery of products by people applying social networking to share services and to establish delivery solutions (Ballare and Lin, 2020). Crowdshipping provides an additional end-user or consumer-provided element to the urban logistics ecosystem. There are four types. First, crowd storage is based on the provision of storage space in which crowd resources are applied to identify suitable spaces and locations. Second, crowd local delivery involves the use of apps to link residents willing to transport products with suppliers and consumers. Goods may be delivered by walking, cycling, cars, scooters, public transport, or vans. Third, crowd freight shipping applies an app to connect drivers and potential users who need to have non-standard or oversized items delivered. Fourth, crowd freight forwarding is based on apps used by peers to post their forthcoming travel itineraries and users of the service can also advertise their logistics requirements.

Cities are at a cultural inflection point involving a major escalation in local deliveries. This requires innovations in urban logistics and in the design and management of cities. New technological and operational solutions are being tested that will eventually become integrated into the urban logistics ecosystem. The key challenge is to reduce the number of journeys by increasing fleet utilisation as this will enhance operator margins whilst simultaneously reducing the negative environmental impacts of urban logistics.

Conclusion

COVID-19 led to an acceleration of existing e-commerce trends. Enforced lockdowns forced reluctant e-commerce users to shop online. Suppliers were also forced to innovate and invest in e-commerce and related logistics. Q-commerce emerged as a new form of e-commerce based on speed as the primary differentiator. The shift towards multilocational work also transformed the geography of local demand with some demand shifting towards the employees' place of residence and away from the workplace.

Urban logistics plays an increasingly important role in underpinning liveability and livelihoods. Nevertheless, transportation is central to urban logistics, and this then results in air and noise pollution and contributes to congestion. Trade-offs need to be made between creating liveable cities and neighbourhoods and the negative externalities derived from urban logistics. This trade-off includes enhancing fleet utilisation as this would reduce the number of journeys and would also be reflected in carrier margins. The urban logistics industry is highly competitive with tight margins that are impacted by fuel price increases. This suggests that all urban logistics operators must innovate to reduce journey costs and enhance margins, but at the same time reduce negative environmental impacts.

Consumer behavioural change is required, combined with technological and organisational innovations, to increase fleet utilisation of urban logistics providers and overall efficiency whilst minimising environmental impacts. Microhubs will play an important role in high-density and high-demand areas with high delivery volumes. In addition, robots, or automated ground vehicles (AGVs) and drones will become increasingly common as customers and suppliers accept these as alternative delivery modes. Home deliveries will continue to increase in response to the on-going restructuring of consumer behaviour. All this means that COVID-19 accelerated existing e-commerce trends and has acted as a cultural inflection point that has altered the direction of travel of the urban logistics industry.

Acknowledgements

The research reported here was funded by the National Environment Research Council (NERC) and comes from the West Midlands Air Quality Improvement Programme Project (grant number: NE/S003487/1).

References

Alvarez and Marsal (2020), *The Shape of Retail: Consumers and the New Normal*, Alvarez and Marsal: London

Andersen, M.S. (2007), 'An introductory note on the environmental economics of the circular economy', *Sustainability Science*, 2, 1: 133–140

Andres, L., Bryson, J., and Moawad, P., (2021), 'Temporary urbanisms as policy alternatives to enhance health and well-being in the post-pandemic city', *Current Environmental Health Reports*, http://dx.doi.org/10.1007/s40572-021-00314-8

Andres, L., Bryson, J. R., Mehanna, H. and Moawad, P., (2022), 'Learning from COVID-19 and planning post-pandemic cities to reduce pathogen transmission pathways', *Town Planning Review*, https://doi.org/10.3828/tpr.2022.5

Arup (2021), *Future of Urban Logistics*, Arup, accessed 1 May 2022, available at https://www.arup.com/perspectives/publications/research/section/future-of-urban-logistics

Ballare, S. and Lin, J. (2020), 'Investigating the use of microhubs and crowdshipping for last mile delivery', *Transportation Research Procedia*, 46: 277–284,

Brydges, T. (2021), 'Closing the loop on take, make, waste: investigating circular economy practices in the Swedish fashion industry', *Journal of Cleaner Production*, 293: 126245

Bryson, J.R., Andres, L, Ersoy, A. and Reardon, L. (Ed.) (2021), *Living with Pandemics: Places, People and Policy*, Edward Elgar: Cheltenham

Bryson, J.R. (2021), 'COVID-19 and the immediate and longer-term impacts on the retail and hospitality industries: darks stores and turnover-based rental models', in Bryson, J.R., Andres, L., Ersoy, A. and Reardon, L. (Ed.), *Living with Pandemics: Places, People and Policy*, Edward Elgar: Cheltenham, 202–216

Bryson, J.R. (2022), 'Reading manufacturing firms and new research agendas: scalar-plasticity, value/risk and the emergence of Jenga Capitalism', in Bryson, J.R., Billing, C., Graves, W. and Yeung G. (Eds) *A Research Agenda for Manufacturing Industries in the Global Economy*, Edward Elgar: Cheltenham: 211–243

Bryson, J.R., Andres, L, Ersoy, A. and Reardon, L. (Ed) (2021), *Living with Pandemics: Places, People and Policy*, Edward Elgar: Cheltenham

Bryson, J.R., and Vanchan, V. (2020), 'Covid-19 and alternative conceptualisations of value and risk in GPN research', *Tijdschrift voor Economische en Sociale Geografie*, 111, 3: 530–542

Bryson, J. R., Vanchan, V. and Zhou, S. (2021), 'Risk management and reduction in global supply chains and production networks: reshoring and rightshoring versus offshoring', in Berry, C., Froud, J. & Barker, T. (Eds). Newcastle upon Tyne: Agenda Publishing: 115–126

Delivery Hero, (2021), *Annual Financial Statement and Combined Management Report*, Delivery Hero, Berlin

Deloison T., Hannon E., Huber A., Heid B., Klink C., Sahay R. and Christoph Wolff C. (2020), The future of the last-mile ecosystem, *World Economic Forum*, accessed 25 April 2022, available at https://www.weforum.org/reports/the-future-of-the-last-mile-ecosystem

Department for Transport, (2017), *Road Traffic Estimates Great Britain, 2016*, accessed 18 April 2022, available at https://assets.publishing.service.gov.uk/government/uploads/system/uploads/attachment_data/file/611304/annual-road-traffic-estimates-2016.pdf

Department for Transport (2021a), *Road Traffic Estimates: Great Britain 2020*, accessed 18 April 2022, available at https://assets.publishing.service.gov.uk/government/uploads/system/uploads/attachment_data/file/1028165/road-traffic-estimates-in-great-britain-2020.pdf

Department for Transport (2021b), *Provisional Road Traffic Estimates Great Britain: July 2020 to June 2021*, accessed 18 April 2022, available at https://assets.publishing.service.gov.uk/government/uploads/system/uploads/attachment_data/file/1021177/provisional-road-traffic-estimates-gb-jul-2020-to-jun-2021.pdf

Department for Transport (2021c), *Final Van Statistics April 2019-March 2020*, accessed 5 May 2022, available at https://assets.publishing.service.gov.uk/government/uploads/system/uploads/attachment_data/file/1065072/van-statistics-2019-to-2020.pdf

European Commission, (2021), *2030 Digital Compass: The European Way for the Digital Decade*, European Commission COM(2021) 118 final, accessed 17 March 2022, available at https://eur-lex.europa.eu/legalcontent/en/TXT/?uri=CELEX:52021DC0118

Hern, A. (2020), 'Robots deliver food in Milton Keyners under coronavirus lockdown', *The Guardian*, Sunday 12 April.

Kumar, A. (2021), 'Germany's green party accuses Russia of 'playing poker' with gas prices amid energy crisis', *Republicworld.com*, accessed 16 May 2022, available at https://www.republicworld.com/world-news/europe/germanys-green-party-accuses-russia-of-playing-poker-with-gas-prices-amid-energy-crisis.html

Logistics UK (2020), 'Logistics workers recognised as key to economic success', Logistics UK, accessed 15 April 2022, available at https://logistics.org.uk/media/press-releases/2020/march/logistics-workers-recognised-as-key-to-economic-su

Suguna, M., Shah, B., Raj, S. K., and Suresh, M. (2021), A study on the influential factors of the last mile delivery projects during Covid-19 era. *Operations Management Research*, 1–14. Advance online publication. https://doi.org/10.1007/s12063-021-00214-y

Transport for London (2015), 'What are the Main trends and development affecting van traffic in London?', *Roads Task Force, Technical Note 5*, accessed 26 April 2022, available at https://content.tfl.gov.uk/technical-note-05-what-are-the-main-trends-and-developments-affecting-van-traffic.pdf

INDEX

Note: **Bold** page numbers refer to tables; *italic* page numbers refer to figures and page numbers followed by "n" denote endnotes.

Abel, S. 257
Aditjandra, P. 271
ADS-B *see* Automatic Dependent Surveillance-Broadcast (ADS-B)
advertisement: engaging local agencies and community associations in 313–315; in Facebook 239
AFLEET *see* Alternative Fuel Life Cycle Environmental and Economic Transportation (AFLEET)
African Development Bank 353
AFTs *see* alternative fuel trucks (AFTs)
agent-based models (ABMs) 79, 85–86n1, 272, 273
Agility 361n3
AGVs *see* automated ground vehicles (AGVs)
air hub 191
air pollution 15, 46, 51, 56, 107, 114, 116, 175, 177, 178, 203, 251, 284, 295, 305, 364, 367, 368, 370, 372, 398, 399, 403
air quality 9, 34, 37, 111, 130, 147, 153, 156, 180, 241, 245, 252, 287, 288, 295, 299, 368, 370, 371, 398, 399
Akgün, E. Z. 69, 299, 301, 302n1
ALARP *see* as low as reasonably possible (ALARP)
Albertsons 149
Aldi 240
Alexander, B. 135, 136
algorithmic management 154, 380–382
ALICE/ERTRAC 20
AliExpress 135
Allen, J. 62, 63, 65, 68, 218, 296, 301

Alliance for Logistics Innovation through Collaboration in Europe (ALICE) 253
Allianz Research 141
Allplants 151
Alternative Fuel Life Cycle Environmental and Economic Transportation (AFLEET) 343
alternative fuels 10, 178, 184, 268, 287, 333–348
alternative fuel trucks (AFTs) 338, **339**
alternative fuel vehicles 184, 337, 338
alternative storage areas 181, *182*
Amazon 85, 138, 140–142, 164, 190, 239, 241, 255, 260, 339; Alexa 149; Amazon Flex 11, 379–381; facility locations 193–194; parcel delivery 110; spatial planning 258
Amsterdam Vaart! project 182
Amukele, T. K. 76–77
Anand, N. 300
ANPR (Automated Number Plate Recognition) cameras 254, 261, 262, **262**
Appetito 138
Apple, iTunes 239
AreaDUM 257, 261
Argonne National Laboratory: Alternative Fuel Life Cycle Environmental and Economic Transportation (AFLEET) 343
Arslan, A. 216
Arvidsson, N. 92
Asda 151
aseptic cancer medicines 76
ASIF rule 336, *336*
as low as reasonably possible (ALARP) 79
ASOS (A's Seen on Screen) 126
Assmann, T. 63, 243

Index

Augmented Reality 163
Australian GECA Standard 18
Australia Post 241
automated ground vehicles (AGVs) 401
Automatic Dependent Surveillance-Broadcast (ADS-B) 81
automating information and product access 163–164
autonomous mobile locker 241

B2B *see* business-to-business (B2B)
B2C *see* business-to-consumer (B2C)
Bairro 139
Baptista, P. 215
battery electric truck (BET) 338–342, 344, 347
battery electric vehicles (BEVs) 241–242, 246
BAU *see* business-as-usual (BAU)
BCCC *see* Brussels Construction Consolidation Centre (BCCC)
Beer Boat 48
BEHALA 48
behavior change 113, 115, 283, 288
behavioural analysis 274
Behrends, S. 45, 55, 56
Behrendt, F. 243
Belliard, L. 254
Ben Mohamed, I. 211, 212
BESTUFS *see* Best Urban Freight Solutions (BESTUFS)
Best Urban Freight Solutions (BESTUFS) **20**
BET *see* battery electric truck (BET)
BEVs *see* battery electric vehicles (BEVs)
Biba 125
Bickel, P. 109
Bierlaire, M. 213
big data: analytics 164; storage and processing 226
bike lanes 242–243
BIM *see* Building Information Modelling (BIM)
BioNTech 165
Birtchnell, T. 328
Björgen, A. 271
Blanquart, C. 200
Blazquez, M. B. 135, 136
Blinkit (formerly Grofers) 138
blitzscaling 140
Blue Apron 151
BNP Paribas Real Estate 139–140
Boccia, M. 212
BOGIDS (buy online, get it delivered from store) 137
bogus self-employment 375, 379
Bóna, K. 66
BOPIS/BOPS (buy online pick-up in store) 137
Bounie, N. 200
Braithwaite, A. 154
Breen, L. 161

Brexit 121
Briel, F. von 135
Bristol & Bath Freight Consolidation Centre 296
Browne, M. 66, 298, 299, 306
Brussels Construction Consolidation Centre (BCCC) 183
Bruzzone, F. 97
Building Information Modelling (BIM) 183, 184
Büközkan, G. 219
Buldeo Rai, H. 109, 111, 113
business-as-usual (BAU) 83, 113, 114, *114*
business-to-business (B2B) 13, 65, 397
business-to-consumer (B2C) 13, 55, 65, 107, 397
Buyk 139
BVLOS (Beyond-Visual-Line-of-Sight) 72, 79, 80, 82

C2B *see* consumer to a business (C2B)
CAA *see* Civil Aviation Authority (CAA)
Cajoo 140–142
California Air Resource Board 287
Canada: dark stores 138; law in 379
Cano, M. B. 136
carbon-neutral 273, 327
Carbon Neutral Construction Service Innovation Challenge 183
Careem 142
cargo bike 5, 6, 55, 59, 60, 63–64, 66–69, 93, 130, 139, 153, 202, 203, 210, 213–215, 219, 240, 242–245, 255, 257, 260, 295, 296, 298, 299, 302, 306, 313, 315–318; contribution to wider economic, social and environmental goals **64**; employment of 63, 70; logistics **60**
cargo cycles 37–38
cargo e-bike 9, 239, 306, 312–313, 316–318, *317*
Cargo Hitching 91
CarGoTram 47, 100, 244
cargo tricycle 59, **60**, 63
Carrefour 135, 141; Bringo 141
Carson City, Los Angeles 371, 372
Carter, D. N. 96
cashier-less stores 135
Casino 135, 141, 244
Cavallaro, F. 96–97
CAVs *see* connected and autonomous vehicles (CAVs)
CCC *see* construction consolidation centres (CCC)
CE *see* Circular Economy (CE)
Chae, B. K. 96
Chakravarty, A. K. 327
Chan, D. 392
Change Foods 151
Chartered Institute of Logistics and Transport (CILT UK): Women in Logistics and Transport (WiLAT) 392

Index

Charter for Sustainable Urban Logistics 253
Chicago Metropolitan Agency for Planning 258
China: clean delivery trucks and vans 255; consumer spending 134; dark stores 138; fast fashion, rise of 125; freight incentives 288
Chop Chop 141
Cidell, J. 199
CILT UK *see* Chartered Institute of Logistics and Transport (CILT UK)
Circular Economy (CE) 402; 9Rs of 168
CityCargo 244
city logistics (CL) 155, 176, 219; initiatives 7, 184
Civil Aviation Authority (CAA) 80
CIVITAS 19, **20**
CL *see* city logistics (CL)
clean delivery vehicles 9, 252, 255, 262
climate change 9–11, 21, 46, 63, 108, 109, 114, 116, 128, 131, 167, 168, 203, 241, 242, 251, 252, 282, 290, 323–330, 399, 402; and freight transport 326; impact of 327–329, *329*; threat of 335; urban logistics and 326–327
climate science 324–325, *325*
CLOCS *see* Construction Logistics and Community Safety (CLOCS) scheme
Cloud Computing 163
CloudKitchens 151
CLPs *see* Construction Logistics Plans (CLPs)
Coca-Cola 339
Cohen, T. 73
collaboration 9, 19, 68, 141, 149, 163, 217, 219, 253, 299, 313, 372; green supply chain 164; horizontal 218; between involved parties 312; operational 37; stakeholder 37; urban logistics 271
Collection-Delivery Points 269
commercial 5, 19, 27–29, 31, 33, 34, 37, 40, 59, 60, 64, 66, 67, 69, 72, 77, 80–83, 85, 108, 122, 125, 129, 139, 140, 142, 153, 154, 156, 199, 203, 234, 241, 251, 252, 254, 255, 258, 286–288, 290, 296, 299, 308, 310, 313, 315–317, 339, 356, 360, 364, 366, 369, 370, 388, 391, 392, 398
"Common but Differentiated Responsibilities" principles 327–328
co-modality 8, 238–239, 243–246, 268
Complex Adaptive System 276n1
computing technology 8, 225–236, *226*; control in smart city 232–234, **233**; convergence into urban logistics system 229–231; digital twins, for collaborative innovation 234–235, **235**; innovations in 226–227, **230**; into logistics systems, impact pathways of 227–229, *228*
Concept of Operations for European UTM Systems (CORUS) 80

concept stores 137
connected and autonomous vehicles (CAVs) 27
construction 175–184; city logistics 176; delivery plans 7, 176; flows 50, 51, 56; future directions of 183–184; initiatives 178–183; Multi-Actor Multi-Criteria Analysis 177; social cost–benefit analysis 177–178; sustainability ratings 183
construction consolidation centres (CCC) 177–179, 183
Construction Logistics and Community Safety (CLOCS) scheme 39, 180
Construction Logistics Plans (CLPs) 179–180
construction supply chain management (CSCM) 175
consumers' habits 140
consumer to a business (C2B) 13
Contardo, C. 212
Convention on International Civil Aviation (the Chicago Convention), Annex 18 77
Cook It Up 151
Co-op 151
CoopCycle 152
COP *see* Glasgow Conference of the Parties (COP)
corporate social responsibility (CSR) 54
CORUS *see* Concept of Operations for European UTM Systems (CORUS)
cost: competitiveness 15; first–last mile **92**; minimization 193
COVID-19: longer-term impacts on urban logistics 395–404; and online grocery shopping 152
Crainic, T. G. 212
Crow, A. 255
crowdshipping 96, 403
crowdsourced deliveries 111
crowdsourcing 137, 379, 380
CSCM *see* construction supply chain management (CSCM)
CSR *see* corporate social responsibility (CSR)
Cuda, R. 212
curbside management and deliveries 257
cyber-physical systems 8, 227
cycle logistics 5, 59–70, 255; bottom up *versus* top down 67–68; company culture and key individuals, importance of 68–70; complementarity of 68; critical factors to 'success' and main constraints 67; current Constraints of 69; definition of 59–60; future prospects of 69–70; need of 61–64, *62*, *63*, **64**; operating range of 60–61, **61**; technical equipment 60, **60**; in urban context 64–66, *65*; as viable business model 66–68
cyclists 180
cyclo-logistics solutions *214*

Index

DAA *see* Detect-And-Avoid (DAA) system
Dablanc, L. 62, 270–271
Daganzo, C. 211
Daki 140
dangerous goods 73, 74; regulations for drone payloads, implications of 77–78
Dangerous Goods regulations for drone payloads, implications of 77–78, 84, 85
Danielis, R. 300
Dar es Salaam, Tanzania: urban freight, growth of 333–334, *334*
dark kitchens 29, 33, 140, 149, 156, 400
Darkstore 209
dark stores 6, 149, 156, 239–240, 335, 400; international press, systematic analysis of 138–142; omnichannel retail and store 135–137; in Paris 142–144, *143*, *144*; as post-pandemic omnichannel strategy 134–145
Darvish, M. 212
data management 183; in health logistics 164–165
DB Schenker 353
DCMs *see* Discrete-Choice Models (DCMs)
DCs *see* distribution centres (DCs)
Debrie, J. 355
decarbonisation 275, 402; availability of 338–339; challenges to 347–348; of freight transport 10, 54, 260, 333–348; local policies 346–347, **346**, *347*; measurement of 337–338; national policy 345–346, **345**; operational considerations for 338; options for 336; public policy 344–345; strategies, alternative fuel 337
decision support software 226–227
De Lange, K. 244
Deliveroo 11, 135, 140, 150, 151, 154, 240, 381–382; Deliveroo Editions 151; Deliveroo Hop 141
delivery: curbside management 257; home 6, 29, 55, 66, 107–109, 111, 115, 124, 127, 130, 131, 134, 148, 151–154, 208, 239–241, 327–329, 334, 359, 397, 399, 401, 404; urban 6, 122, 131, 214, 218, 244, 255, 282–285, 287, 289–292, 305, 316, 327, 328, 334, 360, 397, 400, 401
Delivery Hero 141, 150
demand volatility 121, 127
Denmark: parking pricing 286; pilot program of lockers 305
De Souza, R. 271
Detect-And-Avoid (DAA) system 81
DHL 48, 49, 70, 85, 209, 243, 255, 260, 296; CityHub 238; meter cube boxes 245, *245*, 246
digital assortment extension 137
digital food platforms 149

digitalisation 7, 8, 164, 165, 225–229, 233, 236, 323, 399; of healthcare supply chains 162–163; innovations in urban logistics **230**
digital shelf extension 137
digital twins 163, 219, 227, 231, 234–236, **235**; for collaborative innovation 234–235, **235**
Dija 141
Dijkstra, L. 115
Direct Vision Standards 39
Discrete-Choice Models (DCMs) 272, 273
'Distribuild' initiative 48
distribution: carbon-neutral urban freight 232, 273; spatial 194–196, *194*
distribution centres (DCs) 296–297
DoorDash 141, 150, 152, 153; DoorDash Kitchens 151
DPD 70, 242
drones 72–86; adherence to client quality assurance requirements when transporting sensitive payloads 75–77; air and ground risks on route planning and optimisation, implications of 78–79; cost implications of utilising 83–85, *84*; payloads, Dangerous Goods regulations for 77–78; public acceptance of 73–74; relative to service demand, payload capabilities of 74–75, *75*; service reliability for 82–83; shared airspace 80–82, *81*; Third-Party Risks to 79
Drucker, P. 122, 123
DS-VRPTWs *see* Dynamic and Stochastic VRP with Time Window problems (DS-VRPTWs)
dualization 204
Duggan, J. 381
Duisport 48
Dynamic and Stochastic VRP with Time Window problems (DS-VRPTWs) 213

EASA *see* European Union Aviation Safety Agency (EASA)
Eat24 152
Eboli, L. 96
EC *see* Electronic Conspicuity (EC); European Commission (EC)
e-commerce 6, 8, 107–112, 225, 239, 400; fast and free home delivery 108; innovations 260; last mile and global supply chain 109; multiple stakeholders 109–111, **110**; penetration rate, by region *108*; solutions 111–112; structure of stakeholder groups in *110*; sustainability 108–109
economic development 15, 147, 251, 252, 275, 282, 328, 351, 353, 356, 365
economic situation 128
Ecozone, Mechelen (Belgium) 107–118
efficiency improvement 336–337
e-fulfillment center 191, 193

410

Index

Egypt: dry port project 353; Ministry of Transport 353
Elbert, R. 215
electric commercial vehicles 241–242
electric vans 33
electric vehicle 6, 32, 33, 48, 52, 111, 113, 116, 130, 177, 201, 239, 241, 242, 291, 292, 328, 337, 342, 343, 398
electrolysis 343
Electronic Conspicuity (EC) 81, 82
Elite Sweets 151
Elkington, J. 68
Emerging Senegal Plan 353
Employment Standards Act (Ontario) 378
ENCLOSE 19
end-to-end logistics 45, 54, 76, 123, 163
Enterprise Resource Planning (ERP) 183–184
environmental impacts 6, 56, 73, 94, 98, 109, 122, 176, 179, 180, 184, 218, 287, 296, 298, 330, 335–336, *335*, 364, 365, 367, 370, 372, 373, 401–404; of logistics in megacities 367–369; long-term 369; medium-term 368, *368*; short-term 368
Environmental Protection Agency (EPA) 282, 289
EPA *see* Environmental Protection Agency (EPA)
Equal Pay International Coalition 389
E-retailers 108, 110
ERP *see* Enterprise Resource Planning (ERP)
ETP-Alice vision 217
E-Tram 47
European Bank for Reconstruction and Development 353
European Commission (EC) 19, 94, 98, 107, 209; Green Paper on Urban Mobility 91, 100; on sustainability 109
European Investment Bank 353
European Union (EU) 252, 263n1, 268, 326, 328; carbon-neutral urban freight distribution 232, 273, 327; climate neutrality 108–109; Energy Performance in Building regulations 328
European Union Aviation Safety Agency (EASA) 74
European U-Space 80
Europresse, darkstores in 138
ex-ante policy acceptability 9, 269
experience stores 135, 137
externalities 8–10, 14–17, 63, 91–93, 182, 189, 190, 194, 198–200, 204, 218, 231, 282–287, 291, 292, 300, 369, 371, 372; among supply chain agents, allocation of 289–290; negative 14, 16, 92, 93, 98, 177, 198, 217, 295, 365, 397, 403; positive 199

FAA *see* Federal Aviation Authority (FAA)
facility location problem (FLP) 211, 213
facility locations 7, 8, 189–204; externality 194; factors 193–194; logistics clusterization 199–200, *199, 201*; logistics sprawl 197–198, *198*; proximity logistics 201–203; spatial hysteresis 204; trends in spatial distribution 194–196, *194*; typology 190–193, *191, 192*
false self-employment 375–376
Fancy 141
Farham, M. S. 212
fast delivery hub 192
fast fashion 6; rise of 124–128
FCV *see* fuel cell vehicle (FCV)
Federal Aviation Authority (FAA) 80, 81
Federal Highway Administration (FHWA) 289
Federal Logistics Association (BVL) 389
FedEx 70, 241, 260, 339, 402
female participation in urban logistics, enhancement of 391–392
Fenix 141
FHWA *see* Federal Highway Administration (FHWA)
15-minute city 131, 399
financial crisis of 2007–2008 147
first–last mile (FLM): challenges of 92–94; costs **92**; definition of 92
flagship stores 137
Fleet Operator Recognition Scheme (FORS) 39, 253
Flexe.com 209
Flink 141
FLM *see* first–last mile (FLM)
FLP *see* facility location problem (FLP)
Fontaine, P. 215
food access 147, 150
food digital services **151**
food distribution channels: COVID-19 and online grocery shopping 152; digital platforms and new players 149–152
food logistics 147–156; in cities 155; food distribution channels 149–182; households 152–153; last food miles 153–154; refrigerated vans 154–155; urban food transport system 148–149, *148*
Foodora Market 141
Forest Stewardship Council FSC mark 18
FORS *see* Fleet Operator Recognition Scheme (FORS)
France: Chanteloup Prologis 2 freight village, Moissy-Cramayel *199*; households 153; location of logistics *196*; logistics metropolitan concentration 195; population density *196*; Tramfret 244
Franprix 138
free returns 126

Index

freight: consultation 9, 252; demand management 285; incentives 287–291; mode integration 54; parking pricing 285–286; and passenger transport, integrating 91–100; planning 30, 38, 251, 271, 347; road charging 285; road pricing 9, 285–286, 288–292; stakeholders, consulting with 253; trip generation 30–32; vehicle taxation 286; water 45–57
Freight Forums 253
Freightliner 338
Freight Quality Partnerships 253, 271
Freight Traffic Control 218
freight transport: decarbonisation 333–348; integrated passenger-freight transport 91–100; rail transport 45–57; road 27–40, 54–57; urban 5, 27–40, 45, 176, 183, 184, 227, 232, 272, 274; water 45–57
freight vehicles: taxation 286; urban pricing for 255–256
Fresh Direct 141
Freshippo 151
Frichti 141
Friedrich, C. 215
Friedrich, R. 109
Frito-Lay 339
Fu, J. 97
fuel cell vehicle (FCV) 341, 347

Gao, M. 83
gateways 16, 195, 351–354, 356, 365
Gatta, V. 272, 274, 301
Gauri, D. K. 135, 137
GDPR *see* General Data Protection Regulation (GDPR)
GD-ZES *see* National Green Deal Zero Emission City Logistics (GD-ZES)
gender: bias 391; diversity 11, 387–393; equality 388; gap 388–389; leadership gap 388, 391, 392; mainstreaming 387; neutrality 391; pay gap 388–391, **390**; segregation 388
General Data Protection Regulation (GDPR) 261
geofencing 233
Geographic Information Systems (GIS) 182
George Davies of Next 125
Germany: CarGoTram 47, 100, 244; distance-based road pricing 285; KombiBus scheme 243
Getir 140–144, *143*, *144*, 151, 240
Gevaers, R. 109
Ghana: "Medium-Term Development Policy Framework" (MTDF 2018–2021) 353
GHGs *see* greenhouse gas emissions (GHGs)
Ghilas, V. 94–96
ghost restaurants 400
Giant Eagle 138

gig economy 10–11, 140, 238, 240, 375–383
GIS *see* Geographic Information Systems (GIS)
Giuliano, G. 345
Glasgow Conference of the Parties (COP) 328
Global North 10, 329, 352, 356
Global South 10, 329–330; cities 3, 333, 352, 356, 358–360; on-street logistics 356–358, *358*; trade structure 358–360; urban logistics in 351–361
global warming 324, 329
global warming potential (GWP) 324
Glovo 150
Godard, X. 357
Golini, R. 271–272
Gonzalez-Calderon, C. A. 215
Gonzalez-Feliu, J. 272
Good Distribution Practice (GDP) 75
Goodman, R.W. 109
Google Assistant 149
GoPuff 138, 140–142, 240
Gorillas 138, 140–142, 240
Grab 151
Green Building Council of Australia 183
green consumption emissions 329
greenhouse gas emissions (GHGs) 3, 31–34, 37, 40, 46, 51, 54, 109, 111, 156, 167, 282, 305, 324, 326–328, 333, 334, 336–338, 343, 344, 346–348
Greenhouse Gases, Regulated Emissions, and Energy use in Technologies (GREET) 343
GREET *see* Greenhouse Gases, Regulated Emissions, and Energy use in Technologies (GREET)
Gross Domestic Product (GDP) 291, 397
Gruler, A. 213
Guajardo, M. 218
Guerrero, D. 195, 197
Gunasekaran, A. 96
Guterres, A. 324
GWP *see* global warming potential (GWP)

Hammarby Sjöstad Logistics Centre 179
Hänninen, M. 135
Hanson, S. 345
HCL *see* hyperconnected city logistics (HCL)
healthcare logistics 159–169, *160*; automating information and product access 163–164; challenges to 161–162; data management in 164–165; resilient healthcare supply chains, designing 169; responsive 160–161; sustainability agenda, driving 167–168; talent management in 168–169; vaccine logistics 165–166
healthcare supply chains, digitalisation of 162–163
health logistics, data management in 164–165
health provision, as global agenda 159–160

heavy-duty trucks 340–342, *341*, **342**
heavy goods vehicles (HGVs) 28–30, 33, 34, 39, 40, 54, 55, 179, 296, 388–389, 401; User Levy 288
Heitz, A. 191
HelloFresh 151
Hema Fresh 138
Heuvel, F. P. van den 199
HEVs *see* hydrogen electric vehicles (HEVs)
HGVs *see* heavy goods vehicles (HGVs)
hierarchical location and routing approaches 211–212
HL *see* hyperconnected logistics (HL)
H&M 125
Ho Chi Minh City 353
Hofenk, D. 271
Hofmann, E. 227
Holguín-Veras, J. 56–57
home deliveries 6, 29, 55, 66, 107–109, 111, 115, 124, 127, 130, 131, 134, 148, 151–154, 208, 239–241, 327–329, 334, 359, 397, 399, 401, 404; fast and free 108
Hoover 377
Horizon 2020 CITYLAB project **20**, 274
households 152–153
HPCTP *see* Hunts Point Clean Trucks Program (HPCTP)
humanitarian logistics 166–167
Hunts Point Clean Trucks Program (HPCTP) 288
HVIP *see* Hybrid and Zero-Emission Truck and Bus Voucher Incentive Project (HVIP)
Hybrid and Zero-Emission Truck and Bus Voucher Incentive Project (HVIP) 287
hydrogen electric vehicles (HEVs) 242
hydrogen fuel cell (FC) 338, **339**, 340
Hylton, P. J. 200
hyperconnected city logistics (HCL) 219
hyperconnected logistics (HL) 219
Hyundai 341
Hyzon 341

IBM Institute for Business Value 240
ICAO *see* International Civil Aviation Organisation (ICAO)
ICE *see* internal combustion engine (ICE)
ICL *see* Institute for City Logistics (ICL)
ICLEI, EcoLogistics project **20**
ICT *see* information and communication technologies (ICT)
IEA *see* International Energy Agency (IEA)
IKEA 134
IKI *see* International Climate Initiative (IKI)
Ilıcak, O. 219
ILO *see* International Labour Organization (ILO)
inbound cross dock 191

Independent Worker Union of Great Britain 381
Industry 4.0 8, 227
informal practices 356–358, *358*
information and communication technologies (ICT) 151, 152, 189, 226, 229, 230, 231
INIT 244
inland waterways 7, 48, 53, *53*, 176, 182, 326
Innovation Sandbox programme 80
innovative technologies 163–164, 329
innovative urban freight data collection methods 260–262, **262**
Instacart 151
Institute for City Logistics (ICL) **21**
"insurance value" of metropolises 195
Integrated Passenger Freight Logistics 91
integrated passenger-freight transport (IPFT) 91–100; case studies 98–100, **99**; KPIs, identification of **97**; schemes, evaluation of 96–98
inter- and intra-agency collaboration 312
Intergovernmental Panel on Climate Change (IPCC): Sixth Assessment Report (AR6) 323, 324, 328
internal combustion engine (ICE) 338
International Civil Aviation Organisation (ICAO): 'Technical Instructions for the Safe Transport of Dangerous Goods by Air' (TI) 77, 78
International Climate Initiative (IKI) **20**
International Energy Agency (IEA) 326, 328
International Labour Organization (ILO) 387; Equal Remuneration Convention of 1951 (No. 100) 389
International Post Corporation 134
International Transport Forum (ITF) 3, 32, 326
Internet of Things (IoT) 163
internet retailing 127
IPCC *see* Intergovernmental Panel on Climate Change (IPCC)
IPFT *see* integrated passenger-freight transport (IPFT)
Ishfaq, R. 216
ISO 14001 18
ISO 14024 18
ITF *see* International Transport Forum (ITF)

Jacobsen, S. 212
Jaller, M. 68
Janjevic, M. 211, 299
Jansen, T A. M. 95
Japan: e-commerce, logistics facilities for 202; efficiency improvement 337; Greater Tokyo Area 190; logistics facilities in *191*; Tokyo Metropolitan Area 193, 202
Japan Aerospace Exploration Agency (JAXA) 80
JD.com 241
Jenelius, E. 97

Jiffy 141, 240
Johnston, K. 169
Joint Research Centre Institute for Environment and Sustainability (JRC) 101n1
JOKR 138, 141, 142
JRC *see* Joint Research Centre Institute for Environment and Sustainability (JRC)
Jumbo 141
Just Eat 151

Kalleberg, A. L. 383n3
Katsela, K. 300, 306
Kechir, M. 217
Keeling Curve 324
Kenworth 338
kerb 27
key performance indicators (KPIs) 96, 97, **97**, 213, 231, 391
Kiba-Janiak, M. 69
Kim, N. 213
Kin, B. 352
Kleenex 377
Knoppen, D. 276n1
Kobu, B. 96
Kolasińska-Morawska, K. 391
KombiBus scheme 243
KoMoDo project 217
KPIs *see* key performance indicators (KPIs)
Kravariti, F. 169
Kroger 138

La Belle Vie 141
La Chapelle International 55
Lagorio, A. 300
Lajos Sárdi, D. 66
land use 8, 14–16, 22, 30, 147, 189, 191, 193, 194, 204, 246, 251, 262, 316, 357, 364–367, 371, 372; industrial 31, 33; inefficiency 364, 368; patterns 31, 369, 370; planning 14, 19, 38, 54, 55, 258, 354, 367; policy 190, 367; regulations, in City of Paris 203
land values 140, 365, 367, 369
La Poste Groupe 209
last food mile 147, 149, 150, 153–156
last mile: delivery 28, 29, 32–34, 52, 55, 66, 67, 86, 127, 128, 153, 154, 156, 190, 194, 201–203, 209, 210, 213, 216–218, 241, 258, 305, 306, 333, 396, 401–403; e-commerce 109; environmental impacts of 56; logistics 68, 161, 218, 352
Laura Ashley 125
LCA *see* life cycle analysis (LCA)
LCFS *see* Low Carbon Fuel Standard (LCFS)
Lebeau, P. 300
Lehdonvirta, V. 150
Lenton, T. M. 324–325
Lenz, B. 64, 66, 68

Le Pira, M. 273
Letnik, T. 251
LEZ *see* low-emission zones (LEZ)
LGVs *see* light goods vehicle (LGV)
Li, M. 147
life cycle analysis (LCA) 337–338, 342, *343*, *344*
light goods vehicles (LGVs) 27–30, 38, 39, 62, *63*, 296, 356
Limited Traffic Zone (LTZ) 272
Lindawati 271
Lion 338
Litman, T. 96, 115
living labs (LL) 235, 253, 274, 275
LL *see* living labs (LL)
LLCS *see* London Lorry Control Scheme (LLCS)
local freight station 192
location *see* facility locations
lockers 100, 108, 109, 213, 229, 239, 257, 260, 319, 376, 402; autonomous mobile 241; banks 28, 39, 162; installation 113, 309, 311, *312*; microhub 313; network 6, 111, 113, 115, 118; parcel 9, 110, 111, 115, 191, 211, 273, 305, 306, 308–310, *309*, 313–315, *314*, 318; on public property, permit applications for 311–312, *311*, *312*; sidewalk 315–316
logistics 122–124, 351–353; clusterization 199–200, *199*, *201*; definition of 4, 361n2; facilities 190, 204; hotel 38, 55; hubs 33, 354–356; issues on political agendas, emergence of 353–354; restructuring 366–367; sprawl 15; sustainability measures, hierarchy of **18**; transition 10, 351, 353–354, 356, 360; transition on national scale 353–354; urban (*see* urban logistics); *see also individual entries*
logistics metropolitan concentration 195
Logistics Performance Index (LPI) 351
logistics service providers (LSPs) 9, 161, 295–302
Logistics Sustainability Index 273
Lomax, T. J. 96
London 252; Fleet Operator Recognition Scheme (FORS) 253; Great Ormond St Children's Hospital 162; London Freight Lab 260; non-road freight activity in 54; rail freight 49–52, *50*, *51*, *52*; road transport 27–29, 31, 33, 37–39; water and rail freight flows, integration of 53; water freight in 53, *53*
London Lorry Control Scheme (LLCS) 401
low-emission zones (LEZ) 8, 9, 69, 111, 184, 252–255, **254**, 256, 260–262, 295, 300
Low Carbon Fuel Standard (LCFS) 287
Lowe's 241
Low Traffic Neighbourhoods (LTNs) 129–130
LPI *see* Logistics Performance Index (LPI)
LSPs *see* logistics service providers (LSPs)
LTZ *see* Limited Traffic Zone (LTZ)
Lyft 139

Index

Macharis, C. 111, 253
McKinnon, A. 84
McKinsey 140
Madsen, O. 212
Maes, J. 66
Magic Spoon 151
Mahléné, N. 95, 100
Malik, L. 352, 358
MAMCA *see* Multi-Actor Multi-Criteria Analysis (MAMCA)
Marcucci, E. 272, 300, 301
Mareï, N. 352, 355
marketing: campaigns for parcel lockers 315–316, *315*; engaging local agencies and community associations in 313–315
Martins-Turner, K. 215
Mary Quant 125
Mauritania, urban logistics emergence in 357
Maximum Take Off Mass (MTOM) 79
Mazzulla, G. 96
Medicines and Healthcare products Regulatory Agency (MHRA) 75
medium-duty trucks 339, **340**
megacities: communicate and act at community scale 370–372; definition of 365; environmental impacts of logistics in 367–369, *368*; logistics industry and urban space, interactions between 365–366; logistics restructuring in 366–367; observation and coordination at regional scale 370; policy interventions and responses 369–372; urban logistics in 364–373
Meisen, T. 234
Meituan Waimai 151
Melacini, M. 215–216
Melo, S. 215
mentoring schemes 392
Merchán, D. 211
Merkert, R. 82
meter cube boxes 242–243; on ferries 245–246, *245*
Metro 138
Meyer, M. 96
MHRA *see* Medicines and Healthcare products Regulatory Agency (MHRA)
microhub 306–307, *307*; lockers 313; new strategies/technologies 316; partner agreements 312; partners 312–313
Milkrun 240
Mirhedayatian, S. M. 212
MissFresh 138
Mommens, K. 109
Mon-Marche.fr 139
Monoprix 47, 138
Monte Carlo method 79, 86n1, 213
Montreuil, B. 231

Morocco: international *vs.* metropolitan logistics, in Tangier and Casablanca 355; Ministries of Finance and Equipment 353; Ministry of Planning 353
Morrisons 151
MTOM *see* Maximum Take Off Mass (MTOM)
Multi-Actor Multi-Criteria Analysis (MAMCA) 177, 253, 275–276n1
multichannel retail 134
multi-echelon urban distribution networks 8, 208–220, *209*; challenges to 217–219; fast and green 218; governance of 217–218; hierarchical location and routing approaches 211–212; hyperconnected logistics 219; new paradigms 213–215; omnichannel logistics 215–216; pure mathematical programming approaches 213; simultaneous location-routing approaches 212–213; two-echelon location and routing models 210–211
multi-modality 7, 72–86
multi-modal transport networks 182–183
multiple stakeholders 109–111, *110*
Munoz, J.-M. 354
Muñoz-Villamizar, A. 45, 218
My Bodega Online 139
My Food Bag 151

NAA *see* National Aviation Authority (NAA)
Nagel, K. 215
Nagy, G. 211
Nanyang Technological University 80
NASA *see* National Aeronautics and Space Administration (NASA)
National Aeronautics and Space Administration (NASA) 80
National Aviation Authority (NAA) 77, 78, 80–83; Innovation Sandbox programme 80
National Cooperative Freight Research Program (NCFRP) Project **20**
National Green Deal Zero Emission City Logistics (GD-ZES) 69
NCFRP *see* National Cooperative Freight Research Program (NCFRP) Project
Ndiaye, A. 299
neo-villeiny 375–377, 381, 382
Netherlands, the: Ecostars labeling system 241–242; freight operators' data sharing 261; PIEK program 256
Netscape Navigator 239
New Jersey's Time-of-Day pricing 283
New York City: Commercial Parking/Congestion Pricing program 286; Hunts Point Clean Trucks Program (HPCTP) 288; Off Hour Delivery OHD project 287, 289–291, 371; urban freight, growth of 334
New York Metropolitan Transportation Council (NYMTC) 28

Index

New York Truck Voucher Incentive Program (NYTVIP) 287–288
Next Directory 125
Nguyen, V. P. 212
night deliveries 180
Nikola 338
Nissan eNV200s 242
non-motorized modes 361
NORSULP 19
Norway: environmental impacts 336; Hydrovolt recycling plant 344
Nugent, P. 352
NYMTC *see* New York Metropolitan Transportation Council (NYMTC)
NYTVIP *see* New York Truck Voucher Incentive Program (NYTVIP)

Oakey, A. 76
Ocado 149, 151; Zoom 141
occupational job segregation 388
OECD 353, 389; road, definition of 27
off-hour deliveries (OHD) 284
off-hour deliveries, promotion of 256
Ola 142
Olsson, J. 66
Olvera, D. 361n7
omnichannel logistics 215–216
omnichannel retail 134, 135–137
omnichannel store 135–137, **136**
on-demand and same-day delivery 240–241
online food shopping 155, 156
online grocery shopping 152
Operation Checkout 123
Osorio, C. 213
Otte, T. 234
Ottobots 241
Ottonomy 241

Paddeu, D. 271, 272, 300
Paket Logistik AB 296
Pan, S. 218, 219, 232
Panero, M. A. 300
PANYNJ *see* Port Authority of New York and New Jersey (PANYNJ)
parcel and courier service (PCS) 64
parcel deliveries 107–118; case description 112–113, *112*; consumer movements in 113–114, *114*; methodology 114–115, **115**; results 115–117, *117*
parcel delivery station 192
parcel lockers 9, 110, 111, 115, 191, 211, 273, 305, 306, 308–310, 313–315, *314*, 318; installations of *309*; marketing campaigns for 314–315, *314*
Paris 252; Chapelle "logistics hotel" 259; curbside management and deliveries 257; dark stores 138, 142–144, *143*, *144*; Eiffel Tower 180; logistics and land-use regulations in 203; logistics clusterization 200; Rungis International Market 200
Paris Agreement 108
parking sensors, installation of 313
particulate matter (PM) 178
passenger-cargo flows integration 94–96
Paxsters 242
payload delivery 72
PCS *see* parcel and courier service (PCS)
Penalty Charge Notes (PCNs) 401
PepsiCO 139
Perboli, G. 212
permanent unloading areas 180–181, *181*
permits 311–312, *311*, *312*
Peterbilt 338
Pfizer 165
Physical Internet (PI) 8, 219, 227, 229–232, **232**
Pigou, A. C. 282, 283, 290
pilot studies, success factors for 305–319; collaboration between involved parties 312–313; new strategies/technologies, missing regulations and processes for 315–318; permits and agreements, securing 310–313, *311*, *312*; right location, identifying 306–310
pilot test 305, 306, 318, 319
Pizza Hut 241
place-based change 129–130
planning, for urban logistics 251–263
PLA *see* Port of London Authority (PLA)
platformisation 150, 352
platform work 380, 382
PM *see* particulate matter (PM)
Poelman, H. 115
policy 8–9; acceptability 269–270; implementation 267–276; innovation, support for 259–260; interventions 369–372; levels, interaction with 17; nine best practices 252; recommendations 262–263; responses 369–372; for urban logistics 251–263
POLIS 253
political agendas, logistics issues emergence on 353–354
pop-up stores 137
Port Authority of New York and New Jersey (PANYNJ), time-of-day pricing 283, 288–290
Portes, A. 357
Port of London Authority (PLA) 55
Postmates 152
Potsdamer Platz, Berlin 182
PPP *see* Public Private Partnership (PPP)
precarious employment 380
Primark 125
Prins, C. 213
process replicability 273–274
Prodhon, C. 213

Project Lima shared airspace 81, **81**, 82
Proulhac, L. 195
proximity logistics 201–203
public policy 344–345
Public Private Partnership (PPP) 179
pull-logistics 189
push-logistics 189

Quak, H. 65, 269
Quality-Adjusted Life Year (QALY) 85
quality assurance 75–77
quick commerce (q-commerce) 135, 137–142, 144–145, 201, 258, 263, 335, 400–403

Raicu, R. 272
rail transport 45–57; benefits of 46; examples of 47–48
Rebel Food 151
Red Star Parcels 48
refrigerated vans 154–155
RegioKArgo 244
regulation 77–78, 84, 85, 315–318
reliability 7
Ren, S. 164
retail automation 241
retail behaviour, changing 239–240
retail change 129
retailer power 124
retailing 121–132; challenges to 124–131; fast fashion, rise of 124–128; future of 131–132; logistics and supply chain management 122–124; transformations in 124–128
reverse logistics 7, 95, 100, 127, 168, 178, 359, 402
Rewe 141
Riehle, E. 64, 66, 68
right location, identification of 306–310
risk 78–79
Rivera, L. 199
road, definition of 27
road pricing 282–292
road transport 27–40; barriers to 56–57; challenges to 31–34; developments in 31–34; initiatives to improve 34–39, **35–36**, **36**; operating patterns for 29–30; opportunities for 54–56; trip generation in urban areas 30–31
Robin Food 151
Robomart 241
robot droids 28
Rodrigue, J. P. 191–192
Rönnqvist, M. 218
Rooijen, T. van 65
Ross, C. L. 200
routing 210–213
Royal Seaport Construction Consolidation Centre 179

Rüsch, M. 227

Sainsbury's 151
Salanova, J. M. 272
Salhi, S. 211
SAV *see* Segregated Airspace Volume (SAV)
Savelsbergh, M. 218
Savy, M. 352
SC *see* supply chains (SC)
SCBA *see* social cost–benefit analysis (SCBA)
Schliwa, G. 59, 63, 64, 69
Schulz, V. 245, 246
Schwengerer, M. 212
Scotland, urban consolidation centres 295
SDGs *see* Sustainable Development Goals (SDGs)
Seamless 152
Seattle: Department of Transportation (DOT) 311; Urban Freight Lab of 253, 257; Space Needle 307
Segregated Airspace Volume (SAV) 80
Sekhani, R. 352
self-employed personal trainers (SEPT) 376, 378
Send 240
SEPT *see* self-employed personal trainers (SEPT)
Serafini, S. 96
service evaluation 97
servicing 28, 30
7-Eleven 240
7NOW app 240
SFS *see* ship-from-store (SFS) policy
shared airspace 80–82, **81**
Sheffi, Y. 135–137
Sheth, M. 215
Shiok Meats 151
ship-from-store (SFS) policy 216
ship-to-locations (SL) 208, 209
showrooms 137
SIC *see* Standard Industrial Classification (SIC) code
sidewalk lockers 315–316
simultaneous location-routing approaches 212–213
Singapore: Area Licensing Scheme (ALS) 283; Electronic Road Pricing system (ERP) 255
SL *see* ship-to-locations (SL)
Sluijk, N. 212
small city container 238–246; bike lanes 242–243; co-modality 243–245; electric commercial vehicles 241–242; meter cube box 242–243, 245–246, *245*; on-demand and same-day delivery 240–241; retail automation 241; retail behaviour, changing 239–240
Smart City control: computing technology, role of 232–234, **233**
Smart City Logistics 219
SMR *see* steam methane reforming (SMR)
Snoeck, A. 213

social cost–benefit analysis (SCBA) 177–178
SORA *see* Specific Operational Risk Assessment (SORA)
sortation center 191–192
South Korea, consumer spending 134
space integration 91–100
Space Needle, Seattle 307, *307*
spatial distribution, trends in 194–196
spatial hysteresis 204
spatial planning 257–259
Specific Operational Risk Assessment (SORA) 79
Spoor, J. M. 94, 95
sprawl 15, 197–198, *198*
stakeholder engagement 270–272
stakeholder preferences 272–273
Standard Industrial Classification (SIC) code 390
Starship Technologies 241
Stated Choice Experiments 272
Stathopoulos, A. 272
steam methane reforming (SMR) 343, 344
Sterle, C. 212
Stilgoe, J. 73
Strale, M. 99–100
sub-Saharan Africa 361n7
SUCCESS project 178
Suksri, J. 272
SULPs *see* Sustainable Urban Logistics Plans (SULPs)
SUMP *see* Sustainable Urban Mobility Plan (SUMP)
supply chain agents 284, 287, 289–290, 292
supply chains (SC) 17; digitalisation 164; global, last mile and 109; healthcare, digitalisation of 162–163; management 4, 122–124; reconfiguration 54, 57; resilient healthcare, designing 169; revolution 121
sustainability 7, 10–11, 128; agenda, driving 167–168; e-commerce 108–109; measures, hierarchy of **18**; ratings 183; Triple Bottom Line of Sustainability 167
Sustainable Development Goals (SDGs): SDG 3 159; SDG 5 388
sustainable mobility 32, 273, 275
Sustainable Urban Logistics Plans (SULPs) 19, 263, 273, 274
Sustainable Urban Mobility Plan (SUMP) 19, 273
Sweden: SamCity pilot study 295; SMARTSET project 298; urban consolidation centres 298–299
Swift Express Freight 243–244
Switzerland, Heavy Vehicle Fee (HVF) 256
SWOT analysis 178
Sydney Ferries 239

talent management, in healthcare logistics 168–169
Tang, C. 227
Taniguchi, E. 219, 260
Target 241
Taychakhoonavudh, S. 166
TDA *see* Temporary Danger Area (TDA)
technical analysis 7–8
technological advances 292, 367
technological change 130
Temporary Danger Area (TDA) 80
temporary stores 137
Tesco 124, 140, 141; Tesco Whoosh 141
third places 137
time-distance tolls 285
tipping elements 324, 325
trade structure 358–360
Tramfret 244
Transferability of Urban Logistics Concepts and Practices from a World Wide Perspective (TURBLOG) **20**
Transportation Research Board (TRB): Standing Committee on Urban Freight Transportation (AT025) **21**
Transport Refrigeration Units (TRUs) 154–155
transport/transportation: change 130–131; definition of 4; freight (*see* freight transport); geographies 330; modes 5–6; operation 28, 32, 34, **36**, 37, 38, 66, 91, 94, 96, 126, 153, 154, 156, 200, 202, 326; policy 21, 69, 274; rail 45–57
TRB *see* Transportation Research Board (TRB)
Trentini, A. 95, 100
triple bottom line 68
truck traffic 252, 283–285, 288, 291, 316, 371
TRUs *see* Transport Refrigeration Units (TRUs)
TURBLOG *see* Transferability of Urban Logistics Concepts and Practices from a World Wide Perspective (TURBLOG)
two-echelon Capacitated LRP (2E-CLRP) 212
two-echelon location and routing models 210–211
two-echelon stochastic multi-period capacitated location-routing problem (2E-SM-CLRP) 212
two-echelon vehicle routing problem (2E-VRP) 212
Tyndall, J. 324

UAV Operation and Management System (UOMS) 80
UAV Traffic Management (UTM) 80, 81
Uber 11, 139, 241, 377–379; UberEats 135, 140, 141, 150–152, 154, 240, 261
UCCs *see* urban consolidation centres (UCCs)
UFT *see* urban freight transport (UFT)
UK *see* United Kingdom (UK)

Index

UK Research and Innovation (UKRI) 74
ULAADS *see* Urban Logistics as an On-Demand Service (ULAADS)
ULD *see* unit load device (ULD)
ULLTRA-SIM *see* Urban Logistics Land-use and Traffic Simulator (ULLTRA-SIM)
ultra-low emission vehicles (ULEV) 398–399, 402, 403
uncertainty 56, 77, 128, 165, 193, 213, 215, 327, 341, 380–382
UN Conference on Environment and Development (1992) 327–328
Uncrewed Aerial Vehicles (UAVs) 5, 72
Unilever 139
United Kingdom (UK): Brexit 121, 122, 131; CLOCS (Construction Logistics and Cyclist Safety) 180; consumer spending 134; dark stores 239–240; Department of Health and Social Care 162; Electric Vehicle Charging in Residential and Non-Residential Buildings 328; fast fashion, rise of 125; food distribution channels 151; gender pay gap 389–390, **390**; Greener NHS initiative 167; healthcare logistics 161–162; Heavy Goods Vehicle Road User Levy 288; logistics and supply chain management 123; London (*see* London); NHS England 74, 76, 159, 167; NHS Long Term Plan 161; NHS Supply Chain 159; Office for National Statistics 390; refrigerated vans 154; retailing 122; Swift Express Freight 243–244; vaccine logistics 166; zero-emission vehicles 290
United Nations Conference on the Environment and Development 96
United Nations Department of Economic and Social Affairs 4
United Nations Entity for Gender Equality and the Empowerment of Women 389
United States (US): Bureau of Statistics 365; CAFÉ standards 346; consumer spending 134; dark stores 138; Department of Energy's Argonne Labs 344; Environmental Protection Agency 282, 289; facility locations 190; Federal Corporate Average Fuel Economy standards 337; Federal Highway Administration 339; Greenhouse Gas Emissions 282; health provision 159; online grocery shopping 152; Urban Freight Lab 253, 257, 306
unit load device (ULD) 245
unmanned automated vehicles (UAVs) 260
UOMS *see* UAV Operation and Management System (UOMS)
UPS 209, 260
urban areas 3, 7, 10, 13, 93, 95, 96, *191*, 208, 210, 213–218, 231, 233, 234, 258, 268, 273, 275, 289, 290, 296, 299, 306, 309, 324, 327–329, 335, 347, 365, 366, 396–399, 403; co-modality 243; construction 175, 178, 184; curbside management and deliveries 257; drones in 72, 75, 79, 81; food logistics 147, 149, 153, 154; healthcare 159, 161, 162, 165–167; logistics metropolitan concentration 195; micro-hubs in 209; rail and water freight in 46–49, 51, 54–57; retailing 121, 122, 127–132; road freight pricing in 255; road freight transport in 27–29, 32, 33, 34, 37–40; road freight transport trip generation in 30–31; zero-emission delivery vehicles in 255
urban consolidation centres (UCCs) 9, 60, 67, 201, 213, 269, 295–302; case study 298–299; developments, challenges to 299–301; developments, use of supporting policies for 300–301, **301**; location of *297*; service offerings 296–288, *297*; types of 296–298
urban, definition of 4
urban delivery 6, 122, 131, 214, 218, 244, 255, 282–285, 287, 289–292, 305, 316, 327, 328, 334, 360, 397, 400, 401
Urban Distribution Center 272
urban economy 13, 351–353
urban food plan 149
urban food transport *148*, 149–156
urban form 365, 366, 369
urban freight: data 252, 260–262, **262**; distribution 213, 219, 272, 273; growth of 333–335
Urban Freight 2012 **21**
Urban Freight Lab 253, 257, 306
urban freight transport (UFT) 5, 27–40, 45, 176, 183, 184, 227, 232, 272, 274; policies 300
urban goods transport 136, 352
urban land use 15, 372
urban logistics: charters 253; climate change and 323–330; common problems in 14–17; computing technology 225–236; construction and 175–184; dark stores 134–145; definition of 13–14; ecosystems 399–403; facility locations in 189–204; female participation in 391–392; freight and passenger transport, integrating 91–100; future perspectives of 21–22; gender diversity in 387–393; in Global South 351–361; healthcare and 159–169; improving 17–20; in megacities 364–373; pilot studies, success factors for 305–319; pre-COVID trends 396–399; rail transport and 45–57; research networks **21**; research programmes **20**; and retailing 121–132; road transport and 27–40; role in city economy 13–22; sectors 6–7; start-ups 259–260; transitions and diversification in 360–361; *see also individual entries*
Urban Logistics as an On-Demand Service (ULAADS) **20**

Urban Logistics Land-use and Traffic Simulator (ULLTRA-SIM) 194
urban warehouses 201, 204, 258, 259, 262, 263, 335
Urry, J. 328
US *see* United States (US)
UTM *see* UAV Traffic Management (UTM)

vaccine logistics 165–166
Van Duin, J. H. R. 269
Vanelslander, T. 66
Van Woensel, T. 218
VED *see* Vehicle Excise Duty (VED)
Veelenturf, L. 227
Vehicle Excise Duty (VED) 286, 290
Velasco 162
Velofood 152
Venkatesh, V. 73
vertical take-off and landing (VTOL) drones 74, 83
Ville, S. 300–301
virtual shelf expansion 137
VLOS (Visual-Line-of-Sight) 72
Volkswagen 47
Volvo 338
Volvo Research and Educational Foundations (VREF) **21**
Voly 240
Vuchic, V. R. 96

Waßmuth, K. 218
Walgreens 241, 260
Walmart 138, 240, 241
Walters, A. A. 283
Wang, Y. 92
warehouse platforms (WP) 208, 209
warehouses 3, 4, 6, 7, 31, 33, 39, 111, 123, 126, 135, 137–139, 141, 142, 145, 149, 153, 154, 164, 195, 201, 204, 208, 212, 216, 240, 244, 251, 258, 259, 262, 263, 326, 335, 337, 356, 359, 361, 369, 389, 393, 397, 398, 401
warestores 6, 135, 137, 138
water freight 45–57; barriers to 56–57; benefits of 46; examples of 48–49; opportunities for 54–56

WeChat 142, 151
Weezy 141
WiLAT *see* Women in Logistics and Transport (WiLAT)
WIL *see* women in logistics (WIL)
Wing 260
Winkenbach, M. 211, 213
Wolt 141
women in logistics (WIL) 392
Women in Logistics and Transport (WiLAT) 392
Working for Workers Act (Ontario) 379
World Bank 263; Logistics Performance Index (LPI) 351; World Bank Reports 353
World Conference on Transport Research Special Interest Group in Urban Goods Movement **21**
World Economic Forum (WEF) 227, 305
World Wide Web 239
Woxenius, J. 66
WP *see* warehouse platforms (WP)
Wu, F. 366

Xos 338

Yang, Z. 155
Yeh, A. G. O. 366
Yuan, Q. 198, 369, 370
Yummy 138, 142

Zapp 142, 240
Zara 125, 126, 402
Zepto 138
zero-emission 33, 255
zero-emission trucks (ZETs) 339, 341, 347
zero emission vehicles 34, 93, 253, 286, 288, 290, 295, 338
zero-emission zones (ZEZ) 9, 37, 184, 252–255, **254**, 261, 262
zero-inventory stores 137
Zinn, W. 392
Zipline 74, 75
zoning 257–259
Zürich Cargo Tram 47